HANDBOOKS

BEIJING & SHANGHAI

HELENA IVESON

Contents

Discover Beijing & Shanghai

A visit to Beijing and Shanghai is the first step to unraveling the mystery of China. In China's two most vital and exciting cities, one can experience the country as it takes its place at the forefront of the world stage.

China is a tangled web, from the brash, ultramodern new to the time-honored past. Mao suits and miniskirts, modern metropolises and classic mountain vistas – trying to guess what you'll see next is like trying to keep up with the latest fashions in Shanghai or finding an up-to-date map of Beijing.

Beijing has been at the center of China's tumultuous history for thousands of years – and the 2008 Olympic Games inspired the mother of all makeovers. Towering skyscrapers appear overnight: Beijing changes right before your eyes.

But glimpses of the old city can still be found: In ancient alleys, traditional life continues unchanged. Experiencing Beijing, of course, means a visit to the awesome Forbidden City, but it also means a trip to local shopping centers to see skateboarders with multicolored hair test their newfound freedoms. No other place in the world has Beijing's sights, sounds, and smells, from the noise of a million bicycle bells at rush hour to the wafts of burning incense that fill the air at the Lama Temple.

Where Beijing is refined but laid-back, Shanghai is slick and

sophisticated, keen to impress you with style and charm. It crackles with energy, like New York to the 10th power. After languishing for several decades under heavy government control, in 1992 Shanghai started to come out of its slumber: The market economy was again back in business, and the city has since led China's surging economic growth.

There's a lot to catch up on, and the city is doing it at warp speed. Its contradictory mix of rampant consumerism and communism is dazzling. On the banks of the Huangpu River, some of the tallest buildings in the world look down on historic buildings from the 1920s. In Shanghai, a walk down the Bund admiring these art deco stuccos is essential, but so is slurping steaming noodles in the shadow of a Shanghai skyscraper, or enjoying the newest in art and fine dining. For first-time visitors to Shanghai, the super-slick Maglev train makes for an exhilarating entrance. The Maglev reaches speeds of 270 mph, leaving all other forms of transportation behind.

Welcome to the future. Welcome to Beijing and Shanghai.

Planning Your Trip

WHERE TO GO

Beijing

TIANANMEN

Tiananmen Square—and the country's most prestigious buildings, which surround it—serve as the **spiritual center** of Beijing, and indeed, China. The area is packed with out-of-towners and locals alike, here to pay pilgrimage at the attractions that the country is most proud of: the **Forbidden City,** the Great Hall of the People, the **new National Center for Performing Arts,** and Mao's Mausoleum. To the west of Tiananmen is Zhongnanhai, home to the foremost leaders of the People's Republic of China. Chang'an Jie, one of Beijing's main thoroughfares, runs through central Beijing from east to west. Here you'll see China at its most grand and formal.

HOUHAI TO THE OLYMPIC STADIUM

North of Tiananmen lies Beijing's most **picturesque** district, which, with its **quiet *hutong* streets** and atmospheric Confucius and Lama Temples, has been at the center of Beijing's religious life for centuries. There's plenty to see and explore, and this is the best area to do so by bike. See the imposing **Drum and Bell Towers,** the prettiness of **Houhai Lake,** and the area's counterpoint in the north, the architecturally arresting **Olympic Park:** the iconic **Bird's Nest** stadium and **Water Cube** swimming center, deliberately placed on the same north–south axis as the Forbidden City, illustrating its importance to national pride.

QIANMEN AND TEMPLE OF HEAVEN

The neighborhood south of Tiananmen is a **vibrant** merchant area and tangle of *hutong* alleys. Although many of the historic areas have been demolished in the rush to modernize, the **newly pedestrianized** Qianmen area and remainders of **historic streets** such as Liulichang make the area very popular. The excellent **Planning Exhibition Hall** is here, as is the new **Legation Quarter,** whose

Mao's portrait on display at Tiananmen Gate

collection of trendy bars and restaurants mean to make the area the destination for after-hours entertainment.

CENTRAL BUSINESS DISTRICT

East of Tiananmen is where you'll find many of the best hotels and ritziest shops in the city, because this remains the key financial district in Beijing. Sights may be thin on the ground, but look up to see one of Beijing's newest icons: the CCTV Building, whose crisscross style dominates the skyline alongside the tallest building in Beijing, the new World Trade Center. Pockets of peace also remain, such as the pretty Ritan Park and the lovely Temple of Wisdom Attained, hidden down a maze of alleys.

CHAOYANG DISTRICT AND SANLITUN

This image-conscious area northeast of the Forbidden City is the neighborhood of choice for many of the capital's expats as well as the entertainment center of the city, Sanlitun. Here bars and restaurants varying from student dives to trendy Japanese designer eateries share the same street. Many of Beijing's best boutiques are in this area, as is the Workers' Stadium, which was completely revamped to hold the football competitions at the Olympic Games. In the east lies China's most famous contemporary art district, Dashanzi, complete with small boutiques and cafés; Beijing's biggest city park, Chaoyang Park, with the world's largest Ferris wheel under construction; and a strip of excellent bars and restaurants. It's easy to get to this neighborhood from the airport, thanks to the speedy train link to the Dongzhimen transport center.

CAPITAL MUSEUM AND TEMPLE OF GREAT CHARITY

Once upon a time, few tourists chose to visit this commercial part of Beijing, but the arrival of the superb Capital Museum gave the city a museum to be proud of and visitors a reason to go west. Many companies are also being tempted here, as the government has designated Financial Street as China's equivalent to Wall Street. Away from money-making and skyscrapers, the improving Beijing Zoo is in the north of the area, and two temples that are wrongly overlooked by tourists, the Temple of Great Monarchs and the Temple of Ancient Charity, are also nearby.

a colorful Chaoyang District storefront

UNIVERSITY DISTRICT AND THE SUMMER PALACE

Famous throughout China for its excellent universities and its booming technological scene, this area to the northwest of Tiananmen is a mixed bag of residential and commercial, with a few sights strewn into the mix. On the outskirts of the busy highways is one of Beijing's top attractions, the Summer Palace, and even farther out, the Botanical Gardens and pretty Fragrant Hills are where residents get their fix of fresh air. Thanks to the new subway line, which goes all the way to the Summer Palace, it's never been easier to get around here by public transport.

Excursions from Beijing

The metropolis is surrounded on all sides by lovely countryside and hilly plains,

Summer Palace at twilight

allowing visitors to see a completely different side of China. A trip to Beijing isn't complete without an excursion to the Great Wall, and many sections are within a couple of hours of the capital. Don't expect peace and quiet, though, as these sections are hardly undiscovered: If you're looking for peace and tranquility in a bucolic setting, a weekday trip to the unspoiled Ming dynasty village Cuandixia, to the west of the city, is a must.

Shanghai

THE BUND AND EAST NANJING LU

For first-time tourists, a stroll along the west bank of the Huangpu River to admire the Bund—the most visible reminder of colonial Shanghai—is essential. Encompassing the whole length of the Bund is the famous waterfront promenade, from Broadway Mansions and the Post Office Museum over Suzhou Creek and down the eastern end of Nanjing Lu, one of Shanghai's most famous shopping streets. Local tourists will consider you part of the attraction too! This is also the place to go for the best views of Pudong's exciting skyline. A short taxi ride to the north to Duolun Lu's street-full of preserved row houses will propel you back to 1930s Shanghai.

PEOPLE'S SQUARE AND MUSEUM ROW

The geographical center of Shanghai is linked to the Bund by Nanjing Lu, and after the Bund itself, this is Shanghai's prime tourist destination. People's Park and People's Square both serve as much-needed outdoor space for the city's residents, and cultural must-sees include the world-class Shanghai Museum, two art museums, and the spectacular Grand Theater. The area has some excellent examples of Shanghai architecture, from the art deco Park Hotel to the space-age facades of Tomorrow Square. Foodies flock to Huanghe Food Street, where snack sellers and sit-down restaurants line the streets.

JING'AN AND WEST NANJING LU

Running west of People's Square, this upmarket and bustling neighborhood includes both

Shanghai Museum in People's Square

old meets new in Jing'an

ritzy shopping malls and restaurants and interesting places to visit, such as the gold-covered Jing'an Temple and imposing Ohel Rachel Synagogue, plus the tasty snacks available from the fun and hectic Wujiang Food Street. The western part of one of the city's main and iconic roads, Nanjing Lu, goes through the center of Jing'an, and a crop of new boutique hotels has made this a great place to stay. The Jing'an Transport Terminus is where to catch buses to both airports.

FORMER FRENCH CONCESSION

Despite its not having a huge number of sights, visitors love the low-rise tree-lined streets of the French Concession, which is south of People's Square, for its unique chic atmosphere. This area, which was run by the French during colonial days, has always been popular—as the number of famous people from Chinese history who chose to live here testifies. You can visit preserved mansions and 1930s town houses, and the leafy Fuxing Park provides some greenery, but the main draw of the area is its shops and entertainment options, including the hugely popular Xintiandi complex and the more relaxed Taikang Lu area.

OLD CITY

Shanghai's original "Chinatown"—when Shanghai was divided up into foreign concessions, this was the area designated for and run by the Chinese—lies south of the Bund and was once enclosed by a wall. While that has long since crumbled, the traditional ambiance of the neighborhood still distinguishes it from the rest of the city. It would be a shame if visitors visited only the hugely popular Yu Gardens and Bazaar, which have more than a touch of Disneyland about them. Quiet

lanterns on display in Yu Gardens Bazaar in the Old City

havens exist at Chenxiangge Nunnery and the Confucius Temple. If you take a wander down the area's small alleyways, you can glimpse life going on as it has for centuries for ordinary working-class Shanghainese, as people hang their clothes to dry out on the street and food is prepared communally.

PUDONG

On the other side of the river from Shanghai's other districts, this neighborhood was more muddy bog than financial district 15 years ago—but like Shanghai itself, Pudong has come a long way fast. While much of the area is more commercial than prime tourist destination, the following attractions make Pudong a must: the symbol of Shanghai, the Oriental Pearl Tower; two excellent museums, the Municipal History Museum and Science and Technology Museum; the gorgeous Jinmao Tower; and the brand-new China World Financial Center, whose angular shape cuts the skyline like a knife. The city's international airport is in this district, as is the Maglev terminal, where the world's fastest trains will whiz you to the airport before you've settled into your seat.

Fayu Temple on the island of Putuoshan

Excursions from Shanghai

Shanghai became the world-class city it is because of its proximity to water, and most of the attractions surrounding the city have water at their core, too. West is Suzhou, with its famous canals and stylized gardens, while to the southwest in Zhejiang province, the huge picturesque lake at the city of Hangzhou has attracted visitors for centuries. The many water towns, such as Tongli and Xitang, are filled with original Ming- and Qing-dynasty houses and bridges, which crisscross the town canals. Farther afield lies the Buddhist island Putuoshan, where visitors can get their fix of sunbathing and temple visiting by flying or catching a ferry for a weekend away from the city.

the ultra-high-speed Maglev train

▶ WHEN TO GO

When's the right time to visit? While the two cities are both year-round destinations, fall is the loveliest time to visit. You have as good a chance of seeing clear skies and breezy days in Beijing as you do in spring; but in spring you have the (worsening) sand clouds that sweep in from the plains of Inner Mongolia. From May onward the temperature rises fast. Winters can be dry and glacial (dipping as low as -20°C/-4°F), but in recent years the cold spells have become milder and shorter. Still, if you are used to warm weather, Beijing can be miserably cold in winter but at least the sun is usually out—though with the air pollution, you won't always know it.

Like Beijing, Shanghai is best visited during the spring and fall. Summer is peak season and gets very humid, while from September to November the moderate weather brings out several interesting arts festivals and exhibitions. Winter can be dismal with biting temperatures and rain, but hotel prices will be lower and crowds smaller: Just don't forget the umbrella.

The country now has two national weeklong holiday periods instead of three to relieve some of the congestion that occurs when 1.3 billion people take off for their holidays at the same time. The weeklong national holidays are now during Chinese New Year and the National Day holiday at the beginning of October. Thanks to overemployment and the all-encompassing desire to make money, almost all of China's shops, restaurants, and hotels are open year-round. Some small restaurants and shops may close during Chinese New Year, as their staff head home for the holidays, but all hotels and attractions keep their doors open. While the holiday festivities are great to enjoy and see at least once, the lines everywhere, lack of train and plane tickets, and crowds at attractions may cancel out much of the merriment. Transport prices will also be at their highest, so if you can come at another time, do.

Lanterns are hung from every surface during Chinese New Year.

BEFORE YOU GO

Visas

Everyone who visits China needs a visa. The most common visa is the simple tourist visa, which you must get from the Chinese Embassy in your country. The only exception to this rule is if you are from one of a handful of countries, including the United States and Canada, staying less than 48 hours in China, and have a paper ticket out of the country (e-tickets won't cut it). Tourist visas are also easy to obtain in Hong Kong.

Shanghai's main railway station

Vaccinations

If you are staying in Beijing and/or Shanghai, you don't need to worry about having any inoculations before your trip, aside from the standard Hepatitis A and B, tetanus, polio, and typhoid shots that doctors recommend you have before you travel anywhere. The biggest health problems are the many strains of flu virus that float around, but you can't do much about them aside from following normal standard good-hygiene practices.

Getting There

The Beijing Capital International Airport is 12 miles northeast of the city and now has three terminals, and passengers travel between them by train. After arriving, you have three ways to get to your destination: high-speed train, low-speed bus, or taxi. If you have a lot of luggage, the simplest option is to catch a taxi.

Shanghai has two airports: the newer international Pudong Airport (PVG) 20 miles from the city center and Hongqiao Airport (SHA), which is for domestic flights only and is just six miles from the city center. The coolest way to get to and from the airport is by catching the Maglev train, which will take you to Pudong in just eight minutes. A taxi will likely be cheaper.

If you are flying domestically—from, say, Beijing—try and fly into Hongqiao, which will save at least an hour getting into the city.

What to Take

Chinese people with money like to dress the part and may find the sight of a very scruffily dressed Westerner a bit of an oddity: If you have money—which to most Chinese eyes, all foreigners do—why would you not wear nice clothes? Most restaurants are very casual—the only places you would need to make a little effort are at the cities' most expensive venues. If you hate the idea of being stared at, it's advisable to dress a shade more conservatively than you probably would at home.

If you require medication, bring it from home. Everything from painkillers to sleeping pills are available over the counter without a prescription in China, but there are stories of fake medicine doing a lot of harm to people: It's not worth the risk, no matter how unlikely.

Specialized baby equipment can be found, but bring anything you can't do without from home, as the quality may not be up to par—and bring kid-size chopsticks, which will make it easier for your children to enjoy Chinese food (and which will be hard to find in China). Pack some good maps to complement the ones in this book—those you'll find in Beijing are notoriously inaccurate and will be in Chinese. Wi-Fi in China is good and plentiful—if you will need to work, it's best to bring your laptop, as Internet cafés will be noisy with computer games.

Travel Insurance

Travel insurance covering both medical emergencies and your possessions is vital in China. Emergency services are in no way up to Western standards at public hospitals, and you hear possibly apocryphal stories of people injured in accidents lying by the roadside until the ambulance service, which is run as a business, has been assured that someone will pick up the bill.

Travel insurance should be arranged before you travel. With all policies, check to make sure the coverage is sufficient if you will be carrying high-value items such as laptops and cameras. And make sure to keep all receipts for medical expenses.

Taking a taxi will save you time and sanity.

Money

You can change money just about anywhere; you will just need to show your passport. Save the foreign exchange receipt you will receive, as you may need to show it when changing the money back. Nowadays, the ATM system in both cities is in English and Chinese, so it's easy to pull money out—always keep these receipts, too, as it is not unheard of for machines to debit your card twice. Banks in China are notorious for long lines, which makes using an ATM an even more attractive option—and changing travelers checks is a huge nuisance.

Before you leave, check if your local bank will change RMB (short for *renminbi,* or the people's currency) back into your preferred currency.

Getting Around

The infamously bad traffic in both Shanghai and Beijing can leave people on a tight schedule cursing. While both cities have a veritable maze of subway lines linking many attractions to one another, if you're in a hurry taxis are still the best option.

Access for Travelers with Disabilities

Neither Beijing nor Shanghai is an easy destination for travelers with disabilities—public transportation is basically off-limits as there is next to no wheelchair access, and the heavy traffic on the roads and crowds of people on the sidewalk will be a challenge. Few road crossings have audible alerts, and while some sidewalks will have ridges to help visually impaired people, the many cracks and uneven slabs make walking difficult. It's a good idea to hire a car (with a driver) to get around, which can be arranged by any five-star hotel.

Explore Beijing & Shanghai

▸ TEN DAYS, TWO CITIES

While both cities deserve a month each to fully explore, with a bit of planning and research, you can do the highlights of Beijing and Shanghai in just 10 days, even if you skip the plane and catch the overnight train between the two—to many the 12-hour journey is an exciting experience in itself. You'll see all the sights that the cities are world-famous for, plus get a real feel for their quirks, cuisines, and characters. You'll see for yourself how quickly the cities are changing—and know you'll need to come back.

Although both cities sprawl outward for many miles, Shanghai's and Beijing's areas of interest to most visitors are relatively compact, except for the must-see side trip to the Great Wall while in Beijing. To save time in Beijing, base yourself near Tiananmen Square and the Forbidden City, since that's likely where you'll be spending most of your time. Down south in Shanghai, when time is tight, stay near the Bund: Everyone wants to see the famous skyline opposite in Pudong while enjoying the imposing architecture of the Bund itself—what better way to do it than from your hotel room?

If you're visiting both cities and on a strict schedule, save shopping for Shanghai, which has far superior shops. And don't skimp on taxis in either city—your time and sanity are worth far more than the few RMB you'll save on public transport.

Day 1

As you recover from jet lag, spend the morning walking around the picturesque lake known as Houhai before having your first real Chinese meal at Han Cang, the character-filled restaurant on its bank. After a filling lunch of baked shrimp in salt and braised pork, allow someone else to take the strain and jump onto the back of a rickshaw for a tour of the nearby winding alleys lined with courtyard houses. For more relaxation, a 90-minute foot massage at Bodhi will ease any lingering aches and pains. Snacks and drinks are included, but if you want something more, try nearby restaurant Three Guizhou Men—the spicy dishes will blow away any remaining cobwebs.

the pagoda at the top of Jingshan Park, from the north end of the Forbidden City

FROM THE BUND TO THE BIRD'S NEST: ARCHITECTURAL HIGHLIGHTS

While the two cities can often seem like one huge construction site, and the government rightly faces near-constant criticism for its demolition of many traditional areas, there are still many buildings that serve as symbols of the past, present, and how China wants to present itself to the world in the future – everything from the opulence of Beijing's ancient temples to its futuristic Olympic sites and Shanghai's ultramodern skyscrapers. Architecture fans shouldn't wait too long to get here – the cranes and demolition workers haven't stopped yet.

TRADITIONAL ABODES

Beijing

Hutong

For a look at a fast-disappearing way of life, stroll around the atmospheric *hutong* alleys of **Houhai,** where the ordinary and the elite have lived for centuries. Mandarins who worked at the Forbidden City used to live in the small gray streets near the **Drum and Bell Towers,** where the bang of the tower's drums was a sign it was time to get to work – their workplace, of course, was the traditional home of China's emperors for almost five centuries.

Shanghai

Longtang

Shanghai's equivalent to Beijing's *hutong,* these look like tenements from a town in Northern England. Whole communities lived in grids across the city, and although very few are left now, if you head to the **northern end of the Bund,** behind the Hyatt on the Bund, you'll see a whole block of these houses, looking exactly the same as they have for 100 years.

Shikumen

Also unique to Shanghai are its *shikumen,* which translates as "stone-gated houses"; these blended traditional Asian and Western features. For a look at a prettified version, go to the **Shikumen Open House Museum in Xintiandi,** or to see *shikumen* that are still occupied, go to the lovely **Duolun Lu,** which is lined by antique shops and rows of charming lane houses.

RECENT-HISTORY REMINDERS

Beijing

China's parliament building, the **Great Hall of the People,** would not look out of place in Russia during the 1950s, nor would China's **National Museum** – both were built at a time when China and Russia were close allies.

Shanghai

The Bund is a symbol of the city's turbulent history, when Foreign Concessions ruled the waterfront and erected imposing structures using imported material with no regard to local conditions or feng shui – which was considered of vital importance when the Bund's buildings were being built between 1906 and 1937.

SHOWSTOPPERS

Beijing

The dazzling **Bird's Nest** Olympic stadium and iconic **Swimming Center** obviously need to be suitable for sport, but their real function is to show the world how the country sees itself as it rockets through the 21st century. The **CCTV Building** (due to be finished in 2010) in Chaoyang is another example of a confident China. The **National Center for Performing Arts,** next to the Soviet-style architecture of the Great Hall of the People, overshadows the older building both literally and figuratively as a new style of architecture takes center stage.

Shanghai

Perhaps the first sign of this newfound confidence in Shanghai was the **Oriental Pearl Tower,** as brash as the city it represents, while the more elegant designs of the **Jinmao Tower** and the **Shanghai World Financial Center** illustrate a city or even country more at ease with itself.

the traditional Great Hall of the People and the futuristic National Center for Performing Arts

Day 2

Wear flat shoes today: There's going to be plenty of walking. Get up early and go to the political, cultural, and spiritual center of China, Tiananmen Square. If you have time, catch the subway there for the unique experience of climbing the stairs and suddenly finding yourself in such an iconic spot. Depending on your interests and levels of morbidity, a trip to Chairman Mao's Tomb in the center of the square could be in the cards, as could a tour of China's "parliament," The Great Hall of the People, which is to the west. The Forbidden City, however, is an absolute must, for its dramatic history, awesome buildings, and the sheer spectacle of the place. For refreshment, head to nearby Nandachi Jie and eat fried Beijing dumplings at one of the cheap restaurants that line the street, or hit the CourtYard for coffee. If you can cope with some more walking, head to the north end of the Forbidden City and climb the hill in Jingshan Park for a picture-perfect view of the Forbidden City laid out in front of you—plus a glimpse of the space-age National Center for Performing Arts to the right. You can't leave Beijing without at least trying Beijing duck—the pancakes filled with juicy duck glistening with fat may be a heart attack on a plate, but what a way to go. . . . The most upmarket and delicious duck in town is served at Made in China, but if dining in a shabby but atmospheric *hutong* restaurant is more your thing, try Li Qun. Reservations are needed at both places.

Day 3

After a local Chinese breakfast of *jianbing* (egg pancake) and soya milk—available at any hole in the wall—head south to witness the dazzling splendor of the Temple of Heaven, either by taxi or on the new purple line 5 subway. After a relaxing few hours there, shopping fans will find themselves conveniently near Hongqiao market and the excellent DVD and music store nearby. If you're hungry after all that fierce bargaining, there's a coffee stand in the market—or better yet, take a taxi to the Peninsula Hotel in Wangfujing to experience the bliss of dim sum at Huang Ting. For the afternoon, the newly redeveloped Legation Quarter is interesting historically and has some great shops and restaurants to be and be seen in, or if you prefer more traditional sights, head west to the Summer Palace and see where the imperial family used to spend the warmer months away from the city.

CHINESE TRADITIONS: FIREWORKS AND MOON CAKES

China is changing fast – in 2008, the old system of three national weeklong holidays was revised, and now the traditional tomb-sweeping day or Qingming Jie, Dragon Boat Day, and the Mid-Autumn Festival will all be national bank holidays. The revisions were introduced to reduce the huge pressure placed on the transportation system and at tourist attractions caused by practically the whole country going on holiday at the same time. Catch a glimpse of China's traditional festivals before they disappear forever.

CHINESE NEW YEAR (JANUARY OR FEBRUARY)

This is the country's Christmas, Easter, and Thanksgiving rolled into one – and now that the ban has been lifted, expect a noisy **10 days** or so of huge **fireworks** rocketing into the sky in both Beijing and Shanghai. The holiday, which is also known as Spring Festival, starts on the first day of the new moon of the lunar calendar.

Beijing

- **The Drum and Bell Towers:** Near **Houhai,** this is where **local families gather** to celebrate and light firecrackers to scare off any evil spirits.
- **Ditan Park:** Attend one of the **temple fairs,** such as the huge festival held at this park in **Dongcheng District.**

Shanghai

- **Longhua and Jing'an Temples:** Special ceremonies with **chanting monks** and **festive dances** are held here.

LANTERN FESTIVAL (FEBRUARY OR MARCH)

Marking the **end of the New Year holiday** period is this holiday, which falls on the 15th day of the first lunar month. People traditionally hang **red lanterns** outside their houses for luck and let off even more fireworks while eating *tang yuan,* or **sweet dumplings,** by the mouthful.

Beijing

- **Chaoyang Park:** Visit here for a great **fireworks** display.

Shanghai

- **Yu Gardens:** Almost every outside surface of this **classical garden** has a jolly red lantern hanging off it. While it gets very crowded, it's definitely worth visiting for the experience.

QINGMING JIE (EARLY APRIL)

This holiday is celebrated in both cities, and every year more than six million Shanghainese alone go to the **graves** of their dead **ancestors** and give them a spring cleaning. Because of the nature of the occasion, it's **difficult for tourists to take part,** unless they are close friends with a Chinese person who is taking part in the ritual.

DRAGON BOAT DAY (MAY OR JUNE)

It's easy to join in on this holiday, which falls on the fifth day of the fifth lunar month. It **commemorates the death of a poet-statesmen** who drowned himself in protest over the corruption of the state.

Beijing

- **Houhai and Qianhai:** There are always events at these lakes, including **boat races.**

Shanghai

- **Huangpu River:** There's usually a race on the river between Pudong and the Bund; check the **local press** for more details.

MOON FESTIVAL (SEPTEMBER OR OCTOBER)

During the **Mid-Autumn Festival,** as it's also called, the Chinese go **moon-cake** mad, sending just about everyone they know the sickly sweet traditional cakes to celebrate. If you're in China at this time, you'll be expected to eat at least a few of these cakes.

Check listings magazines and the *China Daily* newspaper for details.

relaxing in Ritan Park

Day 4

The Olympics may be over, but the awesome architecture of the stadiums and sports centers still convey their drama and excitement. Take a taxi or the subway to the Bird's Nest in the north of the city for a glimpse of its fascinating design. Also in the Olympic Park, don't miss the Australian-designed swimming center, the Water Cube, scene of so many Olympic highlights. When lunch calls, jump in a taxi to nearby Comptoirs de France Bakery—its hot chocolates are world-class themselves, or try an authentic ham and cheese baguette. Continuing your architecture tour, hop into another taxi and drive past fabulously twisted CCTV Building, due to be completed in 2010. Once here, you could choose to hit the shops at Ritan Office Building or the nearby Jimmy & Tommy, which is great for men, or instead walk through the largest park in the city center, Ritan Park. In the evening, go for a show: Experience the highly dramatic and serious offerings of the National Center for Performing Arts (itself an architectural spectacle), or for something less sober, the kung fu fighting in *The Legend of Kung Fu* thrills kids—and grown-ups.

Day 5

In the morning, head to Lama Temple, the city's largest Buddhist temple and certainly one of its most atmospheric. After an hour or two of seeing the yellow-robed monks and the 18-foot sandalwood statue of the Maitreya Buddha, choose between the cozy courtyard café. The Vineyard to the north, or, slightly farther across the ring road, the noisy and fun Chinese restaurant Jin Ding Xuan, which serves good dim sum—both are within walking distance. After lunch head back toward the temple, but instead cut down the interesting street that runs off the main road. On your right will be the highly underrated Confucius Temple and imperial college Guozijian, once China's highest institute of learning, where scholars crammed to become civil servants at the emperor's command. Take a break under the cypress trees; these two little-visited sights provide an oasis from Beijing's fast pace and crowds. In the evening, choose between the refashioned Beijing cuisine at the glamorous and expensive Whampoa Club, or, for those on a tighter budget, more traditional Beijing-style fare in pretty surroundings at Xiao Wang Fu in Ritan Park.

Day 6

Either book yourself on a tour or hire a car and go to the Mutianyu section of the Great Wall, which is a good choice for people short of time. After seeing the wall snake up mountains and plunge down into valleys, you'll find that the Schoolhouse restaurant is a good place for Western carb-filled food, or try the traditional Beijing cuisine available at its sister restaurant next door. After lunch head back to Beijing, where you have a little time before catching the train to Shanghai—the four trains that leave daily depart between 6 and 8 P.M. If you're flying instead, relax and enjoy a meal in Dali's beautiful courtyard in Houhai before walking 10 minutes and settling in at the cozy and relaxed No Name Bar, also in Houhai.

Day 7

On your first day in Shanghai, and only if it's a clear day, head to Pudong and go up the Jinmao Tower, or the brand-new Shanghai World Financial Center next door. Only by approaching the clouds can you understand the scale of this hectic metropolis of 18 million people. After coming back down to earth, walk along the Riverside Promenade and stop here for a coffee, or catch the weird and wonderful Sightseeing Tunnel back to the Bund side and take advantage of one of the lunchtime set menus at Jean Georges, Laris, or the cheaper option, New Heights at Three on the Bund. Walk off your lunch by strolling along the Bund from north to south, stopping off outside the Peace Hotel and peeking into the former HSBC building, or let an expert from the Walk Shanghai walking group guide you. As the sun sets, round off your first day in Shanghai with a cocktail at art deco haven the Glamour Bar, or, for a younger, buzzier crowd, the bar at the Captain's Hostel: Both places have killer views.

Day 8

Today revolves around the People's Park area—wear comfortable shoes, as it's best to walk. Stroll past the elderly people who gather to do tai chi in People's Square and spend a couple of hours at Shanghai Museum to get a sense of the sheer scale of Chinese culture. For art that's more cutting-edge, the Museum of Contemporary Art is a 10-minute walk away, in People's Park itself. Here you are conveniently near the Middle Eastern restaurant Barbarossa, but for something more Shanghai, walk along the west side of the Park Hotel to Huanghe Food Street and find the famous steamed pork dumplings at Jia Jia Tang Bao at number 90—just look for a line. Appetite sated, visit the Urban Planning Exhibition Hall, with its model on how Shanghai will look in 2020 plus re-creations of its past; it lies within walking distance. While Nanjing Lu is overrated, a quick walk down the pedestrianized street is worthwhile for a sense of the scale of capitalism here—just ignore the touts and watch your bag. After a body or foot massage at one of the many branches of Dragonfly, decide whether you want to go luxurious or local for dinner: For a dramatic, decadent dinner, book Jade at 36; for more traditional Shanghainese cuisine, try 1221. Then head into the Former French Concession and try Enoteca for a relaxing glass of wine.

the surreal Shanghai Sightseeing Tunnel, under the Huangpu River

FROM DUMPLINGS TO DUCK: A SAVORY SAMPLER

dumplings

China takes food very seriously. Local restaurants are loud, bright, and not usually places to dwell in after your meal, though there are a welcome few that combine gourmet food and a great ambience.

BEIJING

Beijing Duck

- **Huajia Yiyuan:** the ultimate Beijing dining experience, with a **good traditional duck,** a wide selection of local snacks, and hearty sweet and sour dishes.
- **Made in China:** the city's **most refined duck,** with prices to match.
- **Li Qun: *hutong*** restaurant that specializes in the duck Beijing is famous for.
- **Da Dong:** more **upmarket and glitzy,** with ginger and sugar concoctions to smear in the paper-thin pancakes, in addition to the usual tangy hoisin sauce.

Regional Chinese

- **Three Guizhou Men:** tangy and addictive Guizhou-style food in a **cool and classy** atmosphere – don't miss the chili-covered rack of ribs or the Guizhou cold noodle salad.
- **Xinjiang Government Restaurant:** The baked naan bread, robust chicken stews, and lamb kebabs may not seem Chinese, but the spicy meaty dishes, which derive from Xinjiang, in the far west of China, are **delectable, especially during winter.**
- **Crescent Moon Xinjiang Restaurant:** a **cheap but hearty** feast at this brightly lit spot, where many people finish off their meal with a drag on a apple-scented *shisha* pipe.

Street Eats

In Beijing, there's nothing quite like an evening stroll down **Donghuamen Food Market,** where a long row of stalls sell their weird and wonderful wares, as well as fine examples of **traditional Beijing snacks** and noodles.

Comfort Food

- **Panino Teca** in Sanlitun: Beijing's best **Italian-style sandwiches** – wash 'em down with an excellent café latte.

SHANGHAI

Upmarket Shanghainese

- **1221:** elegant surroundings and **refined Shanghainese** cuisine.
- **Crystal Jade:** amazing *la mian,* or **pulled noodles** – choose between the fiery peanut-flavored broth or the mild option, flavored with fried leek oil.

Fine Dining

- **Jade on 36:** sexy and stylish, with a glittering view of the Bund – **a special treat** that's as cosmopolitan and impressive as Shanghai itself.

Street Eats

- **Jia Jia Tang Bao:** for my money – and judging by the lines, for lots of locals too – the place to head for freshly steamed basketfuls of ***xiaolongbao,* or steamed pork dumplings,** which come with a scorching mouthful of broth inside the wrappers.
- **Yang's Fry Dumplings:** for cheaper and **perhaps more delicious *shengjian,*** which are the same dumplings fried rather than steamed – take them away or take them upstairs and sit at one of the rickety tables and chairs.

Comfort Food

- **Whisk:** Charming Shanghai café with **great pastas and salads** – but the devil in you might just go straight for the chocolate brownies.

the lovely streets of the French Concession

Day 9

The best time to experience the historic Yu Gardens and its surroundings is first thing in the morning, before the crowds pack the small space and the touts open shop. After visiting the garden and bazaar, spend half an hour at the quiet Buddhist temple Chenxiangge Nunnery before enjoying a quick stand-up lunch at Sipailou Food Street, where vendors sell hearty grub for a few RMB—or for something more refined, the Old Shanghai Teahouse is a great place to rest, sip tea, and snack on Shanghai dim sum. To shake things up a bit, catch a cab to Moganshan Art District near the Shanghai train station and spend a few hours taking in the most cutting-edge Chinese artists and the delights of an antiques store called, what else, Art Deco. Jade Buddha Temple is nearby if you have time for a quick detour. In the evening, book tickets for the acrobats at the Shanghai Center, followed by a burger at Gourmet Café or local dishes at Wo Jia—or for something more glitzy and child-friendly, head to Circus World, sit back, and enjoy the show.

Day 10

Your last day will be spent in the Former French Concession, the best place in Shanghai for walking and soaking up the city's atmosphere. Spend the morning at Xintiandi and enjoy a coffee and pastry at Paul patisserie before spending an hour in the charming Shikumen Open House Museum showcasing this uniquely Shanghainese home. For lunch, adventurous diners prepared to point and try anything should head a few blocks to the dowdy but delicious Lan Ting, or KABB in Xintiandi is a great lunch spot for casual American dining. In the afternoon, after a quick stop off at Fuxing Park, wander down the tree-lined shopping streets of Xinle Lu, Changle Lu, and Julu Lu, pausing at the Mansion Hotel for afternoon tea. Press on to Taikang Lu Arts Center for more arty shops, galleries, and cafés before rounding off your stay in Shanghai with a predinner drink at the gorgeous Face Bar and dinner at its Thai or Indian restaurant, or for the best Chinese dumplings in stylish surroundings, head to Din Tai Fung in Xintiandi.

BEIJING FOR BUSINESS

Day 1

After jumping on the high-speed rail-link from the airport or booking the airport transfer service whose staff meet you at the gate, check in to the Kerry Center Hotel if you need to base yourself in the CBD. If you have meetings in the west of town, staying at the sleek and sophisticated Intercontinental Financial Street will save you vital taxi time. If you have the day off to recover from jet lag, head to Bodhi for an excellent foot massage, and when hunger strikes, not too far from either hotel is the Grand Hyatt's superb restaurant Made in China. The sophisticated venue rewrote the open-kitchen rules by having diners feast on its delicious roast duck right in the middle of the action, albeit protected by glass walls. After dinner, head to Bed Bar and sip an excellent *mojito* while relaxing on the antique *kang* beds, or head to the Kerry Center's bar Centro, one of the city's best cocktail lounges.

Day 2

If you have time for sightseeing, do the big one: the Forbidden City. Follow a speedy hour there with lunch at Han Cang in pretty Houhai, or if you have to head back to the office for lunch, order some Motorola and 119 sushi rolls from trendy eatery Hatsune. If you can escape in the afternoon, jump in a taxi to the Temple of Heaven. If you don't have time to do the full circuit, enter at the east gate and see the main sights. If you're staying at the Kerry Center, the slick pan-Asian antique-filled surroundings of Face Bar is a cool venue nearby for predinner drinks before dining at its upscale Indian restaurant Hazara or its Chinese eatery Jia, with its traditional Qing dynasty tables and chairs. But if you're in the west of town, try the Whampoa Club's stylish reinterpretations of Beijing classic dishes, or book the chef's table and enjoy the decadent and delicious contemporary cuisine at the Blu Lobster.

Day 3

If you're pushed for time, ask your hotel to organize a car to take you around the Olympic Park to see the iconic Bird's Nest and Water Cube up close before heading northeast to see the CCTV Building, known to the city's cab drivers as the Baggy Trousers. Xiao Wang Fu in Ritan Park is a great lunch spot, though if you need to work through lunch with your laptop in front of you, the Bookworm has free Wi-Fi. Ask your concierge to see if there are any shows on at the National Center for the Performing Arts. If so, after the performance, walk across Tiananmen Square and

The Bookworm is one of the capital's most relaxing bars.

round off your night at the Legation Quarter complex, where the old American Embassy compound houses a collection of top restaurants, an art gallery, and a nightclub, Boujis.

Day 4

If you have finished your work and have an afternoon and night to spare, head out of town and reserve a room at the Commune at the Great Wall or the Red Capital Ranch. Both places are about 90 minutes from the capital and are interesting in different ways: The Commune is fascinating for architecture buffs and the Ranch for its eccentric mix of rustic Tibetan antiques. Once there, enjoy getting away from it all at their private sections of the Great Wall, away from postcard sellers and other hassles. From both places, Beijing's airport is about an hour away.

the Temple of Heaven's Hall of Prayer for Good Harvests

SHANGHAI FOR BUSINESS

Day 1

Most business travelers situate themselves in Pudong—if you are one of them, the St Regis is the best hotel this side of the river and nearest the international airport. After check-in, leave your personal butler to unpack while you head to Dragonfly Massage and enjoy the Happy Landing massage, its two-hour remedy for jet lag. Once revived, stay in Pudong and head up the Jinmao Tower for some awesome views before cocktails at Jade on 36 in the Shangri-la Hotel. Follow that with a sensuous dinner at its award-winning restaurant. Or for Shanghainese, Ye Shanghai offers great food and floor-to-ceiling views across the Bund.

Pudong's exciting skyline

Day 2

If you have meetings all morning, console yourself with the excellent business lunch at art deco–style eatery M on the Bund before a guided tour along the historic riverfront led by one of the expert guides from Walk Shanghai. If you have a spare hour in the afternoon, head to the Shanghai Museum for a dash of culture before continuing the art deco theme at the sophisticated Glamour Bar, famous for expertly made martinis. Then slip over the road to the gorgeous Three on the Bund, where, after a quick dash through

THE TREASURE HUNT

If shopping were a sport, China would have had an extra gold medal at the Olympics – no one excels at the buying and selling of goods like the Chinese. And if you buy like a local, you'll come away with a suitcase bursting with items to treasure.

BEIJING

Antiques and "Antiques"

- **Panjiayuan:** One of the biggest and best antiques and "antiques" markets in the country – as always, bargain hard.
- **Shilibadian:** If you enjoy sifting through copper to find some gold and can hold your own in Mandarin (no one speaks English) – and can find your way there (it's a 20-minute journey from the CBD) – this is a treasure trove of furniture, carvings, and statues.
- **Radiance:** A great option if you are prepared to pay extra for one-stop shopping of renovated gleaming furniture – and it has a huge range of antique carpets too.

Souvenirs

- **Shard Box:** All clothes markets also sell the standard souvenirs, but for something different, try these dinky jewelry boxes with lids made from pieces of porcelain smashed during the Cultural Revolution; any woman in your life will love them.

the cute and covetable slippers at Suzhou Cobblers

- **Plastered:** For something younger and funkier, try these witty T-shirts – and be sure to stroll around the trendy **Nanluoguxiang** street for more great buys.

Clothing

If you have time to hit only one neighborhood, make it Sanlitun.

- **Red Phoenix:** Intimate boutique showcasing tailored glamour inspired by imperial designs.
- **3.3 shopping center:** The fourth floor is

the designer shops, you should enjoy the light Mod-Oz food at the trendy and upscale white-marble restaurant Laris, which is complete with its own oyster bar and sophisticated cocktail lounge, called Vault.

Day 3

Get up early and head to Yu Gardens in the Old City: The walled garden and surroundings are much more appealing when not rammed with tour groups. Perhaps a working lunch is necessary: If so, head to Din Tai Fung in Xintiandi for excellent *xiaolongbao* before caffeinating at Paul, which has wireless Internet access. While in Xintiandi, spend an absorbing 40 minutes in the Shikumen Open House Museum learning about the history of this most Shanghainese type of architecture. Stay in the French Concession for dinner and drinks: The 1930s charm of Yongfu Elite cannot be beat for a predinner tipple, especially during summer, when you can relax in

full of tailors ready to whip up whatever you fancy.

- **Wu Ba:** In the same building, on the ground floor, you'll find womenswear heaven here.
- **The Village:** This is next door: yet more designer clothes and boutiques.
- **Nali Mall:** Across the road is this locals' favorite for hip boutiques.

SHANGHAI

Souvenirs

- **Suzhou Cobblers:** Great souvenirs and gifts can be found at this almost-too-cute shop near the Bund: Its slippers, shoes, and bags come in clashing-colors silk from Suzhou.
- **Brocade Country:** More wonderful fabrics can be found here, including throws, clothes, and baby slings made by members of the Miao ethnic minority.

Clothing

The Shanghainese take great pride in being the most stylish people in China, and their boutiques are ubiquitous – selling everything from the cheap and cheerful, to the latest weird and wonderful designs, to understated sophistication.

- **Hongqiao International Pearl City:** Here you'll find the cheap T-shirts, ties, and shirts that tourists buy by the bagful and a whole floor of pearls awaiting you on the fourth floor.
- **Shirt Flag:** Head to one of the branches of this chain for more fashionable T-shirts and dresses.
- **insh:** For more cutting-edge, distinctly Shanghainese wear, this modern boutique in Taikang Lu is the place.

Xintiandi

If shopping time is limited, this area is full of interesting destinations.

- **Annabel Lee:** The cute silk purses here make great gifts – especially for yourself!
- **Shanghai Trio:** Its delightful (if expensive) designs include great bags and kids' stuff.
- **Shanghai Museum store:** This branch of the museum store sells lovely books and bags inspired by its collections. A few minutes' walk away is the most atmospheric women's boutique in the French Concession, **Roof 603 at Leaf.**

Home

- **Banmoo:** Tiny, ultrastylish homeware store in the French Concession.
- **Dongtai Lu antique market:** Toward the end of the day you're likely to get a good price at this street bazaar for that must-have copy of Mao's *Little Red Book* or that Buddha statue that the seller swears is older than time itself. . . .

the garden and then dine at nearby Japanese eatery Haiku, enjoying its funky California-style sushi rolls.

Day 4

If contemporary art is your thing, in the morning head to Moganshan Lu Art District for a browse-and-shopping session: The perfect souvenir might also be found in antique store Art Deco in the center of the complex. Business matters might take priority on your last day, but if you need to shop, Bund 18 is a gorgeous place to browse—and if the time is right, Bar Rouge is where the hip like to party, on the open-air roof terrace with fabulous views across to Pudong. For a more sophisticated venue, try dark and sexy Vue Bar in the Hyatt on the Bund. Your last meal deserves to be special: Choose luxurious haute cuisine at French eatery Jean Georges, where the views over Pudong compete with the glamorous interior of the restaurant.

CHINA WITH CHILDREN

Though many of Beijing and Shanghai's most famous attractions, such as the Forbidden City and the Bund, might produce a bit of a yawn from kids who aren't into history, there are plenty of other activities to entertain travelers of all ages. The Chinese love children, so they should be prepared to receive plenty of attention and the odd prod and poke from well-meaning adults who find Western kids incredibly cute. The one-child policy, under which Chinese couples have been restricted to having just one child from 1979, has produced a generation of "little emperors" and "little empresses," carrying the hopes and dreams of one set of parents and two sets of doting grandparents—which has in turn resulted in plenty of options to keep pampered kids occupied.

Of course, your kids must try traditional Chinese food, and kid-size chopsticks will make mealtimes easier; however, they're not easy to find in Beijing, so bring some with you if possible. Very few Chinese restaurants provide high chairs and children's changing areas, but most Western restaurants will, and both cities have plenty of these for that little taste of home.

Beijing

DAY 1

Chinese parks are where local families take their offspring to burn off some energy, so do the same and in Beijing, head to Ritan Park for the funny rides, the rock-climbing wall, and the exercise park, a sort of outside gymnasium—something of a novelty for Western kids. The kite flying will also amuse kids, especially if they can have a turn—most people are only too happy to oblige. To add in some history for the adults while keeping the kids happy, a climb up Jingshan Park to look out over the Forbidden City is a must—and in the park, look out for people singing and playing games of feather ball. Perhaps your kids would like to join in! Afterward, head to Comptoirs de France, which kids rate very highly thanks to the most gorgeous ice cream and hot chocolate in the world.

DAY 2

Even the most world-weary child can't fail to enjoy the Great Wall, and the Mutianyu section is probably the most kid-friendly, with cable cars to allow you to enjoy the pretty views and exciting slides for getting back

The Great Wall: The Mutianyu section is the most kid-friendly.

pedicabs ready to head out on a tour of Houhai Lake

down again in a hurry. In the evening, entertain the whole family with *The Legend of Kung Fu* at the Red Theater; or if that's sold out, the acrobatics at Chaoyang Theater are a good second choice. Afterward, check out Grandma's Kitchen for all-American food such as burgers and milkshakes.

DAY 3

Go early to avoid the crowds at the Blue Zoo aquarium, part of the Worker's Stadium complex. The main attraction is a 420-foot moving walkway that swirls around underneath the main tank, with sharks swimming overhead and other creatures swimming by. Then have some fun afterward with China's favorite pastime, karaoke—or KTV, as it's known here. Party World, Beijing's most popular karaoke spot, has lots of child-friendly pop songs. It's cheaper if you go before 6 P.M.—and there's free food!

DAY 4

Girls into glitter will love the cheap manicures and pedicures available for peanuts at Yaxiu Market in Sanlitun: While they get twinkly stickers and nail art painted onto their fingers and toes, you can do a shopping dash around the market. Then check out pretty Houhai Lake, another great place suitable for all the family: You can reserve a pedicab tour with the excellent China Culture Club to ensure an English-speaking tour guide, or you can rent one of the hilarious duck-style boats and get your kids to row with all their might while you relax for a change! That evening, experience one of Beijing's most entertaining restaurants for older children, thanks to its after-dinner entertainment: Red Rose Xinjiang Restaurant. If your kids like being on stage, they are welcome to join the snake-hipped dancing girls and shake their stuff. The only thing most kids (and adults) won't like are the toilets.

Shanghai

DAY 1

Even if the idea of trudging around a museum usually makes your kids break out in a cold sweat, the excellent Shanghai Science and Technology Museum will entertain even the most reluctant of children. Afterward, reward them (or punish them, if they are of a certain age and embarrassed by doing something so dorky) by renting tandem bicycles at nearby Century Park: Girls might enjoy

Kids love the weird and wonderful Oriental Pearl Tower.

watching the processions of brides there for their wedding photos. Next up is the weird and wonderfulness of the Oriental Pearl Tower—children can't fail to be impressed by the giddy heights of the city's tallest skyscrapers, and they can also learn something about Shanghai's history at the Shanghai Municipal History Museum on the ground floor. Nearby eats can be found at the Super Brand Shopping Mall. In the evening, the Cirque du Soleil–inspired show *Circus World* is brilliant family entertainment—make reservations for seats nearest the action.

DAY 2

The relative wildness of Gongqing Forest Park may entertain children bored of cityscapes and traffic jams: It's a good place to take a picnic or use one of the barbecue pits, as the food available on-site isn't great. After a full day there, older children might enjoy a foot massage at Jade Massage or a manicure at Dragonfly in the evening, or there's always a trip to the local karaoke palace to while away a few hours singing very loudly. The most child-friendly restaurant in Shanghai is Din Tai Fung, where you can order half-size child portions of the speciality, *xiaolongbao* dumplings. The restaurant and the restrooms are spotless, and there's even a small toy area and an entertaining DVD on in the background.

DAY 3

For more bizarre entertainment, try the sightseeing tunnel underneath the Huangpu River—or some kids may prefer to see the river from the top, by boat. Just don't do the boring 3.5-hour-long cruise! For lunch, street food such as Xinjiang-style lamb kebabs are kid-friendly, with their bite-size pieces of meat, but if your kids have had enough of Chinese food, the hearty and familiar fare at one of the branches of Blue Frog or KABB in Xintiandi is tasty, and the staff are very friendly. Anyone of any age with a sweet tooth will love the retro-style café Whisk, with its chocolate-based menu of treats.

BEIJING

As Beijing leads China to its place at the center of the world stage, the speed of change is exhilarating. But Beijing has been at the center of China's tumultuous history for thousands of years, from the first settlements in the 3rd century B.C. to the invasion of Mongolian warlord Genghis Kahn in 1215; from Mao's triumphant proclamation of the People's Republic of China in 1949 to the tragic events 40 years later in Tiananmen Square. Nowadays, visitors from just 10 years ago will not recognize the city Beijing has become.

Beijing's charm lies in its citizens' ability to simultaneously embrace their city's astonishing future and its legendary past – from teenage punks listening to rock music at 3 A.M. in bars overlooking the Forbidden City to old men practicing tai chi in the city's parks at dawn. Watching the sun set on the Forbidden City from the summit of Jingshan Park is an astonishing and overlooked spectacle, as is seeing your Beijing duck, glossy with molasses, roasting in a wood-burning oven in an untouristy back-street restaurant – just as they have for the past 100 years.

SIGHTS

China's capital has been a place of intrigue to travelers through the centuries, the city's name a byword for mystery and exoticism. Marco Polo, back in the 13th century, was struck by the city's classical wonders "past all possibility" while nowadays it is the city's striking modernity—the futuristic CCTV Building, the twisted splendor of the Olympic Stadium—that surprises visitors who come expecting the bland grayness of the Mao era. Really, Beijing encompasses them all: the classical, the futuristic, in addition to many drab reminders of the country's tumultuous 20th century.

This varied history has left behind a wealth of historical sights with the majority near the historic center Tiananmen, and there is something to see whatever direction you wander from the world's biggest square. But try not to overlook the less-well-known temples and attractions where you can escape the crowds. But whatever time of year you come, do expect crowds: Tourist numbers are growing by an average of 15 percent each year and in 2008, more than 500,000 overseas and one million domestic travelers were expected. Already the world's fourth-most-popular tourist destination, the country is expected to move to second within a decade and China is forecast to overtake the United States as the world's most-visited country by 2020. But don't worry if the swarms of people start to overwhelm you: Beijing has a few off-the-beaten-track attractions, such as the Military Museum, where you can rent plastic rifles and join in the shootin' fun, and the fascinating Urban Planning Hall with its exhibitions showcasing what the government has

HIGHLIGHTS

LOOK FOR ☾ TO FIND RECOMMENDED SIGHTS.

☾ **Best Address:** The **Forbidden City** allows a glimpse into how China's sons of heaven passed the time with their guards, servants, mandarins, eunuchs, concubines, families . . . (page 37).

☾ **Best Design for Upsetting the Neighbors:** The **National Center for Performing Arts**'s controversial space-age design has single-handedly put the staid buildings around Tiananmen in the shade (page 40).

☾ **Best Student Hangout:** The **Confucius Temple and Guozijian** is a beautiful refuge in the middle of the city and a great place to take kids moaning about their exams: Compared to imperial scholars, they don't know the meaning of hard work (page 42).

☾ **Best Place for People-Watching:** The lakes known collectively as **Houhai** are a great place to kick back with a cappuccino or beer at one of the many terraces up among the curved rooftops and watch local hipsters, fishermen, and lake swimmers in action (page 44).

☾ **Best Restoration:** The **Legation Quarter** illustrates where nightlife in Beijing is heading with the century-old former U.S. Embassy converted into the city's ritziest dining, arts, and entertainment venue (page 47).

☾ **Best Stroll in the Park:** Away from the awesome temple buildings, the **Temple of Heaven**'s grounds are perfect for wandering among the cypress trees and finding a secluded corner (page 49).

☾ **Best Jaw-Dropping Architecture:** The architect said he was not sure whether the twisted design was even possible, but the **New CCTV Building** seems to be holding itself up nicely and has become one of the city's newest landmarks in the process (page 50).

☾ **Best Art Lesson:** Beijing's museums used to be out-and-out awful, but with the opening of the **Beijing Capital Museum** gone are the days of dusty exhibits and boring displays (page 52).

☾ **Best Place for Boating in Summer and Ice-Skating in Winter:** The **Summer Palace** was where emperors came and relaxed and now you can do the same against the wonderful backdrop of Longevity Hill (page 54).

☾ **Best Symbol of the New China:** The **National Stadium** is the capital's newest icon, where national pride soars from the Bird's Nest (page 56).

the Olympic Bird's Nest Stadium

in store for the capital. Peaceful corners such as the quiet garden at Song Qingling's Residence and wandering through the quiet *hutong* streets can also provide a place for weary travelers to catch their breaths.

Beijing's topography of flat plains is terrifically helpful to travelers looking to navigate around a city of 15 million. The concentric ring roads that loop round the city and the wide-open avenues and straight roads make for easy passage if not quick journeys in the snarled-up traffic. The new subway lines, though, have hugely improved getting around and about—it's a world of difference since 2006.

But it's not just transport that has changed: Even the most familiar of sights have, too. As part of the city's preparations for the Olympics, many major attractions, including the Forbidden City and the Temple of Heaven, were given major makeovers: Just before the opening ceremony, the bamboo scaffolding was removed, the paint was dry, and many monuments were once again ready to impress and intrigue. The resilient capital has reinvented itself once again.

Tiananmen

Map 1

(Tiān'ānmén 天安门)

Be prepared to do plenty of walking if you want to do justice to the myriad of sights that make up the Tiananmen area, but it's worth it: No matter what direction you travel, you see sometimes sublime and always interesting examples of Chinese architecture from through the ages. North from the square is the glorious red-walled imperial Forbidden City, hidden away from commoners for hundreds of years. To the east down Chang'an Jie is the century-old French-style Beijing Hotel; the solemn and imposing Great Hall of the People, which clearly displays its Russian lineage, is to the west of the square; and at both the north and south ends lie huge and commanding gates that all visitors to Beijing once had to pass through to gain access to the city.

BEIHAI PARK

(BĚIHǍI GŌNGYUÁN 北海公园)

1 Wenjin Jie, 6403 1102

HOURS: Daily 6 A.M.-10 P.M.

COST: 20RMB, students 10RMB, last ticket sold 30 minutes before closing

Lovely in all seasons, this huge park, which was originally built for Genghis Khan's grandson Kublai, is one of the oldest imperial gardens in the world. It is centered around a lake that one can boat on during summer and ice-skate on in winter. Initially built in the 10th century, the park was part of the Forbidden City, but since 1925, it is open to the public, which uses the park from dawn until dusk. Most of the park buildings were constructed during Emperor Qianlong's reign (1736–1796) during the Qing dynasty. The eye-catching Buddhist-style White Pagoda on Qiongdao Island in the middle of the lake is worth exploring. In addition to the lake, the lovely landscaped gardens complete with hills, pavilions, halls, temples, and covered corridors are equally attractive.

CHAIRMAN MAO'S MEMORIAL HALL

(MÁOZHǓXÍ JÌNIÀNTÁNG 毛主席纪念堂)

Center of Tiananmen Square, 6513 2255

HOURS: Tues.-Sun. 8:30-11:30 A.M., extended hours Tues. and Thurs. 2-4 P.M., July-Aug. A.M. only

COST: Free

His teachings and philosophies may have long been forgotten by the majority of Chinese more interested in mammon than Mao, but the Great Helmsman's mausoleum is still a sober place of pilgrimage, though whether that will change anytime soon is anyone's guess. Work on the mausoleum began straight after Mao's death in 1976—despite his wishes to be cremated—and completed a year later. Although the queues of people can stretch almost across the square during public holidays, the atmosphere is one of reflection and somberness: Laughing and joking will not go down well. The actual building looks like an overgrown school gymnasium plonked down in the middle of the square; inside, the actual room where Mao lies in state on a bed covered in a crystalline sarcophagus and surrounded by flowers is dimly lit, and you cannot stop and get a good look as security guards will usher you on. At Mao's death, China did not have the embalming technologies needed to preserve Mao's body for public display and was forced to turn to Vietnam for help. However, the effectiveness of the embalming is subject to debate because there is significant controversy over whether the body is real. The body is on display for at most a few hours each day—with further restrictions during summer-fueling speculation that if the body is real, it is decaying rapidly. Whether you find the actual sight creepy or not, witnessing people's genuine displays of emotion is an interesting experience, as is seeing the plastic flowers that can be rented and laid down near his body before they are swept away and rented again to the next lot of people. After all the somberness, you end up in a cheap and tacky market where you can buy any amount of Mao memorabilia.

CHINA NATIONAL MUSEUM (ZHŌNGGUÓ GUÓJIĀ BÓWÙGUǍN 中国国家博物馆)

East side of Tiananmen Square, 8447 4914, www.nationalmuseum.cn

HOURS: unknown

COST: unknown

The imposing national museum on the east side of Tiananmen was to be closed until 2010 as the museum receives a well-overdue major upgrade. Built in the same era as the Great Hall of the People, which is opposite, the museum was a dusty old-fashioned relic of the past and in no way a good conduit for displaying China's 5,000 years of history. If the new

EMPEROR YONGLE

Perhaps the greatest of all Chinese emperors, Yongle was the third emperor of the Ming dynasty and is remembered by the Chinese for his achievements in developing Chinese culture, especially in Beijing, and expanding Chinese influence, as well as for his despotic streak. He was born in 1360 and became the prince of Yan, responsible for keeping the region surrounding Beijing safe from the Mongol hordes. When his nephew succeeded to the throne, the prince seized the crown and became emperor after his nephew disappeared in a mysterious palace fire. Yongle brutally purged China of the previous emperor's supporters and destroyed all records of the four-year reign to establish himself as the legitimate successor to the Ming dynasty. A prominent historian refused to acknowledge the emperor, so he was murdered along with every single generation of his family and his students and peers: 873 people in all, the legend goes.

Yongle expanded China's sphere of influence by sending out ships of exploration, most notably the explorer Zheng He, who may have reached the United States, and he unified the country, keeping the empire safe from its many enemies. He is also forever associated with the city of Beijing: He transferred China's capital from Nanjing to where it is now, and he personally planned the Forbidden City, the huge network of buildings in which government offices, officials, and the imperial family itself lived – which was the political capital of China for the next 500 years. Yongle also had the Grand Canal repaired and reopened to provision the new capital of Beijing in the north with a steady flow of supplies.

Before his death Yongle selected a peaceful resting place where he envisaged himself and all his successors lying in eternity. His tomb, called Changling, is the central and largest mausoleum of the Ming Tombs – it resembles a miniature Forbidden City and it is well worth a visit to see the tomb with its huge bronze statue of one of China's most famous historical figures.

FORBIDDEN CITY (GÙGŌNG 故宫)

Entering from the south gate from Tiananmen Square, visitors first pass under Mao's portrait and through Tiananmen Gate and into the next courtyard, the largest square in the palace complex; it serves as the entrance to the Forbidden City and it's where you will find the ticket office plus a whole host of hawkers selling postcards and books. And don't be confused by the signs that say Palace Museum – you are at the right place. The audio tour is just about worth it for 40RMB plus a 100RMB deposit, but if you have a guidebook you don't really need it. Young people may come up to you and ask if you'd like a personal tour guide – these guys get mixed reports as their grasp of history is not perfect, but if you do choose to have a guide, agree on a price right away. If coming by taxi, it's best to be dropped off at the east or north gate as taxis can't stop on Tiananmen Square.

MERIDIAN GATE (WŬMÉN 午门)

After going through the ticket and security check, follow the swarms of tourists through the narrow passageway through the center of this gate, which was built in 1420. While silent now, bells and drums in the gate tower used to be sounded when the emperor attended important ceremonies. Just inside the gate, in the large stone courtyard between this gate and the next, criminals who had offended the Forbidden City's occupants were executed in the shadow of the imposing and forbidding gate.

GATE OF SUPREME HARMONY (TÀIHÉMÉN 太和门)

This gate is guarded by a couple of bronze lions that symbolize different aspects of imperial life: To the west is the male lion with its front right paw resting on a ball, symbolizing imperial power over the world, and to the east is a lioness with her paw on a lion cub, representing a growing family and an imperial lineage stretching off into the future.

HALL OF COMPLETE HARMONY (TÀIHÉDIÀN 太和殿)

This hall was covered in scaffolding for two years, but now the bamboo poles have been removed and the hall, the biggest in the complex and the first hall of the three that make up the Forbidden City's more ceremonial outer court, is considered the single most impressive piece of architecture in the palace. Here is where important ceremonies were held: to celebrate a new emperor's ascention to the throne, birthdays, weddings, winter solstice, Chinese New Year, and announcements of war. From the 14th to the early 20th century, the hall was the most important building in Chinese politics. Twenty-four emperors ascended the sandalwood throne, which stands on a two-meter-high platform in the center of the hall, surrounded by six gold-lacquered pillars carved with dragons. Look up to the ceiling and see the huge pearl known as the Xuanyuan Mirror. Legend has it that the pearl would be able to detect any pretender to the crown and would fall and kill any usurper who was making himself comfortable on the throne. Hundreds of years later, warlord Yuan Shikai, who attempted to take the throne after the forced abdication of the last emperor Puyi in 1911, was so afraid that the pearl would strike him dead that he ordered the throne to be moved slightly backward and not directly below the pearl, and it remains there today.

HALL OF CENTRAL HARMONY (ZHŌNGHÉDIÀN 中和殿)

Think of this hall as the world's grandest rehearsal room, as this is where the emperors prepared for the ceremonies that marked court life. Before the annual procession down to the Temple of Heaven, the emperor would practice his speech here. This smallest of the three main halls in the Outer Court was originally built in 1420 and restored in 1627 and again in 1765.

HALL OF PRESERVING HARMONY (BǍOHÉDIÀN 保和殿)

While the previous hall was for rehearsals, there were no second chances in this hall, which struck fear into students desperate to enter the royal court: This is where the

(continues on page 36)

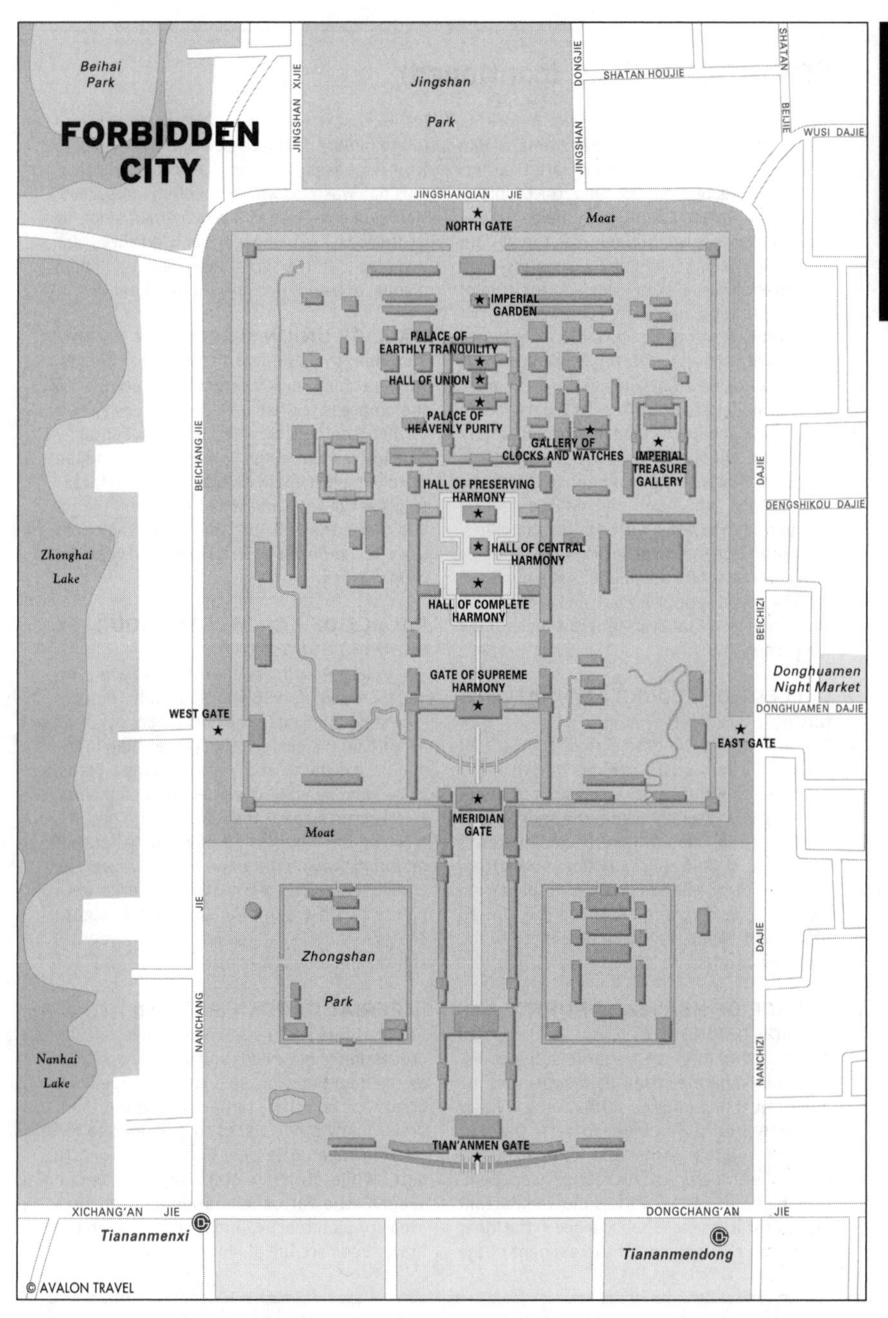
FORBIDDEN CITY
Beihai Park
Jingshan Park
JINGSHAN XIJIE
JINGSHAN DONGJIE
SHATAN HOUJIE
SHATAN BEIJIE
WUSI DAJIE
JINGSHANQIAN JIE
NORTH GATE
Moat
IMPERIAL GARDEN
PALACE OF EARTHLY TRANQUILITY
HALL OF UNION
PALACE OF HEAVENLY PURITY
GALLERY OF CLOCKS AND WATCHES
IMPERIAL TREASURE GALLERY
HALL OF PRESERVING HARMONY
HALL OF CENTRAL HARMONY
HALL OF COMPLETE HARMONY
GATE OF SUPREME HARMONY
BEICHANG JIE
DENGSHIKOU DAJIE
BEICHIZI DAJIE
Zhonghai Lake
Donghuamen Night Market
DONGHUAMEN DAJIE
WEST GATE
EAST GATE
MERIDIAN GATE
Moat
Zhongshan Park
NANCHANG JIE
NANCHIZI DAJIE
Nanhai Lake
TIAN'ANMEN GATE
XICHANG'AN JIE
DONGCHANG'AN JIE
Tiananmenxi
Tiananmendong
© AVALON TRAVEL

FORBIDDEN CITY (continued)

imperial examinations were held. Before its use as the most important examination room in the land, emperors often prepared for ceremonies here, but in 1789, Emperor Qianlong moved the Palace Examination here. He and future emperors would honor the top 10 candidates by reading their papers, and those who passed the palace exam received the title of doctor, assuring their status and wealth.

If by this stage you'd like a break, between the Hall of Preserving Harmony and the next gate is a coffee shop and rest area. It used to be a Starbucks but after a TV personality began a campaign to clear the Forbidden City of foreign influences, the coffee shop lost its license – the current incumbent sells Chinese coffee only. While one can have a certain amount of sympathy with the campaigners, the argument that Starbucks was somehow adversely affecting the image of the buildings can't be taken seriously when an Olympic souvenir shop full of tacky products is just around the corner.

GALLERY OF CLOCKS AND WATCHES (ZHŌNGBIĂO GUĂN 钟表馆)

The gallery, on the east side of the Gate of Heavenly Purity, costs an extra 10RMB and is really worth visiting only if the sight of about 200 clocks and watches from the imperial collection is appealing to you. The collection is composed of Chinese-made timepieces from through the ages and classic examples from Switzerland, England, France, the United States and Japan that were presented to the emperor as gifts.

PALACE OF HEAVENLY PURITY (QIÁNQĪNG GŌNG 乾清宫)

After walking through the large stone courtyard that separates the Outer Court and the Inner Court and passing through the Gate of Heavenly Purity, you'll get to here, the first hall of three that comprise the inner palace where the emperor and his retinue lived. Befitting the home of the world's most important man but still the most public place in the Inner Court, the hall is the most extravagant of the lot. Here emperors would sit on the throne in the middle of the palace and hear reports from ambassadors and visiting dignitaries. This hall was also where questions of succession were answered as the incumbent emperor wrote down the name of his chosen successor and placed it in a secret box hidden behind a plaque, to be opened only upon his death.

HALL OF UNION (JIĀOTÀIDIÀN 交泰殿)

This hall, the smallest of the inner courts, was first built in 1420 and was given over to the empress for her use. She would receive formal greetings here and be waited upon by concubines and eunuchs – uncastrated men were not allowed anywhere near the empress to preserve the sanctity of the royal bloodline. Inside the hall, you can still see the boxes used for imperial seals and a 200-year-old bronze clock.

PALACE OF EARTHLY TRANQUILITY (KŪNNÍNG GŌNG 坤宁宫)

This palace was first built in 1420 but was completely rebuilt in 1655 and is the only Manchurian-style building in the Forbidden City, with its gate on the eastern side rather than in the middle. It is the most private of all the halls as, in the Qing dynasty, it was where the emperor and empress spent their wedding night. Afterward, the emperor would move to another bedroom, leaving the empress to this one. The chamber was painted red and lanterns were painted with traditional Double Happiness characters, 双喜 – if you look closely you can still see the unrestored bridal bed.

IMPERIAL GARDEN (HUĀYUÁN 花园)

Some visitors find the seemingly never-ending procession of huge halls and imposing palaces on the daunting side, so if you're in need of a break (and now that Starbucks has gone, there aren't many other places to go), head to the relaxing Imperial Gardens just inside the north gate. While during winter the grounds can seem a little bare, the gnarled ancient trees are very picturesque, and in the summer, the flower beds are full of blooms. There are also plenty of small halls, rock gardens, and pagodas where you can escape from the crowds.

IMPERIAL TREASURE GALLERY

(GÙGŌNG HUÀLÁNG 故宫画廊)

Sometimes visitors complain that they thought there would be more to see in the actual halls and palaces – in fact, most of the treasure that wasn't carted off to Taiwan by the fleeing nationalists at the end of China's civil war is in here, not in the actual palace buildings. You have to pay an extra 10RMB for access to the gallery and unlike the Gallery of Clocks and Watches, this is definitely worth the money. The gallery consists of three imperial palaces that have been turned into three exhibition halls, each containing priceless artifacts such as dinner sets made of gold, silver, and jade. The dinner sets were mostly made of silver as it was believed the silver would turn black if anyone were attempting to poison the emperor. Other exhibits include imperial seals, incense burners and other religious vessels and bowls, and jade and bejeweled gifts given to the emperor or from him to his favorite concubines.

National Capital Museum is anything to go by, the revamped National Museum will be high-tech and well designed and have (one hopes) banished the old-fashioned English captions full of terms such as "foreign invaders" and "colonial oppressors." The museum's south, north, and west wings were being updated while new buildings were being constructed in the east to allow more of the 620,000 exhibits to be displayed.

FORBIDDEN CITY (GÙGŌNG 故宫)

North of Tiananmen Square, 6513 2255, www.dpm.org.cn

HOURS: Oct.-Apr. daily 8:30 A.M.-4:30 P.M., Apr.-Oct. daily 8:30 A.M.-5 P.M.

COST: 60RMB, children under 1.2m free, last ticket sold 30 minutes before closing, 40RMB audio tour

Considered Beijing's must-see attraction, the sheer spectacle of burnt-crimson 20-foot walls, towering gates, and magnificent ceremonial halls used by 24 emperors through the ages is indeed a highlight of any trip—it's just a shame that the crowds can sometimes be overwhelming. Today, the Forbidden City is a public museum and UNESCO World Heritage Site, but originally, the Ming dynasty masterpiece was a private home, albeit the home to China's sons of heaven and built as a monument to the power and glory of the empire, meant to intimidate all who entered. Even now, the structure's high walls and grandiose ceremonial halls, plus the sheer size of the place—the whole complex is 900 meters long and 750 meters wide with more than 9,700 rooms—can leave visitors feeling overwhelmed.

In the early 1400s, the third Ming Emperor Yongle moved the capital of China to Beijing, and he began construction of a new Forbidden City that would include the imperial palace complex. If you enter through the south gate immediately opposite Tiananmen Square, you progress through Tiananmen Gate, which has been in its present form since 1651, through the passageway under Mao's portrait. (Every once in a while, the portrait is the target of some foolhardy protest: In 2007, a man threw a lit object at the picture that set part of it on fire before he was promptly arrested and the portrait replaced by another.) It was from this gate that Mao addressed the crowds in Tiananmen Square and announced the formation of the PRC. Just follow the crowds and make your way into the next huge open square: You buy your tickets on the left-hand side near the next imposing gate, the Meridian Gate. Once you are through that, you are in the actual Forbidden City.

The complex has faced more than its fair share of drama and intrigue. After the fall of the Qing dynasty in 1911, the priceless imperial collections of jewelry, art, and artifacts were plundered

© HELENA IVESON

the Palace of Heavenly Purity inside the Forbidden City

by pilfering eunuchs who had left imperial service. Remaining property was then spirited away to the city of Nanjing when the Japanese invaded, and the Kuomintang took 4,000 crates worth of treasure to Taiwan after the country's civil war, which followed World War II. Then during the Cultural Revolution, Red Guards marched to the palace and were set to destroy this discredited symbol of feudalism before the country's premier Zhou Enlai ordered troops to defend it. For the next five years, the palace remained closed until it was opened the year before Richard Nixon's historic visit in 1971.

To visitors, especially on a hot crowded day, the Forbidden City can seem an endless parade of identical buildings (and now that Starbucks was forced to close its branch within the city walls, there isn't even anywhere to get a cup of coffee), but the trick is to not try and see too much in one day and take your time in exploring quiet niches. If you leave by the east gate, be sure to follow the moat around heading north: The route takes you around the gray walls of the Forbidden City and is one of the most picturesque and romantic walks to be found in Beijing, especially at night. And if you get tired, a public sightseeing electric bus will take you around the complex for 1RMB.

GREAT HALL OF THE PEOPLE

(RÉNMÍNDÀHUÌTÁNG 人民大会堂)

West side of Tiananmen Square, 6309 6156

HOURS: Daily if not in session 8:30 A.M.–3:30 P.M.

COST: 30RMB, students 15RMB

The huge Soviet-style complex is used for legislative and ceremonial activities and serves as the country's "congress" for the Communist Party's annual meeting. It was built in September 1959 as one of the "10 Great Constructions" completed for the 10th anniversary of the People's Republic. Legend has it that it was built in 10 months by volunteers. Originally, the building was to be completely Soviet in style, but because of a Sino-Soviet cooling of relations, the planned Russian-style cupolas were scrapped and traditional Chinese-style eaves were built instead. One can't help feel that whichever way the building's style went, designers were going for imposing rather than attractive. Inside the building, each province, special administrative

Tiananmen Gate, with its iconic portrait of Mao

region, and autonomous region of China has its hall and is supposed to display the unique characteristics and style of the province, though to this heathen, they all look much the same: The actual rooms you get to see alternate. The highlight of the tour, for political animals anyway, is the main 10,000-seat auditorium: If you're visiting, you'll be given a pair of plastic covers to wear over your shoes in case you mark the carpets. You cannot take any bags in with you: Deposit them at the "depositary" for a nominal fee next door to the ticket office, which is 200 meters south of the main entrance.

JINGSHAN PARK

(JǏNGSHĀN GŌNGYUÁN 景山公园)

Jingshanqian Jie, 6404 4071

HOURS: Daily 6 A.M.-10 P.M.

COST: 5RMB

Across the road from the north gate of the Forbidden City and on the central axis of Beijing, this park and its central hill were formed in 1420 from the soil dug out from the moat around the palace. Handily, the hill helped the Forbidden City's feng shui, protecting the emperors from the icy cold northern winds. The park is famous among the Chinese as it was where the last Ming Emperor Chongzhen hung himself from a tree as Manchu troops approached the city walls. Nowadays, it's a peaceful place full of well-established trees and greenery with a trail running around the bottom of the hill. If your legs can manage the short climb, be sure to head to the pagoda at the top of the hill: If you're there in the early evening, the views down to the Forbidden City with the sun's setting behind the burnt-crimson walls are indescribably lovely.

NATIONAL ART MUSEUM OF CHINA

(ZHŌNGGUÓ MĚISHÙGUǍN 中国美术馆)

1 Wusi Dajie, 6401 7076, 6401 2252, www.namoc.org

HOURS: Tues.-Sun. 8:30 A.M.-4 P.M.

COST: 20RMB

At the top end of Wangfujing, this huge and drafty building may not look too appealing from the inside but persevere as inside the museum regularly stages interesting if conservative exhibitions showcasing the best art from around China as well as traveling exhibitions from abroad (recently, 52 works from grand masters from the Prado in Madrid). Unsurprisingly, given its resemblance to the Great Hall of the People and the National Museum, the art museum is another of the 10 grand buildings constructed to commemorate 10 years since the founding of the PRC. The museum was completed in 1962 and still carries Mao Zedong's calligraphy above the entrance. Despite recent renovation, the museum is still lacking in signage and printed information, but its bright and airy space has five floors with 15 different exhibition halls so you're sure to find something interesting. The permanent exhibitions offer conventional Chinese art, so expect plenty of scroll paintings on traditional themes such as mountains and water. Choose the time of your visit wisely—toward the end of the day is best as crowds do build up to see the exhibitions. This museum, being state run, caters to a conservative crowd: For more contemporary art, go to the Dashanzi art district in Chaoyang District.

NATIONAL CENTER FOR PERFORMING ARTS (GUÓJIĀ DÀ JÙYUÀN 国家大剧院)

Xichang'an Jie, 6655 0000, www.chncpa.org

HOURS: 10 A.M.-end of show

COST: Building admission free, tickets start at 50RMB

You can't miss this enormous glass and titanium structure's innovative design, which has breathed new life into this historic part of Beijing. Some absolutely hate the design, which stands out in the area for being more space-age than Stalinist. The $400 million theater was designed by French architect Paul Andreu, who also designed Charles De Gaulle International Airport in Paris. Directly across from the Great Hall of the People and Tiananmen Square, the theater outdoes the two historical and political symbols of the capital. After a decade of controversy over its design, location, and budget, it finally opened in September 2007. The building itself awes its audiences, who have to first pass under a giant moat, with its state-of-the-art stage mechanics and acoustics. Inside, there are three halls—a 2,416-seat opera house, 2,017-seat concert hall, and 1,040-seat theater—and the spaces are pleasant if somewhat anticlimactic after the exterior. Don't expect good intermission drinks as there isn't much more than a coffee stand. Do visit for the glorious architectural feats and the world's finest orchestras, operas, and musicals.

TIANANMEN SQUARE (TIĀN'ĀNMÉN 天安门)

Tiananmen Square, Chang'an Jie, 6524 3322

HOURS: Daily 6 A.M.-9 P.M.

COST: Free

Named after the Tiananmen, or Gate of Heavenly Peace, that marks the entrance to the Forbidden City, the square symbolizes different things to different people. While in Western eyes, the world's biggest public square will be forever synonymous with the student protests that ended in death for countless hundreds if not thousands in 1989, to the Chinese, the concreted plaza designed to hold a million people is mainly a place for flying kites, standing to attention for the daily flag-raising and lowering ceremonies, and watching the world go by.

During the Qing dynasty, the area served as a walkway between ministry buildings; it was not until 1949 that it was enlarged to the current size of 440,000 square meters and flanked by the Soviet-style buildings that were built to celebrate the 10th anniversary of the People's Republic of China. On the west side of the square is the Great Hall of the People, and directly opposite it on the east side is the National Museum of China.

Many of China's most important historical moments have played out on the square, such as the May Fourth Movement on May 4, 1919, which fueled the birth of the Communist Party; Mao Zedong's proclamation of the People's Republic of China on October 1, 1949; many mass rallies with Red Guards waving their *Little Red Book*s during the Cultural Revolution; and the 1989 student protests on the night of June 4, 1989. Young people had occupied the square for three weeks calling for democracy, until the army put an end to it by ruthlessly firing on thousands of unarmed citizens.

Whatever your feelings about the place's history, you may find it hard to get excited about

© HELENA IVESON

the world's biggest square: Tiananmen Square

such a blank and concreted area, especially during winter when the wind whips straight through. If flying kites doesn't thrill you, try instead to spot the many plainclothes police officers constantly there to keep an eye out for potential troublemakers. The square used to be a popular place for courting couples to stroll around at dusk, but for security reasons, it is now closed at night.

ZHONGNANHAI (ZHŌNGNÁNHǍI 中南海)

Xi Chang'an Jie

The United States has the White House, and China has Zhongnanhai, home to China's top leaders and the headquarters for the Communist Party. The complex is as mysterious to the Chinese public now as the Forbidden City was when it was occupied by emperors. While not a tourist attraction in itself—it's closed to the public, and photography is forbidden in places, such as at the main gate—even from the outside of the mysterious complex, you can get a sense of the power wielded inside behind its vermilion walls. Before liberation in 1949, Zhongnanhai was the municipal government headquarters, and China's first premier, Zhou Enlai, ordered the compound's dilapidated buildings to be repaired and converted them to their current use. The building's main entrance has been the site of protests that have led to some of the defining moments in Chinese modern history, from Red Guards' demanding in 1967 the ousting of then-President Liu Shaoqi, whom they thought a traitor to the revolution, to the 1989 student protests that were ignored and then bloodily quashed during the Tiananmen Massacre. Controversial religious group the Falun Gong also staged a protest here in 1999 before being promptly banned and persecuted by the state. The slogans visible from the main Chang'an Jie gate say, "long live the great Communist Party of China" and "long live the invincible Mao Zedong Thought."

ZHONGSHAN PARK (ZHŌNGSHĀN GŌNGYUÁN 中山公园)

West of the Tiananmen Gate, 6605 5431

HOURS: Summer daily 6 A.M.-9 P.M., winter daily 6:30 A.M.-8 P.M.

COST: 3RMB

If the crowds at the Forbidden City become

too much, take a break in this formal but inviting park immediately to the west of the complex, named after Sun Yat-sen, revered by many Chinese as the "father of modern China." It was originally for the emperor's personal use and part of the Forbidden City; in 1421, Emperor Yongle ordered the Shejitan altar to be built here, for sacrifices to the God of Grain. The emperor visited twice a year: in the spring, to bring a good harvest, and in the autumn for thanksgiving. In 1914, the altar grounds became a public park, and in 1928 they were renamed in memory of China's first great revolutionary political leader, Sun Zhongshan (also known as Sun Yat-sen). In addition to taking time to explore the wide sweeping tree-lined walkways and small pagodas dotted around, be sure to rent a boat and paddle along the Forbidden City's moat for some excellent views accessible only by water. For an even quieter place to recharge your batteries, be sure to walk through lush Changpu River Park (daily 6 A.M.–10 P.M., free) on the other side of the Forbidden City. Split into two parts on either side of Nanchizi Jie, the park was reopened in 2003 after being ignominiously used as a storage facility for the Forbidden City in the 1960s. The park has a river running through it and is much more beautiful in the summer when the flowers are out.

Houhai to the Olympic Stadium — Map 2

(Hòuhǎi, Àolínpǐkè tǐyùchǎn 后海, 奥林匹克体育场)

CONFUCIUS TEMPLE AND GUOZIJIAN (KǑNGMIÀO, GUÓZǏJIÀN 孔庙 国子监)

13 Guozijian Jie, 8402 7224

HOURS: Daily 9 A.M.-5 P.M.

COST: 10RMB, students 3RMB

This quiet but impressive temple and the attached imperial college Guozijian is a wonderful oasis away from the hustle and bustle of Beijing. The temple commemorates China's best-known philosopher, who, after being officially denounced and ignored during the turmoil of the Cultural Revolution, is now experiencing resurgence in popularity with the sage's philosophies again taught in schools. First built in 1302, the complex has been knocked down and renovated throughout its history and the main hall has been freshly repainted. While some visitors prefer the unrenovated gently fading buildings, the newly painted buildings are bright and inviting. The temple's courtyard is full of stele commemorating the scholars who passed the imperial exam during the Qing, Ming, and part of the Yuan dynasties: Unfortunately you cannot read the characters on the stele any more because of weathering. Those students took the exams next door in Guozijian just to the west of the temple. This was the highest institute of learning in China's educational system and served as a "cramming" school for the imperial exam. By 1462, the school had 13,000 students who got to study in the stunning central hall, which resembles the Hall of Prayer for Good Harvests at the Temple of Heaven with its pointed ornate roof topped by a golden center point. The square hall, which has been freshly painted, is enclosed by a small moat and the gardens surrounding the moat serve as a beautiful place to while away an hour among the well-established cypress trees with birds warbling away. These two sights receive relatively few visitors, so if you need a break from the crowds but want to still experience imperial architecture, head here.

DRUM AND BELL TOWERS (GǓLÓU, ZHŌNGLÓU 鼓楼钟楼)

Di'ananmen Dajie, 6401 2674

HOURS: Daily 9 A.M.-5:30 P.M.

COST: 20RMB Drum Tower, 15RMB Bell Tower

These two mighty structures that dwarf the area's *hutong* alleys and houses once served as the capital's timepieces for the court officials who used to live in the area. The two buildings date

HERE TODAY, *HUTONG* TOMORROW

The Chinese don't do preservation well. The city has changed beyond belief in the last decade without too many complaints from local residents, but now people are waking up to the fact that unless people start doing something about it, the local *hutong* – the small residential alleys that give Beijing so much character – and the courtyard homes that line the alleys will soon be a distant memory, bulldozed to make way for new office buildings and anonymous-looking blocks of flats.

Hutong means "water well" in Mongolian and as no building was allowed to overshadow the Forbidden City, the low-level single-story courtyards spread out from the center to cover the city. Each family courtyard, called *siheyuan* in Chinese, consists of an enclosed inward-looking rectangular compound with just one entrance at the southeast and windows facing in toward the courtyard rather than out toward the street. The buildings always face south because it's meant to be good feng shui. And the inner door is never aligned with the outer door so as to stop ghosts from entering. Each structure is topped with gray roof tiles, and they are so tightly packed that no structure shows itself fully. The Chinese believe the true beauty of a *siheyuan* is in the whole, the way it fits together, reflecting traditional Chinese ways of thinking. Yet only one-third of Beijing's ancient *hutong* still exist; most have been demolished or heavily damaged. Areas such as Qianmen to the south of Tiananmen Square used to house some of Beijing's oldest traditional courtyards and were the city's merchants' quarters, some dating from the 13th century, but many are gone, removed to make way for new developments.

It must be said that some Chinese who lived in these picturesque but run-down homes were thrilled when the character *chāi* 拆, which means "demolish," was painted on their walls and they were free to use the compensation money to buy a brand-new apartment full of the latest modern conveniences, but many historians and social campaigners bemoan the end of the close community networks that were a result of sharing communal courtyards and toilets and washing facilities.

Records show that there were 3,679 *hutong* in the 1980s. That figure has dropped by more than 40 percent, with up to 600 *hutong* destroyed each year. When the government finally realized that at least some of old Beijing should exist for visitors during the Olympics, it introduced restoration guidelines, necessitating that *hutong* are rebuilt with original materials and retain their gray color. The interior toilets of many courtyard houses are being rebuilt, and communal toilets have been upgraded. Nothing, it seems, will stand in the way of progress in Beijing, so go and see some *hutong* while you still can – in the famous alleys near Houhai or the historically preserved Dongsi *hutong* off Chaoyangmen Wai Dajie.

only from the 1800s but similar structures have stood on the site since the 13th century, when a Yuan dynasty city makeover saw all the capital's important buildings placed on a north-south axis. The two towers used to boom out a morning bell and a dusk drum to keep people running like clockwork. Today, in the age of digital watches and mobile phones, the Drum Tower is not needed for its original function, but it still houses 25 drums that are beaten for visitors roughly every 30 minutes. Just north of the Drum Tower is the brick and stone Bell Tower with its 500-year-old bronze bell: Alongside it are two two-meter-long wooden logs that you can pay to ram into the bell for a satisfying ring. Both towers offer superb views of the surrounding *hutong* and over Houhai: If it's really clear, you can see the Forbidden City on the same north–south axis, and on a clear day armed with binoculars you can see the Olympic Stadium to the north. The Drum and Bell Bar on the western side of the courtyard between the two towers is a popular place for a beer and pizza and a great place to check out the neighborhood. Once all the tour buses have departed, the area reverts to a local hangout with kids playing in the streets and old people gathered around mah-jongg tables.

HOUHAI (HÒUHǍI 后海)

Di'anmen Xidajie, opposite the north gate of Beihai Park

When Kublai Khan reshaped the city as his capital in the 13th century, he enlarged existing ponds to form the chain of lakes that now run through its center. This body of water became an imperial pleasure palace and was part of the network of imperial canals that once allowed royals to boat all the way to the Summer Palace. Now, this trio of lakes, which are now collectively known as Houhai despite that's being the name of just the middle lake, are a pleasure ground for Beijing residents. This area is one of Beijing's most picturesque, with willows trailing around the water's edge, though there were worrying signs that that may be about to change. Up until recently, the only action used to be a few boats on the lake, quiet music from the No Name Bar, or the public dancing sessions in which you'd see people come out and waltz of an evening. Nowadays, Houhai at night is lit up by the neon lights from the hundreds of bars and restaurants around the lake that broadcast a variety of conflicting music blaring for all to hear. If you walk around after dark be wary of the pedicab drivers, who move at quite a speed. During the day, however, Houhai's charm is still self-evident the farther away you get from Yinding Qiao or Silver Ingot Bridge (the epicenter of the action): Look out for the arched stone bridges and intricate animal sculptures on canal walls and be sure to wander around the back streets, where life continues as it has for hundreds of years. Or kick back on one of the many bars' rooftop terraces and watch the world go by. In summer, some swim in the lakes but I'd strongly recommend boating instead unless you want a dose of diarrhea, and in winter, look out for Beijing's famed ice swimmers, who strip down to their trunks and dive into the icy waters. If Houhai is too noisy, go to the much more serene Xihai, where you'll see plenty of fishermen around the shore. On the northern edge of this lake is a hill with Huitongci, a Buddhist temple, on the top. It may look ancient, but it has been there only since 1988, after the original, which was built in 1403, was nearly demolished to make way for an underground station.

Yinding Qiao, or Silver Ingot Bridge, at Houhai

LAMA TEMPLE (YŌNGHÉ GŌNG 雍和宫)

12 Yonghegong Dajie, 6404 4499

HOURS: Daily 9 A.M.-4:30 P.M.

COST: 25RMB, 20RMB audio tour

This splendidly atmospheric temple is one of Beijing's more unusual, having started life as a residence for a Qing dynasty prince who later became Emperor Yongzheng. The owner's status explains why the complex has golden roof tiles: an honor for those of royal blood only. After the death of the prince, a large portion of the palace was turned over to the monks, and it is still an active lamasery, home to the Yellow Sect of Buddhism, the same sect as the Dalai Lama—though how much religious freedom the monks enjoy is debatable (in August 2007

© HELENA IVESON
The Lama Temple is the most important place of worship for the city's Buddhists.

China's atheist leaders banned Tibet's living Buddhas from reincarnation without their permission). Here is where the government swore in its puppet Panchen Lama after the Dalai Lama's choice, a nine-year-old boy, was spirited away by the Chinese government in 1995 (he has not been seen since). The lamasery is a large complex made up of courtyards, prayer halls, and statues, and it is experiencing a resurgence in popularity with many young people who line up to pay their respects in front of the many Buddhas. The main attraction, however, in the last building of the complex, is the 18-meter-high sandalwood statue of Maitreya, a messianic Buddhist figure. It is made from a single piece of wood that was given to Emperor Qianlong by the Dalai Lama in 1750. While the crowds can limit the peacefulness of the place, if you can see the temple first thing in the morning or just before it shuts, the temple can be absolutely haunting with the chanting of monks and incense wafting in the breeze. And don't throw away your ticket: It is actually a fully functioning VCD that makes a nice souvenir.

SONG QINGLING'S RESIDENCE
(SÒNG QÌNGLÍNG GÙJŪ 宋庆龄庆居)
46 Houhai Beiyan, 6404 4205
HOURS: Daily 9 A.M.–5 P.M.
COST: 20RMB

Song Qingling, perhaps China's most revered woman, was one of the Songs: three sisters who with their husbands were among China's most significant political figures in the early 20th century. She spent her later years at her residence on the eastern bank of Houhai, and it is now a place of pilgrimage to her many fans—few foreign tourists seem to visit. Born into a wealthy and liberal family, Qingling was educated in the United States and came back to marry Sun Yatsen, the founder of the Republic of China. As the exhibition inside the residence makes clear, Qingling was heavily involved with the struggle against the Japanese and indeed with Chinese politics until her death in 1981—two weeks before which she was named honorary president of the People's Republic of China, the only person ever to hold this title. The residence's garden is a delightful place to wander around with rock gardens to clamber up and covered walkways

AN OLYMPIC EFFECT

The transformation of China's capital in time for the Olympics has been astonishing. To name a few major events, the city has seen the completion of a dozen Olympic sports centers; a whole host of new underground lines; a massive airport terminal plus high-speed rail link to the city; the colossal egg-shaped Grand National Theater; and the building of everything from fancy shopping centers to designer hotels. But what about social change?

When Beijing was awarded the Olympics in 2001, its bid had emphasized that the Olympics would lead to much-needed urban renewal and how much ordinary people wanted the games to change perceptions of China – often on the receiving end of negative headlines – and to improve their own lives. Human-rights organizations and politicians have applied pressure on the International Olympic Committee to use the games as a lever to improve China's human-rights record, with the idea being that the media attention would have a positive impact on the human-rights situation in China. The protests that accompanied the running of the Olympic torch were an attempt to bring to light China's unkept promises.

While life has undoubtedly gotten more convenient for the city's residents, it is easy to forget that China is a one-party state in which any form of opposition will be brutally suppressed, and that there is no media freedom – with the more than 20,000 journalists at the Games, Beijing tightened control over information instead of lifting media restrictions as promised. In the months leading up to the Games, several dissidents were jailed, including a former factory worker who collected 10,000 signatures in support of an online petition titled "We Want Human Rights, Not the Olympics." There are no political parties aside from the Communist Party, and groups who stand up to the government – whether they are the religious sect the Falun Gong, Free Tibet activists, or social campaigners – are banned and their members face long prison sentences or worse.

Yet many ordinary people would argue that there is change in the air, that they now have freedoms that were unheard-of just a decade ago, and that China needs to develop at its own pace, not when the rest of the world wills it. China is still considered a mysterious place, and with the huge numbers of tourists expected – China was poised to be the world's number-one destination by 2010 – more and more people will be able to see for themselves what life in China is like. Perhaps that is what the ultimate legacy of the Olympics will be.

around the peaceful small lake in the center. Inside the residence, look out for some offbeat memorabilia as well as the lovely gnarled crabapple trees in the courtyard. Several of her rooms have been preserved, such as the bedroom and study, and although it's all a bit musty, it's an interesting spot to learn about one of China's most beloved figures. Rather incongruously given the peaceful atmosphere, there's an army barracks next door.

Qianmen and Temple of Heaven Map 3

(Qiánmén, Tiāntán 前门, 天坛)

BEIJING PLANNING EXHIBITION HALL

(ZHǍNLǍN GUǍN 展览馆)

20 Qianmen Dongdajie, 6702 4559

HOURS: Tues.-Sun. 9 A.M.-4 P.M.

COST: 30RMB

Don't let the staid name put you off: Trust me—it's definitely worth a look for a glimpse into the future of Beijing. Given the often chaotic state of the city with construction sites everywhere you look, you may not have thought that there is much of a plan behind the city's development, but as this museum shows, there certainly is. The highlight of the tour is a massive scale model of what Beijing will look like 10 years from now: You can walk over the model and find out, as some residents have, that their apartments aren't featured, a sure sign that their homes will be demolished sooner rather than later. It's worth paying the extra charge and watching the Zhang Yimou–directed 3D film on the city's past that swoops through 1,000 years of history. On the first floor, there's a photographic display of what Beijing used to be like before the rush to demolish and develop: an attractive collection of rambling *hutong* and courtyard houses. For some reason (perhaps to thwart would-be vandals who wish to protest their houses' demolition?) you have to deposit your bags at the ticket office.

LEGATION QUARTER

(GŌNGBIÀNGUǍN 公便馆)

23 Qianmen Dongdajie, www.legationquarter.com

Beijing's equivalent of the upmarket elegance of the Bund, the Legation Quarter has transformed the former Qing dynasty–era American Embassy compound, just yards away from Tiananmen Square, into an entertainment complex, complete with designer restaurants including Maison Boulud, a French concept restaurant by award-winning chef Daniel Boulud from New York; a repertory theater; a contemporary art center; and an outpost of the London nightclub Boujis, popular with the younger Royals. The complex has been opened by the owner of the long-running and exclusive restaurant The CourtYard, and similarly, this place doesn't come cheap—bring your corporate credit card if you have one. To some local residents, the only downside is the complex's location, as it is far from the entertainment districts in Sanlitun and Chaoyang Park, but for a glamorous evening to remember, it's worth jumping in a taxi and heading across town to.

LIULICHANG (LIÚLICHǍNG 琉璃厂)

Liulichang Dongjie

This is where the glazed tiles that covered the roofs of the imperial palaces were made, and though the kiln was extinguished in Emperor Qianlong's reign, it has continued to be called Liulichang, or glazed tiles factory. The area developed into a calligraphy and arts street when students, keen to win a position as a Mandarin serving the emperor, came from across the country to prepare for exams in calligraphy and poetry. Many sold their works to pay for food and their keep, and stores emerged selling paper, brushes, and ink to academics in the area. Nowadays, the street is fairly touristy and a few shops have been blighted with terrible Disney–style renovations, but part of the charm of the area is finding it: You have to navigate yourself around winding *hutong* and will probably encounter more than one dead-end before you find the street. It is difficult to distinguish among the many antiques shops and scroll-painting stores, but if you bargain hard, you can come away with more Chinese souvenirs than you can shake a stick at, including jade (possibly fake), ink scrolls, name chops (seals used to prove identity on documents), folk art, and wood carvings.

OX STREET MOSQUE

(NIÚJIĒ QĪNGZHĒNSÌ 牛街清真寺)

88 Niu Jie, 6353 2564

HOURS: Daily 6 A.M.-7 P.M.

COST: 10RMB

A shadow of its former self thanks to relentless urban renewal, the once-vibrant local Muslim area, which has been in existence for more than 1,000 years and was once full of restaurants and traders, now has only its mosque. Built in A.D. 996, Niujie Mosque is the oldest and largest place of worship in Beijing for the city's estimated 250,000 Muslims. The building itself is an interesting blend of Islamic and Chinese styles. Unless you know what you're looking for, it would be easy to walk past the building as from the outside it resembles a traditional Chinese temple with its elaborate eaves, but inside you'll find typical minarets, swirling Arabic scrolls, and Islamic art work. If all the paintwork looks a bit new, the mosque only recently reopened after an upgrade—just the latest in the mosque's many transformations. In 1442, the whole site was rebuilt,

BEIJING'S BUILDINGS

While the city often seems like one huge construction site, and the government rightly faces near-constant criticism for its demolition of many traditional areas, there are still many buildings that serve as symbols of the past, present, and how China wants to present itself to the world in the future – everything from the opulence of Beijing's ancient temples to its futuristic Olympic sites. Architecture fans shouldn't wait too long to get here – the cranes and demolition workers haven't stopped yet.

TRADITIONAL ABODES

For a look at a fast-disappearing way of life, all visitors to Beijing should stroll around the atmospheric *hutong* alleys near Houhai, where the ordinary and the elite have lived for centuries. Mandarins who worked at the Forbidden City used to live in the small gray streets around the Drum and Bell Towers, where they used the bang of the tower's drums as a sign it was time to get to work-their workplace, of course, was the traditional home of China's emperors for almost five centuries. While the last emperor Puyi was evicted in 1924, the inner court, which served as the private residence, is open to the public.

REMINDERS FROM THE RECENT PAST

China's recent history can be read through the architecture of its buildings. China's parliament building, the Great Hall of the People, would not look out of place in Russia during the 1950s, nor would China's national museum – both were built at a time when China and Russia were close allies.

SHOWSTOPPERS

Beijing's Olympic stadiums obviously need to be suitable for sport, but their real function is to show the world, which still sees China as a backward country of temples and ugly Soviet architecture, how the country sees itself as it rockets through the 21st century. In Beijing, the dazzling Bird's Nest Olympic stadium and iconic swimming center will go down as glittering examples of Olympic buildings, and the CCTV Building under construction in Chaoyang is another example of a confident China. The National Center for Performing Arts, next to the Soviet-style architecture of the Great Hall of the People, overshadows the older building both literally and figuratively as a new style of architecture takes center stage.

and in 1696 it was expanded. Today, just as then, men gathered in the prayer hall, and as this is a place for reflection, camera-wielding non-Muslims won't be given a warm welcome. Instead, go to the courtyard garden to see the tombs of the founder of the mosque and of two sheikhs from Central Asia and Persia who visited Beijing in the 13th century. The friendly man at the gate will lend you some MC Hammer–style baggy pants if you're not appropriately attired.

QIANMEN (QIÁNMÉN 前门)

Qianmen Dajie, south of Tiananmen Square

Shopping is an essential part of visiting Beijing: Here in Qianmen, you're back at the source—the city's first shopping district, which dates from the early 15th century. During the Qing dynasty there were strict codes about how the city was laid out, and this area was designated merchants' quarters: Silk makers, traditional pharmacies, and cobblers all flourished here and still do. The area is also the birthplace of Peking duck and, adding to the atmosphere, was the home to Peking opera and acrobatic troupes. Qianmen was closed for a year, reopening in May 2008, as the government restored the area to its 1930s charm. Now it's fully pedestrianized and has *dangdang,* or jaunty trolley buses, to transport you from one end to the other. Look out for the '30s-style street lamps—a nice touch. The old-world focus aside, authorities are hoping the area becomes popular with a new generation of shoppers, so hidden among the Chinese brands of years past are Adidas and Starbucks.

the awesome Hall of Prayer for Good Harvests at the Temple of Heaven

TEMPLE OF HEAVEN (TIĀNTÁN 天坛)

Yongdingmennei Dajie (West Gate), 6702 8866

HOURS: Daily 6 A.M.-8 P.M. park, 8 A.M.-6 P.M. sites

COST: 35RMB combined ticket, 15RMB park

Beijing's two central UNESCO Heritage Sites vie for the most visitors, but in my book, the Temple of Heaven is truly the capital's must-see sight. Founded in the first half of the 15th century, its fine buildings set in relatively quiet and mammoth gardens are a lovely combination. Here you'll find Beijing on a human scale and at its best: the elderly opera singers who gather by the covered walkways for an afternoon singalong session, local families who use the park for picnics, and a steady crowd of enthusiastic local and foreign tourists. Ming and Qing emperors left the Forbidden City to come here four times a year to offer sacrifices to the gods and to pray, and along with them tens of thousands of courtiers, soldiers, and officials proceeded in great ceremony through Tiananmen, south through Qianmen, and down to the complex beyond the southern gates of the city, with commoners forbidden to open their shutters and cast their eyes on the procession on pain of death. A sense of occasion can still be felt if you reenact the emperors' journey through the south gate, straight to the Round Altar traditionally held to be the center of the world, to the Imperial Vault of Heaven with its Echo Wall, and then, to the grand finale, the wondrous Hall of Prayer for Good Harvests. Made entirely of wood and without a single nail, the building rises imperiously and is truly fit of an emperor. The whole complex is well cared for and unlike many tourist attractions, has not been blighted by rampant commercialization. When you have seen all the many sights in the park, be sure to wander around the tree-lined paths where it's possible to find yourself alone despite being in one of the city's busiest attractions.

Central Business District

Map 4

(Zhōngyāng shāngwù qū 中央商务区)

NEW CCTV BUILDING
(XĪN ZHŌNGYĀNGDIÀNSHÌTÁI DÀSHÀ 新中央电视台大厦)

32 Dongsanhuan Lu

Scheduled for completion in 2009, this building is, according to Dutch architect Rem Koolhaas, the most structurally complicated he's ever designed. Some 230 meters high, its steel structure forms a continuous spatial loop climbing up and around the volume of the building. Inside this complex structural web, there will be a "media village" (more like a city actually), complete with places to eat and play, and a sensational public viewing gallery. It is a roller coaster of radical ideas. The tower is already a local landmark and has more than a few nicknames—taxi drivers call it Baggy Trousers, an allusion to the double tower connected at the top. It will be headquarters for CCTV, or China Central Television, China's state-run television station—firmly overshadowing the old CCTV Building in the west of the city (Sihuan Xi Lu), which used to be Beijing's tallest structure. (While the old tower's observation deck at 238 meters is open to the public—for a costly 50RMB—there isn't much to look at, as sights in that part of town are far and few between.) Next door to the new tower is the 115,000-square-meter Television Cultural Center, which includes a hotel, a visitors center, a large public theater, and exhibition spaces.

RITAN PARK (RÌTÁN 日坛)

6 Ritan Beilu, 6561 6301

HOURS: Daily 6 A.M.-8 P.M.

COST: Free

Beijing's nicest central park is a great place to stretch your legs and engage in some serious people-watching, whether they're the Russian traders who hang out in this area, staff from the many embassies in the area looking important, or locals practicing their morning tai chi. It was built in 1530, and a succession of Ming and Qing dynasty emperors came here to the Altar of the Sun to make sacrifices to the gods. The altar in the middle of a round stone pavilion still exists (and is somewhat blasphemously used as an open-air arena for events such as World Cup soccer matches) as does the atmospheric Slaughter Pavilion, where the sacrificial offerings were prepared. Despite the bloody history, the park is lovely and peaceful and full of child-friendly activities such as miniature golf, climbing frames, and miniature speedboats for rent at one of the many ponds. Be sure to head to the middle of the park and climb to the pagoda for a good view of some of the new developments being built in the area, and after that, go to the open-air Stone Boat Bar, which overlooks a large pond that has fishermen at work at all times of the day. (You can rent rods too if the urge bites.)

TEMPLE OF WISDOM ATTAINED
(ZHÌHUÀHSÌ 质化寺)

5 Lumicang Hutong, 6525 0072

HOURS: Daily 6 A.M.-6 P.M.

COST: 20RMB

Part of the joy of this temple is finding it, hidden down a quiet winding *hutong* off one of Beijing's busiest streets. The poetically named Buddhist Temple of Wisdom Attained was first built in 1443, when it was the ancestral temple of Wang Zhen, the power-hungry chief eunuch of Emperor Zhengtong. Now the temple is considered the largest and finest example of Buddhist architecture from the period. It was not until 1742 that it was converted into a temple and became well known for its musical monks. After suffering the embarrassment of being turned into a beer factory during the Japanese occupation of Beijing, it has since been beautifully restored. The temple contains several leafy courtyards and temple buildings and is surprisingly long. In the 1930s, the ceiling of one of the prayer halls, the Tagatha Hall, was shipped to America and put on display at the Philadelphia Museum of Art, but its main feature of 9,999 Buddhas of all shapes and sizes remains.

WORKERS' STADIUM
(GŌNGRÉN TǏYÙCHǍNG 工人体育场)
Gongti Beilu, 6593 6221
Once Beijing's only international-standard stadium, this complex with tennis courts and outdoor pool has been firmly thrust into the shadow by the Bird's Nest in the north. First opened in 1961 for a world Ping-Pong tournament, its 1960s style was probably outdated from 1962 and was urgently in need of updating: Thanks to the Olympics, that's exactly what it received, closing for two years before reopening to hold some of the soccer matches in 2008. Thankfully, the renovation didn't include the removal of the many "uplifting" statues dotted around the complex; they are similar to the works outside Mao's Mausoleum in Tiananmen Square (think triumphant athletes wielding flowers with their arms aloft). This area has become something of a key nightlife destination with some good restaurants, such as Three Guizhou Men, nearby and several of Beijing's superclubs near enough that you can hear the bass thump. There are also some more low-key bars, such as the Pavilion, opposite the East Gate.

© HELENA IVESON
one of the uplifting Soviet-style statues at the Workers' Stadium

Chaoyang District and Sanlitun — Map 4

(Cháoyáng qū, Sānlǐtún 朝阳区, 三里屯)

BLUE ZOO
(LÁNSE DÒNGWÙYUÁN 富国海底世界)
South Gate, Workers' Stadium, Gongti Nanlu, Chaoyang District, 6593 5263, www.blue-zoo.com
HOURS: Daily 8 A.M.–8 P.M.
COST: 100RMB adults, 50RMB children under 12
For some reason, few families know about this small but well-laid-out aquarium, which is part of the Workers' Stadium complex. The highlight is a 120-meter (394-foot) see-through tunnel—which kids will love as it allows them to get up close and personal with a whole variety of weird and wonderful sea creatures, including baby sharks. It's perhaps not as educational as it could be—there's definitely a lack of information available in English—but it's a fun place for kids interested in creatures of the deep. If you want to get even closer, for 380RMB you can scuba dive for half an hour, but keep in mind that the instructors don't speak good English.

CHAOYANG PARK AND THE BEIJING GREAT WHEEL
(CHÁOYÁNG GŌNGYUÁN, DÀGUĀN LǍNCHĒ 朝阳公园, 大观览车)
1 Nongzhanguan Nanlu, 6506 5409
HOURS: Daily 6 A.M.–10 P.M.
COST: 5RMB, students 2.5RMB
Beijing's biggest park—the venue for beach volleyball events during the Olympics—is something of a mixed bag. There are certainly plenty of areas to stroll around, and the northwestern part has large grassy areas and copious flower beds, but plenty of the rest is an

urban wasteland with nothing really to look at. The outdoor swimming pool is a popular spot for locals in the summer (and a bargain too at only 15RMB), but the amusement park has seen better days. The park really comes alive, though, when it holds the annual Beijing Pop Festival over a weekend every September and is full of music fans raring to go. The new Ferris wheel, the Beijing Great Wheel, which is set to be (of course) the world's biggest—208 meters (682 feet) high to commemorate the 2008 Olympics—will add another reason to come to the park. The city had originally intended to have the landmark wheel completed and opened to tourists ahead of the Games; however, the project was delayed several times to improve its design, and it's now scheduled to open in 2009. Near the park's west gate is a collection of bars and restaurants that rival Sanlitun's selection: Try the new Block 8 Complex, with its great sushi bar alongside an Italian restaurant.

SANLITUN (SĀNLǏTÚN 三里屯)

Sanlitun Lu, www.newsanlitun.com.cn

No matter how many different areas the government designates as entertainment areas, punters can't stop flocking to Sanlitun for its bars and restaurants, which span the scale from studenty dive bars that offer mixed drinks for 5RMB to upmarket cocktail bars that attract Beijing's beautiful people. The main northern strip caters more to Chinese patrons than foreign visitors with karaoke, the odd pole dancer, and Filipino bands as well as beggars, fake CD sellers, and lady bar touts, but at the southern end and near Tongli Studios there are some of the best bars in the city. Appalling some of the city's expat residents, the government is on a mission to gentrify the area and make it into more of a shopping and restaurant destination than a place for boozing and carousing. Whether the ritzy new developments, including a five-star boutique hotel will benefit or detract from the area's charm is hard to say.

Capital Museum and Temple of Great Charity Map 5

(Běijīng Shǒudū bówùguǎn, Guǎngjīsì 北京首都博物馆, 广积寺)

BEIJING CAPITAL MUSEUM (BĚIJĪNG SHǑUDŪ BÓWÙGUǍN 北京首都博物馆)

16 Fuxingmenwai Dajie, 6337 0491, www.capitalmuseum.org.cn

HOURS: Tues.-Sun. 9 A.M.-5 P.M.

COST: 30RMB, students 15RMB

With the opening of this striking and well-planned space, the bar for future museums in the capital has been firmly—admittedly up until now, it was barely off the ground. Here though, dingy galleries and incomprehensive English are nowhere to be found: This is Beijing's first world-class museum and it showcases the best of Chinese art. Unlike most of Beijing's new striking buildings, this complex, which opened in December 2006, was designed by a Chinese architect: the vice director of the China Architectural Design Research Institute. The huge main hall is similar in style to London's Tate Modern: Natural light floods in onto the massive six-story bronze cylinder that rests at a jaunty angle. The actual exhibitions, which are sorted by theme, are no less striking and include 200,000 exhibits of jade, bronzes, porcelain, and paintings with full English explanations. In addition to the permanent displays, there is always a traveling exhibition, which recently has varied from Brit-art from the 1990s, artifacts from the British Museum, and ancient Greek relics from the Louvre in Paris.

BEIJING ZOO (BĚIJĪNG DÒNGWÙYUÁN 北京动物园)

137 Xixhimenwai Dajie, 6831 4411, www.bjzoo.com

HOURS: Winter daily 7:30 A.M.-5 P.M., summer daily 8:30 A.M.-6 P.M.

COST: 15RMB, students 8RMB, 5RMB panda house

A few years ago, the zoo would have been off-limits to sensitive souls as the conditions were really quite awful, with animals looking understimulated and living in unsanitary conditions. Attitudes toward animals aren't always kind: Many Chinese see nothing wrong with the animal Olympics held in Shanghai, where kangaroos take part in boxing matches, yet attitudes do seem to be slowly changing, probably because of the rise in numbers of people having pets. The conditions at the zoo are definitely on the up as the new chimpanzee and panda houses testify. The star attractions are of course the pandas, though bear in mind that they are not the most active of animals so you might not see them do anything more than snore the day away. Away from the panda house, there is a vast collection of animals and the leafy compound that was once the private garden of a Qing dynasty aristocrat is a pleasant venue for a stroll. At the northern end of the zoo is the modern and well-equipped Beijing Aquarium (18B Gaoliangqiao Xie Jie, 6217 6655, www.bj-sea.com), where entrance costs 100RMB for adults but two accompanying children get in for free. The Sea World–style shows featuring dolphins and seals are good fun, though, and the illuminating exhibitions on sharks and coral reefs are very informative.

MILITARY MUSEUM

(JŪNSHÌ BÓWÙGUǍN 军事博物馆)

9 Fuxing Lu, 6686 6244

HOURS: Daily 8 A.M.-5:30 P.M.

COST: Free

Don't come looking for some sensitive politically correct museum on peace as much as war, as you definitely won't find it here: What you will find inside the large Stalinist building is a central hall where kids play shoot 'em up video games among the missiles, rocket launchers, and memorabilia from China's military exercises in the past, including captured American flags and spy planes. There is war memorabilia from the past 5,000 years while other exhibits look to the future, the latest being a display of high-tech weaponry, a heavy emphasis on outer space, and young army women in uniform who pose with visitors to mark the 80th anniversary of the army's founding. If despite all these artifacts your revolutionary fervor is still lacking, the displays of social-realist artwork, including a massive portrait of all of China's recent leaders plus Marx, Lenin, and Stalin(!), greeting your arrival, might do the trick.

TEMPLE OF ANCIENT MONARCHS

(LÌDÀIDÌWÁNG MIÀO 历代帝王庙)

Xisi, Fuchengmennei Dajie, 6616 0907

HOURS: Daily 8 A.M.-4:30 P.M.

COST: Free

This surprisingly large temple is for some reason not on the standard tourist itinerary—an oversight given the complex's beauty and size. The temple looks as good as new despite being more than 500 years old thanks to recent sympathetic restoration work. The complex has been well restored and is one of only three imperial temples in the city, built in 1530 for the emperor and his successors to worship the gods, powerful ancestors, and former emperors. The names of 188 monarchs and 80 individuals who had rendered outstanding service throughout the Ming and Qing dynasties are listed near the entrance: It's still possible to make out the characters of their names. Inside the complex, the Temple of Jingde Chongsheng, the main hall, is one of the biggest ancient buildings preserved in Beijing.

TEMPLE OF GREAT CHARITY

(GUǍNGJĪSÌ 广积寺)

Xisi, Fuchengmennei Dajie, 6616 0907

HOURS: Daily 8 A.M.-4:30 P.M.

COST: Free

This little Buddhist temple was built in the Jin dynasty, making it more than 800 years old, and although now it's a peaceful place, it has seen more than its fair share of devastating events. The worst was a fire in January 1934 that destroyed dozens of halls, countless valuable objects, and more than 100 volumes of the Fahuajing, a Buddhist scripture. The temple is still a center of Buddhist learning and serves as the headquarters of the Chinese Buddhist Association. Take some time to explore the restored worship halls and the unusual paintings above each door. In the Hall of the Heavenly King there is a statue of Maiteya Buddha, cast during the Ming dynasty, that has survived and looks almost as good as new.

University District and the Summer Palace (Dàxué qū, Yíhéyuán 大学区, 颐和园) Map 6

BEIJING UNIVERSITY (BĚIDÀ 北大)

1 Yiheyuan Lu, 6275 1230, www.pku.edu.cn

As the sight of many hopeful Chinese families taking photographs of their child in front of the university's gates testifies, Beijing University is the country's, and indeed one of Asia's, most prestigious universities: Entrance goes a long way in securing a student's future. The university was established in 1898, making it the country's oldest, and there are now more than 30,000 students. The students here have a reputation for brains as well as activism: Many of the students and lecturers who took part in the Tiananmen protests came from here. The campus is a nice place for a stroll—and popular with young student couples—being the former site of Qing dynasty royal gardens. In addition to lakes and a marble boat similar to the grand example at the Summer Palace, there are many leafy pathways that wind around traditional buildings, over low bridges, and under willow trees. Mao Zedong was a librarian here; other famous names linked to the university include Wang Dan, the leader of the Tiananmen protests. Nearby is Beijing University's main rival Tsinghua (Chengfu Lu), considered the capital's MIT, but the grounds aren't as nice to walk around.

OLD SUMMER PALACE (YUÁNMÍNGYUÁN 圆明园)

28 Qinghua Xilu, 6262 8501

HOURS: Daily 7 A.M.-7 P.M.

COST: 10RMB park, 15RB ruins, students 5RMB

You may wonder how it's possible to ruin ruins but a recent renovation job at the Old Summer Palace has made the place more of interest historically than as the romantic and somewhat desolate place it once was. The original palace was built in the 12th century as a secondary home for the emperor and his court during the summer when the closeted Imperial City in the center of town was sweltering. The complex was then hugely expanded by Emperor Qianlong, who ordered the gardens to be expanded into the size they are now. As the many signs around the site forcefully remind you, in 1860, furious with the Chinese for having the temerity to expel foreign forces from their soil, Britain's Lord Elgin ordered the destruction of the palace that was once known as "the Versailles of the East." Then, in 1900, the once-proud compound was again plundered by the Allied Forces of the Eight Powers before local warlords and bandits stole or destroyed what was left. Visitors should treat the complex as a park despite its palace label and take time to wander around; sadly, it is nearly impossible to imagine what the buildings actually looked like. The ruins were up until recently left wild and reverting back to nature with trees and plants growing around them, but they have since been restored, rearranged, and placed in concrete.

SUMMER PALACE (YÍHÉYUÁN 颐和园)

Yiheyuan Lu, 6288 1144

HOURS: Daily 6:30 A.M.-8 P.M.

COST: 30RMB, students 15RMB

This wonderfully large complex, on the slope of a hill and next to a lake, was once the summer retreat for imperial families: Now it's where ordinary people came for relaxation and fresh air. Yiheyuan means "garden of restful peace" and despite the huge number of tourists it attracts, it is possible to escape the crowds thanks to the size of the grounds. Like the Old Summer Palace, this complex was also twice sacked by foreign troops but unlike the other gardens was rebuilt in all its former glory. The site is dominated by the picturesque Kunming Lake, which is used for boating in summer and ice-skating in winter. The long walk around the water's edge is punctuated by ornate pagodas; the marble boat built by the notorious Empress Dowager Cixi that used up the Chinese naval budget at a time when the fleet was being decimated by the

Japanese; and the Hall of Jade Ripples, which is where the empress placed her nephew under house arrest for plotting against her. Away from the lake, head to the temple atop Longevity Hill for amazing views of the buildings below. A new and unwanted addition to the site is the kitschy Little Suzhou Water Town. Frankly, do not bother: Instead choose to leave the grounds à la emperor and catch a canal boat to Yuyuantan Park in the west of the city.

Greater Beijing — Map 7

BEIJING BOTANICAL GARDENS (ZHÍWÙYUÁN 植物园)

Wofo Si Lu, Xiangshan, 6259 1283
HOURS: Summer daily 6 A.M.-8 P.M., winter daily 7 A.M.-7 P.M.
COST: 55RMB for all-inclusive ticket to park, conservatory, and temple

Lying at the foot of Fragrant Hills, this huge park, which doesn't attract anywhere near the same number of visitors as its more famous neighbor, is home to 4,000 species of plants and functions as both a tourist attraction and research center. During the Cultural Revolution, the place fell into ruin with many plants destroyed and its collection of rare trees cut down for firewood. Even now, the gardens have not fully recovered from the turmoil of the time, but there is still plenty to see on a sunny day. The highlight is undoubtedly the huge conservatory, built in 1999, which lies in the center of the grounds; if you visit during winter, it makes a welcome change to the city's frigid air with a temperature of 30°C (86°F). The conservatory contains more than 1,500 plants on its three floors with different areas representing different climates from around the world. The garden grounds are also great with a huge number of themed gardens to explore. At the north end of the grounds is Wofosi, or the poetically named Sleeping Buddha Temple, called so because of the massive bronze statue that was built in 1321. Take a picnic, find a shaded area, and relax for a few hours.

DASHANZI (DÀSHÀNZǏ 大山子)

4 Jiuxianqiao Lu

Despite the fact that the kilometer-square block that forms the art district is already bursting to the seams with contemporary galleries, barely a week passes before a new one opens with a whopping big party. Beijing's bourgeois are migrating to the area almost as fast as the galleries, setting up home in designer loft apartments. It's all a far cry from the area's proletariat past when in the 1950s the area was established as a factory zone for producing industrial parts: The factories are still there, but instead of automobile parts, it's art on sale at often-eye-watering prices (everything is priced in US$, which clearly illustrates the type of clientele they cater to). Still, if you can avoid tripping over an art student photographing plumes of smoke coming out of factory pipes, it's an interesting place to wander with some lovely cafés and bars (Pause Café has great coffee and Vincent's Café is straight out of Paris). For photography, check out 798 Photo Gallery and next door the 798 Warehouse, which regularly stages exhibitions and the odd rave in its large open space. There are also plenty of huge statues and artwork dotted around the place outside the actual galleries (to take the art to the people) so keep your eyes peeled. With the area constantly changing, it's worth buying a map of the area from any local gallery or shop.

FRAGRANT HILLS (XIĀNGSHĀN 香山)

Xiangshan, 6259 1155
HOURS: Summer daily 6 A.M.-7 P.M., winter daily 6 A.M.-6:30 P.M.
COST: 10RMB, students 5RMB

Ten kilometers from the city center is this former royal hunting ground, which dates from 1168. Much of the park's layout is credited to Emperor Qianlong, circa 1745. In 1860 and 1900, English and French troops wreaked havoc on the park, but today you'll find a fun public park that on a blue-sky day allows fine views of the city from the craggy summit. The park is packed during fall, when the whole city turns out to see the maple leaves turn—other times of the year can be just as pretty, and then you can walk around without feeling as if you are in a convoy. The energetic can do the steep one-hour walk to the top; the less enthusiastic can let a chairlift take the strain. Either way, the path to the summit has many pagodas and fine buildings to look at—the highlight is the Azure Temple by the north gate; it was built in 1331 by two powerful eunuchs. If you wish to extend your stay, you can check into the Fragrant Hills Hotel (tel. 6259 1166), which is a blend of Chinese and Western architecture styles and which was designed by I. M. Pei, whose works include the pyramid at the Louvre and the Bank of China Building in Hong Kong.

NATIONAL STADIUM (ÀOLÍNPǏKÈ TǏYÙCHǍNG 奥林匹克体育场)

Olympic Park, Beisihuan Lu

HOURS: unknown

COST: unknown

Move over, Forbidden City: The 91,000-seat National Stadium, designed by Swiss architects Herzog and de Meuron, is one of Beijing's iconic sights. Nicknamed the Bird's Nest for its tangle of steel, the structure dwarfs everything around it. More than 5,000 workers toiled away day and night on the $386 million stadium to get it ready for the Olympic Games. Equally eye-catching is the "Water Cube," more formally known as the National Aquatics Center. Resembling a giant ice cube, the $125 million water-sports venue seated 11,000 spectators during the Games. Aside from these two showcase buildings, look out for Digital Beijing, the only building on the site designed by a Chinese architect, Zhu Pei. Resembling the motherboard of a computer, it is the control and data center for the Games. When the park opened to the public in April 2008, many spectators were disappointed with the lack of concession stands and with squat toilets only in the restrooms, but the superb and architecturally fascinating venues soon make visitors forget minor gripes. Post-Olympics, the Stadium will stage national and international sports events. A special line of the subway system was built to help ease the traffic heading to the Olympic Park—as the park is adjacent to a very busy stretch of the fourth ring road, visitors are advised to use the subway.

RESTAURANTS

Leave the General Tso's chicken behind you, practice those chopstick skills, and venture out into Beijing's thriving restaurant scene. From steaming bowls of *jiaozi* dumplings to blow-that-budget destination dining, Beijing has it all—just don't expect any fortune cookies at the end of your meal.

You won't be lacking in choice, as the capital has around 60,000 restaurants to choose from. China's many different types of regional cuisines are available, from Xinjiang restaurants with their lamb kebabs and naan bread from the west of the country, to Guizhou province's tangy and addictive sour fish soup, and Yunnan restaurants serving plates of ham and goats' cheese in a style as foreign to Beijingers as it is to you. If you're adventurous and keen to try as many different types of Chinese cuisine as possible, here is the place to do it as no other city can compete with the variety on offer.

As for the most famous dish of all, Beijing duck, with its assortment of pancakes and dipping sauces, can be an overrated greasy waste of calories or a juicy, crispy treat that could be one of the most memorable meals of your trip. A favorite treat for emperors dating from hundreds of years ago, the dish was introduced to the masses when the last emperor fell in 1911, leaving Imperial Palace chefs without a job. They opened up their own duck restaurants and the dish has been a staple ever since.

Moscow was the first foreign restaurant in Beijing, opening its doors in 1954 and serving Russian staples to its Communist counterparts. Nowadays, though, the variety is astonishing, with one street in Sanlitun having a Brazilian

HIGHLIGHTS

LOOK FOR ☾ TO FIND RECOMMENDED RESTAURANTS.

☾ **Best Snacks:** Beijing's most famous snack destination, **Donghuamen Food Market** (page 59), may have cornered the market for weird and wonderful nibbles, but the juicy lamb kebabs at **Crescent Moon Xinjiang Restaurant** take some beating (page 63).

☾ **Best Place for Delicious Dim Sum:** Every lunchtime, the Peninsula Palace Hotel's Cantonese restaurant **Huang Ting** is full of homesick Hong Kong expats ordering steamers of the city's most delicious dumplings (page 60).

☾ **Best Duck:** You can't go home without trying it, and **Li Qun** may be firmly on the tourist trail, but the atmospheric if ramshackle venue serves some of Beijing's best birds (page 66).

☾ **Best Taste of China's Regional Cuisine:** The arty venue and spicy Guizhou food served at **Three Guizhou Men** attracts more than their fair share of fans who leave happy, if sweaty, thanks to the liberal use of chilis (page 70).

☾ **Best Coffee and Cake: Comptoirs de France Bakery** has added some much-needed ooh la la to Beijing's bakery scene with its delicious chocolate cakes, freshly baked *pain au raison*, and large café lattes served in elegant glasses (page 71).

☾ **Best Courtyard:** It's a tie between the beautifully designed and elegant fine-dining destination **Whampoa Club** (page 73) and the cozy and laid-back courtyard at **Dali,** where you can eat under the stars as the restaurant cat plays under your table (page 63).

☾ **Best Sunday Brunch:** It may be out toward the airport, but **The Orchard** is Ground Zero for expats on the weekend looking for freshly made salads, platters of roast meats, and seafood in a lovely rustic venue surrounded by apple trees (page 76).

© HELENA IVESON

In winter, look out for candied fruit sold all over town.

restaurant next door to a tapas venue opposite a Serbian sandwich shop 100 meters from a Palestinian café. In recent years, standards have gone through the roof (once all fruit salads came with tomatoes and cakes were puffy wastes of time filled with fake cream), though don't be surprised if everything comes at once or your empty plate is whisked away before your companion has finished: That's just how people eat in China.

The city has several key restaurant areas: For a good mix of Chinese and Western restaurants head to Sanlitun, and the closer to the CBD you get the more fancy and expensive the restaurants become. Houhai and Nanluoguxiang have a great mix of bargain-priced places from pizza to lamb kebabs, and on every street you'll find seasonal snacks for a few RMB. Courtyard restaurants are one of the most celebrated aspects of dining in Beijing—few experiences can beat dining on *hao chi,* or good food, in an atmospheric, well-preserved courtyard set on a quiet *hutong.*

Whatever you feel like, you're in luck even if you're on the tightest of budgets as prices are low compared with those in Western countries, and service charges are nearly unknown. Yes, standards of hygiene and decoration at the back-alley dumpling dive may not be up to what you're used to, but as long as your food is served very hot, dining in even the cheapest of places should be absolutely fine: All restaurants were warned to improve standards in the run up to the Olympics (though we can't always say the same for the bathroom facilities). If you can ignore the plastic covers on the tables and lack of atmosphere, the food will usually make it worth your while.

PRICE KEY

- $ Entrées less than US$10 (75RMB)
- $$ Entrées between US$10-20 (75-150 RMB)
- $$$ Entrées more than US$20 (150RMB)

Tiananmen

Map 1

TRADITIONAL BEIJING STYLE

DONGHUAMEN FOOD MARKET $

Donghuamen Dajie

HOURS: Daily 5-11 P.M.

This night market in Wangfujing is a great place for a wander in the evening with hundreds of open-air stalls specializing in Beijing snacks. I'd say skip the more dubious skewers—scorpions and sea-horses, anyone?—and try the Beijing noodles or dumplings or the spicy cumin and chili-spiced lamb kebabs from Xinjiang province. The market does attract both foreign and Chinese tourists as well as the odd local so expect scrums around the most popular stalls. Prices are now set so you don't need to worry about being gouged.

MADE IN CHINA $$$

Grand Hyatt, 1 Dongchang'an Jie, 8518 1234, ext. 3608

HOURS: Daily 11:30 A.M.-2:30 P.M., 5:30-10 P.M.

Anywhere else in the world, hotel dining smacks of a lack of imagination, but in Beijing, some rank among the city's best options for a great meal. Leader of the pack is the Grand Hyatt's Made in China, which frequently wins accolades from both local magazines and restaurant guides. The open kitchen and funky and sleek venue are great, but the real star of the show is the food—with the succulent Beijing duck a must-order. Other great dishes are northern specialties like beggar's chicken—in which the meat is wrapped in leaves and slowly roasted—and even if you have tried *jiaozi* dumplings elsewhere and not liked them, give these ones a go.

24 HOUR RESTAURANT $

88 Nanchizi Dajie, no phone

HOURS: Daily 24 hours

Small backstreet snack-food restaurants vie for custom all along leafy Nanchizi Dajie, which runs along the eastern side of the Forbidden City. Expect grubby communal tables, plastic covering the tablecloths, and gruff service but in return, you'll enjoy a speedy hearty feast for less than 15RMB a person. Try the pan-fried pork dumplings or *guo tie,* which are fried in a huge open-air wok at the 24-hour dumpling joint or the beef noodles and stir-fried mixed vegetables at the similarly unnamed place next door.

REGIONAL CHINESE

CHING PAVILION $$

76 Donghuamen Dajie, 6523 8775, ext. 76

HOURS: Daily 11 A.M.-midnight

Just a minute's walk from the eastern gate of

© HELENA IVESON

Snacks abound at Donghuamen Food Market.

the Forbidden City, Ching Pavilion is a good place to break for a meal. The sleek eatery has three floors of dining rooms and lounges with a highly, perhaps overdesigned, interior, while the menu offers a fusion of different Chinese cuisines and a few Western dishes—one popular order is the free bread with a green-tea pesto dipping sauce, and be sure to try the coconut rice pudding.

HUANG TING $$

B2 Peninsula Palace Hotel, 8 Jinyu Hutong, 8516 2888, ext. 6707

HOURS: Daily 11:30 A.M.-2:30 P.M., 6-10 P.M.

Another standout restaurant in an unlikely shopping mall setting is Huang Ting, one of Beijing's most lovely venues. The best dim sum in the city is served by stylish waitresses in *qipaos* in a slate-gray interior decorated with salvaged stonework from demolished courtyard houses and Ming dynasty antiques. Ignore the pages of abalone and shark's fin soup on the menu and stick to the classic dim sum that brings in the moneyed crowd after a hard morning's shopping at the Peninsula Mall. The shrimp and pork Sieu Mai are exquisite, as are the crab meat dumplings in supreme soup. It's a little more expensive than most dim sum venues, but by far, the best quality in town.

MY HUMBLE HOUSE $$

1/F, West Building 3, Oriental Plaza, 1 Dongchang'an Jie, 8518 8811

HOURS: Daily 11 A.M.-2:30 P.M., 5:30-10:30 P.M.

My Humble House may be set in a shopping mall, but once you pass through its doors into the dramatic light-filled atrium and see the chic and minimalist design, you'll forget the crowds and bustle. Perhaps it's the feng shui'ed design that makes the place seem peaceful. The menu changes constantly but if you're lucky, the superb prawns and the beef and potato stew come highly recommended. Part of a very small chain from Singapore, this house is not a humble but a dazzling place to experience excellent fusion Chinese cuisine.

REGIONAL CUISINE IN THE CAPITAL

Think Chinese food is all about stir-fries and rice? Well, think again, as befitting a country of 1.3 billion people, there's a lot of variation when it comes to food in China. Beijing is the best place in the country to try your pick of the wide assortment of different Chinese cuisines available, so even if you're not planning to travel out of the city, you can still go on a whirlwind gastronomic tour without going beyond the fifth ring road. Here in Beijing, each of the country's 22 provinces and five autonomous areas have local government offices that have served bona fide versions of local dishes for decades, as have private restaurants opened by local migrants. Spicy food aficionados must try **Chuan Ban** in the Sichuan municipal government office: It's always crowded but it's worth waiting for a taste of what real Sichuan food should be like. Many first-timers confronted by baked naan bread, robust chicken stews, and lamb kebabs in a Xinjiang restaurant aren't sure how to classify the food – as it certainly doesn't seem Chinese. Leaving aside the political questions over whether Xinjiang, in the far west of China, should be a part of the country, the spicy meaty dishes are delectable, especially during winter. Head for a cheap but hearty feast at the brightly lit **Crescent Moon Xinjiang Restaurant,** where many people finish off their meals with a drag on a apple-scented *shisha* pipe. Near Beijing Zoo is the **Xinjiang Government restaurant,** with its huge noisy hall, lamb kebabs as big as a baby's arm, fragrant chunks of naan bread, and where everything comes with lamb in it – be warned, this is not the place for vegetarians. Much more meat-free friendly is **Yunteng Binguan,** the cheerful restaurant in the Yunnan government provincial office, just south of the Red Gate Gallery. Vegetarians will love the many exotic mushroom dishes, deep-fried potato balls, and salads, while meat eaters love the ribs cooked in bamboo and the specialties: goat's cheese and the most delicious chicken soup, called *qiguo ji,* imaginable.

If, however, you are keen on ambience as well as authenticity, a whole crop of more upmarket minority restaurants have opened. If you love spicy food, you may become addicted to the tangy Guizhou-style food at **Three Guizhou Men,** which also has a cool and classy atmosphere, with one of the owner's artwork dotted around the dining room. Don't miss the chili-covered rack of ribs, though for lunch you might want something lighter, so go for the Guizhou cold noodle salad. From **Dali,** which has earned kudos for its beautiful courtyard and for the freshness of its ingredients (see the *Houhai to the Olympic Stadium* section for more details), to the delicious Zhejiang cuisine at artist Ai Weiwei's urban-chic restaurant **Qu Nar,** to arty **South Silk Road** serving Yunnan staples in stylish surroundings, business has never been better for upscale minority dining. From its rustic and funky surroundings, **In and Out** brings dishes from picturesque Lijiang to the heart of Sanlitun, and it is full of happy diners every night. The *ningmeng niu pian* (lemon beef), *toudou ni* (crushed potato), and *Lijiang wei doufou* (Lijiang flavor tofu) are the restaurant's biggest crowd pleasers.

- **Chuan Ban** (5 Gongyuan Toutiao, Jianguomennei Dajie, CBD, 6512 2277, ext. 6101 10:30 A.M.-10 P.M.)
- **Xinjiang Government restaurant** (7 Sanlihe, Western Beijing, 6833 5599 11 A.M.-10 P.M.)
- **Yunteng Binguan** (7 Huashi Beili, Dongqu, Chongwen district, 6711 3322, ext. 7105 11 A.M.-10 P.M.)
- **Qu Nar** (16 Dongsanhuan Beilu, Chaoyang, 6508 1597 4 P.M.-2 A.M.)
- **South Silk Road** (19 Lotus Lane, Shichahai, Houhai, 6615 5515 11 A.M.-midnight)
- **In and Out** (1 Sanlitun Beixiaojie, next to Jenny Lou's Supermarket, CBD and Sanlitun, 8454 0086 11 A.M.-11 P.M.)

BEIJING DUCK

Beijing's most famous dish, good old *kaoya*, or roast duck, has been the dish to serve on special occasions for nearly 1,000 years. At first, the rich and expensive duck was the exclusive preserve of the imperial court: During the Yuan dynasty in the 14th century, the recipe was in imperial kitchen inspector Hu Sihui's cookbook: *The Complete Recipes for Dishes and Beverages*. The bird remained restricted to an elite few throughout the subsequent Ming and Qing dynasties as only wealthy households would have had the oven needed to cook it. Even though an oven is still a rarity in most Beijing households, shops that sell ready-roasted ducks have helped it become a staple city dish and you can even buy freeze-packed oven-ready birds to take home with you at the airport.

There is always a sense of occasion when you eat duck: The bird is usually carved in front of guests at the table (to ensure you get the whole bird as it is expensive), and the flesh and fat are presented to diners. The bones are then returned to the kitchen to be turned into soup or bagged up so you can take them home to boil. Hearts, livers, and, in some cases, tongues can be served as side dishes, but these can be something of an acquired taste.

Now the best part – the eating. Simply take a pancake and fill it with a few slices of spring onion, a piece of fatty skin, and a chunk of meat dipped in the dark plum sauce, and then roll it and eat. If you need a lesson, wait staff are usually on hand to show off their skills – the most dexterous can roll a pancake with their chopsticks.

While many local restaurants serve duck, go somewhere that specializes in it, such as the *hutong* restaurant **Li Qun,** which has special ovens that use wood from fruit trees because they produce little smoke and subtly flavor the meat, or the more upmarket and glitzy **Da Dong,** which in addition to the usual tangy hoisin dipping sauce has ginger and sugar concoctions to smear in the paper-thin pancakes.

CAFÉS AND CHEAP EATS

GRANDMA'S KITCHEN $

47-2 Nanchizi Dajie, 6528 2790

HOURS: Daily 10 A.M.-11 P.M.

For a taste of home, Grandma's is a long-term favorite that provides well-priced American comfort food to large crowds of expat families and tourists who can't stand another bowl of rice. The breakfast burritos are a filling way to start the day, washed down with unlimited coffee while you relax in the cozy, brightly wall-papered country-style surroundings. This is another handy pit stop when you're pummeling the pavements around the Forbidden City as a slice of carrot or the legendary apple cake will pep you up in no time, as will a flick through the American magazine collection. There are two other locations: 11 Xiushui Nanjie near the Friendship Store and B/0103 Jianwai Soho, 39 Dongsanhuan near Guomao.

INTERNATIONAL

THE COURTYARD $$$

95 Donghuamen Dajie, 6526 8883, restaurant@courtyard.net.cn

HOURS: Daily 6-9:30 P.M.

For a long time Beijing's only destination-dining venue, The CourtYard has kept up with newer places thanks to its good if a shade overpriced fusion food in a stark white modern venue that makes full use of its location overlooking the Forbidden City. Expect to be surrounded by couples gazing into each other's eyes: This is Beijing's premier date restaurant. The views at night when the Forbidden City's burnt-red walls are lit up provide the perfect backdrop for artful dishes such as pork chops braised with prunes and Sichuan sausage. After dinner be sure to go to the cutting-edge modern art gallery downstairs (see the *Arts and Leisure* chapter), or relax in the intimate cigar room on the top floor.

Houhai to the Olympic Stadium

Map 2

TRADITIONAL BEIJING STYLE

HUAJIA YIYUAN $

235 Dongzhimen Neidajie, 6405 1908

HOURS: Daily 10:30 A.M.-6:30 A.M.

For a fun, genuine *renao* (busy and noisy—just how the locals like it) experience, this is a great destination for Beijing staple dishes. One of two locations (the other quieter and more modern branch is 400 meters east), the restaurant is set on atmospheric lantern-lined Gui Jie or Ghost Street: Look out for the ornate Chinese gate as there is no English sign. No reservations are taken so it may be a while before you dine but hang tight as eventually you'll be taken to one of the courtyards in the sprawling venue, which seems to go back for miles. There is a good English menu: Try the Beijing duck, which doesn't come with the usual theatrics but is very tasty, or the spicy and messy crawfish; you'll be pleased that staff hand you plastic gloves to use while eating.

REGIONAL CHINESE

CRESCENT MOON XINJIANG RESTAURANT $

16 Dongsi Liutiao, 100m west of Chaonei Beixiaojie, 6400 5281

HOURS: Daily 10 A.M.-11:30 P.M.

This is possibly the best (and most hygienic) Xinjiang joint in town, thanks to its chunky lamb kebabs, hearty spicy chicken and potato stew with delicious naan bread, and homemade yogurt to cool down the heat. The friendly staff, who come from Xinjiang province, make this gem as authentic as it gets, though the location can be nuisance to find as it's down a dark alley—look out for the English sign. The moustached manager who's always there sucking on a hookah is something of a local tourist attraction, too. If only it would improve the toilets, this place would be near perfect.

DALI $$

67 Xiaojingchang Hutong, Gulou Dong Dajie, 8404 1430

HOURS: Daily 11 A.M.-2 P.M., 6-11 P.M.

Easily one of the most beautiful courtyard restaurants in Beijing, this lovely and laid-back venue serves spicy and unusual dishes from Yunnan province in southwest China. Don't worry about not knowing what to order: That problem has been taken away as it offers a range of set menus only. The food doesn't quite live up to the surroundings but despite this, the atmosphere and pleasant staff sees the place often full: Be sure to make reservations and enjoy what will be a great evening.

HAN CENG $

Shichahai Dongan, 6404 2259

HOURS: Daily 11 A.M.-3:30 P.M., 5-10:30 P.M.

This rustic attractive venue serves food from the Hakka ethnic minority who settled in Southern China, and Han Ceng nightly attracts crowds keen for its earthy and hearty specialties, such as prawns on a stick baked in salt. Get a table on the second floor and enjoy a great view of the lakes while escaping the noise of the first floor, with its squawking birds in cages and good-natured but shouting waitresses yelling out orders. It attracts a mixed crowd of hipsters off to the local bars after dinner and plenty of couples on dates. The toilets could do with an update, though.

JIN DING XUAN $

77 Heping Xijie, north of Yonghegong Qiao, 6429 6888

HOURS: Daily 24 hours

It's so popular that at nearly any time of the day, be prepared to wait at the flagship restaurant of this Cantonese chain. It specialises in dim sum though practically anything is available on the pages of the book-size menu, which has good English-language translations and pictures. It's open 24/7, and locals come to gobble shrimp dumplings, stewed beef with

Jin Ding Xuan is open 24 hours for Chinese classics.

radish, and spare ribs with black bean sauce just to name a few. Be warned: Don't come if you have a headache, as the noise and bustle on any of the four floors will have you reaching for the Advil.

PAPER $$

138 Gulou Dongdajie, 8401 5080

HOURS: Daily 4 P.M.-midnight

It can be difficult to find Chinese food that's not dripping in oil, so this is the place to head when you need clean, healthy flavors. The signature of this stark-white trendy place is its revolving 16-course "clean-eating" meal of Chinese and Southeast Asian flavors. The owner of long-term favorite Café Sambal has designed a very attractive and cool space: The first floor features a bar and tables while the second floor has comfy white couches. It's not all about healthy living, though: This is one of the few Chinese restaurants with an extensive wine list.

PRIVATE KITCHEN $

44 Xiguan Hutong, Dongsi Beidajie, 6400 1280

HOURS: Daily 11 A.M.-11 P.M.

Bohemian in style, this lovely Guizhou restaurant down a residential alley is a real joy, from its tiny dining rooms off a central courtyard decorated with the stunning embroidery of Yao minority women from Guizhou province to the delicious spicy food. The English menu helps you navigate your way around what may be unfamiliar cuisine, but you can't go wrong with the specialities such as sour fish soup, flagged on the menu as a five-star choice! Be sure to try the homemade rice wine, which for once is deliciously fruity rather than more akin to gasoline.

THE SOURCE $$

14 Banchang Hutong, next door to the Lusongyuan Hotel, Kuan Jie, 6400 3736

HOURS: Daily 10:30 A.M.-10:30 P.M.

This is the place to head for spicy Szechuan food, one of the most addictive types of Chinese food around. The owner is something of a local celebrity in the art world and she's converted the small courtyard beautifully. The twisting corridors leading to relaxed antique-filled surroundings are something of a contrast to the robust and fiery food. In summer, be sure to reserve a table outside. It offers set menus only but will adapt them as necessary and if you're lucky it will have the stir-fried chicken with bamboo.

CAFÉS AND CHEAP EATS

VINEYARD CAFÉ $$

31 Wudaoying Hutong, off Yonghegong Dajie, 6402 7961, www.vineyardcafe.cn

HOURS: Daily 11 A.M.-10 P.M.

Five minutes' walk from the Lama Temple, this converted courtyard restaurant down an obscure *hutong* is a great place to recaffeinate and refuel on Western staples. Run by three Englishmen, the long menu offers basic but well-executed pasta dishes, square thin pizzas, and full English breakfasts on the weekends, when the place is packed. Throughout the day the shaded courtyard attracts many expat freelancers who make use of the free Wi-Fi, magazines, and good coffee in the relaxing surroundings.

XIAO XIN'S CAFÉ $

103 Nanluogu Xiang, 6403 6956

HOURS: Daily 9 A.M.-2 A.M.

Chef Xiao Xin's homemade cheesecakes have a very loyal following though I think they're overrated—try the muffins instead. On the boutique and café-lined alley of Nanluoguxiang, the small and cozy place complete with books and goldfish pond is great for relaxing on a cold day while eating freshly baked cakes washed down by a latte—don't bother with the savory dishes, though; sweet is the specialty here. Many expats and travelers bring their laptops and enjoy the Wi-Fi while watching the world go by in the alley outside.

INTERNATIONAL

CAFÉ DE LA POSTE $$

58 Yonghegong Dajie, 6402 7047, www.cafedelaposte.com.cn

HOURS: Daily 11 A.M.-1:30 P.M., 6 P.M.-1 A.M.

Five minutes south of the Lama Temple and its incense sellers is this lively French bistro crammed full of homesick French expats who peruse the chalkboard menu while chain-smoking their Gitanes. The specialty is steak, with the chef buying and cutting all the meat himself, making for cuts you might otherwise find only in a butcher's kitchen. The house wine is the result of a venture between French knowhow and Chinese grapes, and well worth trying. Everything is incredibly reasonably priced and the French staff are charming in a slightly disorganized way. Its deli next door sells nice bread and wine.

CAFÉ SAMBAL $$

43 Doufuchi Hutong, Jiugulou Dajie, 6400 4875

HOURS: Daily noon-midnight

Look out for two red lanterns and step into the cozy courtyard with a mix of antique and modern furnishings. Its excellent but small-portioned food, such as the Beef Rendang and delicious Chilli Crab, have ensured that for many, Café Sambal is Beijing's default option for Malaysian food. Run by a local gourmet with three restaurants and Bed Bar round the corner to his name, the restaurant's candle-lit tables and relaxed atmosphere make this a cool place to dine, though it's best to be relaxed about the service too, as when the place is busy—as it often is—food can take a while to arrive.

HUTONG PIZZA $

9 Yindingqiao Hutong on the west bank of Houhai, 6617 5916

HOURS: Daily 11 A.M.-11 P.M.

This lovely Beijing courtyard restaurant complete with indoor fishpond serves square thin-crust sophisticated pizzas with style. The relaxed venue is a charming place that attracts a mixed crowd, there to while away the hours over the delectable margarita, though if you like pizza overflowing with toppings, you may be a bit crestfallen. For thin-crust fans, though, this place can't be beat and even including drinks, the check is always surprisingly low. If you're carb loading, try the stuffed potato skins as a starter. The restaurant can be difficult to find but from Yinding Bridge between Houhai and Qianhai head over the bridge from Kourouji restaurant and keep going straight for 100 meters.

Hutong Pizza on the banks of Houhai

TRAKTIRR PUSHKIN RUSSIAN CUISINE RESTAURANT $

5-15 Dongzhimen Neidajie, 8407 8158

HOURS: Daily 9 A.M.-2 A.M.

Around the corner from the huge and imposing Russian Embassy, this rustic restaurant offers steaks as big as the plate covered with bacon and Chicken Kievs the size of a missile for mere rubles. This is where embassy staff come to eat generous portions washed down by Russian beer or vodka alongside crowds of locals as Russian cuisine has become very trendy, but this is certainly not the place to come if you're a vegetarian on a diet. Later on in the evening, there are live performances of Russian classics that after a shot or two of vodka seem quite enjoyable.

Qianmen and Temple of Heaven — Map 3

Traditional Beijing Style

LI QUN $$

11 Beixiangfeng, Zhengyi Nanlu, Qianmen Dongdajie, 6702 5681

HOURS: Daily 10 A.M.-10 P.M.

Now firmly on the tourist trail, this backstreet courtyard restaurant packs people in on the hunt for Beijing's best bird. If you get lost ask any local "Li Qun zai nar?" and he or she will point you to it. The duck roasts in a fiery oven the size of a small boat as you walk in and join the line to wait for a seat (if you haven't made reservations and sometimes even if you have). The duck is admittedly delicious but the rest of the menu is just adequate and the place's popularity often means service is lackadaisical. And why, oh why, doesn't it upgrade the awful toilets?

QUANJUDE $$$

32 Qianmen Dajie, 6701 1379

HOURS: Daily 24 hours

For well more than 100 years, the venerable Quanjude has been slicing up Beijing duck

© HELENA IVESON

the entrance to Li Qun, one of the capital's most famous duck restaurants using its own secret recipe, but we wish we knew the secret for this place's popularity. This, the original location, has the original tiny restaurant appearing almost as a little shrine at the back of the modern two-story restaurant that serves 5,000 meals a day. It is overpriced, boringly decorated, and overcrowded, but if you can stomach all that, the duck is tasty enough. Don't bother with anything but the main event though, as the side dishes (off cuts such as hearts and tongues) don't often appeal to travelers.

Central Business District Map 4

TRADITIONAL BEIJING STYLE

DA DONG ROAST DUCK RESTAURANT $$$

Building 3, Tuanjiehu Beikou, southeast corner of Changhong Bridge, 6582 2892

HOURS: Daily 11 A.M.-10 P.M.

Another very well-regarded duck restaurant, Da Dong is conveniently located on the third ring road near Sanlitun and appeals to people who aren't keen on a more atmospheric but possibly unhygienic backstreet duck restaurant. This place is upmarket, bright, and clean, and though prices are considerably higher than at those backstreet spots, the food is great and very professionally presented. Aside from the main event (which they claim is less fatty than their competition), other items on the menu are great, especially the seafood. Expect a wait if you don't make a reservation, but at least your wait is made painless by sparkling wine at no extra charge. There is now a second branch farther west into the city at A22 Nanxincang International Building, Dongsi Shitiao, which is a little flashier, but the duck is more expensive.

DIN TAI FUNG $

24 Xinyuan Xili Zhongjie, northwest of Yu Yang Hotel, 6462 4502, www.dintaifung.com.cn

HOURS: Daily 11:30 A.M.-10 P.M.

I don't know how it does it, but this venue's *xiaolongbao,* or pork soup dumplings wrapped in paper-thin skins, are completely addictive, and judging by the crowds, I'm not the only one who thinks so. The huge steamers full of dumplings plus the efficient and friendly service and sleek modern design are flawless. Aside from the dumplings, the fried sliced pork with egg-fried rice is delicious, as is the double-boiled chicken soup. It's also a candidate for best toilet in Beijing (Chinese restaurant category). There is another branch at the Shin Kong Place shopping center on Dawang Lu.

THE EAST IS RED $

266 Baijialou, Dongwuhuan, 6574 8289

HOURS: Daily 9 A.M.-2:30 P.M., 4-9:30 P.M.

If you haven't come to Beijing to eat pizza, but another evening of duck doesn't appeal to you either, this is an experience not to be missed. It's named after China's de facto anthem during the Cultural Revolution, and patrons can expect Old Beijing–style meat and potatoes fare, with a hearty dose of rousing live performances meant to get the patriotic tears flowing. You'll be served (and need) plenty of *baijiu,* the local brew, which comes with quite a kick—that combined with the marvelously kitschy decor will make you think you're hallucinating.

ORIENT KING OF DUMPLINGS $

Building 14, Chaoyangmen Nanxiaojie, opposite Jinyuan Hotel, 6527 2042

HOURS: Daily 10 A.M.-10 P.M.

For dumpling lovers who don't dine in dives, this is a great place to try: It's clean and bright and has an English menu, which lists over 30 types of dumplings, from traditional options like pork and scallion to the more adventurous, like carrot and ginger. The staff will ask if you want them steamed, boiled, or fried—I suggest trying all different ways and seeing what you prefer. You can afford to, at these prices.

It's more of a fast-food place than somewhere to linger, but for a filling, unbelievably cheap meal, it can't be beat.

XIAO WANG FU $$

Inside Ritan Park, near the north entrance, Ritan Bei Lu, 8561 7859

HOURS: Daily 11 A.M.-2 P.M., 5-10 P.M.

This small chain of home-style Beijing restaurants has long been a favorite for diners who like their Chinese food unchallenging and similar to what's served up back home—and there's nothing wrong with that. The owners know exactly what their customers want—English menus, familiar dishes, English-speaking staff, and nice surroundings—and they do an admirable job in providing just that. There is, of course, a premium for this, but as its loyal fans testify, it's worth it. The restaurant itself is lovely—it's at the north end of Ritan Park in an attractive two-story building. In summer, be sure to sit outside on the roof terrace and enjoy the view.

REGIONAL CHINESE

CHINA LOUNGE $$

Workers' Stadium South Gate, Gongti Nan Lu, 6501 1166

HOURS: Daily 11 A.M.-midnight

This opulent Chinese restaurant and lounge is a great place to see the city's yuppies dine en masse. In the popular entertainment district surrounding Gongti, China Lounge is the most posh option, and while the selection of regional Chinese cuisine on offer is good, it's outshone by the amount of bling worn by diners and the restaurant's luxurious decor. It's not as expensive as you'd expect, with classic dishes like stir-fried chicken with mushrooms just 58RMB, but prices for more exotic fare, especially fish dishes, can be pricey.

GREEN T HOUSE $$$

6 Gongti Xilu, north of the Gongti 100 Bowling Alley, 6552 8310, www.green-t-house.com

HOURS: Daily 11 A.M.-2 P.M., 6-11 P.M.

You'll either love or hate its food and dramatic, modern art decor: Either way, prepare for a unique evening with cuisine that tries to blur the line between food and art at sky-high prices. All dishes involve tea in some form or another, and the cushioned banquette seating and dramatic table settings are the ideal backdrop to dishes such as Kiss Me, Don't Say Goodbye, a dark chocolate-jasmine fondant, or Snow Flake Yogurt Soup, made of light and creamy cucumbers and delectable grilled prawns, with a glass of iced apple tea. It must be said that this restaurant attracts more business travelers on corporate credit cards than locals and expats.

QIN TANG FU $

59 Chaoyangmen Nanxiaojie, 6559 8135

HOURS: Daily 11 A.M.-2:30 P.M., 5-10 P.M.

There are several interesting minority cuisine restaurants along this street, but this gets the highest ratings because of its delicious repertoire of Shaanxi province food and cute rustic surroundings. The area is known for its hard long winters, so expect filling food of thick noodles and bread for a few RMB. The staple dish is *pao mo,* which is a delicious lamb soup into whose broth you break pieces of bread to soften and soak up the delicious juices, but the *rou jiamo* known as Chinese hamburgers are also excellent. The tables and chairs are oddly low to the ground, perhaps to prevent you from spilling as you slurp.

CAFÉS AND CHEAP EATS

GL CAFÉ $

19 Jianguomenwai Dajie, beside the St Regis Hotel, 6532 8282

HOURS: Daily 24 hours

For fast food, ignore the boring American chains and head to 24-hour eatery GL Café for cheap and cheerful Cantonese grub. Think of it as an Asian version of TGI Fridays (which is actually across the road). Grab a booth and study the huge menu—this isn't a restaurant for the indecisive. The noisy but friendly atmosphere is fun, and be sure to try the roasted barbeque meat platter—Chinese comfort food at its finest. Wash it all down with iced malted drinks like Ovaltine and Horlicks, a Hong

STREET EATS

With the large number of fancy high-rolling venues that have opened their doors in the capital, it's easy to overlook the huge number of street eats that have kept Beijingers going for, in some cases, centuries. Some of the city's best bites can be found in the most unlikely of places, and as long as you choose a busy stall with high turnover, you should be fine. The bigger problem can be trying to track these snacks down because with the city's fast development, the government has decided that snack sellers don't fit the city's new image. But there's always **Donghuamen Food Market,** where a long row of stalls sell their weird and wonderful wares and fine examples of traditional Beijing snacks and noodles.

- *Jianbing* – This is the thing to eat for breakfast on a cold day; first the vendor makes a pancake, and then it's sprinkled with cilantro and scallions before a chunk of fried dough is placed in the middle covered by an egg. Add a slick of chili sauce and it's ready to go.
- *Doujiang* – Generations of Chinese have been brought up on soybean milk, and the best version is the sweetened option. You'll see these cartons in practically every stall and they can be zapped in a microwave, making them good on a cold day.
- *Youtiao* – These are so popular with the Chinese that even branches of KFC have started selling these savory deep-fried doughnuts.
- *Chuan'r* – Ubiquitous on Chinese streets, these lamb kebabs sprinkled with chili and cumin are everyone's first choice of snack, especially after a drink or three.
- *Mala Tang* – If you have a delicate stomach, this may be best avoided, as you can't guarantee how long the skewers of meat and vegetables have been in the huge pots of spicy soup that are a common sight around the city.
- *Rou Jiamo* – Also known as Chinese hamburgers, these bread rolls are stuffed with a braised pork and onion mixture to be gobbled up on the run.

Kong specialty. There's also a branch at the China World Trade Center.

INTERNATIONAL

ALAMEDA $$

Sanlitun Lu, inside Nali Market, 6417 8084

HOURS: Daily 11:30 A.M.-10:30 A.M.

When Alameda opened, you could almost hear the sighs of relief from expats: At last there was a lovely venue serving contemporary Western food at moderate prices. A multiple award winner three years running, Alameda is now considered a reliable rather than exciting choice and you get the feeling that its popularity is more a reflection on Beijing's relatively sparse offerings of good Western food than on the place itself. Still, the short menu changes daily depending on what catches the eye of the head chef, but there's always a delicious steak on offer as well as more innovative offerings. You have to make reservations.

CAFÉ EUROPA $$

1113, Building 11, Jianwai Soho, 5869 5663

HOURS: Daily 11:30 A.M.-11:30 P.M.

If this sleek, upmarket, but relaxed eatery was in the center of the city, it would be booked solid every night; instead it is in the labyrinth of apartment towers that make up the development Jianwai Soho—which, while only a 10-minute taxi ride from Sanlitun, is far away enough to put off some. But that's good news for its local crowd of regulars, who love the European-style menu prepared by a fabulous Australian chef. The menu changes regularly, but there is always some artfully arranged pasta dishes as well as a seafood platter that is famously good. The chocolate mousse is a must-order. Add to all this one of Beijing's best wine lists, and this is a very nice place to be, especially in summer when you can sit outside on the patio.

HATSUNE $$

2/F, Heqiao Building, Building C, A8 Guanghua Lu, 6581 3939

HOURS: Daily 11:30 A.M.-2 P.M., 5:30-10 P.M.

Always packed and winning awards from local dining magazines, Hatsune does Californian-style Japanese food superbly. Traditionalists may not appreciate the Beijing-duck California rolls, but everyone else does. When you go to this trendy but unpretentious place—be sure to reserve a table; it's one of the few places in Beijing where you'll need a reservation for both lunch and dinner—order both the magnificent 119 spicy tuna rolls as well as the Motorola rolls. They are amazing. At lunchtime, the bento boxes are stuffed full of different treats and a great value. The owner has recently opened a second venture called Haiku (in Chaoyang by the west gate of Chaoyang Park), and a third opened at The Village in Sanlitun in 2008.

HAZARA $$

Face, 26 Dong Cao Yuan, Gongti Nanlu, near the Cervantes Institute, 6551 6788, www.facebars.com

HOURS: Daily 5:30-11 P.M.

This is where Beijing's yuppies head for Friday-night Indian: Expect a tasteful but pricy evening in one of the city's most stunning venues. Some gripe about the small portions of the northern Indian food, but dishes such as the cashew nut lamb curry are so rich that it's probably a good thing. The red-walled dining room displays beautiful antiques from all over Asia and the beautifully laid tables are meant for lingering. If you don't want Indian, there are two other upmarket restaurants offering Thai and contemporary Chinese in the same glamorous complex.

Chaoyang District and Sanlitun

Map 4

REGIONAL CHINESE

BELLAGIO $

6 Gongti Xilu, 6551 3533

HOURS: Daily 11 A.M.-5 A.M.

Catering to a young nightclubbing crowd, this Taiwanese restaurant is stylish and buzzy and well known in Beijing for the fashionable waitresses with regulation short and snappy haircuts. It features huge windows, high ceilings, and comfortable chairs, and you're there to be seen as much as to eat though the Taiwanese staples such as beef noodle soup and stir-fried chicken with chilis that are tasty and a shade less greasy than normal. For dessert, try the famous leaning towers of shaved ice smothered with sweet toppings.

THREE GUIZHOU MEN $

3rd Floor, 8 Gongti Xilu behind Bellagio, 6551 8517

HOURS: Daily 24 hours

Leading the charge for upmarket minority cuisine restaurants, this widely popular place is much loved for its bohemian air and authentic cuisine. Named after the three Guizhou men who started it and who are often in attendance, the place reflects the region's culinary links with Southeast Asia in arty stylish surroundings. Expect excellent spicy food—if you're not a fan, make sure to tell the staff to tone it down a little. The huge plate of braised ribs slathered with chilis and garlic is melt-in-the-mouth perfect as are the cold noodle salads in piquant sauces. There are other branches at Building 7, Jianwai Soho and 6 Guanghua Xilu.

XINJIANG RED ROSE $$

7 Xiang Xingfu Yicun, opposite the north gate of Workers' Stadium behind The Olive Restaurant, 6415 5741

HOURS: Daily 11 A.M.-11 P.M.

You can't miss this venue with its garish minaret plastered onto the roof and that lack of subtlety sets the tone for the rest of the evening: Expect hearty Xinjiang food in a very boisterous atmosphere. The excellent *dapanji* (chicken with handmade noodles and vegetables), roast goat, or the ever-popular lamb kebabs will fill you up in no time, but then you can work it off by joining the beautiful dancing girls on stage—and be warned, you may not have a choice. It's a shade overpriced and the toilets are awful, but it's still a good place for a lively evening.

CAFÉS AND CHEAP EATS

COMPTOIRS DE FRANCE BAKERY $

East Lake Villas, 35 Dongzhimenwai Dajie, 6461 1525

HOURS: Daily 7:30 A.M.-9 P.M.

This is Beijing's number one destination for freshly baked goods, whether it's for the artisan breads, the array of exquisitely made French pastries, or homemade chocolates. It also serves lunch but we'd choose the superb *pain au raison* over any salad any day of the week. The venue is nothing exciting as it's in the reception area of an apartment complex, but try to get one of the two comfy booths, and once you try the killer hot chocolate served by real French staff who utter cheery *bonjours,* everything else will fade in importance.

DAREEN'S COFFEE $

26 Sanlitun Lu, no phone

HOURS: Daily 9 A.M.-11 P.M.

The Palestinian owner has been in China since the early 1980s and his small and scruffy café attracts many fans of Middle Eastern food for falafel, hummus, zingy tabbouleh, and possibly Beijing's best coffee, served strong and potent. The savory items seem to be more consistently good than the cakes, but for such reasonable prices, you can afford to try just about anything; nothing on the menu is more than 50RMB. The staff can be lackadaisical and during busy lunchtimes, service can collapse altogether, but the really good food keeps people coming.

PANINO TECA $

1 Sanlitun Beixiaojie near Sanlitun Xiliu Jie, 8454 1797

HOURS: Daily 8 A.M.-10:30 P.M.

Simply put, this light and airy Italian café serves Beijing's best sandwich. The affable Italian owner who runs the upmarket eatery Assaggi next door branched out to this venue

Expect a meat feast and raucous dancing at Xinjiang Red Rose

SMOKE-FREE RESTAURANTS IN BEIJING

Fancy a side of nicotine alongside your noodles? If so, you're in the right country: The Chinese are by far the world's most prolific smokers, and they have no problem lighting up just about anywhere. More than 350 million people smoke in China, and visitors coming from countries that have smoking bans in bars and restaurants may find eating in a smoky atmosphere something of a drag.

The Chinese government promised that the Olympics would be smoke-free, and while smoking in taxis was banned in October 2007 and there has been an effort to ban smoking in schools, hospitals, and government offices, opposition to a ban in bars and restaurants is so fierce that the government backtracked; instead, all restaurants are supposed to have separate sections for smokers and non-smokers.

Beijing's first smoke-free restaurant almost went out of business as a result. After it banned smoking, Szechuan chain Meizhou Dongpo's business dropped to "about 80 percent of that enjoyed by other restaurants across the street," its manager told the *China Daily* newspaper. Beijing authorities have written to 30,000 restaurants asking them to put smoking bans in place, but not a single one has taken up the suggestion, the paper said.

As of this writing, however, smoke-free restaurants are limited to this tiny number:

- Red Capital Club (No. 66 Dongsi Jiutiao, Dongcheng District, 8401 6152)
- Pure Lotus (10 Nongzhan Nanli, Chaoyang Park, 6592 3267)
- All Starbucks branches
- Sizzler (1/F, International Club, 21 Jianguomen Wai Dajie, next to the St Regis Hotel, CBD, 6532 0475)

These restaurants have nonsmoking sections:

- Alameda (page 69)
- TGI Fridays (1/F, Building C, CITIC Plaza, 19 Jianguomen Wai Dajie, CBD, 8526 3388)
- Din Tai Fung (page 67)
- The CourtYard (page 62)
- Café Europa (page 69)
- Passby Bar (page 83)

in 2007 and the place has been packed ever since. The huge windows allow everyone to see you tucking in: I recommend the parma ham, eggplant, and olive ciabatta, which is superb, as is the coffee, and desserts are provided by the French bakery Comptoirs so leave room. You have to arrive early or late to avoid spending your lunch hour waiting for a table.

ILLY CAFÉ $

30 Sanlitun Lu, 6413 0345

HOURS: Daily 8 A.M.–8 P.M.

Farther north from Dareen's on the same tree-lined street is this other cute café, which sells possibly the best egg tarts in the world: You must try them. The Peruvian chef and her Portuguese husband offer exotic baked treats and killer coffee in their small charming venue, which has some magazines in the back. It's a good place to while away an hour especially as there is free Wi-Fi. The Spanish churros, which come with thick hot chocolate for dipping, make for an awesome if bloating breakfast.

INTERNATIONAL

MARE $$

14 Xindong Lu, 300m north of Gongti Bei Lu, 6416 5431

HOURS: Daily 11:30 A.M.–11:30 P.M.

With its excellent lunch menu, this upmarket Spanish eatery attracts the business crowd for lunch during the week and couples smooching over tapas in the evenings. The staff are excellent and very stylishly attired, and thanks to the comfortable seating and relaxing ambience, Mare is a prime place to have a romantic night on the town. Some complain that the food isn't particularly authentic, but even if it's not identical to tapas served on

Las Ramblas in Barcelona, it's still excellent. The free bruschetta is lovely and be sure to try the beef tournedos with blue cheese sauce and the chocolate lava pudding, perhaps the city's best dessert.

MOREL'S $$

5 Xinzhong Jie, Gongti Bei Lu, 6416-8802

HOURS: Daily 11:30 A.M.-2:30 P.M., 5:30-10:30 P.M.

This long-term favorite is a bustling Belgian home-style eatery complete with rustic wooden furniture and checked tablecloths. Here you will find some of Beijing's best steaks and mussels, and there are always seasonal specials to try, like white asparagus in the spring. If you can tear yourself away from ordering the fillet steak and frites, more "grandmother"-style dishes, like braised chicory, are delicious. Try and save room for the awesome desserts, especially the waffles topped with cherries and whipped cream, or for the huge menu of Belgian beers.

Capital Museum and Temple of Great Charity Map 5

REGIONAL CHINESE

BAI FAMILY MANSION $$

29 Suzhou Jie, 6265 4186

HOURS: Daily 11 A.M.-9:30 P.M.

From the moment you're greeted by staff dressed in traditional Manchu outfits, it's hard to escape the feeling you've traveled in a time machine back to the time of Qing dynasty. The spectacular setting was once home to a prince and now is a fitting setting to the stylish menu, which re-creates traditional Chinese dishes from around the country. The names of dishes are on the poetic side—try the Smiling Concubine, a salad of flower petals, as a starter and be sure to try the *gongbao* chicken, which is less sweet and more interesting than the norm (this is the dish that General Tso's chicken originated from!). Peking Opera acts take place during the evenings.

DAI ETHNIC FLAVOR RESTAURANT $

16 Minzu Daxue Beilu, Weigongcun, 6848 3189

HOURS: Daily 11 A.M.-10:30 P.M.

This place may be a 30-minute ride from the center of town, but that doesn't stop people from traveling across the city to experience the wonderful Dai minority food from Yunnan province here for unbelievably low prices. Dai cuisine is as different from regular Chinese food as can be; it is more similar to Thai with its tropical ingredients such as lemongrass, bamboo, and pineapples. You'll probably have to wait in line outside before even getting into the steamy packed dining room. There you'll find plastic covers on tables and an English menu of sorts (be sure to try first item on the menu, the braised pork shoulder). The pineapple rice and deep-fried potato balls with a delectable dip are other must-orders. Don't worry about your lack of Mandarin: Most of the staff don't speak it either but use the Dai dialect.

LU LU $$

9 Fuxing Lu, 50m west of the Military Museum, 6357 6981

HOURS: Daily 11:30 A.M.-2:30 P.M., 5:30-10:30 P.M.

This is the Beijing branch of a famous Shanghainese chain that serves southern specialities in faux art deco surroundings—locals love the glitz and glam, but we prefer to head here for excellent steamers-full of *xiaolongbao* dumplings, arguably Shanghai's most addictive dish. Happily, they are also one of the cheapest items on the menu as the rest are full of prized ingredients such as shark's fin and abalone. We advise you to stick to the Shanghainese dim sum and the hot and sour soup—filling, delicious, and healthy—and then head next door to the surreally entertaining Military Museum.

WHAMPOA CLUB $$$

Jia 23 Jinrong Dajie, 8808 8828

HOURS: Daily 11:30 A.M.-10 P.M.

Shanghai's Whampoa Club has long had

© WHAMPOA CLUB

the glamorous dining room at Whampoa Club

critics salivating, and now the chef Jerome Leung has come north, setting up shop in one of the few courtyards left in Financial Street, Beijing's answer to Wall Street. Leung's unique selling point is his reinvention of local cuisine set in beautiful surroundings akin to a private members' club. Guests enter the courtyard and go down a glorious staircase decorated with candlelit birdcages before entering the sexy and sophisticated dining room. It's more of a nighttime venue than a lunch spot because of the atmosphere, but the chef is trying to make it more daytime-friendly by having afternoon tea. As for dinner, the sticky, soy-braised fish and the mouthwateringly tender beef tenderloin with pistachio nuts are excellent, though at prices that would make locals giggle.

INTERNATIONAL

BLU LOBSTER $$$

Shangri-La Hotel, 29 Zizhuyuan Lu, 6841 2211, ext. 6727

HOURS: Daily 11:30 A.M.-2:30 P.M., 5:30-11:30 P.M.

Irish chef Brian McKenna—a veteran of several Michelin-star restaurants in the United Kingdom—has brought cutting-edge international cuisine to the Shangri-La Hotel. The decor may disappoint, resembling that of an upscale airport lounge, but the food is revelatory. While the restaurant offers a full suite of à la carte options, it's best to forget the expense and go for the full tasting menu, which offers course after mouthwatering course of strange and unprecedented gastronomic delights, including oysters garnished with passion fruit foam and foie gras spread on Rice Krispies. One of Beijing's most comprehensive wine lists makes up for the decision not to match a wine with each course. An expensive but revelatory treat.

KIEV $$

13 Puhui Nanli, Yuyuantan Nanlu, 6828 3482

HOURS: Daily 11 A.M.-11 P.M.

For a unique evening for Beijing or indeed anywhere else in the world, head here for very reasonably priced boozy vodka-marinated lamb kebabs and the indulgent Kiev pudding while stars of Ukraine's opera scene in military uniforms saunter among the tables belting out tunes accompanied by harpsichords. Sounds weird and it is, but it's oddly enjoyable. The grandma's kitchen-style wooden furniture, TVs showing Ukrainian shows, and fake grapevines that line the wall all add to the entertaining ambience.

STEAK EXCHANGE $$$

5th Floor, Intercontinental Financial Street, 11 Jinrong Dajie, 5852 5888

HOURS: Daily 11:30 A.M.-2 P.M., 5:30-10:30 P.M.

Catering to meat-loving business travelers staying on the western side of town, this classy and discreet restaurant, tucked behind the Intercontinental's main eatery, is the place to go for steak. All the meat is imported from the States and Australia, and this of course doesn't come cheap: Most of the clientele are traveling on expense accounts. It's not all business, though—when the lights are turned down, this can be a great place for a dinner date, with its high ceilings and enormous glass wine rack. And it's impossible not to share a dessert after all that meat—even if the portions of classics like New York style cheesecake are nearly as big as the table.

University District and the Summer Palace Map 6

CAFÉS AND CHEAP EATS

LUSH $

2/F, Building 1, Huaqingjiayuan, Chengfu Lu, Wudaokou, 8286 3566, www.lushbeijing.com

HOURS: Daily 24 hours

Ground Zero for the area's huge contingent of foreign students learning Chinese, this friendly hangout run by Americans does a great job dealing with the crowds that pack the place around the clock. An eatery by day serving mouthwatering sandwiches, breakfasts, and milk shakes, it becomes a hopping bar at night with special events scheduled throughout the week, including open-mic nights, live music, and movie nights. It's not innovative or superb food, but fresh and filling, and the friendly staff and cool music add to the fun.

SCULPTING IN TIME $

1, Building 12, Huaqingjiayuan, Chengfu Lu, Wudaokou 8286 7026

HOURS: Daily 9 A.M.-2 A.M.

Another laid-back option in Wudaokou is this branch of a small local chain run by a Taiwanese expat. Though the Western food is just a bit above mediocre, a mixed crowd of expats, students, and locals still flock to this artsy café for its laid-back atmosphere and free Wi-Fi. The sandwiches are on the bland side, but people still stake out territory in the upstairs area. The breakfast sets are excellent value and the good lattes make up for unstellar muffins.

Greater Beijing

Map 7

LOTUS IN MOONLIGHT $$

12 Liufang Nanli, 6465 3299

HOURS: Daily 11 A.M.-10 P.M.

Despite a long Buddhist tradition for vegetarianism in China, people who don't eat meat can find eating here difficult as many Chinese restaurants use meat stock and oils for flavorings. But that won't happen at this dedicated vegetarian restaurant, which serves healthy fare in a relaxed atmosphere using high-quality ingredients. Specialties include food made up to look like meat and fish, such as the spicy "fish" made from wheat germ but tasting nearly identical to the real thing. The candlelight, lotus symbols, and Buddhist statues make for a peaceful experience and to complete the healthy feel, no alcohol or smoking are allowed.

THE ORCHARD $$$

Hegezhuang Village, Shunyi, phone 6433 6270 for directions

HOURS: Tues.-Sun. noon.-2:30 P.M., 6-9 P.M.

A unique venue, The Orchard is a lovely relaxing restaurant set in its own orchard way out of town toward the airport. The fact that people are prepared to brave the traffic to get to this haven is a sign of how good the reasonably priced Western food is. It's run by an American woman and her Chinese husband who use their own organic produce as much as possible, including fish from their own lake—try the trout if it's available but everything is seasonal so food runs out. The Sunday brunch is an excellent deal with a buffet spread that always includes a traditional roast, and catering to their clientele well, they provide a separate children's buffet and play area to keep the little darlings happy.

NIGHTLIFE

When the sun goes down in Beijing, you have plenty of choices regarding how to keep yourself entertained. Want to rock out to Beijing punk music? No problem. Get dressed up for a more sophisticated evening at a classical concert? That's fine. Want to gasp and giggle at an acrobatic show? Available every night of the week. From designer cocktail bars to run-down dives serving only Tsingtao beer, there's a table waiting for you.

Visitors to Beijing can now enjoy the kind of nightlife options available in any capital city around the world, but really, it was not ever thus: Beijing's scene used to be practically nonexistent. In the 1980s, when night fell, Beijing was deserted. The few visitors who ventured out could see approved Beijing opera and acrobatic shows in decrepit theaters, stick to their overpriced and underwhelming hotel bar, or search for the first bar opened outside of a hotel, Frank's Place, which was allowed to serve only foreigners. How times have changed. Over the last couple decades, an influx of expats helped to drive the nightlife scene forward, as did a whole new generation of Chinese youths, keen to experience some glamour and good times for themselves.

Even as recently as a decade ago, Beijingers viewed the high life of Shanghai and Hong Kong with ill-disguised envy. But, as in every other area, Beijing is catching up fast and its nightlife, driven partly by expats but also by well-to-do Chinese youth looking for ways to cut loose, is every bit as energetic and diverse as the rest of the city.

Different districts cater to different people:

HIGHLIGHTS

LOOK FOR ☾ TO FIND RECOMMENDED NIGHTLIFE.

☾ **Best Place for a Beer in the *Hutong:*** There are few places nicer on a summer's day than the rooftop terrace at the **Drum and Bell,** where you can watch the world go cycling by (page 80).

☾ **Best Place for People-Watching "Chuppies" (Chinese Yuppies):** They're all at **LAN** air kissing each other while checking out other people's outfits and drinking lychee margaritas. And when watching that gets boring, check out the place's spectacularly demented design (page 82).

☾ **Best Bar for a Laid-Back Drink: No Name Bar** single-handedly made Houhai a nightlife mecca but the area's original bar is still ahead of the competition (page 82).

☾ **Best Cocktail Bar:** Despite its bizarre location in a run-down hotel, **Q Bar** attracts a fun crowd that parties on the large terrace in the summer, lychee martini in hand (page 83).

☾ **Best Bar on a Summer's Day:** Set in pretty Ritan Park, **Stone Boat Bar** offers good drinks and charming views from open-air tables overlooking a lake (page 84).

☾ **Coolest Design and Music Policy:** Grown-up groovers will enjoy the music at **Song Music Bar and Kitchen,** Beijing's most sophisticated venue for cool music, which attracts a fun crowd (page 87).

☾ **Best Place to See Chinese Punks at Play:** The expertly run **D-22** is where to head for cutting-edge live music in the capital (page 88).

© HELENA IVESON

the terrace at Q Bar, the best place in town for cocktails

Wudaokou is cheap and dynamic and packed full of students; Sanlitun's neon and loud music attract young (and not-so-young) expats; Houhai's elegance draws well-to-do Chinese bar goers and tourists; Nanguoluxiang is for expats who want to drink cappuccinos and cabernet sauvignon in a traditional Chinese *hutong.* The list goes on. And nightlife is not nearly as segregated as it used to be: Nowadays, Chinese and foreigners party together at bars, live music venues, museums, and everywhere in between.

While in some ways the scene is still feeling its way with service and drinks quality not always the best, it's lively, fun, and affordable. Bars do, though, like restaurants, come and go in Beijing, so it's worth checking the local listings magazines such as *Time Out* or *The Beijinger* for the most up-to-date information. Venues face a few threats from different sources: If a place gets too popular, landlords try to hike the rent, causing places to move or close down, and every few years, there's a government crackdown against what is usually termed "unhealthy activities"—in other words, staying out late and partying all night. When this happens, the revelry just moves to a different place.

Bars and Lounges

APERITIVO

43 Sanlitun Beijie Nanlu, Sanlitun, next to Tongli Studios, 6417 7793

Map 4

This is definitely the most grown-up option in the somewhat rough-and-ready Sanlitun, and nearly everyone enjoying a drink in Aperitivo is European, there because the small place's minimalist decoration and stylish high wooden tables and chairs remind them of a bar back in Italy or France. The wine list is particularly strong with a great selection by the glass, and snacks such as bruschetta keep in with the Euro theme. During warmer months the outside tables are the place to be with a wall of shrubbery keeping the rest of the world out as you sip on the house cocktail. The only bugbear is that the service can be indifferent and staff a little forgetful.

BED TAPAS AND BAR

17 Zhangwang Hutong, Jiugulou Dajie, 300m south of Gulou Bridge, 8400 1554

Map 2

Strange as it may seem now, in the past bar owners didn't make the most of their courtyard venues, believing that people wanted more of a Western vibe. But this pioneering *hutong* bar, whose entrance is marked by two red lanterns and is run by the owner of the nearby Café

THE BEST BARS FOR . . .

- **Sport** – As long as smokiness and staff a shade too eager don't put you off, **The Den** (A4 Gongti Donglu, next to the City Hotel, Sanlitun, 6592 6290) has kept Beijing sports fans happy for way longer than a decade. All big games from the worlds of soccer, the NFL, and rugby are shown on its big-screen TVs and the cut-price pizzas and beers keep the mostly older clientele happy. This place used to be known for its prostitutes but it seems to have cleaned up its act.
- **Meeting golf buddies** – Another more upmarket sports bar is **The Pavilion** (Gongti Xi Lu, opposite Workers' Stadium West Gate, Chaoyang, 6507 2617). It is frequented by many die-hard Beijing expats and also doubles as the 19th hole for the golfing fraternity. Its unobtrusive flat-screen TVs blend in with the upmarket well-lit bar, which serves plenty of wine by the glass and beer on tap, and in the summer, the beer garden is the place to be in Beijing.
- **Getting down with the kids** – The two-story unpretentious **The Rickshaw** (corner of Sanlitun Nanlu and Gongti Beilu, Sanlitun, 6500 4330), open 24 hours, is owned by an Aussie and managed by an American and is a fun and lively place to make a few new friends and play pool, but if you're over 30, you might be one of the oldest there. Its burritos win top marks as do the friendly and enthusiastic staff.
- **A Belgian beer** – **The Tree** (43 Bei Sanlitun, behind 3.3 Mall, 6415 1954, www.treebeijing.com) offers an excellent selection of Belgian beer to accompany its tasty thin-crust pizzas, considered some of Beijing's best. The relaxed atmosphere, occasional jazz nights, and low-lit attractive bar area with plenty of seating bring in a nightly crowd.
- **Fab views over the Forbidden City** – **Palace View,** the 10th-floor open-air bar at the Grand Hotel (35 Dong Chang'an Jie, Tiananmen, 6513 7788), has the most fantastic views as the sun sets over the palace complex and Tiananmen Square. Unfortunately open only in the summer, it's definitely worth seeking out. Drinks are run-of-the-mill, but that's not why you're here.

Sambal, makes the most of its courtyard setting and draws in a well-dressed crowd with its warren of secluded rooms with *kang*-style beds to lounge on. The bar is considered Beijing's best venue for mojitos and sangria, though in winter, when the bar seems just as cool as if you were outdoors, you may want a stiffer drink to keep out the chill.

CENTRO

Kerry Centre Hotel, 1 Guanghua Lu, 6561 8833, ext. 42

Map 4

When Centro opened in 2003, Beijing's bar scene got a much-needed shot of glamour; now the upscale lounge is one of many such venues but it keeps the crowds coming thanks to its generous happy hour and keen-to-party vibe. Drinkers here tend to be older and some, because it's in a hotel, just passing through, but the majority of drinkers are loyal local and expat fans enjoying a glass of Moët or one of the specialty cocktails—be warned, Centro makes them strong. It seems to employ only wannabe models as wait staff who may look good but aren't always the friendliest of types. Most nights from 9 P.M. there is a jazz singer crooning away, but occasionally on the weekends, it gets in a DJ to make it more of a party.

CJW

L-137, The Place, 9 Guanghua Lu, 6587 1222

Map 4

The sister bar to the version in Shanghai, CJW aims to attract high-rolling customers looking for somewhere classy and grown-up to dance the night away, albeit in a shopping mall. The house band, fronted by a genuinely talented Vegas jazz singer, is great at getting people off their seats, and other pluses are the excellent service and stylish gray and blue interior with very comfy sofas to relax into when you're worn out from dancing. But then again, that's as it should be considering the high prices and—unusual for Beijing—a service charge. The C in the title stands for cigars but it should refer to cocktails as they are mixed expertly, not just thrown together like in so many places. From the balcony, there's a good view of the mall's unique selling point: a huge LCD screen that is supposed to be the biggest in Asia.

DRUM AND BELL

41 Zhonglouwan Hutong, between the Drum and Bell Towers, Gulou Dongdajie, 8403 3600

Map 2

Cozy and low-key, the much-loved Drum and Bell is a great place to hang out in all seasons. In summer, enjoy the rooftop terrace's views of the two towers on either side of the bar; in winter, cozy up downstairs in one of the many snug rooms on the ground floor. Drinks are averagely priced and average in general, and running somewhat counter to its laid-back grown-up vibe for most of the week, its Sunday special of all-you-can-drink cocktails and beer for just 50RMB makes the Drum and Bell a regular haunt for groups of friends. The pizza by the slice is useful for soaking up excess alcohol. Be careful when using the distinctly average bathroom as it's a tiny space.

GOOSE 'N' DUCK

East side of Chaoyang Park, S1, Green Lake International Tower, 5928 3045

Map 4

Without doubt the most bizarre bar in Beijing if not the world (where else can you find archery, a baseball batting cage, huge screens showing live sports, a live band, and an on-site brewery?), the Goose, as it's known to its fans, is one of a kind. While it has more than its fair share of older male expats looking to forget they are in China, there's also usually a sprinkling of families there as the kids enjoy all the sports while the parents get the chance to have a drink in peace. The Canadian owner has put together a huge menu of both food and drinks at wallet-friendly prices—it's just a shame the bar is all by itself at the far end of Chaoyang Park, over the fourth ring road.

i-ULTRA LOUNGE

8 Chaoyang Xi Lu, just behind Micheng Club, 6508 8585, www.block8.cn

Map 4

More Shanghai than Beijing in attitude and

BEIJING'S FAVORITE DRINKS

While in Beijing, be sure to try once (and that is probably all you'll wish to after tasting it) China's spirit of choice, the potent booze called *báijiǔ*, which means white alcohol. Many a business traveler has spent the morning cursing the drink after being obligated at a business dinner to drink too many shots to count of the noxious spirit that tastes akin to gasoline. The Chinese, especially in the cold north, love to down bottles of this grain alcohol, which can often be near an eye-watering 100 percent alcohol. If this alone weren't enough alone to put you off, many restaurants fill their bottles of *báijiǔ* with twigs, herbs, and even dead animals as they are believed to be a health tonic! If you can, ignore the 10RMB bottles and drink only China's top *báijiǔ* brand, Moutai: It may not taste that much better, but at least it will be unadulterated.

Less offensive and distinctly Chinese is the party people's drink of choice: Chivas and green tea, the Beijing equivalent to vodka and Red Bull. The new middle class has fueled a boom for Chivas, and other whiskey companies are also flocking to the capital to promote their brands. Apparently a Taiwanese bartender created the drink by adding the sweet tea to the Chivas to take the sting out of the whiskey and make it more suitable for the Chinese palate. Whoever he was, he created a monster and now Beijing and Shanghai bars and clubs are full of *dàkuǎn*, or rich Chinese men, who order multiple bottles of the whiskey at a time and drink it ostentatiously to show off exactly how rich they are.

If you're more a beer drinker than anything else, relax: Beijing has plenty of options to work your way through. Aside from China's biggest beer brand, Tsingtao, which dates from 1903, when Germans ran the city of Qingdao and started their own brewery, Beijing has Beijing Beer (Běijīng Píjiǔ) and Yanjing Beer (Yānjīng Píjiǔ). To figure out the popular local brew, just watch what the locals drink on the streets at the barbecue vendors'. A word of warning, though: Most Chinese beer drinkers like their beer warm. If you want it cold, you'll have to ask.

vibe, i-Ultra's striking design attracts the beautiful people in droves; they just love striking a pose as they saunter down the catwalk-style entrance. The bar is sandwiched between two good restaurants, Haiku (sister restaurant to Hatsune) and the Italian eatery Mediterraneano: People tend to eat there and then move into the purple and gray lounge to sip on an expensive but well-made cocktail. For somewhere with such classy aspirations, though, it has a very odd music policy: Last time I was there, Dire Straits was booming out. Staff are well trained and friendly, and in the summer, the exhibitionist in you may enjoy the rooftop beach, where stripping off is very much encouraged.

JAZZ-YA

18 Sanlitun Beilu, Nali Mini Mall, Sanlitun, 6415 1227

Map 4

Styled as a Japanese *izakaya,* or a Japanese bar that also serves food, this place down an alley off the seedy main street in Sanlitun is a stylish refuge from the action outside. Some find the huge unobtrusive door difficult to open—you slide it! Then after a walk down a darkened pathway that makes you feel as if you're pounding a catwalk, you finally get to the action. Not that there's usually much going on as the place is very low-key (there is jazz at different times but the place seems to follow its own schedule), but that's what its fans like, plus the well-made cocktails, especially the legendary Long Island Iced Tea and the large range of sake. The Japanese food gets mixed reviews but the fusion pizzas are excellent—and necessary if only to soak up the strong drinks.

LA BAIE DES ANGES

Nanguanfang Hutong next to Hutong Pizza, Houhai, 6657 1605, www.la-baie-des-anges.com

Map 2

Opened by a pair of French expats keen to

re-create a Parisian wine bar down a winding alley in Houhai, this place's regular crowd of young European drinkers shows that they've got it right. From the outside, the bar looks nothing special, but persevere as inside the cozy venue has huge skylights that allow the light to stream in during the day. A large range of wines are available by the glass, and unsurprisingly there's a French bent to the list. The reasonable prices and convivial loungelike atmosphere enlivened by acid jazz make this a perfect place to start or finish a night. It does get smoky, however.

LAN

4/F Twin Towers, B12 Jianguomenwai Dajie,
5109 6012 and 5109 6013, www.lanbeijing.com
Map 4

Two years in the making, Beijing's biggest bar, club, and restaurant opened its doors to its delighted crowd in 2007. Its Philippe Starck–designed interior is why the word "eclectic" was invented: There's a cigar lounge, oyster bar, and extravagant nightclub area, in addition to what must count as Beijing's most glamorous toilets, bar none. Though there is a restaurant, the Szechuan food is incredibly unreliable: Do as most do and pile in dressed in your fancy duds to sip bubbly alongside Beijing's beautiful people while house DJs spin low-key house music. Unusually for Beijing, there's a service charge.

© HELENA IVESON

the baroque and bejeweled bar at LAN

LOONG BAR

2F, JW Marriott Hotel Beijing, 83 Jianguo Lu,
5908 8995
Map 4

The name of the bar at the JW Marriott means dragon in Mandarin, and the designers have gone all out with the theme, featuring glass dragon sculptures on the shelves, a crystal dragon hovering over the bar, painted dragon-inspired flourishes on the walls, and a marble bar that undulates like one. Even if the hammering home of the theme gets on your nerves, the excellent drinks list will soothe them; it includes a fine array of cocktails you won't see anywhere else, such as the signature drink, the Lomohito, the bar's take on the traditional mojito. And the excellent leather-backed bucket seats are wonderful to slink into.

NO NAME BAR

3 Qianhai Dongyan, next door to Nuage restaurant,
6401 8541
Map 2

Low-key, mellow, and friendly, this bar started the whole nightlife scene around Houhai in the 1990s; it is still going strong and is still the best of the bunch. During the day, the brightly colored venue with plants in every corner is a delightful place for hanging out with a Vietnamese coffee in one of the wicker chairs near the window overlooking the lakes; at night, the subdued lighting, eclectic soundtrack, and extensive drink menu, including a couple of wines by the glass, attract a laid-back crowd of expats and local hipsters. Try to nab one of the tables overlooking the lake for great people-spotting.

PADDY O'SHEA'S

28 Dongzhimenwai Dajie, opposite the Australian Embassy, 6415 6389

Map 4

Beijing's most authentic Irish pub—well, as authentic as it can be 10,000 miles from Dublin—was an instant success when it opened at the beginning of 2008, appealing to homesick expats and locals keen to experience some craic at the Irish-run establishment. The bar's wooden furniture-filled space is cosy in winter and the perfect place to sup on a pint of the capital's best draft Guinness and other Irish favorites. There are four plasma screens showing live sports dotted around the place and a popular pool table, and on weekends, the second floor is turned into a cheesy disco, fittingly named Shenanigans. There is traditional Irish food but the stews aren't a patch on the real thing, unfortunately.

PASSBY BAR

108 Nanluogu Xiang, 8403 8004, www.passbybar.com

Map 2

If only all bars could get it as right as Passby does with its lovely *hutong* location, pretty courtyard, friendly atmosphere, and reasonable prices. A longtime favorite, the bar was one of the first to open on Nanluoguxiang and attracts a mixed crowd keen to enjoy the house wine among the rustic, bohemian decor with its photographic displays of Tibet. A new terrace on the roof opened in 2007 and guests can get free Wi-Fi access alongside their Tsingtao. It also serves food but the mainly Italian menu is the place's one uneven aspect: Pasta dishes are small, pizzas are middling, but the homemade warm bread and sublime eggplant and ricotta salad are excellent. There's no toilet, but the public one across the street is perhaps the cleanest in China.

Q BAR

6/F, Eastern Hotel, corner of Sanlitun Nanlu and Gongti Nanlu, 6595 9239, www.qbarbeijing.com

Map 4

This is the third venue in three years for celebrated local mixologists, George and Echo

© HELENA IVESON

a sign along the always buzzy Nanluogu Xiang

(the two previous bars were demolished), but their fans like this lively and stylish bar with its clever cocktails. The thirty-something clientele pours in because of its central Sanlitun location that's still far enough away from the rowdy student bars, but the wait for drinks does become a bit of a bore. Cocktails are very strong, though, so you might find you need just the one dragon fruit margarita. One night a week—now Thursday—is Gay Night.

SADDLE CANTINA

2/F, Nali Studios Patio, 81 Sanlitun Bei Lu, Sanlitun, 5208 6005, www.beijingsaddle.com

Map 4

This laidback bar and restaurant specializes in sombreros, margaritas, and burritos—and on a sunny day, their open-air terrace is an excellent place to be, especially if the BBQ is up and running. The Cantina is the newest project from the owners of the popular if rowdy bar the Rickshaw, but this edition is less frat-boy and more grown-up. Tequila fans will love the strong margaritas, as well as the selection of top-grade Mexican tequila, and food-wise, the fresh tortilla chips and wide selection of salsas are great ways to soak up the alcohol.

STONE BOAT BAR

Southwest corner of Ritan Park on the east end of the lake, 6 Ritan Beilu, 6501 9986

Map 4

The best outside venue in Beijing for a quiet and relaxed glass of wine, bar none, the Stone Boat is many people's favorite bar in the world. It sounds odd—it is a faux Qing dynasty boat by the side of a lake in pretty Ritan Park—but its regular live-music nights, carefully selected but limited wine list, and well-priced beers and snacks mean the place is full of people, often journalists whose offices are nearby, engaged in earnest conversation. There's free Wi-Fi too and the friendly staff make a mean café latte, so you can stay all day if the mood takes you.

© HELENA IVESON

Stone Boat Bar in picturesque Ritan Park

12SQM

1, Nanluogu Xiang, on the corner with Fuxiang Hutong, 6402 1554

Map 2

Beijing's smallest bar—yes, the name refers to the floor space—is also one of the city's friendliest thanks to its owners, who pride themselves on providing good music, and considering the size, an amazing range of reasonably priced Australian wine and imported beer. There's only one table and comfy sofa in the converted *hutong* home, which makes it really feel like a home away from home—be warned, time can slip by very quickly here—not good if you have sights to see! If you get hungry, the Aussie owners can rustle up some meat pies. The bar, for reasons of ventilation, is nonsmoking and although there's no toilet, there are (nice) public facilities across the alley.

Nightclubs and KTV

Since 2005, the scene at the Workers' Stadium has exploded with superclub after superclub opening their doors to queues of wealthy hip Chinese. And you can't come to China and not have a go at China's number one evening entertainment, KTV, or karaoke—don't worry; you can warble away to English songs.

ABSENT NIGHTCLUB

B1/F, 12 Huasheng Building, Yabao Lu, 5120 6538

Map 4

Yabao Lu is Ground Zero for Beijing's large community of Russian expats, and this is the place to see them in action: Expect copious shots of vodka, glitzy floor shows, the odd fistfight, and a suspicious number of single women in furry knee-high boots strutting on the dance floor—in short, a hilarious night if you're in the mood, hellish if you're not. Evenings here don't kick off until late, say after midnight, and that is when people start sauntering down the neon-lit escalator. Choose a booth near the stage for the best views of the feather-clad boys and girls who make up the floor show, and if you're lucky, they will do their near-perfect reenactment of the finale to the film *Dirty Dancing*. Do as the Russians do and wash down your vodka shots with a slice of dark bread and some salted cucumber—they swear it wards off hangovers.

THE BANK

Gongti Donglu opposite Gate 9 of the Workers' Stadium, 6553 6698

Map 4

This glitzy nightclub/lounge/restaurant/opulent KTV lounge opened in 2007, can hold 1,500 people, and is usually full—that tells you how big the appetite is for partygoing in Beijing these days. Three marble-filled floors of excess make the place just as jaw-dropping on the inside as out, and you can practically see the piles of money that have been spent on the neo-Gothic, mirrored, velvety, and bejeweled interior—it's either your thing or not. While the interior attracts most attention, the music hasn't been forgotten with the DJ booth raised up high and surrounded by gargantuan video screens. Drinks are expensive for Beijing, but the high-spending well-dressed crowd doesn't seem to mind, and how else is The Bank going to recoup all that money?

CARGO

6 Gongti Xilu, Gongti West Gate, 6551 6898

Map 4

A spin-off of much-loved Club Mix, which was knocked down much to the disgust of Beijing clubbers, this club, which glows with neon inside and out, has been remodeled and remodeled, both physically and musically, before finally settling upon its current course of mainstream house. Probably the best option among the Gongti row of clubs, Cargo's auditory-stimulated LED wall attracts Chinese high rollers, trendy partygoers, and a steady crowd of foreign clubbers with its regular Loaded parties, featuring B-list foreign DJs plus the odd class act.

CHINA DOLL

6/F, 3.3 Shopping Mall, Sanlitun Lu, 6417 4699

Map 4

China Doll, which recently moved to its new incarnation on the top floor of the 3.3

The bars in Sanlitun may not look like much, but for a cheap beer they're a fun option.

GAY BEIJING

Not so long ago, the Communist government classified homosexuality as a mental illness and persecuted both gay men and women. But if you check out Beijing's top gay club, Destination, any night of the week, you'll soon see that things have dramatically changed. Gay communities are springing up in Beijing, Shanghai, and other large cities across China. This isn't to say the streets are full of out and proud gays – the situation is similar to that of the U.S. military's attitude: Don't ask, don't tell. There are plenty of bars, clubs, and saunas out there catering to the pink RMB, but they aren't allowed to promote themselves. No official law says they can't, but places will get raided if they are advertised too openly. While this may seem restrictive to people in the West, homosexuals in China don't seem to be too bothered, perhaps because they know how things used to be. "It gets freer every year," says Bernie, a forty-something Beijing resident quoted in *Time* magazine. "And every year more and more gays come out of the closet. In Beijing and the big cities, you can see couples walking around the shopping malls holding hands. In the smaller cities some people are still underground, but even there, I hear it's getting better all the time."

Beijing's most popular gay club for the last few years has been glamorous **Destination** (7 Gongti Bei Lu, opposite the West Gate of Workers' Stadium, 6551 5138), where a mostly male crowd made up of trendy young Chinese, expats, and visitors keen to experience the Beijing gay scene come to dance and be seen. Plenty of women come here, too – it's very friendly. Just around the corner is **Pipe,** a central point for the city's lesbian scene. There's usually a drag show at some point during the evening – unfortunately it's open only on Saturday nights (Gongti Nan Lu, 6593 7756). For more places, check out www.utopia-asia.com/beijbars.htm.

shopping mall, is smack in the middle of Sanlitun and has added some class to an area better known for packed dive bars dishing out 5RMB booze to student revelers. Many clubs in Beijing go for an over-the-top industrialist look, but China Doll, thanks to its female owner, is more feminine—it's a womblike underwater sanctuary, highlighted by looped footage of a naked mermaid writhing in a pool—a sexy piece of entertainment that pulls in a well-dressed crowd. The music policy is very house, and this is a great place to see local DJs in action. The cheapest beer is 35RMB, shooters are two-for-one after midnight, and there's no cover.

MIX

Inside Workers' Stadium North Gate, Gongti Beilu, 6530 2889

Map 4

One of the city's most successful and loud dance clubs, the Mix empire just grows and grows, taking over all the surrounding buildings as local hip-hop fans can't get enough of the place. Most of the crowd is young and into looking good as much as moving to the music, though the place does get some good international DJs passing through. This is a prime pickup spot so don't be surprised if you're constantly looked up and down. Interestingly, hip-hop appeals to the wealthy set in China so the drink of choice is Chivas and Green Tea. If you get the chance, peek into one of the private rooms, which cost a staggering 80,000RMB a night, and see the rich at play.

PARTYWORLD

1-2/F, Prime Tower, 22 Chaoyangmenwai Dajie, 6588 3333

Map 4

Beijing's most popular venue for crooning away does away with the sleaze factor that is often in evidence in other karaoke venues—Partyworld looks more like a luxury hotel than anything else. This location has 130 rooms costing around 100RMB an hour, which sounds a hell of a lot, but at peak times, such as late at night, you might find yourself waiting for a room. There's a long list of Western songs of the Beatles and Madonna persuasion but one of the most amusing aspects is the bargain-basement videos that go along with the songs; they all seem to have been made for about $5 in Russia. If singing away has given you an appetite, there's a free buffet at 11 P.M. Oh, and be sure to peek into rooms and watch the Chinese in action: Karaoke is taken very seriously here, and if you're invited in to listen, you must sit quietly and then give a rousing round of applause afterward.

SANGRIA CLUB

Haojun Jie (Lucky Street) next door to Elisa's Italian Restaurant, 5867 0248

Map 7

This Spanish-themed bar and salsa club is spread over two floors, which isn't obvious from the scruffy entrance outside as it's completely underground. The place has been opened by the owner of a popular Middle Eastern restaurant, but the branching out to all things Andalusian has been successful judging by all the Spaniards partying here. The namesake drink is fantastic, featuring fresh apples and a dash of cinnamon, and the tapas menu will refuel you after a salsa around the dance floor, encouraged by the enthusiastic live band.

SONG MUSIC BAR AND KITCHEN

B108, The Place, 9 Guanghua Lu, 6587 1311, www.songbeijing.cn

Map 4

When Song opened at the beginning of 2008, bar-goers and clubbers fed up with overly loud music and an overwhelming crush of people finally had somewhere grown-up and cool to party. It may be in the basement of a shopping mall, but ignore that and head here to this medium-size bar and enjoy the visually stunning decor; its wooden-ridged interior is designed to resemble the terraced rice fields of southern China—sounds good but it's really effective. The white walls have videos projected on them by the often-full dance floor, where people are enjoying a range of music styles from electronica to avant-garde jazz, but if you're there to drink, there are plenty of places to sit and sip on a well-made cosmo or imported beer. All this style comes at a very reasonable price, too—no wonder it's always busy.

THE WORLD OF SUZY WONG

1A Chaoyang Gongyuan Xi Men, above the Four Seasons Japanese Restaurant, 6590 3377, www.suziewong.com.cn

Map 4

This enduring dress-to-impress club decked out like an old opium den still packs in patrons keen to dance the night away to some of the best house music in town. The later it gets, the more of a meat market it feels, and foreign men may find themselves unusually appealing to the working girls who congregate here. While the upstairs dance area is small, Touch on the first floor gives the high-rolling, beautiful-people crowd more room to see and be seen, while the terrace above is as popular as ever. Every Wednesday is Ladies-Only Night, when women are served free drinks by hunky boxer short–wearing men until 11 P.M., when male customers are allowed in.

Live Music

Once upon a time, Beijing opera was your only choice for live music, and while that can be nice every once in a while, it would not be music to your ears every single weekend. But along came *yaogun,* or rock and roll, whose popularity owes something to the gritty edginess so integral to the Beijing character. In addition to rock and punk, the city has a couple of excellent jazz bars for a more mellow evening.

CD JAZZ CAFÉ

16 Nongzhanguanlu, Dongsanhuan, next to Great Wall Sheraton Hotel, 6506 8288

Map 4

With portraits of jazz greats hanging on the walls, CD Jazz Café fills up with mostly Chinese chain-smoking, cappuccino-sipping fans here for the live music played every Saturday and Sunday. The bar was set up by horn player Liu Yuan, who used to tour with one of China's best-known rock bands; now he's into more mellow music, and the café's intimate atmosphere with its small stage and hushed crowds quietly foot tapping to the house jazz band is the perfect place to sit back and relax and listen. Swing classes are also held here: Call for details.

CLUB OBIWAN

4, Xiyan, Xihai, Shichahai, 200m from Jishuitan Subway Station, 6617 3231, www.clubobiwan.com.cn

Map 2

It takes a lot to drag downtown dwellers out of their comfort zone, but Club Obiwan is doing a roaring trade and has made itself a much-loved staple of the nightlife scene by being all things to all people. Set in a *hutong* off Jishuitan, this three-story affair is sleek and sexy with dim red lighting, polished wooden floors, comfortable couches, and broad dance floors. Late at night, there's a party atmosphere with different DJs on two floors, and every Thursday evening, there's a movie shown with a special dinner menu that's themed according to the film. During the day, the free wireless and good coffee attract patrons, and at any time of the day, the views from the top floor over the lake are fabulous.

COCO BANANA

1/F, 8 Gongti Xilu, down an alley on the north side of Bellagio Restaurant, 8599 9999

Map 4

One of the hottest places for mainstream Chinese-style clubbing is this spot. From the outside it's difficult to distinguish it from the rest of the clubs in this area, but inside it's more upscale. After walking through a room filled with feather boas hanging from the ceiling and being eyed by the beefy security guys, you'll find yourself in the main room, where barmen will be mixing drinks à la Tom Cruise in *Cocktail,* fog will be swirling around you, and cheesy dance music will be blaring. As long as you're not expecting the latest in music and are prepared to squeeze yourself onto the tiny dance floor, you'll have a blast.

D-22

242 Chengfu Lu, halfway between Wudaokou Subway Station and Peking University East Gate, 6265 3177, www.d22beijing.com

Map 6

Much to this low-key bar's surprise, it won listing magazine *The Beijinger*'s Bar of the Year award just a year after it opened, a sign of how much the live music scene needed something fresh. The bar in the student district of Wudaokou has a mission: to support talented young musicians and artists in Beijing and to invite visiting experimental musicians to perform with local musicians. The club, which holds 200, serves beer and basic mixed drinks, and has a nice upstairs lounge. Its live sound system—one of the best in China—encourages people to make the trek across town. The American owner has perfect muso credentials and all profits go back into the local music scene.

EAST SHORE LIVE JAZZ CAFÉ

2/F, 2 Qianhai Dongyan, just to the west of the post office on Dianmenwai Dajie, 8403 2131

Map 2

Ignore the drab exterior, as inside you'll find a sophisticated gem of a venue with great decor—the dark wood paneling and floor-to-ceiling windows offer great views of the lake Qianhai, and there are intense musicians on the intimate stage and a room full of jazz enthusiasts enjoying a smoke. Run by saxophonist Liu Yue (who is usually in action on Saturday nights), it's the most authentic jazz venue in town, featuring mostly Chinese acts from Thursday to Sunday with no cover charge. It does get very smoky, but if you can cope with that, you'll have a great toe-tapping evening.

MAO LIVE

111 Gulou Dongdajie, 6402 5080, www.maolive.com

Map 2

Smoky and cavernous and right at home among the guitar stores along this road, MAO makes a statement with its logo, featuring the famous hairline of a certain chairman, and with its industrial iron-riveted façade. The venue is run by a cool Japanese record label and it's clear it knows what it is doing with the killer sound system. Here is where Beijing's more alternative-music fans play and hang out, lured by bands that you won't hear anywhere else and a plentiful supply of cheap drinks.

STAR LIVE

3/F, Tango, Hepingli Xijie, near Yonghe Gong, 6425 5677, www.thestarlive.com

Map 2

This midsize live-music venue is on the third floor of one of the city's most popular clubs, Tango, and it usually has at least one act on every weekend whooping it up. Music fans consider it to have one of the best sound systems and setups in town and its shows are a very mixed bag—in 2008, international acts such as Faithless and James Blunt appeared here, in addition to local samba groups, Chinese punk bands, and local and foreign DJs. The venue can hold up to 1,200 rowdy fans and considering it has one of the most annoying methods of buying drinks ever—you have to buy vouchers and then exchange them for something from the limited selection of booze—crowds can build up. At least the lockers outside are free!

WHITE RABBIT

C2 Haoyun Jie (Lucky Street), 133 2112 3678

Map 7

When you see this club's name and logo, you might think it's going to be the latest project from Hugh Hefner, but with its industrial minimalist look, it couldn't be further from Playboy bunnies and glamour. The club is behind a discreet door along one of the city's designated entertainment streets, and once you get in, you'll experience Beijing's cutting-edge music scene. The place is financed and managed by local DJs and musicians, and here's where to go for a taste of what China's musos are into—right now electronic music and drum 'n' bass dominates, filling its black-lit rooms with booming beats.

YUGONG YISHAN

3-2 Zhangzizhong Lu, 6404 2711

Map 2

The first location was knocked down in 2007, but Yugong Yishan has risen from the ashes to reclaim its place as the most eclectic and well-run venue in town. The owners are keen to host live music acts, DJs, rock, jazz, improv, and seemingly anything else: In one week I saw a banjo-playing American singer and a Chinese punk band thrashing around the stage. The new venue is a huge improvement with the large bar, nice bathrooms, and upscale interior—remnants of the venue's previous incarnation as a ritzy nightclub—but the sign is a bit discreet and it's easy to whiz past in a taxi. Cover charges vary but are usually around 50RMB.

ARTS AND LEISURE

Beijing is now firmly on the touring schedules for performing arts companies from around the world keen to join the rush to China. The futuristic egg—the cocoon-shaped titanium and glass National Center for Performing Arts—is also an attraction in itself and performers are lining up to be staged there, including in fall 2008 a Mandarin-language version of the hit Broadway show *Les Miserables*.

Visitors can't fail to notice that China is not completely English-language friendly and while Beijing is the center of China's vibrant independent film and theater scene, finding performances with English subtitles isn't always easy. But persevere and read the local listing magazines, and you'll be rewarded by the city's small but lively avant-garde scene. Be aware, though, that etiquette isn't the same as back home, with talking, calling out, and getting up from your seat everyday occurrences in theaters and concert halls.

Fortunately music transcends language difficulties, and the city attracts more than its fair share of Chinese and international performers. Virtuoso pianist Lang Lang often performs here when not traveling the world, but a whole host of lesser-known musicians perform nightly, whether in small jazz bars or concert halls seating thousands.

The contemporary arts scene is also thriving, with avant-garde Chinese art being sold for millions of dollars in auction houses around the world, and in any given month, you're likely to find an arts festival under way. So, the lights of the city are firmly back on and the cultural drought is over, so fill up on the best Beijing has to offer.

HIGHLIGHTS

LOOK FOR TO FIND RECOMMENDED ARTS AND ACTIVITIES.

Best Theater: When it comes to theater-going, "The Egg," properly known as the **National Center for Performing Arts,** wipes out the competition thanks to its imposing controversial design and awesome cutting-edge acoustics (page 92).

Best Place to Make a Song and Dance of It: Whether you're a tourist or living here, everyone loves the drumming, dancing, and all-around entertainment on offer at ***Legend of Kung Fu*** (page 94).

Best Art and Architecture: Chinese art is smoking-hot right now and while plenty of galleries in Beijing contain cutting-edge contemporary design, only at the **Red Gate Gallery** can you wander around admiring the art in a Ming dynasty watchtower (page 96).

Best Traditional Celebration: Expect firecrackers, mountains of lucky food, and cheesy TV shows galore if you're in Beijing during **Chinese New Year**: It's just like Christmas apart from the dumplings (page 101).

Best Jogging Route: It was fit for emperors and their summer strolls, and now the **Summer Palace** offers modern-day Lycra wearers beautiful views along shaded lakeside footpaths (page 104).

Best Cycle Tour: The backstreet half-day tours run by **Cycle China** combine decent exercise with a history lesson on *hutong,* the capital's iconic alleys (page 105).

Best Place to Get Olympic Tips from a Champ: The swimming pool at **Kerry Sports Center** is where multigold medalist Michael Phelps trains when he's in town (page 105).

Best Place to Stretch and Relax: It's difficult to find peace and quiet in Beijing, but the only sounds you'll hear at **Yoga Yard** are birdsongs on the stereo and a few gentle oms (page 108).

Best Way to Take a Hike: The fitness fanatics at **Beijing U-Do Adventure** will put you through your paces when they guide you through a deserted section of the Great Wall (page 109).

Best Place to Have Someone Else Stretch and Relax You: After the jogging, swimming, and cycling tours above, head to **Bodhi** and get one of its expert masseuses to rub your aching limbs back to life (page 111).

© HELENA IVESON

the National Center for Performing Arts, a.k.a. "The Egg"

Beijing has always had the venues but they were let down by stodgy, state-run programming with all performances acting as government propaganda. As with nearly everything else, the rigidity has been loosened and a wide variety of live entertainment is available. Now, acrobats might not be considered high culture, but they definitely put some bounce into the Beijing experience. Most venues will stage a mixture of drama, music, and dance, but a few, such as Tianqiao Theater, specialize in one type of performance, in this case dance. Tickets can be arranged through your hotel or through the excellent English-language website www.piao.com.cn.

If the thought of all this culture sounds intellectually exhausting, there are plenty of other options to keep you entertained, whether it be a stroll in one of the capital's parks, a workout at a well-equipped gym, or a round of golf. And in a city where the pace of life can tire the most go-getting of travelers, a bargain-priced massage is the perfect way to end a long demanding day.

The Arts

THEATER

BEIJING EXHIBITION THEATRE

135 Xixhimenwai Dajie, 6835 4455

Map 5

There's no need to go to Russia for Soviet design: This venue, built back in 1954, is one of Beijing's prime symbols of the once-warm relationship between the two countries. The performances here run the whole gamut—Chinese ballet, Western opera, musicals (*42nd Street* in November 2007, for example), the odd international pop group, such as the Black Eyed Peas, and the mild-mannered saxophonist Kenny G, who is hugely popular in China. The drafty auditorium can seat more than 2,000 people. There are usually plenty of ticket touts hanging around, but speaking from bitter experience, I advise it's best not to buy from them.

CAPITAL THEATER

22 Wangfujing Dajie, 6524 9847

Map 1

Before the era of "The Egg," this was Beijing's main theater, but it can't compete with the modernity and cool factor of the new upstart. There is no denying it: The 2,128-seat purpose-built venue at the northern end of Wangfujing's busy shopping street is looking its age. Still, in addition to being the home of the respected Chinese-language People's Theater Group, it still regularly hosts visiting groups from the United States and Britain, including Northern Broadside's acclaimed *The Tempest* in 2007. It is a relatively small space, and there is no need to buy one of the more expensive tickets as even the cheap seats give you an adequate view of the action.

NATIONAL CENTER FOR PERFORMING ARTS

Xi Chang'an Jie, 6655 0000, www.chncpa.org

Map 1

This theater promises to be one of the jewels of Beijing's performing-arts venues, and possibly of the world's. "The Egg" holds three theaters encased in titanium and glass, forming a huge sphere hovering above a man-made lake and surrounded by gardens. It remains to be seen how cutting-edge the programming will be: One of the first stage shows was to be a Chinese-language version of Cameron Mackintosh's *Les Miserables.* However, the first performance in the main 2,416-seat opera house was of a revolutionary ballet called *The Red Detachment of Women* in September 2007, nearly 10 years after the Chinese government selected French architect Paul Andreu—an unbelievably long time in a city where buildings are erected at warp speed, but controversy over the style of the building caused the slow process. (See the *Sights* chapter for more information on the theater.)

© HELENA IVESON

Ritan Park is popular at any time of day.

TIANQIAO THEATRE

30 Beiwei Lu, 8315 6300

Map 3

The original venue was built in the 1950s with the purpose of staging edifying revolutionary ballet, but thanks to a complete overhaul in 2001, which admittedly did leave the venue looking like a shopping mall, this is now Beijing's premier venue for opera and dance. The theater, near the Temple of Heaven, is the home of the National Ballet of China and the Beijing Acrobatic Troupe of China and in addition to more conventional offerings, it also stages more cutting-edge modern dance: Pina Bausch's troupe was a recent visitor. Although there are few signs of it now, Tianqiao, the name of the neighborhood the theater is in, is where many folk art and dance styles originated in the Yuan dynasty in the 13th century.

SYMPHONY

BEIJING CONCERT HALL

Liubukou, 1 Beixinhua Jie, 6610 8092

Map 1

Experience orchestral and chamber music concerts from the China National Symphony Orchestra, the China Opera Symphony Orchestra, the China Traditional Music Ensemble, and the Oriental Song and Dance Troupe at the Beijing Concert Hall. Whether the music is Asian or Western, classic or modern, you will likely be impressed. Shows nightly and on weekend afternoons.

CENTRAL CONSERVATORY OF MUSIC

43 Baojia Jie, 6642 5702

Map 1

It may be a little worn around the edges but the concert hall at the Central Conservatory of Music is one of the more atmospheric performance spaces around Beijing. Tacked onto a traditional Beijing courtyard house, this medium-size hall hosts performances by local and international virtuosi and conservatory students.

FORBIDDEN CITY CONCERT HALL

Inside Zhongshan Park, Xichang'an Jie, 6559 8285

Map 1

Despite the name of the concert hall, it's not

in the Forbidden City but in Zhongshan Park, which is immediately adjacent. Leave plenty of time to get here as the hall is at least a 10-minute walk from any of the park's entrance gates. Once you arrive, you'll find a purpose-built bland-looking but brightly lit venue with an adequate bar and souvenir area. It's definitely worth paying for stall seats, as acoustics in the back are god-awful, a shame considering the quality of performers who can be seen here.

POLY THEATER

1/F Poly Plaza, 14 Dongzhimen Nandajie, 6500 1188, www.polytheatre.com

Map 4

This theater has a great location opposite the Dongsishitiao subway stop near the Workers' Stadium, and it is the city's biggest venue for classical music and visiting theater groups. Many of the gala events for the Beijing Music Festival are staged here, as was recently something slightly more lowbrow, the staging of *Mamma Mia!* The huge lobby has some overpriced restaurants and a bar, but if you have time before your performance, head to the Poly Art museum in the same building, which is surprisingly undervisited considering the wealth of relics on offer, some of which date from the Shang dynasty.

ACROBATICS AND DANCE

ACROBATICS

Chaoyang Theater, 36 Dongsanhuan Beilu, 6506 0838, www.bjcyjc.com

Map 4

Of course it's touristy, but despite being on the pricey side for a threadbare theater, its thrills and spills come so quickly that it keeps you entertained. The skits come thick and fast with Chinese clowns and young acrobats performing "How do they do that?" tricks: The English subtitles aren't really necessary. The stage and some of the costumes could do with an update—perhaps if they were, the audiences would be larger—as it is, don't bother with anything but the cheapest ticket and edge nearer the stage when the lights go down.

BEIJING ACROBATIC TROUPE OF CHINA

Tianqiao Theatre, 30 Beiwei Lu, 8315 6300

Map 3

The troupe, founded in 1950, is still considered the best in China. They often take their show on the road and have visited more than 80 countries, wowing their audience with plate-spinning, contortions, clowning around, and snippets from Peking opera and kung fu. They perform at Beijing's premier venue for opera and dance.

LEGEND OF KUNG FU

Red Theater, 44 Xingfu Dajie, 6714 2473, www.legendofkungfu.com

Map 3

The newest and best of the current crop of performances aimed at tourists, this show, which has toured all around the world, is the one to choose if you can see only one. Unlike some of the more faded theaters, this one was purpose-built; the sound and lighting are uniformly excellent and all seats have a good view. The actual story of a boy who becomes a kung fu legend is entertaining, but even if the narrative loses its appeal, the miniskits in which performers use a trapeze and the acrobatics will keep your attention. Afterward, you can have your photo taken in the foyer with your favorite performer.

ART GALLERIES

If Chinese art is judged by market prices alone, China has well and truly arrived on the arts scene. Staggering amounts of money are paid for works from the mainland. In 2007, a painting by avant-garde artist Yue Minjun based on the 1989 Tiananmen Square protests fetched just under $6 million at a Sotheby's sale in London, a record for contemporary Chinese art at auction. So while you're in town, have a stroll around some of the art areas that have sprung up: Who knows, you might pick up something that will be worth millions. . . .

Most galleries are in clusters on the outskirts of down, and if you are a real enthusiast, it would be worth arranging a taxi for the day to take you to the different areas (see the

THE CONTEMPORARY ART SCENE

Contemporary Chinese art is hot in the West and shows no sign of cooling down anytime soon. Anything "Chinese" seems to sell – one legendary story in the art world is that of a French artist in Beijing whose work started selling only when he started signing off with Chinese characters.

Here are some of the art world's key figures:

- **Ai Weiwei** – One of the most significant Chinese conceptual and performance artists, Ai has gained international recognition for his role as agent provocateur. He was asked to collaborate with the celebrated Swiss architectural firm Herzog and de Meuron to enter the design competition for the Olympic National Stadium, known as the Bird's Nest, but Ai instead boycotted the opening ceremony to protest the way the government is using the games to whip up nationalism.
- **Yue Minjun** – Based in Shanghai, Yue is famous for his widely smiling portraits (self- and otherwise) – one of which, *Execution*, became in 2007 the most expensive work of Chinese contemporary art ever sold.
- **Gu Dexin** – Maybe the most radical of the bunch, Gu became known in the late 1980s for his alien portraits and his experiments with plastics and other materials. He reshapes, or rejects, accepted ideas of what art is with his unconventional methods and ideas – meat as sex object, to name one example.
- **Zhu Wei** – Born in 1966, the Beijing-born and -based Zhu joined China's People's Liberation Army before becoming a leading figure in the art world. He is known for his subtly quizzical critique of politics and society in a rapidly evolving China, and he produces a lot of work in China's quintessentially classical artistic medium, ink on paper.
- **Song Kun** – Part of the N12 collective, she is considered one of the best artists in China under 30 – educated after the Cultural Revolution, in a time of intense urban and economic development. As a result, her work is more personal than the often-political work of her predecessors – such as "It's My Life," a series of 365 paintings that reflect a year in her life.
- **Wen Leng** – Wen is one of the most successful artists working out of Beijing – and another member of the N12 collective – who works in different media, including oil painting, animation works, and photography.
- **Zhang Xiaogang** – Zhang's paintings have made him one of the most expensive Chinese avant-garde artists around. He was a member of China's '85 New Wave art movement, which is credited for bringing Chinese art to international attention, and sparking a new wave of domestic creativity.

Excursions from Beijing chapter for details on arranging a car or ask your hotel to do so). And if you're in town in fall, be sure to check out the DIAF Art festival (see *Festivals and Events* in this chapter for more information).

CAOCHANGDI

319 Caochangdi, phone 6526 8882 for directions, **Map 7**

As 798, also known as Dashanzi (the name of the district it is in; see next listing)—Beijing's premier art destination—got extremely popular, many artists who were formerly based in 798 were forced to leave and ended up here at this new small community 5km north of their previous home in Chaoyang. It is difficult to find, there are not as many galleries here, and the work is more challenging, so unless you are a serious collector, we'd advise sticking to the more accessible 798. The galleries here change even more frequently than at 798 so check out *Time Out Beijing* to see if any exhibitions here are of interest. Most galleries are open 11 A.M.–5 P.M., Tuesday to Sunday.

THE COURTYARD GALLERY

B1/F, 95 Donghuamen Dajie, 6526 8882, www.courtyard-gallery.com
HOURS: Daily 11 A.M.-9 P.M.
Map 1

Downstairs from the swanky restaurant of the same name and across from the Forbidden City's east gate, this small gallery attracts plenty of foreign buyers to its exhibitions of emerging and midcareer artists. Despite being one of the oldest galleries in the city—it dates from 1996—the owners are keeping it cutting-edge with a new gallery at Caochangdi that is big enough for installation and multimedia art. As at the Red Gate, art here is expensive, but it goes with the territory given that the restaurant is also expense account-priced.

DASHANZI

2 Jiuxianqiao Lu. The complex has two entrances marked by large "798" signs. Choose either one and when you walk past the security guards, you will see a map explaining the layout.
Map 7

The Bauhaus-style factories that make up Beijing's premier art district, popularly known as 798, are now so well known that the area has become a tourist attraction in its own right. Although the most avant-garde galleries have moved on to newer pastures, head here on a sunny afternoon and enjoy a relaxed afternoon of wandering broken up by a coffee or snack at one of the trendy cafés. Galleries come and go: The best advice is to buy a map at the first gallery you see and use that to guide you around the maze of venues, or pick up a copy of *Time Out Beijing,* which has excellent art listings. Below is a tiny selection of what's on offer. When you visit, avoid coming on a Monday as many of the galleries will be closed. (For more information, see the *Sights* chapter.)

RED GATE GALLERY

Levels 1 and 4, Dongbianmen Watchtower, Chongwenmen, 6525 1005, www.redgategallery.com
HOURS: Daily 10 A.M.-5 P.M.
Map 4

The charismatic Australian owner opened the gallery in 1991 and what a location it is, with art spread over two floors of an imposing Ming dynasty watchtower near the center of the city. You have to pay 10RMB to enter the grounds but it's money well spent. It puts on around eight solo shows of more well-established artists every year and all the art from the current exhibition can be seen on its website, so you can check whether you're interested before you go. Be warned before you fall in love with something: The art here is always expensive and priced in U.S. dollars. It also has a gallery in Dashanzi.

COURTESY OF RED GATE GALLERY

The Red Gate Gallery is set in the imposing Dongbianmen Watchtower.

798 PHOTO GALLERY

4 Jiuxianqiao Lu, 6438 1784, www.798photogallery.cn
HOURS: Daily 10 A.M.-7 P.M.
Map 7

This small but excellent gallery opened in 2003 and changes its displays every month: Past exhibitions have varied from photos of some of the last women in China with bound feet, children journeying across mountains to get to school every day, to legendary American photographer Lawrence Schiller's snaps of Marilyn

Monroe and America in the 1960s. The gallery sells posters and prints plus a good selection of photography books.

798 SPACE

4 Jiuxianqiao Lu, 6438 4862, www.798space.com

HOURS: Daily 10 A.M.-7 P.M.

Map 7

798 Space's huge exhibition hall is what sets this gallery apart: Nowhere else has the space to stage the huge installations that are done here. The exhibitions change frequently but if the art on the walls doesn't grab you, look overhead for the Communist slogans written in Mao red that say "Abide by Mao" and "Long Live the Party." Its café, the Old Factory, makes a reviving cup of coffee.

CINEMAS

CHERRY LANE MOVIES

Kent Center, 29 Liangmaqiao Lu, east of Yansha Bridge, 135 0125 1303, www.cherrylanemovies.com.cn

Map 7

Foreign fans of Chinese art films breathed a sigh of relief when Cherry Lane opened its doors. The one-screen cinema is run by a Chinese movie enthusiast and is open only on Friday and Saturday nights, and most films are shown only once, so you have to check the website frequently—signing up for the weekly email is a good idea. Only Chinese films are screened with English subtitles and in addition to being a comfortable space, it's a good place to meet like-minded people as most hang out in the bar afterward.

EAST GATE CINEMA

B1, Building B, East Gate Plaza, 9 Dongzhong Jie, 6418 5930, www.dhyc.cn

Map 4

This cinema may be small and on the expensive side, but with four screens showing the latest Chinese plus a few mainstream English-language films and a central location, it's one of Beijing's most popular. Tickets range from 60–80RMB: Go for the cheapest as there seems to be no real difference in seats. Snacks are meager, but there is a Subway and SPR Coffee shop within the complex. Aim to get to the less busy, earlier screen times as sometimes the number of people talking both to each other and on their cell phones can be excruciating.

WANDA INTERNATIONAL CINEPLEX

3/F, Building 8, Wanda Plaza, 93 Jianguo Lu, 5960 3399, www.wandafilm.com

Map 4

Beijing's newest multiplex was supposed to be a Warner Cinema but the deal fell through. No matter: It looks like a standard multiplex with blaring music, neon signs everywhere, and all the popcorn and nachos you can munch on. There's usually at least one English-language film on—if you're watching a Chinese film, make sure there are English subtitles as not all showings will have them. Standard tickets are 60RMB—VIP tickets aren't worth the extra. For even more sensory overload, there's a noisy arcade full of shoot-'em-up games.

Festivals and Events

At any time of year, there are plenty of events to choose from in Beijing, from avant-garde arts festivals that rival those in New York and London to the traditional festival days unique to Chinese culture, such as the surprisingly cheerful tomb-sweeping day and the brightly lit temples and streets during the Lantern Festival. These holidays are based on the lunar calendar, so their dates change every year.

By far the best time to be here for nontraditional festivals is in the fall, when the majority of interesting cultural events are held, whether you're seeking classical music, contemporary art, or the latest bands to rock out to. Dates change every year, so the best way to find out what's going on is to check out the many monthly English-language magazines available—a sure sign of the variety of entertainment on offer is the number of magazines needed to list them all.

When it comes to making reservations, save your blood pressure and avoid contacting the actual box offices as staff will rarely speak English. You could ask your hotel to help out or instead, go to www.piao.com.cn, an English-language ordering service that will deliver tickets anywhere in Beijing for free.

SPRING

GODDESS OF MERCY GUANYIN'S BIRTHDAY

Guangji Temple, 25 Fuchengmennei Dajie, 6513 3549

Map 5

With so many Chinese being Buddhist, the

SPRING FESTIVAL CHAOS

It couldn't have come at a worse time for China's migrant workers: In 2008, freak snowstorms – the worst for 50 years – hit southern and central China as tens of millions of people tried to board trains and buses to get home for Spring Festival, also known as Chinese New Year, China's most important holiday. The brutal weather led to at least 50 deaths – 25 in a bus crash on an icy road in Guizhou province – and crippled transport links, scuppering holiday plans and delaying coal and food deliveries, water supplies, and cutting whole towns off.

For many of China's 200 million migrant workers, the Spring Festival is the only holiday they get all year and the only chance they have to see their families. Tempers flared at train stations across the country as the people were told there was no hope of their reaching their destinations. And in an unheard-of move, Prime Minister Wen Jiabao rushed to Changsha Railway Station in Hunan province to apologize and promised the thousands of stranded passengers that they would be home for Spring Festival.

The problem of transport congestion during national holidays is an annual headache and is getting increasingly serious with greater numbers of migrant workers. In 2008, 178.6 million people wanted to travel during the holiday compared with 156 million in 2007. The government has taken some measures to help – it has changed the dates of national holidays to make Spring Festival three days longer, expanded train services, fixed the prices of tickets, and started schemes to help migrant workers buy tickets. But, in 2008, to no avail.

The country's infrastructure is to blame for a lot of the disaster, said an article in the *South China Morning Post*. "The snowstorms have cruelly exposed weaknesses in the country's infrastructure, which has failed to keep up with the rapid pace of development – particularly the stressed national railway grid." It adds that the chaos may spark civil unrest. "The crisis and its social and economic costs must be brought under control soon. Otherwise the implications could be far-reaching," it warns.

birthday of one of the religion's most popular gods is a colorful affair. Also known as the Goddess of Mercy, her big day is celebrated in the city's Buddhist temples on the 19th day of the second month of the lunar calendar. The biggest celebration is always at Guangji Si: If you come, you'll witness about 2,000 Buddhists chanting as one with smoking incense adding to the atmosphere.

LANTERN FESTIVAL

Marking the end of the New Year holiday period, this traditional festival falls on the 15th day of the first moon of the lunar year, which varies between February and March: In 2009, it falls on February 9, in 2010, February 28. The lighting of bright red lanterns dates from the Han dynasty and, like other traditional days, is enjoying something of a resurgence with paper lanterns being sold and displayed all around the city in addition to organized events in places such as Chaoyang Park (which hosts a great fireworks display). People traditionally hang red lanterns outside their houses for luck and let off even more fireworks while eating *tang yuan,* or sweet dumplings, by the mouthful. As always, festival days are a good excuse for gluttony, so do try some *tangyuan,* glutinous rice balls filled with a sweet black sesame paste.

QING MING FESTIVAL

This festival's name translates as grave-sweeping day, and while it has the potential for misery, it's generally treated as a fun family day out. Families head to the burial grounds of their departed loved ones and give the graves a good spring cleaning. Some more traditional families take miniature paper versions of cars, money, and more modern must-haves such as laptops and leave them on the graves to keep their loved ones amused in the afterlife.

SUMMER

DRAGON BOAT FESTIVAL

Taoranting Park, 19 Taiping Jie, 6351 1596

Map 3

Another traditional holiday based on the lunar

Lanterns abound during the Lantern Festival.

calendar, the Dragon Boat Festival falls on the fifth day of the fifth lunar month, in May or June. The day commemorates a poet called Qu Yuan who in 278 B.C. drowned himself in protest of the amount of corruption in the imperial court. You can watch dragon boats on many of the city's lakes but the main event is in Taoranting Park. As always with Chinese festivals, there is a traditional snack to eat on the day: This time try *zongzi,* which is triangles of glutinous rice stuffed with meat or dried fruit and steamed in bamboo leaves.

MAY DAY

May Day is the second of China's three week-long holidays, so expect crowds and good-natured chaos at shopping centers, tourist attractions, and on the streets. Flights and train tickets are nearly impossible to find, and once you get to wherever you're going it's liable to be packed, so the best advice is to stay in Beijing and take advantage of one of the discounted packages that the city's five-star hotels offer at this time.

MEET IN BEIJING ARTS FESTIVAL

Various venues, 6494 1107, www.meetinbeijing.cn

The annual Meet in Beijing Festival is usually held during May and has become one of China's best-known festivals showcasing international acts since its inception in 2000. The 2006 festival staged performances by more than 50 artistic troupes from more than 20 countries and regions. In 2007 Barcelona Company La Fura Dels Baus and director Jürgen Müller performed at the festival.

FALL

BEIJING MUSIC FESTIVAL

Various venues, 6593 0250, www.bmf.org.cn

The most established festival in the capital, the Beijing Music Festival is still going strong and its interesting lineups ensure that Beijing's classical music fans circle the date in their calendars. The format of the festival, held in late autumn, usually sees two or three huge soloists, a couple of international orchestras, and the China Philharmonic in different venues throughout the capital. In 2007, local piano prodigy Lang Lang dominated the show, alongside conductor Daniel Barenboim and the Singapore Symphony Orchestra. In all more than 1,000 musicians were playing in more than 30 performances.

BEIJING POP FESTIVAL

Chaoyang Park, 1 Nongzhan Nanlu, 6506 5409, www.beijingpopfestival.com

Map 4

Ignore the word pop in the title of this festival, a highlight for Beijing gig-goers, as the acts it attracts are usually anything but. In 2007, Nine Inch Nails and Public Enemy were on the same bills as local Chinese punk and rock bands and rock legend Cui Jian. Unfortunately, the two-day event suffers from security overkill, which is nothing to do with the organizers, but it does affect the atmosphere somewhat and the policy of forbidding people from bringing in not just beer but water is also ridiculous. Still, on a Sunday afternoon, it's definitely worth checking out as this type of festival, which has been going since 2005, doesn't happen here too often.

CHINA OPEN

Beijing Tennis Centre, 50 Tiantan Lu, www.chinaopen.cn

Map 7

Despite Chinese audiences' not always following tennis etiquette (think cameras, talking on cell phones, and calling out), it's definitely worth visiting the Open's brand-new high-tech stadium south of Qianmen. The Open attracts a fair sprinkling of stars: Fernando Gonzalez won the men's singles in 2007 and Ágnes Szávay beat Jelena Janković in the women's. Tennis as a spectator sport hasn't really caught on yet with the Chinese, so there are no problems getting tickets.

DANGDAI INTERNATIONAL ART FESTIVAL

Various venues, Dashanzi, 2 Jiuxianiqiao Lu, www.diaf.org

Map 4

The art scene's marquee event started in 2004

and has single-handedly raised the profile of contemporary Chinese art both at home and abroad. In 2007, more than 160,000 visitors milled around the galleries in Dashanzi on highly recommended guided art walks, attending lectures and gallery openings and watching conceptual performance art. The festival has now spread beyond Dashanzi to other, more obscure art districts, so if you can get a guided tour to these areas, don't hesitate. Every year the theme, venues, and type of art on display change: Check the website for up-to-date information.

MID-AUTUMN FESTIVAL

Love them or hate them—and most foreigners hate them—expect box after box of sweet heavy cakes if you're in China for the Mid-Autumn Festival, which is celebrated in the eighth month of the lunar calendar on the day when the moon is at its brightest. At least the fillings of the Chinese equivalent of Christmas cake have changed from the traditional bean paste, which dates from the 14th century when, as legend has it, plans for the uprising that got rid of the Mongols were hidden in cakes: Now you can get anything from centers of chocolate to those with green-tea ice cream.

NATIONAL DAY

The third of the weeklong national holidays celebrates the founding of the People's Republic on October 1, 1949. Rumors were that this holiday would soon be scrapped and instead there would be more single-day holidays throughout the year, but as of now, National Day continues. Unlike Chinese New Year, this holiday is one for spending time visiting places and shopping, so expect the streets to be very busy, especially at major sights such as Tiananmen Square and the Forbidden City.

WINTER

CHINESE NEW YEAR

For the Chinese, this is Christmas, Thanksgiving, and July Fourth rolled into one—and now that the ban has been lifted, expect a noisy 10 days or so of huge fireworks rocketing into the sky. The holiday, which is also known as Spring Festival, starts on the first day of the new moon of the lunar calendar. Everyone in the country is supposed to get a weeklong holiday to be with family, so with millions of people on the move, trains, buses, and planes are jam-packed. Despite popular opinion, it's a great time to hole up and be in Beijing: The actual city is much quieter than normal, traffic is a breeze, and all sights are open as normal. If you're lucky enough to score an invitation to a Chinese family's celebration, expect to be fed platefuls of dumplings and other dishes considered lucky, and you might get a *hong bao,* or red envelope with a few 100RMB in it. Other than with the big family meals, many Chinese celebrate by taking the family to a temple fair, which will have fairground rides, plenty of food, and the odd dragon dance parade. There are fairs at most temples, but the biggest is at Ditan Park, or the Altar of the Earth (12 Yonghegong Dajie, 6404 4499).

Sports and Recreation

A small event called the Olympics saw public interest in sports speed up as quickly as a runner nearing the finish line in the 100-meters final. While once all there was to Chinese sport was the so-called soft events, such as table tennis and badminton, which are still hugely popular, Olympic gold medals from hurdler Liu Xiang and tennis players Sun Tiantain and Li Ting in the women's doubles saw interest grow in sports that the Chinese haven't previously excelled in.

Government money is being pumped into recreational areas, not least of which the many new Olympic venues that will now be enjoyed by the less Olympian among us. The growing obesity problem—52 percent of locals are classified as overweight or obese, according to government statistics—has meant more parks' being built with outdoor public gym equipment and table tennis courts.

Unfortunately, many pastimes such as yoga and going to an indoor gym can be more expensive than doing so back home. Activities such as these are considered status symbols: If you can afford to spend 150RMB on a yoga class, you've made it! This is all very well, but it does make keeping in shape a drain on your wallet, especially as sometimes you really shouldn't be running outside because of the air pollution. On days when you can't see farther than 200 meters away, pay to use a gym!

Apart from these problems, there is plenty of scope for keeping active. Whether you want to watch or participate, a growing number of Beijingers—from grandma practicing kung fu in the park to her grandson sweating it out in an expensive gym—are making every day the Olympics in Beijing.

PARKS

The government wants Beijing residents to be no farther than 500 meters from a park by 2010, and 60 new open spaces were built before the Olympics. As you travel around the city in a taxi, parks spring up in unexpected areas such as underneath flyovers and by the sides of busy roads. This is because public space is at such a premium, and with most people living in tower blocks, people use parks like their own backyards—for picnics, sports, or for a quick snooze on a park bench—which makes them a great place to see a slice of Beijing life. Unfortunately, the all-too-tempting grass, which is something of a rarity in the city, is usually covered with warning signs saying Keep Off. Because it is so sporadic, grass is seen as more akin to a precious flower than the ubiquitous plant it is elsewhere, but fortunately there are a few places where you can avoid the wrath of security guards and spread out a picnic blanket.

Many of Beijing's parks serve duel purposes. Not only are many of them prime tourist attractions full of ancient monuments and historical interest, but parks also function as public places where people come to hang out and meet friends. Parks aren't just for exercise, though a lot of that goes on, whether it's people using the public gym equipment or playing badminton in any free area possible. Older people bring their pet birds in cages and hang out or play loud and competitive games of mah-jongg with crowds of people standing around to give advice.

BEIHAI PARK

1 Weijin Jie, 6403 1102

HOURS: Daily 6 A.M.-10 P.M.

Map 1

A park that is busy year-round with tourists and locals, this huge complex is centered around a lake on which one can boat during summer and ice-skate in winter. There aren't as many other activities here as there are in other parks, but the long circumference of the lake takes a good hour or so to walk around. As you stroll around, be sure to stop at one of the pagodas on the water's edge as there are usually groups of Beijing opera singers practicing hitting the notes.

BEIJING BOTANICAL GARDENS

Wofo Si Lu, Xiangshan, 6259 1283

HOURS: Summer daily 6 A.M.-8 P.M., winter daily 7 A.M.-7 P.M.

Map 7

It's worth traveling for 40 minutes out of the city to head to this much-underused space full of lakes, wooded areas, flower beds, and green open spaces. This huge park is one of the few places where you can have a picnic undisturbed by overzealous security guards as it's easy to find somewhere secluded. It would take days to cover the whole site, especially if you intend to enter the conservatory and look at the tropical plants. Look out for the scores of newly married couples in full wedding attire roaming around the park and posing for their wedding photos.

CHAOYANG PARK

1 Nongzhanguan Nanlu, 6506 5409

HOURS: Daily 6 A.M.-10 P.M.

Map 4

Central Park it isn't no matter how much authorities would like to suggest that it is, but Beijing's largest park in the center of town is good for keeping fit. Joggers power around the lakes in the western part of the park, and swimmers enjoy one of the city's few outdoor public pools near the south gate for a bargain 15RMB. One pool is purely for lanes, but the other attracts families on a day out with kids enjoying the fountains and shallow waters to splash around in. There is also a private tennis center on the grounds where you can rent courts for an expensive 240RMB an hour.

RITAN PARK

6 Ritan Beilu, 6561 6301

HOURS: Daily 6 A.M.-9 P.M.

Map 4

Ritan is one of the few central places in town where you can work up a sweat, whether it is a gentle one as you copy people practicing tai chi early in the morning or something more active such as trying to reach the top of Beijing's one and only central climbing wall. The miniature golf course is looking a bit sorry for itself

chilling out in Ritan Park

these days but the lovely shady location makes it a haven on a hot day. In the middle of the square park is a small hill with a pagoda on top that seems to function as a meeting place for the retired; they may be keen to practice their English with you.

SUMMER PALACE

Yiheyuan Lu, 6288 1144

HOURS: Daily 6:30 A.M.–8 P.M.

Map 6

The beautiful location saw the Summer Palace used as a summer retreat for imperial families: Now it's where ordinary people came for relaxation, long walks, and fresh air. Many people go jogging round Kunming Lake as the complex is far enough out of the city that the air feels fresh. Families and couples go boating in summer and in winter, and a whole industry around ice-skating appears with people renting out their skates for a few RMB. If you're not too sure of your skills, you can also rent ice chairs—a chair with blades at the bottom: You sit on it and push yourself along with ski poles.

BIKE RENTAL

The city is as flat as a pancake so don't bother with gears, but do bother with a cycling helmet as cars are increasingly taking priority over two wheels and driving standards are appalling. China has the highest rate of road accidents and deaths from car crashes in the world. If at all possible, stick to roads with separate cycle lanes and go slow as the Chinese do. Also remember that Beijing is not the bike-stealing hell it once was, but you should still leave your locked bike only at a bike park with an attendant—it will cost about 0.5RMB—a bargain for your peace of mind.

BICYCLE KINGDOM

B428, North Garden Office, Oriental Plaza, 218 Wangfujing Dajie, 133 8140 0738, www.bicyclekingdom.com

HOURS: Daily 24 hours (but call first)

Map 1

For good-quality bikes at reasonable rates, check out Bicycle Kingdom's well-designed website, which also serves as a good resource for

The ever-present bike repair men can be life-savers.

cycling enthusiasts in the city with maps listing bike lanes and suggested routes. It will deliver bikes to your hotel and rates start at 100RMB a day but go down if you rent bikes for longer periods. Helmets are 10RMB a day. If you'd rather follow an expert, Bicycle Kingdom offers a range of tours, including a reasonably priced half-day tour of the city's Olympic venues.

CYCLE CHINA

12 Jingshan Dongjie opposite Jingshan Park's east gate, 6402 5653, www.cyclechina.com

HOURS: Mon.-Sat. 9 A.M.-6 P.M.

Map 1

The amiable manager, Jeff Guo, has branched out from just providing bikes: Now he offers good-value cycle tours in both Beijing and to other destinations, such as the walled city of Pingyao an overnight train ride away. The company is very well established and the half-day *hutong* tours are highly recommended. Ask if Jeff will be the tour guide as he knows his history and will point out interesting places, such as the backstreet brothels that were in action hundreds of years ago.

FORBIDDEN CITY BIKES

Jingdu Hotel, 63 Nanchizi Dajie, 6525 0598

HOURS: Daily 10 A.M.-6 P.M.

Map 1

There aren't very many places to rent bikes around the Forbidden City, but this hotel rents out reasonable-quality bikes: Look out for the English sign. They don't speak any English at reception, however, but they'll know what you want. You have to leave a deposit of 300RMB and rental costs 15RMB for half a day or 30RMB for 24 hours. Unfortunately they don't have any helmets and do check the bike carefully before you rent it.

HOUHAI BIKE HIRE

Shichahai Dongan, opposite Han Ceng Restaurant, Houhai, no phone

HOURS: Daily 9 A.M.-6 P.M.

Map 2

If you'd rather propel yourself around the lake and *hutong* surrounding Houhai than sit in the back of a pedicab, here's a good place to pick up cheap and cheerful bikes. Don't expect anything flashy, but as long as you check the bike and take it out on a little test run before handing over any money, the bikes should be fine. You have to leave a deposit of 200RMB and then it costs around 30RMB per day. It doesn't have cycle helmets, however.

GYMS

Gyms and health clubs are big business in Beijing and indeed China as the country's moneyed middle classes turn their back on tai chi in public places to sweat it out in a fancy club. Membership fees tend to be as expensive or even more than in the West though facilities aren't generally as good once you get outside five-star hotels. The Chinese like plenty of loud music blaring as they pound the treadmill so bring some headphones if you want more of a peaceful workout. With a few exceptions listed below, most of the cheaper gyms won't have any English speakers at reception, which can be frustrating, so heading to the more expensive options can be easier if you don't speak Mandarin.

CHINA WORLD FITNESS CENTER

China World Hotel, 1 Jianguomenwai Dajie, 6505 2266, ext. 33

HOURS: Daily 6 A.M.-11 P.M.

Map 4

This well-managed and popular fitness center attracts plenty of local expats with its indoor tennis courts, squash courts, pool, state-of-the-art gym, and Beijing's most sumptuous changing rooms. A new class starts nearly every hour, with offerings varying from Pilates to aqua-aerobics. Day passes are available for 150RMB, which includes access to the restful spa area with whirlpool bath and sauna, while a year costs 15,000RMB.

KERRY SPORTS CENTER

2/F, Kerry Centre Hotel, 1 Guanghua Lu, 6561 8833, ext. 6465

HOURS: Daily 6 A.M.-11 P.M.

Map 4

Olympic swimmer Michael Phelps stays at

the Kerry Centre Hotel to use the celebrated 35m swimming pool in what's probably the city's best gym. There's a well-equipped gym with every machine you could need, plus outdoor tennis courts on the roof. Current membership costs run to 16,000RMB for a year though off-season discounts are available. Otherwise you need to check into the hotel to get access the gym as unfortunately it doesn't offer day passes.

NIRVANA FITNESS

2 Gongren Tiyuchang Beilu, next door to the Great Dragon Hotel, 6597 2008

HOURS: Daily 10 A.M.-11 P.M.

Map 4

Probably the most well-established and professional club outside of a hotel, Nirvana's central location is a plus. The gym prides itself on the number of classes it offers, and these combined with the good swimming pool and equipment-filled gym make up for the changing rooms, which could do with an update. Annual membership costs anywhere from 5,000 to 10,000RMB depending on the deals available and, according to some irritated expats, how good your Chinese is. Day passes are available.

SWIMMING POOLS

Swimming is very popular in Beijing, although because of the frigid winters, almost all pools are indoors. Some bad news for fashionistas: Swimming caps are compulsory except in hotel pools and even then, some overzealous lifeguards will bring you one to wear. They are supposed to be worn for hygiene reasons though if health were the number-one concern, I wish lifeguards would automatically ban people who cough and sneeze in the pool as unfortunately this is a common problem. If that doesn't put you off, there are a few good public pools where that kind of behavior is frowned upon, but if you're worried about germs, the private hotel pools, though obviously much more expensive, are much stricter about behavior so you would be better off heading there.

CHAOYANG PARK POOL

HOURS: Daily 6 A.M.-10 P.M.; closed Sept.-April

Map 4

One of the city's few outdoor public pools, near the south gate, is a bargain for 15RMB. One pool is lanes only, but the other attracts families with kids playing in fountains and shallow waters.

DONGDAN INDOOR SWIMMING POOL

2A Dahua Lu, 6523 1241

HOURS: Mon. noon-10 P.M., Tues.-Sun. 10 A.M.-10 P.M.

Map 4

Just off Jianguomenwai Dajie, which leads to Tiananmen Square, this is Beijing's most central pool and is attached to a public sports center that is often full of students playing basketball after school. Facilities are clean if basic and considering a swim costs just 30RMB, good value for the money. Be sure to bring your swimming cap.

TUANJIEHU PARK POOL

16 Tuanjiehu Nan Lu, 8597 3603

HOURS: Daily 10 A.M.-8 P.M., closed Sept.-Apr.

Map 4

As long as you don't come here expecting to swim laps, you'll have a fun time at this kitschy central pool with wave machines and slide in the middle of this neighborhood park. It's only open in the summer (dates change yearly—phone and check) and on the weekends, your 30RMB entrance ticket gives you three hours of pool time, though during the week, your ticket lasts all day and the place is near empty.

GOLF

Golf is taking off in China, appealing as a sport for high-spending bigwigs, or *dakuans* as they are known in Chinese. Several player-designed courses exist, including those by Colin Montgomerie, Nick Faldo, and Jack Nicklaus, and players such as Zhang Lianwei are attracting new fans to the sport.

Costs are high but no longer as horrendous as they used to be, and even on the most expensive of courses, you can rent a bucket of balls for an hour on the driving range for around 50RMB. Rightly or wrongly, the sport has become something of a symbol of the wide divide between rich and poor in China, with some critics calling golf "green opium" as it ruins green fields that should be used for agriculture.

BEIJING CBD INTERNATIONAL GOLF CLUB

99 Gaobeidian Lu, 6738 4801, www.h-cgolf.com

Map 4

The 18-hole championship-class course is just an eight-minute drive from the Central Business District and is very exclusive. Sometimes members of the public are allowed to play; it's best to phone and check. If you're allowed in, the course is distinguished by its large water areas and long bunkers. The Volvo China Open was held here in 2008.

CHAOYANG KOSAIDO GOLF CLUB

Tuanjiehu Xiaoqu, Shangsi Lu, 200m east of Changhong Bridge, 6501 8584

Map 4

This course is also very central, just 200 meters from Sanlitun. It opened back in 1987 when few locals would have even have heard of golf, but nowadays, most golfers here are middle-class Chinese keen to improve their swings. You can't expect huge expanses of green as it's so central, but the short nine-hole course and low fees make this a popular choice. The driving range is very busy in the evenings, and whenever you play, don't forget to wear a shirt with a collar or you will have to borrow one from the club.

TENNIS

Tennis, like golf, is a status-symbol sport for China's elite. Tennis clubs are expensive and exclusive, and well-kept public courts are few and far between. The sport did, however, receive a massive boost at the 2004 Olympics in Athens when Sun Tiantian and Li Ting won, to everyone's surprise, the women's doubles gold medal. Since then several other female players have made the WTA top 50. This success is spurring the game's growth, but for now badminton and table-tennis courts are a far more common sight than tennis.

CHAOYANG PARK TENNIS CLUB

1a Nongzhanguan Nanlu, 6501 0953

HOURS: Daily 8 A.M.-10 P.M.

Map 4

This large upscale tennis club with both indoor and outdoor courts lets nonmembers play but for a high price: Courts are 400RMB at peak times and 300RMB during the day. Changing rooms aren't as good as you'd expect for these prices but the clay courts are spotless. Lessons are available but there are very few English-speaking coaches you so will need to make an appointment.

THE KERRY SPORTS CENTER

2/F, Kerry Centre Hotel, 1 Guanghua Lu, 6561 8833, ext. 6465

HOURS: Daily 7 A.M.-11 P.M.

Map 4

Probably the most popular courts in Beijing, the two indoor courts are part of the Kerry Sports Center and are as equally professional as the rest of the facilities. Courts cost 200RMB an hour and an in-house pro is available for lessons. The playing surface is hard.

WORKERS' STADIUM TENNIS COURTS

Workers' Stadium North Gate, Gongti Beilu, 6502 5757

HOURS: Daily dawn-dusk

Map 4

If you don't mind the odd pothole and a few piles of leaves on the court, the Workers' Stadium has three open-air courts for a bargain 40RMB an hour. Because they are slightly difficult to find (go through the North Gate and turn left and follow the ground's perimeter for 300m), there is rarely anyone playing on them. If they are locked, rattle on the gate, and the caretaker will come and open them.

YOGA AND PILATES

More relatively new arrivals to China, yoga and Pilates are catching on fast with the city's body-conscious fitness fans. Again, because they are trendy and seen as exclusive forms of exercise, expect to pay the same kind of prices or more than you would in the United States. Most people take classes in their gyms but there are a few places dedicated to either yoga or Pilates and these are where you will find the most professional teachers. You may have to try a few before you find the right style for you—Chinese yoga teachers can be more like sergeants major than relaxing influences—but persevere as more and more venues are opening.

PACIFIC CENTURY CLUB

2A Gongti Beilu, south of Pacific Century Place, 6539 3434, pacificcenturyclub.googlepages.com

HOURS: Daily 10 A.M.–11:30 A.M.

Map 4

One of the few places to offer a full set of Pilates equipment rather than just a workout on a mat, this centrally situated gym offers small private classes for 100RMB an hour three times a week. Private lessons with a qualified trainer and physiotherapist cost around 450RMB an hour. Don't expect an easy workout—your body will likely not forgive you for a few days. The same venue also offers hot yoga every evening.

YOGA YARD

17 Gongti Beilu, Floor 6, behind The Olive Restaurant, 6413 0774, www.yogayard.com

HOURS: Daily 8 A.M.–8 P.M.

Map 4

Much beloved of a mixed group of local enthusiasts and expats keen to keep up their practice, Yoga Yard was started by two Americans in 2002 and they have moved three times to bigger premises to try to keep up with demand and now offer more than 45 classes a week. Their latest home consists of two light and airy studios and much-improved changing rooms. Teachers speak both English and Chinese and in addition to regular hatha yoga, offer pre- and postnatal yoga and classes for kids. If you can, go to a lunchtime class rather than one in the evenings, as after office hours, you'll find yourself doing the upward-facing dog a few inches from the person opposite.

© HELENA IVESON

Stretch and relax at Yoga Yard near Sanlitun.

HIKING

Truth be told, Beijing can be a frustrating place for outdoor types. The horror stories about the city's pollution levels are true—before the Olympics, the International Olympic Committee said it was possible that the marathon would be postponed or moved because of the city's air quality. (The IOC later announced that they think the humidity will actually be more of a problem than the pollution for the athletes.)

So, when the air quality is awful, do what many do and get out of town for a renewing hike in the country a couple of hours out of town. Catering to people keen to make their escapes, there are a number of hiking groups that organize country walks on weekends.

If you have your own transport or wish to rent a car for the day, the excellent book *Hiking Around Beijing* (Foreign Languages Press) was written by three keen hikers and comes with useful maps and driving instructions.

BEIJING HIKERS

139 100 25516, www.beijinghikers.com

Every weekend, this very well-organized group takes a bus load of mostly expats out to some of the hills surrounding Beijing that are relatively inaccessible to people unfamiliar with the area. During holiday periods, it offers overnight hikes to places such as abandoned Ming villages. Hikes vary in difficulty—do check the website to find out what level of hike it is offering that weekend. Having said that, even the most difficult is manageable if you are basically fit. The group organizes hot drinks and snacks, but you do need to bring your lunch. The group is somewhat a victim of its own success as sometimes upward of 60 people will be walking with you, so don't expect a peaceful wilderness experience, but for 200RMB for the day, Beijing Hikers is an excellent value.

BEIJING U-DO ADVENTURE

5120 5887, www.udoadventure.com

Run by two mountaineering enthusiasts, one Chinese, one American, this hiking and mountaineering club takes small groups on "guided adventures" both in Beijing and around the country. Every weekend it goes to an off-the-beaten-track section of the Great Wall, and during holiday periods, run amazing weeklong treks in Xinjiang and Szechuan provinces. Day trips cost 300RMB but group sizes are kept small.

SKIING

To be blunt, Aspen it ain't. While skiing in Beijing can make for a great day out during the winter, the slopes on offer a couple of hours from Beijing are definitely modest by international standards. If you are a seasoned ski bunny, you may find the experience frustrating, but for beginners or irregular skiers, the unchallenging slopes can be a great place to practice.

Crowds can be heavy, especially during holiday periods, and remember that most of your fellow skiers will be Chinese novices who often don't know how to stop, so watch out! Après-ski culture hasn't taken root—instead of a steaming cup of mulled wine to warm your blood, the nearest alternative on offer will be green tea and Tsingtao beer. Every year, Beijing listings magazine *The Beijinger* runs day trips to the ski slopes and they are always excellent value and a fun day out.

There may be problems ahead for Beijing's ski slopes as recent record-setting high temperatures (January and February 2007 were the warmest in 167 years) and northern China's chronic water shortage woes has seen the government ban any more slopes from being built because of environmental concerns.

NANSHAN SKI VILLAGE

Shengshuitou Village, Henanzhai Town, Miyun County, 6445 0991, www.nanshanski.com

Map 7

Though more than 60 miles from the center of Beijing, Nanshan is probably the most professional of the local slopes with 10 well-groomed trails plus a fully equipped snowboard park with half pipe, six rails, and four kickers. It's very popular with expats and if you're new to skiing or snowboarding, this is the place to learn as tuition is available from English-speaking and foreign instructors and they use only high-quality Burton gear. As at many of the slopes around the city, the pricing policy is somewhat Byzantine with separate fees charged for entrance to the park, hiring of equipment, and lift passes. If you can buy an all-inclusive ticket, do so as it saves time and much hassle.

QIAOBO ICE AND SNOW WORLD

Chaobai River National Forest Park, Mapo, Shunyi District, 8497 2568, www.qbski.com

Map 7

Even on a sweltering summer's day, it's now possible to hit the slopes thanks to the city's first and only indoor ski resort, started up by China's first gold-medal winner in the Winter Olympics. Inside a huge dome are two ski slopes, one for beginners and the other for more advanced skiers.

SHIJINGLONG SKI RESORT

Zhongyanfang Village, Zhangshanying Town, Yanqing County, 6919 1617, www.sjlski.com

Map 7

Another popular resort that saw nearly 100,000 people ski there during its last three-month season, Shijinglong offers the city's longest if not the most challenging slopes on mainly artificial snow. In 2007 it added an intermediate run, a widened advance run, and two lifts, which should help with the lines at the lifts. If only it would sort out its chaotic system of renting equipment; as lines build up, people push in and tempers can flare.

SPECTATOR SPORTS

Aside from that two-week period of the Olympics, local sports fanatics don't have much fun when it comes to live action. As befits a capital city, there are several soccer and basketball teams that compete in the national leagues—if only they were any good. Beijing Guo'an is the city's soccer team, but fans have become disillusioned thanks to the match-fixing scandals, poor performances, and an upswing in crowd violence. The amusingly named Beijing Ducks are the capital's premier basketball team, and they finished a lowly 10th in the last Chinese basketball league rankings.

But if watching these two teams doesn't appeal to you, every year more and more international-standard competitions make their way to the capital, and their numbers will only increase thanks to the high standard of facilities left over from Beijing 2008.

BEIJING MARATHON AND GREAT WALL MARATHON

8525 1200, ext. 843, www.beijing-marathon.com, www.great-wall-marathon.com

Every year in October, runners start from Tiananmen Square before hitting the streets of Beijing and ending up at the Olympic Park. After terrible publicity in 2004, when two runners died and the media blamed the organizers for the lack of water and first-aid stations, organization has much improved. But some runners still complain about the starting line as four different events start at the same time—everyone pushes and shoves like they do on the subway—and the major part of the route, although it starts and finishes in iconic places, is along unattractive roads.

Marathon runners really hit the wall during the Great Wall Marathon, which is held every year in May on a stretch of the wall in Hebei province. If a marathon weren't difficult enough, a quarter of the route is on the actual wall and the rest of the course goes through farmland and tiny picturesque villages. Marathons are one of the few occasions when it is considered perfectly fair for foreigners to pay much more than locals—for the most recent Beijing Marathon, locals paid 100RMB while foreigners paid $100.

CHINA OPEN (GOLF)

99 Gaobeidian Lu, 6738 4801, www.volvochinaopen.com

Map 4

The Volvo China Open, China's premier golf tournament, alternates between Shanghai and Beijing: In 2008, it was Beijing's turn, at the Beijing CBD International Golf Club. The Open is trisanctioned by the Asian Tour,

OLYMPIC VENUES

Beijing built or revamped 37 venues in time for the Olympic Games, and the most high-profile are at the Olympic Park, the National Stadium, and the National Aquatics Center, a.k.a. The Water Cube – the rest of the venues are dotted about the city center and outskirts. The Wukesong Indoor Stadium was built specially for the Games and has a capacity of 18,000. At the 2008 Olympics, the indoor stadium hosted the basketball competitions. Chaoyang Park hosted beach volleyball (originally this sport was to be held on Tiananmen Square, but that idea was quietly shelved), while the Workers' Stadium on Gongti Bei Lu hosted football, and the Workers' Gymnasium hosted boxing. In the east of the city, the Capital Indoor Stadium hosted the volleyball events. For more information on the Olympic venues, go to the Games' official website: www.beijing2008.com.

European Tour, and China Golf Association and offers $2 million in prize money. The 18-hole championship-class course is the only tournament-player course in Asia designed by one of the world's top designers, Brit Stenson.

CHINA OPEN (TENNIS)

Beijing Tennis Center, 1 Guangcai Lu, www.chinaopen.com.cn

Map 7

China's premier tennis tournament started in 2004, and Chinese sports authorities want the Open to be considered one of the big grand slams in 10 years' time. While big names do show—Venus and Serena Williams, Amelie Mauresmo, and Nikolay Davydenko have been recent attendees—organizers haven't yet worked out how to attract the crowds. It doesn't help that the tennis center is south of the Temple of Heaven and it takes about an hour to get there from the center to town because of traffic. The occasional player gets frustrated by people in the audience yelling out and talking on their cell phones, but the facilities are good, though there is only one main show court.

WORLD SNOOKER CHINA OPEN

Peking University Student's Gymnasium, 11 Xi Lu, Bei Sanhuan, 6275 1230, tickets from www.piao.com.cn

Map 6

For one week in March, 32 world-class players thrill local fans by bringing their cues to Beijing, where the game is getting more and more popular. Ronnie O'Sullivan, Steven Hendry, and of course China's young prodigy Ding Junhui have all made an appearance in recent years and players report that crowd behavior is getting better as people learn that they shouldn't be shouting at the players at crucial moments.

MASSAGE

It's both affordable and professional: Don't leave town without experiencing traditional Chinese massage, a special treat given Beijing is not always the most relaxing of destinations. Choose carefully what kind of style you want as the cheapest places will not be relaxing but more medicinal, but you come out walking a bit taller and sometimes, long-standing aches and pains magically disappear.

Massage parlors here, like in many parts of the world, are often a front for prostitution. Basically, if it looks seedy, it will be, and given that there's the odd crackdown now and then, they are best avoided.

BODHI

17 Gongti Beilu, behind The Olive Restaurant, 6413 0226, www.bodhi.com.cn

HOURS: Daily 11 A.M.–12:30 A.M.

Map 4

Bridging the gap between ultraexpensive hotel massage and ultrabasic blind massage parlors, Bodhi and Oriental Taipan below offer a variety of decadent massages in a soothing, modern setting for moderate prices. Bodhi is Thai-themed and stylish: Look out for the beautiful glass-covered stairway with a gurgling pond as you enter the lobby, where the attendants will greet you in English and Chinese and will ask if you prefer a male or female masseuse. The 90-minute foot massage is a wonderful way to spend time and free snacks and drinks plus cable TV add to the pleasure. Monday to Thursday before 4 P.M. massages are reduced from 158RMB to 98RMB: a steal.

KANGLONG HEALTH MASSAGE

33 Sanlitun, directly behind Yaxiu Market, 6417 9587

HOURS: Daily 11 A.M.-9 P.M.

Map 4

Massage students from overseas come to study with Mr. Man Kaijun, who merely has to lightly run his hands over your body to be able to pinpoint exactly where you have problems. This, however, is not massage for the sensitive, as believe me, it will hurt. Thirty minutes of kneading, stretching, and digging in fingertips into painful areas is usually enough, but afterward, it's a bit like childbirth—you don't remember the pain because you're left with something good—in this case, a pain-free back or ache-free muscles. Thirty minutes costs 80RMB and no English is spoken, but the staff will know why you are there.

ORIENTAL TAIPAN

1 Xindong Lu, 8532 2177, www.taipan.com.cn

HOURS: Daily 10 A.M.-2 A.M.

Map 4

A small Beijing chain of midmarket massage spas, the relaxing and quiet venues are full of darkened corridors and small ponds with low-level music playing in the background. Therapists don't always speak English but silence is best anyway! The spa has just started offering a range of facials and other beauty treatments such as manicures and waxing. The 90-minute Chinese massage is great value—you change into a pyjama suit and lie on a special massage table—and afterward you can indulge with the free food, drinks, and cable TV.

ZHEN SONG BLIND MASSAGE CENTER

13 Shun Yuan Li, Xinyuan Jie, 8448 3238

OPEN: Daily 10:30 A.M.-midnight

Map 2

Traditionally, massage as an occupation was reserved for the blind. For no-frills body massage, this spartan but spotless place can't be beat. For 36RMB, you'll receive a thorough *tui na* traditional Chinese massage. The style's hands-on approach is meant to bring the body into balance through manipulation of muscles using hands, elbows, and the odd hammer (it doesn't hurt). Zhen Song is a world away from relaxing—expect communal rooms and lots of talking—but afterward, you'll come out a few inches taller and as relaxed as a baby. No English is spoken (though look out for the English sign) but the language of *ouch!* and *argh!* is universal.

SHOPS

Just a couple of decades ago, tourists in China were forced to shop in practically different worlds. Locals got to buy what they could (which was not much) in local shops while overseas visitors were allowed to buy from only one store, optimistically called the Friendship Store, which accepted only foreign currency certificates. Now that capitalism is king, the city's people shop as one, and whether you're born and bred here, or here for a week, it's a rare person who doesn't give in and buy, buy, buy.

The Chinese are making up for valuable lost shopping time as fast as the cash registers can handle. Despite low average incomes—in Beijing the average is just 2,000RMB a month—China as a whole is now the third-biggest consumer of luxury goods with 12 percent of worldwide sales, up from 1 percent in 2003. You'll find all the big designers here, from Alberta Ferrara to Zegna, but because of the high taxes the government imposes, prices will be cheaper back home. Instead walk past those stores and head off the beaten track to the smaller boutiques, where you'll find bargains galore. It has to be said, though, that if there's one area in which Shanghai beats Beijing hands down, it's shopping. The capital just can't compete with its southern rival's individualist and stylish boutiques: Instead Beijingers prefer markets and shopping centers. If you're visiting both cities and shopping is your priority, it would be wise to budget your time so you can have more shopping hours in Shanghai.

The concept of intellectual property rights appeared in Chinese dictionaries only in 2000 and while the issue of rampant piracy

HIGHLIGHTS

LOOK FOR [icon] TO FIND RECOMMENDED SHOPS.

Best Place for Bargain-Priced Basics: You won't find anything cutting edge at **Jimmy & Tommy Foreign Trade Fashion Club,** but if you've had enough of dejectedly looking around markets where everything is for minipeople, head here and feel better (page 116).

Best Place for Iconic and Ironic Clothing: Backpackers, locals, and expats alike flock to **Plastered T-Shirts** for the cute and funny T-shirts: They make great souvenirs for less than 100RMB (page 117).

Best Dressmaker for Your Red-Carpet Moment: If you have the time and money, the expert tailor at **The Red Phoenix** will design an item of beauty that will celebrate your good features while camouflaging the not-so-good (page 117).

Best Boutique: For fashionable women's wear, **Wu Ba** has an excellent range of designer threads and more individual items that look catwalk friendly but are bargain priced (page 119).

Best Souvenir for Your Mother: The **Shard Box,** with its gorgeous jewelry boxes, would please any woman in your life – and while you're there, get something made to put in it (page 119).

Best Place for Fakes: Who knows how long the flagrant disregard for intellectual property rights will continue, but it will be a sad day for shoppers when markets such as **Jiayi Market** are forced to clear their knockoff handbags off the shelves for good (page 124).

Best Place for a Rummage: From jade to jewelry, embroidered fabric to art, **Panjiayuan** will be like Christmas, Thanksgiving, and birthdays all rolled into one for flea market lovers (page 125).

Best Place to Splurge: Mall rats are spoiled for choice in Beijing, but for all the sky-high-priced designer labels you can name, head to **Season's Place** armed with a bulging wallet (page 127).

Plastered T-shirts make quirky souvenirs.

SHOP LIKE A LOCAL

If shopping were a sport, China would have had an extra gold medal at the Olympics – no one excels at the buying and selling of goods like the Chinese. And if you buy like a local, you'll come away with a suitcase bursting with items to treasure.

ANTIQUES AND "ANTIQUES"

While some markets in Beijing are overrun with tourists, **Panjiayuan** isn't one of them, despite being one of the biggest and best antiques and "antiques" markets in the country. First head to the outdoors area, where vendors from the countryside spread out their wares: Items here are cheaper than in the actual market, though as always, bargain hard. If you are prepared to pay extra for one-stop shopping of renovated gleaming furniture, **Radiance** is a great option, and it has a huge range of antique carpets too. If you enjoy sifting through copper to find some gold, check out **Shilibadian,** a treasure trove of furniture, carvings, and statues. (It's not for everyone: No one speaks English, and since it's a 20-minute drive from the CBD, you'll have to negotiate transportation back into town unless you book a car for the day. Taxi drivers don't always know how to get there, so be sure to take a telephone number of one of the area's antiques stores so that they can direct you.)

CLOTHES

All clothes markets also sell the standard souvenirs, but for something different, try the **Shard Box;** any woman in your life will love the dinky jewelry boxes with their lids made from pieces of porcelain smashed during the Cultural Revolution. For something younger and funkier, try the witty wearables from **Plastered T-Shirts,** and be sure to stroll around the trendy **Nanluoguxiang** street for more great buys.

If you have time to go to only one area, make it **Sanlitun.** You'll find women's-wear heaven at **Wu Ba** on the ground floor of the 3.3 shopping center. Next door, you have **The Village,** with its designer clothes and boutiques – or cross the road to **Nali Mall,** an enclave of small boutiques where hip Beijingers love to go.

has the U.S. government gnashing its teeth, it does make for some great bargains! Pirated DVDs, CDs, and Louis Vuitton handbags are one thing, but the rampant copying extends to everything, including antiques, souvenirs, and, more worryingly, medicine—bring any prescription medicine with you. Less seriously, the best advice is always to buy something because you like it, not because you have been assured by an honest-looking shop assistant that it is valuable.

If you're limited with time, restrict yourself to two areas: Sanlitun and Houhai/Nanluoguxiang (Nanluoguxiang is just a 10-minute walk from the lake). These two neighborhoods have the city's largest share of interesting boutiques, with the Ritan Park district a close third.

If you're a mall rat, you're spoiled for choice. Most upwardly mobile residents of the city are huge fans of midrange-brand heaven The Place (with the city's first branch of the European favorite for funky clothes, Zara), while designer-label hunters flock to Lane Crawford on Financial Street in the west (the only reason to go to the area, some say rather sniffily).

Markets are cash only, but midprice stores and up will all take credit cards. When you buy, check your new purchase carefully as if you need to return anything, prepare yourself for an arduous battle, even in the more expensive stores.

Whether you are after souvenir pearls, antique furniture, or forgotten travel essentials, they can be found here: You just need to bargain like a local. The city's legendary surly service in shops is thankfully something of a relic of the past, but be prepared for "hands on" attempts to get you to part with your money. Take everything with good humor and try to enjoy the bargaining process: It's a game! From Ming furniture to Mao tack-o-rama, it's here in all its glory: After all, if it gets made, it's made in China.

Clothes and Shoes

Large sizes can be a problem with even the most average Western woman's being XXL: You can't take it personally. For men, it's even more of an issue: Anyone taller than six feet or with size 11+ feet needs to head to import/export shops such as Jimmy & Tommy, which have larger sizes.

Jimmy & Tommy can't be beat for basics.

HUGEWAVE

3139, 3.3 Shopping Center, 33 Sanlitun Lu, 5136 5759

HOURS: Daily 10 A.M.–8 P.M.

Map 4

The savior of many Western-sized shoe fanatics in Beijing, this store may be small, but it's packed with more Steve Madden and Aldo brand shoes than you could wear in a lifetime. The stylish smiley owner will discount a little, but the marked prices are usually in the ballpark as to what you will pay: around 250RMB for shoes and 700RMB for good-quality leather knee-high boots. Men aren't left out either: There's a good range of both casual and formal shoes varying from suede sneakers to expensive-looking leather loafers.

JIMMY & TOMMY FOREIGN TRADE FASHION CLUB

14 Dongdaqaio Lu, 100m south of Guanghua Lu, 6591 1286

HOURS: Daily 10 A.M.–9:30 P.M.

Map 4

If clothes shopping thus far has been a frustrating experience with the bargaining too hard and the clothes too small, the rows and rows of casual fashions in Western sizes at Jimmy & Tommy may be a balm to your soul. For once, men have it better than women and menswear dominates. Tightly packed rails filled with Ralph Lauren shirts, Abercrombie and Fitch sweaters, and Gap chinos are bargain priced—around 70RMB for a shirt, for example—and absolutely no bargaining is accepted. It's also good for men's shoes.

LONG.COM SHOES

Inside Nali Mall, Sanlitun Lu, 8643 2880

HOURS: Daily 9 A.M.–9 P.M.

Map 4

This store, with its two rooms of Western-size shoes, boots, and sneakers is reason alone to head to the area, and all the goodies are available in Western sizes. It stocks a variety of Nine West, Calvin Klein, and the Japanese cult brand Fin as well as whatever else the staff can lay their hands on. A whole room is devoted to men's shoes (mostly casual trainer style). The staff know that thanks to their sheer variety of products, varying from 50RMB flip-flops to 1,000RMB Calvin Klein boots, that people will come so they make no effort whatsoever when it comes to service. And the store isn't online no matter what its name may suggest.

© HELENA IVESON

rows and rows of shoes at Long.com

NOISE

Building 42, Sanlitun Houjie, opposite Tongli Studios, 6417 5451

HOURS: Tues.-Sun. 11 A.M.-9 P.M.

Map 4

For funky T-shirts and gifts, Noise, run by a Singaporean and Chinese combo, is a must-visit. The arty T-shirts bearing funky designs or sly slogans (Smile if You're Gay, for one) cost 250RMB and cotton retro-style bags made from recycled material are under 200RMB. There's also a brightly colored fashionable range of gifts, from swirling patterned mouse mats to arty books and notepads. In case you can't see the store, look up—it's on the second floor up a rickety staircase above a hair salon and next to a tattoo area (it's that kind of area).

PLASTERED T-SHIRTS

61 Nanluogu Xiang, 139 1020 5721, www.plastered.com.cn

HOURS: Daily 9 A.M.-7 P.M.

Map 2

Plastered is a one-stop shop for tongue-in-cheek slogan T-shirts beloved of Beijing hipsters. The British design combo have been producing and selling their lively interpretations of old Beijing symbols—think subway tickets and pictures of the favorite foreigner dish, *gongbao* chicken—from their *hutong* store in Beijing since 2005. Their special Olympic range was a best-seller, with people fighting over their most popular propaganda-style athletes in action. All T-shirts come in a range of fitted styles for men, women, and kids and are screen-printed onto 100 percent cotton shirts in a rainbow of colors.

THE RED PHOENIX

1/F Building 30, Sanlitun Houjie, opposite Tongli Studios, 6416 4423

HOURS: Mon.-Sat. 9 A.M.- 6 P.M.

Map 4

For the perfect wedding dress or red-carpet occasion (surely we all have one in our lives?), self-taught designer Gui Lin will produce the Chinese-inspired outfit of your dreams, which will fit perfectly thanks to the numerous fittings she insists on. Local film stars and pop singers can occasionally be spotted here and with prices running into the thousands, a big budget is needed. As well as made-to-measure

SUITS YOU, SIR

Ever fancied having clothes tailored just for you? In Beijing it doesn't have to be a distant dream to be able to afford having a suit or dress made to measure; many people bypass the regular stores and either have clothes copied or go to a tailor with a picture of something they have in mind. An important piece of advice, though, is not to get carried away and order a whole new wardrobe: Start small and find a tailor you can trust. Many a customer has come out of a store disappointed with his or her new clothes and if you are here for only a limited amount of time, go to a tailor early in your trip to allow time for multiple fittings.

For cheap and cheerful tailoring, try **Lisa Tailor Shop** in the 3.3 Shopping Mall in Sanlitun. The cheerful Lisa has a good selection of material and is used to foreign visitors who need a very fast turnaround time. A men's tuxedo will cost 700RMB, including material, and can be ready in three days. Of course, in that timeframe and for that price, no one's going to think you've been shopping in Armani, but when money's tight, this place offers good value for money. Similar-quality tailors can be found in **Yaxiu Market** on the third floor.

If money is not a consideration and you have a few weeks to spare, go where society wives and rich locals go and head to **Red Phoenix** in Sanlitun or to **Jeannie Fei** in the Kerry Center Mall attached to the Kerry Center Hotel. Jeannie is originally from Hong Kong and offers sumptuous fabrics and the very latest sewing techniques. After designing whatever item your heart desires, she will whip up a complete prototype before sending off the garment to be properly made. Prices range according to fabrics and complexity but expect to pay about 4,000RMB for a silk business suit.

- **Lisa Tailor Shop** (5011, 5/F, 3.3 Shopping Mall, Sanlitun Lu, Sanlitun, 139 1079 8183)
- **Jeannie Fei** (1/F Kerry Center Mall, 1 Guanghua Lu, Central Business District, 8529 9489)

garments, she has a number of off-the-rack pieces: Unfortunately the dramatic high-collared slinky velvet dress that she uses as decoration at the entrance isn't for sale.

RITAN OFFICE BUILDING

15A Guanghua Lu, 8561 9559

HOURS: Daily 10 A.M.-8 P.M.

Map 4

If the idea of trawling through markets leaves you cold, but you're still looking for bargains, this staple of the shopping scene offers a huge range of small boutiques in small rooms over three floors. It's much less stressful than the bigger markets in town though the assistants could rouse themselves to show a bit more interest. It would take a whole afternoon to do the place justice: If time is limited try Room 2022 for U.S. brand names such as Ralph Lauren and Tommy Hilfiger. Room 3024 looks mysterious as the door is often closed, but ignore that and you'll find a treasure trove of designer bags. A Marc Jacobs tote leather bag was 800RMB without bargaining: It's up to you to decide if it's genuine but if it's not, the goods are pretty close. Room 2024 has factory samples and rejects from the British brand Monsoon: Think hippie-chic long dresses and comfortable long cardigans that, unusually, come in different sizes.

VIVIENNE TAM

WB101, China World Shopping Center, 1 Jianguomenwai Dajie, 6505 0767

HOURS: Daily 9:30 A.M.-9 P.M.

Map 4

Ladies, if you're in the market for designer labels, try one of China's handful of international successes and, in my mind, the most wearable (Shanghai Tang's clothes, the other well-known label, are a little too like Chinese fancy dress). The Cantonese-born designer does not have the fame she deserves, so that means you won't see her clothes on all your friends. While colors are muted, the chinoiserie designs, including kitschy Chinese prints on luxury fabrics as well as more sedate and grown-up cashmere evening dresses with cutouts similar to the style you see on Ming dynasty furniture, are lovely if expensive, but the clothes are beautifully made. China chic indeed.

WU BA

1118, 3.3 Shopping Center, 33 Sanlitun Lu, 5136 5530

HOURS: Daily 10 A.M.-8 P.M.

Map 4

Wu Ba's mixture of homegrown floaty fashions and Western-designer factory samples make it a prime destination for Beijing's fashionistas looking for something stylish on a budget. It's nice to not have to rummage through piles of rubbish before chancing on something pretty, and the roomy changing rooms, a rarity in Beijing, are an extra bonus. Recently Marni and Chloe coats have been spotted and cost around 600RMB, but their color-coordinated rows of clothes often have much cheaper items too. There's no English sign: Go out of the back door of 3.3 and it's on your right.

Accessories and Jewelry

BEIJING FINE JEWELERS

A6 Gongren Tiyuchang Donglu, opposite East Gate of Workers' Stadium, 6592 7118

HOURS: Daily 10 A.M.-6:30 P.M.

Map 4

This deceptively large store, which has photos of Venus Williams buying up the place on its walls, is made up of different rooms on two levels filled with silver or gold, as well as a whole room filled with precious stones ready to be chosen and made into whatever your heart desires. There's no pressure from the helpful sales assistants, probably as the store knows that that's what its large numbers of repeat visitors like. It has great sales every year, including one before Christmas, and this is a great time to buy its ready-made copies of Cartier and other famous designs. It also has a small selection of jewelry that uses Chinese characters and motifs. A second branch has opened 100 meters north at the China View Shopping Mall.

SHARD BOX

1 Ritan Beilu, northeast of Ritan Park, 8561 3712

HOURS: Daily 9 A.M.-7 P.M.

Map 4

When you're stuck for gifts, the Shard Box is the default option for people looking for something traditional and beautiful. The hammered silver or wooden jewelry boxes, which vary from ring size (starting at 30RMB) to huge and heavy, are decorated with fragments of pottery that—the store claims—were saved during the violence of the Cultural Revolution. Whether that's true or not, they are lovely additions to anyone's dressing table and the helpful staff are very patient. The store also sells jewelry, which tends to be on the garish side, though it can make anything to order and prices are very reasonable: A pair of turquoise and 18-karat gold earrings cost 800RMB.

SHARON'S STORE

4201, 4th Floor, Hongqiao Market, Tiantan Donglu, 6713 3354

HOURS: Daily 8:30 A.M.-7 P.M.

Map 3

The world of pearls can be mystifying to nonexperts looking for something pretty, and given that at Hongqiao Market, rows of rows of identical-looking cultured pearls are on offer at stalls manned by overzealous assistants, give your blood pressure a break and head here, where expats and locals in the know go. It has a good selection of freshwater pearls in an array of colors and sizes and the staff will tell you what is good quality and what's not. A simple string will cost about 75RMB. However, if you relish the hunt and are keen to practice your bargaining skills, venture forth to the rest of the stalls.

© HELENA IVESON

the Shard Box's collections of jewelry boxes

Souvenirs

ARTOPAL

Dashanzi 798 Art District, 4 Jiuxianqiao Lu, 8459 9335, www.artopal.in

Map 7

If the sky-high prices at Dashanzi aren't for you, but you crave a piece of contemporary Chinese art, this funky shop brings art (back) to the masses. The small store tucked opposite At Café is a treasure trove of gift cards, T-shirts and cotton bags, all emblazoned with the work of the most famous artists in the country, such as the kitschy Luo Brothers and the surrealist Zhang Xiaogang. Head here to buy great souvenirs for art fans—and unlike most pieces in this area, everything is priced in RMB, not dollars.

BANNERMAN TANG'S TOYS AND CRAFTS

38 Guozijian Jie, 8404 7179

HOURS: Daily 9 A.M.-7 P.M.

Map 2

Down the same alley as the Confucius Temple, this quaint toy store run by friendly descendants of a legendary Qing dynasty toymaker is enchanting. The colorful clay puppets, Peking Opera masks, and tiny clay figures are a world away from today's high-tech gizmos and all the more charming for it. Perhaps your own children will not be so enamored over something that doesn't emit beeps or move, but adults seem to find the very reasonably priced hand-painted figures a captivating symbol of another time.

GRIFTED

32 Nanluogu Xiang, 6406 2716, www.grifted.com.cn

HOURS: Daily 10 A.M.-10 P.M.

Map 2

Catering to the increasing number of backpackers and locals drawn to this interesting street, this brightly lit and friendly shop fills the need for smart and sassy souvenirs that aren't like the same old ones you see everywhere. It offers quirky T-shirts, retro notebooks, prints of works from Chinese contemporary artists, and beaded jewelry that might be a little too much on the hippie side for some. Stock is sourced and handcrafted locally and many of the very reasonably priced items are one-offs.

SOUVENIRS: THE GOOD, THE BAD, AND THE UGLY

China may be shopping central, but it's also Tack-o-rama Plaza when it comes to souvenirs to take home for your friends and loved ones. If you are after ugly or just plain weird, Beijing's markets are the place to go. And we know someone is buying these – otherwise no one would be selling the following lovely items that are all available at Hongqiao Market.

- Plastic pandas with eyes that flash – The stuff of nightmares.
- Jade pendants in the shape of China – Who would wear this?
- Shiny satin blue ties covered with pink dragons – This is not dressing to impress.
- Massive Mao vases in red that play patriotic music when you move it – I'm all for a little patriotic kitsch, but this is too much.

fun and funky souvenirs available at Grifted

Antiques and Artwork

GAOBEIDIAN

Off Dongsihuan Lu; turn right at the Gaobeidian exit of the Jingtong Expressway, call 8579 2458 for directions
HOURS: Daily 9 A.M.-6 P.M.
Map 7

More than 300 stores are spread around the dusty streets that make up Gaobeidian, 15 minutes east of Guomao, where mainly reproduction furniture is mingled with (a small amount of) genuine antiques. A large number of foreign wholesalers come here and buy crate loads and as it's no longer off the beaten track for tourists, prices have risen, but as long as it's not a freezing day (all stores are drafty and unheated), it's a great place to browse. It's unlikely that you'll find anything rare gathering dust: No matter what sellers say, goods are most likely to be *fanggu,* or antique reproductions, or *laomu xinzuo,* new furniture made with antique materials. It's best to just wander around, but look out for Lily's Antiques (8579 2458) and Lu Ban Gudian (8575 6516) as they both have good reputations.

LIANGMA ANTIQUE MARKET

27 Liangmaqiao Lu, 6467 9664
HOURS: Daily 9 A.M.-7 P.M.
Map 7

For some reason, this market in Chaoyang district is often empty: bad for the sellers, but good for us hagglers. It's full of sectioned-off stalls that usually specialize in something, whether it is porcelain, dusty antiques, or furniture. As always, buyer beware and bargain ruthlessly. For furniture, Jenny at Jingding Classical Wooden Art Factory (Stall B31, 6432 2622) is helpful, speaks great English, and can arrange shipping. Adorable 100-year-old hand-painted bookcases were for sale for 2,000RMB. Ho Ho Hang (B21, 6437 1989) is more upmarket and more expensive and offers restored Ming and Qing dynasty furniture. After you're shopped out, take your bargains to Belgian restaurant Morels, which is 50 meters east, and revive yourself with some waffles.

SHIBALIDIAN

Lujiaying, Shibalidian, first exit off Jingtang Expressway, call 8769 6180 for directions

HOURS: Daily 9 A.M.-7 P.M.

Map 7

It may be a nightmare to find—all of Beijing's taxi drivers seem to be unaware of its existence—but persevere if you want to get to the source that supplies all the other antiques stores in the city. It's similar to Gaobeidian; here you'll find a veritable village of furniture sellers who will all insist that their wares are from their country towns and are genuine antiques: As always, buyer beware. You'll come across some amazing sights, such as towering Buddhas and crumbling courtyard doors that used to keep out intruders. The sellers can ship, but if you're in the market for something smaller, there are plenty of camphor chests and carvings that would liven up your home. Feng Yi Ge Gudian Jiaju (8769 6180) has a warehouse full of interesting and covetable items: A new bedside table made with antique wood cost 600RMB and an early 1900s chest was 500RMB. If you're keen to come here, it would be worth hiring a taxi to drop you off and pick you up as it's difficult to arrange transport back.

TIBETAN ANTIQUES AND CARPETS

A8 Gongren Tiyuchang Donglu, opposite Workers' Stadium East Gate, 6501 8258

HOURS: Daily 10 A.M.-6 P.M.

Map 4

If a trip to Tibet isn't on your itinerary but you covet the region's furniture and carpets, this small cozy store is a good place to start. In addition to the more rustic Tibetan style of carpet, it sells handcrafted antique carpets from all over China, including rugs from Muslim oasis towns in Xinjiang. Though prices are high—expect to pay in excess of several thousand RMB—consider it an investment for your grandchildren. If you're a real connoisseur or want to look at a wider variety, the shop's owner, Zhang Yongzhi, has a warehouse nearby at Sanyuan Qiao, which is nearly impossible to find by yourself. If you want to go—and I highly recommend it—call him at 6468 2429 or 139 0100 5150 and he can direct a taxi. He does not speak English.

TORANA GALLERY

Kempinski Hotel, 50 Liangmaqiao Lu, 6465 3388, ext. 5542, www.toranahouse.com

HOURS: Daily 10 A.M.-10 P.M.

Map 7

The intricate Tibetan carpets at Torana, a favorite of well-to-do expats, are simply gorgeous. The mainly new carpets, which are all handmade in Tibet in contemporary designs, are unfussy and stylish—and expensive. Compared to what you would pay in the West, though, and given that you are helping support the continuation and development of traditional textile crafts, they make wonderful souvenirs. Prices start at 6,000RMB and all can be shipped at cost price. If they are beyond your budget, there is also a small selection of Tibetan cashmere for sale and occasionally art exhibitions of work from Tibet and Nepal.

Arts and Crafts

DARA

17 Gongren Tiyuchang Beilu, opposite the North Gate of Workers' Stadium, 6417 9365

Map 4

If you're fed up with traipsing around markets and are looking for a modern aesthetic rather than Ming dynasty ripoffs, Dara blends Chinese, Southeast Asian, and European designs into refined and inspired ensembles. Besides furniture, this trendy expat favorite sells antique accessories, pottery, silk cushion covers, and embroidered fabrics that can be made into bedspreads or curtains to give your home a taste of the exotic. You can meet with the store's designer to discuss customized products for your home; they can be shipped abroad. It has a larger showroom with more furniture in Dashanzi Art District.

RADIANCE

9 Kaifa Lu, Xi Baixinzhuang, Houshayu, Shunyi, 8049 6400, wwwradiancechina.com

HOURS: Daily 9 A.M.-6:30 P.M.

Map 7

The American owner has created a one-stop shop for people who break out into a cold sweat at the thought of traipsing around lots of shops. You will pay for the privilege, though, as prices for its rooms full of Chinese-style furniture, pottery, household decorations, and carpets are higher than if you were to go to individual shops. Another negative is that the store is way out of town toward the airport, but still, people keep coming as the quality for everything is very high. Taking pride of place in my house is my rustic Xinjiang carpet bought from here and I've never seen another one similar.

Books and Music

THE BOOKWORM

Building 4, Nan Sanlitun Lu, 6586 9507, www.beijingbookworm.com

HOURS: Daily 9 A.M.-2 A.M.

Map 4

In addition to being Ground Zero for arty expats for its café and bar, the beloved worm is still fulfilling its original function of keeping English speakers supplied with reading material. It's a lending library (membership for six months is 200RMB and allows you to take out three books at a time), and there is a great selection of books to buy, from best-sellers to all the books on China—from travel guides to business books—that you could read, and prices are only slightly higher than buying at home. Check the website for authors' talks as the very-well-connected manager gets an amazing array of people here, including Thomas Friedman and novelist Ma Jian. There are also up-to-date and well-priced magazines and guidebooks, arty notebooks, and even a small selection of jewelry. No wonder people spend all day here.

CHATERHOUSE BOOKTRADER

B107, The Place, 9 Guanghua Lu, 6587 1328

HOURS: Daily 9 A.M.-10 P.M.

Map 4

The Bookworm's only real competition is in the basement of shopping center The Place and is the city's only stand-alone bookstore selling English-language books and magazines. It has a few comfy chairs for you to sit in and browse the excellent selection, but unlike at the Bookworm, you come here for the books only—there's no atmosphere and not even any music. The staff are helpful, though, and can order items in, but don't bother with the magazines: For some reason, they're usually out of date and very expensive.

DVD STORE

4 Xiang, at Sanlitun Lu

HOURS: Daily 2 P.M.-2 A.M.

Map 4

Its central Sanlitun location among all the bars and boutiques ensures that this unnamed

DVD and CD store gets heavy traffic. It has all the latest TV series boxed sets and DVDs with discs starting at 10RMB for good-quality copies. Unfortunately, some films turn out to be in Russian (that's where they are copied), so ask whether the film is in English or not. While American chart toppers dominate, it does have a reasonable selection of foreign films, though do check that they are subtitled; some are not, which is extremely irritating when you sit down to watch it. The CD selection isn't quite so varied.

DVD STORE

48 Tiantan Donglu, 6717 6419

HOURS: Daily 9 A.M.-7:30 P.M.

Map 3

If you've been at Hongqiao or the Temple of Heaven and are looking for some more down-to-earth pleasures such as the latest Hollywood blockbuster, check out this store, which has been here for years. You might not be able to find it at first as it keeps a discreet profile to avoid police on one of their frequent antipiracy campaigns—look under the KFC and you'll see a small sign saying DVD. Inside is a cornucopia of DVDs and CDs. Customers flick through a folder and write down the titles they want and then the assistants go out to the back and find them. CDs are on the shelves and cover everything from Britney to Bob Dylan. DVD 9s (these have the extra features) are 15RMB; CDs are 20RMB and upward.

FOREIGN LANGUAGES BOOKSTORE

235 Wangfujing Dajie, 6512 6811

HOURS: Daily 9 A.M.-10 P.M.

Map 1

This is the oldest of the three bookstores listed, but it shouldn't be overlooked, especially if you're staying near Tiananmen—it is actually the only real reason to go to the city's former top shopping street, Wangfujing, which now pales in comparison with other, hipper areas. It has the largest selection of books available and its diversity (randomness?) makes it a good place to browse. It's not relaxing—there's nowhere to sit and terrible bright lighting, but for children's and young adults' books, nonfiction and art books, it's definitely worth taking a look. It also has a good range of Chinese dictionaries and study books.

Markets

HONGQIAO MARKET

Tiantan Donglu, opposite east gate of Temple of Heaven, 6713 3354

HOURS: Daily 8:30 A.M.-7 P.M.

Map 3

The busiest tourist market of them all, Hongqiao is, depending on your attitude toward overbearing shop assistants, irritating or bursting with bargaining opportunities. The atmosphere has gotten more pleasant thanks to the removal of the fish market in the basement (the whole place smelled) and a fresh lick of paint in time for the Olympics, and now there's a coffee takeaway supplied by Dareen's Coffee, but in my view the sellers could turn down the hard sell a fraction: I've taken to wearing my iPod and not listening. The sheer volume of products, though, is hard to beat—the basement has electronics, the first floor has watches, and the second floor is overflowing with bags and shoes and some clothes. Most of the pearls for sale on the third floor are low quality (it is possible to get a simple one-strand necklace for 15RMB), so as always in markets, buy because you like it, not because you think it's valuable. The fourth floor has more-upmarket pearls like those in stores such as Sharon's. Bargain hard for everything—go for 10 percent of the asking price!

JIAYI MARKET

3A Xinyuan Nanlu, opposite Kunlun Hotel, 8451 1810

HOURS: Daily 10 A.M.-9 P.M.

Map 7

After a major spruce up, this market offers a

more upmarket and relaxing shopping experience than Yaxiu and Hongqiao but with the same possibility of bagging bargains and it doesn't get as many foreign tourists. Instead of stalls, there are small boutiques, and the men's and women's clothes are not just the same name brands you get everywhere. Dig deep and you'll find everything from Victoria's Secret lingerie to Max Mara dresses. There is a good selection of "event" outfits that come without the usual feathers and sparkles. This is also a good place for "designer" handbags, though there is the occasional crackdown when all the bags are cleared from the shelves.

NALI MALL

Sanlitun Lu, 6413 2663

HOURS: Daily 11:30 A.M.-8 P.M.

Map 4

If the large tourist markets leave you overwhelmed and in search of more fashionable wear, check out this small warren of boutiques that make up Nali. Stores include those that sell both original designs as well as Chinese-made designer labels such as BCBG, Marni, and Marc Jacobs, though it's nearly impossible to tell if they are genuine or not. You can bargain a little here, but don't expect to get more than 10–20 percent off. One shop sells beautiful clothes made from Vietnamese fabric, and at the end is where you'll find shoe heaven Long.com. If you need reviving, grab a Serbian chicken sandwich from the kiosk at the entrance.

PANJIAYUAN

Panjiayuan Qiao, 6775 2405

HOURS: Mon.-Fri. 8:30 A.M.-6 P.M., Sat.-Sun. 4:30 A.M.-6:30 P.M.

Map 7

One for flea market aficionados, this is the mother of all markets. Home to thousands of sellers who scour the countryside in search of what they claim are antiques, family heirlooms, and curios, this is the place to go for everything from 1930s *qipaos,* jade, embroidery, art, furniture, and almost literally everything in between. In the past when a family fell on hard times, the shame of being forced to hock the family furniture meant that sellers came to Panjiayuan very early in the morning to avoid being seen. Even though the market is now seven days a week, the tradition of taking a torch with you and arriving as early as 4:30 A.M. to snatch up the good stuff still holds. If that's too early, don't worry but try to get there in the morning. The undercover stalls tend to be more expensive than the real country folk who turn up and lay out their goods on the floor—I'd try these people first and as always bargain as if your life depended on it. Under the roof, look out for the women in traditional headwear selling ornate embroidery from Guizhou province.

© HELENA IVESON

antiques on display at Panjiayuan

YAXIU MARKET

58 Gongren Tiyuchang Beilu, 6416 8945

HOURS: Daily 9 A.M.-7 P.M.

Map 4

This market is less busy than Hongqiao—but only just, as evidenced by the coaches of tourists that now pull up in front of the market. But if you time your visit well—either at the beginning or the end of the day—Yaxiu is cheap and cheerful and offers bargain hunters treasures galore if you're ruthless when it comes to haggling. The "Tiffany" jewelry makes great gifts and for men, there are all the ties, "North Face" jackets, and "Ralph Lauren" shirts you could stuff in a suitcase. There is a good underwear section and shoes and bag selection on the ground floor, and when your feet have given up the ghost, have a pedicure and manicure at one of the professional and speedy salons on the fourth floor. For some reason the neon sign on the front of the building says Yashow.

ZUOJIA CHAOWAI FURNITURE WAREHOUSE

43 Huawei Beili, 6770 6402

HOURS: Daily 10 A.M.-5:30 P.M.

Map 7

Chaowai is never particularly busy, which is surprising considering this is the place for Chinese enameled furniture and other affordable chinoiserie. The warehouse is crammed with stalls that mostly sell imitation antique furniture, so it is a good place to come if you want to decorate your home affordably. The four stories are a pleasant place to walk around for ideas and the stall holders are low pressure and happy for you to browse. It is possible to bargain a little: 10–15 percent off is the norm. Wangyou Antique Furniture is a good stall, as is Ho Ho Hang. The warehouse also has numerous shipping agents to whisk your new purchases away. If you're not shopped out, it's a good idea to combine a visit here with the sprawling Panjiayuan as they're in the same area: From Panjiayuan head south for 200 meters back toward Guomao.

Shopping Malls

CHINA WORLD SHOPPING MALL

1 Jianguomenwai Dajie, 6505 2288

HOURS: Daily 9 A.M.-9 P.M.

Map 4

If you can deal with the claustrophobic layout and irritating lack of signage and have mountains of cash that you're desperate to off-load, welcome to China World Shopping Mall. If you ever find a map when you're here, you'll see that the place is a who's who of designer fashion labels, including Louis Vuitton, Marc by Marc Jacobs, Tommy Hilfiger, and Gucci. Slightly more down to earth, there are a branch of Watson's Chemists, cosmetics giant Sephora, a row of midrange stores, including CK Jeans, and—perhaps a good place to deposit the kids—an ice rink. Food options include a branch of Cantonese specialists GL Café, Subway, and Starbucks. Beijing's tallest building, the third phase of the China World Trade Center, should be finished in September 2008 and promises even more designer-label heaven—with 73 stories and 300,000 square meters of floor space.

THE MALLS AT ORIENTAL PLAZA

1 Dongchang'an Jie, 8518 6363, www.orientalplaza.com

HOURS: Daily 9:30 A.M.-10 P.M.

Map 1

When Oriental Plaza opened in the 1990s it was the first shopping mall of its kind—upmarket, covering a whole block on its prime location near Tiananmen Square and filled with a wide variety of stores from top-of-the-line to midmarket labels. It was so different that it became something of a tourist attraction, and despite the competition now it still attracts hordes of tourists because of its location. It's busy day and night, and even people who don't shop enjoy the huge variety of food outlets, from a food court to expensive venues such as my Humble House, and the popular cinema. Now that the complex's west wing has been completed, it's boasting a host of new brands and stores (Omega, Cerruti 1881, Nina Ricci, and Ports, among others) to go with the shiny new look.

THE PLACE

9a Guanghua Lu, 8595 1755, www.theplace.cn

HOURS: Daily 10 A.M.–10 P.M.

Map 4

In a crowded market such as Beijing's, it's difficult for mid-range to high-end malls to stand out, but The Place does and not just because of its silly name. In the center of its two wings is the world's longest LCD screen, which projects different footage every night and has become something of an attraction in itself, with taxi drivers pulling in to watch when they don't have fares. Inside the mall, you'll find more down-to-earth shopping delights, such as Beijing's first Zara clothes store, which brought well-priced fashion to the masses, Chaterhouse Book store, MAC cosmetics, and French Connection.

SEASON'S PLACE

2 Jinchengfang Dong Jie, 6622 0888, www.seasonsplace.com

HOURS: Daily 9 A.M. –9 P.M.

Map 5

The very latest shopping mall to open for AMEX carriers, this is Financial Street's prime shopping destination and has China's nouveau riche fighting their way across the city in their chauffeured Mercs to get there. Five floors of brands await you under the beautifully designed glass roofed mall, and 50 percent of the stores are new to the Beijing market. Lane Crawford is Hong Kong's most fabulous department store—its Beijing branch is surrounded by Versace, Louis Vuitton, Hugo Boss, Gucci...and that's just the ground floor. The Ritz-Carlton Hotel is attached too if you need to lie down after spending all that cash, and there's also the futuristic restaurant Sebu, which is run by the same management as LAN Club.

SHIN KONG PLACE

87 Jianguo Lu, northeast of Dawang Bridge, 6530 5888, www.shinkong-place.com

HOURS: Daily 10 A.M.–10 P.M.

Map 4

In the west of the city you have Season's Place, in the east, you have Shin Kong Place: two shopping malls that opened in 2007 to much fanfare. In addition to luxury brands such as Bottega Venezia, Prada, and Gucci, in its seven stories Shin Kong Place has Beijing's best food court as well as glamorous and expensive Fauchon, France's premier food emporium, which covers a mind-boggling four floors with a deli, café, bakery, and expensive restaurant, all done up in its trademark pink and silver. The mall makes for a pleasant afternoon shopping session as it never gets crowded (it's just too expensive for most).

3.3 SHOPPING MALL

33 Sanlitun Lu, 6417 8886, www.3d3.cn

HOURS: Daily 9 A.M.–10 P.M.

Map 4

The first step in the attempt to transform Sanlitun from seedy to glitzy was the opening in 2006 of this shopping mall that spans five floors and is filled with small boutiques specializing in women's fashion. The mall's attempt to be upmarket is somewhat hindered by the hip-hop music blaring as you approach the building, but inside is a bit quieter. The range of clothes here is excellent but prices can be high and there's little bargaining. Items are usually one-offs, which means one size only: If you're of a more Western-size shape, shopping here might be a frustrating experience. On the ground floor, check out the well-organized racks at Wu Ba, and on the third floor at 3139, the highly covetable Steve Madden and Aldo high heels and flats can be yours for around 250RMB. Men generally get a raw deal when it comes to good-quality interesting clothing in China but the boutiques on the fourth floor are the best around. The fifth floor is given over to tailors: Liang Yi Tailor Shop (5035, 5th Floor, 5136 5360) has been around for a while and will knock up a man's suit for 700RMB, including what is claimed to be cashmere fabric. Made-to-measure shirts take about three days and will cost about 70RMB. Don't ask for anything too fancy, though: There's a limit to the kind of effects you can achieve in such a short timeframe.

THE VILLAGE AT SANLITUN

Sanlitun Lu, corner of Gongti Beilu

HOURS: Daily 10 A.M.-10 P.M.

Map 4

Due to start opening at the end of June 2008, this will be a 53,000-square-meter, 19-building development that aims to reinvent the neighborhood. The south zone will cover a retail area of 72,000 square meters, featuring 11 four-story retail blocks and a multiple-function hall; and the 48,000-square-meter north zone, scheduled to open six months after the south side does in June, will have eight four-story retail blocks targeting high-end international brands, and a 100-room boutique hotel.

Department Stores

LANE CRAWFORD

Season's Place, 2 Jinchengfang Dong Jie, 6622 0808, www.lanecrawford.com

HOURS: Daily 9 A.M. -9 P.M.

Map 5

An integral part of Season's Place shopping mall on Financial Street, the Beijing edition of this Hong Kong department store cost $38 million and offers a whopping 600 designer brands, including Stella McCartney and Marni. The store has firmly raised the shopping experience in Beijing—this place is in a different universe, with its personal shopper service, cutting-edge multi-media displays, and gorgeous packaging. Just make sure you bring a wallet-full of credit cards.

PACIFIC CENTURY PLACE

A2 Gongren Tiyuchang Beilu, 6539 3888

HOURS: Daily 10 A.M.-10 P.M.

Map 4

This department store in Sanlitun is a good one-stop shop for everything from (expensive) groceries, including a good selection of Japanese food, to underwear, cosmetics, housewares, and clothes. You'll find midmarket foreign brands such as Esprit and jewelry makers Pilgrim and a whole host of Chinese brands that are worth perusing. Prices are fixed and despite in every other way looking like a modern department store, it still has the old-fashioned way of paying, in which you take your bill to a central pay point, pay, get your reciept stamped, and then go pick up your goodies.

HOTELS

Business is booming for the capital's hotels. Not so long ago, checking into a Beijing hotel meant checking out your patience. Forget a warm welcome after a long flight; guests were often greeted with service with a scowl, no matter how much money their drab room was costing. Even as recently as 2003, visitors had to stay in designated hotels and could not legally stay in a Chinese friend's home or rent their own apartment. But, it's something of a new dawn for hotels in the capital: Tourist numbers are growing by an average of 15 percent each year and more than 500,000 overseas and one million domestic travelers were expected in 2008. By then, the Beijing Municipal Bureau of Tourism expected the number of hotels to have grown to more than 800, from the present 548, including 37 five-star hotels. The Olympics spurred a hotel-building frenzy and now there's no need to stay at run-down state-run hotels—the only options around a decade ago.

As the city's attractions are spread out over such a wide area, choosing wisely where to base yourself is critical unless you want to spend hours in Beijing's torturous traffic. If you're here on business, the upmarket hotels in the Central Business District around Guomao are a sensible place to rest your head, but be aware that many companies are moving out west. In a bid to take on Shanghai's reputation as the business center of China, the government is pushing investment into an area known as Financial Street in the west of Beijing. This is where you will find three of Beijing's newest five-star hotels: the Westin, the Ritz-Carlton,

COURTESY OF RAFFLES BEIJING

HIGHLIGHTS

LOOK FOR ◖ TO FIND RECOMMENDED HOTELS.

◖ **Best Budget Bed:** A stone's throw from the Forbidden City and down an atmospheric alley, the **Peking Guest House** is full of character and charm (page 132).

◖ **Best Service:** While the hotel's exterior doesn't live up to expectations, inside the **Peninsula** the faultless service delivered with a deft touch does and is on par with that of any of the best hotels in the world (page 133).

◖ **Most Historic Hotel:** Since the 1900s **Raffles Beijing Hotel** has seen famous names such as Charles de Gaulle and George Bernard Shaw check in, and thanks to a multimillion dollar refit, the hotel is once again a city landmark with its beautiful lobby and distinguished Writers Bar (page 133).

◖ **Most Fun Location:** Few visitors don't find the gentrified street of Nanluogu Xiang with its mixture of cozy cafés and artisan shops fun, and the boutique hotel **Guxiang 20** is right in the heart of the action (page 135).

◖ **Cutest Place to Lay Your Head:** Busting with character thanks to its gorgeously compact reception room and two-story bedrooms, **Hutong Ren** is achingly adorable (aside from the squat toilets) (page 136).

◖ **Best Romantic Getaway:** The stylish and secluded courtyard lit with glowing red lanterns at night make **Hotel de Cour SL** the place to go for honeymoons and romantic reunions (page 138).

◖ **Best Place for a Business Trip:** **Intercontinental Financial Street** is for adults only with its dark and sleek reception, sophisticated rooms, and terrific they've-thought-of-everything business facilities (page 140).

© PENINSULA HOTEL

the Peninsula hotel near Wangfujing and the Forbidden City

PRICE KEY

$ Under US$50 (370RMB)
$$ US$50-100 (370-740RMB)
$$$ US$100-150 (740-1,100RMB)
$$$$ Over US$150 (1,900RMB)

and the Intercontinental. Be warned that although China is trying to sell this area as the country's answer to Wall Street, there aren't many people around and good restaurants (aside from the Whampoa Club) are in short supply, though these hotels' restaurants are a cut above normal hotel dining.

For a more unusual stay, Beijing's historic courtyard hotels are a superb experience. Usually set in interesting *hutong* streets near the Forbidden City, Houhai, or the *hutong* around Dongsi in Chaoyang District, here's where you'll get a taste of old Beijing. Usually small, all rooms should face into a courtyard that will often have tables and chairs for you to relax. Some of the more expensive courtyard hotels have good facilities with all the latest toys such as wireless Internet and plasma screens, but usually you will have to accept that in exchange for your quiet and picturesque room, you might have to put up with bad plumbing and no Internet access. But when the birds are singing in the courtyard right outside your room, that's a pretty fair deal.

Some of Beijing's best no-frills accommodations are also set on *hutong* streets and here you'll get a taste of the past for minimum cost. Western-style youth hostels are a relatively new concept but are fast catching on and many are in some of Beijing's most interesting and historic areas. The only problem with them is that they are often not near subway stops and trudging down alleys with a heavy suitcase can be a nuisance. If you've just arrived at the airport or train station, I would strongly recommend arranging transportation with the place you are staying as it's usually reasonably priced and is a fail-safe way of ensuring you get to where you're going, and if it's midnight on a cold winter's night, you're not going to be wanting to wander around unlit alleys. Wherever you stay, always remember to collect a business card (*mingpian*) so that if you do get lost, a taxi driver can call the hotel for directions.

For people who have traveled around China, the cost of accommodation in Beijing can be a bit of a shock with more expensive hotels listing their prices in U.S. dollars—always a bad sign—and then charging a 15 percent service charge. Remember, though, that this is China, where bargaining is par for the course. You should never pay the full rack rate—nobody does—especially if you are staying for a few nights. It's always better to make reservations, especially during peak holiday seasons. During China's three national holidays, vacationers may get a pleasant surprise when it comes to room rates at hotels aimed at business travelers. Holiday time means few of their regular guests check in, so hotels often run good promotions for these days. Before you do make reservations, check discount travel websites such as www.elong.net or www.sinohotel.com as there can be some excellent deals.

You would expect people working in hotels that attract foreign visitors to have a good grasp of English, but this isn't always the case. The most expensive hotels and the cheapest catering to foreign backpackers are usually full of well-trained English speakers, but for some reason, staff at midrange hotels aren't always particularly skilled at the language: Be prepared for pointing, miming, and thumbing through a dictionary.

Tiananmen

Map 1

GRAND HYATT $$$$

1 Dongchang'an Jie, 8518 1234,
www.beijing.grand.hyatt.com

Expect to see plenty of sharp-suited execs on business trips if you stay here as the Hyatt is in Oriental Plaza, where many international companies have their China base. With these customers in mind, the service is slick and adult oriented—aside from the fantastic resort-style pool complete with waterfalls, there aren't many facilities for children. Rooms have recently been refurbished and while standard rooms are small for the price, plenty of extras are hidden from view and the color scheme is relaxing without being bland and the subdued lighting adds to the effect. Don't miss the duck at its flagship restaurant Made in China; it is considered one of Beijing's best birds—it's expensive, but if you're staying here, price is obviously not a concern.

HOTEL KAPOK $$$

16 Donghuamen Dajie, Dongcheng District, 6525 9988
www.hotelkapok.com

Beijing's first real boutique hotel, the Hotel Kapok opened in 2006 and is as different as can be from traditional courtyard accommodations. Nicknamed "The Blur" thanks to its glowing gridlike exterior meant to resemble jade, the hotel was designed by China's best-known architect, Zhu Pei, and enjoys a great location between Wangfujing and the Forbidden City. The most attractive feature is the predominantly white reception area, which includes a central, bamboo-filled courtyard that reaches up through the floors to the sky. The lobby bar is minimalist, though the effect is somewhat ruined by the plastic menus and indifferent service. The minimalist theme continues in the rooms but they still have a warm ambience and all come equipped with flat-screen TVs and covetable toiletries.

PEKING GUEST HOUSE $

5 Beichizi Dajie, Beichizi 2 Tiao, 6526 8855,
pekinghostel@yahoo.com.cn

This hidden gem is tucked down an alley 200 meters from the Forbidden City. The tiny courtyard hostel opened only in 2006 but is often fully booked thanks to good customer reviews that praise the helpful staff and superb location. The hostel has both clean and neat dorm rooms and small doubles but the best features are the wooden-beamed reception area and café dotted with potted plants and the outdoor courtyard, which is a great place to rest with a book and coffee after walking around the sights. Other features include free wireless Internet and the staff are very security conscious—you have to be buzzed in at all times.

© HELENA IVESON

the cozy reception room at the Peking Guest House

PENINSULA $$$$

8 Jinyu Hutong, 8516 2888,
www.beijing.peninsula.com

Probably Beijing's most expensive bed, the Beijing Peninsula is let down by its entrance (if it feels as if you're entering a shopping mall, that's because you are, albeit Beijing's ritziest) and the hotel exterior, but all is forgiven when you experience the service and standard of rooms. Staff speak impeccable English and supply service with a deft touch, a rare thing in China. Rooms aren't huge but the Peninsula is way ahead of the competition when it comes to electronics with plasma-screen TVs and DVD players and MP3-compatible music system electronics tucked away in every room: In fact every drawer reveals something new, whether it's a fax machine or DVD selection. Its pre-Olympics facelift saw $35 million lavished on the hotel, and sky-high room rates will see the hotel fast recoup the costs. The final phase, a spa—with 12 state-of-the-art treatment rooms, which will be part of the hotel's third-floor wellness, health, and fitness facility—opened in time for the Olympics. Unique to the hotel, the Peninsula Academy program invites guests to learn to make dumplings with the in-house chef, visit the "wild" Great Wall, or learn antique appreciation from an expert before venturing to the markets.

RAFFLES BEIJING HOTEL $$$$

33 Dongchang'an Jie, 6526 3388, beijing.raffles.com

Just five minutes' walk from Tiananmen Square, this hotel is the city's only hotel with a history. It originally opened in 1917 and was the place to be seen for movers and shakers and, thanks to a full renovation by the world-famous Raffles chain in 2006, is now aiming to attract the same kind of upmarket clientele who don't mind paying its eye-watering prices. The hotel boasts a glorious lobby—if you can't afford a room, splash out on afternoon tea for two—but in some cases rooms don't quite match the promise, though they are still attractive with classic furniture. The ballroom and Writers Bar both hark from the hotel's heyday and offer a similar ambience to the

the historic facade of Raffles Beijing Hotel

Raffles Hotel in Singapore, while a classy pool and signature Amrita gym have brought facilities back up to date.

SUPER 8 BIRD'S NEST $

Building Number 8, Anhui, North Block, 5140 2266,
www.super8.com

You can travel thousands of miles and you can't escape Super 8s: Yes, they're now in China. Part of the Asian Games Village in the Olympic complex, Super 8 Bird's Nest has 61 guest rooms at budget prices. Built in 2007, rooms are modern, clean, and offer a good range of facilities, including cable TV and free Internet access, though given the quality of the furnishings they will probably not age well. It's not stylish but if you need to be based near the Olympic complex, options aren't great in this area anyway. It's often full of Chinese business travelers and not many foreign visitors check in, but if you're looking for a real hotel with modern amenities for backpacking prices, the Super 8 can't be beat.

EXTENDED STAYS IN THE CAPITAL

In addition to **Tai Yue Suites** in Sanlitun, there are plenty of other options where you can rent an apartment for anything from a day upward in Beijing. The serviced apartments at the **Ascott Residence** (108b Jianguo Lu, CBD, 400 820 1028, www.the-ascott.com), opposite the World Trade Center, are luxurious and the two-bedroom option is great for families – rates there start at 1,200RMB a night. The **Henderson Center** (18 Jianguomen Nei Dajie, 6518 3228, www.hld.com/english/property/china/beijing/index.htm), which has a good location on Beijing's grandest avenue near Tiananmen Square, is a cheaper alternative with a one-bedroom costing 7,870RMB a month, a two-bedroom, 10,500RMB. Alternatively, the listings magazine *The Beijinger* has a great classified section for short-term rentals on its website at www.thebeijinger.com, or try the website www.sublet.com to rent directly from an apartment owner. If you're keen to sample real-life Beijing-style or are on a very tight budget, consider a homestay, in which you stay with a Chinese family. You may be expected to teach a bit of English to the family, but in return you'll really experience ordinary life in way that most visitors would never get the chance to. One organization is **Beijing Homestay Agency** (www.beijinghomestayagency.com), which charges around 2,800RMB a month, and there are more on the website www.thebeijinger.com.

TANGYUE HOTEL $

54 Donghuamen Dajie, 6525 2510

If you're on a budget and looking to stay in a hotel a stone's throw from the Forbidden City, Tangyue Hotel is just the thing for the young at heart. It's often full with independent travelers, so you would expect the staff to speak better English than they do. This is certainly not some anonymous bland hotel, which is made obvious from the garish entrance, and the reception desk looks like a beached whale. Every one of the 66 rooms is individually decorated, from the unfortunately brothel-red (including round bed and red net curtains) to the surprisingly stylish. There is a small business center but staying in such a historic area means you'll probably not be inclined to stay in photocopying. If all the colors give you a headache, the relaxing and reasonably priced Dragonfly spa is just doors away.

TIANXIANG COURTYARD HOTEL $$

16 Shijinhuayuan Hutong, Bei Dongsi Dajie, 8403 2831, fax 8403 1831

Set down a residential alley off a busy shopping street, this is a newly converted courtyard hotel and is another former home of a Chinese general. It's amazingly peaceful considering the central location with rooms all looking out onto one of the three attractive leafy courtyards with birds in cages twittering away. Some of the double rooms have traditional *kang* beds, which are great to look at though if you're on the large side, they will be a bit of a squeeze. Most rooms have just a walk-in shower though the most expensive double also has a corner bath. The English-speaking manager, George, is a friendly guy, and he'll probably invite you to have a cup of green tea as you sit in the courtyard enjoying the peace and quiet.

Houhai to the Olympic Stadium

Map 2

BAMBOO GARDEN HOTEL $$

24 Xiaoshiqiao Hutong, Jiugulou Dajie, 6403 2229, www.bbgh.com.cn

This hotel is also well established and attracts many foreign visitors keen to stay in a place with some history in a lovely traditional location near the lakes at Houhai. The original central building was built for a head eunuch from the Qing dynasty, though new wings have been added around the central bamboo garden. Rooms are a mixed bunch, unfortunately, and if you're making reservations from abroad through its website, you might be disappointed with what you are allocated, and because the hotel is often full, it might be difficult to change on arrival. Go for the suites if you have the cash: They have the best furniture and lovely views over the garden.

BEIJING BACKPACKERS $

85 Nanluogu Xiang, 8400 2429, downtown@backpackingchina.com

This cheerful hostel opened in 2005 and immediately filled Beijing's gaping hole for cut-price but well-situated rooms. This is a great place to stay for people on a tight budget: It's halfway down the city's most funky *hutong,* with relaxed bars and boutiques nestled among traditional courtyard houses and backstreet restaurants, and within walking distance from Houhai and Beihai Park. The English-speaking staff cater well to their clientele, offering clean, basic rooms (mostly dorms but a few doubles too) and bathrooms, and a welcoming coffee shop and Western restaurant where you can swap books and meet fellow travelers.

GUXIANG 20 $$

20 Nanluogu Xiang, 6400 5566, www.guxiang20.com

Set on Beijing's most gentrified *hutong,* Guxiang 20 is a new purpose-built boutique hotel with more style than you would expect at these prices in an excellent setting. The reception areas are welcoming and filled with bamboo and lead into the upmarket restaurant, which serves traditional Guangdong food (the street has plenty

HOTELS

Guests love Beijing Backpackers hostel along trendy Nanluogu Xiang.

of other options). Its 28 rooms don't match the old-worldy exterior; a modern designer aesthetic is firmly in control. Expect a charcoal and beige color scheme, flat-screen plasma TVs hanging on the walls, and wireless Internet. Staff are still learning the ropes so service is not seamless but there are a few English speakers on the staff who will try their best.

HUTONG REN $

71 Ju'er Hutong, off Nanluogu Xiang, 8402 5238, www.bb-china.com

A real hidden gem, Hutong Ren is full of character: It's one of those all-too-rare finds in China. Run by a brother and sister, the guesthouse has five rooms: two singles that are fine, if bare, and three doubles that have a small sitting area and bathroom on the ground floor and a Japanese tatami bed upstairs. All rooms face the small enclosed courtyard full of leafy plants and books. As the place is so small, it's not somewhere to get rowdy—this place seems to attract a slighter older crowd than most budget accommodations. Not much English is spoken but that's easily forgiven when the owners are so relaxed and friendly. The only drawback—and to some people it will be a major one—is that toilets are old-style squatters.

LUSONGYUAN HOTEL $$

22 Banchan Hutong, Kuan Jie, 6404 0436, lsyhotel@263.net

Guests here get to experience a great neighborhood that may be very traditional but is just minutes from the bars and boutiques of Nanluogu Xiang. Foreign tourists flock to the Lusongyuan, originally built in the Qing dynasty, looking for a good value place with character. They generally find it, though some gripe about the slightly shabby rooms, and don't reserve a single room unless you like sleeping in what used to be a cupboard. Still, the sunny courtyard complete with caged birds singing in the sun makes up for small irritations and as this is one of the most well-established hotels, the staff know what tourists want and cater to them well with information and tours.

RED LANTERN HOUSE $

5 Zhengjue Hutong, Xinjie Kou, 6616 9477, lindyguo@hotmail.com

This is a small homely place around a converted enclosed courtyard with goldfish pond and is definitely a challenge to find, but persevere if you want the genuine *hutong* experience: This is the only hostel in this area—most courtyards are people's houses. The hostel is excellent value and its simple but spotless rooms get good reviews for budget travelers. The owners, very keen to give visitors a good impression of Beijing, go that extra mile in helping you and are very security conscious, with CCTV in the public areas and with the door locked at midnight—after that you'll have to pound on the doors. The traditional Chinese decor doesn't extend to the bedrooms (and be warned, there are only two toilets and showers so expect lines if the hostel is full) but they are acceptable and well heated—very important come January.

Red Lantern House is a stylish budget option.

HOTELS

Qianmen and Temple of Heaven — Map 3

FAR EAST INTERNATIONAL YOUTH HOSTEL $

90 Tieshuxie Jie, 5195 8811, www.fareastyh.com

This well-established hostel in a converted courtyard is in a great location tucked down a historic *hutong* near Qianmen and the Hepingmen subway stop and sees a steady crowd of backpackers. It is part of the two-star Far East Hotel opposite, and you can upgrade to rooms there, but the hostel dorms overlooking the courtyard are much more interesting though colder and farther away from the spartan bathrooms. Included in the price are free access to a washing machine, book rental, and half an hour of free Internet access every day, and the friendly staff stuff your pockets with useful maps, useful as the location down the *hutong* can be a bit tricky to navigate as the whole area seems to be permanently under construction.

JIANGUO QIANMEN HOTEL $$$

175 Yong'an Lu, 6301 6688, www.qianmenhotel.com

This hotel's unique selling points are the Beijing opera actors who get dolled up in the bright and airy foyer every night to perform in the hotel's own theater and provide an hour's worth of entertainment, which is just as well since the local area isn't exactly brimming with sights. For an upmarket hotel, the standard of English is surprisingly poor. The free breakfast buffet gets good reviews as do the spacious and well-lit rooms but the whole place, built in the 1950s, could do with a revamp to bring it into the 21st century—the wear and tear in the room's bedding and upholstery lets the place down.

365 INN $

55 Dazhalan Xijie, 6354 1107, www.365hostel.com.cn

This place is a lively slice of backpacker heaven in the unlikely setting of bustling Qianmen. At the hostel's Sakura restaurant, you can fill up on pretty good pizzas and Yunnan coffee (there is also MSG-free Chinese food, but it's a little expensive) as you watch the world go by. The hostel was once the residence of a 20th-century warlord, but it is now filled with rough wooden furniture and easy-listening music catering to the young Western twenty-something crowd. Dorms are good value while the doubles aren't quite so much and bathrooms are fine if a little dark. Staff can arrange airport pickups and offer the standard tours to the Great Wall.

Central Business District — Map 4

CHINA WORLD HOTEL $$$$

1 Jianguomenwai Dajie, 6505 2266, www.shangri-la.com/chinaworld

Up until recently, this was Beijing's only real five-star hotel but competition from newer venues has forced the hotel to raise its game. Millions of dollars were spent on the glitzy and opulent lobby, which you'll either love or hate. The hotel is huge with 716 rooms so there is a limit to how personalized the service can be, but for these prices, you'd hope for a little more effort from staff. Rooms and suites are dark because of all the wooden paneling, but the Italian marble bathrooms are relaxing. Most of your fellow guests will be business travelers so expect corporate prices in the hotel's five restaurants and bars, and broadband is expensive at 140RMB a day. Aria is the China World's superb bar and restaurant if you're keen to splurge.

HAOYUAN HOTEL $$

53 Shijia Hutong, 6512 5557, www.haoyuanhotel.com

The Haoyuan's main attraction is the sense of peacefulness you can enjoy lounging in the courtyard despite being just minutes from the crowded chaos at Wangfujing. All 14 rooms combine practicality—think comfortable beds and modern TV sets—with attractive antique desks and wardrobes. Poky bathrooms let the rooms down a little, but the pleasant English-speaking staff do their best to deal with guest gripes. Breakfast is included but it's nothing to get excited about as it's toast and coffee—fine in summer but in winter, you'll want something a little heartier.

HOTEL DE COUR SL $$$

70 Yan Yue Hutong, 6512 8020,
www.hotelcotecoursl.com

Beijing's newest and ritziest boutique hotel, the oddly named Hotel de Cour SL offers plenty of charm and style in exchange for very high prices. The hotel has 14 rooms facing onto the garden, all tastefully and individually decorated and successfully fusing modern amenities with stylish antique surroundings—the mosaic bathrooms and huge showerheads are lovely. In whatever room you choose, a peaceful night's sleep is helped by double glazing, goosedown duvets, and luxurious linen. At night, the central courtyard is lit up with red lanterns and looks like a film set, though if the weather is too cold for sitting outside, the resident's only lounge has plenty of contemporary artwork to enjoy.

KERRY CENTRE HOTEL $$$

1 Guanghua Lu, 6561 8833,
www.shangri-la.com/en/property/beijing/kerrycentre

The Kerry opened in 1999 and is wearing very well, attracting a mixed crowd of business travelers, tourists, and plenty of visiting sports stars (this is where the soccer team Manchester United stays on tour) because of the great pool and gym. Staff seem to try a little harder than in other venues and if you reserve the airport transfer service, you'll be escorted through immigration, all the way to and from the gate. The hotel's bar, Centro, regularly wins best bar in Beijing awards for its cool design and great cocktails but the stylishly attired staff lose points for snootiness. The 487 rooms are large and well-laid-out if not particularly flashy. The only real problem with the hotel is that it's in the middle of a construction site and there aren't many attractions or local restaurants you can walk to. But if you're happy to get taxis wherever you go, this is a great choice, and you're staying 200 meters from Beijing's newest icon, the CCTV Building.

RED CAPITAL RESIDENCE $$$

9 Dongsi 6 Tiao, 8403 5308,
www.redcapitalclub.com.cn

To be blunt, guests who stay here either love it or hate it. Some rave about the experience of living out your Chinese fantasies in an historic venue filled with memorabilia from Revolutionary days and the hotel's intimate size with just five themed rooms around a central courtyard, but others complain about the uncomfortable beds, chilliness in winter, and the lack of English spoken by staff. So, do not go to the Residence expecting five-star comforts: It's a unique experience but you pay a premium for it, as rates are too high considering the level of service and facilities. But if atmosphere is more important to you than say, a plasma TV screen, go—and what other hotel has an underground bomb-shelter bar?

SIHE HOTEL $$

5 Dengcao Hutong, Dongsi Nan Jie, 5169 3555

Sihe Hotel was built for a warlord, and just as it probably served as a haven of tranquility then, that's what it is still like today. *Siheyuan* is the Chinese word for the traditional houses in which rooms are built around a central yard: Once each room was the home for a different family, but now these places make great hotels. Sihe is not as quaint as it could be as the freshly painted bright-red walls are a little garish, but the big attraction here is the central courtyard, which is lit at night by lanterns, and noise is kept out thanks to the thick walls. There are only 12 rooms and their best feature is the sleek modern bathrooms, which are a vast improvement on the freezing-cold ones the hotel had in the past. It's excellent value for the money and sees a steady stream of mostly foreign visitors, so be sure to make reservations.

ST REGIS $$$$

21 Jianguomenwai Dajie, 6460 6688,
www.stregis.com/beijing

If the idea of staying at the same hotel that George W. Bush and Tony Blair use when they're in town is appealing, check into the St Regis. Rivaling the Peninsula in terms of service and the bottom line, the St Regis attracts heads of state, business travelers, and the odd high-roller tourist. Its 273 rooms and suites are relaxing in beiges and cream, and staff here have plenty of experience in dealing with demanding VIP guests and speak English better than anyone else in town. The gym and pool are more for racking up laps than for relaxing, but the glass enclosure allows nice views of the garden.

TRADERS $$

1 Jianguomenwai Dajie, 6505 2277,
www.shangri-la.com/en/property/beijing/traders

Part of the ritzy Shangri-La chain of hotels, Traders pitches itself as the cheaper alternative to the more glamorous China World Hotel next door (they share gym facilities, which is a great bonus) and is very popular with business travelers. It's not an attractive building—it was built in the 1970s—but inside, the lobby and reception areas are all about the bottom line—everything is clean and blandly corporate and money hasn't been spent on glitz. The staff are very efficient, and thanks to its location in the heart of the Central Business District near the Guomao subway stop, you don't have to deal with the city's traffic. Rooms are again blandly corporate but have broadband Internet access, neat bathrooms, and plenty of desk space.

Chaoyang District and Sanlitun

Map 4

TAI YUE SUITES $$

16 Nan Sanlitun Lu, 85952277, 6508 7257

This is situated at the quiet end of Sanlitun Lu, and the largest share of Beijing's bars and clubs are within stumbling distance. Staying here at this modern hotel aimed at business travelers is a good choice for visitors who want to be central but actual sights are thin on the ground. Rooms vary from neat studios to large two-bedroom suites suitable for families (under 18s stay for free), and rooms come with a reasonable kitchen, satellite TV, and free broadband. The decor is fine if anonymous with plenty of glass fixtures and light colors. Many people stay here on extended visits and good deals can be negotiated.

ZHAOLONG YOUTH HOSTEL $

2 Gongren Tiyuchang Beilu, 6597 2666,
yhzl@zhaolonghotel.com.cn

Tucked behind the Zhaolong hotel proper in an unprepossessing alley, the hostel is in the city's major entertainment area of Sanlitun though far enough away from the action for its mostly Western backpacker guests to get a good night's sleep if that's what they'd prefer. The hostel's utilitarian dorms and double rooms are looking their age a little and its run-of-the-mill backpacker-friendly facilities are nothing exciting, but fitness fanatics can use the main hotel's gym for free: Then you can indulge without guilt in the hostel's bargain-priced breakfast buffet.

Capital Museum and Temple of Great Charity Map 5

FRIENDSHIP HOTEL $$$

1 Zhongguancun Nandajie, 6849 8080,
www.bjfriendshiphotel.com

If you are interested in modern Chinese history, you may enjoy a stay here. It was built in the 1950s for visitors sympathetic to the Communist cause, and guests would immediately have felt at home in the Stalinist-style architecture. While the main building is something of an eyesore and overlooks a permanently busy main road, most of the 1,700 rooms are in small blocks dotted around a very attractive tree-lined campus: It does feel as if you're back at the university but with nicer rooms. With a swimming pool and tennis court, this hotel makes a good base to relax after frantic sightseeing at the Summer Palace, and there's even a TGI Fridays for a taste of Americana.

INTERCONTINENTAL FINANCIAL STREET $$$$

11 Jinrong Dajie, 5852 5888,
www.intercontinental.com/icbeijing

Most people who stay here are on business, but the extra-cool touches such as the funky X-Change bar and superb Sunday brunches make the hotel a popular destination for Beijing's expats. The hotel's interior is dark and sleek and staff dressed in slinky black silk *qipaos* or suits are there to greet you when you enter the surprisingly low-key reception. The rooms have big squishy beds, brown marble bathrooms, and flat-screen TVs, and views from rooms facing east are good as Beihai Park and the Forbidden City can be seen in the distance (notwithstanding Beijing's smog). The spa is another perk, offering a range of luxurious massages and treatments for a touch-too-high prices.

SHANGRI-LA HOTEL $$$$

29 Zizhuyuan Lu, 6841 2211,
www.shangri-la.com/beijing

The Shangri-La chain is a major player in Beijing, and thanks to a $72 million upgrade in time for the Olympics, this, its flagship hotel, is always busy despite its out-of-the-way location, being near neither the CBD nor near any tourist attractions or subway stop. It is, however,

The sleek Intercontinental Financial Street is for grown-ups only.

a considerable jump in price from its sister hotel, Kerry Centre, which is much newer, and the gym, rooms, and other facilities don't justify it. If you need to be in this area, stay and reserve one of the newer Valley wing rooms, which are more spacious and smarter than in the Garden wing. And do not under any circumstances miss a meal at the superb restaurant Blu Lobster, known for its exciting contemporary cuisine.

TEMPLESIDE HOUSE HOSTEL $

2 Tiao, Liu He Hutong, Fuchengmennei Jie, 6615 7797, www.templeside.com

A real find—and I don't exaggerate, it is a real find as there aren't any signs to help you find this lovely hostel. It is down an unmarked *hutong* near Financial Street and one of the capital's nicest temples, the Temple of Great Charity. The owners speak fluent English and opened the eight-room hostel in 2006. The twin and double rooms are surprisingly well furnished and toilets and showers are perhaps the most modern and clean seen in a Beijing hostel. The leafy courtyard is turned into an alfresco TV area and meeting point in the summer. The owners include a cooked breakfast in the price and will order food in for you from local mom-and-pop restaurants. Because of the place's popularity, they have opened a new sister courtyard hotel 10 minutes' walk away.

THE WESTIN BEIJING $$$$

9b Jinrong Dajie, 6606 8866, westin.com/beijingfinancial

The Westin opened in March 2007 and while it may be part of the massive Starwood corporation, the hotel prides itself on providing small touches to make the place a haven for travelers. Reviving drinks are available in the understated lobby, and in the 453 rooms, colors are muted and the beds are self-described as "heavenly"—and available to buy if you have a spare 15,000RMB. Standard rooms seem bigger than they are as they are relatively open plan with glass walls allowing plenty of light into the bathrooms. There you'll find fresh orchids, and for an extra fee, bathologists will come and run you a themed bath before an in-room massage. Because of the hotel's emphasis on health, the spa is a big deal and the gym has up-to-the-minute equipment, which is a good thing considering the view overlooking a road is very uninspiring. The chain opened the Westin Chaoyang in August 2008.

University District and the Summer Palace Map 6

FURAMAXPRESS $$

ZhongGuanCun, 68 North 4th Ring West Road, 5898 6688 and 5898 6689, www.furamaxpress.com

This is a new and trendy hotel designed to appeal to sophisticated travelers though one suspects that the brightly colored furniture won't wear well and the business facilities aren't quite up to scratch. If you're on a budget, though, and need to be in Beijing's "Silicon Valley"—ZhongGuanCun—or near Beida or Tsinghua Universities, this is an ideal place to rest your head. Both the lobby and the 238 rooms are very bright and while rooms are comfortable and functional, they're certainly not glamorous. Still, free broadband and clean and better than you'd expect bathrooms make this a good budget pick.

EXCURSIONS FROM BEIJING

Beijing is endlessly interesting, but relaxing? Not so much. If the traffic, pollution, crowds, and the hammering of construction workers around the clock begin to bug you, Beijing offers several worthwhile excursions into the countryside that leave the capital's 17 million residents firmly behind you. And it's only by getting some perspective that you realize how Beijing and definitely Shanghai are very much atypical of China: Only a handful of other cities in the country have experienced anything like their warp-speed development and by leaving the two metropolises behind, you'll see how different life is in smaller cities such as Chengde and Beidaihe—only three hours or so away from Beijing, but 10 years behind.

Even if you are in Beijing for only a short time, do make the effort to see a bit of the countryside. After all, coming to China and not seeing one of the true wonders of the world, the Great Wall, would be a true howler—try explaining that to your friends back home—especially as sections of the structure lie within a couple of hours of the capital.

Aside from the truly impressive sight of the Great Wall as it snakes its way over mountains and down into valleys, beaches and the preserved beauty of a Ming dynasty village are all within a couple of hours of traveling time. While Beijing is overflowing with sights and attractions, the crowds are increasingly a problem, but while certain parts of the Great Wall are rammed with people between the ramparts, other sections that do not get as much publicity rarely see tourists, so you get to walk the wall without being followed at every step by postcard sellers carrying "I climbed the Great

© DANIEL SANDERSON

HIGHLIGHTS

LOOK FOR ☾ TO FIND RECOMMENDED SIGHTS, ACTIVITIES, DINING, AND LODGING.

☾ **Best Day Trip from Beijing:** If you can see only one section of the Great Wall, make a day of it and go to **Simatai**. It is not one of the world's wonders for nothing: You shouldn't miss the Great Wall for all the tea in China (page 146).

☾ **Best place for peace and quiet:** The tranquil courtyard houses that make up the preserved Ming Dynasty **village of Cuandixia** are a wonderful place to kick back and relax in fresh air (page 150).

☾ **Best Garden Fit for an Emperor:** **Chengde Mountain Resort** is worth the three-hour journey from the capital to enjoy its relaxing mixture of formal gardens, leafy wild areas, and peaceful lakes (page 152).

perhaps China's most iconic sight, the Great Wall

Wall" T-shirts and thrusting them in your face. So for a change of pace and people, Beijing's surroundings are well worth an exploration.

PLANNING YOUR TIME

Beijing is a sprawling city, so planning to leave it takes time and effort. For Beijing's urbanites, spoiled by cheap taxis and an increasingly good subway system, getting on a decrepit bus and getting stuck in traffic is unfortunately par for the course if you don't have or rent your own car: Only by first braving the jam-packed highways beyond the fifth ring road do you do get to earn the right to enjoy some fresh air and tranquility. For some reason, Beijing's bus system to outlying areas has not been updated and modernized like the rest of the city's transportation—while the city itself got another four subway lines and a high-speed train link to the airport, day-trippers still have to contend with old buses without seatbelts and fellow passengers' smoking throughout the journey. For this reason, it makes sense to rent a private car and costs are generally very reasonable. If you make only one trip beyond the city limits it should be to the Great Wall, and depending on which section of the wall you wish to go to, a good car with seatbelts will cost around 400RMB a day. If you're on a tighter budget and want someone else to organize the trip for you, youth hostels run minibus trips to different sections and cost about 250RMB including entrance.

Those with a bit more time on their hands should visit the peaceful Ming dynasty village Cuandixia for a taste of how life in China used to be, and while if you hire a car you can do the trip in one (long) day, part of the fun is staying overnight in a courtyard bed-and-breakfast for the genuine rustic experience.

It's important to consider the weather when deciding where to go, as even just a couple of hours away from Beijing the temperature is considerably lower during the winter. Staying in an unheated courtyard in Cuandixia may lose its appeal when you're shivering all night. Temperature is less of a problem when you're at the Great Wall as long as you're planning to actually climb it, as scaling the guard towers will soon have you breaking into a sweat. Going in winter means fewer crowds as well as a greater chance of its being a sunny day, as Beijing gets most of its sunshine during the winter and on a crisp, clear day, views of the countryside surrounding the wall can be astounding—just watch your step in case the wall's stone steps are icy.

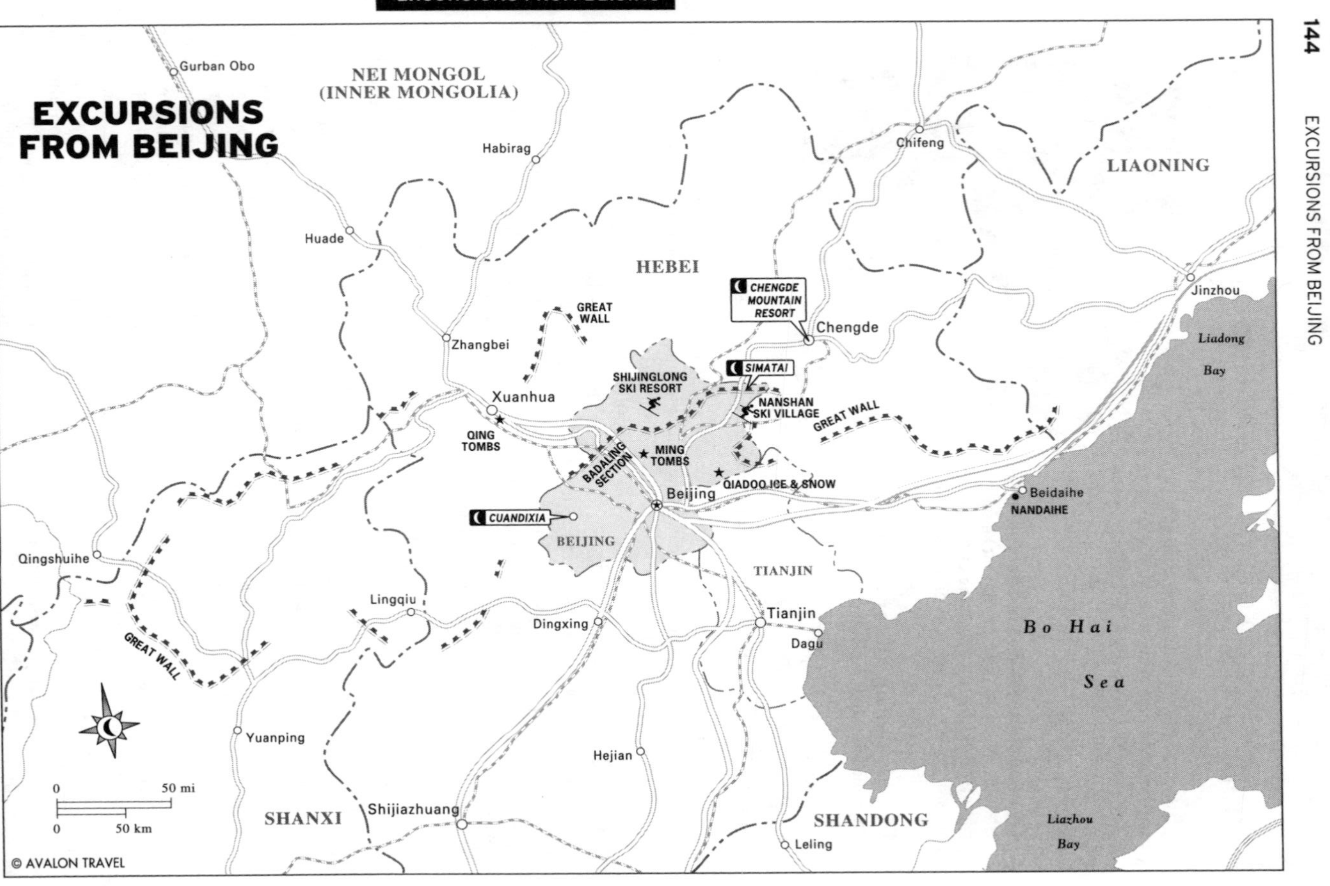

EXCURSIONS FROM BEIJING
Gurban Obo
NEI MONGOL (INNER MONGOLIA)
Habirag
Chifeng
LIAONING
Huade
HEBEI
CHENGDE MOUNTAIN RESORT
Jinzhou
Chengde
Liadong Bay
GREAT WALL
Zhangbei
SIMATAI
SHIJINGLONG SKI RESORT
NANSHAN SKI VILLAGE
GREAT WALL
Xuanhua
QING TOMBS
BADALING SECTION
MING TOMBS
QIADOO ICE & SNOW
Beijing
Beidaihe
NANDAIHE
CUANDIXIA
BEIJING
Qingshuihe
TIANJIN
Lingqiu
Tianjin
Dingxing
Dagu
Bo Hai
GREAT WALL
Sea
Yuanping
Hejian
0
50 mi
0
50 km
SHANXI
Shijiazhuang
SHANDONG
Liazhou Bay
Leling
© AVALON TRAVEL

Great Wall (Chángchéng 长城)

Winding its way across the northern edge of China, from the coastal city of Shanghaiguan in the east to long-gone sections underneath the sand in the Taklaman Desert in the west, the Great Wall has been mythologized like no other sight in China. Popular opinion has it that the wall is one long structure (it's not—its many sections were built by different dynasties during the course of 2,000 years, and it shrank and grew) and that it is the only man-made structure to be seen from space ("The Earth looked very beautiful from space, but I did not see our Great Wall," said China's first astronaut, Yang Liwei, after orbiting Earth in 2003). And while the wall is of course just bricks and mortar, it's a rare visitor who doesn't find the sight incredible as it zigzags its way over undulating mountains.

With tourists allowed to clamber up it, it's easy to forget that the structure is ancient (most of the sections around Beijing were built by the Ming dynasty and are the newest parts at 400–600 years old) and years of government disinterest and uncontrolled tourism have taken their toll. Large sections have been, to the Chinese government's eyes, repaired and improved, to critics' eyes, knocked down and rebuilt with unnecessary handrails, slides, and cable cars to whiz you off the wall. Depending on your fitness and the time you have free for a visit, if possible make a whole day of it and travel to one of the farthest sections, such as Jinshanling, Huanghua, or Simatai. The two sections closest to Beijing, Badaling and Mutianyu, are where visiting dignitaries are whizzed for the obligatory photo-op and where you'll find the most crowds, facilities, and add-ons such as cable cars. For more of a genuine unreconstructed wall experience, the farther away you go from the capital, the more you will be rewarded.

EXCLUSIVE GETAWAYS

In addition to the **Commune at the Great Wall,** other upmarket escapes from Beijing have sprung up to cater to China's burgeoning middle classes looking for a quick break from the city. One of the most popular is **The Red Capital Ranch** (28 Xiaguandi village, Yanxi town, Huairou district, 8401 8886, www.redcapitalclub.com.cn), which is owned by the American entrepreneur who runs the Red Capital Residence in the city itself. As with the Commune, a key attraction is the lodge's proximity to the Great Wall; each of its 10 rustic rooms enjoys stunning views, but while the Commune's architecture is cutting-edge, the ranch is an eccentric mixture of Manchurian hunting lodge and Tibetan decor. The place gets great reviews for its romantic ambience and hiking opportunities on a private stretch of the wall, though some think it's a little expensive at $200 a night, but for a one-off experience, its uniqueness makes it an intriguing place to stay.

BADALING SECTION (BĀDÁLǏNG 八达岭)

If you're on a whistle-stop tour of Beijing, it's possible to jump in a taxi or bus, get to Badaling in a little more than an hour, spend a couple of hours walking the wall with the crowds of other tourists and trinket sellers, and then head back to another sight such as the Ming Tombs in the afternoon. It's overvisited but if you have only a few hours to spare, it's a convenient place to see the wall. Beijing expats can be very sniffy about Badaling and its more than 10,000 tourists a day, but it's quick and easy to get to, and when you don't have the luxury of time, that's what you need.

Sights

This is the first section officially opened to tourists, and visitors have descended on

Badaling (Badaling Expressway Exit 17, Yanqing County, 6912 2222, www.badaling.gov.cn, daily 6:30 A.M.–7 P.M., 45RMB) since 1957. You climb onto the wall by entering the Ming dynasty–era gate, where you can turn either left or right and climb the wall up the gently sloping mountain with handrails on either side of the wall. If you're not a gym regular, head up the right side, as it is a little easier, though for the easiest journey of them all, the cable car will take you up for an extra 40RMB one-way, 60RMB return. In addition to the great views across leafy terrain, there is also a museum of Chinese history, including a photo gallery and the Great Wall Circle Vision Theater, a 360-degree amphitheater where you can see a 15-minute film on the history and legends of the wall.

Food

Your options here are limited to the predictable overpriced noodle and dumpling restaurants to the more surreal sight of a cardboard cutout of Colonel Sanders inviting you into KFC for some finger-lickin' chicken. There is also a Starbucks for that shot of caffeine you need to spur you on and a California Beef Noodle King USA, a popular noodle fast-food restaurant. My advice is to visit one of Beijing's French bakeries, such as Comptoir, and make every one of your fellow tourists jealous by unwrapping a *pain au raison* and ham and cheese baguette. Well, sometimes, the authentic options just aren't much fun.

Accommodations

For a unique experience combining the Great Wall and amazing man-made architecture, a stay at the **Commune at the Great Wall** (Badaling Expressway Great Wall exit/Exit 16 at Shuiguan, Yanqing County, 8118 1888, fax 8118 1866, www.communebythegreatwall.com/en, 2,100RMB double) may go down as the highlight of your trip. On a beautiful leafy site 15 minutes from Badaling, two Chinese property developers commissioned 11 of Asia's hottest architects to design 11 villas that served as a museum of modern Asian architecture in the early 1990s. Now the Commune is in the hands of the Kempinski hotel chain and with its own private section of the wall, the hotel appeals to moneyed expats looking to escape the city while staying in interesting modernist accommodations. Be warned, though, that it is still a commune albeit a very expensive one: The villas have been divided into separate bedrooms so while you have your own sleeping accommodations and bathroom, you will most likely have to share the kitchen, balconies, and living rooms with other people.

Recreation

BEIJING PINE VALLEY

Pine Valley Resort, Nankou Town, 8979 6868, www.pinevalley.com.cn

This high-end 18-hole course near the Badaling section of the Great Wall caters to China's elite. The two courses were designed by Jack Nicklaus and cover 1,000 acres of perfectly manicured green. These, with the huge clubhouse, equestrian center, resort-style hotel, and spa, make Pine Valley the most popular and aesthetically pleasing course in the area. Of course this kind of place doesn't come cheap, but day rates of 1,000RMB are good value given the standard of the facilities.

Getting There and Around

Your options depend on how big your wallet is. The impecunious can catch Bus 919 from Deshengmen bus station (12RMB) or take Tour Bus 1 from Qianmen. A metered taxi will cost about 180RMB, while a private driver in a nice car with seatbelts will be around 400RMB round-trip.

SIMATAI SECTION
(SĪMǍTÁI 司马台)

Simatai, 70 miles out of town, is a good compromise between the crowds but ease of Badaling and the unreconstructed wall and difficulty of Huanghua. Don't be misled by what tough-talking backpackers or tour guides say—this is by no means unconstructed wild wall—it's just that compared to Badaling, it's longer, steeper, and less crowded.

the Simatai section of the Great Wall in the snow

Sights

Simatai (Gubeikou, Miyun County, 6903 1051, www.simatai-greatwall.net, daily 8 A.M.–5 P.M., 40RMB) is staggeringly pretty and made up of two steep initial sections separated by a river with an Indiana Jones–style chain bridge linking them. To visit the eastern section, walk up the steep but well-preserved paths and turrets, passing through 15 watchtowers; there is also the option of a chairlift that takes visitors partway up, cutting out most of the steeper climbs. Coming down, you can either stroll back, though your knees may not thank you, or if you're up for something a little speedier, pay 35RMB and fasten yourself into the flying fox, which sees you speed over a river and down to the entrance area in a matter of seconds.

More hearty folk can choose to make a day of it and head west for the 10km walk all the way to another section of the wall called Jinshanling. If you choose this option, you will have to buy another ticket for the second section of wall—there is no getting around it. While long, the hike is made easier by stopping at the watchtowers, which occur at regular intervals and where you can soak up the view. There will be water sellers and postcard vendors all the way along and you might be grateful to them for lugging water up there when the sun is beating down on a hot day. Most of the sellers are local villagers trying to make an extra buck, and who can begrudge them that? Many hostels in Beijing offer this trek: see Peking Backpackers for more details.

Food and Accommodations

Head to the parking area and you'll find a range of uninspiring fast-food choices. Or go to the hostel. As mentioned before, bring your own food if you're fussy!

Catering to the backpacker crowd, **Simatai Youth Hostel** (Simatai Great Wall Scenic Area, Miyun County, 6903 5311, 260–280RMB private room, 70RMB mixed dorm) has probably one of the best views of any hostel, overlooking the wall as it winds its way up the mountainside. Renovated in 2005, it's not a cozy place, but all rooms open onto a courtyard, and for somewhere cheap to lay your head after a hike, it's a good deal. It also serves (a shade overpriced) food.

Getting There and Around

Simatai is farther away than Badaling but the effort to get there is worth it. The cheapest option is to catch Bus 980 from Dongzhimen to Miyun Zhongdian station, the final stop, and then take a taxi from there. A taxi all the way from Beijing and back will cost about 600RMB. On weekends and holidays, a luxury bus from Qianmen leaves at 8:30 A.M. and returns at 3 P.M. for 85RMB.

MUTIANYU SECTION

(MÙTIÁNYÙ 慕田浴)

Only another 15 minutes or so farther than Badaling from Beijing, Mutianyu has been renovated and thrust into the limelight by the government as it seeks to take the pressure of hundreds and thousands of tourists a year away from Badaling. It is arguably more attractive and thanks to a recent ban on postcard sellers (though not drinks sellers), a little more peaceful.

Sights

The 2.5km stretch that makes up Mutianyu (Mutianyu town, Huairou District, 6162 6505, www.mutianyugreatwall.net, daily 7 A.M.–6:30 P.M., 35RMB) has 22 different watchtowers to explore and aim for—if you manage to see all of them, you've done far better than most people. This section was built during the Ming dynasty and then rebuilt by the current dynasty—there are handrails, slides down the wall, and cable cars galore. But the cable car was good enough for President Clinton when he visited in 1998 and it does enable the less fit and active to have quick access to the wonderful views from the peak of the wall.

Food and Accommodations

A whole cottage industry is developing in Mutianyu with a company run by one American and one Chinese businessman opening several restaurants and bed-and-breakfasts—and about time too as options up until now have been very limited. Their Western restaurant, **The Schoolhouse** (Mutianyu town, Huairou District, 6162 6505, www.theschoolhouseatmutianyu.com, daily 7 A.M.–10:30 P.M., main courses 50RMB), which serves light mainly Italian food using local ingredients is the only venue open—you'll find it just before you get to Mutianyu—but during the course of 2008, several converted village houses were renovated to become rustic bed-and-breakfasts or Chinese restaurants. Go to their website www.mutianyugreatwall.net for more information. The organization is intent on sustainable tourism using local resources and staff as much as possible, so it's worth taking a look at what it offers as it blends its properties into the existing village community.

Getting There and Around

Take Bus 916 from Dongzhimen to the stop Huairou city (Huairou shiqu). From there, use your best bargaining powers to get a taxi for the remaining 17km—you'll have done well if you get a lift for around 35RMB. A taxi all the way from Beijing will cost around 400RMB.

If you're looking to rent a private car for the day to the Great Wall or indeed any other destination, here are some suggestions. Mr. Song speaks good English and charges 400RMB a day for his spotless Volkswagen with—and this is fancy—English magazines and free water. He can be reached at 138 0111 8554. Driver John will take you to Mutianyu for 450RMB—for other destinations, give him a call at 131 4688 9929. Cycle China can arrange a van plus driver for up to 10 people for 700RMB a day to Mutianyu and 950RMB to Simatai. Contact it at 6402 5653 or via the website www.cyclechina.com.

Ming Tombs (Shísānlíng 十三陵)

To the northwest of Beijing 50km are the UNESCO World Heritage–listed Ming Tombs, the final resting place for 13 emperors and the largest imperial burial site in the world. The complex has of late undergone considerable restoration work, which can be on the garish side, and for now only three tombs (*ling* in Mandarin, so *shi san ling* means 13 tombs) are open to the public. The tombs encompass 40 square kilometers, surrounded by an ornate wall. Each tomb sits at the foot of its own hill, linked to the other tombs by a road called the Sacred Way, which is where the imperial coffins made their way to their final destination. After you walk through the imposing stone archway, which dates from the 15th century and marks the start of the procession route, the 7km path is lined with statues of animals and celestial objects and provides a pretty backdrop to the place despite the crowds. The only irritation at the site, aside from its being a mainstay on the tourist circuit with tour groups shuttling in for an hour before gathering everyone up and then depositing them at the Great Wall, is that you have to buy separate entrance tickets for each tomb and the Sacred Way—it adds up.

SIGHTS

The highlight of the Ming Tombs is **Changling** (6076 1334, daily 8:30 A.M.–5 P.M., 45RMB), Emperor Yongle's tomb. He designated that this is where he and his ancestors would lie early in the 15th century. His complex is like a miniature Forbidden City (which he also had built) with its dark crimson palaces and wooden halls, and it is a fitting memorial to an emperor whose achievements included the rebuilding of Beijing, the dispatching of the largest fleet of ships to explore the world ever seen, and the reunification of the Chinese empire. The restored tomb is in great condition, and don't miss the central hall, which has been converted into a small museum of exhumed treasures.

Another mausoleum, **Dingling** (6076 1424, daily 8:30 A.M.–5 P.M., 65RMB) was the final resting place of Emperor Wangli and his two wives, and it was the last tomb to be rediscovered in 1956. The huge marble complex is mostly underground and as you descend to the tomb, look out for his matching set of spirit luggage to help him along his way. The real coffins have been removed as has much of the atmosphere, but the original marble thrones are still there, and Chinese visitors throw wads of notes onto them, hoping to bribe the emperor's ghost.

The final tomb open is **Zhaoling** (6076 1435, daily 8:30 A.M.–5 P.M. , 30RMB), home to Emperor Zhu Zaigou. He was the 12th Ming emperor and was buried in 1572 with three of his empresses after reigning for just six years. The Zhaoling mausoleum was the first tomb to be restored to its original condition, but the real highlight here is wandering around the atmospheric ruins outside the tomb.

RECREATION

BEIJING INTERNATIONAL GOLF COURSE

North side of the Ming Tomb Reservoir, 6076 2288

This highly rated Japanese-designed course offers lovely views of the Ming Tomb Reservoir and the heavily forested Yan Shan and Tianshou Mountains as you make your way around the course that is situated a solid 30 miles from Beijing. There is plenty of water surrounding the par-72, 6,991-yard course and the large greens are surrounded by plenty of out-of-bounds markers that keep it challenging. Membership is 23,000RMB a year but day rates range between 800RMB and 1,400RMB depending on the day of the week.

GETTING THERE AND AROUND

There are tourist buses that leave from the Qianmen bus ranks—Buses 1–5 will take you there for 50RMB and some then go on to Badaling. The journey to the tombs takes about two hours. Alternatively, rent a private car for the day for around 400RMB. The tombs are quite a way from each other, so wear good walking shoes or flag down the tourist buses, which resemble golf carts.

Eastern Qing Tombs (Qīngxīlíng 清西陵)

The Ming Tombs may be better known, but you get more imperial bodies for your buck if you sidestep the crowds and head east to the Qing Tombs. China's last feudal empire buried five emperors, 15 empresses, 136 concubines, three princes, and two princesses here, and the last burial was just over 70 years ago when an imperial concubine died in 1935. The tombs are in a valley at the foot of Changduan Mountain, and their gold-tiled roofs surrounded by pine trees make an attractive picture. Four imperial tombs and two tombs for empresses are open to the public.

SIGHTS

Jingling is the tomb of Emperor Kangxi and is surprisingly modest compared to Cixi's highly decorated tomb, but it is a more beautiful setting. The spirit way leading to the tomb has an elegant five-arch bridge; the guardian figures are placed on an unusual curve quite close to the tomb itself and are more decorated than those at earlier tombs.

Yuling, final home to Emperor Qianlong, was blasted open and plundered by a Chinese warlord in 1928, and though it was an act of utmost desecration, now mere commoners such as we can explore the interior of the vault. The chamber is made from a series of rooms separated by three-ton solid marble doors, with Buddha figures and Tibetan scripture engraved on walls and ceilings.

GETTING THERE AND AROUND

The tombs are 140km east from the capital and the most straightforward way to get there is to hire a driver. If you're watching every cent and want to go by public transport, catch a bus headed for Zunhua from the Sihui long-distance bus station, which is just south of the Sihui underground stop. Get off at Shimen and then catch a taxi for 10RMB to the tombs.

Cuandixia (Cuàndǐxia 爨底下)

This wonderfully unspoiled Ming dynasty village surrounded by jagged mountains is a great weekend trip from Beijing for people looking for the charming China of the past. It's on an ancient trade route, and merchants used to rest there before embarking on their journey to Beijing. When the road became redundant in the 1950s, Cuandixia's fortunes declined, but the lack of development had the unintentional effect of preserving the village's 70 courtyards gathered at the bottom of the hill and moving up the terrain. You can do it in a day trip but it's best to stay overnight in a family home: Rooms are simple but clean. While film crews and tourists are heading here in increasing numbers, it's still more of a trickle than a flood, though during national holiday periods, get here early to secure a bed.

SIGHTS

Village

The village of Cuandixia (Cuandixia village, Zhaitang town, Mentougou District, 6981 9333, daily, 10RMB) is a living museum of traditional Ming architecture with winding alleys leading to different courtyard homes that offer interesting sights if you peep through into their private areas. There's no need to be shy: Villagers are glad you're here! Look out for family wells that are still in use and the huge millstones that villagers use for milling wheat. If you walk in the surrounding hills, the village looks like one large fort with its interlacing roofs and picture-perfect stone wall surrounding the buildings. Their grayness is enlivened by red lanterns and faded Cultural Revolution–era posters—it really is an arresting sight.

FOOD AND ACCOMMODATIONS

Villagers offer food and accommodations (don't worry about looking for a place: They will find you) for the princely sum of around 30RMB per person. For this, you'll sleep on a traditional *kang* bed—toasty warm in winter—and all the fresh home-cooked simple food you can be force-fed—expect some chicken dishes and plenty of fresh stir-fried vegetables. Be warned that the toilets are usually rough and ready and occasionally unnervingly communal. And don't expect to sleep in: The roosters that could be sharing your courtyard might wake you at sunrise, but it's all part of the fun.

GETTING THERE AND AROUND

The village is 64km away from Beijing and you have a few options for getting there. You can take the subway to the western end of line 1 at Pingguoyuan and then take Bus 929 (three hours, 8RMB) to the village entrance, or you can negotiate a taxi from there for about 100RMB. If you want a private car to take you there and back in a day, expect to pay about 400RMB. Or if you stay the night, a private car will again charge about 400RMB to pick you and return you to the city. Several Beijing tour groups run overnight trips to Cuandixia, but it really is easy enough to sort it out yourself. Contact Cycle China at www.cyclechina.com or West China Adventure Tours at inquiry@westchina.net.cn for details.

Tianjin (Tiānjīn 天津)

Beijing's often-overlooked neighbor 140km away with its 10 million people is worth a visit for good food and Foreign Concessions architecture if you are setting up residence in Beijing for a while; if you are here for only a short trip, there are other places more worthy of your time.

Tianjin's coastal location has made it an important city and fortress for more than 1,000 years, and its significance did not go unnoticed by Western powers keen to begin trading with China. Tianjin profited heavily from trading with Great Britain in the 1880s, but the two Opium Wars, which both times left China defeated, saw Britain force the country to open several ports, including Tianjin, to Western interests. Foreign Concessions sprang up and today, the Western and Russian architecture in pockets throughout the city makes Tianjin worth a visit if you have time on your hands. For more detailed information on Tianjin's history or to arrange a very worthwhile tour with an English-speaking guide, go to www.discovertianjin.org, the unusually informative website for the Tianjin Museum of Modern History. Aside from the interesting architectural examples, Tianjin seems like any other fast-developing Chinese city with its central business district full of glitzy skyscrapers and shopping malls, and the huge industrial port has made it one of the country's richest cities.

GETTING THERE AND AROUND

The easiest way to get to Tianjin is to make use of the brand-new elevated train link from Beijing South Railway Station, which opened at the beginning of 2008. The 115km journey takes just 30 minutes with departures every five minutes during rush hour. If you'd prefer to travel by private car, the journey will take about two hours depending on traffic and cost about 300RMB each way.

Beidaihe and Nandaihe (Běidàihé, Nándàihé 北戴河, 南戴河)

Nicknamed by tongue-in-cheek expats the Beijing Riviera, these two towns have been a favorite getaway from the city since the 1890s, when English engineers came across the small fishing town. Expats made use of the hills and built beach houses where they sipped gin and tonics after frolicking in the sea. After Chairman Mao gave it the nod of approval, the resort became the destination for Communist Party members escaping from the pressure of work and even now, the beachfront is dotted with "sanatoriums" dedicated to steelworkers, teachers, and miners. Chinese beach culture is interesting, with the whole family setting up tents to sit in while wearing head-to-toe swimming suits to keep out of the sun, but visitors used to the glitz of Miami or the beauty of South Beach in the Hamptons will probably want to get the next train out of here. If you live in Beijing, it is worth heading here on a sunny day, but be warned, half of Beijing may be doing the same thing. Aside from the kitschy beach atmosphere, the other main interesting feature is the number of Russians on holiday here (signs are in Cyrillic and if you're caucasian everyone will assume you are from there too). One has to wonder what Russian beaches are like if people think it's worth getting on a plane to get here.

© HELENA IVESON

the beach at Beidaihe, two hours from Beijing

GETTING THERE AND AROUND

Beidaihe, overlooking the Bohai Sea, is 253km away from Beijing. Nine double-decker trains leave the capital daily and the journey takes just under three hours. The train station is about 10km out of town, but public buses are frequent or a taxi will cost about 30RMB. A car all the way there from Beijing will cost at least 800RMB.

Chengde (Chéngdé 承德)

While many cities in China have not preserved their pasts, Chengde's imperial past has left the city filled with magnificent examples of imperial architecture that make it well worth the journey from Beijing.

Chengde was just another northern village until Emperor Kangxi came across it during a hunting trip in the final years of the 17th century. Now it is a UNESCO World Heritage Site thanks to the magnificent Mountain Resort, one of the largest intact imperial gardens in China, and the Eight Outer Monasteries that were built to please and appease visiting dignitaries of different religions from across the Chinese empire. The actual town is not at all interesting and seems at least a decade behind Beijing, so stick to the sights.

SIGHTS

Chengde Mountain Resort (Bìshǔ Shānzhuāng 避暑山庄)

Wanting to escape Beijing's humid summers is

nothing new: Even the emperors were keen to get out of town. Kangxi ordered the construction of the Mountain Resort (center of town, Chengde, daily 5:30 A.M.–6:30 P.M., 90RMB) in 1703, and the walled 1,500-acre complex is now largely as it would have been then with its temples, pagodas, and leafy gardens perfect for wandering. The understated and elegant complex was so appealing to the emperor and his court that Mandarins complained (in secret) that the emperor spent too much time there and neglected the matters of court. Instead of conducting business in Beijing, dignitaries used to come to Chengde and stay in palaces that Kangxi had built to awe guests with the extravagance of the empire. The resort can be seen as comprising China's architectural greatest hits of the 17th century, with many of the complex's buildings being replicas of temples and towers built in other parts of the country. But even if you're not fascinated by the minute differences between different types of pagoda, the park is a wonderful place to relax for a few hours in relative seclusion enjoying the resort's lakes, grassy meadows, and wooded areas: You might even see some deer. Although the resort receives a lot of visitors, it does not attract as many foreign tourists as it deserves.

© HELENA IVESON

Chengde's temples make the journey from Beijing worthwhile.

Eight Outer Monasteries

(Wài Bā Miào 外八庙)

Chengde's Eight Outer Monasteries are the second reason to visit the city: Each temple represents the architectural style of a different Chinese minority group, so you can see Buddhist, Mongolian, and Manchu styles all in one place. For a country that does not seem to always respect the culture of its minority groups now, interestingly the construction of the temples seems to reflect a more enlightened time when diversity was encouraged. The Eight Outer Monasteries are grouped in two different areas: on the eastern and northern slopes of the Mountain Resort close to the Wulie River. The eastern temples of Anyuan Si, Pule Si, and Puren can be reached by Bus 10 from the Mountain Resort, and the northern temples of Putuozongcheng Miao, Ximifushou, Puning Si, Puyou, and Shuxiang are on the route of Bus 6 from the same place. Unfortunately, you have to buy separate tickets for all the temples.

The towering **Puning Si** (Puning Si Lu, daily 8:30 A.M.–4:30 P.M., 50RMB) is the most popular of the temples, probably because it is the most exotic to the Han Chinese. The building is an interesting blend of traditional Chinese and Tibetan, and unlike the other temples is still a place of worship: Look out for the monks in their red robes. Despite being so Tibetan, the temple was actually built in 1755 to commemorate a victory over a troublesome Mongolian force. Aside from watching the monks at prayer, don't miss at the rear of the building the awe-inspiring 72-foot-tall statue of Guanyin, a Buddhist deity, the tallest wooden statue in the world, and pay the extra 10RMB to climb up three levels to get a good view of the Buddha's face.

The largest of the temples, the **Putuozongcheng Miao** (Shizhigou Lu, daily 8 A.M.–6 P.M., 40RMB) is also Tibetan in style and modeled on perhaps the most famous Tibetan building of them all, the Potala Palace in Lhasa. It is opulent throughout with brightly colored walls and interiors. The main temple building is three stories high and surrounding it are three floors of mildly interesting Tibetan artifacts. Don't miss the magnificent view from the inner courtyard.

Pule Si (daily 8 A.M.–5:30 P.M., 30RMB), or Temple of Universal Happiness, was built in 1766, and its main building looks very similar to Beijing's Temple of Heaven. Its golden roof is wonderful to behold, and you get a fantastic view of the surrounding countryside and mountains from within. Interestingly, this is a Tantric Buddhist temple and so, as Sting should be forever grateful for, this is where the idea of tantric sex comes from. You can't miss the main shrine where two Buddhas are making love but throughout there are statues of deities engaged in acrobatic sex acts. The temple is also next to **Anyuan Si** temple, which has some beautiful frescoes within its walls. The temple is rarely open, so you have to slip past the security guards and peek inside.

FOOD

Fittingly given Chengde's history as a royal hunting ground, many local restaurants specialize in wild game. Venison, rabbit, and pheasant are available at many restaurants near the Mountain Resort, though few people will speak English outside of hotels. If big chunks of mutton are more to your taste, the Mongolian Yurts Hotel is open to nonresidents.

ACCOMMODATIONS

You haven't come to Chengde for the quality of its accommodations, but these two places are fine for a night. The more adventurous will enjoy the **Mongolian Yurts Hotel** (Mountain Resort, 0314 216 3094, 300RMB yurt) in the grounds of the Mountain Resort. Think of it as upmarket camping as you don't rent a room but a yurt, which is a traditional Mongolian-style circular tent. While yurts on the Mongolian plains are easily movable, these are permanent and filled with modern appliances and have running water and electricity. Meals are again Mongolian style so expect plenty of mutton in the giant dining yurt. The hotel is closed November–March as it is too cold. If you come then, try the more robust **Mountain Resort Hotel** (11 Lizhengmen, 0314 209 1188, www.hemvhotel.com, 500RMB double), which has a great location opposite the main gate of the Mountain resort. The location is the main thing the hotel has going for it, as despite the impressive lobby, rooms are uninspiring though clean enough. Staff here can organize English-speaking guides to take you around the sights.

GETTING THERE AND AROUND

Chengde is 250km from Beijing and the best way to get here is by train. The fastest train leaves Beijing at 7:16 A.M. and arrives at 11:15 A.M. Splash out on a soft seat: The comfortable if frilly cushioned seats are worth the extra 30RMB.

SHANGHAI

Shanghai is full-on and frantic, offering the most modern in fashion and food – at a pace that can sometimes leave even Beijingers in the dust. The city's glamorous art deco architecture and ultramodern skyscrapers dazzle the eyes and the mind: There's a reason this city is often featured in movies set in the future!

At the start of the 20th century, Shanghai was the Republic of China's intellectual, cultural, and economic powerhouse. The brazen Pearl of the Orient was soon the third-largest financial center in the world, ranking after London and New York City, and the largest commercial city in the Far East. But after the Communist takeover in 1949, the good times, the jazz, and the glamour were over – until in 1992 Shanghai's fortunes changed once more and the city again emerged as the country's economic center. Since then, Shanghai has led China's staggering economic evolution.

On the banks of the Huangpu River, the brash skyscrapers of Pudong, some of the tallest buildings in the world, look down on the past, symbolized by the Bund's historic buildings that date from the 1920s. Here is where the future meets its precedents and where tourists stand and gape at how far the city has come.

COURTESY OF HYATT ON THE BUND

SIGHTS

Even the most hard-core fans of Shanghai would say Beijing has the upper hand when it comes to famous attractions that are known the world over. Shanghai is more a city of vicarious pleasures than postcard images: It's a young city that doesn't particularly care to preserve its past. Eating and shopping are what the Shanghainese love to do, not touring dusty old relics of the past—that cuts into fun time! So for visitors, it may sometimes seem as though there's not an awful lot to do, but trust me, there is; it's just that there's no equivalent of the Forbidden City within this city. But must-see Shanghai sights, such as the Bund and the Pudong skyline, will keep photo snappers happy, and museums such as the Shikumen Open House Museum and the renowned Shanghai Museum and people-watching in Xintiandi or at Taikang Lu will keep the most active of tourists occupied for a week.

Unlike in Beijing, with its simple structure of ring roads and straight avenues, in Shanghai it sometimes feels as if the street planners were on a mission to confuse. There is of course a reason for this: When the city had international concessions in the early 20th century with different areas run by the British, French, and, fancy this, the Chinese—none of the different local governments were in a hurry to organize the city. So Shanghai can be confusing even for a local and as you whiz by on one of the many flyovers, or speed through a tunnel, it can be nearly impossible to work out where you are even with a map, and what map can keep up with the pace of change here? On the other hand, sights of interest to tourists are handily

COURTESY OF HYATT ON THE BUND

HIGHLIGHTS

LOOK FOR ☾ TO FIND RECOMMENDED SIGHTS.

☾ **Best Glimpse of Shanghai's Past and Future:** Join the camera-wielding crowds and stroll down **the Bund,** the riverside promenade that was the heart of colonial Shanghai and now faces the glittering future represented by the Pudong skyline (page 158).

☾ **Best Collection of Chinese Art:** Visitors could spend days looking at the priceless treasures on display at **Shanghai Museum,** some of them dating from the 21st century B.C., but the great layout lends itself to quick visits, too (page 163).

☾ **Best City Park: Fuxing Park** was once known as French Park: Now it's open to all and is busy around the clock, with people gathering there for exercise at dawn when all the party-goers who love the clubs in the park are heading home (page 165).

☾ **Best Journey Back into the Past:** The **Shikumen Open House Museum** may be small, but its illuminating re-creation of a traditional house from 1930s Shanghai allows visitors to imagine themselves back in the Jazz Age (page 167).

☾ **Best Place for a Leisurely Stroll:** The galleries, boutiques, and coffee shops dotted along the alleys that make up the **Taikang Lu Arts Center** are a superb place to refuel, relax, and max out the credit card (page 167).

☾ **Best Place for People-Watching:** Everyone comes to the shopping and entertainment destination that is **Xintiandi,** whether it's rich Shanghainese picking up the latest fashions, expats for Sunday brunch, or wide-eyed domestic tourists keen to see one of Shanghai's symbols of success for themselves (page 168).

☾ **Best Place for Reflection:** If Shanghai's rampant thirst for capitalism leaves you gasping for air, the peaceful **Chenxiangge Nunnery** in the Old City is a quiet haven from consumerism (page 168).

☾ **Best Skyscrapers to Savor:** In a land where architecture is hit-and-miss, the **Jinmao Tower** and the latest upstart, the **Shanghai World Financial Center,** are great to look at, and to look from, with their views from above the clouds: Just mind those eardrums during the elevator ride to the top (pages 170 and 172).

© ELYSE SINGLETON

Jinmao Tower

often grouped together, and if you're a walker, Shanghai is the best city in China for pedestrians. A wander around the former French Concession is a fab way to while away a few hours, slipping in some sights between coffee and shopping breaks. People's Square has some of China's best museums, which are a must for museum buffs at any time and good for rainy days for everyone else, and a stroll along the heart of colonial Shanghai, the Bund, stopping off at any one of the historic buildings, is a must in any weather. For more Chinese influence, head south of the Bund to the Old City, where the faux historical architecture at the Yu Gardens bazaar, the interesting gardens, and excellent people-watching opportunities—of locals going about the same way of life as they have for centuries—attract thousands of visitors a day. For viewing opportunities of a different kind, catch the subway to Pudong as the never-ending spread of skyscrapers compete to be the tallest and attract the greatest number of visitors to its observation desks—the newest contender is the Shanghai World Financial Center, the third-highest building in the world.

So you won't spend all your time in museums and ancient temples in Shanghai: Some of the most memorable sights are the newest. The World Expo in 2010 is spurring on Shanghai much in the same way as the Olympics did in Beijing, and the city is getting spruced up and shiny in readiness.

The Bund and East Nanjing Lu — Map 9

(Wàitān, Dōng Nánjīng Lù 外滩和南京路)

THE BUND (WÀITĀN 外滩)

Zhongshan Dongyilu

Visitors from both home and abroad flock to the Bund, and who can blame them? The stately procession of ornate stone buildings, facing across the river the ultramodern skyline in Pudong, is the ultimate symbol of the city. Before the British arrived, the riverfront was just a muddy towpath, but from the 1880s onward, the street was widened, renamed (the word "bund" is an Anglo-Indian word driven from "band," which means embankment in Hindustani), and smartened up. The stately buildings line up one after the other and together make an arresting sight with their diverse architecture and mix of Western and Chinese decoration. From the north end, look out for the Astor House Hotel, which was the Far East's most deluxe hotel before the Peace Hotel opened at number 20. Immediately adjacent you have the Russian Consulate, which is one of the very few buildings still being used for its original function. You can't mistake the Peace Hotel for any other building; it is a couple of doors up from the former home of one of China's most important newspapers, the *North China Daily News*. At number 13, you'll find the old Customs House and then the neoclassical former HSBC bank headquarters at number 12. And when so many people berate the Shanghainese for not preserving more of their city, it's worth remembering that every building on the Bund has survived China's tumultuous 20th century. The walk along the river is a great way to see them all, though you may trip over the other tourists doing exactly the same thing. Anyone who looks foreign is also likely to be asked to pose in a photo with out-of-towners keen to record themselves with an exotic foreigner: The first few times are sweetly flattering, the next 10 times, slightly irritating: Be warned! For the best photos, visit at dusk.

BUND HISTORICAL MUSEUM (WÀITĀN BÓWÙGUǍN 外滩博物馆)

1 Zhongshan Dongyilu, Huangpu Park, 6321 6542

HOURS: Daily 9 A.M.-4 P.M.

COST: Free

Underneath the ugly tower that is the Monument to the People's Heroes is this small museum with a diverting selection of photographs of the Bund through the ages. It won't take you long to look

THE HISTORY IS IN THE ARCHITECTURE

As in many a modern metropolis, Shanghai's history can be seen in its architecture.

Shanghai's equivalent to Beijing's *hutong* is *longtang,* which look like tenements from a town in Northern England. Whole communities lived in grids across the city, and although very few are left now, if you head to the northern end of the Bund, behind the Hyatt on the Bund, you'll see a whole block of these houses, looking exactly the same as they have for 100 years. Another unique feature of Shanghai is its *shikumen,* which translates as "stone-gated houses"; these blended traditional Asian and Western features. For a look at a prettified version, go to the Shikumen Open House Museum in Xintiandi; or to see *shikumen* that are still occupied, go to the lovely Duolun Jie, which is lined by antique shops and rows of charming lane houses.

The Bund in Shanghai is a symbol of the city's turbulent history, representing a time when Foreign Concessions ruled the waterfront and erected imposing structures using imported material with no regard to local conditions or feng shui – which was considered of vital importance when the Bund's buildings were being built between 1906 and 1937.

Perhaps the first sign of China's newfound confidence in Shanghai was the Oriental Pearl Tower, which was completed in 1995 and is as brash as the city it represents. It's also the tallest TV tower in Asia (and third-tallest in the world). The more elegant designs of the Jinmao Tower, completed in 1997, and the Shanghai World Financial Center, completed in July 2008, illustrate a city – or even country – more at ease with itself.

one of the many Colonial buildings along the Bund

at all the photos, and it's definitely worth doing if you're fed up with crowds as there never seems to be anyone here. Well, apart from one person: There is usually a man present who will talk you through the exhibits; he is interesting enough but at the end, he will herd you to an overpriced Chinese calligraphy gallery that can take a while to extricate yourself from.

FORMER HONG KONG AND SHANGHAI BANK BUILDING

(XIĀNGGǍNG SHÀNGHǍI YÍNHÁNG 香港上海银行)

12 Zhongshan Dongyilu

On a row filled with stylish and impressive buildings with stone facades, the former headquarters of the Hong Kong and Shanghai Bank dominates: incidentally, just what the architects were instructed to do. The building was finished in 1923 and its sheer width, imposing dome, bronze lions at the front (these are copies; the originals are in the Shanghai Municipal History Museum in the Oriental Pearl Tower), and inside, the rotunda filled with Italian mosaics, make this building a must-visit. The former tenants are long gone; now a Chinese bank uses the building. Unfortunately you have to be content with photographing the exterior only as security guards will not let you take photos inside.

© HELENA IVESON

the stunning Former Hong Kong and Shanghai Bank Building on the Bund

HUANGPU RIVER (HUÁNGPǓJIĀNG 黄浦江)
Planes may be more convenient and trains a lot cheaper, but neither mode can match the glamour and history of cruising into Shanghai via the Huangpu River, which separates the Bund and the space-age buildings of Pudong. Few passenger liners cruise up the river these days, though that might be about to change with the building of a new passenger ferry terminal: The Shanghai Post International Cruise Terminal (Dong Daming Lu, Hongkou District) officially opened in August 2008, and its bubble-shaped glass building cost more than US$200 million. The owners say it will be one of the most advanced passenger terminals in the world, and it will make Shanghai the first Chinese mainland city with berths for large international cruises. Shanghai is still China's busiest port, so ferries, barges, steamers, and pleasure boats weave up and down the river throughout the day and night. If you wish to join the river traffic, know that most tour boats depart from the Bund side at the south end (see *Sports and Recreation* in the *Arts and Leisure* chapter for more details). If you want to remain a landlubber, watch the procession during the day from either side of the Bund (though the Pudong side is less packed), but at night, the Shangri-La's bar Jade on 36 is the place to be.

NANJING LU (NÁNJĪNG LÙ 南京路)
Nanjing Donglu
This was once considered China's premier shopping destination, but the main reason now for visiting is not for the shops (there's a much better selection elsewhere) but for the unmatched atmosphere as throngs of local tourists mill around wide-eyed at all the neon and glitz. Nanjing Lu's heyday was in the early 1900s: Then the street was the place to go, with ritzy department stores filled with foreign and domestic goodies next door to restaurants, entertainment centers, and cinemas. The party stopped here, though, as it did everywhere after World War II and since then state-run stores have dominated the promenade and still do. The many old buildings are being replaced, but before they go, look out for what was once the largest shopping center in the country, the famed Shanghai No. 1 Department Store at number 800, and the former Wing On Department store at number 635. The Bund end allows traffic and this is where you'll find most of the touts selling fake Rolexes—as you head in from the river, the street becomes pedestrianized. If you run out of energy, an electric train will sedately transport you down the strip.

PEACE HOTEL (HÉPÍNG FÀNDIÀN 和平饭店)
20 Nanjing Donglu, 6321 6888,
www.shanghaipeacehotel.com
The Peace Hotel is receiving a much-needed three-year $65 million facelift that promises to return the shabby old matron to the glamorous starlet of the Shanghai scene she once was. Until the hotel reopens in 2010, when it will be partly owned by the luxury hotel operator Fairmont Hotels, visitors will have to be satisfied looking at its exterior, which still dominates the Bund with its dark green roof contrasting with the more stately buildings beside it. Originally known as the Cathay Hotel, the hotel was finished in 1929; its owner, Sir Victor Sassoon, the

scion of one of the city's most wealthy families, wanted the hotel to serve as "the Claridge's of the East." And indeed it did, with glamorous stars such as Douglas Fairbanks, Charlie Chaplin, and Noel Coward all passing through the art deco doors. The hotel was badly in need of tasteful renovation: Fingers crossed that that is what she receives.

SHANGHAI POST MUSEUM

(SHÀNGHǍI YÓUJÚ BÓWÙGUǍN 上海邮局博物馆)

250 Beisuzhou Lu, near Sichuan Beilu, 6362 9898

HOURS: Wed., Thurs., Sat., Sun. 9 A.M.-4 P.M.

COST: 10RMB

This little-known recently opened museum, set inside the impressive Shanghai District Post Office building, which dates from 1931, rewards the intrepid visitor. It may sound boring—and admittedly the displays of old stamps won't appeal to everyone—but if you're interested in architecture, this is a great place to spend an hour. The surprisingly sympathetic renovations, including the hugely impressive atrium, are superb, and the building also has an actual post office on the second floor in case you want to send some postcards home. And don't forget to go up to the roof garden, where you will find wonderful views over Shanghai's skyline, though of course this being China, you're not allowed on the grass!

SHANGHAI SIGHTSEEING TUNNEL

(WÀITĀN RÉNHÁNG GUĀNGUĀNG SUÌDÀO 外滩人行观光隧道)

Between Pudong and the Bund

HOURS: Daily 8 A.M.-10 P.M.

COST: 35RMB single, 45RMB return

Frankly, it's debatable whether this, perhaps the most surreal experience available in Shanghai, should be recommended. Some people, perhaps the ones who had a great time in the 1960s, may love the trippy psychedelic journey under the river where luminous fish come out of the walls. Kids also seem to like it, but some adults will just hate it, but in some ways, it is a fitting journey to the weird and wonderful architecture in Pudong—suddenly the Oriental Pearl Tower seems restrained. The packed entrances on either side of the tunnel, with slot machines and noisy arcade games, are prime pickpocket venues, so do keep a close eye on your things.

THREE ON THE BUND

(WÀITĀN SĀNHÀO 外滩三号)

3 Zhongshan Dongyilu, www.threeonthebund.com

While the Bund used to be a wasteland when it came to eating and drinking, this new development, complete with a swanky array of designer stores and expensive spa, is a tourist attraction in its own right. All the restaurants are worth a look with their completely different exteriors (the staff won't mind; they're used to it) and use of the dramatic space with glorious views over the river. The gorgeous building, which dates from 1916, has been totally renovated inside by American architect Michael Graves but the art deco touches are still much in evidence. Three used to be a social club for the British, but nowadays anyone can get in—if you can pay for it, of course.... (See the *Food* and *Shopping* chapters for more details.)

People's Square and Museum Row Map 10

(Rénmín Guǎngchǎng, Shànghǎi Bówùguǎn 人民广场, 上海博物馆)

PARK HOTEL (GUÓJÌ FÀNDIÀN 国际饭店)

170 Nanjing Xilu, 6327 5225, www.parkhotel.com.cn

In terms of art deco architecture, the Park Hotel is the area's premier sight thanks to its brooding presence in the skyline, which it dominates despite the array of futuristic skyscrapers nearby. The hotel opened to the public in 1934 and has remained a hotel to this day. (See the *Accommodations* chapter for more details.)

PEOPLE'S PARK (RÉNMÍN GŌNGYUÁN 人民公园)

231 Nanjing Xilu, 6372 0626

HOURS: Daily 6 A.M.–6 P.M.

COST: 2RMB

The whole area surrounding People's Park, a large open space hemmed in by art deco buildings and futuristic skyscrapers, brings tourists to its attractions and crowds of locals to shop in the packed underground mall and meet friends and fly kites in the evenings outside the museum near the center. The park started off life as a center of the colonialist social scene: the Shanghai racecourse. The course was built in 1862 and expats would gather every year in spring and fall for a day at the races until the Japanese occupation in 1941. After this time the area had a more sinister purpose: During the Japanese occupation, it was used to hold prisoners of war, and later during the Cultural Revolution in the 1960s, Mao's Red Guards took over the square and forced their enemies to take part in self-criticism sessions, which often turned violent. Now, though, it's difficult to imagine violence in the square as there are plenty of green leafy areas on either side of the mammoth Renmin Dadao that runs through the middle. On the weekends, look out on the northern side of the park for the crowds of concerned parents who gather trying to set up their too-busy offspring

Shanghai Museum in People's Square

with romantic dates. The signs and flyers you'll see them carrying list their children's characteristics, such as age, job, and salary—all too important in capitalism-crazy Shanghai. While the area doesn't have the beauty or tranquility of, say, Central Park or even Ritan Park in Beijing, it's a fun place to watch the Shanghainese at what counts for resting here.

SHANGHAI ART MUSEUM

(SHÀNGHǍI MĚISHÙ ZHǍNLǍN 上海美术展览馆)

325 Nanjing Xilu, 6327 2829, www.sh-artmuseum.org.cn

HOURS: Daily 9 A.M.–5 P.M.

COST: 20RMB

The art museum, in the northeastern corner of People's Park, used to serve as the racing course clubhouse and dates from the 1930s. There are still a few relics from its glamorous past: Look out for the iron horse heads along the balustrade. The art is very traditional with romantic landscapes and patriotic paintings everywhere, but one hopes the renovations lead to a freshening up of the displays. There is also Kathleen's 5, a well-regarded though pricy restaurant on the top floor, but if you're looking for something more casual, café and Middle Eastern restaurant Barbarossa is 200 meters away.

SHANGHAI MUSEUM

(SHÀNGHǍI BÓWÙGUǍN 上海博物馆)

201 Renmin Dadao, 6372 3500, www.shanghaimuseum.net

HOURS: Daily 9 A.M.–5 P.M. or Sat. to 7 P.M.

COST: 20RMB

You can't miss the city's most popular museum when you're in the area or whizzing past in a taxi on the nearby overpass, as the building itself is an architectural gem, built to resemble a *ding,* an ancient bronze cooking vessel. Inaugurated in 1996, the $50 million museum is a must-visit for people interested in Chinese art. Inside its floors are jam-packed with more than 120,000 exhibits, including Chinese bronzes, ceramics, coins, and calligraphy, but although the English signs are professional and meaningful, unless you have an expert eye you may not get much out of the calligraphy. Much more accessible thanks to their bright colors and interesting designs is the exhibition of minority handicrafts. The audio tour is a relatively pricey 60RMB but well worth it for the insight into the exhibits. If you're keen to see the inside of the Shanghai Theater and the art museum, which are all in the vicinity, buy the 50RMB combined ticket.

© HELENA IVESON

the Shanghai Museum of Contemporary Art (MOCA) in People's Park

SHANGHAI MUSEUM OF CONTEMPORARY ART (MOCA)

(SHÀNGHǍI DĀNGDÀI YÌSHÙ GUǍN 上海当代艺术馆)

Inside People's Park, 231 Nanjing Xilu, 6327 1257, www.mocashanghai.org

HOURS: Daily 9 A.M.–5 P.M.

COST: 20RMB

This museum, set in People's Park, is one of Shanghai's newest museums, built in 2005; the cutting-edge design of the building, which is primarily made from glass and in fact used to be the park's greenhouse, and its interesting exhibits make this a nice counterpoint to the more staid main art museum nearby. Recent exhibitions include the works of Gaudi and a fun exhibition on sport as art sponsored by Adidas. As the contemporary art scene is still relatively small—even with all the headlines about Chinese art—the number of exhibits is still quite small. I recommend having a quick whiz around, stop at the excellent museum shop for postcards and posters, and then have a cup of coffee in the attractive in-house café or head out to the excellent Barbarossa restaurant, which overlooks the park's main pond.

URBAN PLANNING CENTER

(CHÉNGSHÌ GUĪHUÀ ZHŌNGXĪN 城市规划中心)
100 Renmin Dadao, 6372 2077
HOURS: Daily 9 A.M.–5 P.M.
COST: 30RMB

It may sound as dull as ditch water, but this huge multistory building in the eastern corner of the square is definitely worth visiting for a look back into Shanghai's past and a glance into its future. The best floors are the second and fourth: The second has an excellent display of photos of Shanghai from throughout the last century, including pictures of the Bund when it was just a muddy riverbank. On the fourth floor, the huge to-scale model of how the whole city will look in 2020 is jaw dropping and is a great way to get a sense of how huge the city is as it edges toward its high rise–filled future. The exhibitions dedicated to the 2010 World Expo are not as interesting to foreign visitors and are mostly only in Chinese, but if you do go in, look out for the pictures of happy-looking residents being forced out of their homes to make way for the Expo buildings: The protests at the time suggested not everyone was happy to go....

Jing'an and West Nanjing Lu

Map 11

(Jìng'ān, Nánjīng Xī Lù 静安, 南京西路)

JING'AN TEMPLE (JÌNGĀN SÌ 静安寺)

1686 Nanjing Xilu, 6256 6366
HOURS: Daily 7:30 A.M.–5 P.M.
COST: 5RMB

Its Chinese name may mean peace and tranquility, but these things are difficult to find at the city's oldest shrine (older than Shanghai itself!), which is popular with tourists and locals alike. You wouldn't think it from the freshly painted exterior, but the temple dates from A.D. 247: It housed China's first Buddhist organization in 1912 and then, more ignominiously, was converted into a plastics factory during the Cultural Revolution. It wasn't until 1983 that the building reverted to its religious function, but the garish decoration and crowds mean it's difficult to get any sense of peace. The 3.8-meter jade Buddha at the center of the Jade Buddha Hall is interesting, though. One of the most interesting aspects of the temple is the number of fortune-tellers who line the street by the entrance: Unfortunately, they seem to be Chinese speakers only, but surely

SIGHTS

Jing'an Temple, Shanghai's oldest shrine

by the time you read this, some entrepreneurial type will have cottoned on that there is money to be made from telling the fortunes of tourists.

OHEL RACHEL SYNAGOGUE

(YÓUTÀI JIÀOSHÌ 犹太教室)

500 Shanxi Beilu

In its heyday, the Jewish community in Shanghai had seven synagogues; now there are just two and neither is open to the public. This, the most impressive with its imposing pillars and huge stone wall, was built in 1920 to accommodate the community of Baghdadi Jews by a member of the hugely wealthy Sassoon family, Jacob Sassoon, in memory of his wife Rachel. When the Jews left in 1949, the synagogue was used as a Communist center and a stable. It wasn't until 1999, when then–U.S. Secretary of State Madeleine Albright visited the city and asked to see the synagogue, that the city began to take an interest again. The current Jewish community opened a small museum called the Shanghai Jewish Refugees Museum in 2007 that houses art, furniture and pictures from the 1920s and 1930s.

Former French Concession Map 12

(Fǎguó Huāyuán 法国花园)

FORMER RESIDENCE OF SUN YATSEN

(SŪN ZHŌNGSHĀN GÙJŪ 孙中山 故居)

7 Xiangshan Lu, 6437 2954

HOURS: Daily 9 A.M.–4:30 P.M.

COST: 8RMB

Near Fuxing Park's southwest end is the former residence of the man considered the father of modern China, Sun Yat-sen. What is most striking about the house set along an ordinary row of European-style houses on what was known as Rue Molière is its simplicity and austereness considering the number of historic moments that occurred here when Sun founded the Kuomintang Party. The house was paid for by donations from overseas Chinese and the inside has remained basically the same from the 1930s, with the furniture looking particularly small to modern eyes and an interesting array of photos and memorabilia, including Sun's swords and a pair of his glasses. Even if you're not remotely interested in the man himself, the house is worth a peek as it is well preserved and the garden is lovely to stroll in. For more historic houses, the first premier of China Zhou Enlai's former residence is 200 meters down the road.

FUXING PARK

(FÙXĪNG GŌNGYUÁN 复兴公园)

2 Gaolan Lu, 6372 6083

HOURS: Daily 6 A.M.–6 P.M.

Along with People's Park, this is one of Shanghai's most popular central open-air spaces to people-watch, exercise, or, if you're an elderly local, meet with your friends for a lively game of mah-jongg. The area was originally a private estate before being bought for the use of foreign residents; it was popularly known as French Park because of the number of French who used it and its similarity to Parisian parks with its rose garden and rows of tall trees throughout. Nowadays, though, the actual green areas are small. It all changes from peaceful daytime activity when the sun goes down, as the elderly go home to bed, and the young hipsters of the city come out to play at one of the many restaurants and clubs dotted around the park. One wonders what the founder of Communism, Karl Marx, who has a statue in the park dedicated to him, would make of it all. The park is now free to enter.

SHANGHAI ARTS AND CRAFTS MUSEUM
(SHÀNGHǍI GŌNGYÌ MĚISHÙ BÓWÙGUǍN 上海工艺美术博物馆)
9 Fenyang Lu, 6431 4074
HOURS: Daily 9 A.M.-4 P.M.
COST: 8RMB

If you've had enough of the area's cafés and restaurants and need some cultural stimulation, head to this institute, which houses an interesting group of Chinese artisans. Visitors can watch the artists at work in different studios, whether it's calligraphy, weaving, kite making, or carving. While this would be of real interest only to people with an appreciation for arts and crafts (and at times you have to wonder if the artisans are here only to herd you into overpriced gift shops), it's doubtful you would see Chinese political needlepoint portraiture to hang in your

PRESERVING THE PAST: *SHIKUMEN*

A striking feature of Shanghainese architecture, *shikumen* are tenement houses dating from the 1900s that were built by Western landlords for Chinese tenants in the city's Foreign Concessions. In the 1860s, to escape from the upheavals of the Taiping Rebellion, a large number of refugees flooded into Shanghai from the nearby provinces. Many of these refugees headed to Foreign Concessions, which were relatively safer compared to other parts of the city. Targeting this influx of middle and lower middle class Chinese migrants, Western landlords started building *shikumen* houses in the Foreign Concessions. Like *hutong* in Beijing, *shikumen* are a symbol of the city's past that are increasingly under threat from the nonstop tide of development.

Shikumen, which means a "stone gate house," blend European elements, such as slate-gray bricks and French windows, with Chinese features, such as courtyards and stone gates. Each *shikumen* had a large stone gate to keep out intruders and prying eyes. If you gained entrance, behind the gate you would find a courtyard, and farther inside was a living room. Then there was the back courtyard reserved for family use, a kitchen, and back door. To the sides of the courtyard and the living room were the right- and left-wing rooms and on the second floor would be the family's bedrooms. *Shikumen* houses were terraced and built on narrow lanes with their gates facing the main lane. At the end of the lane, there usually was a bigger gate that separated the neighborhood from others. A large block would have hundreds of households, and the closed structure of the neighborhoods with multiple layers of gates and walls was popular among migrants longing for security and safety in chaotic colonial Shanghai.

In 1949, when the Communists took over, there were about 9,000 *shikumen* neighborhoods, which covered 64 percent of the city. As money dried up in Shanghai and the government turned on symbols of its foreign-controlled "feudal" past, most *shikumen* houses deteriorated quickly through lack of repair and overcrowding. The population in Shanghai grew and grew, and the *shikumen* houses, which were originally designed for single-family use, were divided and subdivided. People had to share common kitchens and bathrooms, and overcrowding was rife. By the early 1990s, a large proportion of *shikumen* houses built in the early 20th century had become densely packed slums with poor sanitary conditions.

During Shanghai's frenzied urban development in the 1990s, many old neighborhoods and historical sites were bulldozed to make space for modern buildings. Shanghai's most famous *shikumen* conversion is the Xintiandi complex. While some love the area, some hate it, but many recognize that this may be the only way that *shikumen* are kept for a new generation. Before the redevelopment, the area was a spread of dilapidated *shikumen* houses – many were cleared while others were converted into shops and restaurants. For a glimpse of what living in a *shikumen* was like for a middle-class Chinese family, do go to the Shikumen Museum in Xintiandi, a meticulous reenactment of a long-lost way of life.

© HELENA IVESON
a mansion in the Former French Concession

dining room anywhere else, but here it is. The actual villa, which dates from 1905, is a real French renaissance treasure and was designed by prolific architect Ladislaus Hudec. Its lovely garden, curving staircase, and white stuccoed walls once housed Shanghai's first Communist mayor.

SHIKUMEN OPEN HOUSE MUSEUM (SHÍKÙMÉN BÓWÙGUǍN 石库门博物馆)

25, Lane 181, Taicang Lu, North Block, Xintiandi, 3307 0337

HOURS: Daily 10 A.M.–10 P.M.

COST: 20RMB

For some culture amid all the cafés, this much-overlooked museum is one of the best in the city—and you're likely to be the only person there as everyone else in Xintiandi is too busy shopping or eating. The museum is wonderfully atmospheric and is not a museum in a traditional sense as there are few historical explanations. Instead it's more like a private home from the past where you're free to wander around and peer into the kitchen cupboards and perch on the tiny antique furniture and look at the gramophone records. The top floor is more educational with information on the history of *shikumen* and the restoration of Xintiandi, as well as a pictorial "day in the life" of a wealthy Shanghainese family in the 1930s. It's all absorbing.

TAIKANG LU ARTS CENTER (TÀIKĀNG LÙ YÌSHÙ ZHŌNGXĪN 太康路艺术中心)

Taikang Lu

Shanghai's art and shopping fans head to this narrow collection of lanes that combine to be a treasure trove filled with tiny clothing boutiques, cafés, art galleries, restaurants, and bars. Like Xintiandi, Taikang Lu offers shops that are decidedly upscale but unlike Xintiandi, among all the trendiness local residents are still living in the delightfully crumbling lane houses. The Taikang Lu area first developed as an inexpensive warehouse district for up-and-coming artists, but now in addition to art there's something for everyone, whether it's a fab cappuccino or a one-off cashmere sweater. Check out the antipodal café Bohemia for a delicious piece of chocolate cake to spur you on your stroll.

XINTIANDI (XĪNTIĀNDÌ 新天地)

Corner of Taicang Lu and Madang Lu, 6311 2288, www.xintiandi.com

When the old neighborhood of *shikumen* lane houses dating from the 1920s was turned into the upmarket shopping, restaurant, and entertainment complex Xintiandi, many feared the worst. But nowadays most critics have changed their opinions, recognizing that the complex has breathed new life into the area instead of ruining it. The architect has summed up why it's so popular: The Chinese love it because they think it's Western, and Westerners love it because they think it's Chinese. The place is packed day and night, whether it's expats eating eggs Benedict every weekend at Kabb or Chinese teenage sweethearts heading to the cinema, while well-off locals peruse the chi-chi boutiques. This is a symbol of the new Shanghai, a fusion of old and new, East and West. For my money, Xintiandi is a great one-stop shopping and eating destination that is definitely one of Shanghai's highlights and even if you're not in the mood for spending in the boutiques, it's great for people-watching.

Old City

Map 13

(Lǎo Chéng 老城)

CHENXIANGGE NUNNERY (CHÉNXIANGGÉ 沉香阁)

29 Chenxiangge Lu, 6320 4000

HOURS: Daily 7 A.M.-4 P.M.

COST: 5RMB

This quiet Buddhist temple feels worlds away from the madness of Yu Yuan despite being just a minute's walk away. Shaven-headed nuns in their slate-gray robes have been here since the temple was built more than 400 years ago, and as the birds perch in the ornamental trees in the well-kept courtyards and incense wafts in the air, it feels as if life here hasn't changed all that much. Near the entrance, the Hall of Heavenly Kings contains a myriad of Buddhas inside its yellow walls, but it's the next colorful hall, where the nuns regularly kneel and chant in front of a huge statue of Buddha surrounded by nine arhat, that is the most charming. Don't forget to go upstairs to see the golden statue of Guanyin, the Goddess of Mercy.

CONFUCIUS TEMPLE (KǑNGMIÀO 孔庙)

215 Wenmiao Lu

HOURS: Daily 9 A.M.-5 P.M.

COST: 10RMB

Among all the tourist frenzy in the Old City are some quiet havens, including the Chenxiangge nunnery and this temple dedicated to Confucius. Shanghai has had a temple dedicated to one of the country's most revered philosophers for more than 700 years, but this current example has been around only since 1855 and was most recently restored in 1999 to celebrate his 2,550th birthday. Unfortunately much of the temple's contents are reproductions thanks to the ravages of the Red Guards during the Cultural Revolution, but one original feature near the entrance is a three-story, 66-foot pagoda dedicated to the god of liberal arts. Look out for a statue of Confucius flanked by two disciples and his two favorite musical instruments, a drum and set of bells, and for people, especially students, continuing the old custom of writing wishes on slips of paper and tying them to boards or trees using red ribbon. What the old sage would have made of all the chaos of the area, who knows?

DANFENG LU (DĀNFÈNG LÙ 丹凤路)

Danfeng Lu

It's easy to think that all the Old City has to offer is Yu Yuan and somewhat tacky souvenir shops, but if you walk a few minutes away from the center, you'll find the real old city on streets such as this one. Here, as you walk under the washing that's hanging out to dry from nearly all of the lane houses and see housewives washing their vegetables for the next family meal in the outside sinks, you get the sense that despite the glitz of Shanghai, this is actually how many, if not most, people still live. You may get a few friendly stares and people will assume you are lost as you wander down the alley, but it's refreshing to see no souvenir shops but a few local butchers selling their wares.

SHANGHAI OLD STREET (SHÀNGHǍI JIǓJIĒ 上海久街)

Central Fangbang Lu

Adjacent to the madness at Yu Garden Bazaar is the slightly—and I mean slightly—quieter shopping street known to the Chinese by its proper name of Fangbang Lu despite the government's attempts to have it officially known as Old Street. The area is meant to be a re-creation of shops from the late Qing dynasty, but this can be difficult to see under all the souvenir claptrap. Some of the houses are actually more than 100 years old and they are easy enough to spot. Once you have bought all the carved name chops and propaganda posters you can carry, do leave the main tourist drag and find some of the unprettified parts for a look at the real Shanghai, where snack stalls line the alleys and residents hang all their washing on the street. For more shopping continue to Fuyou Antiques market for some hard bargaining.

© HELENA IVESON

Yu Gardens in the Old City

YU GARDENS (YÙYUÁN 豫园)

218 Anren Jie, 6373 7522

HOURS: Daily 8:30 A.M.-5:30 P.M.

COST: 40RMB

Oh, the humanity! As it's almost always packed wall-to-wall with tourists, the charm of the historic garden and the attached bazaar is now sadly difficult to see—a pity given that many think the gardens are comparable to the classic gardens of Suzhou. The site was founded in 1559 by wealthy Ming dynasty officials and it was not until 1577 that the gardens were completed—18 years later. They have been twice ransacked—once by the British and once by the French as a reprisal during the Taiping Uprising. It was not until 1952 that they were fully restored, a process that took five years, and they are now a prime example of Ming garden design. Natural is not a quality that the Ming admired when it came to gardens; instead of plants and trees, corridors, rock gardens, stone bridges, and pavilions took priority.

YU GARDENS BAZAAR

Once all the crowds have poured out of the Yu Gardens, they swamp this Disneyfied Chinatown within China: Unlike Xintiandi, this is one reconstruction job lacking in taste. In addition to souvenir shops, not one but two Starbucks, and more tourists and peddlers than you can imagine, there's also the famous two-story Huxinting Tea House, which has served a cup or two to Bill Clinton and the queen of England among millions of others—whether they footed the bill for the overpriced tea on offer here is unknown. People also flock to the Bridge of Nine Turnings, whose twists and turns are meant to ward off evil spirits, which are said to travel only in straight lines. When you leave the area, it's a good idea to walk away for a few hundred meters before catching a taxi as price gouging is common here.

Pudong

Map 14

(Pǔdōng 浦东)

CHINA SEX CULTURE MUSEUM

(ZHŌNGHUÁ XÌNG WÉNHUÀ JIÀNKĀNG JIÀOYÙZHǍN 中华性文化健教育展)

Bund Sightseeing Tunnel, 2789 Riverside Ave., 5888 6000

HOURS: Daily 8 A.M.-10:30 P.M.

COST: 20RMB

Part of the Bund sightseeing tunnel complex, this small but interesting enough exhibition is not reason enough to go to Pudong, but while you're here, head in for an insight into sexual behavior throughout China's long history, including sections on the repression of women, with the shoes women used to hobble about in with bound feet. Exhibits vary from the blunt-looking knife used to castrate eunuchs, copulating figures made from clay that date from the 7th century, and some odds and ends that may give you nightmares. The English captions aren't perfect but more than enough to give you the idea. Don't bother with the aquatic exhibition next door with its sad collection of lonely (alive) turtles and stuffed fish.

© ELYSE SINGLETON

the pagoda-like Jinmao Tower in Pudong

JINMAO TOWER

(JĪNMÀO DÀSHÀ 金贸大厦)

88 Shiji Dadao, 5047 5101

HOURS: Daily 8:30 A.M.-10 P.M.

COST: 50RMB

Some may prefer the Oriental Pearl Tower as the more fitting symbol of Shanghai, but for my money, the Jinmao is the more attractive and exciting building with its pagoda-shaped exterior that goes up and up and up. . . . In addition to being hugely attractive, the building also has great feng shui: The tower has 88 floors because 8 is a lucky number to the Chinese. If you are lucky too and your wallet is bulging, you can enjoy the views from your bedroom at the Grand Hyatt, which is the highest hotel in the world, but mere mortals can pay 50RMB and head to the observation floor on the 88th floor, which is accessible through a different entrance than the hotel. The more impecunious can sneak into the hotel and admire the view for free but you may be intercepted by hotel staff. Of course the Jinmao has been knocked off its perch as China's tallest building by the latest upstart, the Shanghai World Financial Center, which is literally a few feet away.

ORIENTAL PEARL TOWER

(DŌNGFĀNG MÍNGZHŪ GUǍNGBŌ DIÀNSHÌ TǍ 东方明珠广播电视塔)

1 Shiji Dadao, 5879 1888

HOURS: Daily 8 A.M.-9:30 P.M.

COST: 70RMB-180RMB

Everything about this Shanghainese icon is extreme, from its lengthy Chinese name to its eye-catching (and utterly garish) centerpiece, a bright pink pearl that serves as the

Whatever you may think of the Oriental Pearl Tower, it certainly stands out.

main viewing platform overlooking the Bund (through the smog). While many visitors dislike it, it's worth bearing in mind that it was finished in 1994, when China was desperate to catch up with the rest of the world, and it is a symbol of that extraordinary time. The main pearl is 1,535 feet (468 meters) high, and there are two other minipearl observation decks if the crowds are too big on the main one. The pricing is very complicated with costs dependent on how high you go, whether you want a meal, and (it seems) whether the ticket sellers are having a good day or not. The tower's nearby neighbor, the Jinmao Tower, has a less complicated pricing structure and is a bit taller, but the Pearl Tower has the added attraction of the Shanghai Municipal History Museum in the lowest pearl.

RIVERSIDE PROMENADE

(BĪNJIĀNG DÀDÀO 濒江大道)

Binjiang Dadao

HOURS: Daily 6:30 A.M.-11 P.M.

One of the best reasons to travel to Pudong if you're not staying there is to look back at where you have come from, thanks to the classic views of the gray and sober Bund across the river. This new 2.5-km walkway is much quieter than the chaos on the other side—few tourists seem to venture over—and there is plenty of attractive greenery lining the route with barges and pleasure boats patroling the river from dawn to dusk. There's a good selection of coffee shops and bars (Starbucks and Paulaner Brauhaus to name a couple). As if you could miss it, the looming Pearl Tower is directly behind you.

SHANGHAI MUNICIPAL HISTORY MUSEUM

(SHÀNGHǍI CHÉNGSHÌ LÌSHǏ FĀZHǍN CHÉNLIÈGUǍN 上海城市历史发展陈列馆)

Gate 4, Oriental Pearl Tower, 1 Shiji Dadao, 5879 3003

HOURS: Daily 8 A.M.-9:30 P.M.

COST: 35RMB

Compared to most of the dusty museums in China, this well-organized and interesting museum is definitely worth a visit for a thorough lesson on Shanghai's past, even if you don't have any desire to go up the Pearl Tower. The museum is very well done and great for both adults and any kids in tow as the many realistic models of Shanghai's historical streets give the visitor an eye into what life was like before private cars and skyscrapers ruled Shanghai. Don't miss the diorama of the Bund with a day-to-night lighting feature that includes honking streetcar sounds.

SHANGHAI SCIENCE AND TECHNOLOGY MUSEUM

(SHÀNGHǍI KĒXUÉ GUǍN 上海 科学馆)

2000 Shiji Dadao near Dingxiang Lu, 6862 2000, www.sstm.org.cn

HOURS: Tues.-Sun. 9 A.M.-5 P.M.

COST: 60RMB

This futuristic museum, about 20 minutes' drive from the river, is a great place to take children in a city not exactly brimming with suitable activities. It opened in 2001 and it's very interactive and educational. Attractions include an indoor rainforest with more than 300 types of plants, sound and light shows, and a space navigation center that is always packed with Chinese kids who want to be taikonauts (Mandarin for astronauts), thanks to the country's recent explorations into outer space. If you want to see something at the huge Imax 3D cinema—and if the human body show is on, go; it's excellent—tickets cost an extra 40RMB. Bear in mind that the museum gets packed on weekends and lines of fractious children (and parents) build up. If your children still have some excess energy, take them to the nearby Century Park, or if you're in the market for fakes, head to A. P. Xinyang Fashion and Gifts Market, inside the museum metro stop.

SHANGHAI WORLD FINANCIAL CENTER

(SHÀNGHǍI HUÁNQIÚ JĪNRÓNG ZHŌNGXĪN 上海环球金融中心)

Block Z4-1, Lujiazui Finance and Trade Zone Center, Pudong

HOURS and COST:

See http://www.swfc-observatory.com/

The skyscraper, which usurps the nearby 421-meter Jinmao Tower as the tallest on the Chinese mainland, was to be finished and put into commercial use in late 2008 with, fittingly, the highest rent in the city. Equally as attractive as the Jinmao Tower, the project has had a difficult history starting back in 1997, when the whole idea was put into deep-freeze because of the Asian economic crisis. The building is owned by the Japanese Mori Group, and Chinese newspapers, always touchy about any perceived slight from the Japanese, went on a rampage over the building's original design, in which the top had a circular hole through the middle that to their eyes resembled the rising sun of the Japanese flag. Now, everyone is happy with the trapezoid-shaped hole. There is to be an observation deck on the 100th floor, 472 meters up, which will be world's highest public observation platform. The center's 70 floors of office space is designed to accommodate 12,000 people, with a hotel (the Park Hyatt Shanghai, which opened in 2008), restaurants, conference centers, and—of course—shopping malls.

Greater Shanghai

Map 15

DUOLUN LU (DUŌLÚN LÙ 多伦路)

Duolun Lu, north of Suzhou Creek

Duolun Lu, a 10-minute taxi ride north from the Bund, is in Hongkou District and is an old street boasting some of the city's best examples of old Shanghai-style buildings as well as European villas and mansions. While some buildings have been renovated and jazzed up, many are gently crumbling and are still people's homes. It was once home to some of China's most famous intellectuals, including Lu Xun, Guo Moruo, Mao Dun, and Ye Shentao. It's a great place to shop for handicrafts and antiques, the best of which is Guo Chun Xiang's Curiosity Shop. The street is shaped like a horseshoe and both ends are marked by a large stone gate. On your stroll, look out for Hongde Tang Church, which was built in 1928 and is Shanghai's only Christian church that has Chinese temple-style features. Old Film Coffee, in a lovely two-story town house, makes a great coffee stop, but if you're hungry, come out of the coffee shop and turn right, and you'll find a great street full of cheap Shanghai eats. Art fans also flock to Duolun Lu for the refreshingly challenging exhibitions at China's first state museum for modern art, the Doland Museum of Modern Art (27 Duolun Lu, 6587 2530, www.duolunart.com, Tues.–Sun. 10 A.M.–6 P.M., 10RMB). You can't miss the gallery as the gray modernist building with no windows stands out a mile away.

JADE BUDDHA TEMPLE (YÙFÓSÌ 玉佛寺)

170 Anyuan Lu, 6266 3668

HOURS: Daily 8:30 A.M.-4:30 P.M.

COST: 20RMB (plus 10RMB to see the Jade Buddha)

Shanghai's most famous Buddhist temple is a mere baby, dating from only the beginning of the last century, but despite that it attracts people keen to see the 70 or so monks chanting (be warned that they don't like having their photos taken) and its famous flock of birds fluttering around the trees. It's truly lovely inside with its mustard-colored walls and red ribbons fluttering on the many bonsai trees, and if you time your visit well, you'll witness the monks in their yellow robes chanting in unison—most days there's a service between 1 and 2 P.M. The temple's two gorgeous white jade Buddhas are interesting: The three-ton seated Buddha and a smaller reclining Buddha representing his peaceful death (and ignominiously displayed in the souvenir shop!) were shipped to Shanghai from Burma. Nowadays there is a third Buddha (rumor has it that temple officials thought a bigger Buddha would attract more tourists) that was donated by Singapore, but don't confuse this newer statue for the original. If you get hungry, the temple's vegetarian restaurant attracts hordes of visitors. The only problem with this temple is its mercenary bent: You're not allowed to bring in incense—you have to buy it here—and if you want to photograph the koi carp in the garden at the back, you have to buy fish food! For something completely different, Moganshan Art District is a 15-minute walk away.

LONGHUA TEMPLE (LÓNGHUÀ SÌ 龙华寺)

2853 Longhua Lu, 6457 6327

HOURS: Daily 7 A.M.-5 P.M.

COST: 10RMB

If you're prepared to fight the traffic south, a visit to the city's premier Buddhist temple is worthwhile for the change in pace from Shanghai's frenetic streets. This is the most active Buddhist center and worshippers flock here from all over the city bringing incense. The seven-story wooden pagoda was built more than 1,000 years ago though unfortunately visitors aren't allowed in it. Instead you can search out the many statues dotted around the saffron-colored complex, including a particularly jovial Milefo, or laughing Buddha. If you get hungry, the temple's vegetarian restaurant is excellent though on the surprisingly expensive side.

50 MOGANSHAN LU ART CENTER

(MÒGÀNSHĀN LÙ 莫干山路)

50 Moganshan Lu

For art lovers, a wander through the unofficial arts district at 50 Moganshan Road, popularly known as M50, will be the highlight of their visit to Shanghai. In fact anyone interested in contemporary Chinese culture should visit the galleries that have opened in the dingy factories along Suzhou Creek. The area was transformed in the late 1990s into a collection of minimalist white galleries and studios. It's a compact version of Beijing's 798 Art District, and just like there, there is a big turnover in galleries (for more on the galleries, see the *Arts and Leisure* chapter), but ShangART, the Art Scene Warehouse, and Eastlink are very popular. You'll also find the Timezone art book shop, the awesome Art Deco antique shop, and Madam Mao's Dowry has its warehouse in Eastlink Gallery. There are a few interesting coffee shops: Try the excellent café lattes at the cozy Traveler Coffee Tea Café. M50 is a five-minute taxi ride from Shanghai Train station, and the Jade Buddha Temple is a 15-minute walk away.

PROPAGANDA POSTER ART CENTER

(SHÀNGHǍI XUĀNCHUÁN HUÀ YÌSHÙ ZHŌNGXĪN 上海宣传画艺术中心)

Room BOC, Basement, Block B, 868 Huashan Lu, 6211 1845, www.shanghaipropandaart.com

HOURS: Daily 9 A.M.-4:30 P.M.

COST: 20RMB

For one of Shanghai's more quirky museums, head to the basement of a nondescript apartment block where Yang Peiming has established his own miniature museum, charting three turbulent decades in Chinese history (1949–1979) through colorful propaganda art. The few hundred posters exhibited are a mere fraction of the 5,000 in Yang's personal collection, but they provide insights into misguided political initiatives such as the Great Leap Forward of the late 1950s (which resulted in the most terrible famine in history) and the chaotic Cultural Revolution. You can buy the posters, which cost upward of 800RMB.

RESTAURANTS

The Chinese version of "How are you?" can be translated into English and means "Have you eaten yet?" This gives you an idea of the importance of food to the Chinese—and to the Shanghainese in particular. Thanks to Shanghai's international outlook, the city has the country's best Western restaurants outside of Hong Kong and in greater numbers than in Beijing, but you'll still be able to find a cheap noodle shop in every street: The Shanghainese love to eat and snack shops abound. And because of the numbers of *waidiren,* or Chinese originally hailing from other locations in the country, flocking to Shanghai, China's regional flavors can also be found easily.

Shanghai has more than its fair share of high-faluting dining destinations, most of which are clustered around the Bund and the French Concession. Dining options used to be poor around the Bund area, but now there are glamorous destinations that almost outshine the spectacular views of Pudong. Expensive, yes, but worth it as a special treat? Definitely.

The French Concession's café culture is still much in existence, and many restaurants make the most of their lovely locations by having terraces along the shady tree-lined avenues that make up the area.

In an attempt to clear the streets of the city's much-loved food vendors and impose higher hygiene standards, the government has designated several areas as food streets or snack streets. These are great places to try a range of options and some of the city's best snacks, such as the nearly sacred *xiaolongbao* dumplings and their fried version, *shengjian,* can be found here as can

HIGHLIGHTS

LOOK FOR ☾ TO FIND RECOMMENDED RESTAURANTS.

☾ **Best Reinventions:** Chef Jerome Leung updates and reinvents Shanghainese staples at the **Whampoa Club,** making dishes delicate while still retaining local flavors (page 177).

☾ **Best Traditional Snack: Jia Jia Tang Bao** closed down for a while, devastating fans of its soup dumplings, but it's now reopened and lines for the delicious parcels of pleasure are just as long as before (page 180).

☾ **Most Unlikely Gourmet Destination: Chun** has rules to follow (single diners aren't welcome, for example) and there's no menu, but if you're after top-quality Shanghainese, beat a path to one of its four tables (page 185).

☾ **Best Resting Place:** If you're shopped out at Taikang Lu, rest your weary soul at cute and cozy **Bohemia Café and Bar** and order some of its excellent coffee and cake (page 188).

☾ **Best Place to Sate a Sweet Tooth:** Shanghai used to be a disaster zone for dessert, but **Whisk Choco Café** is ground zero for diners looking for a sugary snack: The cheery chocolate cupcakes are a marvel to behold (page 188).

☾ **Best Inventions:** A meal at **Jade on 36** will leave you speechless: The chef's unconventional cuisine and artistry nearly outshine the spectacular view over the Bund (page 191).

☾ **Best Sense of Style:** A mixed crowd of locals and expats beats a path to the art deco door of **1221,** where its lovely food and superb atmosphere make it a standout (page 192).

© HELENA IVESON

steamers of *xiaolongbao* dumplings

a whole host of kebabs, roasted sweet potatoes, and more noodle dishes than can be mentioned. The Wujiang Food Street north of People's Park is excellent fun for those brave enough to eat food they may not be able to identify, and the Huanghe Food Street near Nanjing Xilu is great for gourmets staying near Jing'an.

The Old City is home to some of China's most famous snack restaurants, but many think they are too busy and too touristy; if you're prepared to wander off the main drag, there are plenty of interesting alleyways with streetside restaurants serving wonton soup to the masses: While hygiene standards can't be guaranteed, the steaming bowls of broth are sure to be tasty. It makes sense to go to stalls that are busy, which ensures a quick turnover of food, and don't eat anything that is not boiling hot.

Strict vegetarians can find it tough going in Shanghai and China in general; as many veggie visitors will tell you, a Shanghai restaurant's idea of meat-free isn't always the same as theirs. Sometimes "vegetarian" dishes will come with small pieces of meat, or cooked in meat stock, even if you have specified otherwise. To avoid this, either go to strict vegetarian restaurants or tell the wait staff that you are Buddhist (wǒshì fójiàotú 我是佛教徒)—that normally does the trick.

Eating is an all-day affair for the Shanghainese, and as many locals don't have adequate cooking facilities, food can be found from first thing in the morning to cater to hungry hordes on their way to work. The prime lunchtime is earlier than in the West, from 11:30 to around 12:30—this is when you'll see most lines for street stalls or restaurant tables. In the evening, peak hours are again slightly earlier, and it's a good idea to make reservations at the more expensive venues and at the small venues, such as Chun, that have only a few tables. To eat at the cheap local restaurants, ask your hotel to help you reserve or try yourself using the phrase book in this book. At these restaurants and at midrange Chinese eateries, the dining experience has its own quirks. When you arrive, there's usually nowhere to put your coat, so the wait staff will cover it with a plastic covering to protect it from spills. Usually only one menu will be given as the most important person takes responsibility for ordering. Don't expect romantic lighting: The lights are turned up high, the music will be loud, and dining is a casual affair—expect people to talk loudly, use their cell phones, and once the meal is over, there's usually a bolt for the door as people don't hang around and linger. In China, you go to a restaurant because of the food, not for the decor. Enjoy the experience and if it's not for you, plenty of more expensive Chinese restaurants with more of a Western ambience are opening. On the plus side, eating out is generally much more inexpensive than in the West. You can fill your stomach with a steamer-full of dumplings for around 4RMB, but even the most expensive Western dining destinations are still cheaper than eating out in a top restaurant in London or New York would be. Oh, and best of all, tipping is unnecessary.

So after experiencing everything from blowout expense-account dining to streetside snacks, many travelers go home licking their lips thinking wistfully of their meals in Shanghai. Do explore the city and be adventurous: You'll never look at Chinese food in the same way again.

PRICE KEY

$ Entrées less than US$10 (75RMB)

$$ Entrées between US$10-20 (75-150 RMB)

$$$ Entrées more than US$20 (150RMB)

$$$$ Entrées more than US$40 (300RMB)

The Bund and East Nanjing Lu — Map 9

TRADITIONAL SHANGHAI STYLE

WHAMPOA CLUB $$$$

5th Floor, Three on the Bund, 6321 3737, www.threeonthebund.com

HOURS: Daily 11:30 A.M.-2:30 P.M. and 5:30-10 P.M.

As soon as the elevator deposits you on the fifth floor of this swanky dining complex, you'll experience a palpable sense of theater as you walk to your table down the long corridor, lined with bronze and gold art deco metal wall hangings, before passing a dazzling floor-to-ceiling pyramid chandelier. So how can the food compete with that plus the view over to Pudong? Well, the Whampoa gives it a good try thanks to its gleaming-white main dining room and the well-trained staff dramatically revealing your food and taking the time to explain what you're eating—and sometimes you will need help deciphering. Jerome Leung's food is at its best when it's a new rendition of traditional Shanghainese food, so the *shenjian* dumplings are excellent with their fried bottoms contrasting nicely with the more doughy

DIFFERENT CENTURY, SAME ADVICE

Carl Crow was an enterprising American businessman who sought to make his fortune in the bright lights of Shanghai. The Missourian arrived in 1911 as the Qing dynasty was disintegrating, and he was soon hired as the editor of the only English-language newspaper in the city, the *North China Daily News*. He took quickly to life in China and established himself as a leading figure of the social scene during the city's heyday. His book, *Handbook for China* (Kelly and Wash, Shanghai, 1933), was reprinted five times and considered the standard reference for visitors to the city. His advice on food still stands now:

> The foreigner in China will miss few of the luxuries of food to which he is accustomed to at home and will find many new delicacies he cannot procure in any other country. Nearly every variety of vegetable known to Europe or America is cultivated in China and in addition there are many native foods which it is a delight to know. . . .
>
> One bit of advice which the traveler will hear over and over again is that he should not eat any food which has not been thoroughly cooked and should especially avoid green salads. . . .
>
> Even the old resident is careful about the water he drinks and will have none which he is not certain has been both filtered and boiled. As the traveler cannot always be certain that this has been done, he will be wise to drink none but bottled waters, of which he will find a variety on sale everywhere.

top layer. The wok-fried pork chop with sour plum sauce is also terrific, but don't bother to save space for dessert. Small parties or couples can reserve the individual tea rooms, which are beautifully decorated and romantically lit.

REGIONAL CHINESE

SHUI YUAN $$

3/F, 1 Yan'an Donglu, near Zhongshan Dong Er Lu, 6330 8098, www.shuiyuan-restaurant.com

HOURS: Daily 11:30 A.M.-2:30 P.M., 6-10 P.M.

This low-lit and sophisticated eatery is one of the few Chinese restaurants on the Bund and interestingly, it is managed by a former peasant from rural Anhui province. Shui Yuan serves traditional cuisine from different provinces but with a much-welcomed healthy twist: All dishes are free of monosodium glutamate, nongreasy, and organic. Restaurants that market themselves as healthy in China tend to be on the bland side, but a taste of the Chengdu-style sliced pork with garlic stops diners in their tracks with its spiciness, but palates are soon calmed by the organic Chinese tea that accompanies meals.

INTERNATIONAL

FINESTRE $$

11F, 15 Zhongshan Dongerlu near Jin Ling Donglu, 6373 4818, www.attica-shanghai.com

HOURS: Daily 5:30-10:30 P.M.

This Mediterranean restaurant is the sister venue to one of Shanghai's best clubs, Attica, and attracts an equally well-dressed crowd that is ready to party. It's definitely not a venue to be considered merely a pit stop, with its location overlooking the bright lights of Pudong and its excellent and well-priced cuisine that makes you want to linger. Reserve one of the intimate booths in the hall or the terrace in summer rather than sitting in the main room as the boom of the bass from the club can be irritating when you're tucking into your traditional antipasti and perfectly cooked steak *frite*.

JEAN GEORGES $$$$

4th Floor, Three on the Bund, 6321 7733, www.threeonthebund.com

HOURS: Daily 11:30 A.M.-2:30 P.M. and 6-10:30 P.M.

Along with Jade on 36, this is the most expensive

venue in Shanghai, and the French food is taken very, very seriously. Jean-Georges Vongerichten is considered something of a legend and this is his only venue outside his original restaurant in New York, where he still spends most of his time. The tone is set when the *qipao*-wearing waitresses part the seductive, long purple drapes as they lead you to the opulent and stylish spacious main dining room, which has plenty of dark wood—try to get one of the slinky banquettes. Seafood and fish dominate the à la carte menu, where the ingredients are listed with no flowery embellishments, and the sea scallops with *raison* and caper compote with caramelized cauliflower are awesome. There is also a tasting menu for an eye-watering 800RMB per person. Even if you're not dining, the sleek and sexy bar is perfect for a cocktail.

LARIS $$$$

6th Floor, Three on the Bund, 6321 9922, www.threeonthebund.com

HOURS: Daily 11:30 A.M.-2:30 P.M. and 6-10:30 P.M.

Instead of the dark and moody interior that so many Shanghai restaurants go for, the antipodean-owned Laris is decorated everywhere you look with bright white and gray marble, which can feel a little on the cold side. However, unlike in many restaurants named after the owner-chef, the warm and exuberant Australian chef David Laris is usually in residence and will often come around to check that you're happy. If you order the lamb loin with pistachio and palm sugar crush with pickled eggplant and bamboo shoot salad, you certainly will be, as long as you can afford a blowout meal. The restaurant is also famous for its excellent martinis, which you can also enjoy in the stylish cigar divan and oyster bar. For a special occasion, locals head here for the degustation menu, for which you have to make reservations, but simpler set menus for lunch and dinner are also available.

M ON THE BUND $$

7/F, 5 Zhongshan Dongyilu (at Guangdong Lu), 6350 9988, www.m-restaurantgroup.com

HOURS: Daily 11:30 A.M.-2:30 P.M. and 6-10:30 P.M.

M, as it is fondly known, is a pioneer in Shanghai's fine-dining scene, opening in 1999 when few ventured down to the Bund for a good meal. While it doesn't have the same glam factor as newer arrivals, M's reputation for good if tame modern European food (the crispy suckling pig with Suzhou peaches baked with slivered almonds is excellent), attractive sleek venue, and lovely terrace attracts a mixed crowd of wealthy Chinese, expats, and tourists. Though the menu is limited, there are always specials on offer, and the wine list is fantastic and also changes seasonally. Prices are on the high side so opt for brunch, when a cocktail, starter, and entrée run to 188RMB. If you're dressed up, the 1930s-style Glamour Bar is a great place for a post- or predinner cocktail.

NEW HEIGHTS $$

7th Floor, Three on the Bund, 6321 0909, www.threeonthebund.com

HOURS: Daily 11:30 A.M.-2:30 P.M. and 6-10:30 P.M.

Despite being the most casual option in the ritzy Three on the Bund complex, this fusion eatery has the top floor, the best views, and the only outdoor terrace. If that weren't reason enough to visit, the light and airy room in relaxing colors plus the professional service make this a lovely place to linger. The mellow ambience and sleek decor create an atmosphere that will weaken even the snobbiest of diners. The irreverent menu features "Things That Walk" (steaks and burgers) and "Things That Swim," and the 98RMB buffet available at lunch is a steal. If you have room, order one of the best chocolate cakes in Shanghai, and the pear and red wine tart is both sophisticated and mouthwateringly good.

SUN WITH AQUA $$$

2F, 6 on the Bund, Zhongshan Dongyilu, near Guangdong Lu, 6339 2779

HOURS: Daily 11:30 A.M.-2:30 P.M., 6-11 P.M.

The best Japanese restaurant on the Bund, Sun has an interior of slate, wood, glass, and tatami that's just as restrained and stylish as the food: Just don't fall into the little pool by the entrance. As with all the best sushi restaurants, you can sit on stools and watch the chefs make

© HELENA IVESON

living the high life at Vue in the Hyatt on the Bund

your meal in the semi-open glass kitchen, but for a romantic meal, reserve one of the few tables in the small enclave. Depending on how much you want to remember the evening, try the Sake Tasting Box; and it seems as if almost everyone among the upmarket clientele orders the excellent salt-grilled cod fish. If you don't mind watching fish after eating it, head to the Aquarium Bar afterward with its gigantic wall-to-wall fish tank filled with sharks.

VUE $$

32/F, Hyatt on the Bund, 199 Huangpu Lu, 6393 1234, www.shanghai.bund.hyatt.com

HOURS: Daily 11:30 A.M.-2:30 P.M. and 5:30-10:30 P.M.

Shanghai's newest Bund-based fine-dining venue on the 32nd floor of the Hyatt on the Bund has the stunning views you'd expect, but inside is more surprising, with its casual-chic well-lit ambience a backdrop to its mainly classic French cuisine. The white tuxedo–wearing butlers contrast with the more casual environment, which is decorated like a celebrity chef's kitchen with upmarket colanders and recipe books decorating the walls, but its unique selling point is its show kitchens, where meals such as a classic Caesar salad and lobster bisque are finished off by a chef in front of your table: You get a cooking class as part of your meal. Leave room for the excellent desserts, including the chocolatiest chocolate ice cream imaginable, and for a completely different vibe, go up a floor to the funky bar complete with hot tub on the terrace.

People's Square and Museum Row Map 10

TRADITIONAL SHANGHAI STYLE

JIA JIA TANG BAO

90 Huanghe Lu by Fengyang Lu, 6327 6878

HOURS: Daily 6:30 A.M.-5 P.M.

You certainly don't come to this small eatery on Huanghe Food Street for the ambience (there is none) or a variety of menu options (everyone has the same)—what you come here for is one of the top contenders for Shanghai's best *xiaolongbao* dumplings, here called *tang bao,* or pork soup dumplings. What you do is pay the lady 7RMB, wait for a seat at the Formica communal tables, and eventually receive a steaming steamer-full of delicious dumplings. As always, eat these cautiously, as the boiling soup inside can scald easily. Do like locals do: Hold one on a spoon and gingerly nibble off the top to let the steam out before greedily gobbling it down.

TAI SHENG YUAN $$

50 Huanghe Lu near Fengyang Lu, 6375 0022

HOURS: Daily 11:30 A.M.-4:30 A.M.

For home-style Shanghainese cooked the way your Shanghainese grandmother would if you had one, head to this two-story noisy venue on the corner of Huanghe Food Street. On the

STREET EATS

In Shanghai, fierce opinions abound about where you find the best street food. For my money – and judging by the lines, a whole lot of other people think so too – **Jia Jia Tang Bao** is the place to head for freshly steamed basketfuls of *xiaolong-bao*, or steamed pork dumplings, which come with a scorching mouthful of broth inside the wrappers. And for 7RMB a meal, you won't be breaking the bank. Even cheaper and perhaps more delicious are the same dumplings, fried rather than steamed: *shengjian*. Mrs. Yang at **Yang's Fry Dumplings** will charge you a whopping 4RMB for a portion of crispy dumplings dotted with scallions and sesame seeds – you can either take them away or take them upstairs to one of the rickety tables and chairs.

bilingual menu are traditional favorites such as Shanghainese dim sum, sweet and sour ribs, and *hongshao rou,* or soy sauce–stewed pork that is, after *xiaolongbao,* Shanghai's favorite dish. The staff is friendly and patient, but be warned that all fish dishes are at the market price, so confirm how much items will cost before ordering them.

REGIONAL CHINESE

AI MEI $$

Le Royal Meridien Hotel, 789 Nanjing Donglu near Jiujiang Lu, 3318 9999, ext. 7700

HOURS: Daily 10 A.M.-2:30 P.M. and 5:30-10 P.M.

On the eighth floor of Le Royal Meridien Hotel, guests must first walk through a fish-tank archway to find this stylish dim sum eatery, which, in addition to serving hotel guests, is very popular with Hong Kong expats, so expect what the Chinese love in big restaurants: piped music and a bit of glitz. The stylish waitresses clad in purple *qipao* lead you past the huge glittering chandelier to the elegant dining room. A huge range of traditional dim sum is served during the day, and the shrimp dumplings are a must. On the weekends, it's 25 percent off, so you need to make reservations then. Do try the Hong Kong barbecue dishes on the à la carte menu, and take advantage of the reasonable prices as despite its being in a five-star hotel, there is no service charge.

CAFÉS AND CHEAP EATS

ELEMENT FRESH $

Unit 2, 2nd Floor, Headquarters Building, 168 Xizang Zhonglu, 6361 6556, www.elementfresh.com

HOURS: Daily 8 A.M.-9 P.M.

This friendly local casual eatery was a lifesaver to many an expat when it first opened, serving good Western staples such as healthy salads, sandwiches, and pasta. Since then and in the face of plenty of new competition, it has expanded the menu to include smoothies, excellent breakfasts, especially the big American and Chinese set meals, and a dinner menu. Thanks to the glass floor-to-ceiling windows, the cafés are bright and airy and always packed with office workers at lunchtime: Try to avoid this time or be prepared to wait. It has eight locations, including a large branch in the Shanghai Center: Check the website for details.

SLICE $

1/F Shanghai Times Square, 99 Huaihai Zhonglu, 6386 8588

HOURS: Daily 10 A.M.-10 P.M.

David Laris, Shanghai's very own celebrity chef known for his eponymously named restaurant on the Bund, has opened this well-priced upmarket deli in the huge shopping center Times Square, so if you can't afford Laris, head here for innovative snacks and items to take away. The green walls and retro-style high chairs look great, but it's not the place to lounge for hours as the chairs are hard. Pasta dishes such as fresh egg tagliatelle and sandwiches with names that will either amuse or irritate you ("Beef Me Up, Big Johnny," anyone?), but the organic coffee and delicious coconut cupcakes will revive the most weary of shoppers.

WAGAS $

Hongyi Plaza, G116, 288 Jiujiang Lu, near Nanjing Donglu, 3366 5026, www.wagas.com.cn

HOURS: Daily 6:30 A.M.-11 P.M.

One of eight branches spread across both sides

© HELENA IVESON

freshly baked naan bread from a Xinjiang seller

of the river, this popular homegrown chain was opened by a couple of expats fed up with not being able to find decent healthy Western food. The crowds that congregate daily at all their bright and airy cafés show they're doing something right, though anyone from the West may wonder what the fuss is about. Still, the wraps and salads are especially good and the chain prides itself on its coffee, served by friendly baristas, but some complain that the pasta dishes are usually overcooked. Be prepared to wait at lunchtime for a table as the place gets packed and if you go after 6 P.M., lots of items are reduced in price. Another popular branch is in the CITC center on Nanjing Xilu. If you wish to start a conversation with a Shanghainese café-goer, ask which is better: Wagas or Element Fresh.

XINJIANG TAKEAWAY $

Corner of Guangdong Lu and Zhejiang Zhonglu

HOURS: Daily 24 hours

This area used to be full of Muslim restaurants run by Uighurs from Xinjiang in the far west of China. You'll be able to spot them right away as they look Central Asian rather than Chinese. Nowadays the area has been encroached upon by skyscrapers and other developments, but this corner joint is clinging on, dishing out beautifully decorated naan bread baked in its kiln. Most people buy one of these for a couple of RMB and then a huge amount of *yangrouchuan,* which are the tasty if greasy cumin-flavored lamb kebabs beloved by millions, if not billions, of Chinese.

INTERNATIONAL

BARBAROSSA $$

People's Park, 231 Nanjing Xilu, 6318 0220, www.barbarossa.com.cn

HOURS: Daily 11 A.M.–11 P.M.

In the summer, there are few nicer spots than sitting outside this Middle Eastern–themed restaurant and bar overlooking a lily pond, with small lanterns on the tables, terra-cotta walls, and red net curtains inside. It's a popular casual brunch venue on the weekends and in the evening serves dishes such as spicy lamb salad with harissa dressing. The staff could do with cheering up, though. There are special offers on different drinks or *shisha* pipes every night of the week.

TAJ BEIRUT $

649 Hankou Lu near Zhejiang Zhonglu, 6352 2590

HOURS: Daily 11 A.M.-11 P.M.

Despite this Lebanese restaurant's over-the-top decor, garish lime-green vinyl booths, minarets everywhere you look, and strip mall location just off the People's Square, the food is as home-style as you can get. The Syrian chef produces filling Middle Eastern classics that can't be beat, and nothing on the menu is more than 40RMB. Standard dishes such as creamy hummus and chunky eggplant dips are well done, while the stewed meatballs eaten with bowlfuls of rice topped with pine nuts and fried onion is comfort food at its finest. No alcohol is served, but nearly everyone puffs away on a *shisha* after a meal, including the friendly Lebanese manager.

Jing'an and West Nanjing Lu

Map 11

TRADITIONAL SHANGHAI STYLE

SHANGHAI SCENERY GARDEN RESTAURANT $

466 Changde Lu, by Xinzha Lu, 6289 9999

HOURS: Daily noon-11 P.M.

For delicious *jiaozi* dumplings, China's equivalent of ravioli and staple food for millions, head to this typical Shanghainese eatery with ultrabright lighting and more waitresses than customers. The perennially busy restaurant a 10-minute walk from Jing'an Temple has a wonderful selection of *jiaozi,* so this is a great place in winter. The most popular *jiaozi* are the pork and scallion variety, but vegetarians aren't overlooked with plenty of egg-based and tofu options.

YANG'S FRY DUMPLINGS $

54 Wujiang Lu and 60 Wujiang Lu

HOURS: Daily 6 A.M.-midnight

Mrs. Yang still gets up at 4 A.M. every morning to make her fried soup dumplings herself even though this place is now something of an

fried *shengjian* dumplings speckled with sesame seeds at Yang's Fry

institution. She has two tiny branches, which constantly have people lining up outside, on Wujiang Food Street, which is packed full of snack shops and great for a stroll. For a princely sum of 4RMB, you'll receive four fried crunchy brown *shengjianbao* pork dumplings covered by sesame seeds and scallions: If you're feeling hungry, get a double portion. Be careful, as there is an art to eating these molten-hot goodies: Bite a small hole in the top and slurp out the soup before tackling the pork filling or you'll need to head straight to a dry cleaners to get rid of the soup stains. There are rickety communal tables inside and upstairs, but don't expect anything more fancy than a chair and table.

REGIONAL CHINESE

CHARMANT $

Wanhangdou Lu/Yuyuan Lu, 6378 1298

HOURS: Daily 11 A.M.–1 A.M.

Just north of Jing'an Temple is this constantly bustling and unpretentious Taiwanese restaurant that serves healthy light fare in a simply decorated environment. Taiwanese expats love it for its simple comfort food such as stir-fried vegetables with a tangy Taiwanese dressing and its wonderfully refreshing ice desserts. It's not a vegetarian restaurant, but refreshingly for non-meat eaters, plenty of the menu is vegetarian friendly. It also does good afternoon tea sets when you can try the interesting-tasting bubble milk teas that have small sweets at the bottom.

CAFÉS AND CHEAP EATS

GOURMET CAFÉ $

455 Shanxi Beilu, near Beijing Xilu, 5213 6885, www.gourmet-cafe.com

HOURS: Daily noon–11 P.M.

Some say this newcomer dishes out the best burgers in town, and thanks to its tasty fish-and-chips, this cozy café with free wireless attracts more than its fair share of British expats. With a selection of more than 25 gourmet burger creations, such as the Stand and D'Liver with pan-fried foie gras, and The Bun Laden(!), a vegetarian Middle Eastern–style burger, this

a taste of the exotic at Bali Laguna in Jing'an Park

great venue with very efficient Filipino staff will fill any meat and carb cravings, and it also does a good-value lunch deal that includes one of its healthy and crazily named smoothies.

INTERNATIONAL

BALI LAGUNA $$

1649 Nanjing Xilu, inside Jing'an Park, 6248 6970, www.balilaguna.com

HOURS: Daily 11 A.M.-2:30 P.M., 5:30-10 P.M.

This beautiful Indonesian restaurant may not be the most authentic this side of Jakarta, but its many fans forgive it because of its gracious service with a smile from sarong-wearing staff and its idyllic location overlooking the lily pond in Jing'an Park. As guests enter, they step over a trickling stream with flowers floating in the water, and the rest of the experience is just as relaxing. In summer, reserve a table outside along the water's edge.

ROOMTWENTYEIGHT $$

Urbn Hotel, 183 Jiaozhou Lu, 5172 1300

HOURS: Daily 7 A.M.-10 P.M.

Urbn Hotel's bar and lounge is visually as equally striking as the rest of the whole hotel thanks to its recycled tiles on the walls and marbled walls, and it is run by the hugely popular Wagas group (see the *People's Square and Museum Row* section), though the modern European fare is a step up in price and more complicated than the simple offerings from the café. After free breads and dips, the open kitchen serves dishes such as goat's cheese terrine to start followed by a crispy snapper fillet with grilled asparagus, but if it's on the changing menu, the pine nut and pumpkin risotto is perfect. It's a great place for a romantic but casual dinner and the view over the bamboo-lined garden is lovely, especially if you come for brunch on a sunny day.

Former French Concession — Map 12

TRADITIONAL SHANGHAI STYLE

CHUN $

124 Jinxian Lu, 6256 0301

HOURS: 11 A.M.-9:30 P.M.

From the outside, this restaurant looks as plain as anything, and inside is probably worse, but if you reserve one of the four tables at this home-style Shanghainese restaurant, you will be wowed by the food. Here the chef specializes in *nong you chi jiang*–style (thick oily sweet sauce) food, which tastes much better than it sounds and is basically smartened-up home cooking. The owner-waitress is very old-school and no-nonsense: If you turn up by yourself, she simply won't serve you—you'll have to find some friends. Oh, and there's no menu: You will get whatever she judges suitable and she doesn't speak a word of English. This hasn't stopped world-renowned chefs from making a beeline to her door, though.

CHUSE RENJIA $

212 Wulumuqi Zhonglu near Anfu Lu, 6437 4753

HOURS: Daily noon-2 P.M., 6-11 P.M.

This outstanding and bargain-priced restaurant, like its loyal patrons, is Shanghainese through and through. It's bright, energetic, the staircase is neon, and someone in the room has inevitably had too much *baijiu,* the potent Chinese spirit that is something of an acquired taste. The menu is half in English and poorly translated on an epic scale, but the accommodating staff will never lead you astray. They will probably recommend dishes such as "Mouthful of Spicy Beef" and "Sweet and Sour Mandarin Fish" (Tangsu Loyu), which unlike most Chinese fish dishes is deboned.

LAN TING

107 Songshan Lu, near Xingan Lu, 5306 9650

HOURS: Daily 11 A.M.-10 P.M.

Another home-style restaurant similar to Chun is this tiny place near Xintiandi. It's easy to ignore while you're walking down the street—and but for the small, constant crowd of people waiting outside for space at one of the six tables within, you'd be likely to miss it—there's no English sign. The clientele are not here for the decor (which isn't here anyway) or the service. They're here for its reputation for excellent Shanghainese food; for the outstanding *ji gu jiang,* a sticky, sweet plate of rich chicken in an appropriately thick soy-based sauce, or the *you bao xia,* long-armed river shrimp quickly fried to crisp the shells and render them edible and then tossed in soy and sesame. They're on every tiny table, eyed hungrily by every customer waiting for a table.

1931 $

112 Maoming Nanlu, near Nanchang Lu, 6472 5264

HOURS: Daily 2 P.M.-1 A.M.

If you're pining after Concession-era Shanghai and nostalgia, look no further, though make sure you arrive after 2 P.M. as for some reason it doesn't open its art deco doors until then. The romantic and traditional art deco ambience at 1931 draws in expats and the occasional local crowd with tunes coming from the old-fashioned phonograph, posters, and antique furniture to transport you back in time while you dine, though the food, while fine, does not live up to the surroundings.

REGIONAL CHINESE

CRYSTAL JADE $$

2/F House 6-7, South Block, Xintiandi, Lane 123, Xingye Lu, 6385 8752

HOURS: Daily 11:30 A.M.-3 P.M., 5-10:30 P.M.

This stylish Cantonese eatery is a prime candidate for the best dim sum in Shanghai. In addition to traditional Hong Kong–style miniature treats such as egg tarts, shrimp dumplings, and *shao mai* (traditional dumpling with pork and shrimp), it also caters to growing crowds of young local professionals and families looking

SHANGHAI'S BEST BRUNCHES

The thing to do for plenty of Shanghai residents is to head for brunch on the weekend. In this go-getting city, weekdays are given over to a quick takeaway on the way to work, but it's a different story on Saturday and Sunday when the pace turns leisurely.

Dim sum is hugely popular: **Crystal Jade** in Xintiandi is full of Chinese families dining on steamers filled with Cantonese dumplings such as *har gow* and clattering plates of *cheung fan* and egg tarts. There is also a page of Shanghai-style dim sum such as *xiaolongbao, shengjian,* and *mantou* to get your mouth watering. Another option is The JC Mandarin's Chinese restaurant **Mandarin Pavilion** (3/F, Shanghai JC Mandarin, 1225 Nanjing Xi Lu near Xikang Lu, 6279 1888, ext. 5301, www.shanghaijcmandarin.com), which does a bargain dim sum brunch where 30 different types of small treats are available for 88RMB.

For a more American option, **KABB** is always busy with regulars who love their eggs Benedict and good old American greasy grub, but for a more sophisticated brunch try **Mesa** (748 Julu Lu, near Fuming Lu, Former French Concession, 6289 9108, www.mesa-manifesto.com). This popular restaurant has gained the reputation for the best brunch in Shanghai and offers home-style favorites all weekend, either in the restaurant or al fresco on the outdoor terrace – champagne scrambled eggs, asparagus, tomato and smoked salmon with grilled brioche, anyone? It's good for kids too as there is a special play area. Chuppies (Chinese yuppies) and expats on expense accounts flock to the city's five-star hotels for their all-inclusive champagne brunches. The most popular at the moment is the extravaganza at the **Westin** (88 Henan Zhong Lu, 6335 1888, www.westin.com/shanghai) – an endless array of mouthwatering choices of food from across the world; everything from Japanese sushi to English roasts to Cantonese dim sum is on offer, and live music plays in the background. The place is always packed despite its hefty 418RMB price tag.

for Shanghainese dim sum. The dining room is stylish and despite the crowds, it doesn't get too noisy as there is plenty of room between the tables. While the staff are efficient and service is very quick, a smile would be nice. Despite this, the crowds keep coming for the well-priced excellent food so make reservations.

DIN TAI FUNG $

2/F House 6, South Block, Xintiandi, Lane 123, Xinye Lu, 6385 8378, www.dintaifung.com.cn

HOURS: Daily 11 A.M.-1 A.M.

This may well upset foodies who insist that for the best genuine dining experiences one must suffer in a decrepit unhygienic venue, but the delightful *xiaolongbao* dumplings served at this sleek professional Taiwanese chain are just about the best in town. DTF is as different from a standard dumpling joint as Nobu—NYC's chichi sushi restaurant—is from a sushi boat joint: Both have their moments, but if you're going to have one dumpling experience, head here for the superior taste of the pork, the richness of the soup, and the perfectly thin dumpling wrappers. It now also does half orders when a whole steamer-full isn't quite enough (I suggest trying the *shao mai* as well as the original *xiaolongbao*), though side dishes such as stir-fried bean shoots *(dou miao)* make a great accompaniment, too. There is also a branch in Super Brand Mall in Pudong.

WO JIA $

Building 7, 227 Huashan Lu near Yan'an Xilu, 6279 3985

HOURS: Daily 11 A.M.-2 A.M.

For cheap and cheerful traditional Shanghainese food, this small eatery, called My Home in Mandarin, is a great choice. The owners have been serving huge plates of comfort food since the mid-1980s, and crowd of regulars come back for the home-style specialties such as chicken wings in sweet chili sauce and pomfret fish braised in soy sauce. Staff don't speak much English but are helpful and friendly. If you're in the area, this is a great place to try the kind of food locals eat on a regular basis: fuss free, possibly a little greasy, but delicious. And when dishes cost around 20RMB, it's a great place to experiment.

CAFÉS AND CHEAP EATS

BLUE FROG $

207-06 Maoming Nanlu, 6445 6634, www.bluefrog.com.cn

HOURS: Daily 10 A.M.-1 A.M.

The terra-cotta–colored café and bar is a deservedly popular expat spot that is all things to all people. It's a relaxed hangout during the day with good coffee and free Wi-Fi available as people perch on the high wooden tables, and then its great-value happy hour segues into turning the place into a late-night lounge when the music is turned up and the lights go down. At anytime of day the specialty is burgers—the blue-cheese burger is particularly tasty—and the weekend brunch is popular, especially when the patio doors are open during the summer, with dishes such as Greek omelet with pine nuts and olives on the menu. This is the original location and still the most popular, but check the website for other locations.

© HELENA IVESON

Blue Frog on Maoming Nanlu is relaxed and friendly.

BOHEMIA CAFÉ AND BAR $

42, Lane 248, Taikang Lu, 6415 0065,
www.bohemiashanghai.com
HOURS: Daily 9 A.M.-midnight

Lavazza Coffee lovers flock to this tiny but perfectly formed hangout right in the middle of Taikang Lu, a maze of shops and bars that make up the city's loveliest shopping experience. The delicious-looking cakes are tempting, especially as they come served with a scoop of New Zealand ice cream. Bright and cheery atmosphere combined with the friendly Chinese and antipodean staff attract a good crowd, but be warned, there are few tables. It's also a great casual lunch venue, with interesting meals such as warm beef salad with a light horseradish dressing and artichoke bruschetta on the menu. At night, the vibe changes to funky bar with tea lights balancing on protruding bricks in the wall and lighting up the room.

GUYUAN ANTIQUE TEAHOUSE $$

1315 Fuxing Xilu near Fenyang Lu, 6445 4625
HOURS: Daily 10 A.M.-2 A.M.

This cozy spot on Fuxing Zhonglu transports you back to a different time in China as the teahouse is modeled after a Ming dynasty courtyard and the 200-year-old gateway was transported from Shanxi province. Inside is more traditionally Shanghai with dark wooden furniture, and if you sit by the windows there are some great alcoves for soaking in the afternoon sun sipping tea and munching on free Chinese snacks, including the usual selection of seeds, nuts, and figs. The English-speaking staff will talk you through the teas' different characteristics, though do check prices beforehand as the menu is just in Chinese.

WHISK CHOCO CAFÉ $

1250 Huaihai Zhonglu by Changshu Lu, 5404 7770
HOURS: Daily 7:30 A.M.-11 P.M.

This is Ground Zero for Shanghainese chocoholics, and the friendly guys who run the sleek Italian retro-style café must be making a fortune as the place is permanently packed. As you may have guessed, chocolate is the specialty whether it's to be drunk (try the chocolate shot—four ounces of pure thick hot chocolate) or eaten in the form of a luscious brownie or a giant chocolate cupcake. Don't do what I did, though, and have both and feel decidedly queasy for the rest of the day. Aside from sweet treats, it has a regular menu with an Italian bent. The friendly mainly Filipino staff do an excellent job dealing with the crowds of expat families who pack the place on the weekend.

INTERNATIONAL

A FUTURE PERFECT $$

16, Lane 351, Huashan Lu, 6249 6867,
www.afutureperfect.com.cn
HOURS: Daily 7 A.M.-2 A.M.

Be sure to make reservations as the restaurant's slick service, reasonable prices, and stylish surroundings attract quite a crowd. Unlike the 1930s-style vibe of the attached hotel, the Old House Inn, the restaurant looks to the future with its clean modern lines and bright color scheme. If possible, get a table in the leafy walled courtyard—the modernist plastic seating may look uncomfortable but after an excellently mixed cocktail, you won't notice. Sitting in the dining room, one can see across the walkway to the detached bakery kitchen where A Future Perfect's breads and desserts are made fresh daily. The bar room also hosts two booths that seem to be where the cool crowd likes to perch. The extensive menu is rather whimsical with dish names such as Mary Had a Little Lamb for a braised-lamb dish but you'll soon forgive all when your artfully arranged dish arrives: Try the pork tenderloin with coconut sweet potato and a lime and mango compote. Finish off with a green tea tiramisu and give yourself a pat on the back for finding this gem.

HAIKU $$

28B Taojiang Lu, near Hengshan Lu, 6445 0021
HOURS: Daily 11:30 A.M.-10:30 P.M.

Beijing gourmets are used to having to wait for branches of Shanghai's best restaurants to open up north, but for once, it was Shanghai who was made to wait for a branch of this hugely popular and funky California-style Japanese restaurant. The food is uniformly excellent, and on most tables, you'll find people ordering the 119 spicy tuna roll and the excellent Motorola rolls. Just like in Beijing, the restaurant attracts the young and beautiful, so you need to make reservations, but it's surprisingly inexpensive considering the quality of the food.

KABB $$

House 5, North Block, Xintiandi, Lane 181, Taicang Lu, 3307 0798, www.kabbsh.com

HOURS: Daily 7 A.M.-1 A.M.

Very much a staple of the expat brunch weekend scene, Kabb's American-style comfort food (think burgers, breakfast burritos, and imported U.S. steaks) and relaxed atmosphere make it a pleasant place to while away a few hours at any time of the day. If you can snag a table outside the renovated *shikumen* the restaurant is situated in, you can indulge in some of the best people-watching opportunities in Shanghai. Later in the evening, the restaurant becomes more of a bar and with its deep red banquettes and dark wooden furniture, it's a great place to unwind with one of the reasonably priced glasses of wine.

SUGAR $$

The Collection, Building 2, North Block, Xintiandi, Lane 181, Taicang Lu, 5351 0007, www.thecollectionsh.com

HOURS: Daily 10 A.M.-10 P.M.

Part of The Collection, a trio of brand-new funky venues that have opened in Xintiandi, Sugar is apparently China's first desserts parlor and it's as cool if ultragirly a venue as you could imagine for something sweet and decadent. Everything is made fresh and you can watch the chefs at work in the open kitchen as they combine unlikely ingredients such as blue cheese and chocolate into something gorgeous. While the sweetness of the desserts plus the white-and-peppermint-stripes decor may be a shade over the top for some, others will be cooing with delight. As in the other two venues, a Japanese restaurant called Pure and a funky bar called Cube, smoking is not allowed.

Old City

Map 13

TRADITIONAL SHANGHAI STYLE

NANXIANG STEAMED BUN RESTAURANT $

378 Fuyou Lu, 6355 4206

HOURS: Daily 7:30 A.M.-10 P.M.

Dare we say it, but are the steamed pork dumplings here a little overrated? Judging by the (amazingly orderly) line of people that can loop around the block on the weekends waiting for a takeaway, this may be an unpopular statement, but compared to the wafer-thin wrappings at Din Tai Fung, the dough here is too thick and the juices inside the dumpling too meager. Still, for a takeaway lunch eaten as you perch near the Yu Yuan pond, you can't get much more filling and cheap than 12RMB for 12 dumplings, but do go to the more rarefied Din Tai Fung (see the *Former French Concession* section) and see which style you prefer. At least while you wait, you can watch the dumplings being hand made by manically busy women rolling out the dough, but if you can't be bothered to wait, go upstairs to the canteen-style restaurant.

WU DA NIANG DUMPLINGS $

238 Fuzhou Lu, no phone

HOURS: Daily 8 A.M.-8 P.M.

This branch of the local chain (look out for the Chinese grandmother on the logo) is definitely not the place to linger, being the equivalent of McDonald's to Americans, but its tasty steamed *jiaozi* dumplings are reliably good, filling, and cheap. You pay at the counter and it has an English menu: Try the pork and scallion or egg and tomato. At these prices, though, you could order practically everything and still have change from a 100RMB note—you order by the 50g, or *liang*, and two *liang* will fill up the average diner. The staff will then bring your food to your plastic table, and unlike many *jiaozi* joints, Wu Da Niang prides itself on its hygiene.

CAFÉS AND CHEAP EATS

OLD SHANGHAI TEA HOUSE $

385 Fangbang Zhonglu, 5382 1202

HOURS: Daily 9 A.M.-10 P.M.

This pretty if touristy teahouse is on the second floor above Old Street, and while it may be a little overpriced, it's not outrageously so, and it makes a great place to sip a cup of green tea away from the crowds. It's a tiny place and decorated nicely with antiques and small fans and gramaphones dotted around while 1930s-style jazz plays on the stereo. A cup of tea chosen from the wooden menu costs from 35RMB and a small array of dim sum is also available though it's distinctly average.

SIPAILOU LU FOOD STREET $

Sipailou Lu

HOURS: Daily 24 hours

For a taste of real local snacks, leave Yu Yuan behind you and venture down this unvarnished street where family-run stalls that specialize in local breads, kebabs, dumplings, roasted sweet potatoes, and more can be found night and day. Hygiene can't be guaranteed and you are sure to be on the receiving end of more than a few stares as few foreigners come down here, but it's a great experience and you'll leave full of food for a few RMB. The fried bread stuffed with scallions makes a very tasty breakfast.

© HELENA IVESON

Sipailou Lu Food Street

STARBUCKS $

Yu Gardens Bazaar, 5385 5001

HOURS: Daily 10 A.M.-10 P.M.

There are not one but two branches of the coffee chain that needs no introduction in the center of the bazaar; suffice to say that it's always full of tourists from all countries enjoying a respite from the chaos and hassle that is Yu Yuan! The very friendly staff are also happy to give you directions, as the layout of the bazaar can be confusing.

Pudong

Map 14

TRADITIONAL SHANGHAI STYLE

YÈ SHANGHAI $$

3/F Citigroup Tower, 33 Huanyuanshiqiao Lu, near Fucheng Lu, 5878 5660

HOURS: Daily 11:30 A.M.-2:30 P.M. and 5:30-10:30 P.M.

The upmarket Yè Shanghai, which has sister restaurants in Hong Kong and Tokyo, has changed its normal art deco look to fit in with its futuristic surroundings in Pudong. It's right on the Huangpu River, and the floor-to-ceiling windows offer picture-postcard views of the Bund. Expect distinctive interpretations of classic Shanghai dishes and the cuisines of the surrounding provinces of Zhejiang and Jiangsu: Must-orders include the fried whole king prawns with XO chili sauce (a traditional spicy seafood sauce) and sautéed beef short ribs with black and green peppercorn sauce, washed down with one of the many Shaoxing rice wines on offer. There is another branch near Xintiandi (Lane 181, Taicang Lu, 6311 2323).

CAFÉS AND CHEAP EATS

PAUL $

Thumb Plaza, Ground Floor, Number 8, Lane 199, Fangdian Lu, 5033 5402, www.paulchina.com

HOURS: Daily 7:30 A.M.-10 P.M.

Chi-chi bakery chain Paul has kept Parisians happy with its legendary bread and tarts for more than 100 years in France, and now Shanghai no longer has to go without excellent bread. If the chewy baguettes stacked up high and blackberry tarts laid out invitingly don't convince you that they are worth the price, the glamorous store with its checkered floor and French furniture will. The thick delicious hot chocolate completes the carb-heavy treat. There are more branches in the Shanghai Center, Xintiandi, and in the Village complex on Dongping Lu.

INTERNATIONAL

DANIELI'S $$

39/F, St Regis, 889 Dongfang Lu, 5050 4567, ext. 6370

HOURS: Daily 11:30 A.M.-2:30 P.M., 6-10:30 P.M., brunch Sun. 11:30 A.M.-2:30 P.M.

The St Regis's flagship restaurant proudly displays its awards from local dining magazines, but you can't help feeling the Tuscan-oriented eatery is overhyped. It's made up of two dining rooms on the 39th floor, but a floor-to-ceiling wine cellar between the two keeps both sides intimate. While staff are professional and on hand to answer any questions, service is unsmiling rather than warm. Still, there are nice distances between the tables, which are beautifully laid out with cream tablecloths, the open kitchen is interesting to look at, and the food is tasty, especially the linguine with squid and anchovies and the lamb and rocket sun-dried tomato salad. Its somber atmosphere makes it more suitable for business lunches than romantic rendezvous, especially if you come for lunch and enjoy the very-good-value two-course set menu with coffee for 158RMB.

JADE ON 36 $$$$

36/F, Tower 2, Pudong Shangri-La Hotel, 33 Fucheng Lu, 6882 3636, ext. 280, www.shangri-la.com

HOURS: Daily 6:30-10 P.M.

This is Shanghai's best destination for cutting-edge fine dining, and if you can afford the prices, your taste buds are in for a theatrical and mind-blowing workout. There are a small number of seasonal set menus to choose from, and the French chef Paul Pairet is a believer that food should be challenging, so expect some bizarre combinations of food, texture, and presentation—such as fois gras ice cream as just one example—that work like a charm. Some might consider the food on the pretentious side—this is not the venue for fans of straightforward food—but the charming staff do not take themselves too seriously. The food is so mind-blowing that it almost overshadows what must be a serious contender for Shanghai's best view looking down from the 36th floor onto the Bund.

Greater Shanghai

Map 15

TRADITIONAL SHANGHAI STYLE

1221 $$

1221 Yan'an Xilu, between Panyu Lu and Dingxi Lu, 6213 6585

HOURS: Daily 11 A.M.-2 P.M., 5-11 P.M.

Tucked down an evocative historic lane, 1221 has a loyal following of both locals and expats, which has made reservations essential. The restaurant's fans choose 1221 for its contemporary decor and its signature culinary style: hearty Shanghainese fare that fills a huge bilingual menu. The chef is Cantonese so the food is a little lighter than normal, which is an added bonus. Well, most of it is lighter, but the deep-fried spare ribs, while a heart attack on a plate, are still a must-order for carnivores.

CAFÉS AND CHEAP EATS

HOUSE OF FLOUR $

1/F, Number 2, Shanghai Legend, 635 Bibo Lu near Chunxiao Lu, 5080 6230

HOURS: Daily 7 A.M.-9 P.M.

Carb fans in Shanghai can have a tough time of it, especially over in Pudong, so this little café has made waves with its delicious muffins, cheesecakes, cappuccinos, and deli-style sandwiches. Pudong-based locals come to hang out and make use of the free Wi-Fi, and whoever runs the place has excellent taste in music with no insipid boy bands or teenage pop tarts to be heard. I had a chicken curry masala panini that was excellent—crispy bread and a good curry-tasting filling. If this place were on the other side of the river, it would be permanently packed: As it is, it is a nice and friendly place to eat and sip your coffee.

NIGHTLIFE

Here's one area in which even Beijingers agree that Shanghai has the better of the capital: After years of the Communist Party's basically banning partying—no nightclubs existed in Shanghai until 1992—Shanghai has a wild side once again, and it outshines that of every other Chinese city with perhaps the exception of Hong Kong. The 1930s decadence of opium dens, brothels, and underground gambling joints may be long gone, but no matter where you are based in the city, somewhere interesting will be nearby (except for Pudong!), as nightlife is pretty evenly dispersed across the city.

The scene is very international with plenty of expats running venues and being a major part of the clientele, but increasingly, the Shanghainese are keen to sample Western-style entertainment—go to a nightclub such as Bonbon at 2 A.M. and you'll find it full of Chinese eager to party in rooms complete with go-go dancers who put on wild shows. Some find the atmosphere at the bigger clubs and the more expensive bars more than a little on the pretentious side, with people wearing sunglasses indoors at 2 A.M. looking you up and down to see whether you are wearing the latest fashions, but there are plenty of other options to choose from, whether it be a sports bar to catch up with the latest game, an underground music venue to check out the Chinese music scene, or a friendly neighborhood joint where you can sit down and have a quiet beer, Shanghai-style.

A few years ago, Maoming Nan Lu in the French Concession was the place to go for a wild night, but a police crackdown has left it a

HIGHLIGHTS

LOOK FOR ☾ TO FIND RECOMMENDED NIGHTLIFE.

☾ **Best Bar for Shanghai-Based Sports Fans:** It's loud, brash, and busy, but when beer and keeping up with the NFL are vital, **Big Bamboo** keeps its customers happy (page 196).

☾ **Best Grown-Up Glamour: Glamour Bar** lives up to its name: Upon your arrival smartly dressed doormen usher you into the art deco elevator that takes you to the stunningly decorated cocktail bar with soothing music in the background (page 198).

☾ **Best Bar with Beautiful People and a Beautiful View:** Early during your stay head to **Jade on 36 Bar**: Its sophisticated sexy style will knock your socks off, and the view of the Bund isn't bad, either (page 198).

☾ **Best Place to Drink and Dance:** So many Shanghai clubs are more into posing than dancing, but the well-run **Mao Lounge** allows its young crowd plenty of room to strut its stuff (page 201).

☾ **Best Bar for Smoky Soul Sessions:** When it's all about the jazz, man, the gimmick-free subtle charms of **JZ** can't be beaten (page 203).

Glamour Bar lives up to its name.

shadow of its former self with just a few bars, such as the Blue Frog, remaining. Nowadays that scene, with its associated massage joints, flower sellers, and sleazy characters, has moved to Tongren Lu near the Shanghai Center on Nanjing Xilu. Other parts of the French Concession offer a much cooler vibe, as indeed the area always has: As one wag put it during the Foreign Concession era, the British know how to do business, the French know how to live. The areas around Fuxing Xilu and Yongjia Lu have more than their fair share of sophisticated and upmarket bars and lounges that attract a mixed crowd of stylish Shanghainese and in-the-know expats. Perhaps of most interest to short-term visitors, the Bund, which up until a few years ago was a near-wasteland after dark, has plenty of upmarket bars and clubs charging plenty for the spectacular views. Bars vary from the sophisticated—the Glamour Bar, for example—to Bar Rouge, which attracts clubbers looking for a beautiful backdrop to their boozing, to the cheap and cheerful Captain's Hostel bar with another killer view.

Bars and Lounges

A15 BAR

15, Lane 248 Taikang Lu, 6472 0220

Map 12

Don't be put off by this tiny bar/teahouse's lack of floor space: If you go in, you'll see a narrow winding staircase that takes you to a second-floor lounge where comfortable tables and chairs abound, along with a few floor cushions to sit on if you feel like making use of their free video games; laid-back electronica is played at low levels. Unlike some bars in this trendy area, A15 isn't remotely snotty when it comes to service, and staff go out of their way to make you feel at home. The bar caters mainly to hip young Chinese who don't mind splashing out for a martini or two, though it also has a wide range of beers.

AVENUE BAR

101 Wuning Nanlu near Wuding Lu, 5256 2276

Map 11

Avenue Bar is a few blocks north of Jing'an Temple and if you're staying in the area, this is a good friendly low-key place for a relaxed drink. The Shanghainese manager speaks great English and is always happy to chat or take music requests, so even if you've never been before, you're made to feel like a local. Take a seat on one of the sofas or perch up at the wooden bar, but bear in mind that this is primarily a beer-drinking kind of place as there are no wines by the glass and bottles are way overpriced.

BARBAROSSA

People's Park, 231 Nanjing Xilu, 6339 1199, www.barbarossa.com.cn

Map 10

Fans of Middle Eastern chic—think velvet curtains, terra-cotta walls, and mosaics on the floor—will love this venue, which gets busier as the evening gets later: Big groups tend to come and lounge around one of the low tables and puff on a hookah pipe. The excellent drink specials every night of the week before 8 P.M. make this sexy spot a good place to start an evening, too. Locals gripe about the service as staff can be on the inept and unfriendly side, but if you can ignore the attitude, the venue attracts a fun and stylish crowd to party with. (See the *Restaurants* chapter for more details.)

BAR ROUGE

7/F, 18 Zhongshan Dongyilu near Nanjing Donglu, 6339 1199

Map 9

A regular winner of best-bar awards from local magazines, Bar Rouge sits atop the luxurious shopping mall Bund 18 and offers one of the best views of the Bund from its fabulous outside terrace. It's always packed, and the music here lasts late into the night. Expats and Chinese alike crowd the terrace, sitting in the slightly bizarre ship-style booths. The only irritations are the snappy waitresses and the crowds: The dance floor gets packed in the small hours. The drinks are great, however.

© ELYSE SINGLETON

Barbarossa has an excellent location in People's Square.

WHERE TO GET A CHEAP DRINK

If you need a change from Shanghai's glut of expensive cocktail bars filled with beautiful people, try these for size.

The notoriously cheap **Windows Too** (J104, 1699 Nanjing Xi Lu near Huashan Lu, opposite Jing'an Temple, 3214 0351) is affectionately considered the mother of all Shanghai dive bars. If extremely cheap strong mixed drinks (10RMB for most), loud music, and a rowdy crowd of students and expats appeals to you, you will love it – everyone else, especially the over 30s, might find the atmosphere altogether too frat house. This is the original venue in the seedy surroundings of the Jing'an amphitheater, but the Windows chain is spreading fast.

Up the food chain, cool and cavelike **Mural** (697 Yongjia Lu near Hengshan Lu, 6433 5023, www.muralbar.com) offers 100RMB all-you-can-drink nights every Friday. Mural attracts a slightly more sophisticated crowd, thanks to its live music, which varies from salsa to reggae. If all-you-can-drink alcohol isn't enough for you, you can always try its hookah pipes in different flavors as the resident belly dancer does her thing.

Mexican venue **Zapata's** (5 Hengshan Lu near Dongping Lu, 6433 4104, www.zapatas-shanghai.com) is another place for cheap drinks – but mainly if you are of the fairer sex. Its Ladies' Nights every Monday and Wednesday are a Shanghai legend as women can drink free margaritas all night. Even if you're a guy, drinks are cheap, and what with all the free booze flowing, the scene becomes pretty wild as the night goes on.

If the idea of a margarita-fueled crowd isn't appealing, **Diage** (20 Donghu Lu near Huaihai Lu, 5404-5757) is perfect for a sophisticated drinker on a tight budget, thanks to its location in a 19th-century mansion filled with leather couches and velvet curtains. Drinks before 9 P.M. are staggeringly cheap, with mixed drinks available for 15RMB.

BEEDEES

433 Dagu Lu, near Chengdu Beilu, 6327 3160

Map 10

Dagu Lu is becoming increasingly popular with the city's bar-goers who eschew the megabars and clubs that Shanghai has an abundance of, so if you're looking for a quiet drink, go now before it gets too rammed. Beedees is perhaps the best bar on the street if you're looking for a place without pretensions—while not exactly a dive, it comes close in terms of atmosphere, if not decor or music—it's a little too hip for that. It's never crowded—perhaps people think it will be expensive as it looks pricey, with two antique oil lamps at the end of the dark wooden bar shining down on the comfy couches that are long enough to lie down on, but it's not, and during the nightly happy hour, it's a bargain.

BIG BAMBOO

132 Nanyang Lu near Tongren Lu, 6256 2265, www.bigbamboo.cn

Map 11

Shanghai's best sports bar knows exactly what its clientele wants: well-poured draft beer, plenty of entertainment with a shuffleboard table, foosball, two pool tables, and a host of flat-screen and projection TVs showing the latest game, all served by pretty girls in regulation tight uniforms. If this doesn't appeal to you, it's best to steer clear (of the whole street actually, as it is on the seedy side), but if the combination is what you're looking for on a night out, you'll love it. The American menu, served all day with a special brunch menu on the weekends, goes down well thanks to the size of the portions and good renditions of solid American staples. If you want more of the same, Malone's, which attracts a similar if slightly older clientele, is just around the corner at 255 Tongren Lu.

DR BAR

15, North Block, Xintiandi, Lane 181, Taicang Lu, 6311 0358

Map 12

Xintiandi's most understated bar is a relaxing place to sip a cocktail in arty uncrowded surroundings. The bar is partly owned by the designer of the whole complex, and it's easy to spot the attention to detail that's been applied: Look out for the gray slate in the walls. The rest of the venue is equally attractive, but be warned, your fellow drinkers may be on the pretentious side. Ignore them and have a beautifully mixed cocktail, such as the famous lychee cosmopolitan.

EDDY'S BAR

1877 Huaihai Zhonglu, near Tianping Lu, 6282 0521

Map 15

Attracting an older gay clientele who aren't so keen to whoop it up on the nearest dance floor, Eddy's has been a mecca for Shanghai's more discreet gay community for years. No one would claim the place is fashionable, but the cozy, dimly lit, Asian-themed bar is a welcoming place, and the owner is usually around propping up the bar and making first-timers feel welcome. Unlike most gay venues, Eddy's starts to wind down after midnight so don't arrive too late.

ENOTECA

53-57 Anfu Lu, near Changshu Lu, 5404 0050, www.enoteca.com.cn

Map 12

The place to come for oeneophiles, Enoteca is a much-loved wine bar and wine store down a cute street full of interesting boutiques. It specializes in wines from the New World, in particular South America, and it prides itself on its low markups. Guests can buy a bottle in the store and then take it to the classy wine bar/café next door with paying a corkage fee, though if you don't wish to buy a bottle, it also has an excellent selection by the glass to work your way through. The Chinese manager knows his grapes, and Enoteca also offers wine tastings twice a week and was planning to open another branch—check the website.

FACE BAR

118 Ruijin Erlu, 6466 4328, www.facebars.com

Map 12

While Shanghai's cool crowd moved on from Face a while ago, its Asian antique-filled country mansion venue is delightful and ever-popular with visitors and locals who can afford the prices. Few Shanghai experiences can beat lying back on a traditional *kang* daybed surrounded by opulent artifacts as you sip a cocktail, or in summer, relaxing outside on the beautifully manicured lawns hedged in on all sides by skyscrapers. Unfortunately, during the day on weekends, most of Shanghai's expats head here, complete with kids in tow, so stick to the evenings if that's not your thing. Some—with reason—gripe about the unfriendly service: If the staff get on your nerves and you're hungry, don't get the overpriced snacks at the bar but head to one of the excellent restaurants in the mansion—there's a Thai restaurant called Lan Thai and an Indian restaurant called Hazara.

Face Bar still brings in the crowds.

GLAMOUR BAR

6/F Zhongshan Dongyilu, 6350 9988,
www.m-restaurantgroup.com

Map 9

Just like the bar's sister restaurant M, which adjoins the bar, Glamour is packed nightly and unlike so many other bars in the city, has proved itself to be a stayer. Why has this art deco delight lasted? Because its slinky retro-glam lounge is staffed by professionals who brilliantly manage the two striking bars; the killer cocktails, especially the martinis, are reasonably priced for the quality of the venue; and of course the view over the river as it bends is fabulous. While it's not a place to seriously party, it's a perfect venue to get dressed up for and enjoy sipping a sophisticated drink. It's also something of a cultural center as it often holds book readings when visiting authors are in town and an annual literary festival.

HIRO

29, Lane 248, Taikang Lu, 6473 0938

Map 12

A recent arrival to trendy Taikang Lu, this cute Japanese bar is in an exotic corner of the neighborhood, nestled in the back of a Japanese café and below a Thai restaurant, and it's the place to check out some of Japan's favorite spirits, such as sake, *shouchu,* or *umeshu,* most of which are available by the glass. The bar is very small so don't expect a partylike atmosphere, as there are only five bar stools to perch on. The friendly owner will recommend some drinks if you're a beginner when it comes to imbibing Japanese spirits—and beware, they slip down all too easily so be careful when you try to get down from that chair.

THE HUT

385 Yongjia Lu near Taiyuan Lu, 3401 0958

Map 12

If you need a quiet reliable drink a world away from Shanghai's more glamorous offerings but still in a cute venue in the French Concession, head to this neighborhood bar, dimly lit by Tibetan-style lamps. The Hut's orange walls and red bar stools sound awful, but the place pulls it off. Your fellow patrons will be a loyal crowd of local residents and Shanghai Conservatory students there to enjoy a beer or two. If you're lucky, you'll see some of the students get up and perform. All drinks are very affordable, even without the long-running extended happy hour.

JADE ON 36 BAR

Level 36, Grand Tower, Pudong Shangri-La Hotel,
33 Fucheng Lu, 6882 3636

Map 14

Prepare to be wowed by the Shangri-La's stunning and sexy bar on the 36th floor. Even locals are prepared to cross the river to the "Dong," as it's popularly known, to sip one of the innovative cocktails while looking down on the Bund and the passing river traffic. The lights are kept very low, as is the music until around midnight, when the DJ arrives and it becomes more of a party venue. The hugely popular Friday night events are fun and buzzy and apparently attract a lot of local models though it's up to you if that's a bonus or disadvantage. Still, the cocktail list is extensive, the service impressive, and the toilets out of this world.

I LOVE SHANGHAI

155 Zhongshan Dongerlu near Jinling Donglu,
6355 8058

Map 9

This exuberantly named venue is a true original: Where else can you get a Filipino-theme night or a mixed duo providing pole-dancing shows as the mixed audience, looking for a budget night out, cheers them on and sips the free cocktails provided every couple of hours? Unlike most Bund locations, here the emphasis is on fun rather than sophistication; the owners cheerfully admit that it's a dive bar famous for strong cheap Long Island iced teas. If you come during the day, the partying seems like a distant memory as the bar makes a lovely and relaxed afternoon venue with its cozy nooks.

MANIFESTO

748 Julu Lu near Fumin Lu, 6289 9108

Map 12

This seductive watering hole is an extremely pleasant place to grab pre- or postdinner drinks. It was once an electronics factory, and nowadays there is still an industrialist look about the place, as it is dominated by a central three-sided copper bar, but the place has been made comfortable thanks to slouchy leather armchairs and opium beds. Well-heeled Shanghainese martini drinkers love sipping cocktails made from ingredients as varied as lemon balm and anchovy-stuffed olives—try the famous Dirty Manifesto martini. If you're hungry, Manifesto is attached to the restaurant Mesa, which has a modern Australian menu and very popular brunches.

NAPA WINE BAR

57 Jiangyin Lu, 6318 0857

Map 10

Just around the corner from the JW Marriott Hotel, this converted red-brick mansion that opened at the beginning of 2008 is the Shanghai wine lover's home away from home—as long as he or she has a big wallet and has passed the stringent membership requirements meant to keep out all the riffraff. The place operates as a private members' club run by the fine-wine importer ASC, and members prepared to pay the eye-watering prices can maintain their own wines in perfect condition in the club's underground wine cellar or select from 2,000 of the world's best wines. However, if you're just passing through and fancy a high-class glass or two, it has a wine bar that is open to the public and where you too can pretend you're living the colonial dream.

PEOPLE 7

805 Julu Lu, by Fumin Lu, 5404 0707

Map 12

Despite the industrial feel, thanks to its raw concrete walls, People 7 is much less pretentious than you'd think, despite the tricky entrance that requires a little too much insider knowledge to open. The minimalist theme doesn't extend to the bathrooms: We won't spoil the surprise. This is the sister bar to fellow industrial chic venue Shintori, an excellent Japanese restaurant, and offers well-made swish cocktails in a hip venue that really gets going later in the evening—you'll need to reserve a table for Friday and Saturday nights or take your chances with everyone else. This is one of the few places in Shanghai that has lines on busy nights.

PICCONE

1 Taojiang Lu near Dongping Lu, 139 1761 1512

Map 12

Piccone isn't easy to find, which probably helps with its popularity: If you find this bar, which offers live music every day of the week, you too will feel like part of the in crowd. Owned by a French and Japanese duo who have gone all out to make it a relaxed and friendly haven, the venue is spacious—a good thing, as it attracts a loyal crowd of regulars who enjoy inexpensive drinks washed down with snacks ordered from nearby restaurants. The music varies, with local gypsy bands from western China, reggae, and good old blues and rock: Call for details.

PINKHOME

18 Gaolan Lu, between Ruijin Er Lu and Sinan Lu, 5382 0373

Map 12

Shanghai's biggest gay nightlife destination aims to be all things to all men with a bar/restaurant, boutique hotel, and nightclub, all in the same converted historic building near Fuxing Park. The bar and club have the same futuristic decor, and we recommend you do what its many local fans do, which is eat dinner in the fusion restaurant before burning off the calories on the psychedelic dance floor. The place attracts a mixed crowd of urban Chinese men and Western expats looking for fun to a disco soundtrack, and the male dancers wearing next to nothing seem to go down well with the crowd too.

RACKS

5/F, Number 7, South Block, Xintiandi, 6384 2718

Map 12

If an evening out is not complete without a game of pool, head to Xintiandi and Shanghai's first high-end pool bar. The Chinese love pool so you may have to make reservations. The large room on the fifth floor has 16 well-lit pool tables, and when you're not reenacting Paul Newman fantasies, you can relax on brown leather seats and listen to the midtempo music played in the background. At peak hours, prices shoot up, but the standard rate of 88RMB an hour is reasonable, and the place is full of staff keen to rack up the balls for you and generally make your life easy. The helpful service, plus a solid range of imported beers and cocktails—the Sidecar is particularly recommended—make this venue a fun place for a night out.

RED BEAT

3/F, 72 Tongren Lu, 6279 0338

Map 11

It may be surrounded by some of Shanghai's seedier nightlife haunts on the infamous Tongren Lu, but Red Beat is attempting to single-handedly raise the tone of the neighborhood behind the Portman Center. An energetic if somewhat uneven house band tries to get the party started, but most patrons are happy to just drink and listen rather than make their moves on the dance floor. The bar doesn't have the bar girls or the amounts of neon as other bars along the strip; instead the owners have gone for a more simple and tasteful look. Beer and cocktail prices range from a reasonable RMB38–50, making this a good place to chill on a street where options for a quiet drink are limited.

ROOM WITH A VIEW

12/F Xianshi Building, 479 Nanjing Donglu, near Jiujiang Lu, 6352 0256

Map 10

Part loft bar, part art gallery, this is one of Shanghai's few bars that can genuinely call itself arty. The bar area is aiming for a New York City look, with its glass and black leather, but it's gradually becoming a bit shabby, which fits in with the arty bohemian look. For some culture, take your cocktails or beer into the adjoining art gallery, where, depending on the exhibition, you'll find anything from political pop art to huge installations and photography. If there weren't enough going on in the inside, the fine views over the surrounding area are a bonus.

SHANGHAI STUDIO

4, Lane 1950, Huaihai Zhonglu, near Xingguo Lu, 6283 1043, www.shanghai-studio.com

Map 12

This fashionable gay venue might be hard to find, but persevere and head down the flight of stairs behind the unimposing entrance, as it's a fun, quirky place with an extravagantly lit underground maze of tunnels and private rooms, where music is played at levels at which conversation remains possible. In addition to there being a bar open from 9 P.M. every night (there are three dotted around—take your pick), it's also an art gallery with a perhaps not surprising focus on the torsos of young fit men. Most evenings you will find a mix of cool Chinese locals and young expats looking to drink and meet people in a friendly, funky environment.

TARA 57

2F, 57 Fuxing Xilu near Yongfu Lu, 6431 7027

Map 12

A relative newcomer to the cocktail scene, Tara 57's teeny-tiny room above Boona Café and opposite JZ on Fuxing Lu has just four tables, two coat stands, and a few bar stools all set around a well-stocked bar. But small is very, very beautiful in Tara's case; its cocktail menu runs to 150 options, including three brands of the potent spirit absinthe and hard-to-get booze that you won't find anywhere else in Shanghai. Because of the stylish atmosphere and beautifully made drinks, Tara 57 is one of Shanghai's premier destinations for those who know and love their mixed drinks.

Nightclubs

ATTICA

15 Zhongshan Dongerlu, 6373 3588, www.attica-shanghai.com

Map 9

Shanghai's installation of Singapore's popular party spot, Attica, offers a stellar view of the city and an eclectic mix of grooves, but only to those with the bills to back it up. When Paris Hilton was in town, she partied here, so if that thought doesn't put you off, you'll love it. Clubbers mingle on the outdoor patio or shake it up inside the intimate hip-hop pavilion with 360-degree Bund and Pudong views, but you do have to come prepared for the cost: The cover charge is at least 150RMB on weekends. For these kinds of prices drinks should be better, but guests complain that they are very hit-and-miss. Italian restaurant Finestre is in the same building.

BONBON

2/F, Yunhai Tower, 1329 Huaihai Zhonglu, 133 2193 9299, www.clubbonbon.com

Map 12

Clubs in Shanghai come and go, but this place, which has legendary U.K. dance band Godskitchen in the DJ booth, is number one for local club kids. It gets too crowded to dance, it runs out of glasses, and the cover charge is high (drinks are included in the price but only beer and spirits—if you want a soft drink, you have to pay for it), but the range of different rooms means that different kinds of clubbers are catered to, with one room usually playing hip-hop and another house, and the sound system gets top marks. People get very dressed up to come here and it has a reputation as a great place to meet people for some short-term fun.

MAO LOUNGE

46 Yueyang Lu, 6466 7662, www.maoshanghai.com

Map 12

Tucked deep into the French Concession, this lounge/club has the intimate feel of a private members' venue but is open to all as long as you are beautiful, hip, and have the cash to afford to buy drinks by the bottle only. Mao stands for Music Art Oasis and the management is seriously into its music, so expect to hear the latest sounds booming everywhere, including into the garden in back. The raised couches in the bar area underneath a dramatic chandelier are perfect for people-watching, and the mostly European management goes all out to create a buzzy atmosphere.

PARAMOUNT THEATER

218 Yuyuan Lu, near Wanhangdu Lu, 6249 8866

Map 11

Once the most luxuriously appointed art deco dance hall in the Far East and where the 1930s glitterati used to fox-trot in their furs, this theater has been reopened as a nightclub after a lengthy hibernation. The first floor is a run-of-the-mill disco with laser lights, a focus on '80s nights, and an expensive sound system that attracts mostly Chinese clubbers, but I suggest using the elevator (you have to buy a ticket for 80RMB) that will take you up to the fourth floor and back to a different era. Here you'll find some of the original fixtures, such as the huge stage surrounded by belle epoque mirrors and outrageous floral wallpaper, and people ballroom dancing as though the past 70 years haven't happened. It's a surreal experience unique to Shanghai.

THE SHELTER

5 Yongfu Lu near Fuxing Xilu, no phone

Map 12

The French Concession's newest alternative-music venue is definitely worth visiting thanks to its fantastic bomb-bunker venue, and its owners, who have their fingers firmly on the pulse of local nightlife. The design is sleek and simple and the owners have poured money into the sound system, which, judging by the crowds of music fans there on weekends, is paying off. Cover charges and drinks prices are kept low to make it affordable for local Chinese students, and the local DJs know how to please their audience with techno, hip-hop, and early funk dominating on different nights.

VOLAR

99 Yandang Lu, by Nanchang Lu near Fuxing Park, 134 8223 9390, www.volar.com.hk

Map 12

Officially a private members' club on the second floor of the Pudi Boutique hotel, this Phillipe Starck–designed offshoot of the original Hong Kong club is living up to its reputation as the place to go for chilled-out drinking sessions in a nicely hip environment for the wealthy set. The eclectically decorated lounge—Starck must have been inspired by Hitchcock's films judging by the number of stuffed animals—is wacky, but thanks to the good service it doesn't take itself too seriously. And for fans of obscure alcohol, it has positively the best selection of liquor by the bottle in town.

YONGFOO ELITE

200 Yongfu Lu near Hunan Lu, 6471 9181, www.yongfooelite.com

Map 12

Set off one of the French Concession's most picturesque tree-lined streets, Yongfoo is housed in the former British Consulate and is a great venue for a post- or predinner cocktail, but those in the know say the food is average at best. Staff are not particularly friendly either—and you're not allowed to take photos—but the striking venue and antique-filled rooms with crystal chandeliers and comfortable velvet chaise longues transport its well-heeled crowd of regulars—both expats and locals—back to the 1930s.

Live Music

COTTON CLUB

1416 Huaihai Zhonglu near Fuxing Lu, 6437 7110

Map 12

This old-timer much beloved by Shanghai's finger clickers, but no relation to the legendary New York institution, offers unchallenging and soothing mellow sounds. The stage dominates the wood and brass–decorated room, and the stills of jazz greats give the performers something to aspire to. It's popular with both expats and Chinese, mainly because of its consistency: Even if you visit only once every few years, the local band will probably consist of the same performers—some of them have played there for longer than a decade.

4 LIVE

Building 8, 8 Jianguo Lu near Chongqing Nan Lu, 6415 0700

Map 12

This fun and funky bar is now totally dedicated to live music, with mostly local live bands during the week and guest bands on weekends. With black booths along one wall and a stainless-steel bar along the other, this place makes the stage and dance floor the focal point. The layout makes the performers very accessible, while the thumping stereo system turns each show into a visceral experience. Although the crowds on the weekends are such that spilling a drink is highly probable, the prices are such that one can get another without ruining the evening.

HOUSE OF BLUES AND JAZZ

60 Fuzhou Lu, 6437 5270

Map 9

This lovely art deco–themed bar attracts a mixed, slightly older crowd, there to enjoy the bar's high-quality rotating live acts. With a little rock and funk infused into the jazz, this venue's acts definitely get the crowd involved, especially its occasional jam sessions, which bring out some of the city's more talented amateur musicians.

The house has existed in different locations since the original opened in the early 1990s, and the club will be moving from its French Concession locale to the Bund in late 2008.

JZ

46 Fuxing Lu, 6431 0269, www.jzclub.cn

Map 12

This jazz club's motto is "Jazz Made in China," and that's exactly what it is: There are no gimmicks or pretentiousness at this multifloored plush jazz venue; here the music is what matters. The stage is almost as big as the area for the audience, creating a great intimate setting. There's no cover charge and drinks are averagely priced, so the place does get popular—it's best to make reservations. Live shows put on by the regular and visiting musicians are consistently of high quality, and if you feel like taking to the stage, every Monday is open mic night.

LOGO

13 Xingfu Lu, near Fahuazhen Lu, 6281 5646

Map 15

Logo has quickly become a mainstay of Shanghai's alternative-music scene by giving musicians and music lovers somewhere cool to hang out. Here is a great place to see where Chinese music is at the moment, whether it's punk rock, electronic, techno, or roots. Almost every night of the week independently promoted events pack the place, and although musos can often seem too cool for school, it's a friendly down-to-earth place, and drinks are surprisingly reasonable too. Every Sunday is jam session time: Just turn up and join in.

YUYINTANG

1731 Yan'an Xilu, entrance at Kaixuan Lu, 5237-8662, www.yuyintang.org

Map 15

Owner Zhang Haisheng is at the forefront of the Chinese rock-music scene so if you're into loud and raucous rock, expect a good night out at this, the latest incarnation of the club. It can be difficult to find, so make sure you have the telephone number with you, but it's worth the effort to find, as you might just see the next big thing on the small intimate stage, but even if the music on that night isn't to your taste, at least there are weird and wonderful video projections on the walls and the beer is cheap.

021 BAR

2/F, North Bund Commercial Center, 2925 Yangshupu Lu near Dinghai Lu, 6580 1185

Map 15

Yes, as unlikely as it sounds, Shanghai does have a punk-music scene, and 021 Bar is its Ground Zero and as underground as it gets in the Shanghai rock scene. The bar puts on rock and folk shows most weekends at its converted factory location. It also boasts of being the only live-music venue with a hostel, for those blurry nights when you can't face a cab ride home, as punks need a place to sleep in, too: Handy as the bar is a 10-minute taxi ride east from Yangshupu Lu subway station. Rooms are from 50RMB/night. If you're into underground rock, do check this bar out as it offers a genuinely alternative atmosphere that is a breath of fresh air when the Western-style bars in Shanghai start blurring into one.

ARTS AND LEISURE

The performing arts scene in Shanghai is not as vibrant as in Beijing, despite having the glamorous grand-scale venues such as the Grand Theater standing proud in People's Square and the cutting-edge Oriental Arts Center in Pudong. Commercial spectacles such as the latest Broadway musical to visit town are hugely popular and make the most money, squeezing out the more experimental works, which tend to be in Chinese only and therefore inaccessible to the average Western tourist. Huge spectacles such as Circus World and the Shanghai Center Acrobats are deservedly popular and should be seen once—that tends to be enough for most. Hotels and even the cheapest hostels are usually good for arranging tickets, but if you want to do it yourself the Shanghai Cultural Information and Booking Center has an excellent English-language website (www.culture.sh.cn). As for cinemas, it's nearly impossible for them to compete when pirated DVDs will literally be sold on the streets outside for a fraction of the price of a ticket. Another problem for a foreign movie fan is that the government heavily restricts the numbers of foreign films that can be shown, and most Chinese films shown at the cinema will not have subtitles. If you want the experience, though, of a Chinese cinema, head to the UME in Xintiandi and be prepared for incessant phone calls and talking during the film.

Shanghai is making itself felt in the world art market, and the city is seeking to rival both Beijing and Hong Kong as the place to go for contemporary art. In addition to the galleries dotted around the city, the designated art

HIGHLIGHTS

LOOK FOR ☾ TO FIND RECOMMENDED ARTS AND ACTIVITIES.

☾ **Best Night at the Theater:** Its central location, interesting architecture, and awesome acoustics make **Shanghai Grand Theater** the city's best venue for performing arts (page 206).

☾ **Best Place to Keep the Kids Happy:** **Shanghai Circus World**'s show is like a Chinese version of Cirque du Soleil: Kids or the kid in you will love the clowns, spills, and thrills (page 207).

☾ **Best Escape from Shanghai's Smog:** The quiet forested expanses of **Gongqing Forest Park** is only 30 minutes from downtown skyscrapers but feels a world away (page 213).

☾ **Best Place to Rent a Mountain Bike:** **Bodhisattva Mountain Bikes** offers sturdy bikes and helmets to help you survive the urban jungle (page 214).

☾ **Best Place to Mix with the Crowds:** Exercise can be more about seeing and being seen than sweating, except for at the city's biggest public park, **Huangxing Sports Park** (page 217).

☾ **Best Place to Mix with Shanghai's Monied Elite:** Pilates is the in exercise, and the machines at **Synapse Studio** are usually full of Lycra-clad ladies who lunch (page 217).

☾ **How to Combine Keeping Fit with Culture:** The professional tour guides at **Walk Shanghai** will lead you around the most picturesque parts of the city on foot (page 218).

© HELENA IVESON

Shanghai Grand Theater, in People's Square

district at 50 Moganshan Lu is a must-visit for art fans. Most buyers are Western, which explains why the art, which was once in RMB, is now priced in U.S. dollars.

Some things remain a bargain, though, whether it's a free stroll through Fuxing Park to soak up the latest atmosphere or joining a walking tour and listening to an expert talk you through the history of the Bund. This might be the most exercise you get in Shanghai as gyms and exercise facilities, unless you are staying in a good hotel that includes them, can be prohibitively expensive and just not up to the standards you'd enjoy back home. Options are increasing, though, and you'll always be able to find the trendiest and most exclusive of sports, such as Pilates, yoga, and golf, as long as you are prepared to spend a small fortune (in Chinese eyes) on it.

The Arts

THEATER

LYCEUM THEATER

57 Maoming Nanlu, near Changle Lu, 6217 8530

Map 12

This art deco–era theater sitting on a prime corner of French Concession real estate across from the Okura Garden Hotel dates from the 1930s and is one of the oldest in Shanghai still used for its original purpose. It's a small, intimate space and was recently renovated, but although acoustics and seating have been much improved, the original fixtures and fittings didn't survive the refurbishment. Nowadays a vast variety of acts perform here, including Shanghai's international festival chorus, Chinese opera performances, and shows for children. The box office is 50 meters down the street, or book online at Shanghai's cultural center's website, www.culture.sh.cn.

MAJESTIC THEATER

66 Jiangning Lu, 6258 6493

Map 11

This is another art deco theater, but this time behind the ritzy shopping malls of Nanjing Xilu, and unfortunately, only the outside of the building harks from the 1930s. The stark white reception area has been stripped of its features, and the rest of the theater may look more attractive, but an unfriendly security guard wouldn't let us see. The theater mainly shows Chinese-language productions, but occasionally there is an opera show with English subtitles: Phone the box office and check.

SHANGHAI DRAMATIC ARTS CENTRE

288 Anfu Lu near Wukang Lu, 6433 4546, www.china-drama.com

Map 12

With three intimate stages and two rehearsal rooms, this modern and striking arts center presents an award-winning lineup of both local and international companies, including the Royal Shakespeare Company. Despite being a state-owned institution, it regularly has boundary-pushing performances that examine controversial social issues. If you're in the mood for a glass of wine after your dose of culture, walk along this cute street to Enoteca.

SHANGHAI GRAND THEATER

300 Renmin Dadao, 6327 3094 and 6386 8686, www.shgtheatre.com

Map 10

Shanghai's premier venue for opera, musicals, drama, and ballet is in itself a symbol of the city's resurgent arts scene. Its eye-catching design is the work of French architect Jean-Marie Charpentier, and while during the day the modernist design can look a little harsh, at night, thanks to superb lighting, the curved roof looks its best. On any given day, performances in one of the three theaters under its roof can vary from huge productions of Broadway musicals such as *Cats* and *Les Miserables* to traveling orchestras from all over the world. Even if you're not intending to see a performance, do visit the huge soaring foyer, which is very attractive, and tours are available daily 8:30–11 A.M., 1–4 P.M.; and if you need reviving, there's a branch of Coffee Beanery Café on the ground floor.

SYMPHONY

SHANGHAI CONCERT HALL

523 Yan'an Donglu, People's Square, 6386 2836, www.shanghaiconcerthall.org

Map 10

The hall, just south of People's Square, was originally in another location two blocks away, but in 2004, the city council moved it—all 5,650 tons—and placed in a quieter location in the middle of a park. The renowned Shanghai Symphony Orchestra calls the place home, and a regular procession of world-famous musicians takes to the hall's grand stage: Check the hall's English-language website for its current program of events and you can also order tickets online.

SHANGHAI CONSERVATORY OF MUSIC

20 Fenyang Lu, 6431 8756

Map 12

A 2003 renovation made this 780-seat hall a top venue for classical acoustic performances. It hosts visiting Asian and Western musicians and acts as a showcase for the talented students of the conservatory—which includes a music research institute, an elementary school, a middle school, and a music instruments workshop. Performances are held at 7:15 P.M., and the ticket office is to the north of the actual conservatory.

SHANGHAI ORIENTAL ARTS CENTER

425 Dingxiang Lu near Yingchun Lu, 6854 1234

Map 14

This 40,000-square-meter butterfly-shaped feat of architectural artistry opened in 2005 at a cost of more than 1 billion RMB, is among China's most important performance venues, and is one of the main reasons for visiting Pudong. The government built the center in an attempt to develop Pudong culturally alongside the amazing economic development, and it has been very successful: The Kremlin Ballet and Yo-Yo Ma performed in the 2007–2008 season. The five petals are actually five halls: the entrance hall, a state-of-the-art concert hall, the Oriental Performance Hall, the Oriental Opera Hall, and an exhibition hall. At night, the ceiling changes its sparkling colors according to the melodic tunes played inside.

ACROBATICS AND DANCE

SHANGHAI CENTER THEATER

Shanghai Center, 1376 Nanjing Xilu near Xikang Lu, 6279 8948

Map 11

The huge Shanghai Center, which includes the Portman Ritz-Carlton and a host of shops, offices, and purpose-built theater, was finished in 1990 and was Shanghai's first major building to be erected since 1949. The theater is the home of the Shanghai Acrobatic Troupe, which has toured all over the world, and no matter how cheesy the show can be, the plate-spinning, balancing acts, and general bendiness of the young performers is a must-see, especially as it's only an hour long. The show is on every night of the week at 7:30, unless another troupe is in town, and tickets cost 100–200RMB.

SHANGHAI CIRCUS WORLD

2266 Gonghe Xin Lu near Guangzhong Lu, 6652 5468, www.circus-world.com

Map 15

Despite being far north of the center of the city and a 20-minute taxi ride from Shanghai Railway Station, Circus World stills draws

STAGE FIGHT

Just as in so many other areas, there's a huge rivalry between Shanghai and Beijing – just where will Christina Aguilera and other international acts choose to play when they grace China with their presence? In what was a body blow for the capital, Xtina went south. Indeed, 2007 and the beginning of 2008 were bad times for Beijing fans of foreign bands, as Avril Lavigne, Beyoncé, Björk, Maroon 5, and Linkin Park all gave the capital a wide berth while lighting up the Shanghai stages. All Beijing could console itself with was that the reigning babe of ballads, Celine Dion herself, chose to appear in Beijing – and then go to Shanghai.

In particular, 2007 was the year when the floodgates really opened in terms of mainstream foreign bands making it on to China's stages. For the most up-to-date information on who's coming to town in both Beijing and Shanghai, check out **Emma Ticketmaster** (www.emma.cn). Here's a list of the most popular venues for big live acts: The 28,000-capacity **Hongkou Stadium** (444 Dongjiangwan Lu) saw Linkin Park, while in 2006 the Rolling Stones performed at the **Shanghai Grand Stage** (1111 Caoxi Bei Lu), which seats 8,500, and **Shanghai Stadium** (666 Tianyaoqiao Lu) is where Celine Dion took to the stage at the beginning of 2007.

tourists for its performances of *Era: Intersection of Time,* a high-adrenaline action-packed show choreographed by a former Cirque du Soleil staffer. The show has both modern and traditional circus elements, and kids will love it. If you don't wish to take a taxi, there's now a subway stop conveniently called Shanghai Circus World on Line 1.

ART GALLERIES

ART+SHANGHAI

Room 101, Building 75, 1295 Fuxing Zhonglu near Xiangyang Nanlu, 6437 3108, www.artplusshanghai.com

HOURS: Tues.-Sun. 1 P.M.-6 P.M.

Map 12

Hidden at the end of a typical Shanghai-style lane on Fuxing Lu, Art+Shanghai is in the heart of the former French Concession. The four partners of Art+Shanghai, three from France and one from Spain, want the gallery to be a pleasant gathering place for collectors and art lovers as well as a bridge between artists and the public. The gallery opened November 2007 with a group show of five very different Chinese artists—Sun Qi, Li Shiguang, Zhang Wei, An Kun, and Wu Jianjun.

ART SCENE CHINA

2/F, Building 4, 50 Moganshan Lu, 6277 4940, www.artscenechina.com

HOURS: Tues.-Sun. 10:30 A.M.-6:30 P.M.

Map 15

This chic, minimalist 1,800-square-meter space showcases some of the most exciting artists from Shanghai and throughout China, and the curators are interested in creating dialogue between Chinese artists and artists worldwide. The warehouse is closed on Mondays, and it also has a smaller gallery set in a 1930s villa in the French Concession (House 8, Lane 37, Fuxing Xilu, 6437 0631).

EASTLINK

5/F, Building 6, 50 Moganshan Lu, 6276 9932, www.eastlinkgallery.cn

HOURS: Tues.-Sun. 11 A.M.-6 P.M.

Map 15

Eastlink has a pioneering reputation in Shanghai thanks to a spectacularly rude exhibition a few years ago, but more recently, the calligraphy and paintings on display at the huge multiroomed white-walled space were more grown-up. Exhibitions change frequently and include painting, sculpture, video, installation, and performance art, and the curator, Li Liang, is happy to talk you through exhibitions if you make an appointment, and the gallery is very foreigner-friendly (nearly 90 percent of its art is bought by foreign collectors). The gallery also contains a branch of Madam Mao's Dowry antique shop.

1918 ART SPACE

78 Changping Lu, near Suzhou Xilu, 5228 6776, www.1918artspace.com

HOURS: Daily 3 P.M.-6 P.M.

Map 11

This, one of Shanghai's most up-and-coming galleries, recently moved, but despite its not-as-central location, collectors still flock to the warehouse-style space to see its exhibitions of Chinese contemporary art. Every year it holds an exhibition of promising young artists, and this is the time to come here to see what you can expect will be making millions in auctions in a few years' time.

SHANGART

Building 16-18, 50 Moganshan Lu, 6359 3923, www.shanghartgallery.com

HOURS: Daily 10 A.M.-6 P.M.

Map 15

This was one of the first galleries to move into the area, and the owner, Swiss-born Lorenz Helbling, is considered something of a power broker in contemporary Chinese art, representing hot young talents such as Yang Zhenzhong, Yang Fudong, and Wang Guangyi. ShangART was the first gallery in China to show at Art Basel, in 2000. The main gallery holds smaller exhibitions, while the larger H-Space in Building 18 focuses on large-scale conceptual art. Brisk business has allowed Helbling to open another gallery at 800, Guoshun Donglu, and a third that opened in Beijing in 2008 (at 261 Caochangdi, 6432 3202, infobj@shangartgallery.com).

SHANGHAI GALLERY OF ART

3/F, Three on the Bund, 3 Zhongshan Dongyilu, 6321 5757, www.shanghaigalleryofart.com

HOURS: Daily 11 A.M.-11 P.M.

Map 9

Set on the third floor of the same beautiful building as über-glam restaurants Jean Georges and Laris, this 1,000-square-meter space caters to the same people who can afford to dine there, but the staff are friendly enough if you just wish to browse the work of the high-profile Chinese artists the gallery specializes in. Even if the contemporary offerings aren't to your taste—the gallery focuses on video and large installations—its views over the Bund might be.

CINEMAS

SHANGHAI FILM ART CENTER

160 Xinzha Lu, 6280 4088

Map 15

This is the official cinema for the Shanghai International Film Festival, and so it is the most arty of all of Shanghai's multiplexes with the most eclectic selection of films available in Shanghai, though as films are so censored, that's not really saying much. Tickets cost 50–80RMB though they are half price during the day. The nearest metro is Zhongshan Park.

STELLAR CINEMA CITY

8F, Super Brand Mall, 168 LujiaZui Xilu, 5047 8022

Map 14

If you're dying for a movie in Pudong, this is your best option. It has plenty of screens, and like UME, is foreigner friendly with one film always having the original English dialogue or subtitles. For night owls, every night after 9 P.M. it offers 50 percent off.

UME INTERNATIONAL COMPLEX

5/F, South Block, Xintiandi, 6373 3333

Map 12

On the fifth floor of the Xintiandi shopping center, the American-style mainstream cinema UME is always packed. It has four screens and always has one film in either the original English or with English subtitles. Cinema-going is an expensive treat considering that DVDs are available for less than one-eighth of the price of a prime-time ticket here, though during the day, prices lower considerably and the crowds are smaller. Tickets are half price on weekends before noon and on Tuesdays before 7 P.M. In addition to traditional American snacks at the refreshments counter, you can also get more local snacks such as green-tea ice cream and fried dumplings.

Festivals and Events

While you might expect the money-conscious and cosmopolitan Shanghainese to spurn traditional Chinese festivals, events like the Qing Ming Festival and the temple fairs are more popular than ever. Of course, modern Shanghai doesn't just look to the past for their festivals and celebrations: Events like the ShContemporary, which brings together the best in contemporary art, and the Shanghai eArts Festival, which celebrates digital art, are as cutting-edge as they come. Of course, art and culture aren't the only ways to spend time in Shanghai, there's plenty of major sporting events to watch—see *Spectator Sports* for more details on watching sportsmen and women do their stuff.

SPRING

LONGHUA TEMPLE FAIR

Longhua Temple, 2853 Longhua Lu near Longhua Park, 6456 6085

Map 15

To see a different side of Shanghai, go to the Longhua Temple Fair, where the crowds of devout Buddhists are something to behold. Every April—the exact date depends on the lunar calendar—the entire temple area is packed with stalls selling snacks and crafts, while local groups perform opera and give musical shows. The Buddhist temple fair dates from the Ming dynasty and is the largest of its kind in Shanghai. The temple is elaborately decorated for the occasion, and it is said that dragons visit the temple to grant people's wishes.

QING MING FESTIVAL

During the grave-sweeping festival, Shanghai radio stations have special traffic broadcasts because of the numbers of people heading to the cemeteries of their loved ones to give the graves a good spring cleaning. While it has the potential for misery, it's generally treated as a fun family day out. Some more-traditional families take miniature paper versions of cars, money, and more modern must-haves such as laptops and leave them on the graves to keep their loved ones amused in the afterlife.

SUMMER

DRAGON BOAT FESTIVAL

Taoranting Park, 19 Taiping Jie, 6351 1596

Map 9

Another traditional holiday based on the lunar calendar, the Dragon Boat Festival falls on the fifth day of the fifth lunar month, in May or June. The day commemorates a poet called Qu Yuan who in 278 B.C. drowned himself in protest of the amount of corruption in the imperial court. You can watch dragon-boat races on the Huangpu River. As always with Chinese festivals, there is a traditional snack to eat on the day: This time try *zongzi,* which is triangles of glutinous rice stuffed with meat or dried fruit and steamed in bamboo leaves.

ROCK IT! SUMMER MUSIC CONFERENCE

Dino Beach, 78 Xinzhen Lu, Qibao town, Minhang district, www.urbanon.com

Map 15

The Rock It Dino Beach Rock Festival takes place June 29–July 1 at Dino Beach and caters to the type of music fan who has no interest in the types of acts at the Shanghai International Music Festival—expect punk rock and pop to dominate. In 2007, 36 bands participated in the three-day Rock It! festival and you can buy one-day tickets or a pass for the whole festival.

SHANGHAI INTERNATIONAL FILM FESTIVAL

Various venues, www.siff.com

Map 15

The festival takes place over one week in June, and while Chinese films dominate, there are usually a few foreign entrants, too. The festival started in 1993 and is probably the highlight of the year for local movie fans, as for once the films shown during the festival are uncut—fabulous news as Chinese censors are notorious for their zealousness. The opening and closing galas are usually held at the Shanghai Film Art Center—look out for the stars that will grace the red carpet.

SHANGHAI INTERNATIONAL MUSIC FESTIVAL

Various venues, 6386 8686

Map 10

World-renowned international acts such as the Berlin Philharmonic show up at this annual festival held in May, which showcases a broad variety of different types of music. The first festival was held in the 1960s, though it probably didn't have the kind of pop and world music acts that it now has, alongside more classical fare. The flagship events are held at the Shanghai Grand Theater, but there is plenty going on at other venues during the course of the month: Check the cultural center website for details at www.culture.sh.cn.

FALL

INTERNATIONAL ART, ANTIQUES, AND JEWELRY FAIR

Shanghai Exhibition Center, 1000 Yan'an Zhonglu, www.sfjaf.com

Map 11

Like ShContemporary, this fair started in 2007 and hopes to tap into the growing interest in Chinese art, with 60 exhibiters specializing in antiquities and antiques, paintings and drawings, modern and contemporary art, and fine jewelry. In 2008, the event will be from October 12–19 and will cost 100RMB to get in.

MID-AUTUMN FESTIVAL

Expect box after box of sweet heavy cakes if

you're in China for the Mid-Autumn Festival, which is celebrated in the eighth month of the lunar calendar, on the day when the moon is at its brightest. Most foreigners hate the cakes, but at least the fillings have changed from the traditional bean paste, which dates from the 14th century when supposedly plans for the uprising against the Mongols were hidden in cakes: Now you can get them with centers of anything from chocolate to green-tea ice cream.

NATIONAL DAY

The third of the weeklong national holidays celebrates the founding of the People's Republic on October 1, 1949. This is one of China's major public holidays, so expect crowds everywhere, especially in the main tourist areas, which may be unbearable—unlike Chinese New Year, this holiday is one for spending time visiting places and shopping. If you are traveling to Shanghai during this time, be aware that hotel rooms can rocket in price, and midrange and budget accommodations can become very scarce. Rumors were that this holiday would soon be scrapped and instead there would be more single-day holidays throughout the year, but as of now, National Day continues.

SHANGHAI BIENNALE

www.shanghaibiennale.org

Map 10

Coinciding with the Shanghai International Arts Festival, this event features a wide range of international—and Chinese—artists, upwards of 70 in past years. Based at the Shanghai Art Museum and Museum of Contemporary Art, the biennale has been held every other year during November and December since 1996, and the crowds are growing.

SHANGHAI EARTS FESTIVAL

Various venues, www.shearts.org

China's first festival dedicated to digital arts—and the world's largest—is held over five days in November. The city's best venues are put into action, including MoCA, the Oriental Arts Center, and the Science and Technology Museum in Pudong. The festival aims to open up people's minds to new concepts in art and technology, and judging by the crowds at the 2007 festival, the high-tech gadgetry went down a storm in China's most technologically advanced city.

SHCONTEMPORARY

Shanghai Exhibition Center, 1000 Yan'an Zhonglu, call 3307 0050 for information, www.shcontemporary.info

Map 11

This event, which started in 2007, is China's first truly international, modern, and contemporary art fair and is coordinated by Swiss dealer Pierre Huber and former Art Basel head Lorenzo Rudolf. Thanks to the directors' excellent connections, galleries, dealers, artists, collectors, and art enthusiasts from all around the world were present, and the event is set to be an annual celebration of contemporary art.

WINTER

CHINESE NEW YEAR

For the Chinese, this is Christmas, Thanksgiving, and July Fourth rolled into one—and now that the ban has been lifted, expect a noisy 10 days or so of huge fireworks rocketing into the sky. The holiday, which is also known as Spring Festival, starts on the first day of the new moon of the lunar calendar. Everyone in the country is supposed to get a weeklong holiday to be with their families, so with millions of people on the move, trains, buses, and planes are jam-packed. Despite popular opinion, it's a great time to hole up and be in Shanghai: The actual city is much quieter than normal, traffic is a breeze, and all sights are open as normal. If you're lucky enough to score an invitation to a Chinese family's celebration, expect to be fed platefuls of dumplings and other dishes considered lucky, and you might get a *hong bao,* or red envelope with a few 100RMB in it. Besides the big family meals, many Chinese celebrate by taking the family to a temple fair, which will have fairground rides, plenty of food, and the odd dragon-dance parade. Longhua and Jing'an Temples have special ceremonies with chanting monks and festive dances.

LANTERN FESTIVAL

Marking the end of the New Year holiday period is this holiday, which falls on the 15th day of the first lunar month. People traditionally hang red lanterns outside their houses for luck and let off even more fireworks while eating *tang yuan,* or sweet dumplings, by the mouthful. At Yu Yuan, almost every outside surface of this classical garden has a jolly red lantern hanging off it. While it gets very crowded, it's definitely worth visiting for the experience.

SHANGHAI FASHION WEEK

www.shfashionbridge.com

While it may not have the same buzz as London or New York, it's clear by the increasing numbers of designers who choose to exhibit here every year that the industry is fast evolving. The event started in 2001 and hosts both foreign and local-born designers. Wu Xuekai and Marck Cheng are local names to watch, according to people in the know. Unfortunately, the week is somewhat disjointed, with events all over the city and not enough publicity, but see the website for more details of future years' events.

SHANGHAI INTERNATIONAL ARTS FESTIVAL

Various venues, www.culture.sh.cn for tickets

Visitors and locals alike can enjoy a diverse program of events varying from live music and dance to theater and magic acts as part of the annual Shanghai International Arts Festival. It lasts for an entire month, and events, exhibitions, and entertainment take place in a variety of venues and locations, including the Shanghai Museum and Shanghai Art Museum. The 2007 program also featured 18 art exhibitions, including paintings by Rembrandt and artifacts borrowed from Madrid's famous Prado Museum.

SHANGHAI INTERNATIONAL MARATHON

www.shmarathon.com

Despite the dubious air quality, the well-organized Shanghai Marathon attracts runners from across China and the rest the world. Every year around 18,000 participants take part in either the full marathon, half marathon, or the fun run that goes through the center of the city and down the Bund.

Sports and Recreation

Unsurprisingly, given a certain event in August 2008, Beijing is the focus for sports in China. Despite Shanghai's wealth and its glamorous marquee events such as the Tennis Masters Cup and the Formula 1 Grand Prix, what city can compete with the world's biggest sporting event? Does the city's lively capitalist character mean that locals would prefer a new shopping center to a stadium and parks? Well, they just take up too much land. Perhaps that's slightly unfair as the government is setting aside areas such as Century Park in Pudong, but there is not the same kind of obsession with green spaces that Beijing is going through and parks can be on the sterile side.

The most popular sports in Shanghai are of the more body-conscious and trendy variety: gym going, yoga, and golf. Expect high costs for these types of activities, and you'll be mixing with the movers and shakers of Shanghai so wear your best and most body-conscious outfit if you want to fit right in.

Don't despair, though: If Formula 1 racing or world-class tennis tournaments are energetic enough for you, you'll enjoy these spectacles in Shanghai. If it's your heart you want to get racing, head to one of the city's public parks, where you'll find tennis and football courts as well as tai chi enthusiasts. Most sports from back home are on offer, whether it's the local Hash House Harriers running through the city or homesick baseball fans getting together to talk about the home runs they hit 30 years ago. For the most up-to-date listings, check out the sports pages of magazines *City Weekend* or *That's Shanghai.* And don't miss the chance to combine a bit of exercise with a slice of culture with one of the many walking tours available.

PARKS

CENTURY PARK

1001 Jinxiu Lu

HOURS: Daily 7 A.M.-6 P.M.

COST: 10RMB

Map 14

If it's clean air you are seeking, Shanghai's largest park offers (relatively) fresh air and plenty of green space for kids to play in—the downside is that it's a pretty sterile place, having been in existence for only a few years, and the park is far from the main tourist parts of the city, though it's simple enough to get to using the subway as the park has its own subway stop (Century Park). Inside you'll find a large lake where you can rent electric boats, or, if you're feeling more energetic, rowing boats. There's also a separate children's play area with slides, swings, and climbing walls; it costs an extra 5RMB. My favorite activity is to rent a bike (there are tandems too for up to four people) and cycle round the park to check out the kite fliers and couples in full wedding regalia who flood the park in summer for their wedding photos.

FUXING PARK

2 Gaolan Lu, 6372 6083

HOURS: Daily 6 A.M.-6 P.M.

COST: Free

Map 12

If you need a brush with nature while still being in the center of the city, Fuxing Park's many trees, flowers, and grassy areas is the place to head. Like most parks in China, the green spaces mean all things to all people, but nowhere more so than in Fuxing Park. In the very early morning, tai chi enthusiasts and agile elderly folk use the parks as their exercise spaces, not long after the crowds of young partygoers have vacated the area after hanging out at one of the many clubs and lounges in the park. The children's play area was undergoing a much-needed revamp, so hopefully the slides, swings, and amusement rides will be more suitable for this century than for the last. The tree-lined walkways and nicely manicured lawns make the park a good place for a stroll—unfortunately and as always, you have to stay off the grass if you don't want to be shouted at. (See the *Sights* chapter for more on the park's history.)

GONGQING FOREST PARK

2000 Jungong Lu, 6532 8194, www.shgqsl.com

HOURS: Daily 6 A.M.-5 P.M.

COST: 7RMB

Map 15

When the urban jungle starts to get you down, this huge expanse of green spaces and forests is the place to go, though even here, supposedly soothing music is played on hidden speakers dotted around the park. In addition to grass you can for once walk on, there are plenty of trees and plants to look at, a lake to walk along, and kids will like the horse riding and rock-climbing wall even if the roller coasters and merry-go-rounds are on the tame side. There

© HELENA IVESON

Shanghai's green lungs: Fuxing Park

© HELENA IVESON

shooting the breeze in People's Park

are barbecue pits if you want to bring your own food, which is a good idea as the snack stalls won't dazzle you with their variety. You can rent bikes and boats or if that's too energetic, a shuttle bus will whiz you around the park.

JING'AN PARK

1649 Nanjing Xilu opposite Jing'an Temple

HOURS: Daily 6 A.M.–10 P.M.

COST: Free

Map 11

This attractive expanse of greenery smack bang in the middle of Shanghai's central business district used to be the Bubbling Well Cemetery in the time of Foreign Concessions. Now the pathways are often busy with elderly people doing their morning exercises or fan dances, and in the evening, people gather to sing patriotic opera songs in the pagodas. If hunger pains strike, ignore the amphitheater-like mall at the north end with its cheap shops and snack bars and head to Bali Laguna, which is set by the pretty pond filled with lilies at the southern end of the park. In that area, look out for the men practicing water calligraphy. They practice brushstrokes on the concrete using giant brushes dipped in water. There is not as much for children at this park as there is at others, but a small gated area does have a few rusty swings and slides.

PEOPLE'S PARK

231 Nanjing Xilu, 6372 0626

HOURS: Daily 6 A.M.–6 P.M.

COST: 2RMB

Map 10

Here you'll find plenty of green leafy areas on either side of the mammoth Renmin Dadao that runs through the middle of the park. While the area doesn't have the beauty or tranquility of, say, Central Park or even Ritan Park in Beijing, it's a fun place to watch the Shanghainese at what counts for resting here.

BIKE RENTAL

Unlike the flat expanses of prime concreted road in Beijing, Shanghai's winding and narrow streets and modern flyovers don't exactly lend themselves to cycling. People do, but not nearly in the numbers of Beijingers who take to two wheels. Shanghai is too cut-and-thrust to see people idly cycle—instead they pile onto buses, catch cabs, or drive themselves. It was taken by newspapers as a real sign of the times when the government announced that many roads were going to be closed to cyclists—it couldn't be made clearer that cars were the kings of the road. Not that cyclists are particularly disciplined in Shanghai: If roads are closed to them, people just cycle on the sidewalks instead. If your Chinese experience won't be complete without time on a bike, stick to the French Concession and wear a helmet!

BODHISATTVA MOUNTAIN BIKES

Suite 2308, Building 2, 2918 Zhongshan Beilu, 5266 9013, www.bohdi.com.cn

HOURS: Daily 9 A.M.–7 P.M.

Map 15

Bodhi is a good local professionally run outfit that will bring rental bikes and locks (plus helmets if you pay a nominal extra charge) to your hotel. You can rent by the day (starting from 100RMB a day for a basic model) or longer and unlike most rental places, it offers a wide choice of bikes from standard road runners to tougher mountain bikes. Staff can also provide you with the safest routes through the city and advice on day trips out of the urban jungle.

CYCLE CHINA

1/F, Block 25, Number 1984 Nanjing Xilu, Jing'an, 6248 2146, www.cyclechina.com

HOURS: Daily 9:30 A.M.-6:30 P.M.

Map 11

The Beijing tour company has branched out to Shanghai and offers the same services down south as it does in the north: bike rental and bike tours. Of its Shanghai city options, people really enjoy the half-day Nongtang tour, which takes you through some of the best-preserved tree-lined streets in the city—this costs around 250RMB per person. It also offers worthwhile one-day and two-day tours to local water towns such as Xitang (see *Beyond Shanghai* chapter).

GYMS

ALEXANDER CITY CLUB

Number 6-7, Xintiandi, Lane 123, Xingye Lu near Madang Lu, 5358 1188

HOURS: Daily 6 A.M.-12 A.M.

Map 12

On the third floor of the Xintiandi shopping center is one of Shanghai's best-equipped health clubs—a huge room full of running machines and every other type of equipment with private TVs attached, a sparkling swimming pool, and two rooms for exercise classes. A year-long membership is 5,400RMB, but if you "try out" the club for a day you pay 100RMB.

FITNESS FIRST AT PLAZA 66

B1, Plaza 66, 1266 Nanjing Xilu near Tongren Lu, 6288 0152

HOURS: Daily 7 A.M.-11 P.M.

Map 11

Apparently the world's largest chain, Fitness First's only branch in Shanghai is of international standard with plenty of English speakers on the staff, including some of the muscle-bound personal trainers. In addition to an equipment-packed main room, there is a class area with different options varying from Pilates to boxercise on offer every hour and a spinning room. Afterward, members hang out at the coffee area, or there's a new beauty salon to indulge yourself in. The minimum membership is for three months and costs 500–700RMB a month, depending if you want off-peak or a regular membership.

PHYSICAL GYM

Hong Kong Plaza, 289 Huaihai Zhonglu, 6390 8890, ext. 501

HOURS: Mon.-Sat. 6:30 A.M.-11 P.M.; Sun. 7 A.M.-10 P.M.

Map 12

It's just around the corner from Xintiandi, and you won't miss the gym's advertising, with the buffest Chinese man you'll ever see smiling proudly in his Speedos. The gym itself is cheap and cheerful with year memberships usually on special offer for under 2,000RMB, but a day pass is 100RMB, and a month is 500RMB. For that, you have access to the pool and gym though there are no TVs or towels provided, and the music might be a little too pumping for some.

SWIMMING POOLS

Your best bet for swimming in Shanghai is taking advantage of your hotel pool if you're staying somewhere swish (the Hyatt on the Bund's is particularly cool, as is the Westin's) or paying their day rates to use their facilities. If the high prices are preventive, the city runs a few pools to cater to serious and not-so-serious swimmers. While the sight of someone spitting in the water is thankfully increasingly rare, it does still happen.

DINO BEACH WATER PARK

78 Xinzhen Lu, Qibao town near Gudai Lu, 6478 3333

HOURS: Daily 2 P.M.-11 P.M., June-Sept.

COST: 150RMB

Map 15

The world's largest water wave pool (181 feet

wide by 360 feet long for fact fans)—with miles of slides and rivers to raft down and fake beaches—this water park is a surefire way to cool down kids on a humid Shanghai summer day. The staff organize games of volleyball on the sand and everything from the snack food on offer to the number of lifeguards makes this a very child-friendly venue. Shuttle buses leave from Shanghai Stadium and Xinzhuang Metro Stations daily: Call for details.

JING'AN SPORTS CENTER SWIMMING POOL

151 Kangding Lu near Jiangning Lu, 6272 7277

HOURS: Daily 3:30 P.M.-9 P.M.

COST: 30RMB

Map 11

This pool is a good all-rounder for the kids or the kid in you: There's a wave pool with inflatables, and for the more serious swimmer, there are sectioned-off lanes. Like in all public pools in China, you have to wear a swimming cap—if you don't own one, you can buy one there. The pool has very restricted hours: It's open 3:30–9 P.M. only.

SHANGHAI SWIMMING POOL

1300 Zhongshan Nanerlu, near Tianyaoqiao Lu, 6438 2372

COST: 40RMB

Map 15

Not too far from the Bund is the largest of Shanghai's municipal pools: Expect crowds and compulsory swimming caps (pools in China have an obsession with hair clogging the drains). You are out of luck if you want to swim in the morning as the pool opens 7–9 A.M. for early birds and then closes until 1 P.M.

GOLF

China's most yuppified sport is, unsurprisingly, popular and expensive in image-conscious Shanghai. Sports bar and second home to many a Shanghai-based golfer is the Big Bamboo (see the *Nightlife* chapter); for finding out more about the area's courses and driving ranges, its website www.bigbamboo.cn/golf directory/index.php is a great resource, listing more than 25 courses and advertising golf lessons taught by pros who can help you perfect your swing.

SHANGHAI COUNTRY CLUB

961 Ying Zhu Lu, Zhu Jia Jiao, Qingpu district, 5972 8111, www.shanghaicountryclub.com

Map 15

You would be forgiven for thinking you had been magically transported to England when you arrive at this beautifully manicured 18-hole par-72 course with its Victorian-style clubhouse, but facilities are ultramodern with a fully equipped gym and a course considered the most challenging in the area. The club is a 30-minute drive from downtown Shanghai and it provides round-trip transportation if you phone and make reservations. Nonmembers playing on weekends won't get much change from 1,000RMB, but fees are a little cheaper during the week.

SHANGHAI EAST ASIA GOLF CLUB

135 Jianguo Xilu, 6433 1198

Map 12

Don't be fooled by its name: This is not a golf club but an affordable driving range where you can practice on the cheap without leaving the city center. A bucket of balls costs 100RMB and it has a double-deck practice course with 46 brightly lit practice lanes. Peak hours are after work when office workers blow off steam by whacking some balls.

TOMSON GOLF COURSE

1 Longdong Lu, 5833 8888, www.tomson-golf.com

Map 15

The best aspect of this course is its location in Pudong—no long journeys are necessary to get to the championship-level 18-hole par-72 course which cost $100 million to build. But what you save in taxi costs, you'll lose in course fees as it can be very expensive for nonmembers to play a round on weekends, with prices reaching 1,500RMB. But you would be playing with the movers and shakers of the city on a course that held the Asian Open in 2007.

TENNIS

HUANGXING SPORTS PARK

Intersection of Guoshun Donglu and Shuangyang Lu, 6538 2240

HOURS: Daily 7 A.M.-10 P.M.

Map 15

Shanghai's largest public park opened in January 2008 and has the cheapest courts in town—the top-quality hard courts are just 20RMB an hour, a wonderful change from snooty club fees commonplace everywhere else. In addition to tennis courts, there are basketball, soccer, and even a baseball court. The park has even employed 20 professional coaches to help you perfect your strokes.

SHANGHAI INTERNATIONAL TENNIS CENTER

516 Hengshan Lu, 6415 5588

HOURS: Daily 6:30 A.M.-11:30 P.M.

Map 12

The Tennis Center is part of the Regal International East Asia Hotel and has the best tennis facilities in Shanghai with four indoor courts (300RMB per hour) and seven outdoor (150RMB an hour). It's all very snooty and membership is frighteningly expensive but the facilities, which include a huge pool and gym, are top class. Make reservations and be warned that members often book the courts out weeks in advance.

YOGA AND PILATES

KARMA YOGA

3-4F, Number 172, Pucheng Lu, 5887 3122, www.karmayoga.com.cn

Map 14

Karma Yoga Center in Pudong is a bit more spiritual than the other places offering yoga in Shanghai, so it's a good choice if you want your karma worked on as much as your waist size. Teachers speak both English and Chinese and offer a variety of styles, including hatha, and go out of their way to make beginners feel at home. You can become a member or pay as you go.

SYNAPSE STUDIO

Apartment 1403, Building B, Tomson Center, 188 Zhangyang Lu, 5876 3307, www.synapsestudio.com.cn

Map 14

For stretching without the spirituality, head to Pudong to the only dedicated Pilates studio in Shanghai. The calm and airy studio is small but packed with equipment that the owners imported from the United States, and they also offer mat work classes. Group classes (fewer than five people per class) are 160RMB while private classes are 500RMB.

Y PLUS YOGA CENTER

299-2 Fuxing Xilu near Huashan Lu, 6433 4330, www.yplus.cn

Map 12

Y Plus Yoga is the most established center in Shanghai, offering classes, workshops, and specialty yoga programs. The classes held here are suitable not only for those who possess the experienced yoga-buffed body but also for beginners. You can work through the 26 classic hatha yoga postures in the Hot Yoga series, during which the room is usually maintained at a temperature of 95–100°F—don't do this if you're prone to fainting. The pre- and postnatal classes are very popular, too. Membership fees are expensive but of good value considering the number of classes on offer, and it has special offers a couple of times a year.

WALKING TOUR GROUPS

LUXURY CONCIERGE

www.luxuryconciergechina.com

This local company run by two expats with an obsessive interest in architecture offers three private tours that would be fascinating to culture vultures. The Architecture Shanghai tour takes you around the city's art deco delights, the Art Insider tour showcases Moganshan Art District, and the World of Interiors tour is designed to encourage people to look at interiors with a fresh eye. Aimed at the high-end trendy market, the tours do not come cheap, but they are led by experts in their field.

PETER HIBBARD

hibbard@gingergriffin.com

The British historian who has called Shanghai home since 1986 leads fascinating architectural walking tours, offering tours of the old quarters of Shanghai to small groups of visitors. He is also a member of Save Shanghai Heritage, a group of locals and foreigners that aims to promote the understanding and protection of old Shanghai and hosts 12 historic walking trails around the city.

WALK SHANGHAI

5, Lane 690 Yongjia Lu, 6445 5133, www.walkshanghai.com

Australian architect Anne Warr has been a Shanghai resident for more than a decade, and in addition to writing books about Shanghai's changing architectural styles, she also leads tours around the city. Tours focus on architecture, art, Shanghai's history, or can be tailored to any special interest you may have. Anne is also involved with Explore Shanghai Heritage, a volunteer group that aims to promote the understanding, protection, and care of Shanghai's heritage to all its residents and visitors. The group is producing walking-tour brochures of each of Shanghai's 12 Conservation Areas; the first brochure on the Jewish Ghetto area was published in 2006 and the second brochure on Suzhou Creek published in 2007. To order, check the website.

SPECTATOR SPORTS

FORMULA 1

Shanghai International Circuit, Anting, Jiading, 9682 6999, www.icsh.sh.cn

Map 15

China fought hard to become part of the Formula 1 circuit, and the track 40 minutes out of the city is certainly eye-catching as it is shaped like the Chinese character *shang* 上, the first part of the city's name. Tickets are much cheaper than for other stops on the circuit—they start from 150RMB—and the high-profile sporting event has become a vital part of the Shanghai social calendar, in the fall.

HSBC CHAMPIONS GOLF TOURNAMENT

Sheshan Golf Club, Lane 288, Lin Yin Xin Dadao, call 962288 for tickets

In November 2007, Phil Mickelson won the tournament at Sheshan Golf Club, which is about an hour away from the city center. It was the third year that the $5 million tournament described as Asia's Major took place at Sheshan, and it drew more top 20 players than ever before. In the early

SHANGHAI'S BIG MAN: YAO MING

It was always likely that Houston Rockets center Yao Ming was going to be tall and going to be a basketball player – his parents both played for China's national basketball teams; his mother, Fang Feng Di, is six foot, three inches tall and his father, Yao Zhi Yuan, is six foot, seven inches. But few would have predicted the amount of hero worship the seven-foot, five-inch Yao would inspire from the Chinese, who consider Shanghai's most famous son a legend who has beaten the Americans at their own game.

When Chairman Yao/the Ming dynasty/the Great Wall of Yao – whatever you want to call him – was 10 years old, doctors predicted he would grow to be taller than seven foot. He started on his local Shanghai Sharks team and in 2002 became the first foreigner to be NBA's number one draft pick – and the tallest player in the NBA.

The six-time NBA All-Star has sponsorship deals with several corporations, including Gatorade, Pepsi, Reebok, and McDonald's, but he doesn't get to keep all the $25-30 million he is estimated to earn each year because like all young people who rise through the intense Chinese sports-coaching system, a percentage of his earnings goes to the Chinese government. Unlike his wilder colleagues, Yao isn't exactly known for fast living and tattoos – before his marriage to his childhood sweetheart and fellow national basketball player, Ye Li, he lived in Houston with his parents.

days of the tournament, tickets are 300RMB and rise sharply as the event progresses.

MOTO GP

Shanghai International Circuit, Anting, Jiading, 9682 6999, www.icsh.sh.cn

The flagship MotoGP of China is held at the ultramodern Shanghai International Circuit, which was bankrolled by the government to the tune of $325 million and also holds the Formula 1 Grand Prix. Tickets to all three days cost around $200, and the action kicks off in May.

TENNIS MASTERS CUP

Qi Zhong Stadium, www.masters-cup.com

Every year, the Tennis Masters Cup brings together the eight best male players of the season for a final showdown at the futuristic Qi Zhong stadium in the southwest of the city. Roger Federer won in 2007 at the 15,000-seat Centre Court Stadium, which features a retractable roof in the shape of a magnolia. There are also 16 outdoor courts. The 2008 Cup was to be held November 9–16: For tickets book online at www.piao.com.cn.

MASSAGE

DRAGONFLY

84 Nanchang Lu, 5386 0060, www.dragonfly.net.cn

HOURS: Daily 10 A.M.-2 A.M.

Map 12

Everyone loves Dragonfly, as it stylishly fills the gap between ultrabasic massage available on any street and the expensive hotel spas: A standard Chinese-style full-body massage is 179RMB. As you lie prostrate in a reclining chair, silently professional masseuses will knead away jet lag and general aches and pains, and the darkened rooms and quiet atmosphere (TV is forbidden), wafting of incense, and semilit Chinese lanterns add to the tranquil atmosphere. Bear in mind, though, that the individual massage rooms are tiny and not for the claustrophobic. In addition to basic Chinese massages, it offers packages such as Double Trouble (two therapists at once) and a whole slew of facials, nail treatments, and waxing. Perhaps get your legs waxed and then go for a soothing massage. There are 11 branches all over the city, including in Jingan, Donghu Lu, Xinle Lu, and Dagu Lu: Check the website for details.

GANZHI BLINDMAN'S MASSAGE

1065 Beijing Xilu, near Jiangning Lu, 5228 7621

HOURS: Daily 10 A.M.-1 A.M.

Map 11

If all you want is a good pummeling without the fancy atmosphere and chirping-birds CD on the stereo, this massage parlor in the basement of an apartment block is a great choice. For 48RMB, you can choose from a one-hour body or foot massage that will be carried out by one of the professional blind masseuses. Rooms are spartan but clean, and you don't have to remove any clothes before being stretched and pressed. No one speaks English, but there is a bilingual price list.

GREEN MASSAGE

58 Taicang Lu near Jinan Lu, 5386 0222, www.greenmassage.com.cn

HOURS: Daily 10 A.M.-11:30 P.M.

Map 12

If Jade Massage is full, which often happens because it's so tiny, try this place on the northern side of Xintiandi. It offers the same kind of service: traditional Chinese massage for reasonable prices, but it's not as stylish as Jade and slightly more expensive. A suspicious amount of demolition is going on in the area, so it's best to call ahead to make sure Green Massage is still there.

JADE MASSAGE

367 Zizhong Lu near Madang Lu, 6384 8762, www.jademassage.com.cn

HOURS: Daily 12:30 P.M.-midnight

Map 12

The lights are turned down low at this stylish venue that offers traditional Chinese massage, so be careful you don't tumble down the steep stairs in your postmassage blissed-out state. Jade is very popular because of its nearness to Xintiandi, low prices, and stylishness. The small but perfectly formed harem-style retreat is decorated with floaty chiffon curtains, stone artifacts, and dark wooden furniture. The friendly

COURTESY OF HYATT ON THE BUND

Lay back and relax at Yuan Spa.

English-speaking reception staff will talk you through the options, but the simplest option, the hour-long Chinese massage, is 100RMB.

YOU'S ACUPUNCTURE

1711 Xinzha Lu near Jiaozhou Lu, 5203 1353

HOURS: Daily 9 A.M.–5 P.M.

Map 11

If you can't shake a bad back, or more controversially, want to lose weight, try what many Shanghainese do and undergo a course of acupuncture. For totally English-speaking service, you should head to the Worldlink medical center in the Shanghai Center, but brave souls who have limited funds could try this place, where Dr. You runs the show. He doesn't speak good English, but all you have to do is say what your problem is, lie back, and leave him to it, sticking needles into particular pressure points. One visit is 200RMB.

YUAN SPA

199 Huangpu Lu, 6393 1234, shanghai.bund.hyatt.com

HOURS: Daily 10 A.M.–10:30 P.M.

Map 9

The Hyatt on the Bund's flagship spa and health center takes up a whole floor of the hotel, and the healthy café and juice bar makes it very easy to spend the whole day there—if you have the money, that is. Unlike the Bali-style ambience that many spas go in for, its treatment rooms are bright and practical with each room having its own rainfall shower and bathroom. Each treatment starts with a fabulous short foot massage, and the bliss continues if you then choose the signature Yuan infusion body massage. Prices are high, but included in the price is access to the rest of the health club, including the well-equipped gym and 25m swimming pool.

RIVER CRUISES

HUANGPU RIVER CRUISE

219-239 Zhongshan Dongerlu, 6374 4461

Map 9

The Huangpu River is Shanghai's lifeblood: Without it the city would never have experienced the prosperity it has enjoyed for centuries. The city is still China's largest port, and when the new international ferry terminal is completed in late 2008, there will be even more traffic on the already heavily trafficked waterways. Boats also go past the future site of the 2010 World Expo. If you'd like to join them—and bear in mind the cruises get mixed reports—there are nearly 20 different companies offering different types of cruises. The most reliable is the Huangpu River Cruise company, which offers a one-hour cruise south to the Yuangpu Bridge or a 3.5-hour journey all the way to the Yangtze River. As the sights soon thin out the farther you get out of the city, most people prefer the shorter trip unless the sight of cranes unloading huge shipments is appealing to you. Tickets cost 35RMB for the hour-long trip or 45–100RMB for the longer journey. Exact departure times vary by the season though there are usually departures at least once in the morning, afternoons, and evening: Call for details or head to Jingling pier, which is where the boats depart, and check the notice board there.

SHOPS

Shopping is Shanghai's favorite pastime bar none. Well, maybe eating, but aside from that, nothing comes close. From up-and-coming Chinese clothing brands at bargain basement prices to "antiques" at Dongtai Lu Antique Market, Shanghai has it covered. Boutiques line every street in the French Concession, a procession of flashy expensive malls dominate Nanjing Xilu and Huaihai Lu, while the pedestrian-friendly Nanjing Donglu near the Bund is mainly of interest to Chinese tourists because of the street's historic reputation as a shopping heaven when the rest of the country had next to nothing. Nowadays, the best shops are elsewhere, but it's still worth a stroll to look at the neon. Up until recently there had been next to no shops on the Bund since the area's heyday in the 1930s, but in the past few years, boutiques have moved in, set up shop, and their tills are ringing. Small ultraglamorous malls such as Bund 18 and Three on the Bund are tourist attractions in themselves thanks to their stunning and sympathetically restored architecture. Oh, and their stylish boutiques are worth a look too.

As is soon made obvious by a stroll through the city, fashion is hugely important to Shanghai's trend-crazed residents, with no less than Giorgio Armani proclaiming Shanghai to be the most exciting city in the world. While most Shanghainese like shopping in malls, the tiny stores in the French Concession are the most rewarding. Xinle Lu is worth exploring for small clothing boutiques, as this is where you can see the cutting edge of independent Chinese fashion design: a fascinating glimpse, even if the

HIGHLIGHTS

LOOK FOR [icon] TO FIND RECOMMENDED SHOPS.

Best Shanghai Style: China's most fashionable city has boutiques on every corner, but the tiny **Roof 603 at Leaf** stands out thanks to its stylish women's clothes that hark from the 1930s (page 225).

Best Place for Funky Fashion: The home-grown brand **Shirt Flag** offers cool T-shirts and clothes in unique designs (page 225).

Most Charming Souvenirs: For dinky slippers, shoes, and bags made from traditional Chinese silk head to **Suzhou Cobblers** (page 226).

Most Stylish Packaging: Song Fang Maison de Thé's eye-catching boxes for its vast collection of Chinese teas makes the tea a thing of beauty (page 229).

Best Place for Rummaging: Despite what the stall owners say, next to nothing at **Dongtai Lu Antique Market** is older than you are, but no matter – it's a great place to bargain for a brilliant souvenir (page 231).

Most Distinctive Material: Head to **Brocade Country** for its stunning and brightly colored collections from a Miao ethnic minority village in Guizhou Province (page 234).

Biggest DVD and CD Collections: The shelves at **Even Better Than Movieworld** are full of the latest Hollywood hits (page 236).

Best Place for a Credit Card Blowout: Few shopping malls are as stunning or exclusive as **Bund 18,** and few are as expensive (page 238).

Everything is beautiful at the art deco-era Bund 18.

off-the-rack sizes are often a bit on the small side for overseas visitors. Nearby, Taikang Lu started life as a run-down artists' enclave that took over a derelict candy factory, but now it rates as one of the city's most interesting shopping destinations with a cool collection of tiny boutiques, laid-back cafés, and the odd art gallery lining the tangle of narrow back lanes. The enormously popular Xintiandi is a must-visit for both clothes and home wares . . . the list is nearly endless. No matter what street you go down, there will be something interesting to buy: The only worry is getting it all in your suitcase when you leave. Some tourists still head to Xiangyang Market hoping to find its blend of cheap bags, watches, and clothes, but all they find is a huge hole in the ground as the market has been demolished. Those stall holders have spread to different venues across the city, though some touts have forlornly stayed around the construction site, hoping to stumble across the odd tourist. As always when it comes to fakes, the best advice is buyer beware and bargain hard.

While shopping in Shanghai is a veritable land of opportunity, there are some caveats. Expensive designer labels are actually more expensive here than back home because of high import taxes. Some shoppers find assistants too overwhelming in their attention, clinging onto them when shoppers just want to browse and instead receive what are meant to be helpful suggestions. Shop assistants work on commission, hence the pushiness. As anyone who has been in a Chinese market knows, the constant calling out to attract people's attention and the limpetlike grip can be very irritating. The only thing to do is to do what Chinese people do and ignore it: It may be rude, but when in Rome. . . . On the plus side, clothes, shoes, and bags are cheap, although thanks to the plunging dollar, they're nowhere near the bargains they used to be. But if you look hard, you're sure to find that perfect souvenir or present.

Now, just like in the past, some Chinese come to Shanghai just to shop, and once you see the scale of purchases on offer, you can understand why. As you walk the streets armed with bags, you can practically hear the crackle of 21st-century Chinese consumerism in action.

Clothes and Shoes

H&M

645-659 Huaihai Zhonglu, near Sinan Lu, 5383 8866

HOURS: Daily 10 A.M.-10 P.M.

Map 12

When the Scandinavian cut-price fashion chain opened its first branch in China in Shanghai, thousands of people turned out to see what all the fuss was about. Its four floors haven't quieted down since then, as the cheerful and fashionable clothes are so reasonably priced, it's often cheaper to buy here than at a market. Of course the quality isn't always brilliant, but for basics and accessories as well as the celebrity-designed lines from people like Madonna, H&M can't be beaten. The fact that everything comes in large sizes is also a plus point.

INSH

200 Taikang Lu, 6466 5249, www.insh.com.cn

HOURS: Daily 10 A.M.-9 P.M.

Map 12

Regularly featured in Chinese *Vogue,* insh is a local brand founded by two stylish Shanghainese who trained in Tokyo and specializing in T-shirts, ready-to-wear dresses, and accessories. They aim to make use of Shanghai cultural elements such as local crafts and materials such as silk while innovatively playing with Western and Eastern influences. Even if most of the high fashion fashion isn't to your taste, the I Love Shanghai T-shirts make cute souvenirs. They have five other branches in Shanghai: Check their website for details.

© HELENA IVESON

Taikang Lu in the French Concession is a great place to browse.

MAYUMI SATO

169 Anfu Lu, near Wulumuqi Lu, 5403 3903, www.mayumisato.com

HOURS: Daily 10 A.M.-7 P.M.

Map 12

Despite ongoing antagonism between the Chinese and Japanese, this has not stopped Japanese clothes designers from going down a storm in Shanghai. Miss Sato is Japanese and spent many years in Paris, but she has found her niche in China's most fashion-conscious city, and her boutique is on a great lane lined with similar small-scale shops. She blends a range of fabrics, colors, and styles, with many variations of traditional *qipaos* and kimonos on display at her brightly lit boutique plus a lovely range of scarves, jewelry, and purses. Everything is made from natural materials—wool and mohair, cotton and linen—and this is the new place to go for fashionable feminine wear.

ROOF 603 AT LEAF

347 Zizhong Lu near Madang Lu, 139 0181 3155

HOURS: Daily 10 A.M.-9 P.M.

Map 12

We don't understand the name either, but ignore that and enter this tiny boutique and you'll be rewarded with a mixture of floaty individual vintage and contemporary women's wear. The phonograph plays 1930s-style music and the whole store has a boudoir feel with clothes laid out on an antique art deco bed in the middle. The stylish owner will engage in some friendly bargaining, but prices are very reasonable anyway. The only possible problem is that most of the clothes are from Japan so it's small sizes only. On the same street is one of Shanghai's smartest florists, Secret Garden, and if you need a break from all the shopping, Jade Massage offers excellent foot rubs.

SHANGHAI TANG

59 Maoming Nanlu, 5466 3006, www.shanghaitang.com

HOURS: Daily 10 A.M.-10 P.M.

Map 12

Despite its name, Shanghai Tang actually originated in Hong Kong, but its spiritual home is definitely the Pearl of the Orient, where its flashy bright designs go down a storm. Its kitschy wares, including expensive clothes (which can look a little like fancy dress on foreigners and which proudly say "Made by Chinese") and accessories from umbrellas to cigarette cases, won't be to everyone's taste, but one and all seem to like the ritzy packaging, and the stores are always glamorous with antique furniture and stylish assistants. The company is gunning to be China's foremost luxury brand (despite being owned by a Swiss luxury company!), and with the crowds of well-off locals who fill the stores, it looks as though it is achieving its aim. There are also branches in Xintiandi and the Shangri-La Hotel in Pudong.

SHIRT FLAG

330 Nanchang Lu, between Shanxi Nan Lu and Maoming Lu, 5465 3011, www.shirtflag.com

HOURS: Daily 11 A.M.-10:30 P.M.

Map 12

The goods on offer at this fun boutique were considered cutting-edge a few years ago, but the hand-painted T-shirts and clothes designed by one of the city's best-known graphic

© HELENA IVESON

swanky Shanghai Tang in Xintiandi

artists now have a slew of copiers—well, this is China. . . . Still, the way that slogans from the Cultural Revolution are made witty and ironic and the recycling of propaganda on funky canvas bags emblazoned with red stars have earned the store cult status among Chinese and foreign fashion lovers, especially for men who don't always have it so good in Shanghai when it comes to fashionable wear. And when T-shirts start at 99RMB, why not indulge, especially on the evil-looking panda T-shirt, a great counterbalance to the cutesy panda souvenirs you see everywhere else. There are also branches on Taikang Lu and Moganshan Lu.

SUZHOU COBBLERS

Room 101, 17 Fuzhou Lu, 6321 7087,
www.suzhou-cobblers.com
HOURS: Daily 10 A.M.-6:30 P.M.
Map 9

A must-visit if you're shopping around the Bund, this gorgeous slip of a store is a Shanghainese favorite because of its cute hand-stitched silk slippers; they are often featured in fashion magazines. Suzhou, two hours away from Shanghai, is famous for its silk and owner Denise Huang uses its traditional silk but combined with designs that bring the slippers (suitable for both indoor and outdoor use and costing around 400RMB) up to date. The store now also stocks equally attractive bags—look out for the Mandarin duck bag and some adorable children's clothes: For a larger range try No. 19, a shop that stocks their clothes. All products can be ordered online and shipped abroad.

THE THING

60 Xinle Lu, 5404 3607
HOURS: Daily 10 A.M.-9 P.M.
Map 12

This place is indeed the thing for funky and contemporary local design—expect cool T-shirts (from 100RMB) and excellent accessories, like bags and sneakers, at this locally owned fast-expanding chain, which opened in 2005. The Thing's designers believe that even the cheapest clothes should be well-made and well-designed, and their cool collection of items is worth hunting down.

THREE

2/F, 3 Zhongshan Dongyilu, near Guang Donglu, 6323 3355
HOURS: Daily 11:30 A.M.-10 P.M.
Map 9

With a prime position in the upmarket echelon of Three on the Bund, ladies who lunch at the complex's fabulous restaurant often pop into Three's flagship boutique for the latest designer fashions. Some of the world's most cutting-edge designers—Yohji Yamamoto and John Galliano, for example—are on display in the sparely decorated store. Prices are eye-wateringly high, but that's no surprise considering the store's location and collections. The staff speaks English fluently.

WANG HAND CRAFTS

11 Xianxia Lu, near Yan'an Lu
(west of the French Concession), 6229-3916
HOURS: Daily 10 A.M.-7 P.M.
Map 15

Anyone with above-average-size feet can

KEEPING UP WITH THE *QIPAO*

Shanghai has long enjoyed a reputation as China's most fashionable city, and though many of the combos you will see sported by Shanghainese *xiaojies* (misses) may not be to everyone's taste – white leather boots and puffball skirts are very popular – no one could say fashion here is boring. Shanghai was a place where the East met West, and so did its fashion. Chinese women used to wear a traditional outfit called the *qipao,* which also became known as the cheongsam; it was wide and loose, camouflaging most of the body. But from the 1920s on, thanks to Western tailoring techniques, *qipaos* were more form fitting and revealing, and they became all the rage in the city. Slender with a high cut and made from silk, it contrasted sharply with the traditional *qipao,* and Shanghainese women, who were known for being especially slim, had them made in a succession of styles and colors. In the traditional method of making a *qipao,* the body is measured in more than 30 different places for the best fit.

The *qipao*'s strength was that it could be adapted to the wearer with ease: Slim young women went for the sexy look with thigh-high splits, while other women could go for a more demure look and reveal less skin. Nancy Kwan in the 1960 film *The World of Suzie Wong* made the *qipao* popular in the West with a whole generation of men, and more recently, Maggie Cheung in Wong Kar-wai's movie *In the Mood for Love* dazzled in a variety of elegant yet sexy *qipaos*.

Fashion soon became a secondary concern to Shanghainese women when the 1949 Communist Revolution saw anyone wearing one dismissed as a prostitute or class traitor, and gray and dowdy Mao suits became more appropriate wear. But in recent years the dress has been revived, especially for brides and for special occasions. Ready-made *qipaos* can be found everywhere, but for a perfect fit, a whole strip of tailors along Maoming Nan Lu are waiting to run you up a *qipao,* or try Li Gu Long (205 Changle Lu, French Concession, 5403 1515) which is well known for excellent-quality silk and craftsmanship. Living out your Suzy Wong fantasies won't come cheap, though – here expect to pay around 2,000RMB, while cheaper tailors who don't use the best silk and require only one fitting will charge about 700RMB.

struggle to be well-shod in China, so many in-the-know expats turn to Mr. Wang, who produces custom-made shoes. The Italian-trained shoe expert may not be the cheapest in town, with prices running between 500–900RMB, but considering the range of imported leathers to choose from, they're well worth it. While the designers are good, the best results seem to be when you take in a pair you want to be copied. Unfortunately, quality takes time, so expect to wait at least a week, but for an extra fee, they can courier your new shoes to you.

YOUNIK

2/F, Bund 18, 18 Zhongshan Dongyilu, 6323 8688

HOURS: Daily 10 A.M.-10 P.M.

Map 9

One of the prime destinations in Shanghai's most chi-chi shopping destination, Bund 18, Younik specializes in up-and-coming designers from Shanghai and the rest of China. Plenty of Chinese celebrities shop here for women's clothes and accessories, including handbags and jewelry from names like Jooi and Jiang Qiong Er. It's not a large store, but designs are well-selected and displayed artily, and the store's white walls serve as a blank canvas for the clothes. Bring your credit cards.

Accessories and Jewelry

ANNABEL LEE

1 Lane 8, Zhongshan Dongyilu, 6445 8218,
www.annabel-lee.com

HOURS: Daily 10 A.M.-10 P.M.

Map 9

The name may suggest that it is one person designing these ultrafeminine silky bags and accessories such as scarves and business-card holders, but it's actually a group of international artists who have taken the traditional Chinese craft of embroidery and updated it for the modern consumer. Despite the high quality, beautiful packaging, and stylish stores, the prices are surprisingly reasonable. The silk clutch bags are particularly covetable. The Bund store is the flagship, but there are also smaller outlets in Xintiandi and the Okura Garden Hotel and the Portman Ritz-Carlton.

PEARL CITY

2/F and 3/F, 558 Nanjing Donglu, 6322 9299

HOURS: Daily 10 A.M.-6 P.M.

Map 10

After Pearl's Circles in the Old City, this is Shanghai's biggest pearl market. And though this is a fun place to shop for nice freshwater pearls, don't believe overzealous vendors who try to convince you their pearls are highest-quality. Because there are so many vendors in one spot, it is easy to compare price and quality. Don't think you have to be polite when vendors try and harass you into a sale—do what the Chinese do and completely ignore them if they are too over-zealous. Just take your time, look carefully, and ask lots of questions. One vendor who gets good reviews for her straightforward pricing is Li Ling Ling.

PEARL'S CIRCLES

First Asia Jewelry Plaza, 3rd Floor, 288 Fuyou Lu,
6333 2226

HOURS: Daily 10 A.M.-6 P.M.

Map 13

Pearl's Circles, one of Shanghai's two pearl markets, tops the First Asia Jewelry Plaza near the chaos of Yu Gardens Bazaar, but be warned, it isn't any quieter here. Still if you're looking for pearls of any persuasion, this is the place to come in the Old City, though the number of options in every kind of style you can imagine can overwhelm all but the most dedicated of shoppers. Shanghai is very near the freshwater pearling areas of China, so you can get good deals on these. It's best to do a quick reconnaissance around the floor, and then try to find a vendor in a quiet(er) area who may be more inclined to bargain. Bargain hard here as most vendors have similar freshwater wares, so if the price isn't right in one place, just move on. You can find a ready-to-wear string starting at a measly 20RMB or commission your own designs, which will be ready for you in a matter of minutes.

SHANGHAI TRIO

Unit 5, House 1, North Block, Xintiandi, Lane 181,
Taicang Road, 6355 2974, www.shanghaitrio.com

HOURS: Daily 10 A.M.-10 P.M.

Map 12

In the address book of many Shanghainese, this is the place for excellent-quality accessories that look very Chinese but with a French twist. They use traditional cotton and silk fabrics on 21st-century stuff like cell-phone cases and gorgeous cashmere throws. As well as the luxurious adult range, there are also some fabulous children's clothes worn by Shanghai's best-dressed kids, but the high prices for these—and really, does a child need a cashmere dress?—may be off-putting to some.

TREE

253 Shanxi Lu, near Shaoxing Lu, 5465 4855

HOURS: Daily 10 A.M.-7 P.M.

Map 12

Tree, with its good-quality leather goods, has quickly expanded from a single boutique to a small chain in Shanghai, and it's no surprise: Owner Yang Feng's designs are both affordable and funky. The stores are very low-key, with shop assistants happy to let you browse unaccompanied—look out for the trendy ballet flats in a kaleidoscope of colors as well more masculine items like belts and wallets.

Souvenirs

SONG FANG MAISON DE THÉ

227 Yongjia Lu near Shaanxi Nan Lu, 6433 8283

HOURS: Daily 10 A.M.-6 P.M.

Map 12

This beautiful sliver of a shop with its striking storefront is a tea shop specializing in premium teas from China and tea blends from France, where the owner of the store comes from. Fans love the fancy tea packaging—baby blue tins with a propaganda-style picture of ruddy-faced farmers—but you will be paying high prices for it with teas starting from 70RMB per 50g. The friendly staff take their role of tea educators very seriously and will talk you through the myriad varieties of tea with enthusiasm, and unlike many other tea shops, this one is very accessible to foreign visitors.

© HELENA IVESON

Song Fang Maison de Thé in the French Concession

SHANGHAI SOUVENIRS

In Shanghai, great souvenirs and gifts can be found at the almost too cute **Suzhou Cobblers** near the Bund: Its slippers, shoes, and bags come in clashing-colors silk from Suzhou. More wonderful fabrics can be found at **Brocade Country,** which sells throws, clothes, and baby slings made by members of the Miao ethnic minority. The friendly English-speaking sisters who run the store will delightedly explain their wonderful products.

The Shanghainese take great pride in being the most stylish people in China, and their boutiques are ubiquitous. **Hongqiao Pearl Market** sells the cheap T-shirts, ties, and shirts that tourists buy by the bagful, and a whole floor of pearls awaits you on the fourth floor. For more fashionable T-shirts and dresses, head to one of the branches of **Shirt Flag,** and for more cutting-edge, distinctly Shanghainese wear, **insh** in Taikang Lu is the place.

If shopping time is limited, the **Xintiandi** area is full of interesting destinations. The cute silk purses at **Annabel Lee** make great gifts (especially for yourself!), as do the delightful if expensive designs at **Shanghai Trio** – and there's also the branch of the **Shanghai Museum Art Store,** which sells lovely books and bags inspired by the museum's collections. A few minutes' walk away is the most atmospheric women's boutique in the French Concession, **Roof 603 at Leaf.**

Also in the French Concession is the tiny, ultrastylish housewares store **Banmoo.** From there you're walking distance from **Dongtai Lu Antique Market,** where toward the end of the day you're likely to get a good price for that must-have copy of Mao's *Little Red Book,* or that Buddha statue that the seller swears is older than time itself.

TEA

About 4,000 years ago, the legend goes, Chinese Emperor Shen Nung was sitting underneath a tree as his servant boiled water. Leaves from the tree fell into the water and the emperor decided to sample the infusion. The leaves were from a wild tea tree, and the drink that has sustained the Chinese, and millions of others around the world, was born. Now there are about 8,000 tea varieties in China and despite being threatened by Western coffee franchises such as Starbucks, the rituals associated with buying and drinking tea are becoming increasingly fashionable again. Even though it all comes from the same plant, four kinds of tea are available: white, green, oolong, and black. Their distinctive characteristics derive from the method used to process the leaves.

Shanghai is a great place to buy tea and in addition to specialist shops such as **Song Fang Maison de Thé** and the **Guyuan Antique Tea House,** there are also plenty of wholesale markets, which as well as being cheaper are interesting places to stock up. There are rows and rows of crammed stalls in drafty **Tianshan Tea City** (520 Zhongshan Xi Lu near Yuping Lu, Metro Line 2 and 3 Zhongshan Park Station), where shopkeepers are happy for you to taste their produce. Stalls tend to specialize in a certain type of tea and the most popular at the moment is *pu'er* tea, a type of black tea. Investors and devotees speculate on, collect, and pour fortunes into *pu'er,* and Chinese women believe it will keep them slim. The most popular tea in China is green tea, however, and most black tea is produced for the export market. Green tea is considered very healthy: It's full of antioxidants, and not just antioxidants but polyphenols, which have 100 times the antioxidants of Vitamin C. Studies have linked green tea drinking with a lowered risk of stomach, esophageal, and liver cancers.

The array of different teas at the market is dizzying and so are some of the prices: up to 1,500RMB for a little packet of leaves. While that may sound a lot, in 2006, half a kilo of Dragon's Well leaves from Hangzhou were bought for $100,000.

USHIGOKORO

20 Donghu Lu, near Huaihai Zhonglu, 5404 8085, www.ushigokoro.com

HOURS: Daily 10 A.M.-8 P.M.

Map 12

It's very difficult to know in which category to put this one-of-a-kind store from Japan as what you will find there in any given week could be dramatically different. The great concept is that independent entrepreneurs rent a box, varying from tiny to medium-size, to display their arts and crafts products, and it can be anything—bags, dolls, notebooks, or postcards. Art exhibitions are also held here monthly: Ask the friendly Japanese owner. Last time I was here I picked up some paper coasters emblazoned with a kung fu princess and an Elyse 7 tote with a bright red lantern on it. What will be there next time is impossible to guess.

YAOYANG TEA HOUSE

House 25, Lane 181, North Block, Xintiandi, 6355 6166

HOURS: Daily 10 A.M.-6 P.M.

Map 12

Conveniently situated in the heart of Shanghai's most interesting shopping destination, here's a great place to pick up beautifully packaged rare red or oolong tea. It may be a little expensive, but like at Song Fang, it's beautifully packaged.

Antiques and Artwork

ART DECO

1/F, Building 7, 50 Moganshan Lu, 6277 8927

HOURS: Tues.-Sun. 10 A.M.-8 P.M.

Map 15

A husband-and-wife team has assembled a fab collection of restored furniture from Shanghai's art deco heydays. The large warehouse in the arty Moganshan Lu district attracts collectors from all over the world, and prices are high, but the quality is exceptional. The lovely collection of curvy dark wooden tables with matching chairs is very covetable, and the owners can arrange shipping (most items are far too big for you to carry on a plane). The store is closed on Mondays.

DONGTAI LU ANTIQUE MARKET

Dongtai Lu, off Xizang Lu

HOURS: Daily 9 A.M.-6 P.M.

Map 13

The stalls that line either side of the street may loudly claim they sell antiques, but let's be honest—the real deals will be few and far between. But really, who cares? This is one of Shanghai's premier shopping destinations because you can come away with bags full of Communist kitsch, including posters and Mao's legendary *Little Red Book* at bargain prices. Rummage deep and you'll find embroidered slippers for bound feet, chopsticks, lanterns, porcelain, and figurines, but really, no matter what the vendors say, next to nothing here will be valuable. That shouldn't detract from the fun, though! If you like embroidery, one stall that does stock antiques is Yun Chuan Xiang Gui at number 153. Here you'll find delicately hand-stiched minority clothes from China's diverse range of ethnic minority groups scattered across the country. And while you're at the market, be sure to explore the crumbling residential lanes on either side of the market where Shanghai life continues as it has for centuries.

Buyers can haggle over the old and new in the Old City.

BARGAIN LIKE A LOCAL

Military operations and Shanghai shopping expeditions have much in common.

- **Know your enemy and his or her territory:** If you have a rough idea about the general terrain – how much other people pay for their knockoff Nike sneakers, for example – you are in a much better position when it comes to getting a good price. If you know that someone is quoting a ridiculously high price – such as 400 RMB for a pair of said sneakers – walk away. The vendor has started too high and it's best to try somewhere else.

- **Plan your attack and operate strategically:** Dress for battle – don't go in your best Gucci suit as one look at you and any trader is going to start his or her prices high. If at all possible, look like a student – everyone is used to their whining about lack of cash. This may be a difficult look to pull off if you are older than 40, but at least don't look too well groomed.

- **Pysch-ops:** If you were a trader, who would you give the best price to – someone you thought seemed an OK person, or some rude idiot who shouts and snaps at you? It astounds me that some people act so aggressively in markets and expect to get a good price. Be friendly, smiley, and try to see it as the game it is.

- **A few words of Chinese go a long way:** Again, pysch-ops – if you look like a tourist and can't manage more than *ni hao*, you're going to get tourist prices.

Strategies: If you were a military strategist, you wouldn't use the same battle plan for every situation. For the equally serious matter of bargaining, you must also be prepared to adapt different tactics in your quest for victory. Some tried and tested tactics are the following:

- **The walk away:** When you've got the price down to only half and you want a little bit more off, it's time for the old faithful – the fake "I give up in disgust and I'm off to spend somewhere else" tactic. Obviously the idea is that the shopkeeper will accept your price rather than face the loss of the sale. This ploy works best in less-touristy areas. Success rating: 5/10. Overused so try it judiciously.

- **I like it so much, but I don't have any money:** Effective only if you are in your oldest clothes and have a pained hungry look – the polished among us aren't going to be able to carry this off. You need to emphasize that you really like that bright-pink Tods bag, and then mournfully explain that you don't have much money because you're a student/unemployed/raising 12 children. Needs to be accompanied by winsome charm so the shopkeeper feels pity. Success rating: 4/10. Shopkeepers aren't known for their charity.

- **I will become your best customer:** You need to spin a yarn that if the vendor gives you a good price, you will become his or her number-one customer. By emphasizing that you are a Ralph Lauren polo shirt addict and need a regular fix of the preppy look, you may be able to get cheap, cheap prices. You may have to put your money where your mouth is here and come back a few weeks in a row. Get his or her business card and make the shopkeeper into your new best friend. Success rating: 6/10. Not as well known a technique

Remember, it's a war zone out there and it comes down to survival of the fittest. There is no room for wishy-washy sentiments and visions that by your hard bargaining, you are ensuring that there is no food on the trader's table that night. If the traders are not making any money off the sale, they just won't sell it to you.

FUYOU LU ANTIQUE MARKET
457 Fangbang Zhonglu
HOURS: Daily 9 A.M.-6 P.M.
Map 13

Amid the piles of dross in this five-story flea market, which is also known as Cang Bao Lou, you occasionally rummage your way into finding something choice, but the seriously disinterested staff here aren't going to rouse themselves to help you find what you want—it's all up to you. This building at the end of an old street acts as a wholesale market that supplies a lot of the souvenir shops in the area. The piles of Buddha heads at the front of the market make a good picture but the prices are eye-watering. Upstairs seems to get fewer browsers so staff aren't quite as jaded. Items to look out for include propaganda posters from the 1950s, boxes of yellowing photographs, their surfaces beginning to crack with age, and some marvelous embroidery available at a stall on the right-hand side near the entrance. The fourth floor is great for vintage clothes.

GUO CHUN XIANG'S CURIOSITY SHOP
179-181 Duolun Lu near Sichuan Beilu, 5696 3948
HOURS: Daily 9 A.M.-5 P.M.
Map 15

Happily, store owner Mr. Guo lets people browse at their leisure in his shop, which is ram-packed with everything from 1930s-style beauty boxes, telephones, and phonographs to 1950s biscuit tins stacked up high—and everything in between. There's a great section of posters and old photographs, and if you speak any Chinese, the owner is entertaining when he dismisses almost all of the other markets as offering fakes only. Refreshingly, all items have marked prices, though Mr. Guo will bargain a little.

MADAM MAO'S DOWRY
207 Fumin Lu, near Julu Lu, 5403 3551
HOURS: Daily 10 A.M.-7 P.M.
Map 12

This antique-filled bright-blue store is named after Jiang Qing, Mao's fourth wife, who was one of the Gang of Four who was held responsible for the murderous excesses of the Cultural Revolution and who killed herself after Mao died. While this might seem like an odd choice of person to name a shop after, the name reflects the era of the piles of black-and-white photography, Cultural Revolution propaganda posters, and other Mao-era artifacts available to buy here. The furniture on display is also very covetable though the high prices will put off all but the most enthusiastic buyers—a bust of the man himself costs from 2,000RMB. There is another store at the Eastlink Gallery in the Moganshan Art District (see the *Arts and Leisure* chapter).

PROPAGANDA POSTER ART CENTER
Room BOC, Basement, Block B, 868 Huashan Lu, 6211 1845, www.shanghaipropandaart.com
HOURS: Daily 9:30 A.M.-4:30 P.M.
Map 15

This small quirky museum sells genuine antique propaganda posters from 800RMB each (see the *Sights* chapter for more details).

SHANGHAI ANTIQUE AND CURIO STORE
196-246 Guang Donglu, 6321 4697
HOURS: Daily 9 A.M.-5 P.M.
Map 9

This may look like a dusty relic (which it is), but for antique hunters, it's still worth heading to this huge government-run store a stone's throw from the Westin. Despite appearances, apparently antiques judged not good enough for the Shanghai Museum end up here. All items, including jade, porcelain, metal, furniture, and paintings come with a stamp of authenticity, though be aware that foreigners are not allowed to take anything more than 200 years old out of the country. Although it attracts a lot of tourists, staff leave you alone to browse undisturbed and prices really aren't bad at all.

TORANA HOUSE
164 Anfu Lu, 5404 7787, www.toranahouse.com
HOURS: Daily 10 A.M.-9 P.M.
Map 12

Just like the original store in Beijing, Torana's

collection of beautiful modern and antique Tibetan and Xinjiang carpets are fun to check out even if you're not in the market for one of their expensive pieces. The store owner is a long-term China hand and plows a percentage of the profits back into local Tibetan and Xinjiang communities. Their new designs for 2008 are very abstract—the nicest are based on ancient textile designs from the Silk Road. Even if you can't get to the store, check out their website, as they can ship throughout the world.

Arts and Crafts

BANMOO

264 Madang Lu near Zizhong Lu, 6386 2985, www.banmoo.com

HOURS: Daily 10:30 A.M.-9 P.M.

Map 12

This ultrastylish furniture and accessories store is the place to go for a look at where Chinese design is heading. The tiny brightly lit showroom on a boutique-filled street near Xintiandi is owned by local designer Lu Yongzhong but also shows the work of other up-and-coming designers. Most pieces are one-offs or limited edition and while practical, with items varying from tea sets to chairs, their stylishness will no doubt make them collector's items in the future. The calligraphy series, in which all the products resemble calligraphy brush strokes, are particularly lovely.

© HELENA IVESON

beautiful embroidery at Brocade Country in the French Concession

BLUE SHANGHAI WHITE

Room 103, 17 Fuzhou Lu, 6323 0856, www.blueshanghaiwhite.com

HOURS: Daily 10 A.M.-9 P.M.

Map 9

Fuzhou Lu is rapidly becoming a hot shopping destination thanks to Suzhou Cobblers and this ceramics store just two doors down. The elegant porcelain on display fuses traditional techniques with modern designs and items such as the teacups and vases are very pretty indeed, particularly the new Shikumen variety, which uses Shanghai's famous style of housing as inspiration, and the small variety of wooden furniture with ceramics inlaid. The ceramics are made in Jingdezhen, a town south of Shanghai that has been famous for its porcelain for nearly 1,000 years. There's a larger showroom near People's Square, but you need to make an appointment (1060-23 Yanan Donglu, 6359 6897).

BROCADE COUNTRY

616 Julu Lu near Xiangyang Lu, 6279 2677

HOURS: Daily 10 A.M.-8 P.M.

Map 12

If your travel plans don't run to heading to rural Guizhou province, this tiny boutique run by two sisters stocks a variety of hand-stitched tapestries made by members of the Miao ethnic minority group. The textiles, tablecloths, shoes, and indigenous dresses, some of which are more than 100 years old, will make fans of beautiful embroidery very happy indeed, but there is also plenty for fabulous fashionistas too, as while some of the textiles are untouched, others have been recut and remodeled into contemporary wear such as miniskirts and casual but stylish bags.

CHINESE PRINTED BLUE NANKEEN EXHIBITION HALL

24, Lane 637, Changle Lu, 5403 7947

HOURS: Daily 9 A.M.-5 P.M.

Map 12

Half the fun of this store is actually finding it, as English signs direct you through the twists and turns of an alley full of lane houses with washing hanging out on the street. Once you find the store, you'll discover a room filled with the uniquely regional ware from Shanghai, *nankeen,* or traditional indigo-dyed batik cloth. The fabric is lovely and you can buy everything from umbrellas, throws, and clothes, though sizes available are small. Don't ask if the shop has things in other colors. . . .

DUO YUN XUAN ART SHOP AND GALLERY

422 Nanjing Donglu, 6351 0060

HOURS: Daily 9 A.M.-5 P.M.

Map 10

Something of a relic from the past with its old-fashioned dusty displays and unsmiling, unhelpful staff, this store on the pedestrianized section of Nanjing Lu is still worth looking up, as it's a good place to pick up Chinese souvenir staples. Jade, calligraphy, scrolls, and calligraphy brushes (which in themselves make great souvenirs) are all available here. Refreshingly, shop assistants don't hassle you, all prices are marked, and they are surprisingly reasonable considering that this street is scam central. There's no English sign, but look out for the prominent number and Chinese-style roof.

SHANGHAI MUSEUM ART STORE

Shanghai Museum, 201 Renmin Dadao, 6372 3500, www.shanghaimuseum.net

HOURS: Daily 9 A.M.-5 P.M.

Map 10

After cruising around the displays of China's finest artifacts, be sure to visit the surprisingly excellent museum store (most museums in China don't sell much more than a few postcards). It has high-quality English-language coffee-table books on Chinese art and calligraphy as well as a large selection of ceramics that are imitations of the pieces you might have just been looking at. If these are beyond your price range (and they might be as they often run into thousands of RMB), the nifty Shanghai Museum logo tote bags also make a stylish souvenir. There's a second branch at Xintiandi.

ZEN LIFESTORE

7-1 Dongping Lu, 6437 7390

HOURS: Daily 10 A.M.-7 P.M.

Map 12

Along one of the French Concession's prettiest avenues (look out for the statue of Pushkin erected by refugee White Russians in the 1930s) is Zen, one of many small boutiques and restaurants that line the street. Zen's specialty is ceramics and its range of handcrafted but practical housewares, including vases, pretty bathroom sets, and tableware, are a bargain. It also has a small range of furniture around the back. Have a postshopping cappuccino and pastry at swank bakery Paul, and another of Shanghai's best home-design stores is next door at Simply Life.

Books and Music

BOOK CITY

465 Fuzhou Lu, 6352 2222

HOURS: Daily 9:30 A.M.-9:30 P.M.

Map 10

This giant of a store on a street traditionally known for its bookshops is constantly packed with people using the place more as a library. On all seven floors, everywhere you look, on every available surface, you'll see people engrossed in books. The imported selection is on the top floor (unfortunately there's no elevator for shoppers) and there you will find a reasonable selection of magazines, hardbacks, and paperbacks varying from the latest Harry Potter to Haruki Murakami. The selection can't rival that of Chaterhouse or Garden Books, but prices are lower, with a paperback costing around 70RMB. For some reason, this store always has a lot of beggars outside.

© HELENA IVESON

the best place to buy English books

CHATERHOUSE BOOKTRADER

B1-K, Times Square, 93 Huaihai Zhonglu, 6391 8237

HOURS: Daily 9:30 A.M.-6 P.M.

Map 10

Chaterhouse is where Shanghai's literature-loving set turn for their fix. It's no independent quaint store, but for the latest best-seller or an up-to-date guidebook for reasonable prices, it can't be beat. Unlike many Chinese bookstores, there are chairs so you can sit and browse. At this branch in Times Square, there's a good selection of magazines and Chinese-related literature, but for some reason magazines aren't always as new as you'd think, so check the date. There is another branch located in the Shanghai Center on Nanjing Xilu.

DVD STORE

42 Xinle Lu, 5403 6625

HOURS: Daily 10 A.M.-11 P.M.

Map 12

Handily situated amid the many clothes boutiques on this funky road, this professionally run store is no-nonsense in its offerings: It sells the kind of American movies, boxed sets, and CDs that everyone wants. DVDs are 10RMB each and if you buy a few, you can usually wangle a discount.

EVEN BETTER THAN MOVIEWORLD

407 Dagu Lu, near Shimen Yilu, 6327 0979

HOURS: Daily 24 hours

Map 11

Opposite this popular store is another store called Movieworld, hence the name—just as in the popularity battle between cafés Wagas and Element Fresh, these two DVD stores are also huge rivals. I have to agree that this one is slightly better because of its larger collection of mainstream DVDs, boxed sets, and CDs, as well as a large collection of Chinese movies. Most discs cost 7RMB and CDs start from 15RMB. Perfect for late-night movie watchers, the store is open 24 hours.

GARDEN BOOKS

325 Changle Lu near Shaanxi Nan Lu, 5404 8729

HOURS: Daily 10 A.M.-7 P.M.

Map 12

Garden Books is newer than Chaterhouse and has a café in the building with great coffee—so it's easy to while away an hour or so while flicking through their selection. They are more eclectic than the competition, which can be frustrating when you want a bestseller, but if not, you'll enjoy browsing. They have a particularly good selection of children's books, with over 200 titles and a small play area to allow parents to shop in peace.

HOLLYWOOD

27 Wanghangdou Lu, no phone

HOURS: Daily 10 A.M.-2 A.M.

Map 11

On the western wall of Jing'an Temple—it sounds incongruous but the whole area is a capitalist extravaganza—is this great DVD and CD store. It lives up to its name and sells reliable copies of all the latest U.S. releases, as well as a bulging selection of Chinese movies, but check that they have English subtitles. As long as the police do not shut the place down for copyright infringement, it's open 10 A.M.–midnight.

Markets

A. P. XINYANG FASHION AND GIFTS MARKET

2000 Shiji Dadao, inside Shanghai Science and Technology Museum Metro Station, 6854 2230, www.xinyang-market.com

HOURS: Daily 10 A.M.-6 P.M.

Map 14

If you're staying in Pudong, this oddly named market is a great place to head for the kind of bargains that used to be found at Xiangyang market across the river. Apparently most of the stalls filled with fake bags, clothes, and DVDs have headed here, but the tourists haven't in anywhere near the numbers that used to swamp Xiangyang every day of the week. Because of the lack of bodies, the bargaining opportunities are even better and the indoor clean environment is a definite improvement in inclement weather. As well as the fakes, there are also a smallish number of boutiques selling more interesting clothing and jewelry.

HONGQIAO INTERNATIONAL PEARL CITY

3721 Hongmei Lu near Yan'an Xilu, 6465 0000

HOURS: Daily 9 A.M.-7 P.M.

Map 15

Despite the name, this multistoried market, a 20-minute taxi ride from People's Square, offers a full range of goods aside from pearls, including "North Face" jackets (popularly known as North Fake), touristy T-shirts, "designer" ties, sunglasses, DVDs, and any other pirated goods that the customs agents may confiscate from you (joke! Well, kind of . . .). Now that the infamous Xiangyang Market has been bulldozed, tourists head here for hard bargaining sessions and plastic bags full of booty.

SOUTH BUND FABRIC MARKET

399 Lujiabang Lu near Zhongshan Nan Lu, 6377 7288

HOURS: Daily 9 A.M.-6 P.M.

Map 15

Locals complained when the original fabric market closed, as prices have risen at the new location, but at least now it's inside and much more sensibly laid out. There are hundreds of tailors at this multifloor indoor bazaar, selling copies in cashmere, silk, and cotton of such designers as Giorgio Armani and Prada. They'll copy anything as long as you bring a picture or an original; expect to pay about 300RMB for wool jackets and 500RMB for cashmere—after you bargain hard, that is. The quality is good, but in case you need to come back for adjustments, make sure you head here at the beginning of your stay.

YU GARDENS BAZAAR

218 Anren Lu, 6238 3251

HOURS: Daily 9 A.M.-6 P.M.

Map 13

See the *Sights* chapter for more details, but all you need to know is that every kind of traditional Chinese souvenir from chops to chopsticks can be found here: Whether it will work for you depends on your tolerance levels for constant yells toward you of "hello, hello, look-a, look-a" aimed at you from all angles.

Shopping Malls

BUND 18

18 Zhongshan Dongyilu near Dianchi Lu, 6323 7066, www.bund18.com

HOURS: Daily 10 A.M.-10 P.M.

Map 9

This is set in some prime real estate on the Bund—the building was once the Chartered Bank headquarters—and it's clear as soon as the smartly uniformed doorman holds the door open for you that this is one of Shanghai's classiest retail and dining destinations. What other mall has white marble columns and a trio of violinists serenading you as you spend? And that of course means that prices at the small number of boutiques, such as Cartier, Zegna, and Chinese designer store Younik, are sky high. If you haven't treated yourself enough, try French restaurant Sens and Bund (President Sarkozy went when he was in town), Bar Rouge on the top floor, or the new destination cocktail bar Lounge 1.

MAISON MODE

1312 Huaihai Zhonglu, 6431 0100, www.maisonmode.com

HOURS: Daily 10 A.M.-9 P.M.

Map 12

Maison Mode may have been around since 1994—practically considered prehistoric for Shanghai—but this chic small collection of boutiques is still very popular thanks to its sophisticated brands on offer and great service. It's not cutting-edge but appeals to older affluent shoppers. It has many of the luxury brands favored by Chinese consumers, such as Ermenegildo Zegna, Hugo Boss, Paul and Shark, and Canali on its first floor, as well as more affordable brands BCBG, DKNY, JC Versace, and Just Cavali on the second floor. The mall also recently opened a new branch at Shanghai Times Square.

PLAZA 66

1266 Nanjing Xilu, just east of the Portman Ritz-Carlton, 6279 0910

HOURS: Daily 10 A.M.-10 P.M.

Map 11

The highest end of all Shanghai malls before Bund 18 and Three on the Bund opened, 66 is still the place to go for big spenders thanks to its huge variety of the world's biggest designer labels over five floors. Brands such as Chanel, Harry Winston, Christian Dior, and Prada call 66 home, but even if you're not interested in the ostentatious consumerism on display, it's worth a visit to see China's pampered nouveaux riches maxing the plastic. If you want more of the same, the slightly older CITC Square shopping center is immediately east and has a similar range of upmarket offerings and a useful branch of popular café Wagas in the basement.

SUPER BRAND MALL

168 Lujiazui Xilu near Fucheng Lu, Pudong, 6887 7888, ext. 5555, www.superbrandmall.com

HOURS: Daily 10 A.M.-9 P.M.

Map 14

Some Shanghainese cattily say that this mall that opened in 2002 is the only reason to head to Pudong, but given it's the city's biggest with an excellent range of both shops and restaurants (there are branches of American cafés Element Fresh and Blue Frog plus dumpling specialists Din Tai Fung just for starters), it's a pretty good reason. Thirteen floors of stores

© HELENA IVESON

row upon row of designer boutiques in Xintiandi

await you and refreshingly for Shanghai, prices are not too mind-boggling. Instead of ultra-expensive designer stores, midmarket stores dominate. A very small list includes Skechers, Spanish fashion retailer Zara, Hong Kong store Bossoni, CK Jeans, Chaterhouse Books, Esprit, H&M, Apple Computers, plus a cinema. . . . Make sure you have a few hours to spare before heading here.

THREE ON THE BUND

3 Zhongshan Dongyilu, 6323 3355, www.threeonthebund.com

HOURS: Daily 11:30 A.M.–10 P.M.

Map 9

Pure Shanghai flash in a shopping mall—this is destination shopping at its finest. Doormen keep out the riff-raff, allowing Shanghai's jet set to peruse in peace. The gorgeous 1916 building, which was renovated and designed by American architect Michael Graves, has the city's only Armani store, and Hugo Boss is there too, making this place, for once, a good spot for men to flash the plastic. As well as some of the city's best restaurants, there is also a spa. Despite the gorgeous facade on the Bund, the actual entrance is around the side of the building.

XINTIANDI

283 Huangpi Nanlu, near Xingye Lu, 6311 2288, www.xintiandi.com

HOURS: Daily; shop opening hours vary.

Map 12

See the *Sights* chapter for more details, but if you were born to shop, you must check out this incredibly successful development that uses old *shikumen* houses. There are more than 30 shops to swan around in, plus a cinema, swanky hair salon Vidal Sassoon, and more restaurants than you could eat at during the average stay in Shanghai.

HOTELS

If money is of no matter, then you are in for a great stay in Shanghai. Five-star hotels kitted out with all the latest facilities and extras are already in position on or near the Bund or with prime views from the other side of the river in Pudong, and a lot more were to come in time for the World Expo in 2010. But if money is tighter, accommodation in China's financial capital can be more problematic with a dearth of backpacker-friendly hostels or even midrange hotels where rooms are clean and staff are friendly. You won't find any converted courtyards like you do in Beijing, but if you seek them out, there are a handful of art deco gems and an even smaller number of independent small hotels that are causing a minirevolution.

Pudong has more than its fair share of ritzy hotels catering to business travelers flying in and out of the international airport, but people visiting for a short time who are keen to avoid too much time in the traffic in the tunnel that links the east and west sides would probably prefer to be closer to the action. Anywhere near the Bund makes for a convenient and historic place to stay, though as the Peace Hotel was in the middle of much-needed major renovation, there aren't any five star hotels actually on the main drag of the Bund itself. There are, though, some of the city's most historic venues at the northern end of the Bund, such as the Astor House Hotel and backpacker-friendly Broadway Mansions, and the new Hyatt on the Bund may not be right on the Bund as you'd expect, but it still has fabulous views over both sides of the historic riverfront.

HIGHLIGHTS

LOOK FOR ☾ TO FIND RECOMMENDED HOTELS.

☾ **Best Budget Room:** Its popularity may have led to a downturn in staff attitude, but the dorms at the **Captain's Hostel** can't be beaten on price or cleanliness (page 243).

☾ **Best Views of the Bund:** At the northern end of the Bund, the slick and stylish rooms at the **Hyatt on the Bund** look out onto both the majestic sweep of the Bund and the glitz and neon of Pudong (page 243).

☾ **Best Room to Spend a Rainy Day In:** When it's gloomy out, guests might not want to leave the comfort of **Jia Shanghai,** with all rooms containing Chinese board games, Nintendo Wiis, top-of-the-line music systems and DVD players, plus the afternoon tea and cocktails in the arty lobby (page 247).

☾ **Best Cutting-Edge Design: Urbn Hotel**'s attention to detail is delightful to see: Look out for the recycled mahogany on the floors, the secondhand Suzhou tiles on the walls, the wall of suitcases in reception, and the bamboo-lined courtyard (page 247).

☾ **Best Former French Concession Location:** As long as you have the bucks, the beautiful antique-filled **Mansion Hotel** on the corner of two funky tree-lined streets puts you in the center of the Shanghai's café culture (page 250).

☾ **Best 1930s Chic:** The **Old House Inn**'s creaking staircase leads to charming rooms decorated with antiques rescued from demolished Shanghai houses (page 251).

☾ **Best Service:** If you need to stay in Pudong and can afford the room rates, the **St Regis** offers amazing personal service with each guest assigned an in-the-know butler who can do everything from arranging art gallery tours to ordering in Shanghai's best pizza (page 252).

COURTESY OF JIA SHANGHAI

Chic and stylish rooms at Jia Shanghai make it hard to leave.

The Former French Concession with its tree-lined streets, restaurants, and cafés is a great place to stay and this is where the majority of the more interesting places to stay are situated, from the new ultraluxurious antique-filled Mansion Hotel to more reasonably priced and bursting-with-history hotels such as the Ruijin Guesthouse and the Donghu Hotel. Unfortunately, there aren't any real budget rooms in the area, so backpackers will have to make use of the subway to get here. The People's Square area has been considered a good place to stay for decades since the Park Hotel opened its doors in the 1930s and now because of its proximity to the area's museums and subway system, many visitors choose to base themselves here. Few visitors base themselves in the Old City because options there are very limited for non-Chinese speakers. Up until recently, it has tended to be business travelers only who locate themselves in the Jing'an Temple area, but with the opening of the stylish new boutique hotel Jia and URBN, that is changing, and it's easy to get a sense of the Shanghainese way of life if you stay here, and transport options are great.

Just in time for the estimated 70 million visitors expected to visit Shanghai during the World Expo, a whole slew of new hotels were to open, including on the Bund the latest offering from the Peninsula chain in 2009 and a W Hotel in 2010, and across the water in late 2008, the Park Hyatt will open in Shanghai's brand-new tallest building, the International Trade Center: Expect sky-high prices to go along with sky-high views.

PRICE KEY

$ Under US$50 (370RMB)
$$ US$50-100 (370-740RMB)
$$$ US$100-150 (740-1,100RMB)
$$$$ Over US$150 (1,900RMB)

The Bund and East Nanjing Lu

Map 9

ASTOR HOUSE HOTEL $$

15 Huangpu Lu, 6324 6388, www.astorhousehotel.com

Shanghai's oldest hotel is trying to recapture its 1930s heyday, when the hotel was full of socialites dressed up in their glad rags, so now the hotel, which was also known as the Pujiang and was a backpacker favorite, has closed its dorms, turning them into smart doubles, and it's aiming itself at the higher end of the market. The wonderfully atmospheric dark-wood-paneled lobby gives the mix of both Chinese and foreign guests a taste of the hotel's history and remnants of its illustrious past are easy to find—look out for the wooden floorboards, high ceilings, and faded wallpaper. The hotel is at the far north end of the Bund and has great views over the river if you get a room at the front: It's worth the extra, though discounts on standard rooms can be considerable if money's tight.

© HELENA IVESON

The Astor House Hotel was once the place to party.

BROADWAY MANSIONS $$

20 Beisuzhou Lu, 6324 6260, www.broadwaymansions.com

Dominating the north end of the Bund, Broadway Mansions sternly glares over the river and is considered one of the city's art deco classics. If only the experience of staying here matched up to its exterior, as rooms are a very mixed bag: Some look as though they were last painted when the hotel opened, but others, especially what it terms its business rooms, are filled with all mod cons and are great value. Despite the hotel's being popular with foreign guests, staff don't have great English-speaking skills or much in the way of cooking skills—skip breakfast even if it's included. But if you

THE OLDEST HOTEL IN SHANGHAI: THE ASTOR HOUSE HOTEL

In 1861, American Dewitt Clinton Jansen moved down to Shanghai from Beijing, where he had been working for China Maritime Customs. He bought a small boardinghouse just south of Suzhou Creek that had been opened by the Richards family in 1846 during the Qing dynasty. After Jansen took over, the Richards Hotel became the most modern and luxurious hotel in Shanghai, according to an *Atlantic Monthly* reporter who stayed there. It wasn't until 1857 that the hotel moved to its current location north of the creek and was renamed the Astor House Hotel. The hotel was *the* place to stay in Shanghai and has a number of firsts to its name: It was the first hotel to have electric lighting (1882), the city's first phone call was made here in 1901, and the first stock exchange in China opened here in 1900. In 1907, the hotel was fully revamped in the latest neoclassic baroque style, and in the 1920s the Kadoorie family, one of Shanghai's wealthiest Jewish dynasties, bought the place and made it the place to socialize and sip champagne. A stream of illustrious guests flocked here: Albert Einstein stayed in Room 304 while Charlie Chaplin spent his honeymoon a floor above in Room 404. Like so many places in Shanghai, the party was soon over and the glamour faded throughout the war years and the Communist regime when its chandeliers and stylish grandeur were dismissed as bourgeois folly. While it remained a hotel, it was a rundown shadow of its former self and reinvented itself as a cheap hotel called the Pujiang, beloved to many a backpacker. Someone wised up to the idea that tourists with money to spend would love to stay in such a historical place full of atmosphere, so the hotel has been revamped, is dorm free, and has come almost full circle and is now again called the Astor House.

pay the extra charge and have a room overlooking the Bund, these gripes will seem a small price to pay.

CAPTAIN'S HOSTEL $

37 Fuzhou Lu, 6323 5053, www.captainhostel.com.cn

Sorry, I can't resist: Everything's shipshape at Shanghai's most popular and well-established backpacker hangout. No one could accuse the place of doing the theme halfheartedly: The dorms are known as berths and the budget restaurant is called the mess. The studenty bar on the roof has a view over Pudong worth a fortune—amazingly, drinks are as cheap as you will get in Shanghai, so expect an exuberant crowd of both guests and locals making the most of it. Staff are somewhat jaded but if you ask specific questions, they can usually help, but if that doesn't work, the wall where past guests have written advice and comments will probably be useful. The double rooms are overpriced and of better value elsewhere; it's worth putting up with the dorms (50RMB) if you're on a budget. And considering you are about two minutes' walk from the Bund, this place offers exceptional value.

HYATT ON THE BUND $$$$

199 Huangpu Lu, 6393 1234, shanghai.bund.hyatt.com

This fab hotel that markets itself as offering "casual luxury" is situated on the north end of the Bund, which is a bit of a backwater at present but an area that will come into its own once the international passenger terminal opens in late 2008. Full of contemporary flair and the latest mod cons, the glass-and-steel lobby is more like an airport than a hotel (and was designed by the same company that did Hong Kong Airport). Even the elevators that whiz you up to one of the 631 rooms have great views, and inside the stylish dark-wood-lined and thoughtfully laid-out rooms are all angled to take full advantage of the hotel's best asset—its view down the river. Reserve a river-view room (they are in the higher floors): The west wing has the best views over the Bund, while the east looks onto Pudong. The spa takes up a whole floor with an organic juice bar in a

ART DECO DIGS

If you want to relive Shanghai's glory days, the city still has plenty of art deco hotels to check out and check into. The city was booming in the 1930s, and when new buildings were erected, they had to be the most fashionable around – to appease the Western bankers who ran the city and the new Chinese middle classes. Thus, the city has one of the largest collections of art deco buildings in the world.

Ladislaus Hudec, a Czech architect from Budapest who was sent to Siberia by the Russians, ended up in Shanghai and is considered the city's most preeminent prewar architect. Two of his gems that have survived the citywide craze to demolish and modernize are the 22-story **Park Hotel** overlooking what was once the racecourse and is now People's Park, and the **Museum of Arts and Crafts** in the Former French Concession.

Perhaps the most famous of Shanghai's art deco hotels is the **Peace Hotel** on the Bund, which was under renovation and was to reopen in 2009. Built by Sir Victor Sassoon, it was designed by P&T Architects Limited and known as the Cathay Hotel when it opened in 1929. Members of Shanghai's high society flocked to dance at the famous jazz bar under the hotel's pyramid-shaped green roof while Sassoon himself had the top floor as his private quarters. Sassoon, the Donald Trump of his era, commissioned some of the city's other art deco masterpieces: **Hamilton House** (137 Fuzhou Lu, near Jiangxi Lu, the Bund, 6321 0586, www.hamiltonhouse.com.cn), which has recently been renovated and is now a luxurious French restaurant, the **Metropole Hotel** (180 Jiangxi Lu, 6321 3030, www.cbw.com/hotel/metropole) near the Bund, and the **Jinjiang Hotel** (59 Maoming Nan Lu, French Concession, 6258 2582, jj.jinjianghotels.com). Despite the trauma of war, civil war, and the excesses of Mao and the Cultural Revolution, all these hotels are still standing and still open for business.

lovely setting filled with natural materials such as wood and granite. Dining options are overflowing, with the hotel's signature four-story restaurant and bar, Vue, just one of the choices. The Hyatt became the first five-star chain to have a presence on both sides of the river after this hotel opened in September 2007, and a third was set to open in August 2008 in the Shanghai International Financial Center.

METROPOLE HOTEL $$

180 Jiangxi Lu, 6321 0586,
www.cbw.com/hotel/metropole

Two blocks away from the Bund is this 1930s-era hotel, which you'll easily find thanks to its striking angular exterior. While some guests rave about the location—you are walking distance to both the Bund and People's Square—and rooms for good value if lacking in features, others complain about the curt service and traffic noise as the hotel is on a busy junction, but where in Shanghai isn't noisy? Most guests who stay here are Chinese so expect more of an Asian theme to breakfast than most foreign guests would like, but one excellent aspect is the amount of bargaining you can do for the hotel rooms: Staff seem to relish the process. Try the romantic French restaurant Hamilton House (137 Fuzhou Lu) in a gorgeous building that faces the hotel. The Metropole is soon to undergo the same kind of renovation as the Peace Hotel, but for now the hotel is taking reservations throughout 2008.

MINGTOWN ETOUR YOUTH HOSTEL $

450 Jiangxi Zhonglu, 6329 7889,
mingtown@vip.163.com

If Captain's Hostel and the Broadway Mansions are full, try this place, though it's definitely not up to the same standards as the more established two. It is in a good location, 10 minutes' walk from both People's Square and the Bund, though keep your eyes peeled for signs as it can be tricky to find. Once you get there and find the old building, which has a pond and fish in a central courtyard, you'll find that friendly staff are helpful and there is lots of common space so it is easy to meet people, and facilities such as a kitchen and free washing machine are useful, especially when the food it serves is on the expensive side for backpackers. The six- or four-bed dorms are certainly cheap, but the doubles are warmer, drier, and worth the few extra RMB.

PEACE HOTEL $$$$

Until 2010, the Peace Hotel is undergoing a fabulous facelift; visits will have to be limited to its exterior. See the *Sights* chapter for more information.

VILLAS 1931 BY THE BUND $$

306 Guang Donglu, 6547 1254

This undiscovered gem, five minutes' walk from the Bund and 10 minutes from People's Square, is great value for money. The building—unsurprisingly—dates from 1931 and has been sympathetically renovated; rooms are particularly well decorated with art deco lamps and dark wood paneling on the walls. The standard rooms are not huge but spotlessly clean, but if you pay a little extra and pay for a large room, the two large windows offer a nice view and broadband Internet access is included. There are no English TV channels available, but when you're so near such a exciting part of town, presumably you won't spend that much time in your room.

THE WESTIN $$$$

88 Henan Zhonglu, 6335 1888, www.westin.com/shanghai

Forget subtle: The 570-room Westin attracts attention starting with its distinctive crown roof, continuing with its glitzy open-plan lobby with Vegas-style light effects, and finishing with bright and spacious modern rooms with floor-to-ceiling windows, most with partial views of the Pearl Tower across the river. Choose a room equipped with the trademarked Heavenly Beds in the newer tower, the Grand Tower, which opened in 2006 with its own private lobby and striking artwork in the corridors. The light effects continue in the rooms, with a wall of light turning on as soon as you walk in the room. All the special effects make the rooms interesting but occasionally guests think that style rather than everyday practicality takes priority: Most guests need instructions on how to turn on the taps. Bathrooms are a main feature, though, with deep oversize baths and rainfall showerheads, and out of the bathroom, all rooms have plasma TVs and DVD players. Staff deal with the constant flow of guests well and the hotel's main-lobby buffet restaurant regularly wins awards for its Sunday brunch, though with long lines at the counters, it may be a victim of its own popularity. The gym is brand new and well equipped and the Banyan Tree spa is a restful if pricey place to end the day in style.

© HELENA IVESON

The Peace Hotel is a Shanghai landmark.

People's Square and Museum Row Map 10

JINJIANG YMCA HOTEL $

123 Xizang Nanlu, 6326 1040, www.ymcahotel.com

Across the street from the Shanghai Concert Hall in a dark and moody-looking art deco building, this is an excellent place to stay in terms of location, as People's Square is across the way, and the shopping delights of Huaihai Lu, the Bund, the Old City, and the French Concession are all within walking distance, albeit a good walk to the French Concession. This was Shanghai's original YMCA back in the 1930s and the staff are very old-school: Don't expect an overly warm welcome. They offer dorms, but the single rooms are good value: The rooms are small and slightly gloomy but the bathrooms are surprisingly pleasant.

JW MARRIOTT $$$$

Mingtian Guangchang, 399 Nanjing Xilu, 5359 4969, www.marriott.com

Whatever you think of the architecture, this hotel is certainly eye-catching with its futuristic tower resembling a rocket launcher. Inside, however, the feeling is much more comfortable; the hotel focuses on a home-away-from-home ambience with warm, cozy rooms in moss-green colors and rich woods with textiles you might have in your own home, interesting artwork, and an attention to detail that is lacking in many large corporate chains. Of course the hotel makes great use of its height and position with the restaurants and bar all enjoying fine views over the neon. If you can afford it, stay on the club floor for the best views and access to the excellent club lounge with its charming staff who are full of information on what to do in the city.

LE ROYAL MERIDIEN $$$$

789 Nanjing Donglu, 3318 9999, www.starwoodhotels.com

For some, this five-star hotel's best point is its location on the busy pedestrianized section of Nanjing Lu; for others, the hustle, bustle, and hawkers who will accost you when you approach the hotel can wear you down. It's a shame, but at least the inviting interior, with relaxing waterfalls and lit candles at night in the reception, is calming. It's a good thing there are so many helpful staff members as the layout is very confusing, and guests usually have to change elevators at least once to get to their rooms. Inside the pleasingly bright rooms, L'Occitane toiletries are a nice touch as is the in-room coffee percolators (ground coffee included), but it's a shame about the high daily Internet charges. Rooms are on the small side but thanks to the open-plan layout, don't appear to be, but some find the open-plan bathroom awkward when sharing a room. The hotel certainly knows how to charge, and if the expensive breakfasts don't appeal to you, there is a row of cafés opposite the entrance.

PARK HOTEL $$

170 Nanjing Xilu, 6327 5225, www.parkhotel.com.cn

This brooding building, which is the oldest continuously open hotel in Shanghai, opened its doors in 1934 and is considered one of the city's most iconic art deco icons. With a great location across the road from the attractive Renmin Park and five minutes' walk from the Shanghai Museum and the People's Square metro, this is an excellent midprice option, especially if you can bargain the price down a little. The lobby looks lovely with a grand piano in the middle of a sky-lighted central area, though the area and indeed the corridors smell a little musty. The 250 rooms are perfectly adequate if on the dark side: Even standard rooms come with Internet access and a small bath with shower. Food choices are limited but considering the wealth of options nearby, that's not a problem: Try Barbarossa in the center of People's Park.

YANGTZE HOTEL $$

740 Hankou Lu, 6351 7880, www.e-yangtze.com

Another hotel dating from the 1930s, the Yangtze's art deco charms have faded so it tries to differentiate itself by calling itself a business boutique hotel. Despite queries on how a hotel with 183 rooms can be boutique, the broadband Internet and fax machines in every room certainly make it a good budget room for people on business who want to stay somewhere more interesting than a bland chain. Rooms are on the small side, though: Do try to get one with a balcony for some extra space. If it could update the decor and get rid of the musty smells, this hotel would be a must-stay; as it is, it's good value for people on a budget who want to be near the action.

Jing'an and West Nanjing Lu

Map 11

JIA SHANGHAI $$$$

931 Nanjing Xilu, 6217 9000, www.jiashanghai.com

Describing itself as a "residence" rather than a hotel, the 55-room sister hotel to the superhip Hong Kong hotel Jia, Jia Shanghai opened to much acclaim at the end of 2007. The original structure was built in 1926, but inside the decor is uncompromisingly modern and masculine. The corridors are oddly dark but open onto bright white and achingly cool rooms equipped with the very latest home entertainment systems and small kitchens. While rates are high, especially for a small studio, the hotel throws in a lot of extras, including free Internet access, the use of an iPod, a DVD library, swanky pinchable toiletries, and a tub full of the addictive local White Rabbit candies. Rates include breakfast served in the arty lobby and afternoon tea and cocktails all evening, and the service is flawless and friendly.

COURTESY OF JIA SHANGHAI

Jia Shanghai has a prime position along Nanjing Xilu.

PORTMAN RITZ-CARLTON $$$$

1376 Nanjing Xilu, 6279 8888, www.ritzcarlton.com

The Portman used to be the cream of the crop in Shanghai, but with the spate of glamorous new five-star arrivals, the unglamorous-looking hotel built in 1990 and situated in the upmarket Shanghai Center is not faring well. Its rooms are overpriced and staid looking and are not up to the Ritz's normal standards. The Shanghai rooms, which are on the higher floors, have the better decor and facilities but are even more expensive, as are the hotel's six restaurants and bars. If you need to be here for work, the hotel is very much geared up for business travelers with a good business center with efficient staff. The staff throughout the hotel provide a good if impersonal service. A new Ritz-Carlton was to open in Pudong in 2010—one hopes this hotel will reflect better on the brand.

URBN HOTEL $$$$

183 Jiaozhou Lu near Xinzha Lu, 5153 4600, www.urbnhotels.com

With just 26 rooms, Shanghai's newest and funkiest boutique hotel combines environmental friendliness with its own unique version of Shanghai style. The hotel prides itself on its carbon-neutral status and has used only

© URBN HOTELS

China's first carbon-neutral hotel, Urbn doesn't sacrifice style.

recycled materials—even the hotel's building was a former factory. Once guests walk through the bamboo-lined courtyard and past the reception decorated by real antique suitcases, the corridors on the four floors are lined with bricks taken from demolished factories, and the wood used on the floors and in the rooms is old Chinese mahogany. The expat owners have tried to make the rooms as different from a standard hotel as possible with their sunken baths set in the room, low Asian-style bed, and a step below that a wraparound couch great for lounging on as you watch the massive plasma-screen TV with DVD player. Prices are high, and occasionally, guests feel that style rather than practicality is the order of the day with the modernity striking some as cold, but it's a buzzy place to stay in an interesting part of town.

Former French Concession

Map 12

ANTING VILLA HOTEL $$$

46 Anting Lu near Yongjia Lu, 6433 1188

Still relatively unknown to foreign visitors, this pretty mansion offers excellent-value accommodation on a quiet street in the heart of the French Concession. Rooms are situated in the original 1930s building and in a somewhat garish modern block: Do go for the older rooms with their lovely views overlooking the garden, though you can't help wish more original fittings had been kept as rooms now are pleasant if anonymous. It also offers "digital rooms," which come with broadband Internet, also available in the business center. Staff don't speak fluent English but certainly enough for the average stay, and you'll need no help finding good restaurants and bars in this area as the lively neighborhood is overflowing with them.

DONGHU HOTEL $$$

70 Donghu Lu, 6415 8158, www.donghuhotel.com

The Donghu could be one of the best boutique

hotels in Shanghai; as it is, it's reasonable value for the money but doesn't quite live up to its promise. The hotel has an excellent location with a corner plot set back off central Huaihai Lu and was once the home of notorious gangster Du Yuesheng. The main building does have old world charm, but in the light of new openings such as the Mansion Hotel, the Donghu's old-fashioned ambience is in need of an update. The clean adequate rooms are in different buildings around the grounds: Reserve the garden building rather than the modern wings as they have a lovely view and the most character. Staff don't speak particularly good English, which is surprising as the hotel does get a lot of foreign guests.

88 XINTIANDI $$$$

380 Huangpi Nanlu, 5383 8833, www.88xintiandi.com

Part of the upmarket shopping and retail complex Xintiandi, this boutique hotel aimed at people traveling equipped with corporate credit cards is unfortunately not in a converted *shikumen* house like the many restaurants in the area, but in a modern building that overlooks the attractive park next door. The interior is much more attractive than the exterior, with tasteful antique furniture in the small intimate lobby and staff members dressed in stylish traditional Chinese outfits. The spacious rooms are a relaxing oasis of dark-red walls and more antique furniture but all mod cons are there, hidden behind screens and in cupboards, and there's a minikitchen. Beds are an attractive feature, raised on a platform surrounded by gauze. Even though the 53 rooms are already a little overpriced—and don't bother upgrading for a lake view; it's more of a pond—you're hit with a slew of extras, including a charge if you want to check out late. Some guests mention noise from bars and clubs nearby in the evening: If you think this might be a problem, choose a room with a city view rather than courtyard room.

HENGSHAN MOLLER VILLA $$$

30 Shanxi Nanlu, 6247 8881, www.mollervilla.com

With a building that looks as though it has come straight out of a fairy tale, the Moller

© HELENA IVESON

the whimsical exterior of the Hengshan Moller Villa

Villa is one of Shanghai's most distinctive buildings. This was originally the private residence of Swedish millionaire Eric Moller and its design was apparently inspired by a dream that his daughter had. After lying dormant for decades, it was converted into a hotel in 2002. Unfortunately only a tiny percentage of rooms are in the main building; instead most of the 45 rooms are in a new block next door. The rooms were renovated at the end of 2007 and promised to have better bathrooms and more features such as broadband Internet access, but at least the features in the main building, such as its chandeliers, wooden staircases, and round windows, have been well preserved, and the manicured lawn out front is lovely.

LAPIS CASA BOUTIQUE HOTEL $$$$

68 Taicang Lu, 5382 1600, www.lapiscasahotel.com

In a location to die for a block away from Xintiandi, this small and elegant place opened in May 2007 after its brother and sister owners, who run a popular interior-decoration store, spent two years converting the unassuming building into an antique-filled peaceful haven. Guests enter through large European-style wooden doors before reaching the stone-floored reception, and corridors lined with lovely stained glass lead to the rooms. The 18 guest rooms have different themes though all are from the past, but the favorite (and most expensive) is the corner suite with its 1900s traditional Shanghainese decor, wooden floors, soft lighting, and red carpet. There is also a 1930s-themed stylish bar and restaurant, but it doesn't seem to attract a crowd, probably because of the myriad of other options in the area.

C MANSION HOTEL $$$$

82 Xinle Lu, 5403 9888, www.chinamansionhotel.com

Opened in May 2007, this beautifully renovated 32-room hotel in the heart of the French Concession is a labor of love for the owner, a local businessman, and captures the essence of old Shanghai for eye-wateringly high prices: Rooms are priced in U.S. dollars. The villa in a walled courtyard garden dates from 1932 and you step back in time as you step into the reception area. The building was once owned by an associate of the gangster Du Yuesheng and held some infamous parties: Nowadays it's a place to sip afternoon tea while listening to the original phonograph. All rooms are decorated in the same style with tasteful carpets, artwork, and leafy plants, as well as all business standards such as fax machines and wireless Internet access. Bathrooms have some art deco touches on the walls and a whirlpool bath as standard. The roof terrace has great views over the city though the food is hit-and-miss and overpriced. But if the eye-catching room rates don't put you off the price of the food won't either, and while the Mansion Hotel is firmly at the top of the scale, the excellent staff help to ease the pain of the bill at checkout time.

NO.9 $$$

9, Lane 355, Jianguo Xilu, 6471 9950

Staying here is more like staying in someone's beautiful and surprisingly rustic 1930s house than in a hotel, thanks to its tiny size and personal service. You'll find this delightful bed-and-breakfast with its own walled garden down a lively back lane where life continues in much the same way it has for centuries: Taxi drivers can struggle to find No.9 as it doesn't shout about its existence, so be sure to have its telephone number on you at all times. After a frantic day's sightseeing, your room will feel like a peaceful haven, though it's something of a lottery as to what kind of facilities you'll enjoy as some rooms feature more add-ons than others. The only reason not to enjoy a stay here is if you want the anonymity of a larger hotel: Here everyone will see your comings and goings. If you can afford it, book the penthouse, which is the most private with its own TV room, small kitchenette, and terrace.

OKURA GARDEN HOTEL $$$$

58 Maoming Nanlu, 6415 1111,
www.gardenhotelshanghai.com

With its outstanding location on one of Shanghai's nicest tree-lined shopping streets, combined with the stunning white baroque exterior of the former French Club built in 1926 and lush grounds that served as the community's sports ground, this hotel should be one of Shanghai's best. But it's not quite there, as rooms don't live up to expectations. The reception areas in the original French Club building have some lovely art deco touches, such as original fireplaces and curved staircases, but rooms in the 33-story extension behind it don't come with the same level of style. In 2006, half the rooms were renovated, updating the bathrooms and providing better lighting. All staff speak good English but Japanese is the most popular second language as the hotel is a standard choice for Japanese business travelers (the high-tech Japanese toilets might come as a surprise). The hotel's restaurants are overpriced so don't bother staying in but head out to the local area, which has many of the city's best restaurants.

OLD HOUSE INN $$$

16, Lane 351, Huashan Lu, 6248 6118, www.oldhouse.cn

This delightful converted lane house tucked down a nondescript alley near the Hilton Hotel was a breath of fresh air for the Shanghai hotel scene when it opened in 2005, thanks to its beautifully renovated, small selection of stylish rooms at very reasonable rates. The most expensive room, with an antique four-poster bed and brand-new gray-tiled bathroom, is worth splashing out on for its 1930s elegance with seductive lights and blood-red painted walls giving it a romantic air. As it's such a small hotel, don't expect a business center or gym, but there is an Internet terminal and a few extras available such as airport pickup—worth arranging as few taxi drivers know this place, and it's worth bearing in mind that walls are thin and noise might be a concern to light sleepers. But perhaps best of all, the Old House Inn's restaurant, A Future Perfect, is one of Shanghai's best contemporary restaurants and like the hotel, is very well priced.

PUDI BOUTIQUE HOTEL $$$$

99 Yandang Lu, 5158 5888, www.accorhotels.com

Part of the massive French Mecure hotel chain, the Pudi Boutique Hotel, which opened in 2007, is a great choice for people looking for brand-new facilities in a small stylish hotel. Slightly hard to find, it is next door to Fuxing Park, and there are only 50 rooms, the smallest of which is a very generous 50 square meters, and they are beautifully decorated and offer laid-back luxury with an interesting blend of modern chic and traditional Chinese touches such as fish tanks for good feng shui. Each room has a floor-to-ceiling window—try to book a room overlooking the park—and the bathrooms are relaxing with huge stand-alone tubs. The hotel's bar, restaurant, and gym are on the top floor to take advantage of the views, but don't expect a pumping scene as few people seem to know about the hotel—so far.

Plenty of nostalgia is on offer at the Old House Inn.

RUIJIN GUESTHOUSE $$$

118 Ruijin 2 Lu, 6472 5222,
www.shedi.net.cn/outedi/ruijin/

There are few things nicer in Shanghai than sitting with a drink on the manicured lawns of this venerable hotel, a green oasis in the midst of a sea of skyscrapers. The Ruijin's selling points are its grounds, history, and location and it deserves to be considered a highlight of the Shanghai hotel scene if you can ignore the uneven service (English skills are not great) and the mediocre breakfast that is included in the price. Accommodation is spread around the complex in different buildings; Building 1 is the best option with great bathrooms and was the former Morris estate, but the other villas are equally historic. If you are staying on the weekend during the summer, you are sure to see a Chinese wedding as the place is a very popular venue, and you are stumbling distance from one of the city's best bars, Face, which is part of the complex along with its great though expensive Indian and Thai restaurants.

Pudong

Map 14

GRAND HYATT $$$$

88 Shiji Dadao, 5049 1234, www.hyatt.com

Whatever superlatives you wish to use about this five-star hotel, it deserves them all. Sitting near the top of the imposing Jin Mao Tower, it's the tallest hotel in the world—a fact that you couldn't be unaware of considering the giddying views from rooms and the eardrum-affecting 50-second-long elevator ride to the lobby on the 52nd floor. The excellent multilingual staff have overlooked only one thing—perhaps they should provide sickness pills to deal with the vertigo many people experience when looking up or down at the atrium. The more-expensive rooms overlook the Bund and have floor-to-ceiling windows, but nearly overshadowing the views are the luxurious bathrooms, which also enjoy the same vistas. The only real gripe is that the hotel charges guests a cover charge at its bar on the 87th floor, Cloud 9. Wouldn't you think that at these sky-high prices it wouldn't do that?

PUDONG SHANGRI-LA $$$$

33 Fucheng Lu, 6882 8888, www.shangri-la.com

Shanghai's largest hotel has 950 rooms, jaw-dropping views from its outstanding and glamorous bar and restaurant Jade on 36, and many extras and facilities everywhere you look, including laptop-size room safes with built-in rechargers, TVs in the bathrooms, and best of all, in the executive rooms, electrically controlled blinds that open to reveal floor-to-ceiling views of the Bund with binoculars and a guide to all the buildings you can peer down at. The smaller older tower may be nearer the waterfront, but the new tower has better decoration and on higher floors, fabulous views. The bathrooms are smaller than you expect and plastic looking, but that's a small flaw in an amazing overall package. The Himalayan-themed spa has a whole floor to itself, with just eight incredibly luxurious treatment rooms; a sunken tub containing a sprinkling of rose petals is a central feature. Being so large, the hotel is popular for conferences, but staff try to make the service as personal as possible by assigning concierges and butlers to all executive guests.

ST REGIS $$$$

889 Dongfang Lu, 5050 4567, www.stregis.com/shanghai

The St Regis opened its striking red 40-story building in 2001 and promptly became Shanghai's top destination for discerning travelers who appreciate the small touches that are this hotel's signature. Three floors are for women only and the spacious mirrored bathrooms with separate deep tub and rainfall shower come with Bvlargi toiletries. The only negative is the location—the odd taxi driver might sigh on hearing your destination—but do remember the subway is only a five-minute walk away. The 24-hour butler service prides itself on fulfilling any request and the service is deft, anticipating and friendly from your in-room check-in to when you reluctantly pack your bags. All staff have been extremely well trained. All rooms have the same color scheme of relaxing brown and old gold and come with Bose CD players and DVD players: By the end of 2008, all TVs were to be plasma flat-screens.

The quiet gym is open 24 hours if you're battling jet lag. All guests have access to the lounge on the 40th floor where breakfast (included in the rate) is offered, but be sure to head there at night when your free drinks and canapés come with the excellent views of the neon skyscrapers surrounding you. Butlers will serve as translators on tours. The hotel also organizes regular art exhibitions where guests can meet up-and-coming artists.

Greater Shanghai

Map 15

LINGLONG HOTEL $

939 Yan'an Xilu, 62250360, www.hostelworld.com

Bargain-priced beds are a rare sight in this area, so this small 16-room hotel that was once a private residence dating from the 1930s is a great choice. It is beautifully decorated and spotless throughout if on the old-fashioned side and it feels as if you're staying in someone's home rather than in an anonymous hotel—the only drawback is that it is on a busy street: Look out for the word "Hotel" in English on the outside of the white town house, which looks as if it should be in Surrey, England, not Shanghai. While staff don't speak fluent English, they get top marks for their friendliness and helpfulness. For a bargain-priced hotel room with bags of character with a bathroom en suite in an OK location, the Linglong can't be beaten.

PIER ONE $$$

88 Yichang Lu, 5155 8399, www.pierone-hotel.com

Pier One is part of an arty new development on Suzhou Creek and the first boutique hotel to open in this up-and-coming area near the arty complex at 50 Moganshan Road. Twenty-four rooms fit snugly within the framework of this Ladislaus Hudec–designed gem, and the building's heritage is evident in the uniquely shaped rooms, but you can't help but think it's a mistake that not more of the original features were kept, and the dazzling-white color scheme is a bit on the precious side. The rooms to reserve are the spacious duplexes and extravagant Emperor, Empress, and Concubine-themed suites. The main problem is the distance from town, but those willing to trade city conveniences for lotus-fringed ponds, river views, and arty surroundings now have an interesting option in Pier One.

EXCURSIONS FROM SHANGHAI

For a chance of pace and an escape from the razzle-dazzle of the city, pack a day pack, consult a map, and leave the bright lights of Shanghai behind you. The city has excellent transport links to its neighboring provinces of Zhejiang to the south and Jiangsu to the north and if you can spare a day, it's definitely worth exploring a little.

Water has been the cause of the whole region's wealth and prosperity, and two of China's most popular destinations, Hangzhou and Suzhou, which are both within day-trip distance, have been its biggest winners. You will hear ad nauseam the phrase "In heaven there is paradise, on earth Suzhou and Hangzhou," and you have to admire the confidence of the travel board, as really what cities could live up to that? But if you take these claims with a pinch of salt, you'll be rewarded with a pleasant excursion and a chance to experience a different pace of life, a brush with nature, and, last but not least, the Chinese train system.

Hangzhou's charm lies in its vast body of water on the edge of the city, while Suzhou's number-one attraction, its picturesque gardens, saw its ardent fan, the explorer Marco Polo, dub the city "the Venice of the East"—another phrase you'll see plastered on every surface. Aside from the gardens, its interesting history attracts visitors—dating from the 7th century, the city was the end of the road (river?) for the Grand Canal, considered one of the world's greatest engineering feats.

If these destinations don't appeal to you, both a Buddhist mountain island and the ancient canal town that served as a backdrop for Tom Cruise's

©BARBARA STROTHER

HIGHLIGHTS

LOOK FOR ☾ TO FIND RECOMMENDED SIGHTS, ACTIVITIES, DINING, AND LODGING.

☾ **Best Day Trip from Shanghai:** Thanks to superfast bullet trains, Hangzhou's **Xi Hu** is within easy reach; here you can experience the lake's misty prettiness, which has inspired poets and writers for centuries (page 257).

☾ **Best Place to Combine Beaches and Buddhism:** Putuoshan is becoming increasingly developed, so come now to enjoy its atmospheric **Puji Temple** before kicking back at Thousand Step Beach (page 260).

☾ **Best Place for a Lesson on Feng Shui:** The highly stylized **Garden of the Master of the Nets** in Suzhou is both educational and enchanting (page 262).

© BARBARA STROTHER

Xi Hu in Hangzhou

film *Mission Impossible III* are within a few hours' traveling time. Shanghai is crisscrossed with ancient canals built as inland trade routes during the Ming and Qing dynasties, and sometimes it feels as though the pace of life at these villages, with elderly fishermen out at dawn and traders hawking local specialties door to door, hasn't changed since then. But then, you see the tourists. . . . Some villages have been swamped by day trippers with the most celebrated town of Zhouzhuang now too busy because of unregulated tourism. I suggest skipping this overdeveloped village as crawling around the cobbled streets at a snail's pace because of the crowds is too frustrating. Instead, try Xitang or Tongli, which are slightly farther afield. The island of Putuoshan is best visited over a couple of days as the boat journey alone takes four hours. The Buddhist island is no longer the secret getaway it once was, and now some visitors choose to fly from Shanghai to the nearby island of Zhujiajian and then take the short ferry ride to the island. Wherever you go, ask your hotel for the latest travel information, and it may be best to consider a tour, especially if you're going only for a day trip.

PLANNING YOUR TIME

If time is limited and you can do only one trip out of the city, Hangzhou gets my vote. The city itself is prosperous and as Chinese cities go, attractive, but its stunning lake surrounded by shady gardens and willow trees trailing in the water lives up to most visitors' expectations of China in a way that Shanghai with its brash modernity certainly doesn't. Suzhou is also very popular with tourists, but its beauty can be difficult to appreciate through the crowds. The canal towns are almost as popular and more difficult to get to: If they appeal to you, renting a car for the day from Shanghai is your best option.

Shanghai has two airports, three train stations, two ferry terminals, and bus stations too numerous to mention, so there are many different ways to leave the city: The secret is to make sure you make reservations if at all possible as a lot of other people are also going to be seeking some peace and quiet. If possible, always go to any of the destinations in this chapter during the week, as crowds on weekends, especially in Suzhou, can cause the most dedicated traveler to wilt, especially on a hot, humid day.

The best time to go depends on your destination. The vast majority of the attractions at these places are outdoors, so the dead of winter would not be advisable unless you like your tourist sights cold and overcast, and especially in the case of Suzhou as the gardens

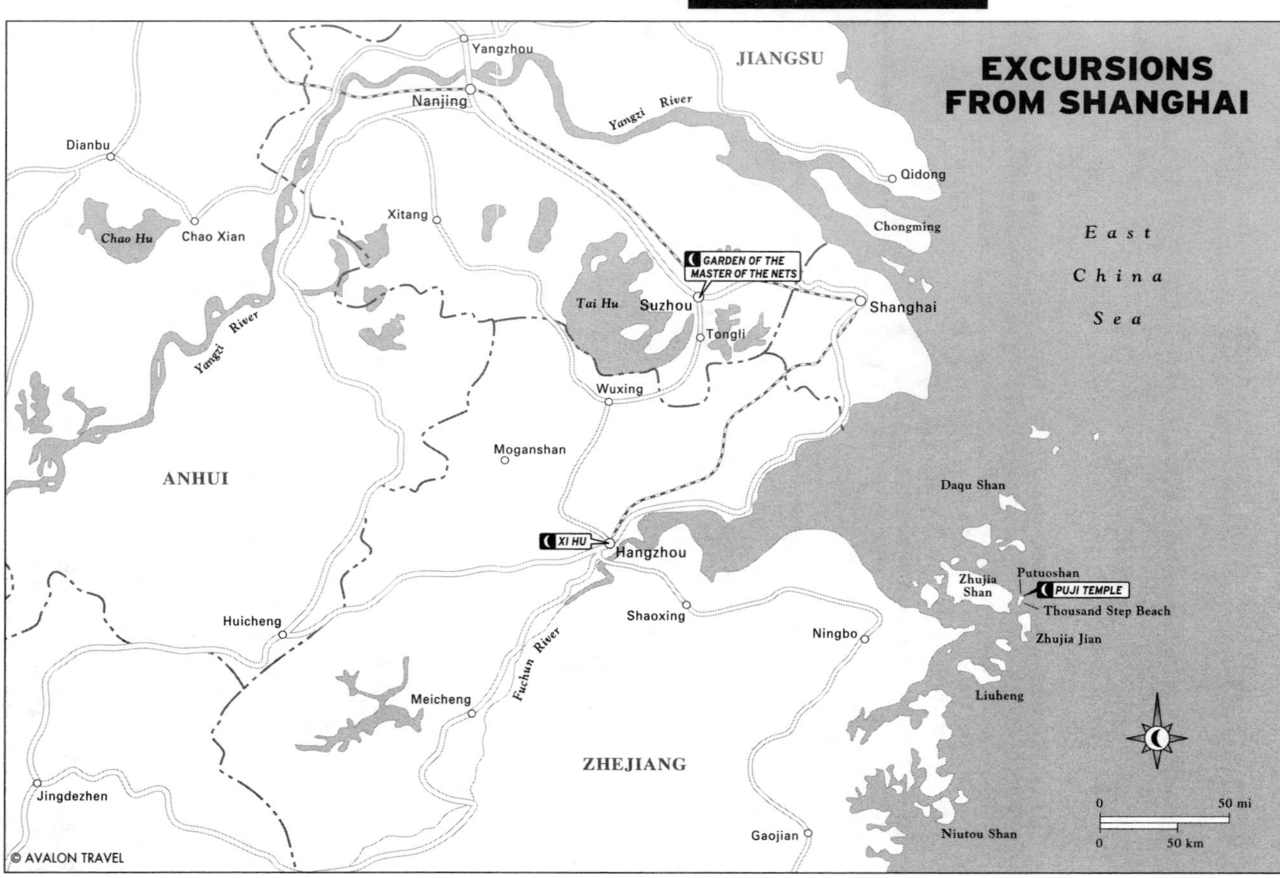
EXCURSIONS FROM SHANGHAI
East China Sea
JIANGSU
Yangzhou
Nanjing
Yangzi River
Dianbu
Chao Hu
Chao Xian
Xitang
Qidong
Chongming
GARDEN OF THE MASTER OF THE NETS
Tai Hu
Suzhou
Shanghai
Tongli
Yangzi River
Wuxing
Moganshan
ANHUI
Daqu Shan
XI HU
Hangzhou
Zhujia Shan
Putuoshan
PUJI TEMPLE
Thousand Step Beach
Huicheng
Shaoxing
Ningbo
Zhujia Jian
Fuchun River
Meicheng
Liuheng
ZHEJIANG
Jingdezhen
0
50 mi
0
50 km
Gaojian
Niutou Shan
© AVALON TRAVEL

won't exactly be looking their best. Spring and fall are the best times to visit all the destinations listed: It won't be too hot, humid, or cold, though it's a good idea to always have an umbrella on you just in case and just as in the region itself, water is not usually far away. If you prefer private transport, the excellent and English-speaking Shanghai Eastern Taxi Service is not prohibitively expensive. Go to www.shanghai-taxi.com for more details.

Hangzhou (Hángzhōu 杭州)

One of China's most popular destinations, the city's beauty has been eulogized for centuries, just like Suzhou. Visitors arriving at the train station may wonder what all the fuss is about, but you can understand its popularity when you first glance at the huge lake called Xi Hu, or West Lake, which has inspired writers and painters for centuries. Local and an increasing amount of international tourists come to Hangzhou not just to see the serene beauty of the lake and breathe some relatively fresh air, but also to see the nearby tea plantations surrounded by hills and lush green forests. There are plenty of antique buildings to stroll through, though as ever in China, they are being knocked down at a frightening pace. Now that there are superfast bullet trains, it's possible to do "Shanghai's garden" in a day trip, or as snooty Hangzhouvians put it when they make the trip in the opposite direction, head to "Hangzhou's Shopping Mall." Hangzhou is hugely popular so if you can, arrange your day trip during the week rather than on weekends, when the trains and lake promenades are packed: This is a city that sees a mind-boggling more than 30 million domestic tourists every year.

SIGHTS

Xi Hu

A short taxi ride from the train station on the western edge of the city is Hangzhou's main sight, the very picturesque Xi Hu. The lake is fringed by hills, shady parks, and caves, and if you came to Hangzhou only to amble or cycle round the lake, it would be a worthwhile trip. The most convenient way to get around the lake's circumference is to rent a bike from the rental stands around the lake—there are 27 stands dotted around so you can't miss them. Every 15 minutes there's a dancing fountain show by Lubin Promenade, but if that's not to your taste, it's worth heading clockwise around the lake to the popular local meeting place for the elderly, who gather here to sing folk songs and play traditional instruments. As you make your way around the lake, don't miss **Leifeng Pagoda** (daily 8 A.M.–4:30 P.M., 5RMB). This octagonal five-story structure was originally built in 975 B.C. It has been rebuilt many times since then, but the open-air ruins of the original building are open for viewing. From there the top floor has upper views across the lake and its islands, lakeside pagodas, and the city in the distance. Don't miss getting onto the water and visiting the three islands dotted around the lake. The trips last around three hours if you visit all the islands and tickets that last all day cost 40RMB. You can spend as much time as you want at each island and the small boats run between all the islands until sunset. The boats leave from Nanshan Lu near the Carrefour superstore.

FOOD

Xihutiandi (south bank of Xi Hu) is Hangzhou's answer to Shanghai's trendy Xintiandi development, home to fancy boutiques and endless rows of restaurants. The whole area is now a major Hangzhou attraction, and the excellent and stylish **Va Bene** (House 8, Xihutiandi, 147 Nanshan Lu, 0571 8702 6333) Italian restaurant is in the center of the complex. Hangzhou food is considered one of the eight regional cuisines of China, and it is lighter and more delicate than Shanghainese cuisine. For traditional Hangzhou specialties, try noisy but fun

Louwailou (30 Gushan Lu, 0571 8796 9023), which has been serving dishes such as West Lake fish and Beggar's Chicken since the 1840s. It's always packed with tourists who enjoy the food and the lovely views over the lake, so make reservations. Hangzhou also has a good night market along Wushan Lu where interesting snacks and unrecognizable things on a stick are barbecued in front of you. Choose the busiest stalls, though, because they have a high turnover of food. Some tourists think that a visit to a teahouse is a highlight of Hangzhou, and I agree: Try **Qing Teng** (Yuanhua Plaza, 278 Nanshan Lu, 0571 8702 2777), one of the oldest teahouses in the city. It is very atmospheric with bamboo furniture and streams running through the tea room, which you cross using elegant wooden bridges. You choose which kind of tea you want (the famous local brew Longjing is 50RMB per person) and then you can eat your fill at the snack buffet for free.

ACCOMMODATIONS

For budget beds, look no farther than **West Lake Youth Hostel** (Number 62–3 Nan Shan Road, 571 8702 7027, www.sinohotels.com, 45RMB dorm, 150RMB double). The hostel is full of old-fashioned character and has a great location on the banks of the lake near Leifeng Pagoda. The 21 double rooms and dorms are bright and spacious though all fittings are a little cheap and cheerful, especially the basic wooden furniture, but this is where travelers to Hangzhou congregate.

Further up the price scale and enjoying a similarly nice though more remote location by the lake is the often-overlooked **Xihu State Guest House** (18 Yang Gong Causeway, 571 8797 9889, www.xihusgh.com, 600RMB double). The guesthouse, which is occasionally used for important government meetings (well, Chinese leaders like nice views, too) has wonderful grounds and views of the lake. Bear in mind that the hotel is not within walking distance of the city center, but who needs to leave when the grounds are this nice and the staff do a great job in making you welcome?

Farther afield is one of China's most luxurious hotels, the **Fuchun Resort** (Fuyang Section, Hangzhou, 571 6346 1111, www.fuchunresort.com, 2,000RMB double). The resort is on a 150-acre site between mountains and the pretty Fuchun River south of Hangzhou. Here you'll find an 18-hole golf course sculpted from the hills of the surrounding tea plantation, a luxurious clubhouse and driving range, a boutique hotel with comprehensive spa, and a group of 48 luxurious villas with private pools. Guests rave about the pavilions set against misty Hangzhou mountains, and the whole place is a fantastic, if very expensive, place to explore.

GETTING THERE AND AROUND

Virtually all foreign tourists travel to Hangzhou by train from Shanghai and superfast bullet trains have whizzed passengers from Shanghai South Railway Station to Hangzhou in around an hour—not bad considering the distance is 170km south. A good schedule for a day trip is to catch the 9:36 A.M. train there and return on the 5:19 P.M. train. A soft-seat first-class ticket costs 63RMB each way. To check departure schedules, ask your hotel or check the website, www.travelchinaguide.com/china-trains. Bullet trains are prefixed with the letter D, and Hangzhou has a dedicated bullet-train waiting lounge on the right-hand side of the waiting hall—it has comfier chairs and a few snacks concessions.

In the city, if you don't wish to use up all your energy walking around the lake, there is a golf buggy–like tourist bus that ferries people around the lake. If you want to travel under your own steam, bikes cost 10RMB an hour or 50RMB for the day, and you have to leave a 200RMB deposit before you can take one of the bright red, yellow, or green bikes for a spin. Distances between attractions aren't long—taxi journeys should not ever cost more than 20RMB unless you are going out to Longjing Tea Village.

OUTSIDE HANGZHOU

The area surrounding Hangzhou is famous for its fine green tea, so if sipping a cup near the source appeals to you, a visit to **Longjing Tea Village** (daily 8:30 A.M.–4:30 P.M.) is a must, as much for the scenery as the brew itself. When you arrive at the village, you'll see local farmers lining the roadside and stirring their tea leaves over roasters with their bare hands. The actual village on the side of a mountain is very pretty, with winding streets and a stream running through the middle. An increasing amount of development is taking place and prices for tea are rising sharply, but the leaves are still much cheaper than what you would pay in the big cities. Unless you are a real connoisseur, though, it's not worth spending a fortune on tea as the differences in taste are too subtle for most people to tell. For more information on tea production, there's a small museum (10RMB) in the village with an adequate amount of English explanations. Longjing is about 12km outside of Hangzhou and it can be reached by taking City Bus 27 or Tourist Bus 3.

Qinghefang Lu (Hefang Jie) is one of those attractions you see only in China, where local tourists prefer the new to the old. It's a reconstruction of a traditional Qing dynasty shopping street that was knocked down to build the reconstruction, if you follow my meaning. It could be horrible, but it's actually quiet charming as there are many little shops that preserve local traditional arts and crafts such as silk, paintings of local beauty spots such as Xi Hu, and embroidery. There are also snack-food vendors lining the wooden street if you get puckish. To find the street, look for the entrance close to Wushan Square at the end of Yanan Nan Lu. If you rent a bike, you can cycle from downtown in about 20 minutes.

Lingyin Temple (1 Fayun Jie, south bank of Xi Hu, 8 A.M.–5 P.M., 30RMB) is a magnificent Buddhist temple whose name translates as the Temple of the Soul's Retreat. The complex boasts a spectacular entrance—a series of caves and hillside grottoes featuring around 350 Buddhist hill carvings, many dating from the 10th century. The incense-filled temple features four grand halls. The 12-meter-high Hall of the 500 Arhats features 500 life-size Buddhist statues. Behind the temple is a cable car that takes passengers up the craggy peak and offers great views over the lake and city. The cable car that takes you to the summit is 20RMB, and the views make this fee completely worth it on a clear day, though bear in mind Hangzhou suffers from the same kind of smog as most Chinese cities. There's also a small café and a viewing platform at the top, with plenty of space to sit and gaze at the views. You reach the cable car by continuing up the road where the temple is situated.

Putuoshan (Pǔtuóshān 普陀山)

Few foreign tourists would expect a mountainous lush island to be a few hours from Shanghai, but the island of Putuoshan is full of surprises with Buddhist temples, quiet beaches, and mountainous surroundings all to be found. Every year a million pilgrims come to this island, which is dedicated to the Buddhist goddess of mercy Guanyin, and increasing numbers of foreign visitors are discovering the island for themselves. The legend goes that Guanyin came to the island in A.D. 916 when a Japanese monk was taking a statue of her from Japan to the Chinese mainland. As he got nearer the mainland, a fierce storm blew up, and the deity appeared to him in a dream and promised the monk would return home to Japan safely if the statue were left on the island. The statue stayed on Putuoshan and remains there to this day in the southeast corner of the island. Buddhism thrived on the island for centuries, and at one point there were three large temple complexes and 88 nunneries. Many of the religious buildings were destroyed during the Cultural Revolution, and now there are just the three temples and a few nunneries. While the island still attracts plenty of pilgrims, their numbers are now matched by bikini- and Speedo-clad tourists seeking some fun in the sun on Thousand Step Beach while munching on freshly caught seafood. Unfortunately, there is a lot of building work going on on the island as tourist authorities seek to turn it into a smaller version of Hainan Island, which is off the south coast of China and hugely popular with Chinese sunseekers. It's cashing in on its newfound popularity, and all arrivals have to pay a 110RMB entrance fee to the island.

© HELENA IVESON

the island of Putuoshan's Thousand Step Beach

SIGHTS

Puji Temple

Situated at the center of Putuoshan, this is the most accessible and famous monastery on the island, and it costs 5RMB to enter. Puji, which is by far the largest of Putuoshan's temples, is situated at the base of a mountainous forest, which is hard to see through the haze from the courtyards' large fire pits, where pilgrims burn incense and pray. The best time to see the temple's monks in action is very early, before 7 A.M., though the temple gets very crowded.

Just more than a mile north is the second-largest temple, **Fayu.** It is much quieter than Puji and the monks are less jaded by tourists. This temple is famous for its delicate wood carvings and you can still read the calligraphy written by Chinese emperors from centuries ago. Parts of the temple date from 1580, though it's been heavily remodeled since then. It is on the left top of the Baihua hill, and you can get there via cable car or by a 20-minute walk up the hill.

For more earthly pleasures, head to nearby **Thousand Step Beach** for sunbathing and a paddle. The sand is nice enough, but I'm not sure full immmersion in the sea is a good idea; if you're feeling brave and it doesn't look too murky, go ahead. During peak season there's an entrance charge to the beach, but you can sometimes avoid that if you simply walk around the entrance to the beach. The beach has facilities such as sun loungers and parasols, quad bikes (off-road buggies) and banana boats for rent. At night, the beach is sometimes used to host karaoke parties—shy singers be warned: If you're spotted, you will definitely be expected to take part! The island's second beach, Hundred Step Beach, is longer and free to enter but no facilities are available.

FOOD

Seafood is plentiful and one of the more worldly highlights of Putuoshan, though you can be gouged over prices. Try one of the bright orange stands on the promenade in the evenings, where the freshest stuff has been caught the same evening, but agree on the prices before you order: Expect to pay 100RMB a head, including cooking charges. Vegetarian food is easy to find, since the island is dominated by Buddhism—all the temples have enjoyable restaurants.

ACCOMMODATIONS

While there is plenty of accommodation to be had, some foreign tourists report that they have been turned away from the cheap local options that local tourists go to—there seems to be some kind of reluctance to house foreigners. To avoid a three-hour walk around the island fruitlessly trying to find somewhere to stay, visit the accommodation bureau at the port. The staff are extremely helpful and provide reliable information on hotels and guesthouses on the island. During national holidays, make room reservations using elong.net or sinohotels.com.

The island's best hotel is the **Putuoshan Hotel** (93 Meicen Lu, 0580 609 2828, 600RMB double), though given the lack of competition, it doesn't seem to be making much of an effort. It resembles a school building from the outside, and inside expect plenty of cheap glitz, but rooms are clean and neat. It's also only a five-minute walk from the pier.

For cheaper, though not that much more cheerful, accommodation, try the **Baibuge Hotel** (209 Puji Lu, 0580 609 2199, 150RMB). The best thing about this place is its proximity to the beach, and though staff aren't particularly interested, the rooms are clean enough for the price. The touts at the pier who offer this hotel wave at you a brochure that is more than a few years out of date, so don't be disappointed!

GETTING THERE AND AROUND

If you're in a hurry, visitors seeking a bit of sunshine in Putuoshan can fly to the island's airport, actually on a neighboring island, from Shanghai's smaller airport, Hongqiao. The flights are operated by China Eastern Airlines—it's easiest to check elong.com for prices and flight times rather than phoning the actual airline. Once you've landed, you then have to catch a taxi to the dock before taking a short speedboat ride to the island. It is of course much easier and quicker to fly, and only slightly more expensive, but the old-fashioned and more environmentally friendly way is to catch a ferry to the island. Don't bother with the slow overnight ferries; instead buy a ticket for the more zippy ferries that do the journey in around four hours. You definitely need to reserve the tickets in advance and bear in mind that the trips are weather dependent: I've turned up at the dock and been told it was too rough to cross. The dock from which the ferries leave is south of Shanghai: Passengers catch a bus from 1588 Waima Lu, which is near Nanpu Bridge; the bus ride is included in the price of the ticket. Tickets cost 225RMB for a first-class ticket and it's worth paying the few RMB extra for first class. To save yourself a trip to the ticket office, which is incredibly difficult to find and very unhelpful, either ask your hotel to get tickets for you, or use China's travel agency CITS (2 Jinling Donglu, 6323 8749), which will reserve them for you for a minimal service charge.

On the island, Putuoshan has an efficient minibus service that links all the island's main attractions, and it costs just 2RMB per journey. You will need to be able to tell the driver your destination, however, so make sure you have the name of your destination written down in characters to show the driver, or master the tones! If weather permits, the island is best explored on foot, so make the most of the opportunity to get some exercise, as most Chinese destinations are not as pedestrian friendly.

Suzhou (Sūzhōu 苏州)

Thanks to its traders, cultural life, and beautiful gardens, Suzhou, 100km west of Shanghai, used to be the most desirable address in China when Shanghai was a sleepy backwater. About 1,400 years ago, the village found itself in the middle of the Grand Canal's north-south axis, the country's main transportation route for trade. Important merchants moved in and transformed Suzhou into a rich and beautiful town crisscrossed by the picturesque canals still used today. Suzhou became a byword for pleasure, with the already ancient city's silk industry further built up and struggling to keep up with the demand for luxurious cloth, and as the numbers of rich merchants increased, the older pillars of the community retired and spent much of their time designing the lavish feng-shui'd gardens that Suzhou is now most famous for.

Suzhou's cultural heyday was a long time ago, however, and on arrival, visitors may struggle to see any remnants of the city's glamorous past. Nowadays the city is a bustling commercial town that has attracted plenty of foreign investment, but unlike a thousand years ago, profits aren't being spent on charming gardens but on ultrabrash office buildings. The local tourist board does rather overstate Suzhou's charms, but there is enough to do for at least a full day trip from Shanghai, and if you have a special interest in the intellectually interesting aesthetics of Chinese gardens, a two-day visit is a good idea. Oh, and in addition to the gardens and silk industry, Suzhou has another claim to fame: Its women are supposed to be the most beautiful in China.

SIGHTS

The Gardens

In a country so overflowing with humanity, gardens were and are private places for the owner's family to seclude themselves in peace, away from prying eyes. But that is where the similarity to Western gardens ends, as you won't find any grassy lawns, beds of begonias, or other features common in the West in the highly prized UNESCO Heritage–listed gardens of Suzhou. Chinese gardens can be difficult to understand as beauty is just one small element of the gardens, and everything is symbolic, from the way a rock is arranged to where a shady tree is situated. The attention to detail is staggering: Visitors are even supposed to follow a certain route via the meandering paths leading to a particular garden that has a particular meaning. The gardens serve as a microcosm of the world with man, the master, arranging nature, which is part of the Taoist philosophy. The importance of nature should not be understated, though, with elements such as water and earth hugely important (hence all the rock gardens).

The city once had more than 100 gardens, but now just a handful remain and have been fully restored and opened to the public. The three gardens considered the best (and therefore the busiest with megaphone-waving tour leaders followed by baseball hat–wearing tourists) are the Garden of the Master of the Nets, the Humble Administrator's Garden, and the Blue Wave Pavilion. Each garden costs 30RMB to visit so costs do add up and unfortunately there isn't an all-inclusive ticket.

GARDEN OF THE MASTER OF THE NETS

The Garden of the Master of the Nets (11 Kuotao Xiang off Shiquan Jie, 521 522 3550, 8 A.M.–4:30 P.M., 30RMB) is the smallest garden, but what it lacks in size, it makes up for in striking beauty, encompassing all the elements of a classic Chinese garden, including a tranquil pond, outdoor pavilion, tastefully decorated rooms, stone bridges, and serene courtyards. The garden, first built in 1140, was abandoned and not restored until it was transformed into the residence of a former official in 1770. The garden still gleams, but the huge crowds who flock here can take away the charm: Come as early or as late in the day as you can.

HUMBLE ADMINISTRATOR'S GARDEN

While the Garden of the Master of the Nets is the smallest, the Humble Administrator's Garden (178 Dongbei Jie, 521 826 7737, 8:15 A.M.–4:15 P.M., 30RMB) is one of the largest. It was built in the 16th century by a retired Ming dynasty official who said he now wished to be a humble man, hence the name of the garden. Water features dominate and are dotted around small forests, hills, and rock formations.

BLUE WAVE PAVILION

The oldest garden in Suzhou is the Blue Wave Pavilion (Shiquan Jie, 7:30 A.M.–5:30 P.M., 30RMB). Unlike the previous two gardens, the Blue Wave Pavilion is not as famous and is more wild and, to some eyes, more attractive for it. It was originally designed for a prince well more than 1,000 years ago, and seeing the weeping willows trail into the many ponds and streams that flow through the garden is lovely.

Other Sights

To see Suzhou as traveling merchants such as Marco Polo did centuries ago, get on the water on a **boat tour.** In the 12th century there were 20 canals winding their way through the city, but the majority have been plugged. Up until recently, the canals were shadows of their former selves, filled with rubbish and smelling awful (a bit like Venice, after all?), but a cleanup campaign has made some major improvements to the remaining canals, and a tour underneath the humpbacked stone bridges and past the canal-side pagodas provides some great Kodak moments. There are a variety of different tour companies, but all follow the same basic loop. All boat tours depart from Guangji Lu.

The city's premier museum, **the Suzhou Silk Museum** (661 Renmin Lu, 512 6757 5666, 8 A.M.–5 P.M., 7RMB) is one of the most interesting in China. The bilingual exhibitions are very informative about the silk industry's 4,000 years of history in Suzhou; they take visitors through the whole process of making silk from the wriggling silkworms to the looms to the finished product. There's also a room full of antique embroidery that shows off the exquisiteness and painstaking skill of the silk spinners of the past. The museum is walking distance north of the train station.

FOOD

Qiantang Teahouse (793 Shiquan Jie, 521 6530 0001) is a warm and inviting place to rest after trampling your way around the gardens—the Garden of the Master of the Nets is nearby. You pay for your tea and waitresses keep refilling your pot with hot water until you can't drink another thing, and then you can help yourself to the free buffet, where you'll find Chinese snacks, appetizers, noodles, and fruit and cakes. In the evenings there are performances of local music.

Glitzy **Songhelou** (141 Guanqian Jie near Renmin Lu, 521 6727 7006) claims to be 2,000 years old and is the most famous restaurant in Suzhou; it once served emperors but now mainly caters to huge foreign tour groups who can afford the delicious, expensive dishes. Seafood dominates the menu and shrimp and freshwater fish, including sweet and sour mandarin fish and braised eel, are the most popular orders.

Deyuelou (27 Taijiang Jie, Guanqiang Lu, 512 6522 6969) also specializes in local dishes but without the glamour of Songhelou. The menu is full of traditional braised and simmered dishes such as pork simmered with crisp bamboo shoots and cherry-flavored pork: wonderful in cold winter months.

ACCOMMODATIONS

Bamboo Grove Hotel (168 Zhuhui Lu, 512 6520 5601, www.bg-hotel.com, 500RMB double through elong.com) doesn't have the best location as it's set in its own garden on a busy main road, but it is still a popular choice, especially with tour groups because it's inexpensive and rates include plenty of extras such as free broadband Internet, use of a pool, and breakfast. Rooms are on the tired side though adequate and spotlessly clean, and the reception staff speak good English and have a wide supply of maps to point you in the right direction of the sights.

Nanlin Hotel (20 Gun Xiu Fang, Shiquan Jie, 512 6801 7888, 500RMB double through elong.com) is deservedly popular with both independent travelers and an increasing number of tour groups. Its modern rooms were recently renovated, making them as attractive as the lovely public areas (though beds are on the rigid side of firm), and the hotel has an amazing buffet breakfast that would put many five-star Shanghai hotels to shame. Its location is excellent, close to the sights and downtown, but if you go the opposite way, the small traditional alleys are great to explore, too.

Nanyuan Guesthouse (249 Shiquan Jie, 512 522 7661, 300RMB) is on a much smaller scale than either the Bamboo Grove or Nanlin Hotel and is set inside secluded grounds near the Humble Administrator's Garden. Rooms are great value for the price, but they have definitely seen better days.

GETTING THERE AND AROUND

The best way to get to Suzhou is on one of the hourly express services that leave Shanghai Railway Station. The journey takes just over an hour, and a one-way ticket is 25RMB—there's no need to make reservations. Check www.travelchinaguide.com/china-trains for the exact schedules. If you'd prefer private transport, round-trip by taxi will cost around 600RMB or renting a car for the day will cost 900RMB. This is not a bad option if there are a few of you traveling together. Ask your hotel for advice and help or contact the English-speaking taxi service Shanghai Eastern Taxi Service (www.shanghai-taxi.com).

Tongli (Tónglǐ 同理)

A two-hour drive from Shanghai, but just half an hour's drive from Suzhou, Tongli is far enough to keep the crowds away from the atmospheric alleyways lining the canals. For such a small place, Tongli has a huge number of stone bridges that crisscross the canal. The charms of the place are best explored by simply walking around and spying on the traditional way of life. You'll see old women spinning silk and their men nearby, getting excited over a game of mah-jongg. The village charges a pricy 80RMB admission but that includes access to the sights listed here; sights are open from 7:45 A.M.–5:30 P.M.

SIGHTS

The main traditional sights are the **Tuisi Yuan Water Garden** and **Jiayin Hall.** UNESCO World Heritage–listed Tuisi Yuan was built in 1886 and during your visit you can wander around the original family's residence and the beautiful landscaped garden. Jiayin Hall is another traditional residence with a quiet courtyard garden in the middle. It was built in 1922 as the residence of famous local scholar and is quieter than Tuisi Yuan. But since 2001, Tongli has had the most unlikely interloper banished from Shanghai: the **Museum of Ancient Chinese Sex Culture.** The collection was put together over many years by a Shanghai University professor, and there are more than 1,600 relics that span more than 9,000 years of Chinese history.

Xitang (Xītáng 西塘)

This charming canal town 90km from Shanghai has not yet been consumed by tourists, though thanks to the star power of Tom Cruise, who filmed scenes from *Mission Impossible III* here, numbers have hugely increased from the trickle they were just a few years ago. During filming, the town was closed for a week, much to the bemusement of locals. There are few sights to speak of, but the town is stunning at dusk when locals hang out red lanterns. Xitang has 122 lanes to explore: Have your cameras ready to capture the classic sights of rural China with the village's stone bridges, traditional gardens, and preserved merchant's mansions all making jaw-droppingly pretty sights. The village now charges tourists 30RMB to wander its streets; sights are open from 7:45 A.M.–5:30 P.M.

SIGHTS

The real pleasure of the place is just to wander aimlessly, but if you need sights to see, **Xiyua Garden** is probably Xitang's main actual attraction. It's a maze of courtyards, rockeries, bonsais, and ponds, and well worth a stroll though. You'll also find many photographers trying to capture the perfect shot of **Wangxian Bridge**. It was built in the Song dynasty more than 1,000 years ago and is named after a Taoist monk who stood guard on the bridge, warding off evil spirits.

GETTING THERE AND AROUND

Most tourists who wish to visit the canal towns hop on one of the dedicated tourist buses that leave from Shanghai Stadium (Gate 5, 666 Tianyao Qiao Lu, 6426 5555). Buses to Tongli leave at 9 A.M. and return at 4:30 P.M., and buses to Xitang leave weekdays at 8:45 A.M. and weekends at 9 A.M. All tickets cost 135RMB per person, including entrance fees to the villages, and take about 90 minutes to reach their destinations. A taxi would cost about 250RMB each way, though ordinary taxis may be reluctant to head so far out of the city so you may have to try a more expensive service, such as Shanghai Eastern Taxi Service (www.shanghai-taxi.com). Also consider Cycle China's tours to Xitang if you feel like getting some pedal power (www.cyclechina.com).

BACKGROUND

The Land

BEIJING

Geography and Climate

The capital is on the northern edge of eastern China, and as it has no coast or major waterways nearby, at first glance it might seem an odd location for a capital city. But many different dynasties chose to base themselves in Beijing, because of its central location between different regions of the country. It's more than 150 miles from the sea, but for centuries traders traversed through the area, which contributed to its development as a trading center, as did the fact that the region has long been rich in natural resources. The city's population is said to be a shade under 16 million, but with an unknown number of migrants who come to the city for work, no one really knows exactly how many people there are in its 6,487 square miles, which are 45m above sea level. Though Beijing proper is on flat land, there are many hills to the west, north, and northwest.

Geographers classify the city as lying in a warm temperate humid/subhumid zone. As residents will attest, this means that in summer all you'll need is the lightest of clothing (average temperatures in July are at 25–26°C (77–79°F), while in winter, when temperatures can drop to below 0° Celsius (32°F), visitors may need to wear everything they've brought to stay warm. In January, average temperatures

hover between -7 to -4°C (19–24°F). At least you won't have to worry about bringing an umbrella, unlike in Shanghai—here annual precipitation is little more than 600mm, with 75 percent of that in summer.

Environmental Issues

China's environmental problems are, or rather should be, the most important issue in China today. Headlines describing the country as one of the world's leading polluting nations are common, especially in reference to air and water pollution. Visitors will encounter heavy amounts of pollution: Even on an ordinary day in the capital, air-pollution levels are almost five times higher than what the World Health Organization considers safe. Bearing in mind that the government is out to impress visitors, it seems astonishing that the all-powerful state has not come to grips with the problem. In Beijing itself, the pollution becomes worse in winter, when residents heat their homes using cheap and plentiful coal. When Beijing won the Olympics in 2001, it promised to hold a "Green Olympics," yet air pollution did not get significantly better before the Games. The government did shut down blast furnaces in the city's biggest steel company to improve air quality and took a million cars off the roads during the Games, but while that may have helped the Olympic athletes, it doesn't really help the city's citizens, who still have to live there after the Games are a distant memory. In 2006, in a shocking survey, Chinese people marked Beijing as just the 15th most livable city in China. The previous year, the city was fourth, but people surveyed reported that the city's pollution and traffic accounted for the drop.

© HELENA IVESON

everyday traffic woes in Beijing

Aside from the terrible air, in spring the capital is increasingly plagued with dust storms caused by desert erosion in the north of the country—in 2008, four separate dust storms wreaked havoc. And despite the Olympic organizers' promise to ensure that tap water was safe to drink across the city by the Games, visitors should not drink tap water. As the Olympics approached, the pledge was reduced to safe drinking water just within the Olympic Village.

SHANGHAI

Geography and Climate

Shanghai is China's biggest and busiest city, with one of the world's largest populations packed into an area of about 2,448 square miles. While the official population is said to be around 17 million, many experts believe it is in actuality three million higher, because of the ever-increasing number of migrants seeking a new life there. Shanghai faces the East China Sea at the mouth of the Yangtze River in central-eastern China, 664 miles from Beijing. The city's name means "on the sea," and while that may not be precisely true, it's certainly bordered by plenty of water. Its neighboring provinces are Jiangsu and Zhejiang, well-known in China for their watery geography. It's because of this advantageous geographic location that Shanghai became the massive river and sea port it still is, one of the world's largest, thanks to the access it provides to the heartlands of China.

While Beijing has very short springs and falls, Shanghai is blessed with four distinct seasons. Winter visitors are likely to encounter gray skies and freezing temperatures, while in the hot and humid summer, average temperatures reach 32° Celsius (90°F) in July and August. The city has an average annual rainfall of 1,200mm, with the majority of precipitation between May and September.

Environmental Issues

Water pollution is one of the major issues in Shanghai, because of the city's proximity to the Yangtze River. This hugely important waterway, which stretches across the length of the country, receives 40 percent of the country's sewage, 80 percent of which is untreated—so don't drink the tap water. Aside from this issue, in three decades seas off Shanghai have risen by 4.53 inches, and occasionally newspaper reports claim that Shanghai will be underwater before too long. Rising sea levels have also led to contamination of drinking-water supplies, according to China's State Oceanic Administration.

It may be less polluted than Beijing, but the air in Shanghai is still considered heavily polluted by world standards. The problem of coal usage has caused major air pollution, and attempts are being made to lower residents' dependence on the fuel source as well as industrial usage. Aside from these forms of pollution, most Shanghainese are more concerned with noise from traffic and constant construction, according to the number of complaints to the Environmental Protection Bureau.

History

China has a whole lot of history behind it—the country dates back to the first millennium B.C.—and a full discourse is beyond the scope of this book, but here's a quick gallop through . . .

ANCIENT CIVILIZATION

Ancient man called the land surrounding present-day Beijing home. In the 1930s, at Zhoukoudian, just under 50km from Beijing, the remains of an early hominid who walked the earth between 500,000 and 300,000 years ago were found. Originally called *Sinanthropus pekinsis,* or Peking Man, the ancient figure is now called by a more familiar name: *Homo erectus.* The first real settlement in the area dates to around 1000 B.C. Beijing was first known as Ji, when during the Warring States period (475–221B.C.) it was a local capital and an international trading post. The city remained a military town and administrative center for more than 1,000 years.

EARLY HISTORY

In the 10th century, the Liao dynasty, who originated from Mongolia, chose the city as their second capital and changed Ji's name to Yanjing. The next dynasty, the Jin, renamed the city Zhongdu, or Central Capital. The Jin was not a very successful dynasty, and within 100 years, in 1215, the legendary Genghis Khan left Mongolia and took over and then destroyed Zhongdu. It wasn't until 1267 that the city was rebuilt under the orders of Genghis's grandson, Kublai Khan. He called his new city, the capital of his vast empire, Dadu, or Great Capital. Dadu was the new capital of the Yuan dynasty and a symbol of China united. Kublai Khan set about constructing a capital city fit for his all-conquering empire by building huge palaces surrounded by artificial lakes, which still exist (Houhai, in the center of the city). A rebellion in 1368 saw the overthrowing of the Yuan: Now the Ming were in charge. The new emperor decided to move his capital to Nanjing in the south, changing the name of Dadu to Beiping, or Northern Peace.

It was the third Ming Emperor, Yongle, who became most closely associated with the northern city: He moved the capital back to Beiping (now called Beijing) and in 1406 ordered the

© HELENA IVESON

an old door-knocker at the Forbidden City

construction of the Forbidden City, which would house the emperor—considered the heavens' representative on earth—for the next 600 years. The city was made the capital once again to keep a closer eye on Mongol invaders, but despite this, the Ming were eventually overthrown by Manchu warriors in the 17th century, and the new dynasty, the Qing, kept power for the next 280 years. Beijing remained their capital, and three of their emperors—Kangxi, Yongzheng, and Qianlong—ensured that the city remained a great one, with new fantastic imperial complexes like the Forbidden City and the emperors' retreat, the Summer Palace, redesigned thanks to the effort of 100,000 workers during the city's golden period in the 18th century.

Shanghai is a much younger city than Beijing, which explains why there are next to no ancient sights to see in the city. Shanghai emerged in the 14th century as a small, prosperous shipping port by the Yangtze and Huangpu River (which nowadays flows through Shanghai, dividing Puxi and Pudong). Fifty thousand people called the walled city home by the end of the 17th century, but befitting a city that has long been considered China's most cosmopolitan, the city was eventually propelled to greatness though foreign trade.

FOREIGN POWERS

The Chinese empire saw their country as the literal and metaphorical center of the world, and their attitude toward outsiders was primarily one of condescension. There had been explorers in China, most famously Marco Polo in the 13th century, but Europeans had only begun to eye China with real interest three centuries later. Religious missionaries came first, swiftly followed by businessmen and diplomats, and China's isolation was brought to an end. Traders brought opium to China from India in the mid-1700s, and the arrival of the drug had enormous consequences for China for centuries. Using disparate tactics including bribes and violence, British opium ships supplied the country's east coast. Within 50 years, opium had penetrated the country—10 percent of the population were users, with British and American importing over 5 million pounds a year.

These amounts weren't enough for the British, though, and in order to ensure their trading links within the country, the British sent gunboats to accompany their opium ships. Qing dynasty troops tried to shut down the drug industry, but were no competition for England's superior firepower. The Chinese were forced to sign the humiliating Treaty of Nanjing in 1842, in which the Chinese acquiesced to all the British demands—Hong Kong was given to Britain "in perpetuity," and the British were allowed to trade and live in five port cities, including Shanghai. The treaty completely changed the city. The British arrived in 1843 and were given a parcel of land, which is now known as the Bund, and were swiftly followed by other foreign countries that set up concessions.

The second opium war began 15 years later, when the British insisted that one of their opium ships was boarded and illegally searched by Qing troops. In swift retaliation, they sailed to Tianjin, a port city near Beijing that was yet to open to foreign trade. Before they attacked, the Chinese surrendered and were forced to sign the Treaty of Tianjin, which allowed foreigners to settle in even more Chinese cities— most humiliating of all, in Beijing itself. Britain's victory in these two Opium Wars had forced China open.

The Qing dynasty was becoming increasingly unpopular, and the nationwide Taiping rebellion, which became one of the bloodiest conflicts in history, hugely affected Shanghai's Foreign Concessions. In 1853, a branch of the rebels menaced the Chinese part of the city and remained in control for 18 months, until a combined force of British, Qing, and French troops—for once united by a common enemy—repelled them. As many as 30 million people are thought to have died across the country as they rebelled against the excesses of the Qing dynasty, and refugees fleeing the violence were offered shelter in the foreign concessions. This wasn't a purely altruistic move, however: The cost of land soared as the city's population swelled, and plenty of people made a fortune in property.

Just 50 years later, the Boxer Rebellion then caused chaos across the country. The rebellion was fueled by hatred for the foreigners, and the embattled Qing dynasty at first covertly helped the rebels, until the rebels themselves grew disgusted with the feebleness and excesses of the crumbling Qing court. In 1900 the Boxers attacked the foreign legation in Beijing, killing the German Ambassador, and in retaliation eight different foreign forces combined into a 20,000-strong army and repelled the rebels in just 10 days. The allies went on to burn down the Summer Palace, an event that has never been forgotten by the Chinese, judging by the amount of plaques in the park decrying the "wicked act." With this humiliation, the Qing dynasty came to an end; the last emperor, Pu Yi, was forced from his imperial throne; and Sun Yat-sen, the man the Chinese consider to be the modern founder of China, took charge of the provisional republican government.

CIVIL WAR

Sun Yat-sen was not at first the unifying figure that he hoped to become. He was very quickly forced from power and fled the country to Taiwan, where he began to build up the Nationalist party, also known as the Kuomintang. China quickly fractured into different regions controlled by warlords, making the country as unstable as it had ever been. The Communist Party, inspired by the changes sweeping so many other countries in the world, grew in popularity; one of Sun's deputies, Chiang Kai-shek, led the Nationalists in joining up with their enemies the Communists to defeat the warlords, clear the country of imperialists, and unite China once again. His troops marched on Shanghai in 1927, and in the lead-up to their arrival, local communists had organized a city-wide strike to help bring the city to a halt. Unknown to the Communists, Chiang had joined up with one of the city's most infamous drug barons, Du Yuesheng. With Du's help, Chiang betrayed his Communist allies and ordered his troops to fire on them, before rounding up 12,000 more and executing them in what became known as "the White Terror."

While Chiang gained nominal control of the country, when war broke out with Japan in 1937, he was not strong enough to rid the country of the invaders alone, so he once again had to join up with the Communists. The Japanese quickly took over much of the north of the country and made their way to Shanghai. They soon occupied the Chinese parts of the city, brutally leaving thousands of civilians dead, and in 1941, invaded the International Settlements. Japan's behavior during the war has never been forgotten by the Chinese, and even now, they generally view the country with suspicion. As foreigners fled Shanghai, taking the glamour of the city and its money with them, while others were forced into prisoner camps, Shanghai's decline commenced. In 1945 the Japanese left, after being beaten by the allies, and the Americans took control of the city for a year before the Nationalists gained control. Chiang never managed to beat the Communists, though, and he fled to Taiwan, taking much of the country's wealth with him—leaving the Communists to march into Shanghai in triumph, where they found a city that was a shadow of its former self. The foreigners had gone, but so had the city's spirit.

THE PEOPLE'S REPUBLIC

Mao Zedong, the son of a peasant farmer who led the Communists to victory over the Nationalists, marched his army into Beijing on January 31, 1949. "Liberation" came on October 1 the same year, when Mao announced the formation of the People's Republic of China—to millions of supporters who had packed Tiananmen Square—declaring: "The Chinese people have stood up." The Communists wanted to redesign Beijing, using their allies, the Soviet Union, as inspiration; they destroyed huge swathes of the city's hutong neighborhoods to built Stalinist palaces like the Great Hall of the People—next door to a Tiananmen Square that was expanded to four times its original size.

While Mao was initially revered as a near God who promised to bring China peace and the end of the tyranny of the past, he quickly inflicted the nation with a succession of policies that were deeply painful to ordinary people. The Great Leap Forward in 1958–1960—when peasants were forced to industrialize at an impossible rate—was an unmitigated disaster that led to famine and an estimated 30 million deaths. Next, and even worse, was the Cultural Revolution, between 1966–1976, which saw the country, for all intents and purposes, collapse. Mao was hoping to recapture the revolutionary fervor of the past, but his policies ended up unleashing chaos as students became Red Guards, intent with flushing out class enemies and fighting against the "four olds": old culture, old customs, old habits, and old ideas. Millions suffered; so-called traitors were beaten, their lives ruined; and an unknown number of people—estimated in the millions—were executed. Historic monuments were also attacked, and in Beijing, many temples and historic sites, such as the Lama Temple, were redesignated as factories.

Shanghai suffered even more than Beijing: It may have been the birthplace of Chinese Communism, as the city was the site of many of the party's earliest meetings, but for Mao, Shanghai was a shameful symbol of foreign decadence. The Cultural Revolution was launched here, and any citizens who had any kind of involvement with "foreign devils" were humiliated in huge rallies that took place in People's Square. Opium addicts were rounded up and imprisoned, as were the city's thousands of prostitutes. The whole city—the whole country—was nervous: Anyone could be denounced—by anyone with a grudge to bear—and they could then be imprisoned, killed, or shipped off to the countryside.

Though he was outwardly still revered, when Mao died in 1976, many people must have sighed with relief. The Party knew it needed a fresh approach. Deng Xiaoping, his successor, began gradually freeing China's economy. The south of the country was chosen for Deng's experiments, and the areas of Guangdong and Shenzhen, both near Hong Kong, changed irrevocably in just a few years as money poured in—while Shanghai remained out of favor.

It wasn't until 1992 that Shanghai's fortunes changed again. Thanks to a new generation of leaders who came from the city—such as future president Jiang Zemin—the party leadership decided to make Shanghai its financial center, while Beijing remained the political center.

Despite this newfound economic freedom, political reforms remained out of the question for ordinary Chinese. In the spring of 1989, the death of Hu Yaobang, a popular Communist Party official, saw students grasp this opportunity to call for reform. Hundreds of thousands occupied Tiananmen Square for two months—and when the protests culminated during a visit to Beijing by Mikhail Gorbachev, the Soviet leader, the Party decided they could not allow the humiliation to go on any longer. Troops were brought in—mainly from other provinces in China, as many Beijing soldiers

© HELENA IVESON

a statue dating back to the 1950s in Shanghai's People's Park

refused to take up arms against their fellow citizens—and on May 20, martial law was declared. On June 4, the order was given to clear the square, and the army fired on the unarmed demonstrators. No one knows for sure how many were killed—but the numbers may have run into the thousands. In the aftermath, hundreds were imprisoned and thousands fled.

Today, the government seems to be banking on the fact that if people have economic freedom, they will not be so concerned with personal and political freedom. In recent times, the people of both Shanghai and Beijing have enjoyed an era of unparalleled prosperity. Having come a long way from living in communal housing and dressing in Mao suits, residents now can live in their own homes, buy their first cars, and chat away on the latest mobile phones. The cities themselves have also changed beyond recognition, thanks to Beijing's Olympic-inspired building boom and Shanghai's rush to modernize—with its proud skyline composed of some of the world's tallest skyscrapers. It should be pointed out, though, that while many people enjoy the new buildings and modern conveniences, many others bemoan the wholesale demolition of traditional neighborhoods that has gone with it. But for most residents, the Olympic Games were a dream come true—winning the right to host the Games was a huge source of national pride. Financially, the Games were expected to lead to 1.8 million new jobs, and residents will benefit from the city's gentrification process for years to come.

Life in Shanghai has also changed immensely, with the city now once again a proud and cosmopolitan place. Foreign companies normally choose to base themselves in the ultra-modern metropolis rather than Beijing, and in 2007, the city was predicted to attract foreign investment of more than $9 billion. Visitors from just a few years ago wouldn't recognize the city, with its high-tech infrastructure, tangle of metro lines, Maglev train link, and high-tech airports.

Government

While it can be easy to forget in the light of the rampant capitalism evident throughout the country, the Chinese Communist Party has an iron-grip over China and is the ultimate source of power. The party allows no opposition, and the secretive and ruthless nature of the organization and its adaptation to a market economy, ending years of a state-run planned economy, have ensured that it is still in power despite turbulent times and frequent political upheavals. The party still oversees and influences many aspects of people's lives, though not to the same overwhelming extent it once did. Where once membership was restricted to government officials and "model workers," the 73 million strong membership now includes businesspeople in its ranks.

The quickest way to get ahead in China is to join the party, but it's not a simple process—and it must be said that the vast majority apply to get the benefits of membership, not because of any ideological passion. People who wish to apply have to get the backing of current members. The prospective member would then be interviewed at length—as would the person's family, work colleagues, and teachers. If they are then accepted, they are placed under probation for a year before final and complete acceptance.

Befitting a party with more members than the population of Britain, the structure of the party is made up of thousands of layers that reach all the way to the top of the party, which is headed by the country's president. The National People's Congress (NPC) comes under the party in terms of power and is made up of unelected representatives from across the country who meet at the Great Hall of the People in Beijing. The country's president is "elected" by the NPC for a five-year term—the current incumbent is Hu Jintao.

While the NPC's meetings are full of pomp and ceremony and covered in great detail by the state media, the NPC has no real power and is a symbolic organization that merely endorses the commands of the Party. Most analysts think that the real decision-making is done by the Communist Party's central committee, which meets in secret. The two newest members of the State Council are Xi Jinping and Li Keqiang, and these two men are considered the front-runners for the Chinese presidency when Hu steps down in 2012. Very little is known about the two men, or indeed about any top Chinese leader.

Economy

It's no secret: The Chinese economy is booming, with China considered the factory of the world. The country has boomed at an unheard-of rate, with an average increase of GDP above 10 percent. Only the United States has a bigger economy, if measured on a purchasing-power parity basis, and in exchange rate terms, the country is only topped by the United States, Japan, and Germany. Many of China's people enjoy a standard of living that was undreamed of a decade or two ago, thanks to annual incomes increasing at a rate of more than 8 percent over the last 30 years. But not everyone has benefited to the same degree (see the *Distribution of Wealth* section for more details).

After state-orchestrated economic disasters such as the Great Leap Forward in the 1960s, the Chinese government under new leader Deng Xiaoping began to reform the centrally planned economy modeled on a Soviet-style system. While for decades the economy was closed off to foreign trade and investment, Deng sought to reverse that and change to a capitalist market economy. Deng would probably not have dreamed that China would ever have become such a major player—and some predict it will eventually become *the* major player. Deng's famous quote, "I don't care whether the cat is black or white as long as it catches mice," shows his pragmatism, in contrast with Mao's ideological approach. Since being introduced, Deng's reforms, carried on by Presidents Jiang Zemin and then Hu Jintao, improved the lives of millions of Chinese in 20 years, reducing the rate of poverty from 53 percent, but rural incomes still lag way behind the income of urban residents (who as a population account for only around 15 percent of Chinese). Deng's reforms saw incredible growth in the southeastern and eastern coastal provinces, but growth then and now has not been uniform, and interior provinces lag behind.

The government refers to its economic system as "socialism with Chinese characteristics," but most economists would classify the economy as firmly capitalist, with less than a third of the economy still under state control, and that percentage is shrinking fast. Any Chinese student can proudly reel off the details about China's entry into the World Trade Organization in 2001, as its importance is taught in every school in the land. Since joining the club, China's exports exceeded America's for the first time in 2007, but the economy has become much less reliant on exports to the United States and more focused on its own domestic demand as a source of growth. As the population becomes richer, it makes sense that China's awesome manufacturing capability will shift focus from the 250 million American consumers toward the 1.3 billion local shoppers. The issue of exports made the headlines in 2007 as a spate of recalls of Chinese-made goods—contaminated toothpaste, dangerous children's toys, and ill-made tires to name a few—seriously tarnished the "Made in China" brand image. The importance of exports to China's economy can't be overstated: Total exports for the first half of 2007 were worth $547.6 billion. Not only are these large-scale recalls embarrassing to China, but the repercussions of these scandals may have long-term consequences far beyond the country's borders. Businesses around the world rely on the country for cheap parts and labor, and consumers have gotten used to China's cheap prices.

Industry and construction account for about 48 percent of China's GDP, with the country ranking third in the world for industrial output. A train ride across China quickly reveals how industrial huge swaths of the country are, whether they are producing coal or mining or iron and steel. If it can be produced, it is being produced somewhere in China.

While Beijing is China's political center, Shanghai has always been considered the leading financial city. Yet some analysts believe that with the opening of Chinese headquarters in Beijing by Goldman Sachs, UBS, and JP Morgan, a shift in the financial center from Shanghai to Beijing may be taking place.

JUDICIAL AND PENAL SYSTEMS

China's legal system, which was codified in 1949, owes much to China's close ally at the time, the Soviet Union. While the system wasn't perfect, at least there was a system: It soon collapsed under attack from Mao Zedong, who wanted to use the law as a way of establishing control and purging his enemies. Instead of Rule of Law, there was Rule of Man, with legal decisions made in private and not revealed to the public. The legal system suffered hugely during the Cultural Revolution, and it wasn't until Mao's death and the arrival of more moderate leaders that it began to improve. By 1981, China had just 5,500 lawyers, up from zero in 1979; now there are estimated to be 110,000.

The current Constitution of the PRC, adopted in 1982, is viewed as the highest source of law in the country, with the Supreme People's Court the highest judicial organ in the land. The judiciary is officially independent but is generally believed to be subject to the Communist Party's control. The party appoints the judges, most of whom are party members and therefore subject to party control. Of late, some party leaders have suggested that the legal system should become more independent, but in practice, that doesn't seem to be happening: There is a conviction rate of 99 percent in the country, and while those found guilty can appeal, there seem to be few cases when a judgment is reversed.

Exact numbers are unknown, as China refuses to release figures, but human rights organizations such as Amnesty International estimate that China executes more people than the rest of the world's countries combined. And people aren't just executed for the most serious crimes like murder—people can be put to death in China for many white-collar crimes, such as fraud and embezzlement. In January 2008, a fraudster was sentenced to death for swindling investors as part of an illegal ant-breeding scheme. Aside from the harshest sentence of all, lengthy prison sentences are the norm at hard-labor prisons. To earn the right to host the Olympic Games, China promised to improve its human rights record, yet dissidents still disappear from their homes. Six months before the Games, China jailed Hu Jia, a human rights activist, who was dragged from his home by state police agents and charged with inciting subversion. His location is unknown, and he is just one of many activists imprisoned in China on what many believe are spurious grounds.

AGRICULTURE

In recent history, Chinese agriculture has frequently suffered due to experimentation for ideological purposes—with disastrous effects. In 1949, China's grain and cotton output was considered far too low to support a nation of its size, so the government carried out wide-ranging land reform. In an attempt to spur enthusiasm and increase production, the government decided to give peasants with little or no land acres to toil over. At the start of the 1950s, the yearly gross output of agriculture increased by an average 4.5 percent. But the worst excesses of the Mao period reversed these increases, as peasants were forced to work together in collectives. During the Great Leap Forward campaign, propaganda posters promised that if everyone pulled together, the country would overtake America in 15–20 years—but the reforms were an unmitigated disaster. The 1959 and 1960 harvests both failed and millions starved. Eventually, the worst excesses of the policy were watered down and the commune system was dismantled, and peasants could once again own their own land.

Nowadays, it's not just consumer goods that are made in China—the country is one of the world's largest producers and consumers of agricultural products. Amazingly, the country feeds a fifth of the world's population on just 7 percent of the world's arable land.

If you spend most of your time in China in Beijing and Shanghai, it's very easy to forget that the majority of Chinese people live in rural areas. While many peasants still earn a living from the soil, as opportunities to leave rural areas and head to the dazzling lights of the cities have increased, more and more people have done exactly that. The farmers that have been left behind—more than 300 million workers—compose about 45 percent of the country's labor force. Perhaps unsurprisingly, China produces more of its national foodstuff—rice—than the rest of the world, and the country also produces huge amounts of wheat, corn, potatoes, tea, pork, and tobacco.

DISTRIBUTION OF WEALTH

Despite the purported Communist ideals, China is no model of equality. While economic reforms since the 1980s have lifted a huge swath of the population out of abject poverty, there are now large disparities in income between urban and rural residents, between different regions, and even among urban residents. But while people who live in the rich eastern cities of Shanghai, Beijing, Qingdao, and Guangzhou in the south are doing very nicely compared to a decade ago, hundreds of millions of people are not doing so well—specifically, the country's peasants in the interior of the country, who number around 800 million. The government fears that if there is to be any kind of rebellion, it will come from these peasants, bitter about how they have been left behind. Urban migration, in which rural residents on the hunt for better jobs and more money head to one of the rich cities, is rising rapidly. There are estimated to be between 80 and 100 million migrant workers in China, and they form the backbone of the economy, doing the dirtiest and most dangerous of jobs. They are the people building the exciting new CCTV building, the Olympic Bird's Nest stadium, and all the other marquee projects changing the faces of Beijing and Shanghai. Life for these people is tough: Most work almost every single day, send back the majority of their pay to their families in the country, and return home only once a year, during the Chinese New Year. To most local Beijingers or Shanghainese, the migrants are an ignored section of society who, despite helping make their cities into the modern and world-class places they have become, are given little credit and often have to work in dangerous conditions for little pay.

People and Culture

As of July 2007, the Chinese population stood at 1,321,851,888—a quarter of the world's population. No wonder Beijing and Shanghai seem crowded. . . . The Han are the main ethnic group, constituting 92 percent of the country. The Han constitute the minority in every region of China aside from Tibet and Xinjiang. There are many other ethnic groups, including the Zhuang, Manchu, Hui, Miao, and the Uyghurs—just a few of the 55 recognized ethnic minorities.

Perhaps the most famous aspect of Chinese demographics is its one-child policy. The government became concerned with the issue in the 1950s, but it was only in 1979 that it introduced its world-famous policy, unique to China. For the vast majority of Chinese people, with few exceptions, only one child is allowed to each couple. Aside from the obvious restrictions to people's freedom of choice, the policy has been judged to be a huge success, with the national birth rate reduced from 5.4 children per woman in the 1970s to the current rate of 1.7 children. The policy has also had an unconsidered effect on Chinese culture, producing generations of little emperors and empresses—children doted on by their parents and two sets of grandparents. More important, because of the age-old preference for boys, the ratio between the sexes is a concern. In the last national census, 116 boys were born for every 100 girls.

Because of the slowing birthrate and the Baby Boomer years, in which people born in the 1950s are on the way to being elderly, China has been officially classed as an aging society. The elderly in China number 149 million, making up more than 11 percent of the nation's population. In less than 50 years, the elderly as a group are predicted to reach 437 million.

CULTURAL DIFFERENCES

When visiting China, it pays to be aware that Chinese customs or practices can be very different from what you've experienced. There are not a lot of cultural hoops to jump through, and people are generally forgiving if someone makes a faux pas, but occasionally visitors get upset by social behavior they see on the street. The concept of personal space means very little to the Chinese—there simply isn't room for everyone—so on crowded subway lines and buses, you may have people inches away from your face. Also, on public transport and in many other areas, such as at public attractions, the concept of lining up is just that—a concept. To most Chinese, it's a fine idea in theory, but China is a country where you have to look after yourself first, so the person who waits patiently at the back gets nothing. This is changing slightly—there are regular days on the Beijing subway when guards order people

© HELENA IVESON

There are more men than women in China – and most of them seem to be playing cards in parks like this one, People's Park in Shanghai.

to line up, but as soon as the guards go, so does any thought of lining up.

Conversely, though people are prepared to shove their armpits in your face on a crowded bus, physical contact between strangers is not common. If you spend any time at an airport you will see that the Chinese are not big on public displays of affection, and you will rarely if ever see couples or relatives kissing or hugging each other in public. When meeting a new person in China, it's most common to just say hello, but increasingly people shake hands, too—wait to see if you are offered a hand. One rule that is generally valid: When in doubt, err on the side of greater formality, as this is unlikely to cause offense. People definitely do not kiss on first meeting unless they are very cosmopolitan and spend lots of time abroad. Yet, again conversely, it's very common to see men and women holding hands with members of the same sex, which doesn't have any kind of gay undertones.

Something that many visitors to China find beyond the pale is the amount of spitting that some people do on the street. It may not be any consolation, but incidences have definitely decreased thanks to public-health and civilized-behavior campaigns. The government knows that public spitting is bad for its image and therefore bad for business, and also bad for health (the arrival of SARS was what triggered the campaign to eradicate the habit). So now, on public transportation, you can see free paper bags being given out for people to spit in. If people don't use the bags, they can be fined 50RMB.

In Western countries, it's common to maintain eye contact when talking with other people, but this is not the case among the Chinese. Because of the more authoritarian nature of Chinese society, people do not always look other people, and especially their superiors, in the eye—it is considered aggressive or defiant. If someone does get angry with you, a sure sign of their feelings is that they engage in a "stare off."

The Chinese will go through a lot to avoid saying "no" to a direct request. This is all to

BEIJING BY THE NUMBERS

- 11 – number of days in Beijing in 2007 when pollution was considered "very unhealthy" by the U.S. Environmental Protection Agency
- 20 – where Beijing lies on the list of the world's most expensive cities for expatriates
- 28 – percentage of only children in Beijing who would like more than one child
- 30 – percentage of Beijing population classified as mobile, in other words, migrant workers and visitors
- 2,074 – number of cars sold every day in Beijing
- 5,500 – number of bottles of champagne sold at the bar i-Ultra Lounge in its first six months of business
- 2.3 million – number of passengers who use the subway every day

do with the concept of "face" and preserving harmony whenever possible. Many etiquette guides, particularly for doing business in China, spend a lot of time addressing the issue, as it's probably the number-one cause of communication difficulties, especially with more "in your face" and direct nationalities like Americans. Instead of merely going on what a person says verbally, people who wish to communicate successfully must become skilled at reading body language and other non-verbal clues.

In certain situations, it's hard to avoid getting angry—China can certainly be a challenging place to travel around at times. If you need to let off steam, bear in mind that the person who will be on the receiving end of your irritation, whether it is a waitress or ticket seller, rarely has any power to change the situation.

In restaurants, if the table is eating home-style and everyone is sharing (which is customary in Chinese restaurants), do not use your chopsticks or the spoon you are eating with to dish your food. Use the serving spoon to dish into your bowl or plate, and then use your spoon or chopsticks to eat. When you have finished your meal, do not stick your chopsticks into your leftovers in your bowl, as this very much unnerves superstitious locals, who believe that it resembles the way mourners place sticks of incense into a bowl during funerals. There is also no shame for foreigners unable to use chopsticks—all restaurants will be able to supply knives and forks. Another consideration while dining is that clearing everything on your plate is not a good thing. If you eat all of your meal, the Chinese will assume you did not receive enough food, that you are still hungry, and that they have been bad hosts.

As in many Asian countries, business cards are a big deal in China. If someone gives a business card to you, you can give him or her face by examining the card properly and treating the actual card with respect. If you are spending any real time in China, it's worth getting some cards made with English on one side and Chinese on the other—the cities are full of printing shops that can do this affordably.

CHANGING TIMES

Despite the government's best efforts to play up the continuity of ancient Confucian values, China's "morality crisis" is a hot topic of public discussion. Decades ago, immorality and infidelity were considered distinctly Western imports, whether in reality or by virtue of propaganda. But the government's increasingly relaxed grip on the private lives of its citizens, coupled with the freedoms afforded by rising incomes, has led to a major cultural shift, with incidence of divorce jumping from 341,000 in 1980 to 1,913,000 in 2006. Visiting prostitutes, whether at one of the fake "hairdressing salons" visible on so many streets in China or at seedy karaoke clubs, is increasingly common. *China-Style Divorce* is one of the most popular shows on mainland television, while *bao*

SHANGHAI BY THE NUMBERS

- 166.84 billion – amount in U.S. dollars of Shanghai's GDP in 2007
- 1,400 – amount in RMB of the average salary in the city
- 3,000 – amount in RMB of a meal for two with wine at Jade on 36
- 2 – number of subway lines Shanghai had in 2000
- 11 – number of subway lines Shanghai will have by 2010
- 50-60 – percentage of plastic surgery patients seen by the Shanghai BK hospital who are students
- 15 – percentage of schoolchildren considered obese, the highest rate in China

er nai—keeping second wives—has become a status symbol among affluent businessmen. China once worried the West's lax morality would flood in as China opened its doors, but the opposite is now happening. Among overseas Chinese communities, most women consider their families "lucky" if their husband's work does not require frequent business trips to China, where infidelity is accepted as a foregone conclusion.

RELIGION

In a 2007 survey, Shanghai university professors found that 31.4 percent of Chinese people over 16 considered themselves religious. If that figure were true nationally, that would mean 300 million people could be described as religious, a huge number considering religion in China has taken decades to recover from the destruction wrought when the Communist Party came to power in 1949. The state was, and is, officially atheist and for years has dismissed organized religion as an outdated feudalistic concept. Communist leaders rejected religion as backward and quickly moved to turn the many houses of worship across China into more "practical" buildings such as factories and communal housing. This was nothing compared to the Cultural Revolution, which tried to completely eliminate religion for good—as just one example, ancient relics such as the thousands of Buddhas in the now UNESCO-protected Longmen Grottos were decapitated, wiping out thousands of years of cultural history.

The darkest days for China's believers only began to come to a close with the end of the Cultural Revolution. In 1978 the country's constitution was changed to guarantee "freedom of religion," but it recognizes only five religions—Buddhism, Catholicism, Islam, Protestantism, and Taoism—and each officially sanctioned church has to operate under the government's direction. There are estimated to be 10 million Catholics in China, but experts estimate that two-thirds of them choose to risk worshiping illegally at underground churches, with only the remaining one-third worshipping at the official state-sanctioned churches. It is this state interference that has led to hostile relations with the Vatican for more than 50 years, though the relationship seems to be improving somewhat.

Buddhism and Taoism have the longest history in China, and these religions like the others suffered very badly during the worst excesses of the Mao regime. But as the government has relaxed its opposition, the numbers of followers have increased dramatically, and many temples across the country have been rebuilt. As the numbers of worshippers at the Lama Temple in Beijing or the Jade Buddha Temple in Shanghai testify, many experts feel that Chinese people are seeking a replacement to Communism as the country moves away from its past. The government has always seen religion as a threat, and the current focus is the banned religious group the Falun Gong. In 1999, 10,000 members gathered in Beijing to protest the government's attitude toward them, and perhaps fearing similar scenes to what last happened when there was a mass protest—in Tiananmen in 1989—the

© HELENA IVESON

Buddhism is once again increasingly popular: Lama Temple, Beijing.

government promptly banned them and started to round up followers. Human Rights groups like Amnesty International accuse the authorities of torture and even the murder of Falun Gong practitioners. Aside from the Falun Gong, the state is seeking to get along with religious leaders and link them to the party cause. At the beginning of 2008, President Hu Jintao was photographed with one of China's main Christian leaders, which led to speculation that government controls would soon relax further. No one, however, can claim that religious freedom really exists in China, given the ongoing harsh treatment of Buddhists in Tibet or Muslims in Xinjiang, where, in Chinese eyes, religion is linked to political activity.

LANGUAGE

Mandarin is by far the most common Chinese dialect, spoken by more than 70 percent of the population—and 850 million people around the world—but Shanghainese and Cantonese aren't far behind, and they are followed by a huge number of more minor dialects. If you are planning to study a dialect, choose Mandarin, as even in regions that speak another dialect, most people will be able to manage a conversation in Mandarin; it is taught in schools across the country, because it is the official standard language used by the People's Republic of China.

All spoken varieties of Chinese use the same written language; therefore, the number "one" is *yi* in Mandarin and *yat* in Cantonese, but they share an identical Chinese character (一). Chinese characters represent meaning. They also have an assigned pronunciation, but this can vary with the Chinese dialects, whereas the meaning doesn't. Early Chinese characters were simply pictures of the things they represented. Through time the pictures became more stylized: Examples of this type of character are 人 *rén,* which means "person" or 山 *shan,* which means "mountain." Characters have changed little in the 2,000 years that they have been in existence, though of course there are now many more characters than there used to be as new words have been developed and entered the language.

The majority of today's characters consist of two components—one pointing to the pronunciation, the other vaguely suggesting the meaning: for example, the character 妈. The right-hand part, 马, is pronounced *mǎ* on its own and suggests the pronunciation of the whole character, which is pronounced *mā.* The left-hand part is also a character in its own right, 女, and it means "female," hinting at the meaning of the whole character, which means "mother." If you think this sounds complicated, it is, but as least the characters you will see in mainland China are simplified versions of the traditional characters that are still used in Hong Kong and Taiwan.

The Arts

LITERATURE

The Chinese have an enormous appetite for literature, dating from the Tang dynasty (618–907), when the introduction of woodblock printing helped popularize literature among the masses. If you go into Beijing's or Shanghai's Book Cities, which are huge book superstores, you will see them jam-packed with readers sitting on the floor or perched wherever they can find a ledge, devouring books. Literature on cell phones is also massively popular with young people, and at the moment Penguin China is working on a deal with a telephone company to put Penguin Classics on phones.

The ongoing problem of censorship affects literature, as it does every other kind of art form in China. According to the acting director of English PEN's Writers in Prison program, Ophelia Field, who was interviewed for the British newspaper *The Guardian,* "China is still one of the worst violators of writers' rights for freedom of expression in the world." The three T's—Tibet, Tiananmen, and Taiwan—are all taboo, alongside the Falun Gong and Uighur cultural rights. "Any time somebody crosses the line to write about any of these issues," says Field, "they're putting themselves at enormous risk."

Chinese literature spans thousands of years, and treatises by figures such as the philosopher Confucius—and Sun Tzu's *The Art of War*—are world-famous. However, because of the obvious language problems, the current cultural life of the Chinese remains a closed book to many in the West—their best-selling authors unfamiliar, their most exciting writers untranslated. Yet just as in the United States and the United Kingdom, Chinese publishing companies produce around 200,000 new titles and new editions a year. Unsurprisingly, it is by far the largest publishing market by volume—officially, about six billion units a year. When you see books sold on the street, most of them will be pirated copies of *Harry Potter* or whatever else is popular, and no one knows how many copies of these are sold.

The Chinese literary world has been described as like a parallel universe, almost invisible to many in the West. Its biggest names are authors such as Su Tong, Jia Pingwa, Han Han, and Annie Baobei, some of whom are earning more than $2 million a year. Only the most adventurous Westerner capable of reading Chinese characters will have ever picked up a copy, as they are not translated into English. For more English translations of contemporary Chinese writers, go to www.paperrepublic.org, the website of a group of Chinese literature aficionados hoping to introduce their favorite writers to the English-speaking world.

FOLK ART

Chinese folk art may not be as important to the Chinese as it was, but some types have been in existence for thousands of years and can be found today, relatively unchanged. Chinese **paper cutting** has existed for thousands of years—the oldest surviving paper cut is from Xinjiang and dates from the 6th century. Paper began as a precious commodity in the Han dynasty, and the cutting up of paper for entertainment was affordable only for nobles in the royal court. Nowadays, visitors can buy mass-produced paper cuts for a few RMB, but the most delicate versions made by hand can be extremely expensive.

One of the oldest forms of folk art in China is **puppetry.** For more than 1,000 years, puppeteers entertained everyone from emperors to peasant children using stories from folk legends and fables. Today, audiences are dwindling. The only place in Beijing to go is the **China Puppet Theater** (1A Anhua Xili, Beisanhuan Lu, Chaoyang, 6425 4798), where performances are in Mandarin only. If you do go, call ahead as the troupe is often on tour.

Another folk art form popular with tourists is the bright and cheerful peasant paintings that can be found at Panjiayuan in Beijing and antiques stores in Shanghai. The pictures show an idealized version of rural life in China, with scenes of animals, traditional holidays, and feasts. The most famous were created by farmers from Jinshan County near Shanghai during the late 1970s. While you are very unlikely to find these on the market, copies are commonplace.

OPERA

Chinese opera is not very accessible to most foreign ears and an increasing number of mainland Chinese ears. For some, a performance will only be an ordeal, with the sounds from the heavily made-up and stylized performers sounding like screeching rather than anything enjoyable. Beijing opera is not as old as you may think, dating from 1790, when Emperor Qianlong was on the throne. If you want to experience the art form yourself, the **Liyuan Theater** in the Jianguo Qianmen Hotel has daily performances, as does the very touristy **Laoshe Tea House,** also in Qianmen (3 Qianmen Xi Dajie, Qianmen, 6304 6334, www.laosheteahouse.com). Shanghai does not have a dedicated opera theater, but the **Yifu Theater** (701 Fuzhou Lu, People's Square, 6351 4668) often stages grand Chinese operas.

FILM

The first recorded screening of a movie occurred in Shanghai on August 11, 1896, but it wasn't until nearly 10 years later that China produced its first home-grown film, a recording of the Beijing Opera's *The Battle of Dingjunshan*. Unsurprisingly, the Chinese film industry centered around China's most cosmopolitan city, Shanghai, the largest city in the Far East at the time. The oldest surviving film from this period is *Laborer's Love,* which was produced in 1922.

China's first cinematic golden age is considered to be the 1930s, when socially conscious films focused on ordinary people's lives and class struggles. Film studios sprang up in Shanghai, Beijing, and Hong Kong. Realizing the enormous influence film had over an often illiterate population, the Nationalists and the Communists both sought to gain control over the major studios. When the Japanese invaded Shanghai, almost every studio fled to Hong Kong, snuffing out the industry until after World War II, when some studios returned. But with the Communist takeover in 1949, motion pictures were soon brought under state control—the government recognized them as an important propaganda tool. In 1951, the Communist Party decreed that there would be no more screenings of pre-1949 Chinese films or Hollywood or Hong Kong productions. Films from this era had to focus on peasants, soldiers, and workers. Chairman Mao's wife, Jiang Qing, took control of the film industry. (In the 1930s she had been on the other side of the screen, as she was then a Shanghai movie actress called Lan Ping.)

The industry's darkest years came between 1966 to 1976, during the Cultural Revolution, when the Beijing Film Academy was forced to close, and Madame Mao blacklisted actors and directors who didn't follow her decrees and completely banned any film that didn't reflect the Party's ideals. It was not until 1978 that the Beijing Film Academy reopened and the film industry as a whole began to slowly restart. Now household names in China, directors Zhang Yimou and Chen Kaige were part of the academy's first intake of new undergraduates. They and their contemporaries became popularly known as the Fifth Generation, because they were in the academy's fifth graduating class. They went on to make *King of Children* (1987), *Ju Dou* (1989), *Farewell My Concubine* (1993), and *Raise the Red Lantern* (1991), which captured the imagination of the domestic market and also became known to art house audiences around the world. When *Red Sorghum* won the Golden Bear in 1988 and Zhang Yimou won the 1992 Golden Lion for *The Story of Qiu Ju,* it was judged a new renaissance for the Chinese film industry. It must be noted that these films, alongside *Farewell My Concubine*, *Ju Dou*, and *Raise the Red Lantern*, were all banned in China, though then as now, fans could easily seek out pirated video copies.

The Tiananmen Square massacre effectively brought to an end this period of

Chinese film, and several prominent filmmakers left China to go into exile in the face of increasing state censorship. The Sixth Generation produced an edgy underground film movement in which films were shot quickly and cheaply by independent filmmakers. Prominent directors from the Sixth Generation include Wang Xiaoshuai *(Beijing Bicycle)*, Jia Zhangke *(Xiao Wu, Unknown Pleasures, Platform, The World)*, Zhang Yuan *(Beijing Bastards, East Palace West Palace)*, and Li Yang *(Blind Shaft)*.

More prominently, in 2000, the multinational production *Crouching Tiger, Hidden Dragon* by Taiwanese director Ang Lee achieved massive success at box offices around the world. Chinese audiences turned their nose up at the film, complaining that it was nothing new, but in the West the film was a smash hit. This was followed by Zhang Yimou's *Hero* in 2002, which featured many of China's leading actors, including Maggie Cheung, Tong Leung, starlet Zhang Ziyi, and martial arts legend Jet Li. Unlike *Crouching Tiger*, the film was a huge hit throughout its home territory and the rest of Asia. It also topped the U.S. box office—a rare event for a foreign-language film. Ang Lee's *Lust, Caution* (2007) has been the latest mainland Chinese-language film to prove a success around the world. Although several minutes of sex scenes were cut from the version shown in China, it still proved a massive success (and people simply downloaded the uncut version online).

ESSENTIALS

Getting There

BEIJING

By Air

It's not just the city center that benefited from a major overhaul thanks to the Olympics: The expanded and updated **Beijing Capital International Airport** (6456 3604, www.bcia.com.cn, PEK) has a new terminal to deal with the expected 83 million passengers a year that will eventually use the airport. The $3.6 billion dragon-shape terminal was designed by British architect Sir Norman Foster and made the airport one of the five busiest in the world. If that size weren't mind-boggling enough, the Civil Aviation Administration of China has already proposed the construction of another, even larger, international airport in the south of Beijing!

For now, though, the current airport is 17 miles northeast of the city, now has three terminals, and passengers travel between them by train. Because the airport is so sprawling nowadays, allow plenty of time to get to the airport, find your terminal, and check in. Unfortunately, if all goes smoothly and you have time to kill, there isn't a great deal to do at the airport—when a Starbucks opened a few years ago, it was the height of excitement to bored travelers used to coffee from vending machines or buying the world's most expensive cans of Coke. There is Internet

© HELENA IVESON

access but not airside, and the shops are very limited, expensive, and dull, and access to English-language media is almost nonexistent. There are currency exchange booths, and expensive left-luggage service, clean toilets, and hotel reservation services, but no general travel-information office. When you arrive at the airport, people may come up to you and gesture you to follow them to check-in, where they will accompany you through the process: Be aware this is not a free service, though if you are running late, it can be a lifesaver as they have connections that will speed you to the front of the line. The going rate is 100RMB. And all departure taxes are now included in the price of your ticket: There have been a few reports of tricksters trying to extort money out of people departing, but the airport police seem to be cracking down on them.

International airlines that fly to Beijing increase almost daily. In North America, Air China, United, Continental, American Airlines, and Northwest all fly direct from several airports throughout the United States to Beijing, and from Europe, BA, Air China, Air France, Lufthansa, KLM, SAS, Austrian Airlines, and Finnair all operate direct flights to Beijing. Direct flights from the United States average at around $1,000, from Europe, about $750. If you are reserving a ticket out of China, be sure to check online travel agency **Elong** (www.elong.net) as it usually has some good offers.

There is now a separate check-in for flights to Shanghai Hongqiao Airport at the front of terminal 1 with the idea that this is quicker than entering the main check-in area. It doesn't cover all flights, so show your ticket and ask or check the departures board, which will tell you where to check in.

When leaving the airport, you have three options: high-speed train, low-speed bus, or taxi. If you have a lot of luggage, the simplest option is still catching a taxi from the official taxi rank, despite the brand-new train. When you enter the arrivals hall, you will probably be approached and offered a taxi, but ignore these people, who will overcharge you, and proceed to the taxi rank that is just outside. A taxi to the city center usually takes about 45 minutes if the traffic is OK and should cost 90–150RMB on the meter, plus a 10RMB compulsory road tax. I have never had any problems with Beijing taxi drivers except at the airport—for some reason, the authorities have not yet cracked down on them, which is odd as it gives such a bad first impression. Insist on drivers' turning on the meter (say *da biao*) and if possible have small bills as sometimes drivers will claim to have no change. If you think you have been overcharged and you are being dropped off at a hotel, don't hesitate to get the hotel involved.

A cheaper alternative is catching the airport bus. There are five different routes, but the most useful is Bus Route 2, which will drop you off at Dongzhimen (in 35 minutes, if traffic is light), where you can connect to the subway, or Bus Route 3, which will drop you off at the railway station. All buses leave every 15 minutes up until the last flight comes in, and a ticket, which you have to buy before you get on the bus from the stall just outside of the terminal, costs 16RMB. Luggage is stored underneath the bus.

The newest option is the high-speed rail link, which follows the same route as the airport expressway but has the shortest journey time at just 16 minutes. The terminus is at Dongzhimen, which connects to the subway system, and the train also stops at Sanyuanqiao Station, which is on Line 10 of the subway system before it reaches the second and third terminals of the airport. If you do not have much luggage, this is the best option, but if you do and then have to take a taxi from Dongzhimen, the total cost of train ticket and taxi will be about the same as if you'd gotten a taxi direct from the airport. Supposedly, starting in 2008, passengers bound for the airport will be able to get boarding passes and check in luggage at Dongzhimen, and they will only have to go through security checks at the airport before taking off. Check with your airline for the latest information.

By Train

Beijing has two main train stations: **Beijing Zhan** (Beijing Zhan Jie, 6563 3262) near Tiananmen, and in the west, **Beijing Xi Zhan** (Lianhuachi Dong Lu, 5182 6253). Both are absolutely enormous: Leave around an hour to get through the huge crowds that are outside the station day and night, to pass through a pointless luggage-scanning area, and to find the right platform.

Trains to domestic cities such as Shanghai and Tianjin and the Trans-Siberian Railway to Russia leave from Beijing Zhan. The station is easy to get on as it is on the subway system and has been smartened up a little recently, and now the ticket office is in a separate area to the right as you look at the station. Very few employees speak English, though if you walk to the last ticket seller at the far end of the ticket office, you will see a small sign: Foreigners Ticket Office. Here the staff will speak rudimentary English. However, I strongly advise you to buy tickets well in advance: You can now buy tickets to Shanghai and Hong Kong up to 28 days in advance on the soft sleeper–only express trains, and for most other destinations, up to 10 days in advance. To save a frustrating trip to the station only to find out tickets are sold out, as they so often are, ask your hotel to assist: Your sanity is well worth the 30–50RMB service fee it will charge. Tickets can be bought online at www.piao.com but it's in Chinese only.

Construction of the new Beijing–Shanghai high-speed railway started at the beginning of 2008 and should be finished in 2013. It will cut traveling time between Shanghai and the capital from 12 hours to less than five. The Shanghai terminal of the new railway was to be built at the Hongqiao Transport Hub.

The station has many snack stores and restaurants and a Chinese copy of KFC, but no one comes to a Chinese railway station expecting gourmet food. All soft-seat ticket holders and any foreigner who happens to wander in, with the right ticket or not, can use the soft-seat waiting room; it's worth seeking out if you have a bit of a wait for its comfy seats and clean(er) toilets.

If you are going to Hong Kong, Tibet, or Xian to see the Terracotta Warriors, your train will leave from Beijing Xi Zhan, which is even bigger than the main station. No matter what, check your departure station carefully: Many a passenger has missed his or her train after turning up at the wrong station. This station is a nuisance to get to: The nearest subway station is the Military Museum and then it's a five-minute taxi ride from there or a long 20-minute walk south from there. There are buses connecting the two stations, though in Chinese only, and there is little room for luggage; or a taxi, from say, Sanlitun, will cost about 70RMB because of the heavy traffic in the area. A high-speed rail-link between the two stations was under construction (due to open mid-2009). There is a foreigners' ticket office on the second floor of this station.

In China, there's no such thing as first class—well, there is, but it's called either a soft seat *(ruan zuo)* for shorter journeys or a soft sleeper *(ruan wo)*. All express trains between Beijing and Shanghai are soft-sleeper only, so you will get a comfortable bed in a four-person private room. Toilets and sinks are at either end of the carriage and there's a choice of a squat or Western toilet. If you want to go one better than that, there are a few deluxe two-bed rooms but again with a communal toilet. If you are going to destinations other than Shanghai, you will have the option of a cheaper hard sleeper *(ying wo)* ticket, for which you will get a bed in an open-plan carriage that is divided up into three-tier rows: Be warned that the lights go off early and come on at the crack of dawn, as does the piped music. For the even more budget minded, you can have the experience in the hard-seat *(ying zuo)* section, where most working-class Chinese will be—here seats are not reserved so it's first come, first served. Take your own food with you if you have high standards: All trains will have a restaurant car (and the Beijing–Shanghai expresses even have a bar) but food is generally overpriced and unappealing.

SHANGHAI

By Air

Shanghai has two airports: the newer international **Pudong Airport** (3848 4500, www.shairport.com) 20 miles from the city center and **Hongqiao Airport** (6268 8918, www.shairport.com), which is for domestic flights only and is just six miles from the city center.

Pudong (PVG) opened in 1999 and was designed by Sir Norman Foster, who also designed the new terminal at Beijing's airport. Befitting its purpose as the entry point to China's most fashionable city, the airport looks great with sweeping curves and high ceilings, but in terms of facilities, it's limited and a boring place to wait with dull shops and little in the way of Internet access for the 27 million passengers who use it every year. Frequent travelers are hoping that the second terminal, a three-story glass structure shaped like a bird with open wings, will not only look good but have the kind of facilities that passengers need. As in all airports in China, departure taxes are now included in the ticket price.

The coolest way to get to and from the airport is by catching the Maglev train (www.smtdc.com), which will take you to the Longyang Subway station in Pudong in just eight minutes traveling at 267mph (430kph). While it's worth experiencing at least once, the long walk between the Maglev station and the subway station is irritating if you have luggage, and if you want to catch a taxi onward, the lines can built up. It costs 50RMB each person, or 80RMB round-trip, so if you are traveling alone and with little luggage it's a good option, but if there is more than one person, a taxi is cheaper. The train has not been as popular as expected and the decision to extend the line all the way to Hongqiao Airport and then onto Hangzhou in time for Expo 2010 has been very unpopular with residents who will be forcibly relocated.

Less sci-fi but probably more practical is a good old taxi from the airport. (Please read *By Air* in the *Beijing* section for more on taxis from airports as the same cautionary tales apply.) A taxi to the Bund will be around 170RMB and take at least an hour, and a taxi to Hongqiao Airport will be more than 200RMB and take even longer. The best option between the airports is Airport Bus 1, which costs 30RMB and takes only a little longer than a taxi and runs every 30 minutes. Other airport buses go to the Jing'an Transport Terminus (Line 2, 19RMB, one hour, every 30 minutes) and to the railway station (Line 5, 18RMB, one hour fifteen minutes, every 30 minutes).

Hongqiao Airport (SHA) is much nearer the city center, so if you are flying domestically from, say, Beijing or Hong Kong, try to fly here as you will save yourself at least an hour when getting into the city. The actual airport is OK, but much older than Pudong. At least it has Internet access, a few overpriced coffee shops, and shops that price their products in dollars.

The easiest way to get to and from the airport is by taxi: From Hongqiao, it will cost about 65RMB to get to the Bund and take 35 minutes in good traffic. There is also an express bus to Jing'an Terminus, which leaves every 25 minutes and costs 4RMB. All transport options are well signposted and as always, avoid going with anyone who makes a beeline for you offering transport: You will always be ripped off. It will all change in 2013 for Hongqiao: Not only will it serve as the terminus for the new high-speed train link to Beijing, it will also have a Maglev station, at least three metro stations, and several bus stations.

By Train

(See *By Train* in the *Beijing* section for information on trains between the two cities.) There are two main stations in Shanghai: **Shanghai Station** (385 Meiyuan Lu, 6317 9090) and **Shanghai South Station** (200 Zhaofeng Lu, 6317 6060). Shanghai Station is the most important to travelers with trains to Beijing, Suzhou, and Tibet, among many other destinations, but eventually, some trains were to be routed to the brand-new South Station, so check your ticket carefully to find where you leave from. Shanghai Station may be the busiest place in the whole city—at any time of the day it is heaving with humanity, not only with people catching a train but also

plenty of river traffic on the Huangpu River

floods of people using the station's subway station, which is the interchange for three different lines. Always leave plenty of time if using the subway, or indeed any method of transport to get to the train station, as you have to walk long distances to get anywhere. There is an orderly taxi point and though lines build up, it's still likely to be easier to get a taxi here than off the congested nearby streets. Be aware that taxis are not allowed to stop in front of the station but are directed to an underground taxi stop.

Shanghai South Station is where to head for bullet trains to Hangzhou and other cities in the south. It looks more like an airport than train station thanks to its huge circular rotunda and airy design. It's easiest to reach by subway, as the station is near but not directly at the intersection of Lines 1 and 3: Just follow the crowds who will head to the station.

By Boat

Few ways of traveling to Shanghai can be finer than cruising up the Huangpu River and disembarking near the Bund, just as people did 100 years ago. Up until recently, the romance was cut short by ships' having to stop in an industrial zone, but the Shanghai Port International Passenger Terminal, just north of the Bund, is due to open in late 2008. International passenger liners will be able to berth at the wharf.

Getting Around

BEIJING

Bus

Eight million people use buses in Beijing every day, but unless you speak some Mandarin or are full of enthusiasm to travel like a local at the expense of speed and efficiency, buses aren't the best way for visitors to get around. Unlike the subway, which is in English and easy to navigate, Beijing's bus routes are just too much like hard work. Destinations are sometimes but not always written in English. So this, plus the fight to get on and off, makes traveling by bus too much hassle. If, however, you are set on it, at least it's cheap, with most fares costing 1RMB. The Beijing Bus website (www.bjbus.com) makes a stab at being useful to English speakers, but unfortunately route maps are in Chinese only.

The only time it pays to take the bus is if you are leaving the city and heading out somewhere, such as to the Great Wall. The most useful terminus is at **Dongzhimen Long-Distance Bus Station** (Dongzhimen Wai Dajie, 6467 4995), which is also connected to the subway system and the high-speed link to the airport.

Subway

Be prepared to push and shove: The Beijing subway is one of the busiest in the world and regularly sees more than three million passengers a day. The good news is that it is rapidly expanding—Beijing has six subway lines and is building five more. The growth spurt was of course because of the Olympics, but the city ain't seen nothing yet, as by 2015, Beijing is to have 19 subway lines; in 2005, it had just two. Stations are both signposted and announced in English and Chinese so traveling underground is a good way to traverse the capital. When Line 5 was opened at the end of 2007, authorities also lowered the price of tickets from an already cheap 3RMB to 2RMB, and considering it's a flat-rate fare, you can travel for well more than an hour between, say, Dongzhimen and Pingguoyuan in the far west, so this may be the best bargain in Beijing. The only time it costs more and goes up to 5RMB is if you transfer to the overground Line 13. The downside is, of course, the numbers of passengers using the service: At rush hour, the crowds can be hideous, but even on a weekend in the middle of the day, it's always busy. The good news is, the machines are finally fully automated—and in English too, so they're very user-friendly.

Taxi

Despite the ever-worsening traffic—more than 400,000 new cars hit the roads in Beijing every year—taxis are still the best option for getting you from A to B. They are plentiful with more than 60,000 at last count, can be hailed just about anywhere (aside from Tiananmen Square), and despite a few recent price rises, very cheap. Flag-fall is 10RMB for four kilometers and then it's 2RMB per kilometer after that. A ride in the city center should always be less than 25RMB. The trade-off for the cheapness is that next to no drivers speak any English, so you will need to practice your Chinese or have your destination written down in characters, not pinyin. Taxi drivers earn very little, aren't always the most educated, and may have trouble reading a map, so it's always a good idea to have the telephone number of where you are going or a Chinese speaker who can help navigate. Smoking is now banned inside the taxi, upsetting many a driver, but unfortunately, spitting out of the window hasn't been. Try to have change for the drivers as they can get irritable if you have only 100RMB—of course they should have change, but having lower-denomination bills will save a whole load of hassle.

SHANGHAI

Bus

As in Beijing, the bus system with its more than 1,000 bus routes can be overwhelming to foreign visitors. Stops and destinations are in Chinese only, which is odd as Shanghai is usually much more English-language friendly. As the buses are not as quick or as comfortable as the air-conditioned subway, avoid the trouble of having to stand, fight your way on or off, and take the subway if price is the main criteria, or a taxi if comfort and speed are.

Subway

The Shanghai metro is one of the youngest in the world. Astonishingly, the first line opened only in 1995, but by the end of 2007 there were 161 stations along eight lines while another two will be finished by the World Expo in 2010, and another 18 are in the pipeline, which would make Shanghai's subway the biggest in the world. Unlike in Beijing, fares depend on how far you travel but range 3–8RMB, but like in Beijing, it sure gets crowded down there and if you are traveling with luggage, the packed trains and long distances walked between interchanges can make for a miserable experience. At least the subway is air-conditioned and well maintained—if you have used the subway in Hong Kong, you will find this is very similar. Passengers buy tickets at one of the vending machines (cash only), or if you are planning to use public transportation a lot, you can buy a *jiaotong* card for a 30RMB deposit, which, after you add money to it, can be used on any form of public transport plus taxis (and you get the deposit back if you turn it back in). Unfortunately the Shanghai Metro authority does not have any English-language website, but an enthusiastic Shanghai subway rider has put together an up-to-date interactive map that can work out your fares and how long your trip should take: www.exploreshanghai.com/metro.

Taxi

If you see a Dazhong taxi—labeled with "Dazhong" on their side—hail it at once, as these are the best and most courteous drivers in Shanghai. The city has more than 45,000 taxis in the streets, though you may dispute that number if you're caught in the rain, when all taxis seem to magically disappear. Unlike in Beijing, you usually have to wait in line for a taxi in Shanghai

© HELENA IVESON

Keep an eye out for these signs when looking for the subway.

at peak times: Many people head to the nearest hotel and join the line, but most hotels have cottoned onto this and now you have to show your hotel key for them to hail a cab for you. Taxis here are slightly more expensive than in Beijing, but they're still affordable, making them usually the most convenient option. The large majority of vehicles are clean and air-conditioned and have an amusing list of do's and don'ts in English to unintentionally amuse you if you get stuck in traffic. Like anywhere else in China, taxi drivers here do not speak English so practice saying your destination in Chinese or have it written down clearly in Chinese characters. When you arrive at your destination, you will probably be asked if you want to pay cash or with a prepaid card; usually it will be cash and just pay what the meter says. It is a good idea to get a receipt just in case you forget something in the car; there's a small chance you will get it back if you get a Chinese speaker to phone the company afterward. Unlike in Beijing, you can call and reserve a taxi, though for now it's for Chinese speakers only: Dazhong taxis (82222).

© HELENA IVESON

Beijing has more than 60,000 taxis.

Visas and Officialdom

VISAS

Everyone who visits China needs a visa of some sort, and the most common visa is the simple tourist visa, which you must get from the Chinese Embassy before you leave for China. The only exception to this rule is if you are from one of a handful of countries, including the United States and Canada, staying less than 48 hours in China, and have a ticket out of the country that you can wave in front of authorities: Etickets won't cut it. The Chinese Embassy in Washington, DC (www.chinese-embassy.org), and its consulates in Chicago, San Francisco, Los Angeles, Houston, and New York organize all sorts of visas. A standard tourist "L" single- or double-entry visa is now a pricey $100 for U.S. citizens, takes four working days, and must be applied for in person or through a friend or visa agent. You must have at least six months remaining on your visa and at least one blank visa page in it, and be careful when filling out the application form as if it has the slightest mistake on it, your application will be sent back to you. If you want your visa processed in one working day, it costs an extra $20. Usually the validity of a single-entry or double-entry "L" visa is 90 days or 180 days from the date of issue. This means you have to enter China no later than 90 days or 180 days from the date of issue; otherwise the visa expires. On an "L" visa, you can stay in China for up to 30 days, though this can easily be extended once you are in China at the Foreign Affairs Office of the Public Security Bureau (2 Andingmen Dongdajie, Mon.–Sat. 8:30 A.M.–4:30 P.M.) near the Lama Temple subway stop in Beijing or in its office in Shanghai (333 Wusong Lu, Mon.–Sat. 9 A.M.–4:30 P.M.).

INSURANCE

Travel insurance covering both medical emergencies and your possessions is vital in China and should be considered an integral part of the cost of your holiday. There is no reciprocal agreement between China and any other country in the world, so if anything goes wrong you are on your own. There is no free health-care service in China and bills can add up very quickly. Both Beijing and Shanghai have public hospitals and top-of-the-range private hospitals, and while public hospitals are fine if you have little or no insurance, if you want to be treated by English-speaking staff in private surroundings with more modern equipment, you should head to one of the private hospitals listed in the *Hospitals and Pharmacies* section.

Travelers should arrange insurance before they travel and websites such as www.travelinsure.com offer instant online quotes, but if in the buildup to the holiday you overlook arranging insurance, try www.worldnomads.com. These independent insurers are one of the very few who will cover you even if you have already left for your trip and policies include evacuation cover. One decision you need to make is whether to buy single-trip insurance or a year policy that will cover multiple trips. If you choose the multiple-trip option, bear in mind that usually trips have to be shorter than 30 days long. With all policies, check to make sure the coverage is sufficient if you are carrying high-value items such as laptops and cameras.

If you lose or have any property stolen, you will almost definitely have to provide your insurers with a statement from the police. Unfortunately this can be a long drawn-out affair and if you do not speak any Mandarin, you should try to involve your hotel to act as a translator or head to the Sanlitun Police Station (see *Police* for more details) where they speak reasonable English. Keep all receipts for medical expenses too—all private hospitals will provide them in English; public hospitals may not.

If you have health insurance, check to see whether it will cover you when you are abroad—most policies do not, but if yours does, you then need to decide whether you need to take out additional coverage to insure your possessions. Even if you're not packing your Gucci jewelry, if you lose your suitcase or travel essentials like your passport, the costs of replacing everything can be immense, so additional travel insurance keeps you better safe than sorry. People who are trying to keep costs down should opt for basic travel insurance, which is for medical emergencies only and loss of passports—Global Nomads (www.globalnomads.com) offers a good no-frills policy.

EMBASSIES AND CONSULATES

The brand-new U.S. Embassy in Beijing, which opened just ahead of the Olympics is in Chaoyang District, north of the Kempinski Hotel. For more information, see beijing.usembassy-china.org.cn. The Canadian Embassy is at 19 Dongzhimenwai Dajie, Chaoyang District, 6532 3536, geo.international.gc.ca/asia/china, and the British Embassy is at 11 Guanghua Lu, Jianguomenwai, CBD, 6532 1961, www.uk.cn. For a full list of all embassies in Beijing, go to www.beijingservice.com/beijingtoolkits/embassies/embassies.htm.

Many countries maintain consulates in Shanghai: The American Consulate is at 1469 Huaihai Zhong Lu, 6433 6880, shanghai.usembassy-china.org.cn, the British Consulate is at Suite 301, Shanghai Center, 1376 Nanjing Xi Lu, 6279 8103, www.uk.cn, and the Canadian Consulate is at Suite 604, West Tower, Shanghai Center, Number 1376 Nanjing Xi Lu, 6279 8400, geo.international.gc.ca/asia/china.

POLICE

The branch of the police that deals with tourists is the Public Security Bureau, recognizable by the dark navy-blue uniforms. In major tourist destinations such as Tiananmen Square, you may strike it lucky and find a police officer who speaks some

Police are always stationed at Tiananmen Square.

English, but the vast majority don't, which is not very reassuring if things go wrong and you are a victim of a crime or need to make a stolen-property report for your travel insurance. The emergency number is 110, but again few people answering will speak any English. If necessary, involve your hotel or a Chinese-speaking friend to translate, or go to the Sanlitun police station, which, because of its location in the center of the expat universe in Beijing, has several helpful officers who speak good English. In Shanghai, there is a large branch of the PSB at People's Square—499 Nanjing Xi Lu, 6386 2999. If you can avoid it, try not to have any kind of involvement with the police as they are not exactly known for their efficiency in the vast majority of cases. You are supposed to register with the police on arrival in China—your hotel is responsible for that if you are staying in one, but if you are staying with a friend, you're supposed to do it yourself—99.9 percent of people don't bother and nothing comes of it.

Conduct and Customs

GENERAL ETIQUETTE

A lot of time has been spent by people examining the issue and importance of the concept of face, or *guanxi,* to the Chinese, but most of it is common sense and actually can be applied to practically all people. After all, what person likes being made to look a fool? However, while many people can laugh it off, perhaps the Chinese are more attached to the concept than others, so keep it in mind in both personal and professional dealings. Confrontation and criticism toward a Chinese person are not going to win you any friends—what you think of as straightforward American-style constructive criticism in China can come across as out-and-out offensiveness. Instead of being straightforward, the Chinese prefer to couch their criticism or make suggestions rather than give orders. Some people advise travelers to China to never get angry or complain when things go wrong as it will backfire: I'm of the opinion that nowadays you should complain without hesitation without resorting to shouting and getting seriously angry—it might not get you very far but surely you will feel better for it.

Staring is not considered rude in China so be prepared for stares and comments, even in cosmopolitan Shanghai and Beijing. Foreigners will get attention wherever they go and as you leave the city limits, the amount will increase immeasurably. It is usually not local Beijingers or Shanghainese who will be having a good old look, but people from other provinces, where foreigners are as rare as a Chinese nonsmoker. Another habits that can be difficult for foreign visitors to understand is spitting—it will be a rare day in China when you don't see someone having a good old clearing out at least once a day. The idea behind it is that it is better out than in, but thanks to health campaigns in the aftermath of the SARS outbreak, spitting had seemed to be dying out, but unfortunately the unsightly habit seems to have been undergoing a resurgence of late—perhaps the Olympics and the government's concern for showing off China's best face to the world will bring an end to having to watch where you're going as you walk down a phlegm-dotted sidewalk.

TERMS OF ADDRESS

Chinese names can be very difficult for a foreign visitor to decipher. Here family names are given first and then comes the first name, so for the current president, Hu Jintao, Hu is his family name and Jintao is his first name. But if you met him strolling down Wangfujing in Beijing, it would not be a good idea to introduce yourself by using his first name: The Chinese use a huge number of titles, both formal and informal, such as Wang Laoshi (teacher Wang), Mao Jingli (Manager Mao), Xiao Xu (little Xu), or Lao Li (old Li). The best advice is to simply ask people what you should call them. Only the closest of friends use a person's first name without any kind of title with it.

TABLE MANNERS

Eating is one of the great pleasures in China and if you are aware of a few pointers before you chow down, your experience will be all the more enhanced. Now that you have traveled thousands of miles from home, your dining experience will be totally different from what you will be used to. Chinese food is served family style with communal dishes in the middle of the table, and you shouldn't use the same chopsticks to serve yourself that you then use to eat your food—use a different serving set for hygienic reasons. Chopsticks should not be stuck into your bowl of rice, as it resembles incense in an urn as it's used during funeral rites.

Be prepared for a noisy experience: Slurping when eating slippery noodles is par for the course and no one will raise an eyebrow, and afterward if you feel the need for a good belch, let it rip: It's a sign you've appreciated your meal. And don't worry about any scattered debris on the table, either. Of course, these are the rules for when you go to a local cheap and cheerful place: If you did this at M on the Bund in Shanghai or a posh restaurant in Beijing, you'd cause a stir.

Wherever you go, the same rules about paying apply: Whoever asked pays. Going dutch is extremely rare and if you really want to pick up the tab, you will have to do the fake going-to-the-restroom trick and hand over the cash or you can just turn up at the restaurant with a gift to show your appreciation.

SMOKING

To add to worries about China's huge air-pollution problem is China's obsession with chain-smoking: One out of three cigarettes smoked in the world are smoked in China. If you're a nonsmoker or hate people's smoking at bars and restaurants, your lungs might not be the only thing getting irritated. If you are a smoker, the low, low prices may tempt you to smoke much more than normal and next to nowhere will you be made to feel unwelcome as a smoker. There is a growing awareness about the damage to people's health caused by cigarettes and smoking is banned on subways, trains, and a growing number of offices, but all this means is that smokers crowd into corridors and into the ends of train carriages and fill those with smoke.

Tips for Travelers

WHAT TO TAKE

Chinese people with money like to dress the part and may find the sight of a very scruffily dressed Westerner a bit of an oddity: If you have money—which to most Chinese eyes, all foreigners do—why would you not wear nice clothes? Most restaurants are very casual—the only places you would need to make a little effort are at the cities' most expensive venues. If you hate the idea of being stared at, it's advisable to dress a shade more conservatively than you probably would at home.

If you require medication, bring it from home. Everything from painkillers to sleeping pills are available over the counter without a prescription in China, but there are stories of fake medicine doing a lot of harm to people: It's not worth the risk, no matter how unlikely.

Specialized baby equipment can be found, but bring anything you can't do without from home, as the quality may not be up to par—and bring kid-size chopsticks, which will make it easier for your children to enjoy Chinese food (and which will be hard to find in China). Pack some good maps to complement the ones in this book—those you'll find in Beijing are notoriously inaccurate and will be in Chinese. Wi-Fi in China is good and plentiful—if you will need to work, it's best to bring your laptop, as Internet cafés will be noisy with computer games.

However, most American appliances can't be used in China without an adapter, as the electrical current is 220 volts. There is not a standard socket system in the country: You will come across both two- and three-pronged round sockets as well as two-pronged flat sockets, so bring a good general adapter, as only the more expensive hotels will have adapters as standard.

OPPORTUNITIES FOR STUDY AND EMPLOYMENT

To many go-getters, China, with its huge virtually untapped markets, is the Promised Land full of opportunity. Every year, more and more people of all ages come to both Beijing and Shanghai looking for adventure and/or hoping to build a career in China. Estimates vary hugely on the number of students, English teachers, and professionals who call these cities home—the most recent survey in Shanghai said there were more than 350,000—but no matter what the figures are: If you judge the expat community by the numbers of magazines aimed at its members or the numbers of exotic restaurants that open each month, the expat community is growing exponentially.

So is there room for you, you may ask? If you speak Chinese your prospects widen considerably, although plenty of people with skills that are in short supply still manage to find work. If you wish to study the language—a good idea as it will let you see if you like the place before you sign any work contracts—there are literally hundreds of universities and language schools keen to help you recognize Chinese tones. Studying at a university is popular because classes are very formal, though classes tend to be on the large side and are much more expensive than private language schools, where hourly rates range 20–120RMB depending on the school. **Peking University** (en.pku.edu.cn) has a very prestigious program, as does **Beijing Language and Culture University** (www.ebclu.net). Bear in mind, though, that you will be in a class full of foreign students so it can be very difficult to submerge yourself in Chinese culture. Popular language schools where you can choose the intensity of study and whether you want private or small-group classes include **Frontiers** (www.frontiers.com.cn) near Dongzhimen and **Executive Mandarin** (www.execmandarin.com) in the CBD. Schools come and go out of favor—for more information, consult the forum at the www.thebeijinger.com website or read the listings magazines for recommendations.

Many people find more casual work through websites such as www.thebeijinger.com in Beijing and in Shanghai, the online classifieds at www.adweekly.cn can be helpful. Here you will find everything from English teaching, modeling, voice-recording work, and random jobs for advertising agencies with pay ranging from 150RMB an hour upward. As the cost of living is very reasonable in Beijing, you can very easily live off these jobs. If you can, however, get employment before you arrive and sign a fat expat contract, you will have the salary to live well in China. Media jobs can be found at www.danwei.org and also check out www.jobsdb.com for employment opportunities in mainland China as well as elsewhere in the region. Many people live in China without having the proper "Z" work visa, which you can get only if your company sponsors you: It's a reasonably drawn-out but simple-enough process that involves a rudimentary medical exam. If you do not have a company to sponsor you, you can't stay on a tourist visa forever, so people get an "F" visa, which is slightly on the shady side but not illegal—it's meant for people living in Hong Kong who wish to travel to the mainland frequently. Every so often you hear of a potential crackdown on this loophole, but for now, people who hold "F" visas are left alone.

ACCESS FOR TRAVELERS WITH DISABILITIES

Neither Beijing nor Shanghai will be easy destinations for travelers with disabilities—an irritating situation considering Beijing hosted the Paralympics in 2008. Public transportation is basically off-limits as there is next to no wheelchair access and the heavy traffic on the roads and crowds of people on the sidewalk can be a challenge at the best of times. Few road crossings have audible alerts and while some sidewalks will have ridges to help visually impaired people, the many cracks and uneven slabs will make walking difficult. This isn't to say that it's all bad: The problems facing travelers with disabilities have been raised at tourism conferences and now many of the more-expensive hotels have adapted rooms. It would be a good idea to rent a car to get around: This can be arranged by any five-star hotel, or you could try Beijing etours (beijing.etours.cn/disabled_travel), which offers special guided tours to the city. *The Disabled Travelers Guide* (www.disabledtravelersguide.com) is full of useful information, too.

TRAVELING WITH CHILDREN

If you want to introduce your child to a completely different culture, pack your bags, get ready for the occasional challenging moment, and you'll have a blast. The Chinese love children, so they should be prepared to receive plenty of attention and the odd prod and poke from well-meaning adults who find Western children incredibly cute. The one-child policy, under which Chinese couples have been restricted to having just one child since 1979, has produced a generation of "little emperors" and "little empresses" carrying the hopes and dreams of one set of parents and two sets of doting grandparents. Aside from the very serious consequences of males' seriously outnumbering females, it has also meant that there are plenty of ways to keep pampered kids occupied (see the *Explore Beijing and Shanghai* chapter for more details). Both cities have plenty of Western restaurants for that little taste of home when your kids have had enough of Chinese food.

WOMEN TRAVELING ALONE

For women used to traveling alone, China can be a breath of fresh air: Any attention tends to be of the interested rather than sleazy variety. The women of these two cosmopolitan cities have a reputation for not taking any nonsense with the result that women can travel freely, of course taking measures that are basic common sense. If you are traveling by taxi, it's a good idea to sit in the back and have a mobile phone with you and the number of your hotel or of a friend who could help out in case of an impenetrable language barrier or other emergency.

GAY AND LESBIAN TRAVELERS

While neither Beijing or Shanghai have huge out-and-proud gay communities, there's enough going on to make you feel, if not at home, entertained. No one will care about your accommodation arrangements if you wish to share a room with your same-sex partner—people are more interested in the pink dollar than anything else. The history of homosexuality in China has had its ups and downs, with there being many recordings of gay relationships in the Forbidden City throughout the ages. Gay men and women have suffered hugely in the past, though, especially when Mao proclaimed the country the People's Republic in 1949. Gay lifestyles were considered decadent and immoral and homosexuals were persecuted relentlessly. The often-quoted fact that the government declassified homosexuality as a mental illness only in 2001 shouldn't be taken as a sign of China's backwardness now—there are no laws against being gay and most of the time, gay bars and clubs are left alone, and while you will certainly attract attention if you are publicly affectionate with your partner, it is very unlikely you would be at the receiving end of anything more than a curious stare. The listings magazine *Time Out* has a Gay and Lesbian section that reviews the current favorite bars and clubs, and Beijing has *Promen*, a networking group for professional gay men (groups.yahoo.com/group/promen), while on www.gay.com, there's a Shanghai-based chatroom.

Health and Safety

Both Beijing and Shanghai are very safe cities, and it's extremely rare for anyone more than the odd pickpocket to set his or her sights on foreign tourists. Quite simply, anyone who commits a crime against a tourist is punished much more harshly than if he or she had done the same thing to a local because authorities see such acts as extremely damaging to the country's reputation. However, the opening of the Olympics in Beijing was marred by the murder of an American by a deranged local who then killed himself; and earlier in the year, a Canadian model was murdered in Shanghai. The start of 2008 also saw bombs in Kunming in Yunnan province and a brutal attack in Kashgar, in which two Uighur men killed 16 policemen with a handmade bomb. These terrible events are all the more shocking as the cities are normally very safe for foreigners, but are a reminder about the need for vigilance. Thanks to cheap taxis, you don't have to walk home by yourself late at night and as there are almost always people on the streets, you'll rarely find yourself alone. There aren't any no-go areas in either city and there are few modern metropolises you can say that about. Of course it still pays to pay attention to your surroundings and use common sense, as foreigners are a target for scams. Don't go off with people you don't know, even if they claim to be friendly art students. They aren't and it's a scam, and you could end up like the recent Swedish businessman who was swindled out of 4,000RMB for a round of coffees in Shanghai!

The more likely danger you will face in China is being in a car accident: Wear seatbelts if at all possible and stop the car if you think the driver is too erratic. The other major concern is pollution, with Beijing in particular judged one of the worst places in the world for the quality of its air. While the long-term effects of living here and breathing in the fumes are unknown, no one should seriously think his or her health will be damaged by a short stay unless he or she already has respiratory problems. Shanghai's air quality is a little better, but it is still considered heavily polluted by U.S. standards. Don't drink the water from the tap in either city: It's not the actual water that is at fault but the old and rusty pipes that it comes through.

If you are staying in Shanghai and Beijing, you don't really need to worry about having any inoculations before your trip aside from the standard Hepatitis A and B, tetanus, polio, and typhoid shots that doctors recommend you have before you travel anywhere. The biggest problem is the many strains of flu virus that float around, but you can't do much about them aside from following normal standard good-hygiene practices. As soap is still irritatingly rare in public and restaurant toilets, it's a good idea to bring some antibacterial hand gel for when you can't wash your hands.

SARS, or Severe Acute Respiratory Syndrome, caused a worldwide panic between November 2002 and July 2003, with 8,096 known infected cases and 774 deaths, the vast majority of which were in mainland China and Hong Kong. Despite the scary headlines, there have not been any recurrences of the virus that killed a significant number of people. If there ever were to be another spate of SARS deaths in these cities, it would be sensible to postpone your trip. While the amount of spitting did decrease in the aftermath, people still do, unfortunately.

As always, use your best judgment—and if you find yourself embroiled in anything serious, immediately involve your embassy.

HOSPITALS AND PHARMACIES

Beijing

Beijing United Family Hospital (2 Jiangtai Lu, Lidu, Chaoyang District, 6433 3960, www.unitedfamilyhospitals.com) is considered Beijing's premier private hospital and if you have good insurance, head here. All staff speak English and in addition to full emergency services, there is an excellent maternity ward. The hospital is about a 20-minute drive from the city center on the way to the airport. In the city itself in Sanlitun is **Beijing International SOS Clinic** (Building 5, BITIC Building, 5 Sanlitun Xiwujie, 6462 9112, www.internationalsos.com.) This is the private clinic of choice for many expats and is a good place to head if you want to talk to a foreign or overseas-trained doctor. Costs are high, however, and you may have to pay upfront as it does not have arrangements with many insurance companies. In addition to a full range of medical services, including a dentist, opticians, physiotherapist, and counseling service, it also has a fully stocked pharmacy that you do not have to be a patient to use. For a cheaper alternative, many believe the foreigners' wing at the public hospital **Peking Union** (1 Shuaifuyuan, Wangfujing, Tiananmen, 6529 5284) is OK—it has 24-hour emergency care and is much more central than Beijing United. If you have full insurance, however, and can get to Beijing United, head there, as the bedside manner of many of the doctors can be on the brusque side and privacy is not high on the agenda. To see a doctor here costs 200RMB and medicine and treatment costs are extra, and payment is cash only.

Shanghai

For nonemergencies and if you're armed with medical insurance, **World Link** (Suite 203, Portman Clinic, 1376 Nanjing Xi Lu, 6279 7688, www.worldlink-shanghai.com) in the

Shanghai Center is conveniently situated and all staff are either from abroad or speak excellent English, with some speaking Spanish, French, and Japanese. World Link offers both medical and dental services, and it also has other clinics spread around the city—check the website for details. At this branch, there is also a unconnected pharmacy next door where staff speak English.

Another expat favorite is **United Family Hospital** (1139 Xianxia Lu, Changning District, 5133 1900, www.unitedfamilyhospitals.com), which like its sister hospital in Beijing, is the best place to head in an emergency armed with your health-insurance policy. It is about 35 minutes' drive out of the city center, however.

There are some recommended cheaper options. **Huashan Hospital** (19th Floor, 12 Wulumuqi Zhong Lu by Huashan Lu, French Concession, 6248 9999) has a dedicated foreigners' wing where staff speak English. Try this if you don't have good insurance or a fully comprehensive policy; it has modern facilities and is part of one of Shanghai's best hospitals.

EMERGENCY SERVICES

If you are in dire need of assistance, the emergency telephone number is **110** for the police. But no one will speak English, so you must find someone to help you if you do not speak Mandarin. Emergency services are in no way up to North American or European standards, and you hear possibly apocryphal stories of people injured in accidents lying by the roadside until the ambulance service, which is run as a business, has been assured that someone will pick up the bill. This is why travel insurance is vital in China. If the worst-case scenarios come true, the best advice is to don't bother calling an ambulance but flag down transportation of any sort and make your way to the nearest international-standard hospital—ambulances will deposit you at the nearest and not necessarily the best hospital.

Information and Services

BEIJING

Tourist and Travel Information

TOURIST CENTERS

You might expect a tourist office to be able to deal with international tourists, but you'd be mistaken: Chinese tourist centers are notoriously useless, are aimed only at local visitors, and generally are only interested in your signing up for an expensive tour on which the tour guide doesn't speak any English. Don't even bother seeking one out: Instead, use this book, local listings magazines, and travel advisory sites such as Trip Advisor.

MAPS

An up-to-date map of Beijing is rare on the ground, though the ones sold at tourist destinations and on the subway for around 5RMB are better than nothing. The listings magazine *City Weekend* has a bilingual pullout that can be useful; otherwise ask your hotel to provide one.

POSTAL SERVICE

There are many post offices across the capital, but head to a big branch, where the clerks will be more used to dealing with foreigners. When you walk in, you'll see English signs that are often nonsensical and there will be lots of different lines: Your best bet is to go to the post office on Gongti Bei Lu opposite the Workers' Stadium, which also has a Western Union and ATM, and head to the left counter that sells stamps, as the clerks speak some English there. Postcards cost 4.5RMB to send, and letters start at 6RMB. (See the *Shanghai* section for advice on parcels.) There is also a huge branch on the second ring road at Yabao Lu, Jianguomen Beidajie, 6512 8114, if that is more convenient. Bring your passport if you need to send parcels.

INTERNET

In 2008, China overtook the United States and now has the largest number of broadband

© HELENA IVESON

These characters indicate an Internet café.

Internet users in the world, and this connectivity makes Beijing an easy place to get online. The vast majority of cafés have free wireless Internet access, including Pass By Bar and Xiao Xin's on Nanluoguxiang, the Bookworm in Sanlitun, and the Stone Boat Bar in Ritan Park, to name just a few. For a more comprehensive list, check out www.danwei.org/China-Guide/Beijing_wifi/wireless_hotspot_beijing.htm. The best advice is just to turn your computer on and see what it picks up—you will normally have plenty of connections to choose from. All hotels, from the cheapest hostels to the most expensive five-star palaces, will have Internet access though more-expensive places are increasingly charging for the privilege. If you don't have your own computer, there is an OK Internet café in the basement of the East Gate Plaza off Dongzhimen Wai, though you will need your passport and high tolerance for noisy computer games. The more relaxing option is to use your hotel's computers and pay around 20RMB at a hostel for an hour to 150RMB at a five-star hotel's business center.

Media

Before the age of the Internet, the Chinese media were heavily controlled and censored. The national news agency Xinhua supplied and still supplies all newspapers with the party line, and few would claim that newspapers were worth the paper they were written on. But times have changed a little—economic reforms have improved the media industry, with many new television channels available, in addition to hundreds of newspapers and magazines. The government's grip on the media has relaxed somewhat, though nowadays journalistic self-censorship is probably more of a problem. National English-language newspapers look like real newspapers and have many fine features, but their journalists are stifled by government control, and mayy encounter severe penalties if they address sensitive political topics, such as democracy or Tibet. If you're desperate for real news, the *South China Morning Post* can be found late in the afternoon at five-star hotels, as can the *International Herald Tribune,* the *Wall Street Journal,* and the *Financial Times.*

© HELENA IVESON

The Chinese love their magazines.

China is struggling to come to grips with the Internet as it's clear that Chinese people have turned to the web to find uncensored news and publish blogs in mind-boggling numbers. The famous "Great Firewall of China" exists, as anyone trying to log onto the BBC will find out, but web-savvy Chinese can usually work around it, for example by finding a proxy server that bypasses the censors. (For more on websites, please see the *Resources* chapter.)

Most midrange and above hotels will have a full array of English-language TV stations showing BBC Worldwide and CNN at the very least. China's very own international English-language channel, CCTV 9, is widely available too and shows news and features from "a Chinese perspective." Like the *China Daily* newspaper, it used to be awful but in recent years, the quality has improved considerably (full disclosure: I used to present a program there!).

TIME OUT BEIJING, WWW.TIMEOUT.COM/BEIJING

Beijing's sassiest monthly magazine is part of the growing international company that publishes magazines in New York and London, and the Beijing offshoot is just as opinionated and fun to read. The Consume sections reveal all the best shops in the city while the nightlife pages are full to the brim with reviews on the latest openings. (Full disclosure: I'm an occasional features writer for them.)

THE BEIJINGER WWW.THEBEIJINGER.COM

The oldest of the crop of Beijing's monthly listings magazines, this started off as young and fun, but it has definitely got staid with age. Its sheer size can't be beaten and it's the best magazine to read for the latest art gallery exhibitions. It also does an "off-the-beaten-track" tourist destination every issue, which is useful when you have exhausted this book's supply!

CHINA DAILY, WWW.CHINADAILY.COM.CN

The country's main English-language daily newspaper started in 1981 and has been considered a propaganda-filled rag for most of its existence. But in recent years and like many state-run enterprises, the newspaper no longer receives government subsidies, so its editors have had to adopt a more commercial approach, making it much more of an interesting read. You still get all the pointless political stories on the front page, but there are usually some interesting features somewhere in the paper.

BEIJING TODAY

This weekly newspaper, which is sold at newspaper stands across the capital, is the best state-media read. Like *Shanghai Star*, it tries to forgo the boring political stories that *China Daily* has to report and instead focuses on more relevant news and features for its local readers. It does occasionally push the censorship envelope with articles on subjects such as Beijing's gay scene and the capital's homeless.

SHANGHAI

Tourist and Travel Information

TOURIST CENTERS

Neither Shanghai nor Beijing yet has an

independent useful travel service for the millions of foreign visitors who descend on the cities every year. Tourist offices see themselves more as travel agents and sell overpriced tours to their mainly Chinese customers: Information in English is still very limited. If you want to try, the main office is at 303 Moling Lu, near the south exit of the railway station, 6353 9920, www.tourinfo.sh.com, but you will receive better information from your hotel concierge, listings magazines, and travel websites such as Trip Advisor—and of course this book! Even if you are not staying at the hotel, you could pick the brains of a hotel concierge—there's no need to make clear you're not staying there. . . .

© HELENA IVESON

Shanghai's jaunty mailboxes

MAPS

While Shanghai has not seen the same number of changes as Beijing in the last few years, an up-to-date map is still essential, especially one that lists the city's subway system, where new lines seem to be opening every six months or so. Aside from the fine maps you will find in this book, you may find you need something larger. The maps that vendors sell at tourist sights such as the Bund are cheap and OK but tend to be aimed at Chinese tourists more than foreigners and so might not always have English translations. The website www.smartshanghai.com has an excellent map of the city that is updated monthly, and it also features a street-finder function. If you'd prefer to have a hard copy as you travel, the biweekly magazine *City Weekend,* which is available at most bars and cafés in the city, has a pullout up-to-date map.

POSTAL SERVICE

The main post office also serves as the Postal Museum at the north end of the Bund (see *Sights*), but more conveniently located branches are situated in Xintiandi (3, Lane 123, Xingye Lu near Madang Lu, French Concession, 6385 7449) and in Jing'an at the Shanghai Center (Suite 355A, East Office Tower, Shanghai Center, 1376 Nanjing Xi Lu, Jing'an, 6279 8044). Here English-speaking staff will help you send postcards, letters, and parcels. If you are sending a parcel, staff will want to have a look through it before they accept it so don't seal it before you get there. China Post is efficient and reasonably priced: Postcards to anywhere in the world cost 4.5RMB and letters from 6RMB. You can of course ask your hotel to post letters too but it will add a service charge.

INTERNET

China is much more wired than the United States or Europe with the vast majority of cafés offering free Internet wireless access. All branches of Element Fresh and Wagas have free Internet access, as do branches of Blue Frog and KABB in Xintiandi, Big Bamboo, and Coffee Bean branches dotted throughout the city. Unfortunately Starbucks branches don't, but that's just another reason to try a more local place. All hotels will have some form of Internet access but unfortunately many five-star hotels are now charging upward of 120RMB a day: If free access is important to you, ask before you reserve your room. If you don't have your own laptop, all expensive hotels will have business centers, but hostels are more affordable: The Captain's Hostel near the Bund has computers for 20RMB an hour. These are much better options than going to a huge earsplittingly loud Internet café full of Chinese youths playing noisy shooting games and that often won't allow foreigners in because of government crackdowns after a number of fatal fires. For a full list of Internet hot spots in Shanghai, go to www.danwei.org/china_information/free_wireless_internet_hot_spo_1.php.

Media

The local Chinese-language media is heavily controlled, as is the state-run *China Daily* English-language newspaper and its Shanghai weekly, *Shanghai Star.* While if you're prepared to weed out the dross about steel production and the recent visit to China by the president of the Faroe Islands, their features can be worth a read. The best English-language media, however, are the magazines and websites listed here: Although all will have a state censor overseeing their output, they get away with far more than Chinese magazines would. Newspapers such as the *South China Morning Post* can be found late in the afternoon at five-star hotels, as can the *International Herald Tribune,* the *Wall Street Journal,* and the *Financial Times.*

SHANGHAIIST, SHANGHAIIST.COM

The Shanghai branch of the international Gothamist sites that are now all over the globe, *shanghaiist* dishes up the dirt on what's happening in Shanghai and to less of an extent, in the rest of China. This is the best source of news about Shanghai bar none.

SH MAGAZINE, WWW.SHMAG.CN

SH is the city's only weekly magazine and considering things change so quickly in Shanghai, it's worth seeking out this free mag for its up-to-date information. *SH* is more about having fun than a serious look at life in Shanghai and its restaurant critic is particularly amusing and spot-on in his opinions—check out his blog on the site.

THAT'S SHANGHAI, WWW.URBANTOMY.COM

This free monthly magazine may not be as good as its Beijing sister, but it's still very much worth a read to find out who the latest big acts to come to Shanghai are and to read reviews of the many new bars and restaurants that spring up every month. The new website is a major improvement if you can't find a copy of the magazine, but considering it has the best distribution of any listings magazine in the city, stroll into practically any hotel, restaurant, or bar, and you will find one.

SHANGHAI STAR, WWW.SHANGHAI-STAR.COM.CN

This is Shanghai's only English-language weekly newspaper and is run by *China Daily.* Despite its staid owner, the paper quite rightly ignores politics as much as it can and concentrates on city news that can be—amazing but true!—interesting. The features can be interesting and it also does a full roundup of news from around the world. The only daily English-language newspaper is state-run *Shanghai Daily,* which like the *Star* is available from hotels and at newspaper stands on the street.

MONEY

Currency and Exchange Rates

The Chinese currency is called *renminbi* (RMB), or the People's Currency in English, but it is popularly known as *kuai,* the Chinese equivalent of bucks. After years of pressure from the United States, the government no longer has a set exchange rate to the dollar but allows it to fluctuate slightly against the dollar, though not nearly enough, according to many economists. At this writing, $1 equals 7RMB. Chinese currency comes in notes varying 1RMB–100RMB, and as many people get paid in cash, that makes for a bricklike pay packet. You can also get 1RMB coins and small denominations (10 *jiao* equals 1RMB), though increasingly as prices rise it's the notes that will come in handy.

Changing Money

You can change money just about anywhere in Beijing and Shanghai, at the airports, hotels, and any bank you come across. Rates will not vary much, though hotels will be the least competitive, and don't bother with the touts who hang outside banks asking you to change money: There's no point in risking it for next to no benefit. You will need your passport to change money, and when it comes to changing it back, you will need to show the foreign-exchange receipt you will have received when first changing the money. Nowadays, the ATM system in both cities is in English and Chinese, which makes it unnecessary to join the lines and use a bank: I would recommend using your cards to pull money out of the wall and having an emergency supply of cash. Always keep your card receipts, though, as it is not unheard-of for machines to debit your card twice. Also be aware when using ATMs that your cash comes out before your card—it's very easy to walk away at that point, leaving your card in the machine for the next customer to dip into if he or she is feeling dishonest. ATMs are of course usually available 24 hours a day, while banks tend to close at 5 P.M. every day. Banks in China are notorious for long lines, which make using an ATM an even more attractive option, and changing travelers checks is a huge nuisance. Withdrawal limits have been raised to 3,000RMB per transaction, but if that is not enough, you can repeat the transaction.

When you leave, you can now exchange money back into your preferred currency at the airports before you go and at an increasing number of countries abroad—a major change as the currency used to be completely useless when taken overseas. Do check before you leave your home country whether your local bank will do so, as you don't want to be left with huge piles of RMB notes that you can't change.

Costs

By world standards, China is a cheap travel destination, but Shanghai and Beijing are all about extremes. Yes, it's possible to eat only 4RMB bowls of noodles and drink 2RMB bottles of Tsingtao at some backstreet bar, but this is also a place where you can drink 150RMB cocktails at a penthouse bar overlooking the Bund in Shanghai before dining at Jean Georges, where you won't receive much change from 4,000RMB for two. So, the costs of your trip will depend on your appetite for splurging. Your main costs every day will be accommodation, and every price range is catered to in both cities. If you have been backpacking in the rest of China, where it is much cheaper, hostel prices might come as a shock, being a whole 50RMB a night for a dorm room, but for most travelers on a budget, both Shanghai and Beijing have plenty of options, and as your budget increases, the number of options does exponentially. As previously mentioned, food can be the biggest bargain in the country but if you want a nice atmosphere and a sit-down meal, prices rise and rise. Imported alcohol, especially wine, is expensive here—in fact anything that is imported is considerably more than what you would pay back home, so if you're trying to keep costs down, you will have to eat and drink locally as much as possible. The cost of admission to the cities' premier attractions such as the Forbidden City and, say, the Oriental Pearl Tower in Shanghai have gone up considerably in recent years, but as the numbers of tourists and middle-class Chinese increase, everyone is jumping on the bandwagon and raising prices. Fortunately, transportation, both within the cities and to and from them, is still the bargain it always was. There are few cities where English teachers and students can travel by taxi as much as they want, subway tickets start from 2RMB, and a 12-hour soft-sleeper train ticket from Beijing to Shanghai is 500RMB. A backpacker can easily get by on 200RMB if staying in a dorm and able to ignore the shops; a more relaxed traveller staying in a midrange hotel, eating at a nice restaurant every night with a few drinks, and the odd look around the shops needs to budget around 1,500RMB a day, while for a five-star traveler, the sky's the limit!

Tipping

China is one of those wonderful countries

where you don't need to tip unless you really feel the need to reward good service. Even then, do it discreetly and not in front of expats who live there as they might turn on you for ruining the status quo for everyone else! A small number of expensive restaurants already add a 10–15 percent service charge (which despite the name, won't go to the actual servers), so check your bill carefully.

Tipping is just not part of the Chinese way of life, though whether that will change with the increasing numbers of foreign tourists post-Olympics is hard to say. But if you are in a taxi or a local restaurant and the bill is not quite a round number, that extra 1 or 2RMB will go a lot further in the hands of a driver or waitress, so it's worth rounding up in those circumstances. Sometimes tour guides hang around afterward waiting for gratuities: They would be appreciated but there would not be any kind of outcry from them if nothing extra was given. Hotel staff don't need tips unless someone has really gone out of his or her way.

RESOURCES

Glossary

PLACES AND DIRECTIONS

Běi (北) north
Dàjiē (大街) avenue
Dàxué (大学) university
Dōng (东) east
Gōng (宫) palace
Gōngyuán (公园) park
Guǎngchǎng (广场) square
Gǔlóu (鼓楼) drum-tower
Hé (河) river
Hútòng (胡同) traditional lanes or alleys in Beijing
Jiāng (江) river
Jiē (街) street
Lǐlòng (里弄) traditional alley houses in Shanghai
Lòngtáng (弄堂) traditional alleys in Shanghai
Lù (路) road
Mén (门) entrance, door, gate
Nán (南) south
Pagoda a tiered tower with multiple eaves
Peking the old English name for Beijing
Qiáo (桥) bridge
Shān (山) hill, mountain
Shìchǎng (市场) market
Shíkùmén (石库门) stone-gated houses in Shanghai
Shuǐ (水) water
Sì (寺) temple
Sìhéyuàn (四合院) a compound with houses around a courtyard; quadrangle
Tiān (天) sky; heaven
Xī (西) west
Zhàn (站) station, stop
Zhōnglóu (钟楼) bell tower

PEOPLE AND HISTORICAL EVENTS

Cultural Revolution A struggle for power within the Communist Party of China that manifested into wide-scale social, political, and economic chaos, and which grew to include large sections of Chinese society and eventually brought the entire country to the brink of civil war.

Dèng Xiǎopíng (邓小平) (1904-1997) Chinese leader who was the most powerful figure in China from the late 1970s until his death in 1997. He abandoned many orthodox Communist doctrines and attempted to incorporate elements of the free-enterprise system into the Chinese economy.

Great Leap Forward (1958-1960) Mao's plan to use China's vast population to rapidly transform the country from a primarily agrarian economy into a modern, industrialized society but which was an unmitigated disaster, with between 14 million and 43 million people believed to have died in the resulting famine.

Hàn (汉) The Han nationality, the main ethnic group in China.

Hú Jǐntāo (胡锦涛) (1942-) The president of China since 2003, Hu has never granted a free-ranging interview so little is known about the man himself.

Jiāng Zémín (1926-) Former president who took over from Deng. Considered a shrewd survivor in Chinese politics and an economic reformer intent on shaking up China's massive state-run industries. Still wields power behind the scenes.

The Long March A massive military retreat 1934-1936 by the forerunners of the PLA led by Mao to evade the pursuit of the Kuomintang army during China's civil war.

Lǎowài (老外) Slightly derogatory term for a foreigner.

Máo Zédōng (毛泽东) (1893-1976) Mao rose to become the preeminent revolutionary theorist, political leader, and statesman of China after the country's civil war. While many still worship the charismatic leader, the official version of Mao's career is that his leadership was essentially right until 1957 but from that point forward it was uneven.

Tóngzhì (同志) Originally meant comrade but nowadays is used in the gay community to mean a gay man.

Uighur Turkic-speaking people who live for the most part in northwestern China in Xinjiang province.

CONCEPTS

Chāi (拆) Demolish, the character seen painted on buildings that means they will soon be knocked down.

Fēngshuǐ (风水) Literally means wind and water, an ancient Chinese art of placement and arrangement of space to achieve harmony with the environment.

Guānxi (关系) Relation, relationship.

Guānyīn (观音) Buddhism Guanyin, the Goddess of Mercy.

Overseas Chinese Chinese people who left the country to live abroad.

Pīnyīn (拼音) The Romanization system used to translate Chinese characters – pinyin means "spell sound."

Pǔtōnghuà (普通话) Mandarin Chinese, literally means "common language."

Qiípáo (旗袍) form-fitting dress with slits to thigh

Rénmín (人民) The People.

Rénmínbì (人民币) Chinese currency, literally means the people's currency, also known as asyuán (元).

Tai Chi Chinese martial art that relieves stress and improves flexibility and balance.

ACRONYMS

CCP Chinese Communist Party

CITS China International Travel Service

PLA People's Liberation Army

PRC People's Republic of China

PSB Public Security Bureau

Mandarin Phrasebook

There are about 50,000 Chinese characters in existence but mastering them may be a little ambitious: Instead use this phrasebook with both pinyin and characters to help you along your way.

PROUNCIATION GUIDE

The main obvious difference between Romance languages and Chinese is characters. See the *Background* chapter for more details on China's unique and ancient system of communication, but for people wanting to learn a few phrases for their trip, the most important thing to know is that the way a character looks bears no relation to how you pronounce it. There are very few shortcuts to learning characters as it comes down to memorization, so in the 1950s, pinyin, which transcribes Chinese characters into a Roman-style alphabet, was created to help people learn Mandarin. Many letters are similar in pronunciation to English, but here's a short guide to the more difficult sounds:

q like the ch in "cheese"
c like the ts in "rats"
r like the s in "leisure"
x like sy
z like the ds in "roads"
zh like j in "jam," but with the tongue curled back slightly
a like the a in "rather"
ai like the i in "high"
ao like the o in "cow"
e like the e in "errr... "
ei like the a in "hay"
i like the ee in "lee," or like the oo in took after c, ch, r, s, sh, z or zh
ian like "yen"
ie like "yeah"
o like the o in "for"
ou like "oh"
u like the u in "flute"
ui like "way"
uo runs "u" and "o" together, u-o, sounds like "wo"
yu Pucker your lips as if to whistle and say "yee," sounds like "y" and the German "ü"
ü like the German "ü"

Tones

Grammar may be simple, but here's the bad news: Chinese is a tonal language, which means that the pitch, or tone, of the pronunciation completely alters a character's meaning. There are four tones in Mandarin: high, rising, falling and then rising, and falling – if that sounds a lot, remember that other Chinese dialects can have as many as nine tones. Tones are the main reason for the difficulty in learning Chinese – unless you get the tones dead-on, people may not have a clue what you are saying, so practice as much as you can.

Grammar

Now for the good news: Chinese grammar is simple. Verbs do not conjugate – in other words, it's just "go" whoever's doing it: I go, you go, he go, etc.), there are no genders, no "the" or "a," and no tenses. Another grammar point that makes Chinese slightly easier than you may at first think is that just like in English it's subject-verb-object. In Mandarin, you say the subject first, then the verb, then the object. So, for example:

I	Wǒ	我
like	xǐhuān	喜欢
China	Zhōngguó	中国

Add it all together to make *Wǒ xǐhuān Zhōngguó,* 我喜欢中国, or *I like China.* If you want to turn this or any other sentence negative, you add bù 不 in front of the verb, so *Wǒ bù xǐhuān Zhōngguó,* 我不喜欢中国, or *I don't love China.* Then, to make it a question, you simply add the character ma 吗 to the end of the sentence: *Nǐ xǐhuān Zhōngguó ma?* 你 喜欢 中国 吗? means *Do you like China?*

BASIC AND COURTEOUS EXPRESSIONS

Hello.	Nǐhǎo	你好
How are you?	Nǐhǎo ma?	你好吗
Very well, thank you.	Hěn hǎo, xièxiè	很 好谢谢
Okay; good.	Hǎo	好
Not okay; bad.	Bù hǎo	不好
So-so.	Bùcuò	不错
And you?	Nǐ ne?	你呢?
Thank you.	Xièxiè	谢谢
Thank you very much.	Xièxiè Nǐ	谢谢你
You're welcome.	Bùkèqi	不客气
Good-bye.	Zàijiàn	再见.
See you later.	Dāi huì ér jiàn	待 会儿见
please	qǐng	请
I don't know.	Wǒ bù zhīdào	我不知道
correct	duì	对
No, not	bù	不
Just a moment, please.	Děng yīhuìr	等一会儿
Excuse me, please (when you're trying to get attention).	Máfan nǐ	麻烦你
I'm sorry.	Duì bùqǐ	对 不起
I don't want it (this, that, these, those).	Búyào	不要
Pleased to meet you.	Hěnhǎo rènshi nǐ	很好认识你
How do you say... in Chinese?	...Zhōngwén zěnme shuō?	中文怎么说?
What is your name?	Nǐ jiào shénme?	你叫什么?
Do you speak English?	Nǐ huì shuō yīngwén mǎ?	你会说英文马?
How long have you studied English?	Nǐ xué yīngyǔ duō jiǔ le?	你 学 英 语 多 久 了?
Your English is very good.	Nǐ de yīngyǔ hěn hǎo	你 的 英 语 很 好

I don't speak Chinese well.	Wǒ bùhuì shuō hěnhǎo de zhōngwén	我不会说很好的中文
I don't understand.	Wǒ bù míngbái	我不明白
Please speak more slowly.	Qǐng shuō de màn yīdiǎn	请 说的慢一点
My name is...	Wǒ jiào...	我叫...
I am American / British / Canadian.	Wǒ shì (měiguórén / yīngguórén /jiānádàrén)	我是（美国人 / 英国人 / 加拿大人）

TERMS OF ADDRESS

On almost all occasions, use the informal version of terms of address. The formal versions tend to be used in advertising and when addressing someone very important.

you (informal)	nǐ	你
you (formal)	nín	您
he/him	tā	他
she/her	tā	她
we/us	wǒmén	我们
you (plural)	nǐmén	你们
they/them	tāmén	他们
Mr., sir	xiānsheng	先生
Mrs., ma'am	nǚshì	女士
miss, young lady	xiǎojiě	小姐
wife	qīzǐ	妻子
husband	zhàngfū	丈夫
friend	péngyǒu	朋友
boyfriend, girlfriend	nánpéngyǒu, nǚpéngyǒu	男朋友，女朋友
son, daughter	ér zi, nǚ ér	儿子，女儿
older brother	gēge	哥哥
older sister	jiějie	姐姐
younger brother	dìdi	弟弟
younger sister	mèimei	妹妹
father, mother	bàba, māma,	爸爸，妈妈

TRANSPORTATION

Where is...?	... zài nali?	...在那里?
Is it far to...?	... yuǎn bù yuǎn?	...远不远?
from... to...	cóng ... dào	...从... 到...
How do you get to...?	... zěnme zǒu?	... 怎 么走?
the bus station/stop	qì chē zhàn	汽 车 站

Is this bus going to...?	Zhèi liàng qìchē qù...mă?	这辆汽车去… 马?
the train station	huŏchēzhàn	火车站
the airport	jīchăng	机场
I'd like a ticket to...	Wŏ xiăngmăi yīzhāng qù... de piào	我想买一张去…的票
soft (hard) seat (sleeper)	ruăn (yìng) zuò (wò)	软(硬)座(卧)
round-trip	láihuí	来回
one-way	dānchéng	单程
What time does it leave/arrive?	Jidiăn kāi/dào?	几点开/到
How long does it take?	Huā duōcháng shíjiān?	花多长时间
I want to get off (at...)	Wŏ xiăng (zài...)xià chē	我想(在...)下车
Get a taxi	Dădī	打的
(Take) underground/subway	(Zuò) dìtiŭ	(坐)地铁
When is the next bus/train?	Xià yìbān chē jidiăn kāi?	下一班车几点开
When is the first/ last bus/train?	Tóu/mò bān chē jidiăn kāi?	头/末班车几点开
reservation	yùdìng	预订
baggage	xínglĭ	行李
I want to go to...	Wŏ xiăng qù...	我 想 去
Do you have a map?	Yŏu dìtú ma?	有地图吗
Stop here, please.	Tíng zhèr	停这儿
the entrance	rùkŏu	入口
the exit	chūkŏu	出口
the ticket office	shòupiàokŏu	售票口
(very) near, far	(hĕn) yuăn, jìn	(很) 远; 近
right	yòu	右
left	zuŏ	左
straight ahead	yīzhí zŏu	一直走
in front	qiánmiàn	前面
beside	zài pángbiān	在 旁边
behind	hòumian	后面
intersection	shízìlùkŏu	十字路口
the stoplight	hónglǚdēng	红绿.灯
At the next junction turn right.	Xià kŏu yòu zhuàn	下口右转
Turn left/right.	Wăng zuŏ (yòu) zhuàn	往左 (右) 转
Use the meter.	dă biăo	打表

Please ask someone for directions.	Wènwen lù ba	问问路吧
Where is the seatbelt?	Ānquándài zài nǎr?	安全带在哪儿?
Please give me the receipt.	Máfan bǎ piào gěi wǒ	麻烦把票给我
street	jiē	街
road	lù	路
bridge	qiáo	桥
address	dìzhǐ	地址
north, south	běi, nán	北南
east, west	dōng, xī	东西

ACCOMMODATIONS

hotel	fàndiàn/jǔudiàn/bīnguǎn	饭店/酒店/宾馆
hostel	kèzhàn/lǚguǎn	客栈/旅馆
single room	dānrénfáng	单人房
double room	shuāngrénfáng	双人房
dormitory room	duōrénfáng	多人房
Are there vacancies?	Yǒu méiyǒu kōng fángjiān?	有没有空房间
Yes, there are/No.	Yǒu / Méiyǒu	有/没有
economy room	pǔtōngfáng	普通房
standard room	biāozhǔn fángjiān	标准房
deluxe suite	háohuá tàofáng	豪华套房
Can I see the room?	Wǒ néng kànkan fángjiān ma?	我能看看房间吗?
How much is the room?	Duōshao qián yītiān?	多少钱一天?
I want to change rooms.	Wǒ xiǎng huàn fángjiān	我想换房间
Are there messages for me?	Yǒu méiyǒu liúhuà?	有没有留话
Is there a hotel namecard?	Yǒu méiyǒu lǚguǎn de míngpiàn?	有没有旅馆的名片
Can I have these clothes washed please?	Kǔyǔbǎ zhè xiē yīfu xǔ gānjìng ma?	可以把这些衣服洗干净吗?
Is there Internet access here/in the room?	Zhèli/fángjiānlǔ néng shàng wǎng ma?	这里/房间里 能上网吗?

FOOD

I'm hungry.	Wǒ è le	我饿了
I'm thirsty.	Wǒ kě le	我渴了
Chinese food	zhōngcān	中餐
Western food	xīcān	西餐

restaurant	cāntīng	餐廳
waiter/waitress	fúwùyuán	服務员
Can I see a menu?	Wǒ néng kàn càidān ma?	我能看看菜单吗?
I'll have that.	Wǒ diǎn neige	我点哪个
Please bring a...	Gěi wǒ lái	给我来
spoon	sháozi	勺子
fork	chāzi	叉子
knife	dāozi	刀子
chopsticks	kuàizi	筷子
napkin	cānjīn	餐巾
beverage	yǐnliào	飲料
glass/cup	bēizi	杯子
bowl	wǎn	碗
plate	pánzi	盤子
I am vegetarian.	Wǒ chī sù.	我吃素.
I cannot eat...	Wǒ bùnéng chī...	我不能吃...
salt	yán	鹽
MSG	wèijīng	味精
pork	zhūròu	豬肉
spicy food	làcài	辣 菜
sugar	táng	糖
Can I have the check?	Mǎidān	买单
coffee	kāfēi	咖啡
tea	chá	茶
water	shuǐ	水
beer	píjiǔ	啤酒
red (white) wine	hóng (bái) jiǔ	红(白) 酒
milk	niúnǎi	牛奶
juice	guǒzhī	果汁
sugar	táng	糖
dim sum	diǎnxīn	点心
snack	xiǎochī	小吃
breakfast	zǎofàn	早饭
lunch	wǔfàn	午饭
dinner	wǎnfàn	晚饭
eggs	jīdàn	鸡蛋
bread	miànbāo	面包

salad	shālā	沙拉
fruit	shuǐguǒ	水果
mango	mángguǒ	芒果
watermelon	xīgua	西瓜
banana	xiāngjiāo	香蕉
apple	píngguǒ	苹果
orange	chénzi	橙子
lemon	níngméng	柠檬
fish	yú	鱼
shrimp	xiā	虾
meat	ròu	肉
chicken	jīròu	鸡肉
pork	zhūròu	猪肉
beef, steak	niúròu, niúpá	牛肉，牛排
lamb/mutton	yángròu	羊肉
stir-fried	chǎo	炒
roasted	kǎo	烤
steamed	qīngzhēng	清蒸
vegetables	shūcài	蔬菜
broccoli	xīlánhuā	西兰花
tomato	xīhóngshì	西红柿
green beans	sìjìdòu	四季豆
tofu	dòufu	豆腐
garlic	dàsuàn	大蒜
soy sauce	jiàngyóu	酱油
vinegar	cù	醋
chili sauce	làjiàng	辣酱
dumplings	shuǐjiǎo	水餃
steamed stuffed bun	bāozi	包子
fried noodles	chǎo miàn	炒麵
steamed white	rice bái fàn	白飯
spicy tofu	má pó dòufu	麻婆豆腐
beef and rice	niúròu fàn	牛肉飯
omelet	dàn bǐng	蛋餅
Beijing duck	běijing kǎoyā	北京烤鴨
pork chop and rice	páigǔ fàn	排骨飯
spring roll	chūnjuǎn	春卷

fish cooked in soy sauce	hóngshāo yú	紅燒魚
fried rice	chǎo fàn	炒飯
egg and vegetable soup	dànhuātāng	蛋花湯
sweet and sour soup	suān là tāng	酸辣湯

SHOPPING AND MONEY

How much is this/that?	Zhè/nà ge duōshǎo qián?	这/那个多少钱
Too expensive!	Tài guile!	太贵了
Can you make it cheaper?	Keyi piányì yì diǎn ma?	可以便宜一点吗
How about ... RMB/yuan?...	...rénmínbì /yuán xíng ma?...	人民币 / 元行吗?
What's that?	Nà shì shénme?	那是什么?
Are there larger (smaller) sizes?	Yǒu méiyǒu dà (xiǎo)hào?	有没有大（小）号?
If you can't make it any cheaper, I just won't buy it!	Bù néng gèng piányì wǒ jiù búyàole!	不能更便宜我就不要了!
Do you accept credit cards?	xìnyòngkǎ shōu bùshōu?	信用卡收不收?
Bank of China	Zhōngguó Yínháng	中国银行
ATM	Zìdòng qǔkuǎnjī	自动取款机
RMB	Rénmínbì	人民币
U.S. dollars	Meiyuán	美元
Euros	Oūyuán	欧元
U.K. pounds	Yīngbàng	英镑
exchange money	Huàn qián	换钱
money	qián	钱
I would like to exchange 200 U.S. dollars.	Wǒ xiǎng duìhuàn liǎngbǎi meiyuán	我想兑换两百美元
travelers checks	lǚxíng zhīpiào	旅行支票
What is the exchange rate?	Duìhuàn lǜ shì duōshǎo?	兑换 旅是多少?
Can you write that down for me?	Nǐ néng bùnéng xiěxiàlai gěi wǒ?	你能不能写下来 给我?

HEALTH AND EMERGENCIES

Help!	Jiùmìng!	救命!
Call the police!	Bàojǐng!	报警!
police	jǐngchá	警察
thief	xiǎotōu	小偷
I'm ill.	Wǒ shēng bìng le	我生病了
I'm injured.	Wǒ shòu shāng le	我受伤了

Can you get me a doctor?	Qǐng bāng wǒ zhǎo yī wèi dàifu	请帮我找一位大夫
Is there a doctor who speaks English here?	Zhèr yǒu huì jiǎng yīngyǔ de dàifu ma?	这儿有会讲英语的大夫吗
health insurance	jiànkāng bǎoxiǎn	健康保险
hospital	Yīyuàn	医院
drugstore	yàodiàn	药店
toilet	cèsuǒ	厕所
male/female	nán/nǚ	男/女
toilet paper	wèishēngzhǚ	卫生纸
bathroom	xǚshǒujiān	洗手间
soap	féizào	肥皂
shampoo	xiāngbō	香波
sanitary towel	wèishēngjīn	卫生巾
tampon	wèishēngmiántiáo	卫生棉条
sunscreen	fángshàiyóu	防晒油
aspirin	Āsīpīlín	阿司匹林
antibiotics	kàngjūnsù	抗菌素
laxative	xièyào	泻药
anti-diarrhea medicine	zhǚxièyào	止泻药
condom	Ānquán tào	安全套
medicine	yào	药
birth-control pills	bìyùnyào	避孕药
toothbrush	yáshuā	牙刷
toothpaste	yágāo	牙膏
dentist	yákē	牙科
toothache	yáténg	牙疼
I have a...	Wǒ...	我...
I need medicine for a...	Wǒ yào zhì ... de yào	我要治... 的药
pain	téng	疼
fever	fāshāo	发烧
a cold	gǎnmào le	感冒了
headache	tóuténg	头疼
stomachache	dùziténg	肚子疼
burn	shāoshāng le	烧伤了
cramp	chōujīn le	抽筋了
vomiting	tù le	吐了

POST OFFICE AND COMMUNICATIONS

post office	yóujú	邮局
(to send a) letter	(jì) xìn	寄信
parcel	yóubāo	邮包
stamp	yóupiào	邮票
envelope	xìnfēng	信封
registered mail	guàhào	挂号
airmail	hángkōng xìn	航空信
surface mail	píngyóu	平邮
postcard	míngxìnpiàn	明信片
post	cúnjú hòulǚng	存局后领
telephone	diànhuà	电话
telephone card	dianhuàkǎ	电话卡
international call	guójì diànhuà	国际电话
public telephone	gōngyòngdiànhuà	公用电话
cell phone	shǒujī	手机
SIM card	SIM kǎ	SIM卡
collect (reverse charges) call	duìfāng fù qián diànhuà	对方付钱电话
computer	diànnǎo	电脑
email	diànziyóujian/email	电子邮件/Email
Internet	Yīntèwǎng	因特网
get online	shàngwǎng	上网
Internet café	wǎng bā	网吧
fax	chuánzhēn	传真

OFFICIALDOM

visa	qiānzhèng	签证
extend a visa	yáncháng qiānzhèng	延长签证
ID	shēnfènzhèng	身份证
passport	hùzhào	护照
boarding pass	dēngjì kǎ	登记卡
Public Security Bureau	gōngānjú	公安局
embassy	dàshǐguǎn	大使馆
customs	hǎiguān	海关

VERBS

Verbs are simple in Mandarin: They don't change according to their subject.

to buy	mǎi	买
I buy, you (he, she) buys	wǒ, nǐ (tā, tā) mǎi	我 你（他，她）买
we buy, you (they) buy	wǒmén, nǐmén mǎi	我们，你们买
to eat	chī	吃
I eat, you (he, she) eats	wǒ, nǐ (tā, tā) chī	我 你（他，她）吃
we eat, you (they) eat	wǒmén, nǐmén chī	我们，你们 吃
to climb a mountain	páshān	爬山
I climb, you (he, she) climbs	wǒ, nǐ (tā, tā) páshān	我 你（他，她）爬山
we climb, you (they) climb	wǒmén, nǐmén páshān	我们，你们 爬山

Instead of changing, Chinese verbs use auxiliary verbs or particles or time words to indicate time:

I ate breakfast this morning.	Wǒ zǎoshàng chī zǎofàn	我早上吃早饭
Yesterday I climbed a mountain.	Wǒ zuótiān páshān	我 昨天 爬山
to go	qù	去
to love	ài	爱
to like	xǐhuān	喜欢
to work	gōngzuò	工作
to want	yào	要
to need	xūyào	需要
to read/see/watch	kàn	看
to study	xué	学
can	néng	能
to write	xiě	写
to repair	xiū	修
to stop	ting	停
to get off (the bus)	xiàchē	下车
to arrive	dào	到
to stay (remain)	tíngliú	停留
to stay (lodge)	zhù	住
to leave/to walk	zǒu	走
to look for	zhǎo	找
to give	gěi	给
to be located	zài	在
to have	yǒu	有
to come	lái	来

NUMBERS

0	líng	〇 or 零
1	yī	一
2 (number)	èr	二
2 (things)	liăng	两
3	sān	三
4	sì	四
5	wŭ	五
6	lìu	六
7	qī	七
8	bā	八
9	jiŭ	九
10	shí	十
11	shíyī	十一
12	shíèr	十二
13	shísān	十三
27	èrshíqī	二十七
100	yībăi	一百
101	yībăilíngyī	一百零一
110	yībăiyīshí	一百一十
114	yībăiyīshísì	一百一十四
1000	yīqiān	一千

TIME

now	xiànzài	现在
today	jīntiān	今天
2:34 P.M.	xìawŭ liăngdiăn sānshísì	下午两点三十四
11 A.M.	shàngwŭ shíyīdiăn zhōng	上午十一点钟
early morning	zăoshàng	早上
morning	shàngwŭ	上午
afternoon	xiàwŭ	下午
evening	wănshàng	晚上
tomorrow	míngtiān	明天
yesterday	zuótiān	昨天
day after tomorrow	hòutiān	后天
day before yesterday	qiántiān	前天
three days later	sāntiān yĭhòu	三天以后
two months ago	liăng gè yuè yĭqián	两个月以前

DAYS AND MONTHS

Monday	xīngqīyī	星期一
Tuesday	xīngqī'èr	星期二
Wednesday	xīngqīsān	星期三
Thursday	xīngqīsì	星期四
Friday	xīngqīwǔ	星期五
Saturday	xīngqīliù	星期六
Sunday	xīngqīrì	星期日
January	yīyuè	一月
February	èr yuè	二月
March	sānyuè	三月
April	sìyuè	四月
May	wǔ yuè	五月
June	liùyuè	六月
July	qī yuè	七月
August	bā yuè	八月
September	jiǔ yuè	九月
October	shí yuè	十月
November	shíyī yuè	十一月
December	shíèr yuè	十二月
a week	xīngqī	星期
a month	yuè	月
a year	nián	年

Suggested Reading

HISTORY AND GENERAL INFORMATION

Aldrich, M. A. *The Search for a Vanishing Beijing.* Hong Kong University Press, 1996. The author is a Beijing resident obsessed with local history and this book serves as an excellent guide and walking tour to the old areas of the Chinese capital. The beautifully written resource is filled with colorful stories and pictures to bring Beijing's past back to life.

Becker, Jasper. *The Chinese.* Oxford University Press, 2002. One of the most well-respected China hands around, Becker has lived and worked as a journalist in China since 1985, and this weighty tome offers excellent observations on the state of the People's Republic of China and the unique characteristics of the country and its people. Becker's newer book, *Dragon Rising,* is aimed more at business travelers looking for insight into dealing with China.

Gifford, Rob. *China Road: A Journey into the Future of a Rising Superpower.* Random House, 2007. NPR's China correspondent went on a six-week journey across China. Leaving from Shanghai, Gifford traveled through remnants of the Silk Road and met a wide range of interesting characters on his way. It's engagingly written, and Gifford uses the hopes and plans of the people he meets to illustrate what the world can expect from China in the future.

Lu, Hanchao. *Beyond the Neon Lights: Everyday Shanghai.* University of California Press, 2004. This may be an academic study, but this engagingly written book on how ordinary people in Shanghai lived through the extraordinary changes that have swept the city in the 20th century is excellent because of its insight. Lu weaves rich documentary data with interviews in this well-rounded portrait of a city and its people.

McGregor, James. *One Billion Customers.* Free Press, 2007. Considered the best book around on doing business in China, the former journalist turned successful businessman tells a different story about a company trying to make it in China and explains where it went right or wrong, before offering his compelling conclusions on what other businesses should learn from others' experiences.

Short, Philip. *Mao: A Life.* Henry Holt and Company, 2000. Newer biographies of China's most controversial leader may be available, but this is still the best, with Short not failing to show both Mao's brilliance and his legendary ruthlessness in this in-depth study complete with many previously unseen photos.

LITERATURE AND FICTION

Chang, Eileen. "Lust, Caution." Anchor Books, 2007. Eileen Chang's short story, "Lust, Caution," was reissued to tie in with the release of Ang Lee's film version. The steamy short story is set in Shanghai in the 1940s when the city was occupied by the Japanese and is half spy thriller, half romance, and tells the story of a young woman who gets swept up in a dangerous game of emotional intrigue with a powerful political figure. Chang lived through this era herself so expect plenty of heady descriptions of a decadent city on the edge of disaster.

DeWoskin, Rachel. *Foreign Babes in Beijing: Behind the Scenes of a New China.* W. W. Norton, 2006. Don't overlook this book on account of its terrible title; it's much more interesting and has much more to say on contemporary China than you'd think. DeWoskin left her native America for an exciting jaunt to Beijing and ended up as a main character on a popular TV show. Her relationships with her Chinese friends and colleagues ring true as do her observations on what modern life is like for young Chinese in the capital.

Gao Xingjian. *Soul Mountain.* Harper Perennial, 2001. Gao won the Nobel Prize for Literature in 2000 for this long and lyrical novel of a dying man's quest for adventure and closure. While some find its lack of focus and structure puzzling, the author's poetic descriptions of the landscape, villagers, priests, and monks the narrator meets on his journey are captivating.

Hessler, Peter. *The Oracle Bones.* Harper Perennial, 2007. Since his first book on China, *River Town,* Hessler has established himself as an author who writes beautifully done narrative nonfiction on China. In *The Oracle Bones,* the Beijing correspondent for *The New Yorker* looks at the country through a kaleidoscopic lens of history, archaeology, language, and contemporary culture.

Ishiguro, Kazuo. *When We Were Orphans.* Faber and Faber, 2005. Ishiguro's main character is detective Christopher Banks, and the novel revolves around events in Banks's childhood in the International Settlement in 1930s Shanghai. But as the way of life in Shanghai comes under attack, Banks's childhood does too when both parents disappear. The dark novel follows Banks's attempts to discover the truth about his parents as he returns to Shanghai to find them and where nothing is as it originally seemed.

Wei Hui. *Shanghai Baby.* Robinson Publishing, 2003. Wei single-handedly started the trend for Chinese women to write about their sex- and drug-filled rock 'n' roll lifestyles in Shanghai. The book was promptly banned in China and if judged on literariness alone it may be found lacking, but for readers who have an outdated view of modest Chinese women, this book will open some eyes and raise some eyebrows.

Internet Resources

GENERAL INFORMATION

www.china-embassy.org

The Chinese embassy's website in the United States may be dominated by turgid announcements on China's concrete industry, but ignore them and head for the visa page for the most up-to-date information on how to apply for the compulsory visa. As of now, visas cost $100 for U.S. citizens.

www.talesofoldchina.com

Run by an old China hand, this website is a great resource for information on what life in China, especially in Shanghai and Beijing, used to be like. If you're interested in Chinese history from 1850 to 1950, this offers a fascinating if not particularly well-laid-out hub of information—there's so much there, including texts of hard-to-find-elsewhere articles, including an American magazine on the rise of Shanghai written in 1935, and a photo gallery so its best to spend a leisurely hour reading through.

http://chinadigitaltimes.net

This a collaborative news portal covering China's social and political transition and its emerging role in the world. If you want to know what's happening in China, subscribe to its daily news list, which will send you a rundown of the latest articles from a wide range of newspapers, websites, and blogs. The excellent site is run by the Graduate School of Journalism at the University of California, Berkeley.

www.china-window.com/china_culture

This site offers interesting information on Chinese culture from Suzhou embroidery to information on much-misunderstood Chinese medicine. While the range of topics is considerable and well written, there are unfortunately few photos or images.

www.chinatoday.com

This is the site to choose for its sheer range of news relating to China from a huge variety of sources as well as good general information on everything from opening hours to the system of government. The portal also comes up with a daily list of mind-boggling figures to do with the PRC, including the news that China has more than 20 million bloggers.

www.chinadaily.com.cn

While people sneer and dismiss this state-run English-language newspaper because of the way it follows only the party line, every journalist in China reads the *China Daily* for insight into what the Communist Party is thinking. The recent redesign of both the paper and website has made them both easier to physically if not mentally read.

www.chinaartspage.com

This site serves the English-speaking artistic community in mainland China, Hong Kong, and Taiwan and there is always plenty of coverage on what's happening in the art scene in Beijing and Shanghai. The well-designed site is a good resource for news and opinion on many different art forms, from film to photography.

http://appetiteforchina.com

Created by Beijing-based food writer Diana Kuan, the website is useful to anyone, whether living in or visiting China, who is interested in learning about the all-important element of eating. In addition to food reviews, she also reveals her own recipes using both Western and Chinese ingredients.

shanghaiist.com

The Shanghai branch of the international Gothamist sites that are now all over the globe, *shanghaiist* dishes up the dirt on what's happening in Shanghai and to less of an extent, in the rest of China. Expect witty and irreverent blogs on everything from gig reviews to where to find warm winter tights.

www.chinesepod.com

Probably the best place on the web to learn Chinese, Chinesepod is run out of Shanghai and offers full programs to increase your level as well as free podcasts to download on useful subjects such as finding a hotel room to chatting up the man or woman of your dreams. You can try the site for free for a week before signing up.

english.sepa.gov.cn

If you're scared easily perhaps you shouldn't look at this site, which shows the level of air pollution in most major Chinese cities. It's run by the government, so some think that the statistics here are underrepresented, which makes it even more frightening. . . . The air quality is ranked into different levels and when it goes over 100, the government recommends you stay indoors.

EVENTS LISTINGS

www.thebeijinger.com

The website of the popular local listing magazine *The Beijinger* is the number-one place to go to find out what's on, job ads, and accommodations. There's also a lively forum where you'll find out the latest gossip in the city as well as where you can find the answers to those difficult questions, such as where do you find bongos in Beijing (really).

www.timeout.com/beijing

The Beijinger's newest rival, the *Time Out* site is much better on bar and restaurant reviews as it uploads all of its reviews from the magazine and is much easier to navigate around, too. There's also a good range of features on what to do in the capital.

www.smartshanghai.com

Shanghai's best listings and reviews site is archly witty and was started by a well-connected girl-around-town. Now it has expanded to cover a few hotels and day trips out of town, but its strength is still its new reviews of bars and restaurants. The public forum is also very lively.

www.piao.com.cn

You can buy tickets for practically any event in Beijing or Shanghai on this English-language website. After ordering your tickets, an English-speaking assistant will phone to check your order and arrange delivery. You pay for tickets when they are delivered.

BEST BLOGS

www.danwei.org

Danwei, which means work unit in Chinese, is a website about media, advertising, and urban life in China run by something of a local celebrity. It's great for finding out what's really going on in China and is one of only a few sites that has translations of articles from the Chinese-language media. In addition to its podcasts and videos, many people make use of the media-jobs section.

blogs.telegraph.co.uk/foreign/richardspencer

The blog of the China correspondent for the British *Daily Telegraph* newspaper is the best of any journalist working in the country. In addition to background to the stories he writes for the main paper, the most interesting parts are his more casual musings on what life is like in Beijing—the smaller stories that wouldn't make the pages of a newspaper.

www.beijingnewspeak.com

Chris O'Brian is a young British journalist who worked for two years for China's state news agency and his blog attracted plenty of attention from people interested in what working in China's propaganda department was really like—frustrating but illuminating at the same time.

www.beijingboyce.com

Beijing-bound hedonists study Beijing Boyce's blog before they venture out into the bars, clubs, and restaurants of Beijing—he's done it, drunk it, and reviewed it on his very witty website. The American writer has an alternative life as the head of an NGO in the capital, but after work is done he can be found in the city's best bars.

TRAVEL

www.elong.net

Both elong and ctrip are engaged in a battle to dominate the huge Chinese travel market, and both offer a very professional English-speaking service. You can look up domestic and international flight schedules and prices, hotel rooms across China, and a small number of package holidays and book them online. You can then either pay on your credit card or pay on delivery (which is free). It often has specially discounted plane tickets at off-peak times.

english.ctrip.com

Elong's main rival offers an equally good service when booking plane tickets or accommodation within mainland China.

www.seat61.com/china.htm

This site run by a volunteer train enthusiast is excellent as a resource, whether you're planning to travel by train either within or to China—or indeed just about any other country in the world. There are good pictures on what the trains are like, up-to-date information on routes and schedules, and information on where you can reserve tickets.

Index

C

D

E

I

JK

T

UV

W

XY

Z

Acknowledgments

I would like to thank my wonderful friends in China for making life in our adopted city so much fun. Thanks to everyone at Avalon Travel for their enthusiasm for this project. Most of all, thanks go to my mother, Francesca, and brother Alex for their love and support.

MOON BEIJING & SHANGHAI
Avalon Travel
a member of the Perseus Books Group
1700 Fourth Street
Berkeley, CA 94710, USA
www.moon.com

Editor: Tiffany Watson
Series Manager: Erin Raber
Copy Editor: Karen Bleske
Graphics Coordinator: Domini Dragoone
Production Coordinator: Darren Alessi
Cover Designer: Domini Dragoone
Map Editors: Albert Angulo, Brice Ticen
Cartographers: Kat Bennett, Lohnes & Wright, Chris Markiewicz
Proofreader: Ellie Behrstock
Indexer: Judy Hunt

ISBN-10: 1-59880-149-X
ISBN-13: 978-1-59880-149-1
ISSN: 1945-2985

Printing History
1st Edition – December 2008
5 4 3 2 1

Front cover photo: The giant red doors to the Forbidden City in Beijing, © Getty Images/Justin Guariglia
Title page photo: The Oriental Pearl Tower dominates the Pudong skyline, © Helena Iveson
Interior front matter photos: pages 2, 4, 5 (top left and bottom photos), 6-9, 10 (top), 13, 14, 16, 18, 20-24, and 27 © Helena Iveson; pages 5 (top right), 11, and 26 © Daniel Sanderson; pages 10 (bottom), 12, and 19 © Barbara Strother; page 28, © Elyse Singleton.

Printed in United States by RR Donnelley

KEEPING CURRENT

If you have a favorite gem you'd like to see included in the next edition, or see anything that needs updating, clarification, or correction, please drop us a line. Send your comments via email to feedback@moon.com, or use the address above.

MAP SYMBOLS

Expressway
Primary Road
Secondary Road
Unpaved Road
Trail
Ferry
Railroad
Pedestrian Walkway
Stairs

Highlight
City/Town
State Capital
National Capital
Point of Interest
Accommodation
Restaurant/Bar
Other Location
Campground

Airfield
Airport
Mountain
Unique Natural Feature
Waterfall
Park
Trailhead
Skiing Area

Golf Course
Parking Area
Archaeological Site
Church
Gas Station
Glacier
Mangrove
Reef
Swamp

CONVERSION TABLES

°C = (°F - 32) / 1.8
°F = (°C x 1.8) + 32
1 inch = 2.54 centimeters (cm)
1 foot = 0.304 meters (m)
1 yard = 0.914 meters
1 mile = 1.6093 kilometers (km)
1 km = 0.6214 miles
1 fathom = 1.8288 m
1 chain = 20.1168 m
1 furlong = 201.168 m
1 acre = 0.4047 hectares
1 sq km = 100 hectares
1 sq mile = 2.59 square km
1 ounce = 28.35 grams
1 pound = 0.4536 kilograms
1 short ton = 0.90718 metric ton
1 short ton = 2,000 pounds
1 long ton = 1.016 metric tons
1 long ton = 2,240 pounds
1 metric ton = 1,000 kilograms
1 quart = 0.94635 liters
1 US gallon = 3.7854 liters
1 Imperial gallon = 4.5459 liters
1 nautical mile = 1.852 km

Beijing Maps

SIGHTS

1 BEIHAI PARK
3 JINGSHAN PARK
5 NATIONAL ART MUSEUM OF CHINA
9 **FORBIDDEN CITY**
19 ZHONGSHAN PARK
32 ZHONGNANHAI
33 **NATIONAL CENTER FOR PERFORMING ARTS**
35 GREAT HALL OF THE PEOPLE
36 TIANANMEN SQUARE
37 CHINA NATIONAL MUSEUM
38 CHAIRMAN MAO'S MEMORIAL HALL

RESTAURANTS

10 THE COURTYARD
12 CHING PAVILION
15 **DONGHUAMEN FOOD MARKET**
17 **HUANG TING**
21 GRANDMA'S KITCHEN
22 24 HOUR RESTAURANT
26 MADE IN CHINA
27 MY HUMBLE HOUSE

ARTS AND LEISURE

2 BEIHAI PARK
4 **CYCLE CHINA**
8 CAPITAL THEATER
11 THE COURTYARD GALLERY
20 FORBIDDEN CITY CONCERT HALL
23 FORBIDDEN CITY BIKES
25 BICYCLE KINGDOM
30 CENTRAL CONSERVATORY OF MUSIC
31 BEIJING CONCERT HALL
34 **NATIONAL CENTER FOR PERFORMING ARTS**

SHOPS

16 FOREIGN LANGUAGES BOOKSTORE
28 THE MALLS AT ORIENTAL PLAZA

HOTELS

6 TIANXIANG COURTYARD HOTEL
7 **PEKING GUEST HOUSE**
13 TANGYUE HOTEL
14 HOTEL KAPOK
18 **PENINSULA**
24 **RAFFLES BEIJING HOTEL**
29 GRAND HYATT

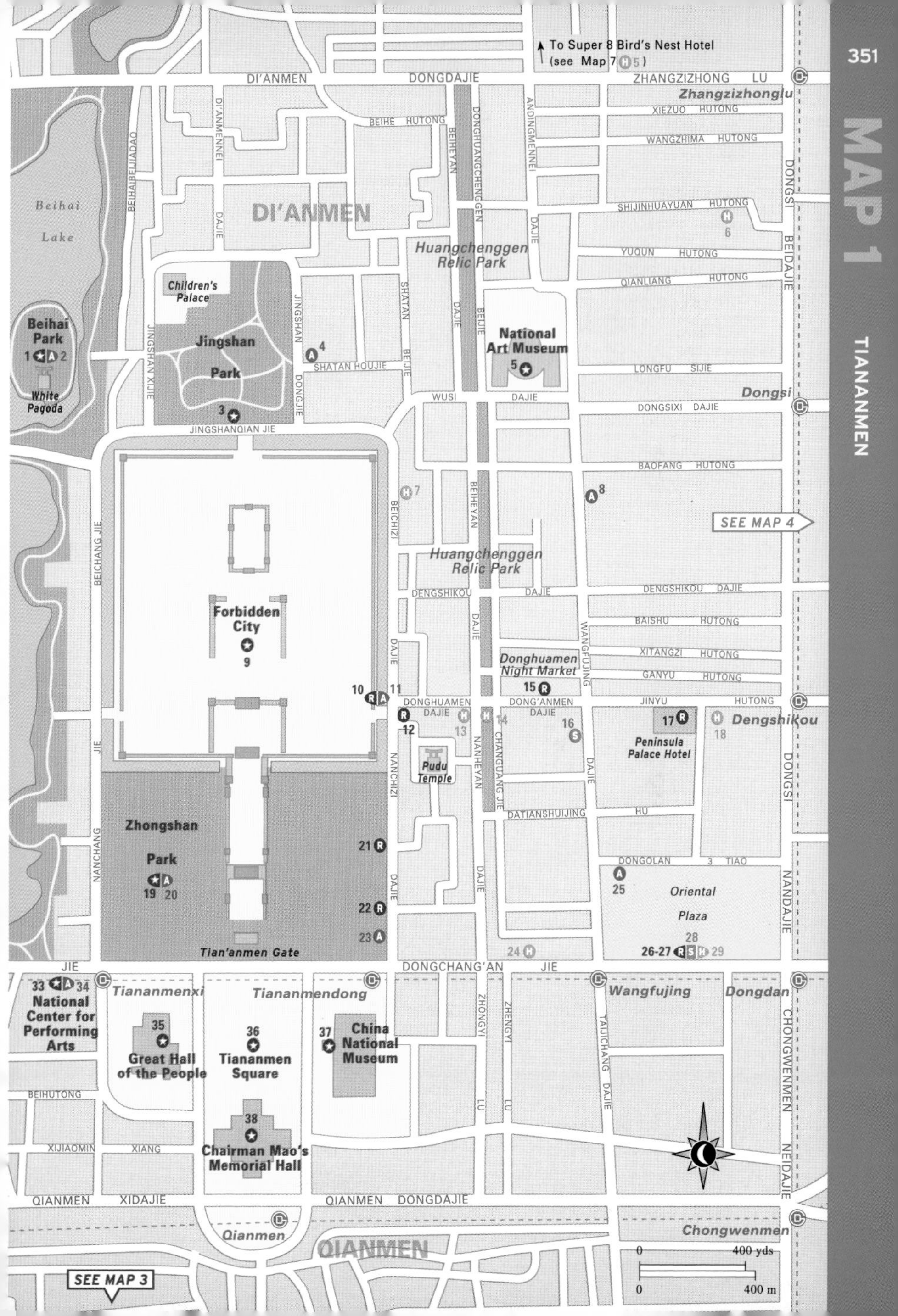
To Super 8 Bird's Nest Hotel (see Map 7 H5)
DI'ANMEN DONGDAJIE
ZHANGZIZHONG LU
Zhangzizhonglu
XIEZUO HUTONG
WANGZHIMA HUTONG
BEIHE HUTONG
DI'ANMENNEI DAJIE
BEIHAIBEIJIADAO
BEIHEYAN
DONGHUANGCHENGGEN
ANDINGMENNEI DAJIE
DONGSI BEIDAJIE
SHIJINHUAYUAN HUTONG
YUQUN HUTONG
QIANLIANG HUTONG
Beihai Lake
DI'ANMEN
Huangchenggen Relic Park
Children's Palace
Beihai Park
White Pagoda
Jingshan Park
JINGSHAN XIJIE
JINGSHAN DONGJIE
SHATAN HOUJIE
SHATAN BEIJIE
DAJIE
National Art Museum
LONGFU SIJIE
WUSI DAJIE
Dongsi
DONGSIXI DAJIE
JINGSHANQIAN JIE
BAOFANG HUTONG
BEICHIZI
SEE MAP 4
BEICHANG JIE
Huangchenggen Relic Park
DENGSHIKOU DAJIE
DENGSHIKOU DAJIE
BAISHU HUTONG
XITANGZI HUTONG
GANYU HUTONG
WANGFUJING DAJIE
Forbidden City
Donghuamen Night Market
DONGHUAMEN DAJIE
DONG'ANMEN DAJIE
JINYU HUTONG
Peninsula Palace Hotel
Dengshikou
Pudu Temple
NANCHIZI DAJIE
NANHEYAN DAJIE
CHANGDUANG JIE
DONGSI NANDAJIE
DATIANSHUIJING HU
Zhongshan Park
NANCHANG JIE
DONGOLAN 3 TIAO
Oriental Plaza
Tian'anmen Gate
DONGCHANG'AN JIE
Tiananmenxi
Tiananmendong
Wangfujing
Dongdan
National Center for Performing Arts
Great Hall of the People
Tiananmen Square
China National Museum
ZHONGYI LU
ZHENGYI LU
TAIJICHANG DAJIE
CHONGWENMEN NEIDAJIE
BEIHUTONG
XIJIAOMIN XIANG
Chairman Mao's Memorial Hall
QIANMEN XIDAJIE
QIANMEN DONGDAJIE
Qianmen
QIANMEN
Chongwenmen
SEE MAP 3
0 400 yds
0 400 m

SIGHTS

- 2 SONG QINGLING'S RESIDENCE
- 7 DRUM AND BELL TOWERS
- 11 **HOUHAI**
- 31 LAMA TEMPLE
- 33 **CONFUCIUS TEMPLE AND GUOZIJIAN**

RESTAURANTS

- 6 CAFÉ SAMBAL
- 10 HUTONG PIZZA
- 12 HAN CENG
- 17 **DALI**
- 19 PAPER
- 23 XIAO XIN'S CAFÉ
- 28 THE SOURCE
- 29 JIN DING XUAN
- 32 VINEYARD CAFÉ
- 35 CAFÉ DE LA POSTE
- 36 HUAJIA YIYUAN
- 37 TRAKTIRR PUSHKIN RUSSIAN CUISINE RESTAURANT
- 38 PRIVATE KITCHEN
- 40 **CRESCENT MOON XINJIANG RESTAURANT**

ARTS AND LEISURE

- 13 HOUHAI BIKE HIRE
- 41 ZHEN SONG BLIND MASSAGE CENTER

NIGHTLIFE

- 1 CLUB OBIWAN
- 5 BED TAPAS AND BAR
- 8 **DRUM AND BELL**
- 9 LA BAIE DES ANGES
- 14 EAST SHORE LIVE JAZZ CAFÉ
- 15 **NO NAME BAR**
- 16 MAO LIVE
- 24 PASSBY BAR
- 26 12SQM
- 30 STAR LIVE
- 39 YUGONG YISHAN

SHOPS

- 18 GRIFTED
- 21 **PLASTERED T-SHIRTS**
- 34 BANNERMAN TANG'S TOYS AND CRAFTS

HOTELS

- 3 RED LANTERN HOUSE
- 4 BAMBOO GARDEN HOTEL
- 20 **GUXIANG 20**
- 22 BEIJING BACKPACKERS
- 25 **HUTONG REN**
- 27 LUSONGYUAN HOTEL

Beijing University of Science & Technology
To National Stadium (Bird Nest)
LONGXIANG LU
BEITUCHENG
Xiongmaohuandao
BEICHEN LU
XITUCHENG LU
WENHUIYUAN BEILU
Beijing National University
XINJIEKOUWAI DAJIE
DESHENGMEN
HUANGSI DAJIE
Rendinghu Lake
XUCYUAN NANLU
DESHENGMANWAI DAJIE
ANDELI BEIJIE
GULOUWAI DAJIE
Rendinghu Park
XIZHIMEN BEIDAJIE
WENHUIYUAN LU
ANDE LU
Jishuitan
Guluodajie
DESHENGMEN DONGDAJIE
Beijing North Railway Station
Xizhimen
XIYAN
Xihai Lake
Song Qingling's Residence
DESHENGMEN XIDAJIE
XIHAINANYAN
GULOU XIDAJIE
HOUHAI BEIYAN
Houhai Lake
GUOWANG HUTONG
ZHANGWANG
DOUFUCHI
JIUGULOU DAJIE
BAOCHAO HUTONG
SEE MAP 5
XINJIEKOU DONGJIE
Drum and Bell Towers
XIZHIMENNEI DAJIE
ZHENGJUE HUTONG
GULOU DONGDAJIE
QIANHAI DONGYAN
XINJIEKOU
DI'ANMENNEI
BEILISHI LU
XIZHIMEN NANDAJIE
XIZHIMEN NANXIAOJIE
NACAOCHANG JIE
LIU XIANG
XINJIEKOU NANDAJIE
FANGZHUANCHANG HUTONG
NANGUANFANG
Qianhai Lake
YU'ER
Houhai
DI'ANMEN XIDAJIE
DI'ANMEN
PING'ANLI XIDAJIE
Beihai Park
XISI BEIDAJIE
XIHUANGCHENGGEN BEIJIE
Chegongzhuang
ZHAODENGYU LU
Beihai Lake
SEE MAP 1

XIAOGUAN
SHAOYAOJU
International Olympic Sports Center
University of International Business & Economics
Huixinxijienankou
Shaoyaoju
Beijing Chemical Technology University
Hepingxiqiao
Guangximen
HEPINGLI
Liuyin Park
Hepinglebeijie
Liufang
Qingnianhu Park
Qingnianhu Lake
Ditan Park
Temple of the Earth
ANDINGMEN
ZUOJIAZHUANG SHANGCHANG
Andingmen
Yonghegong
Lama Temple
Dongzhimen Park
JIAODAOKOU
Confucius Temple and Guozijian
DONGZHIMEN
Dongzhimen
BEIXINGQIAO
Beixinqiao
DONGSI
Zhangzizhonglu
College of Chinese Medicine
Dongsishitiao
Workers' Gymnasium
Beijing Workers' Stadium
DI'ANMEN
SEE MAP 4
BEISANHUAN ZHONGLU
BEISANHUAN DONGLU
ANDINGMEN DONGDAJIE
DONGZHIMENNEI DAJIE
DONGZHIMENWAI DAJIE
GONGREN TIYUCHANG BEILU
DONGSI 10 TIAO
DONGSI 8 TIAO
DONGSI 6 TIAO
ZHANGZIZHONG LU
JIAODAOKOU DONGDAJIE
GUOZIJIAN JIE
XIYANGGUAN HUTONG
BEIXINCANG HUTONG
XIGUAN HUTONG
JU'ER HUTONG
NANLUOGU XIANG
TAIYANGGONG LU
JIAN'ANDONGLO
ANYUAN LU
QINGNIANGOU LU
HEPINGLI BEIJIE
HEPINGLI ZHONGJIE
HEPINGLI NANJIE
ANDE LU
XINDONG LU
DONGZHIMEN BEIDAJIE
CHAOYANGMEN BEIDAJIE
YONGHEGONG DAJIE
DONGSI BEIDAJIE
ANDINGMENWAI DAJIE
ANDINGMENNEI DAJIE

SEE MAP 1
Forbidden City
Zhongshan Park
Nanhai Lake
Tian'anmen Gate
XIDAN
Xidan
Tiananmenxi
Great Hall of the People
Tiananmen Square
Mao's Mausoleum
FUXINGMEN
Xishiku Cathedral
Qianmen
Hepingmen
Xuanwumen
Changchunjie
Qianmen
4
5
SEE MAP 6
Liulichang
6
7
8
9
10
Ox Street Mosque
Tianqiao Theatre
11-12
Tianqiao Bus Terminal
CAISHIKOU
Wanshou Park
HUFANGQIAO
18
Taoranting Park
Temple of Agriculture
Xiannongtan Stadium
Beijing South Railway Station
0
400 yds
0
400 m
FUXINGMENNEI DAJIE
XICHANG'AN JIE
XIDAN BEIDAJIE
FUYOU JIE
NANCHANG JIE
NAOSHIKOU DAJIE
DALIUBUKOU JIE
BEIXINHUA JIE
XUANWUMENNEI DAJIE
XIRONGXIAN HUTONG
XIJIULIANZI HUTONG
GAO BEIHUTONG
XIJIAOMIN XIANG
QIANMEN XIDAJIE
XUANWUMEN DONGDAJIE
XUANWUMEN XIDAJIE
QIANMEN XIHOUHEYANJIE
QIANMEN XIHEANJIE
XIDAMOCHANG
LANGFANGTOU TIAO
QIANMEN DAJIE
LIULICHANG XIJIE
LIULICHANG DONGJIE
NANXINHUA JIE
NANLIU XIANG
BEILIU XIANG
XUANWUMENWAI DAJIE
LAOQIANGGEN JIE
XICAOCHANG JIE
YINGTAOXIE JIE
TIESHUXIE JIE
DAZHALAN XIJIE
SHAAN XIXIANG
MEISHI JIE
LANGSHIDIAN JIE
CHANGCHUN JIE
WEIRAN HUTONG
ZHUSHIKOU XIDAJIE
GUANG'ANMENNEI DAJIE
LUOMASHI DAJIE
QIANMEN DAJIE
LIUXUE LU
XIANGCHANG LU
NIU JIE
SHURO HUTONG
JIAOZI HUTONG
LANMAN HUTONG
JIAJIA HUTONG
FENFANGLIULI JIE
HUIFANG LU
YONG'AN LU
DONGJING LU
NANHENG XIJIE
NANHENG DONGJIE
BEIWEI LU
NANWEI LU
XIANNONGTAN JIE
YONGDINGMENNEI DAJIE
BAIZHIFANG DONGJIE
TAORANTING LU
LONGZHUAHUAI HUTONG
TAIPING JIE
YOU'ANMENNEI DAJIE
LIREN JIE
GAISHIKOU DAJIE
BANBUQIAO
YONGDINGMEN XIJIE
KAIYANG QIAO
YONGDINGMEN XIBINHE LU
YOU'ANMEN DONGBINHE LU

SEE MAP 4
DONGDAN
QIANMEN
CIQIKOU
ZHUSHIKOU
YONGDINGMEN QIAO
Tiananmendong
Wangfujing
Dongdan
Jianguomen
Beijing zhan
Chongwenmen
Ciqikou
Tiantandongmen
Puhuangyu
DONGCHANG'AN JIE
JIANGUOMENNEI
DAJIE
QIANMEN
DONGDAJIE
CHONGWENMEN XIDAJIE
XIXINGLONG JIE
DONGXINGLONG JIE
ZHUSHIKOU
DONGDAJIE
TIANTAN LU
TIYUGUAN LU
LONGTAN LU
YONGDINGMEN
DONGJIE
YONGDINGMEN-DONGBIHE-LU
Dongdan Park
Legation Quarter
Beijing Planning Exhibition Hall
North Heavenly Gate
Hall of Prayer for Good Harvest
Longevity Pavilion
Tiantan (Temple of Heaven) Park
Temple of Heaven
West Heavenly Gate
East Heavenly Gate
Tiantan Stadium
South Heavenly Gate
Red Theater
Longtan Velodrome
Yuandushi Temple
Longtan Lake
Beijing Amusement Park
SIGHTS
1 LEGATION QUARTER
2 BEIJING PLANNING EXHIBITION HALL
4 QIANMEN
6 LIULICHANG
10 OX STREET MOSQUE
17 TEMPLE OF HEAVEN
RESTAURANTS
3 LI QUN
5 QUANJUDE
ARTS AND LEISURE
11 TIANQIAO THEATRE
12 BEIJING ACROBATIC TROUPE OF CHINA
16 LEGEND OF KUNG FU
18 DRAGON BOAT FESTIVAL
SHOPS
13 DVD STORE
14 HONGQIAO MARKET
15 SHARON'S STORE
HOTELS
7 FAR EAST INTERNATIONAL YOUTH HOSTEL
8 365 INN
9 JIANGUO QIANMEN HOTEL

ENTERTAINMENT DISTRICT
Sanlitun
SANLITUN LU
GONGREN TIYUCHANG BEILU
DONGZHIMEN
SEE MAP 2
Dongzhimen
DONGZHIMENWAI DAJIE
BEIXINCANG HUTONG
SEE DETAIL
CHUNXIU LU
XINDONG LU
XIZHONG JIE
DONGZHONG JIE
HAYUNCANG HUTONG
BAIMENCANG HUTONG
XINZHONG JIE
XIANG XINGFU YICUN
Dongsishitiao
GONGREN TIYUCHANG BEILU
DONGSI 10 TIAO
Zhangzizhonglu
DONGSI 9 TIAO
DONGSI 8 TIAO
DONGSI 7 TIAO
DONGSI 6 TIAO
DONGSI 5 TIAO
DONGSI BEIDAJIE
CHAOYANGMEN
College of Chinese Medicine
DONGMENCANG HUTONG
NANMENCANG HUTONG
CHAOYANGMEN BEIDAJIE
Workers' Gymnasium
Workers' Stadium
Blue Zoo
GONGREN TIYUCHANG
GONGTI XILU
GONGREN TIYUCHANG DONGLU
PANJIAPO HUTONG
GONGREN TIYUCHANG NANLU
BEIXIAOJIE
DOUBAN HUTONG
SEE MAP 1
Fuwangfu Temple
Dongsi
Chaoyangmen
CHAOYANGMENNEI DAJIE
CHAOYANGMENWAI DAJIE
YUANLAO HUTONG
Dongyue Temple
GONGREN TIYUCHANG NANLU
DONG CAO YUAN
BEIZHUGAN HUTONG
ZHUGAN HUTONG
LISHI HUTONG
DENGCAO HUTONG
DONGCHENG
BENSI HUTONG
NEIWUBU JIE
SHIJIA HUTONG
Dengshikou
GANMIAN HUTONG
JINBAO JIE
HONGXING HUTONG
DONGTANGZI HUTONG
WAIJIAOBU JIE
XIZONGBU HUTONG
XINKAILU HUTONG
DONGSI NANDAJIE
CHAOYANGMEN
DAFANGJIA HUTONG
Temple of Wisdom Attained
LUMICANG HUTONG
DAYABAO HUTONG
NANXIAOJIE
DONGDAN
DONGZONGBU HUTONG
CHAOYANGMEN NANDAJIE
CHAOYANGMEN NANHEYAN
CHAOWAITOU TIAO
CHAOWAISHINCHANG JIE
SHENLU JIE
FANGCAODI XIJIE
DONGDAQIAO LU
RITAN BEILU
Ritan Park
RITAN LU
RITAN DONGLU
YABAO LU
XIUSHUI DONGJIE
The Place
GUANGHUA LU
XIUSHUI BEIJIE
JIANHUA LU
XIUSHUI NANJIE
JIANGUOMEN BEIDAJIE
JIANGUOMENWAI DAJIE
Jiangguomen
Yonganli
Chaoyang Stadium
Dongdan
CHONGWENMEN NEIDAJIE
XIANYU XIANG
SUZHOU HUTONG
Beijing-Zhan
JIANHUA LU
YONG'ANLI ZHONGJIE
ZHUANCHANG HUTONG
Dongdan Park
Beijing Railway Station
DAHUA LU
SEE MAP 3
Chongwenmen
CHONGWENMEN DONGDAJIE

1, 2, 3, 4, 5, 6, 7-9, 10-11, 12, 13, 14, 15, 16-17, 18, 19, 20, 21, 22, 24, 25, 26, 27, 28, 29, 30, 31, 32-33, 34, 35, 36, 37, 38, 39-40, 41, 42, 43, 44, 45-46, 47, 66, 67, 68, 69, 70, 71, 72, 73, 74, 75, 76, 77, 78, 79, 80, 81, 82, 83-84, 85-86, 87, 103, 104

To Jiayi Market
To Sangria Club and White Rabbit
SIGHTS
4 SANLITUN
36 WORKERS' STADIUM
42 BLUE ZOO
57 CHAOYANG PARK AND BEIJING GREAT WHEEL
72 TEMPLE OF WISDOM ATTAINED
75 RITAN PARK
91 NEW CCTV BUILDING
Nanhu Lake
Museum of Agriculture and Exhibition Centre
Chaoyang Park
SANLITUN
CHAOYANG XI LU
Chaoyang Park and Beijing Great Wheel
Gongtibeilu
GONGREN TIYUCHANG BEILU
NONGZHANGUAN NANLU
Pacific Century Place
TUANJIECHU BEIKOU
RESTAURANTS
1 ILLY CAFÉ
2 DAREEN'S COFFEE
14 ALAMEDA
20 DIN TAI FUNG
21 PANINO TECA
24 COMPTOIRS DE FRANCE BAKERY
26 MARE
29 MOREL'S
31 XINJIANG RED ROSE
39 GREEN T HOUSE
40 BELLAGIO
41 THREE GUIZHOU MEN
43 CHINA LOUNGE
47 HAZARA
53 DA DONG ROAST DUCK RESTAURANT
68 QIN TANG FU
71 ORIENT KING OF DUMPLINGS
77 XIAO WANG FU
82 GL CAFÉ
92 HATSUNE
99 CAFÉ EUROPA
NIGHTLIFE
6 CHINA DOLL
12 APERITIVO
13 SADDLE CANTINA
15 JAZZ-YA
23 CD JAZZ CAFÉ
25 PADDY O'SHEA'S
34 MIX
37 COCO BANANA
38 CARGO
44 THE BANK
55 I-ULTRA LOUNGE
56 THE WORLD OF SUZY WONG
61 GOOSE 'N' DUCK
63 Q BAR
73 PARTYWORLD
74 ABSENT NIGHTCLUB
78 STONE BOAT BAR
83 SONG MUSIC BAR AND KITCHEN
84 CJW
88 CENTRO
98 LAN
101 LOONG BAR
ARTS AND LEISURE
19 KANGLONG HEALTH MASSAGE
22 ORIENTAL TAIPAN
27 EAST GATE CINEMA
28 POLY THEATER
32 YOGA YARD
33 BODHI
35 WORKERS' STADIUM TENNIS COURTS
49 PACIFIC CENTURY CLUB
51 NIRVANA FITNESS
54 CHAOYANG KOSAIDO GOLF CLUB
58 CHAOYANG PARK
59 CHAOYANG PARK POOL
60 CHAOYANG PARK TENNIS CLUB
64 ACROBATICS
65 TUANJIEHU PARK POOL
76 RITAN PARK
89 THE KERRY SPORTS CENTER
94 CHINA WORLD FITNESS CENTER
100 WANDA INTERNATIONAL CINEPLEX
103 DONGDAN INDOOR SWIMMING POOL
104 RED GATE GALLERY
SHOPS
3 DVD STORE
5 THE VILLAGE AT SANLITUN
7 WU BA
8 HUGEWAVE
9 3.3 SHOPPING MALL
10 THE RED PHOENIX
11 NOISE
16 NALI MALL
17 LONG.COM SHOES
18 YAXIU MARKET
30 DARA
45 BEIJING FINE JEWELERS
46 TIBETAN ANTIQUES AND CARPETS
48 THE BOOKWORM
50 PACIFIC CENTURY PLACE
79 RITAN OFFICE BUILDING
80 SHARD BOX
85 THE PLACE
86 CHATERHOUSE BOOKTRADER
87 JIMMY AND TOMMY FOREIGN TRADE FASHION CLUB
95 CHINA WORLD SHOPPING MALL
96 VIVIENNE TAM
102 SHIN KONG PLACE
YAOJIAYUAN LU
BAIJIAZHUANG LU
NANSANLITUN LU
Tuanjiehu Park
TUANJIEHU NANLU
Hujalou
HUJALOU
CHAOYANG BEILU
BEIJIE
GUANDONGDIAN BEIJIE
CHAOYANGMENWAI DAJIE
GUANDONGDIAN NANJIE
DONGSANHUAN BEILU
JINGGUANG QIAO
Kerry Centre
New CCTV Building
Guanghualu
GUANGHUA LU
China World Shopping Center
Wanda Plaza
JIANGUO LU
JINGTONG EXPRESSWAY
Dawangqiao
Guomao
HOTELS
52 ZHAOLONG YOUTH HOSTEL
62 TAI YUE SUITES
66 RED CAPITAL RESIDENCE
67 SIHE HOTEL
69 HOTEL DE COUR SL
70 HAOYUAN HOTEL
81 ST REGIS
90 KERRY CENTRE HOTEL
93 TRADERS
97 CHINA WORLD HOTEL
DABEIYAO
Tonghui River
0 500 yds
0 500 m
Beijing East Railway Station

MAP 5
CAPITAL MUSEUM AND TEMPLE OF GREAT CHARITY
SIGHTS
6 BEIJING ZOO
9 TEMPLE OF ANCIENT MONARCHS
10 TEMPLE OF GREAT CHARITY
20 MILITARY MUSEUM
21 BEIJING CAPITAL MUSEUM
RESTAURANTS
1 BAI FAMILY MANSION
3 DAI ETHNIC FLAVOR RESTAURANT
5 BLU LOBSTER
12 STEAK EXCHANGE
14 WHAMPOA CLUB
18 KIEV
19 LU LU
ARTS AND LEISURE
7 BEIJING EXHIBITION THEATRE
11 GODDESS OF MERCY GUANYIN'S BIRTHDAY
SHOPS
16 LANE CRAWFORD
17 SEASON'S PLACE
HOTELS
2 FRIENDSHIP HOTEL
4 SHANGRI-LA HOTEL
8 TEMPLESIDE HOUSE HOSTEL
13 INTERCONTINENTAL FINANCIAL STREET
15 THE WESTIN BEIJING
SIHAI QIAO
SITONG QIAO
SUZHOU JIE
LANDIANCHANG BEILU
YUANDA LU
WIEGONGCUN
BANJING LU
ZIZHUYUAN LU
LANDIANCHANG NANLU
Zizhuyuan Park
ZIZHU QIAO
BAISHIQIAO
XI SANHUAN BEILU
CHEGONGZHUANG
ZENGGUANG LU
ENJI LU
ENJILI
FUSHI LU
FUCHENG LU
WANSHOU LU
HANGTAIN QIAO
Yuyuan Lake
CUIWEI LU
XI SANHUAN ZHONGLU
HAIDIAN
FUXING LU
Wukesong
Wanshoulu
Gongzhufen
Junshibowuguan
YANGFANGDIAN LU
0 600 yds
0 600 m
LIANHUA QIAO
SEE MAP 6
Beijing West Railway Station

BEI SANHUAN XILU
BEISANHUAN ZHONGLU
Dazhongsi
XITUCHENG LU
Beijing National University
WENHUIYUAN BEILU
XINJIEKOUWAI DAJIE
DESHENGMEN
DESHENGMANWAI DAJIE
SIDAOKOU LU
XUCYUAN NANLU
XUCYUAN NANLU
SEE MAP 2
XIZHIMEN BEIDAJIE
WENHUIYUAN LU
DAHUISI LU
GAOLIANGQIAO LU
North China Jiaotong University
SIDAOKOU LU
ANDE LU
Jishutan
Beijing North Railway Station
DESHENGMEN XIDAJIE
Xihai Lake
GULOU XIDAJIE
Xizhimen
Houhai Lake
Beijing Zoo
6
Beijing Exhibition Theatre
7
XINJIEKOU DONGJIE
XIZHIMENNEI DAJIE
XINJIEKOU
ZHONGGUANCUN NANDAJIE
XIXHIMENWAI DAJIE
XIZHIMENWAI NANLU
BEILISHI LU
XIZHIMEN NANDJIE
XIZHIMEN NANXIAOJIE
NACAOCHANG JIE
LIU XIANG
XINJIEKOU NANDAJIE
SANLIHE LU
XIZHIMEN
DI'ANMEN XIDAJIE
DAJIE
PING'ANLI DAJIE
ZHAODENGYU LU
XISI BEIDAJIE
XIHUANGCHENGGEN BEIJIE
Beihai Park
ZHANLANGUAN LU
Chegongzhuang
Beihai Lake
BAIWANZHUANG DAJIE
KOUZHONG HUTONG
Xishiku Church
GANJIAKOU
XISI
8
9
10
11
FUCHENGMENWAI DAJIE
FUCHENGMENNEI DAJIE
Temple of Ancient Monarchs
Temple of Great Charity
Fuchengmen
FUCHENGMEN
SEE MAP 1
Yuyuantan Park
SANLIHE LU
YUETAN BEIJIE
WUDING HUTONG
TAIPINGQIAO DAJIE
FUYOU JIE
Zhonghai Lake
12
YUETAN NANJIE
DONGLU
YUETAN DAJIE
XICHENG
JINRONG DAJIE
14
13
15
16-17
PUHUI NANLI
18
NANLISHI LU
XIDAN
XIDAN BEIDAJIE
Nanhai Lake
20
Military Museum
SANLIHE
FUXINGMENWAI DAJIE
FUXINGMENWEI DAJIE
XICHANG'AN JIE
Muxidi
21
Beijing Capital Museum
Fuxingmen
XIBIANMENWAI DAJIE
NAOSHIKOU DAJIE
XUANWUMENNEI DAJIE
LU
BEIFENGWO
FUXINGMEN
Xishiku Cathedral
Xuanwumen
XUANWUMEN DONGDAJIE
Changchunjie
Hepingmen
LIANHUACHI DONGLU
SEE MAP 3

SIGHTS
1 SUMMER PALACE
3 OLD SUMMER PALACE
4 BEIJING UNIVERSITY

RESTAURANTS
6 SCULPTING IN TIME
7 LUSH

NIGHTLIFE
5 D-22

ARTS AND LEISURE
2 SUMMER PALACE

HOTELS
8 FURAMAXPRESS

Summer Temple
Summer Palace
Old Summer Palace
Kunming Lake
YANYUAN
BEIWUCUN
ZHONGWU
SIHAI QIAO
ZIZHU QIAO
Bagou
YUQUANSHAN LU
YIHEYUAN LU
KUNMINGHU LU
XINJIANGONGMEN LU
SUZHOU JIE
WANQUANHE LU
BEI SIHUAN XILU
HAIDIAN NANLU
BEIWUCUN LU
LANDIANCHANG BEILU
YUANDA LU
XI-SIHUAN-BEILU
BANJING LU
XINGSHIKOU LU
LANDIANCHANG NANLU
ZIZHUYUAN LU
0 600 yds
0 600 m

SEE MAP 5
SEE MAP 3
Yuanmingyuan Park
QINGHUA DONGLU
Chinghua University
QINGHUAYUAN
ZHONGGUANCUN BEIDAJIE
SHUANGQING LU
Wudoakou
CHENGFU LU
ZAOJUNMIAO LU
Beijing University
Students Gymnasium
ZHONGGUANCUN
Beijing University of Science & Technology
BEI SIHUAN XILU
Qinghuayuanzhan Railway Station
University of Aeronautics & Astronautics
HAIDIAN DAJIE
HUAYUAN BEILU
ZHONGGUANCUN DAJIE
Zhinchunli
Zhinchunlu
HAIDIAN NANLU
ZHICHUN LU
Haidian Huangzhuang
Peoples University of China
SITONG QIAO
SUZHOU JIE
BEI SANHUAN XILU
Dazhongsi
XITUCHENG LU
SIDAOKOU LU
XUCYUAN NANLU
XIZHIMEN BEIDAJIE
WIEGONGCUN
DAHUISI LU
GAOLIANGQIAO LU
North China Jiaotong University
SIDAOKOU LU
Beijing North Railway Station
Xizhimen
Zizhuyuan Park

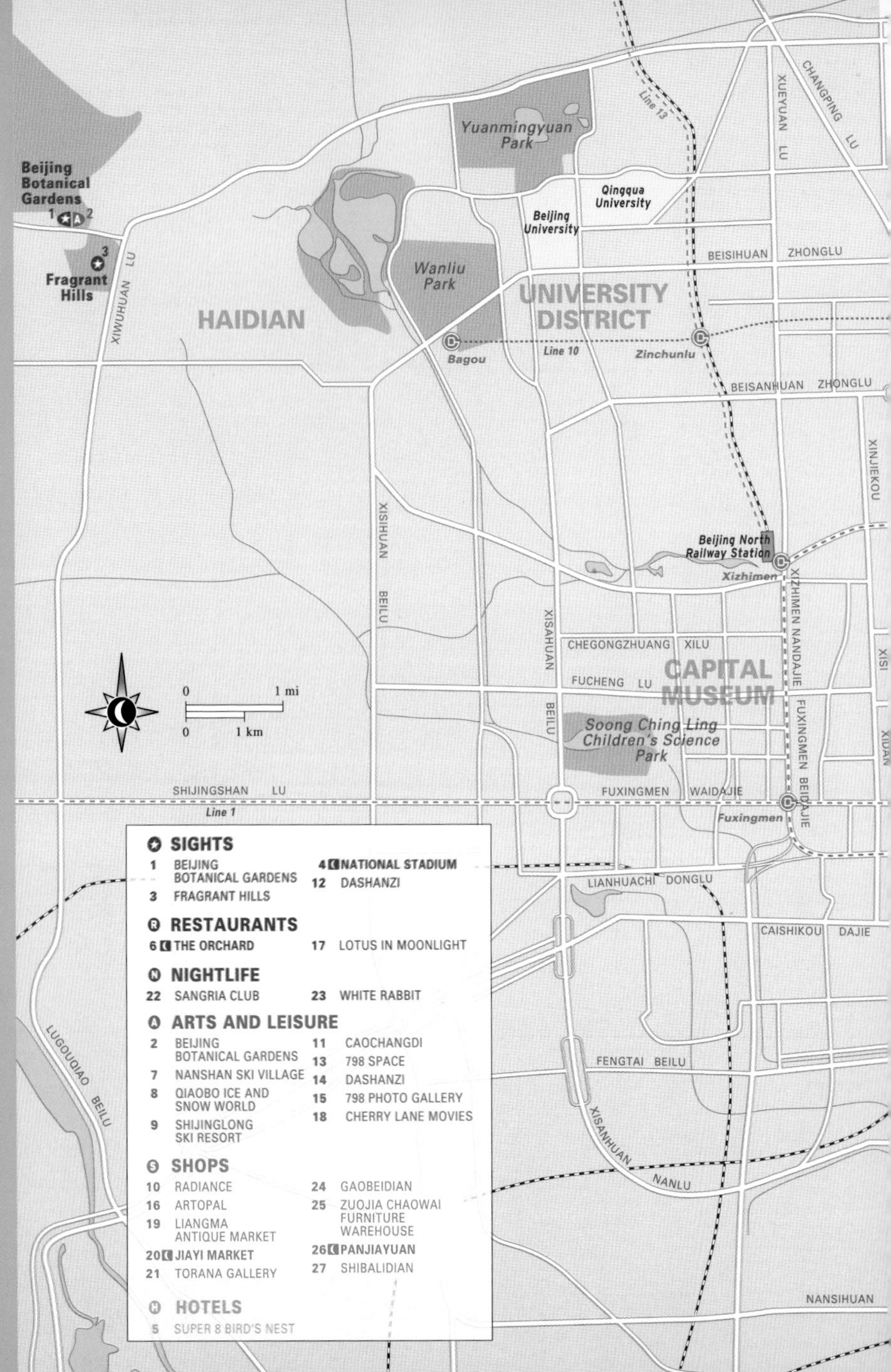
Beijing Botanical Gardens
Fragrant Hills
XIWUHUAN LU
HAIDIAN
Yuanmingyuan Park
Wanliu Park
Qingqua University
Beijing University
UNIVERSITY DISTRICT
Line 13
XUEYUAN LU
CHANGPING LU
BEISIHUAN ZHONGLU
Bagou
Line 10
Zinchunlu
BEISANHUAN ZHONGLU
XINJIEKOU
XISIHUAN BEILU
Beijing North Railway Station
Xizhimen
XIZHIMEN NANDAJIE
XISAHUAN BEILU
CHEGONGZHUANG XILU
CAPITAL MUSEUM
FUCHENG LU
XISI
Soong Ching Ling Children's Science Park
FUXINGMEN BEIDAJIE
XIDAN
SHIJINGSHAN LU
Line 1
FUXINGMEN WAIDAJIE
Fuxingmen
0 1 mi
0 1 km
LIANHUACHI DONGLU
CAISHIKOU DAJIE
LUGOUQIAO BEILU
FENGTAI BEILU
XISANHUAN NANLU
NANSIHUAN
SIGHTS
1 BEIJING BOTANICAL GARDENS
3 FRAGRANT HILLS
4 NATIONAL STADIUM
12 DASHANZI
RESTAURANTS
6 THE ORCHARD
17 LOTUS IN MOONLIGHT
NIGHTLIFE
22 SANGRIA CLUB
23 WHITE RABBIT
ARTS AND LEISURE
2 BEIJING BOTANICAL GARDENS
7 NANSHAN SKI VILLAGE
8 QIAOBO ICE AND SNOW WORLD
9 SHIJINGLONG SKI RESORT
11 CAOCHANGDI
13 798 SPACE
14 DASHANZI
15 798 PHOTO GALLERY
18 CHERRY LANE MOVIES
SHOPS
10 RADIANCE
16 ARTOPAL
19 LIANGMA ANTIQUE MARKET
20 JIAYI MARKET
21 TORANA GALLERY
24 GAOBEIDIAN
25 ZUOJIA CHAOWAI FURNITURE WAREHOUSE
26 PANJIAYUAN
27 SHIBALIDIAN
HOTELS
5 SUPER 8 BIRD'S NEST

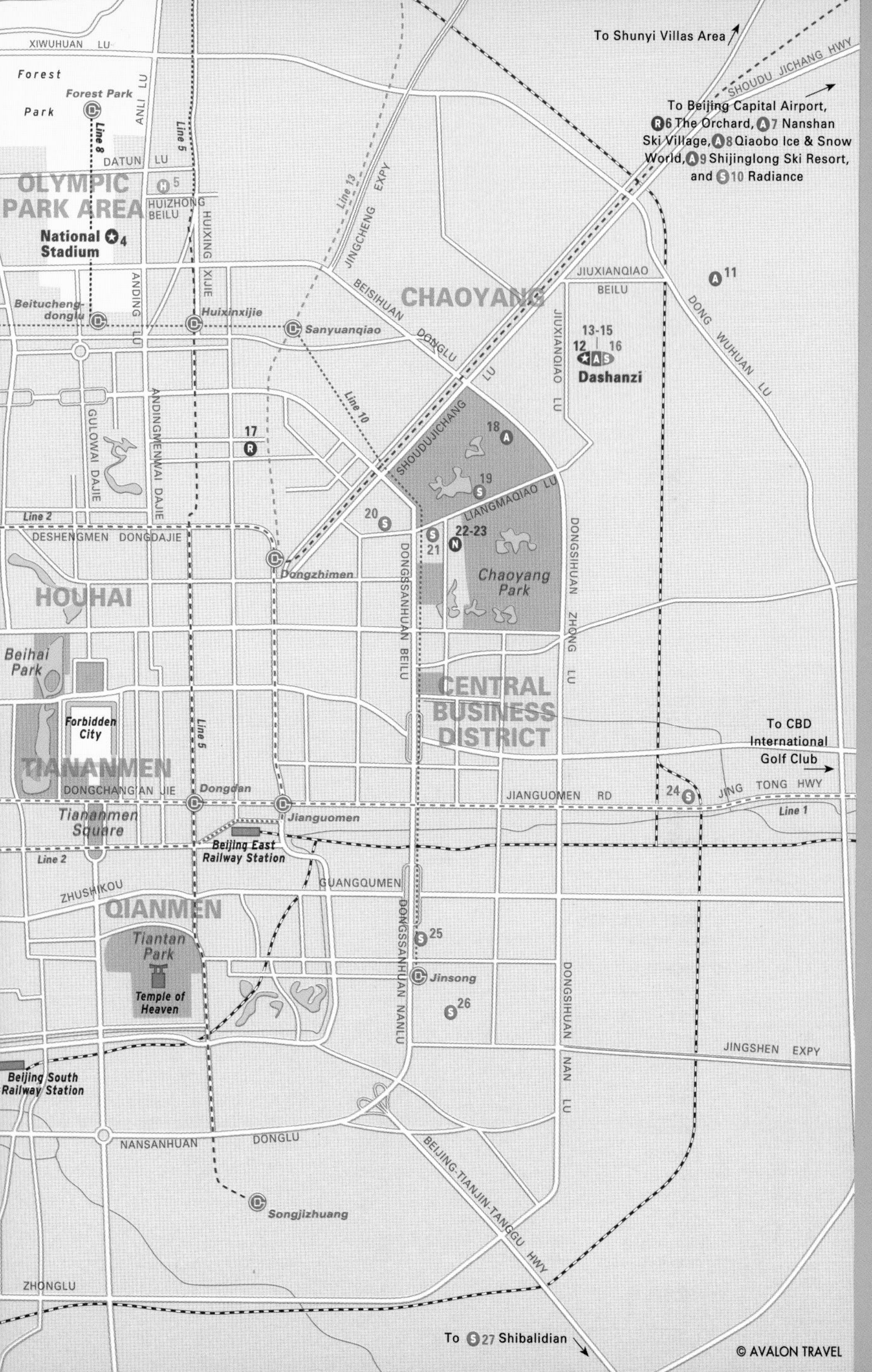
To Shunyi Villas Area
To Beijing Capital Airport, R6 The Orchard, A7 Nanshan Ski Village, A8 Qiaobo Ice & Snow World, A9 Shijinglong Ski Resort, and S10 Radiance
OLYMPIC PARK AREA
National Stadium 4
CHAOYANG
Dashanzi
HOUHAI
Beihai Park
Forbidden City
TIANANMEN
Tiananmen Square
CENTRAL BUSINESS DISTRICT
Chaoyang Park
QIANMEN
Tiantan Park
Temple of Heaven
Beijing East Railway Station
Beijing South Railway Station
To CBD International Golf Club
To S27 Shibalidian
XIWUHUAN LU
DATUN LU
HUIZHONG BEILU
JIUXIANQIAO BEILU
DONG WUHUAN LU
BEISIHUAN DONGLU
SHOUDUJICHANG LU
LIANGMAQIAO LU
DESHENGMEN DONGDAJIE
DONGCHANG'AN JIE
JIANGUOMEN RD
JING TONG HWY
GUANGQUMEN
ZHUSHIKOU
JINGSHEN EXPY
NANSANHUAN DONGLU
BEIJING-TIANJIN-TANGGU HWY
ZHONGLU
SHOUDU JICHANG HWY
JINGCHENG EXPY
Forest Park
Beitucheng-donglu
Huixinxijie
Sanyuanqiao
Dongzhimen
Dongdan
Jianguomen
Jinsong
Songjizhuang
© AVALON TRAVEL

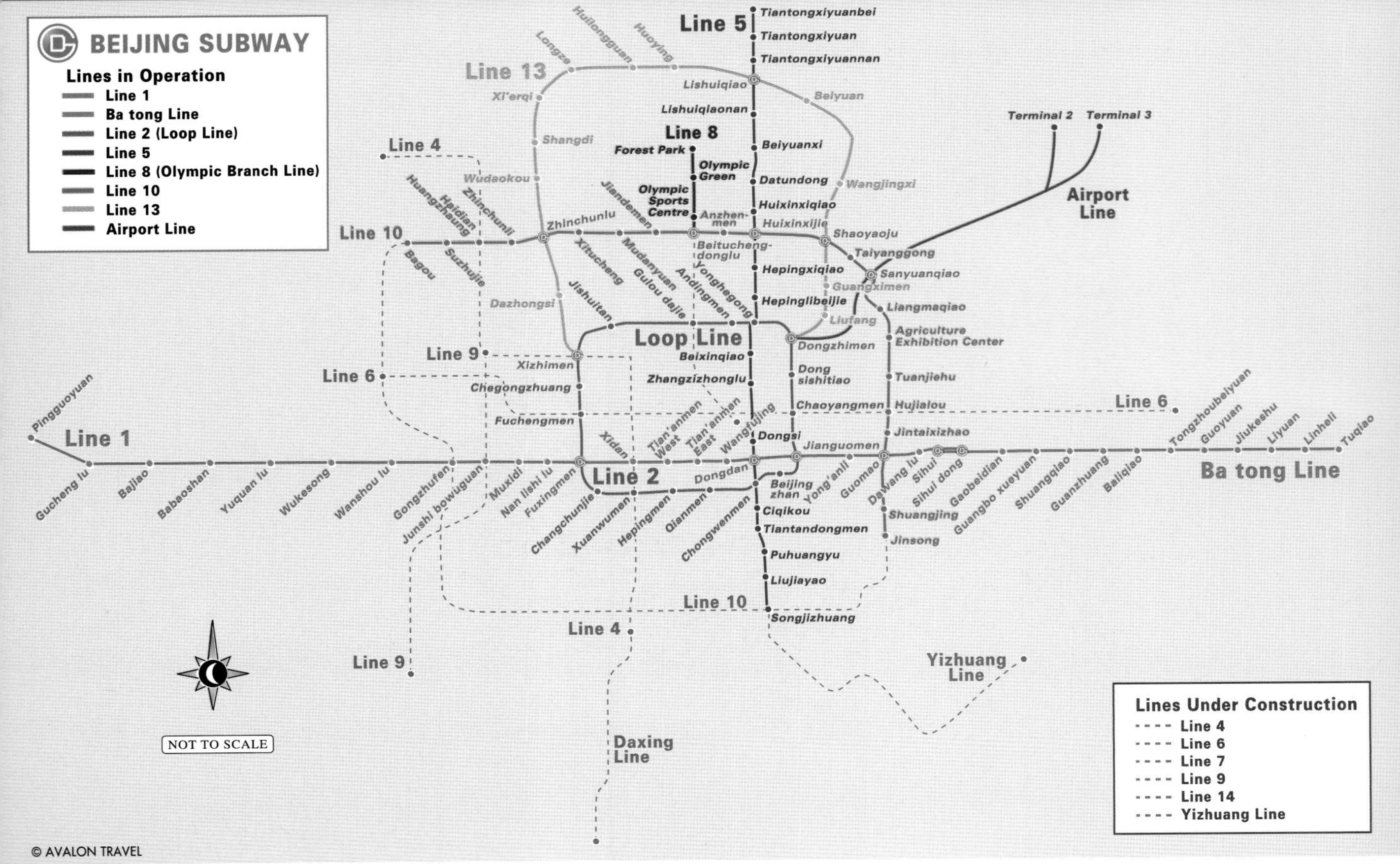

BEIJING SUBWAY
Lines in Operation
Line 1
Ba tong Line
Line 2 (Loop Line)
Line 5
Line 8 (Olympic Branch Line)
Line 10
Line 13
Airport Line
Lines Under Construction
Line 4
Line 6
Line 7
Line 9
Line 14
Yizhuang Line
Line 5
Tiantongxiyuanbei
Tiantongxiyuan
Tiantongxiyuannan
Lishuiqiao
Lishuiqiaonan
Beiyuanxi
Datundong
Huixinxiqiao
Huixinxijie
Beitucheng-donglu
Hepingxiqiao
Hepinglibeijie
Line 13
Longze
Huilongguan
Huoying
Xi'erqi
Beiyuan
Shangdi
Wudaokou
Wangjingxi
Dazhongsi
Shaoyaoju
Guangximen
Liufang
Line 8
Forest Park
Olympic Green
Olympic Sports Centre
Anzhen-men
Line 4
Line 10
Bagou
Huangzhuang
Haidian
Suzhujie
Zhinchunli
Zhinchunlu
Jiandemen
Mudanyuan
Xitucheng
Gulou dajie
Jishuitan
Andingmen
Yonghegong
Taiyanggong
Sanyuanqiao
Liangmaqiao
Agriculture Exhibition Center
Tuanjiehu
Hujialou
Jintaixizhao
Jinsong
Shuangjing
Terminal 2
Terminal 3
Airport Line
Loop Line
Beixinqiao
Zhangzizhonglu
Dongzhimen
Dong sishitiao
Chaoyangmen
Line 9
Line 6
Xizhimen
Chegongzhuang
Fuchengmen
Line 1
Pingguoyuan
Gucheng lu
Bajiao
Babaoshan
Yuquan lu
Wukesong
Wenshou lu
Gongzhufen
Junshi bowuguan
Muxidi
Nan lishi lu
Fuxingmen
Xidan
Tian'anmen West
Tian'anmen East
Wangfujing
Dongsi
Jianguomen
Line 2
Changchunjie
Xuanwumen
Hepingmen
Qianmen
Dongdan
Chongwenmen
Beijing zhan
Yong'anli
Guomao
Dawang lu
Sihui
Sihui dong
Gaobeidian
Guangbo xueyuan
Shuangqiao
Guanzhuang
Baliqiao
Tongzhoubeiyuan
Guoyuan
Jiukeshu
Liyuan
Linheli
Tuqiao
Ba tong Line
Line 6
Ciqikou
Tiantandongmen
Puhuangyu
Liujiayao
Line 10
Songjiazhuang
Line 4
Line 9
Yizhuang Line
Daxing Line
NOT TO SCALE

Shanghai Maps

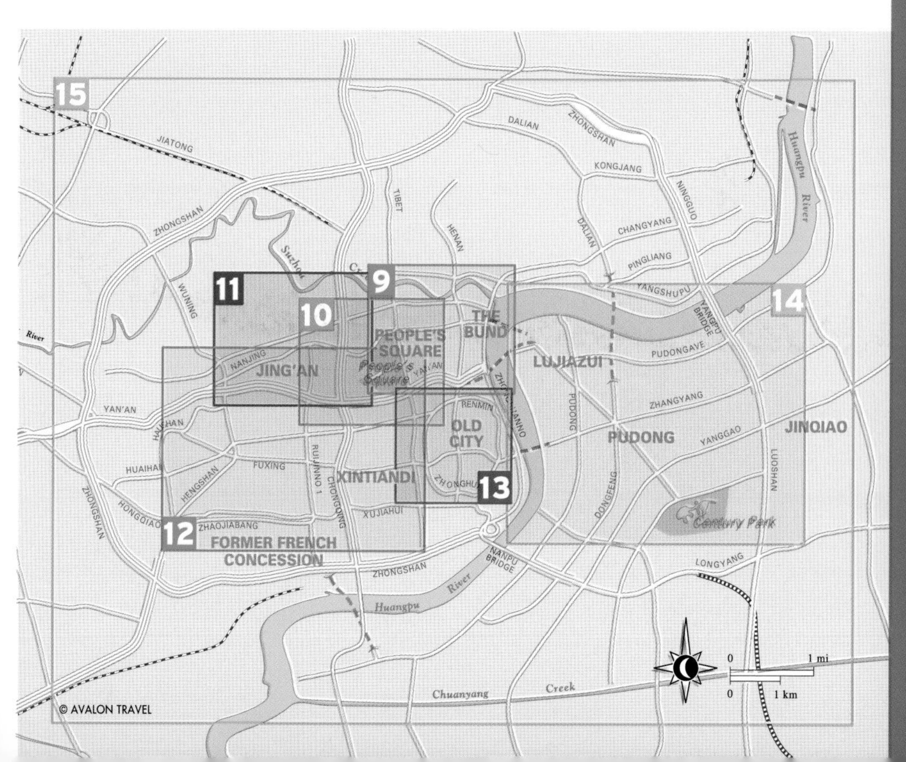

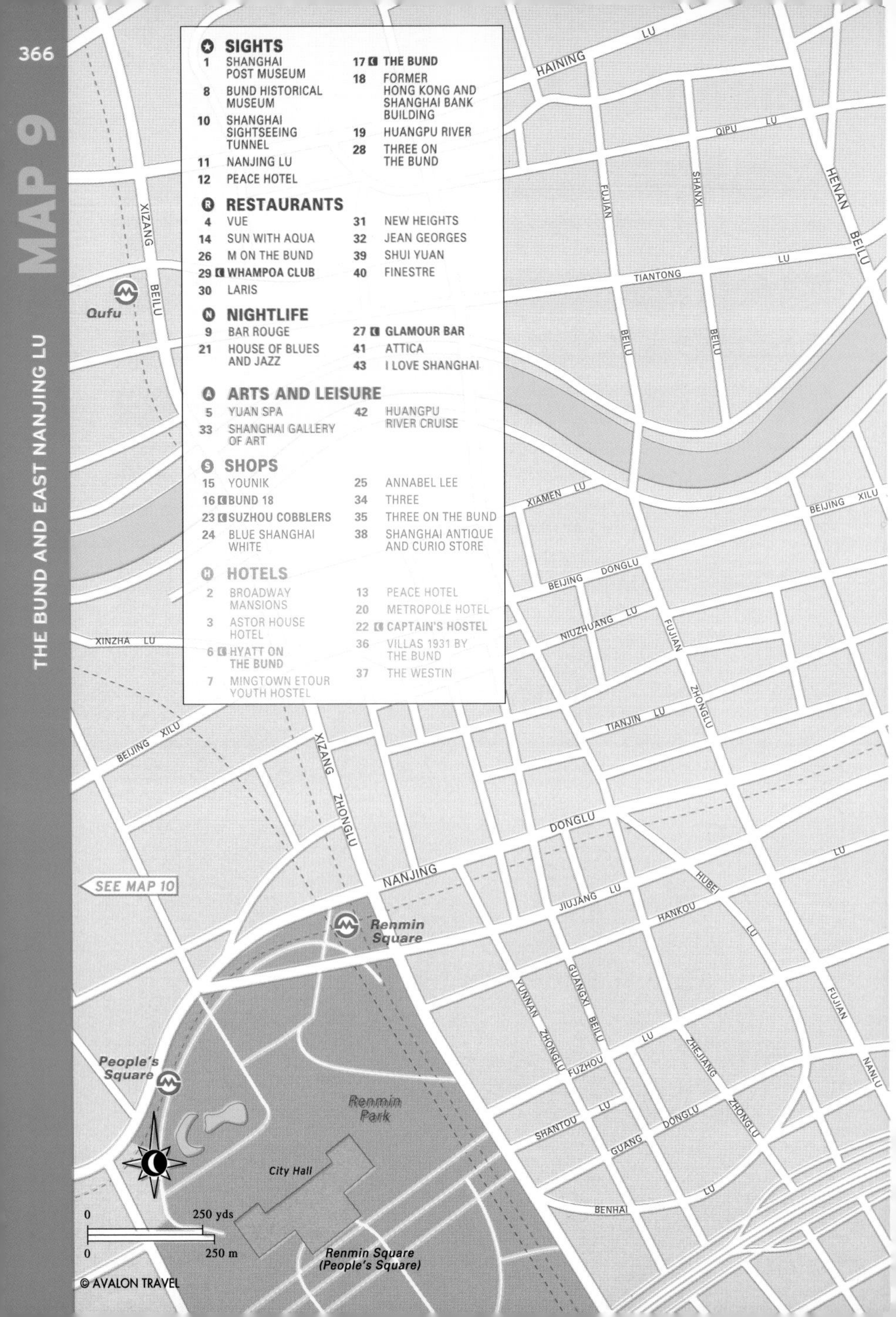
SIGHTS
1 SHANGHAI POST MUSEUM
8 BUND HISTORICAL MUSEUM
10 SHANGHAI SIGHTSEEING TUNNEL
11 NANJING LU
12 PEACE HOTEL
17 THE BUND
18 FORMER HONG KONG AND SHANGHAI BANK BUILDING
19 HUANGPU RIVER
28 THREE ON THE BUND
RESTAURANTS
4 VUE
14 SUN WITH AQUA
26 M ON THE BUND
29 WHAMPOA CLUB
30 LARIS
31 NEW HEIGHTS
32 JEAN GEORGES
39 SHUI YUAN
40 FINESTRE
NIGHTLIFE
9 BAR ROUGE
21 HOUSE OF BLUES AND JAZZ
27 GLAMOUR BAR
41 ATTICA
43 I LOVE SHANGHAI
ARTS AND LEISURE
5 YUAN SPA
33 SHANGHAI GALLERY OF ART
42 HUANGPU RIVER CRUISE
SHOPS
15 YOUNIK
16 BUND 18
23 SUZHOU COBBLERS
24 BLUE SHANGHAI WHITE
25 ANNABEL LEE
34 THREE
35 THREE ON THE BUND
38 SHANGHAI ANTIQUE AND CURIO STORE
HOTELS
2 BROADWAY MANSIONS
3 ASTOR HOUSE HOTEL
6 HYATT ON THE BUND
7 MINGTOWN ETOUR YOUTH HOSTEL
13 PEACE HOTEL
20 METROPOLE HOTEL
22 CAPTAIN'S HOSTEL
36 VILLAS 1931 BY THE BUND
37 THE WESTIN
HAINING LU
QIPU LU
HENAN BEILU
FUJIAN
SHANXI
TIANTONG LU
BEILU
XIZANG BEILU
Qufu
XIAMEN LU
BEIJING XILU
BEIJING DONGLU
NIUZHUANG LU
FUJIAN ZHONGLU
XINZHA LU
TIANJIN LU
XIZANG ZHONGLU
NANJING DONGLU
HUBEI LU
JIUJANG LU
HANKOU LU
SEE MAP 10
Renmin Square
YUNNAN ZHONGLU
GUANGXI BEILU
FUZHOU LU
ZHEJIANG ZHONGLU
FUJIAN
NANLU
SHANTOU LU
GUANG DONGLU
BENHAI LU
People's Square
Renmin Park
City Hall
Renmin Square (People's Square)
0 250 yds
0 250 m
© AVALON TRAVEL

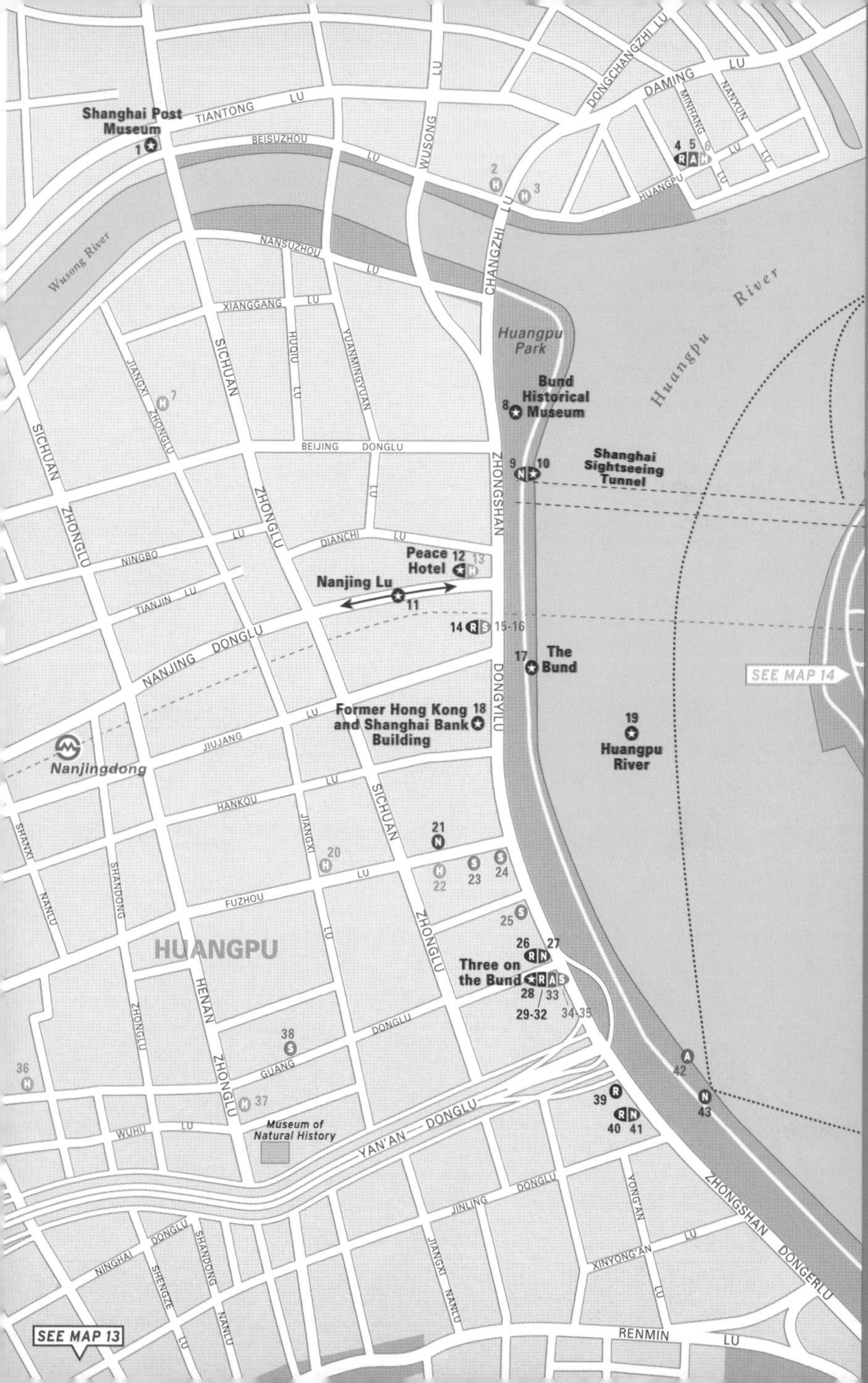

1 Shanghai Post Museum
2
3
4 5 6
7
8 Bund Historical Museum
9 10 Shanghai Sightseeing Tunnel
11 Nanjing Lu
12 Peace Hotel 13
14 15-16
17 The Bund
18 Former Hong Kong and Shanghai Bank Building
19 Huangpu River
20
21
22 23 24
25
26 27
Three on the Bund 28 / 33
29-32 34-35
36
37
38
39
40 41
42
43

Huangpu Park
Huangpu River
Wusong River
HUANGPU
Nanjingdong
Museum of Natural History

TIANTONG LU
BEISUZHOU LU
NANSUZHOU LU
DONGCHANGZHI LU
DAMING LU
MINHANG LU
NANXUN LU
HUANGPU LU
WUSONG LU
CHANGZHI LU
XIANGGANG LU
HUQIU LU
YUANMINGYUAN LU
SICHUAN ZHONGLU
JIANGXI ZHONGLU
BEIJING DONGLU
ZHONGSHAN DONGYILU
DIANCHI LU
NINGBO LU
TIANJIN LU
NANJING DONGLU
JIUJIANG LU
HANKOU LU
FUZHOU LU
SHANXI NANLU
SHANDONG ZHONGLU
HENAN ZHONGLU
GUANG DONGLU
WUHU LU
YAN'AN DONGLU
JINLING DONGLU
NINGHAI DONGLU
SHENGZE LU
SHANDONG NANLU
JIANGXI NANLU
YONG'AN LU
XINYONG'AN LU
ZHONGSHAN DONGERLU
RENMIN LU

SEE MAP 14
SEE MAP 13

SIGHTS

- 7 PARK HOTEL
- 16 PEOPLE'S PARK
- 17 SHANGHAI ART MUSEUM
- 20 SHANGHAI MUSEUM OF CONTEMPORARY ART (MOCA)
- 22 URBAN PLANNING CENTER
- 25 **SHANGHAI MUSEUM**

RESTAURANTS

- 4 WAGAS
- 5 **JIA JIA TANG BAO**
- 6 TAI SHENG YUAN
- 9 AI MEI
- 12 TAJ BEIRUT
- 13 ELEMENT FRESH
- 15 XINJIANG TAKEAWAY
- 18 BARBAROSSA
- 30 SLICE

NIGHTLIFE

- 2 ROOM WITH A VIEW
- 19 BARBAROSSA
- 23 NAPA WINE BAR
- 29 BEEDEES

ARTS AND LEISURE

- 24 **SHANGHAI GRAND THEATER**
- 27 SHANGHAI CONCERT HALL

SHOPS

- 1 DUO YUN XUAN ART SHOP AND GALLERY
- 3 PEARL CITY
- 14 BOOK CITY
- 26 SHANGHAI MUSEUM ART STORE
- 31 CHATERHOUSE BOOKTRADER

HOTELS

- 8 PARK HOTEL
- 10 LE ROYAL MERIDIEN
- 11 YANGTZE HOTEL
- 21 JW MARRIOTT
- 28 JINJIANG YMCA HOTEL

BEIJING XILU
GUIJNG LU
HUANGHE LU
XINCHANG LU
FENGYANG LU
People's Square
Shanghai Art Museum
NANJING DONGLU
HUANGPI BEILU
Shanghai Grand Theater
JIANGYIN LU
CHENDU LU
WEIHAI LU
WUSHENG LU
DAGA LU

SEE MAP 11

SEE MAP 12

0 250 yds
0 250 m

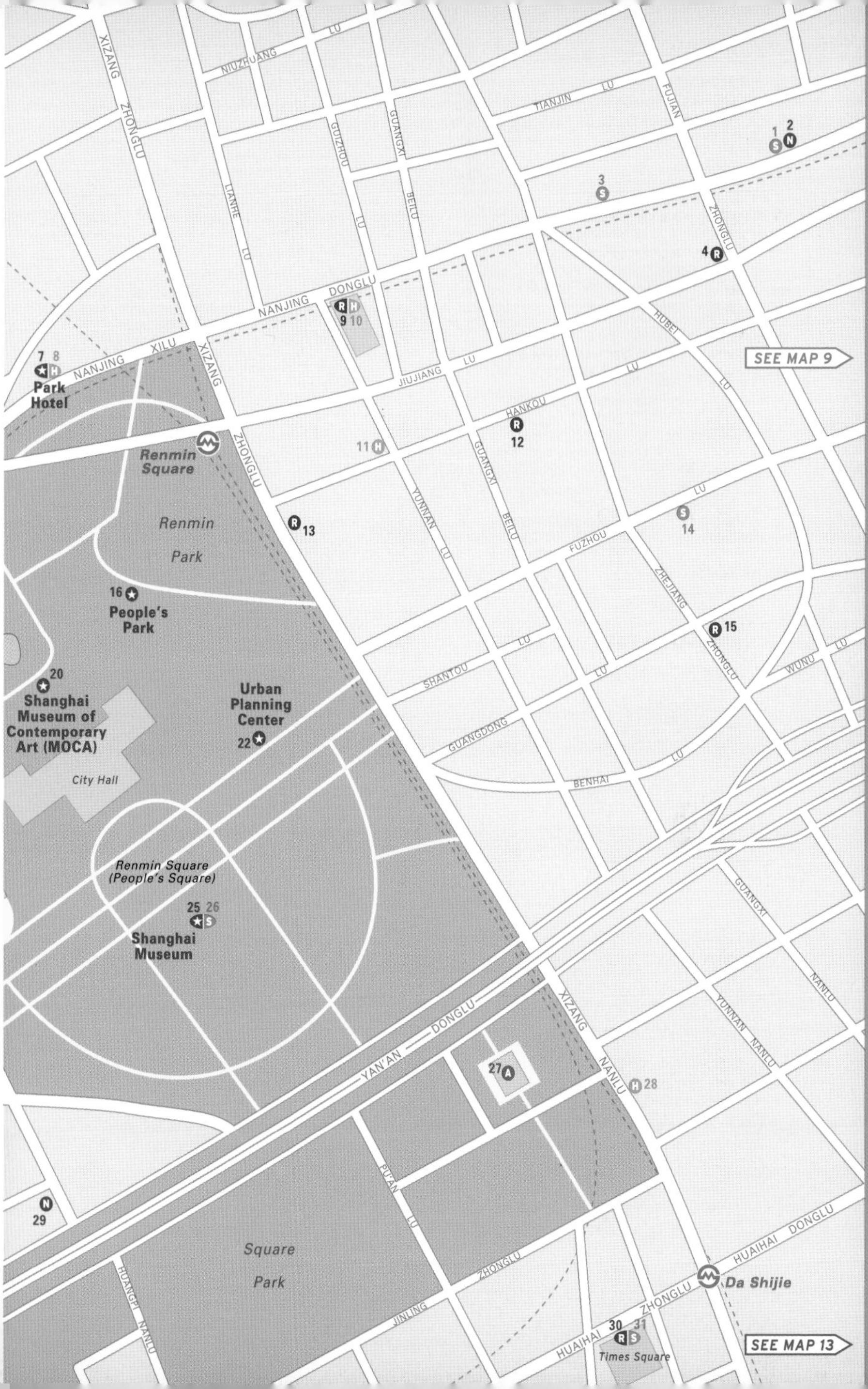

MAP 10

PEOPLE'S SQUARE AND MUSEUM ROW

SEE MAP 9

SEE MAP 13

NIUZHUANG LU
TIANJIN LU
FUJIAN ZHONGLU
XIZANG ZHONGLU
GUIZHOU LU
GUANGXI BEILU
LIANHE LU
NANJING DONGLU
NANJING XILU
HUBEI LU
JIUJIANG LU
HANKOU LU
YUNNAN LU
FUZHOU LU
ZHEJIANG ZHONGLU
SHANTOU LU
WUNU LU
GUANGDONG LU
BENHAI
YAN'AN DONGLU
XIZANG NANLU
GUANGXI NANLU
YUNNAN NANLU
PU'AN LU
HUANGPI NANLU
JINLING ZHONGLU
HUAIHAI ZHONGLU
HUAIHAI DONGLU

1 S
2 N
3 S
4 R
7 8 Park Hotel
9 10 R H
11 H
12 R
13 R
14 S
15 R
16 People's Park
20 Shanghai Museum of Contemporary Art (MOCA)
22 Urban Planning Center
25 26 Shanghai Museum
27 A
28 H
29 N
30 31 R S Times Square

Renmin Square
Renmin Park
City Hall
Renmin Square (People's Square)
Square Park
Da Shijie

SIGHTS
3 OHEL RACHEL SYNAGOGUE
26 JING'AN TEMPLE
RESTAURANTS
4 GOURMET CAFÉ
6 YANG'S FRY DUMPLINGS
8 SHANGHAI SCENERY GARDEN RESTAURANT
10 ROOMTWENTYEIGHT
24 CHARMANT
28 BALI LAGUNA
NIGHTLIFE
9 AVENUE BAR
13 BIG BAMBOO
19 RED BEAT
23 PARAMOUNT THEATER
ARTS AND LEISURE
1 1918 ART SPACE
2 JING'AN SPORTS CENTER SWIMMING POOL
5 GANZHI BLINDMAN'S MASSAGE
12 YOU'S ACUPUNCTURE
15 FITNESS FIRST AT PLAZA 66
16 SHANGHAI CENTER THEATER
17 MAJESTIC THEATER
20 INTERNATIONAL ART, ANTIQUES, AND JEWELRY FAIR
21 SHCONTEMPORARY
27 JING'AN PARK
29 CYCLE CHINA
SHOPS
14 PLAZA 66
22 EVEN BETTER THAN MOVIEWORLD
25 HOLLYWOOD
HOTELS
7 JIA SHANGHAI
11 URBN HOTEL
18 PORTMAN RITZ-CARLTON
XIKANG LU
HAIFANG LU
JIANGNING LU
CHANGPING LU
SHANXI BEILU
KANGDING LU
XIKANG LU
CHANGDE LU
WUDING LU
JIAOZHOU LU
XINZHA LU
WUDING LU
WUNING NANLU
NANYANG LU
Shanghai Center
BEIJING XILU
JIAOZHOU LU
YUYUAN LU
NANJING XILU
TONGREN LU
WANHANGDOU LU
CHANGDE LU
ANYI LU
Jing'an Temple
Jing'an Park
YAN'AN ZHONGLU
YUYUAN LU
WULUMUQI LU
NANJING XILU
Jing'an Temple
0 300 yds
0 300 m

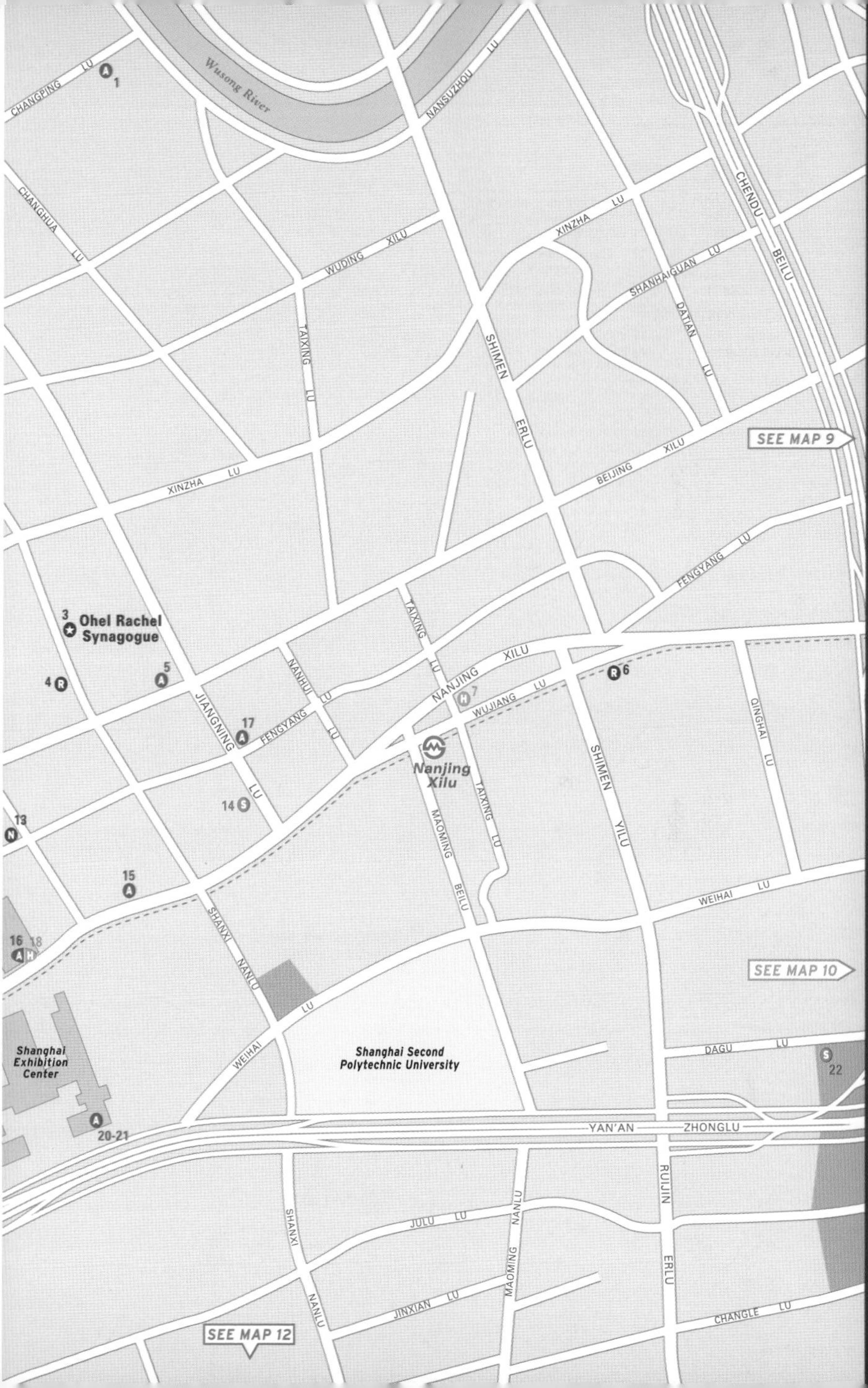

Wusong River
CHANGPING LU
CHANGHUA LU
NANSUZHOU LU
CHENDU BEILU
XINZHA LU
WUDING XILU
SHANHAIGUAN LU
DATIAN LU
TAIXING LU
SHIMEN ERLU
BEIJING XILU
XINZHA LU
FENGYANG LU
TAIXING LU
3 Ohel Rachel Synagogue
4
5
NANHUI LU
NANJING XILU
6
7
WUJIANG LU
JIANGNING LU
17
FENGYANG LU
Nanjing Xilu
14
13
MAOMING BEILU
TAIXING LU
SHIMEN YILU
QINGHAI LU
15
WEIHAI LU
SHANXI NANLU
16
18
WEIHAI LU
Shanghai Exhibition Center
Shanghai Second Polytechnic University
DAGU LU
22
20-21
YAN'AN ZHONGLU
RUIJIN ERLU
JULU LU
SHANXI NANLU
MAOMING NANLU
JINXIAN LU
CHANGLE LU

SEE MAP 9
SEE MAP 10
SEE MAP 12

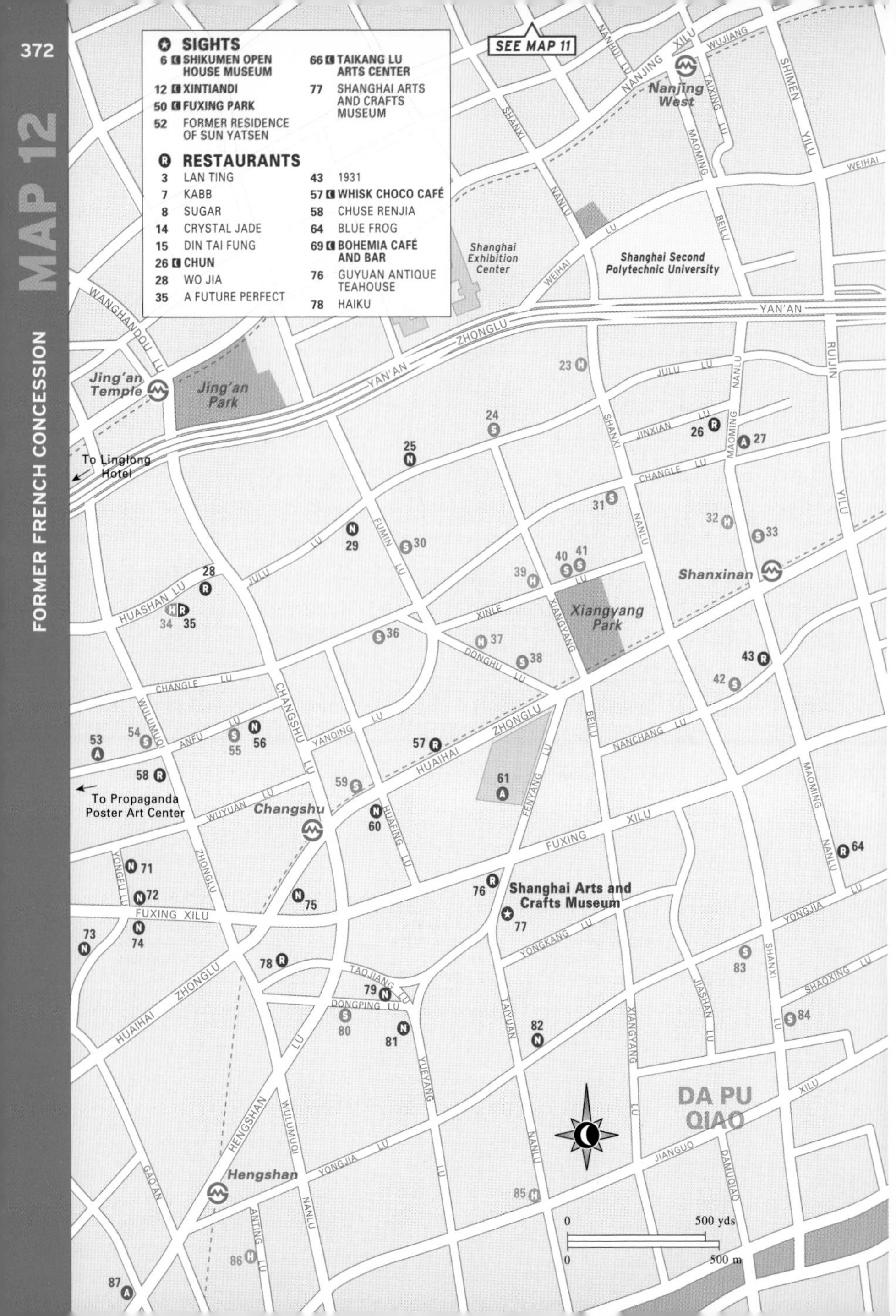
SIGHTS
6 SHIKUMEN OPEN HOUSE MUSEUM
12 XINTIANDI
50 FUXING PARK
52 FORMER RESIDENCE OF SUN YATSEN
66 TAIKANG LU ARTS CENTER
77 SHANGHAI ARTS AND CRAFTS MUSEUM
RESTAURANTS
3 LAN TING
7 KABB
8 SUGAR
14 CRYSTAL JADE
15 DIN TAI FUNG
26 CHUN
28 WO JIA
35 A FUTURE PERFECT
43 1931
57 WHISK CHOCO CAFÉ
58 CHUSE RENJIA
64 BLUE FROG
69 BOHEMIA CAFÉ AND BAR
76 GUYUAN ANTIQUE TEAHOUSE
78 HAIKU
SEE MAP 11
Nanjing West
Jing'an Temple
Jing'an Park
Shanghai Exhibition Center
Shanghai Second Polytechnic University
To Linglong Hotel
Xiangyang Park
Shanxinan
To Propaganda Poster Art Center
Changshu
Shanghai Arts and Crafts Museum
Hengshan
DA PU QIAO
NANJING XILU
WUJIANG
SHIMEN YILU
WEIHAI
YAN'AN ZHONGLU
JULU LU
CHANGLE LU
HUASHAN LU
XINLE LU
DONGHU LU
ANFU LU
WUYUAN LU
HUAIHAI ZHONGLU
FUXING XILU
YONGJIA LU
JIANGUO XILU
SHAOXING LU
CHANGSHU LU
FUMIN LU
SHANXI NANLU
MAOMING NANLU
XIANGYANG LU
RUIJIN YILU
0 500 yds
0 500 m

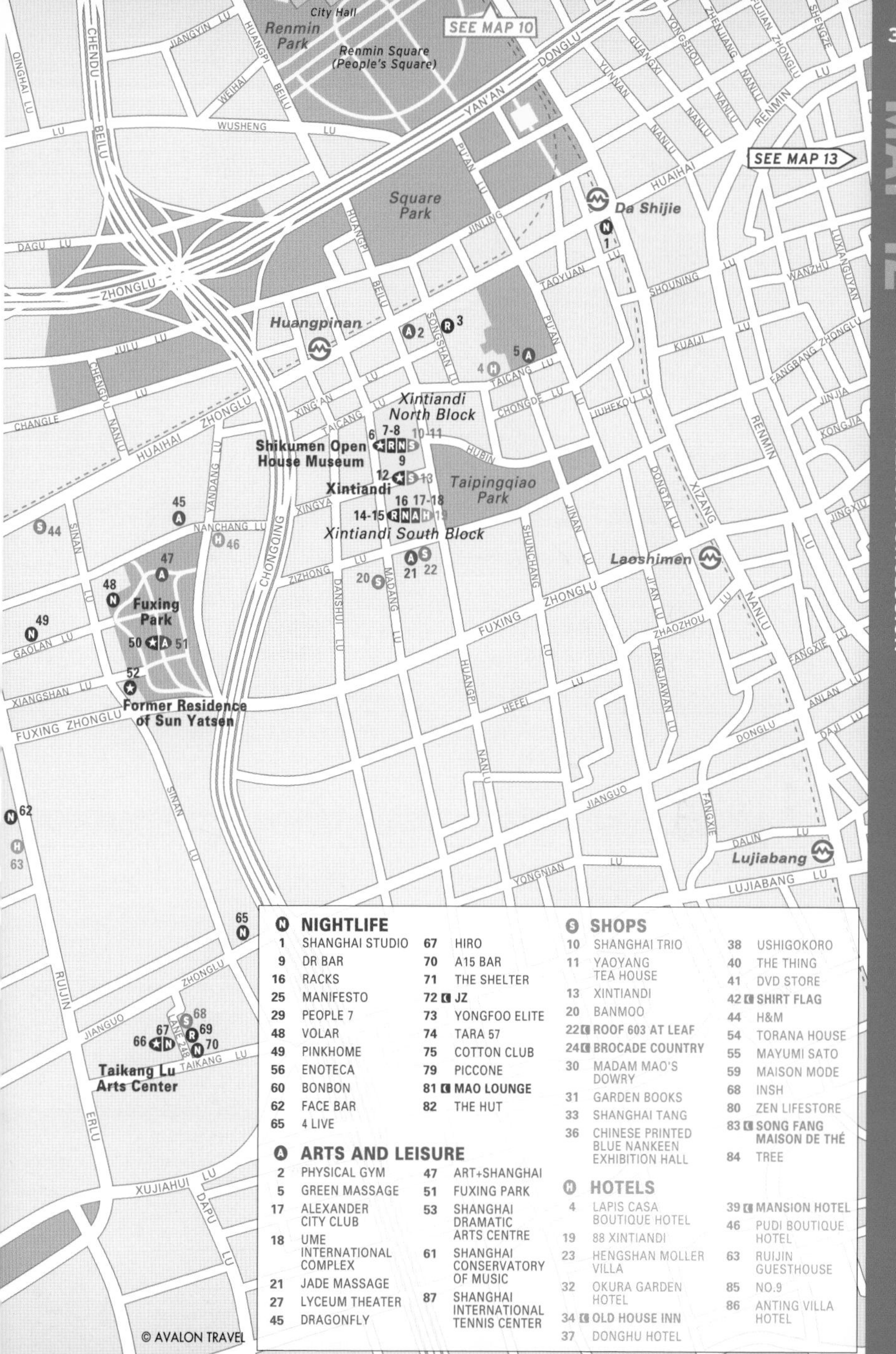
City Hall
Renmin Park
Renmin Square (People's Square)
SEE MAP 10
SEE MAP 13
Square Park
Da Shijie
Huangpinan
Xintiandi North Block
Shikumen Open House Museum
Xintiandi
Taipingqiao Park
Xintiandi South Block
Laoshimen
Fuxing Park
Former Residence of Sun Yatsen
Lujiabang
Taikang Lu Arts Center
YAN'AN DONGLU
HUAIHAI ZHONGLU
FUXING ZHONGLU
CHONGQING
RENMIN LU
XIZANG NANLU
JIANGUO ZHONGLU
LUJIABANG LU
XUJIAHUI LU
RUIJIN
SINAN LU
NIGHTLIFE
1 SHANGHAI STUDIO
9 DR BAR
16 RACKS
25 MANIFESTO
29 PEOPLE 7
48 VOLAR
49 PINKHOME
56 ENOTECA
60 BONBON
62 FACE BAR
65 4 LIVE
67 HIRO
70 A15 BAR
71 THE SHELTER
72 JZ
73 YONGFOO ELITE
74 TARA 57
75 COTTON CLUB
79 PICCONE
81 MAO LOUNGE
82 THE HUT
ARTS AND LEISURE
2 PHYSICAL GYM
5 GREEN MASSAGE
17 ALEXANDER CITY CLUB
18 UME INTERNATIONAL COMPLEX
21 JADE MASSAGE
27 LYCEUM THEATER
45 DRAGONFLY
47 ART+SHANGHAI
51 FUXING PARK
53 SHANGHAI DRAMATIC ARTS CENTRE
61 SHANGHAI CONSERVATORY OF MUSIC
87 SHANGHAI INTERNATIONAL TENNIS CENTER
SHOPS
10 SHANGHAI TRIO
11 YAOYANG TEA HOUSE
13 XINTIANDI
20 BANMOO
22 ROOF 603 AT LEAF
24 BROCADE COUNTRY
30 MADAM MAO'S DOWRY
31 GARDEN BOOKS
33 SHANGHAI TANG
36 CHINESE PRINTED BLUE NANKEEN EXHIBITION HALL
38 USHIGOKORO
40 THE THING
41 DVD STORE
42 SHIRT FLAG
44 H&M
54 TORANA HOUSE
55 MAYUMI SATO
59 MAISON MODE
68 INSH
80 ZEN LIFESTORE
83 SONG FANG MAISON DE THÉ
84 TREE
HOTELS
4 LAPIS CASA BOUTIQUE HOTEL
19 88 XINTIANDI
23 HENGSHAN MOLLER VILLA
32 OKURA GARDEN HOTEL
34 OLD HOUSE INN
37 DONGHU HOTEL
39 MANSION HOTEL
46 PUDI BOUTIQUE HOTEL
63 RUIJIN GUESTHOUSE
85 NO.9
86 ANTING VILLA HOTEL
© AVALON TRAVEL

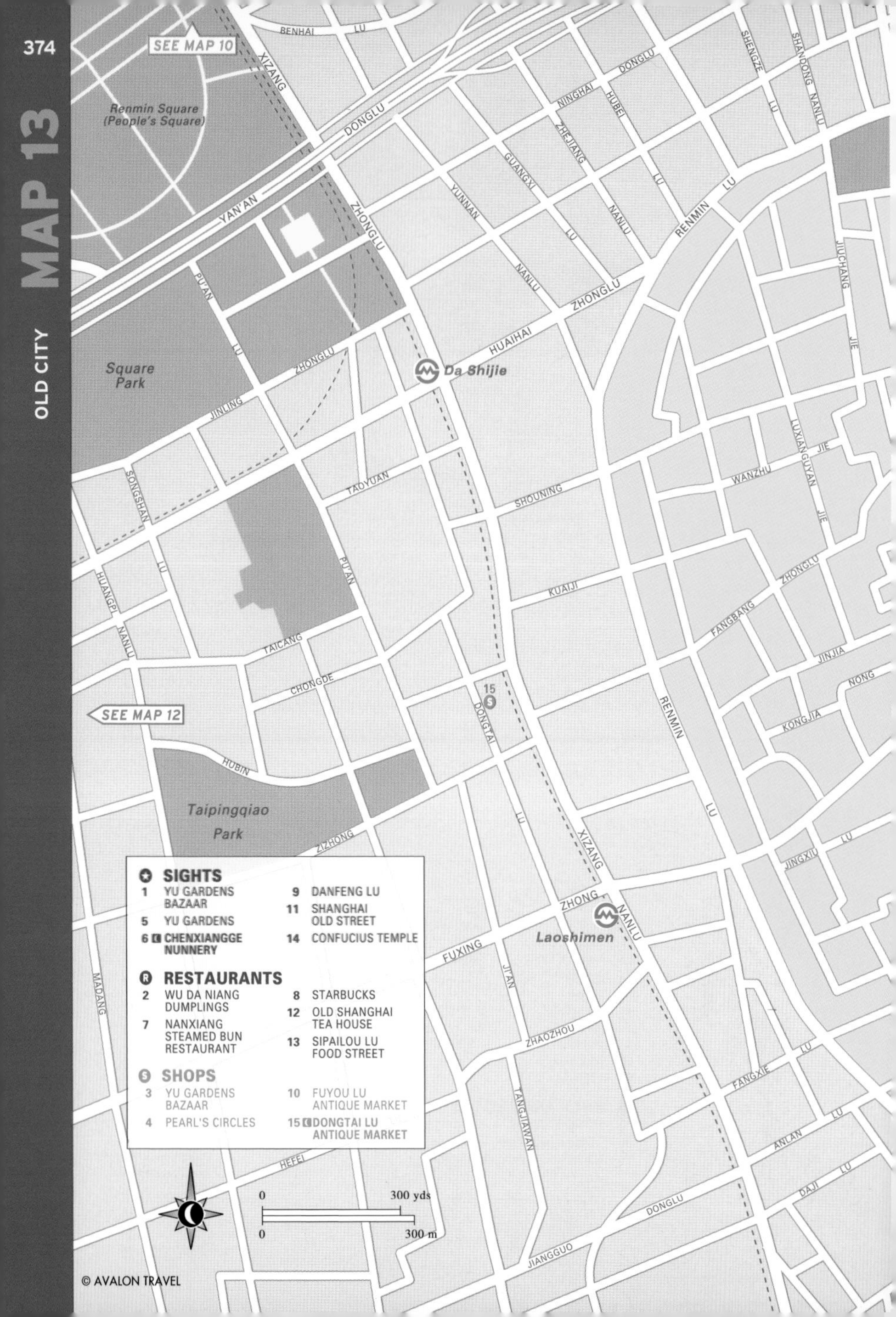
MAP 13
OLD CITY
SEE MAP 10
SEE MAP 12
Renmin Square
(People's Square)
Square
Park
Taipingqiao
Park
Da Shijie
Laoshimen
BENHAI LU
XIZANG
DONGLU
YAN'AN
ZHONGLU
PU'AN
LU
HUAIHAI
ZHONGLU
JINLING
SONGSHAN
TAOYUAN
SHOUNING
HUANGPI
NANLU
TAICANG
CHONGDE
DONGTAI
HUBIN
ZIZHONG
FUXING
ZHONG
NANLU
JI'AN
ZHAOZHOU
TANGJIAWAN
HEFEI
JIANGGUO
DONGLU
MADANG
KUAIJI
RENMIN
LU
FANGBANG
ZHONGLU
JINJIA
NONG
KONGJIA
JINGXIU
FANGXIE
ANLAN
DAJI
WANZHU
JIE
LUXIANGUYAN
JIUCHANG
YUNNAN
GUANGXI
ZHEJIANG
NINGHAI
HUBEI
SHENGZE
SHANDONG NANLU
SIGHTS
1 YU GARDENS BAZAAR
5 YU GARDENS
6 CHENXIANGGE NUNNERY
9 DANFENG LU
11 SHANGHAI OLD STREET
14 CONFUCIUS TEMPLE
RESTAURANTS
2 WU DA NIANG DUMPLINGS
7 NANXIANG STEAMED BUN RESTAURANT
8 STARBUCKS
12 OLD SHANGHAI TEA HOUSE
13 SIPAILOU LU FOOD STREET
SHOPS
3 YU GARDENS BAZAAR
4 PEARL'S CIRCLES
10 FUYOU LU ANTIQUE MARKET
15 DONGTAI LU ANTIQUE MARKET
15
0
300 yds
0
300 m

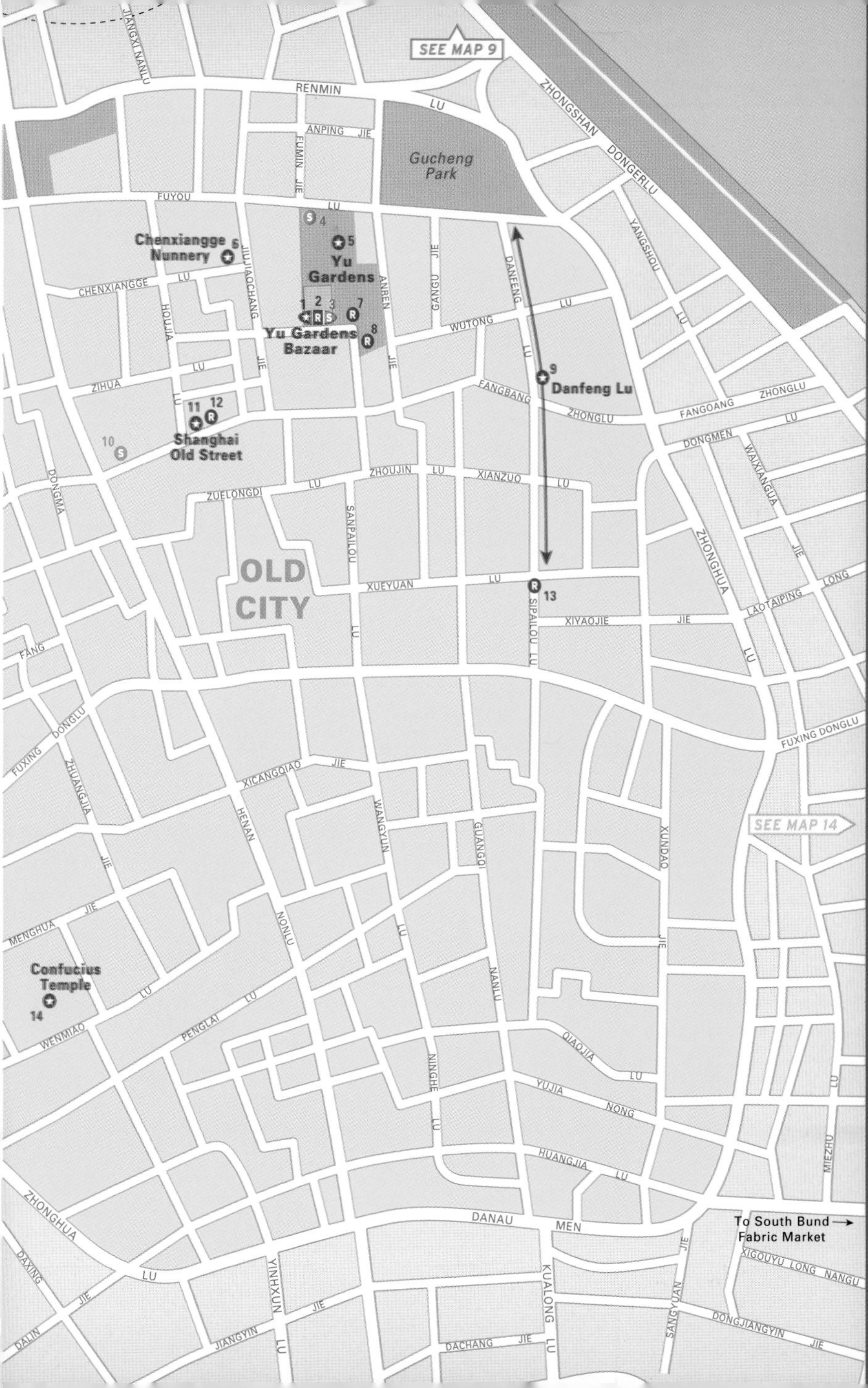

SEE MAP 9
SEE MAP 14

OLD CITY

1 2 3 Yu Gardens Bazaar
4
5 Yu Gardens
6 Chenxiangge Nunnery
7
8
9 Danfeng Lu
10
11 12 Shanghai Old Street
13
14 Confucius Temple

Gucheng Park

To South Bund Fabric Market →

RENMIN LU
ZHONGSHAN DONGERLU
ANPING JIE
FUMIN JIE
FUYOU LU
JIANGXI NANLU
JIUJIAOCHANG JIE
CHENXIANGGE LU
HOUJIA LU
ANREN JIE
GANGU JIE
DANFENG LU
YANGSHOU LU
WUTONG LU
ZIHUA LU
FANGBANG ZHONGLU
FANGOANG ZHONGLU
DONGMEN LU
WAIXIANGUA JIE
ZHOUJIN LU
XIANZUO LU
ZUELONGDI LU
DONGMA
SANPAILOU LU
XUEYUAN LU
SIPAILOU LU
XIYAOJIE JIE
ZHONGHUA LU
LAOTAIPING LONG
FANG
FUXING DONGLU
XICANGQIAO JIE
ZHUANGJIA JIE
HENAN NONLU
WANGYUN LU
GUANGQI NANLU
XUNDAO JIE
MENGHUA JIE
WENMIAO LU
PENGLAI LU
QIAOJIA LU
YUJIA NONG
NINGHE LU
HUANGJIA LU
MIEZHU LU
ZHONGHUA LU
DANAU MEN
DAXING JIE
YINHXUN LU
KUALONG LU
SANGYUAN JIE
XIGOUYU LONG NANGU
DONGJIANGYIN JIE
DALIN
JIANGYIN JIE
DACHANG JIE

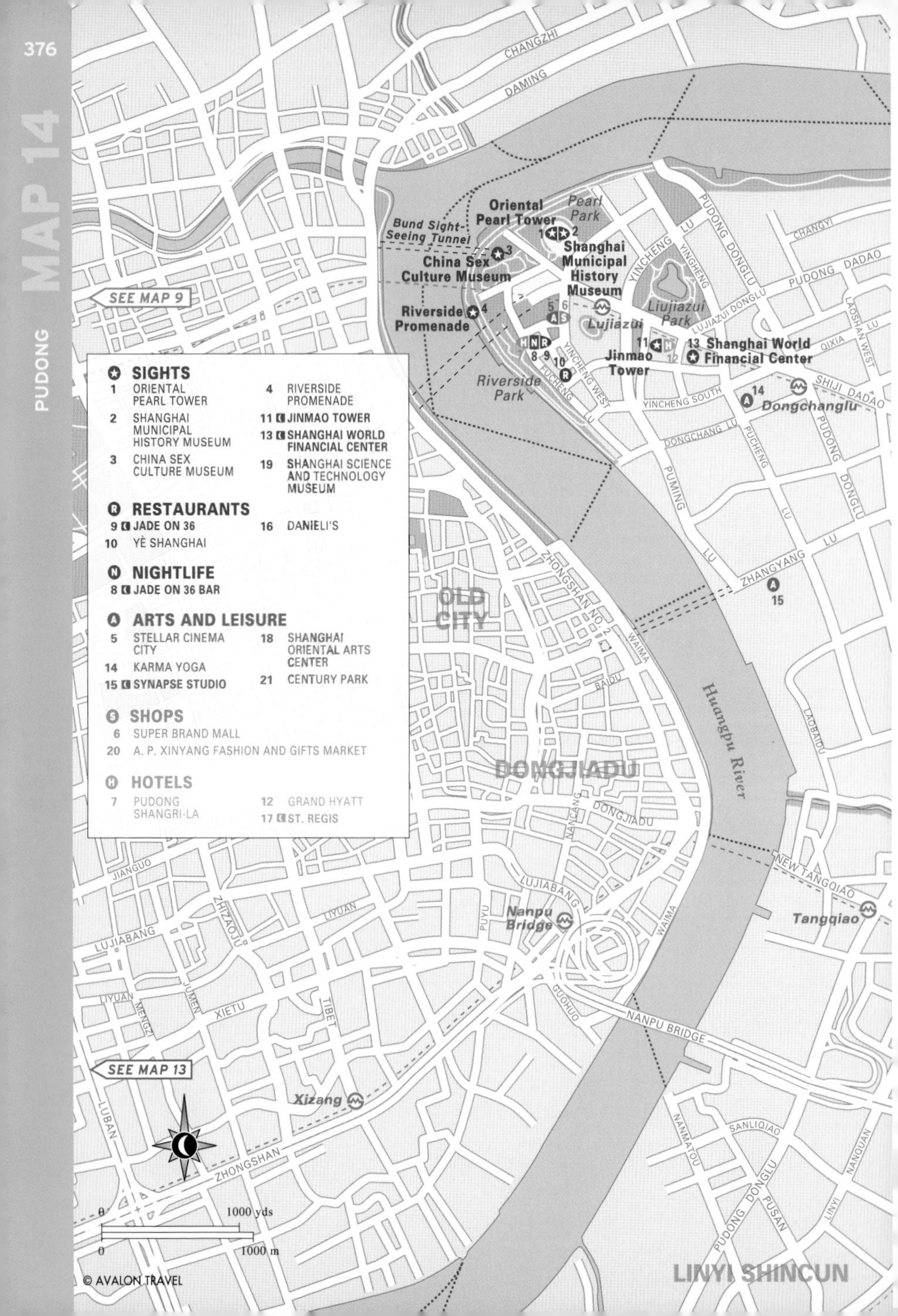
SIGHTS
1 ORIENTAL PEARL TOWER
2 SHANGHAI MUNICIPAL HISTORY MUSEUM
3 CHINA SEX CULTURE MUSEUM
4 RIVERSIDE PROMENADE
11 JINMAO TOWER
13 SHANGHAI WORLD FINANCIAL CENTER
19 SHANGHAI SCIENCE AND TECHNOLOGY MUSEUM
RESTAURANTS
9 JADE ON 36
10 YÈ SHANGHAI
16 DANIELI'S
NIGHTLIFE
8 JADE ON 36 BAR
ARTS AND LEISURE
5 STELLAR CINEMA CITY
14 KARMA YOGA
15 SYNAPSE STUDIO
18 SHANGHAI ORIENTAL ARTS CENTER
21 CENTURY PARK
SHOPS
6 SUPER BRAND MALL
20 A. P. XINYANG FASHION AND GIFTS MARKET
HOTELS
7 PUDONG SHANGRI-LA
12 GRAND HYATT
17 ST. REGIS
SEE MAP 9
SEE MAP 13
Oriental Pearl Tower
Pearl Park
Shanghai Municipal History Museum
Bund Sight-Seeing Tunnel
China Sex Culture Museum
Riverside Promenade
Lujiazui
Liujiazui Park
Shanghai World Financial Center
Jinmao Tower
Riverside Park
Dongchanglu
OLD CITY
DONGJIADU
Huangpu River
Nanpu Bridge
Tangqiao
Xizang
LINYI SHINCUN
CHANGZHI
DAMING
PUDONG DONGLU
YINCHENG
YINGHENG
CHANGYI
PUDONG DADAO
LUJIAZUI DONGLU
LAOSHAN WEST
QIXIA
SHIJI DADAO
YINCHENG SOUTH
YINCHENG WEST
FUCHENG
DONGCHANG LU
PUCHENG
PUMING
PUDONG
DONGLU
ZHANGYANG
ZHONGSHAN NO. 2
WAIMA
BAIDU
LAOBAIDU
NANCANG
DONGJIADU
NEW TANGQIAO
JIANGUO
LUJIABANG
ZHIZAOJU
LIYUAN
PUYU
MENGZI
JUMEN
XIETU
TIBET
GUOHUO
NANPU BRIDGE
LUBAN
ZHONGSHAN
NANMATOU
SANLIQIAO
PUDONG DONGLU
PUSAN
LINYI
NANQUAN
0
1000 yds
1000 m

LUOSHAN XINCUN
LUOSHAN
Huangpu River
GUSHAN
BOSHAN
YANGLING NORTH
DADAO
PUDONG
MIAOPU
JUYE
Pudong Dajie
NEIYUAN XINCUN
Shanghai Maritime University
TAOLIN
LU
Beiyangjing
SHANGCHENG
LU
RUSHAN
DONGFANG
LAOSHAN
SHENJIALONG
LU
Minsheng
ZHANGYANG
DONGILU
LU
Yuanshen Stadium
Yuanshen Sports Centre
YUSHAN
ZHUYUAN XINCUN
JINGNAN SHINCUN
FANGDIAN
Century Avenue
LINGSHAN
LU
WEIFANG
LU
YANGGAO
17 16
MINSHENG
DINGXIANG
LU
WIEFANG XINCUN
FUSHAN
SHIJI
LU
OLD YANGAO
LAOSHAN DONGILU
DADAO
Pudian
18
Shanghai Science & Technology Museum
Pudian
Century Square
19 20
JINXIU
LU
LU
PUDIAN
Century Park
Shanghai Science & Technology Museum
PUDIAN XINCUN
21
PUDONG DONGLU
NANQUAN
ESHAN
LU
LU
YANGGAO
Lancun
HUAMU
LONGJIANG
LANCUN
BAIYANG
Century Park
LU
HUAMU XINCUN
MEIHUA
PUJIAN
LU
MUDAN
LU
NANQUAN
LONGYANG XIAOQU
DONGXIU
JINXIU
YULAN
PUJIAN
LU
Longyang
DONGCHENG XINCUN
Children's Medical Center
LONGDONG
BAIYANG
LONGYANG
LU
HUNAN
DONGFANG
LONGJIANG
LU
YANGGAO
LU
YOUYOU SHINCUN

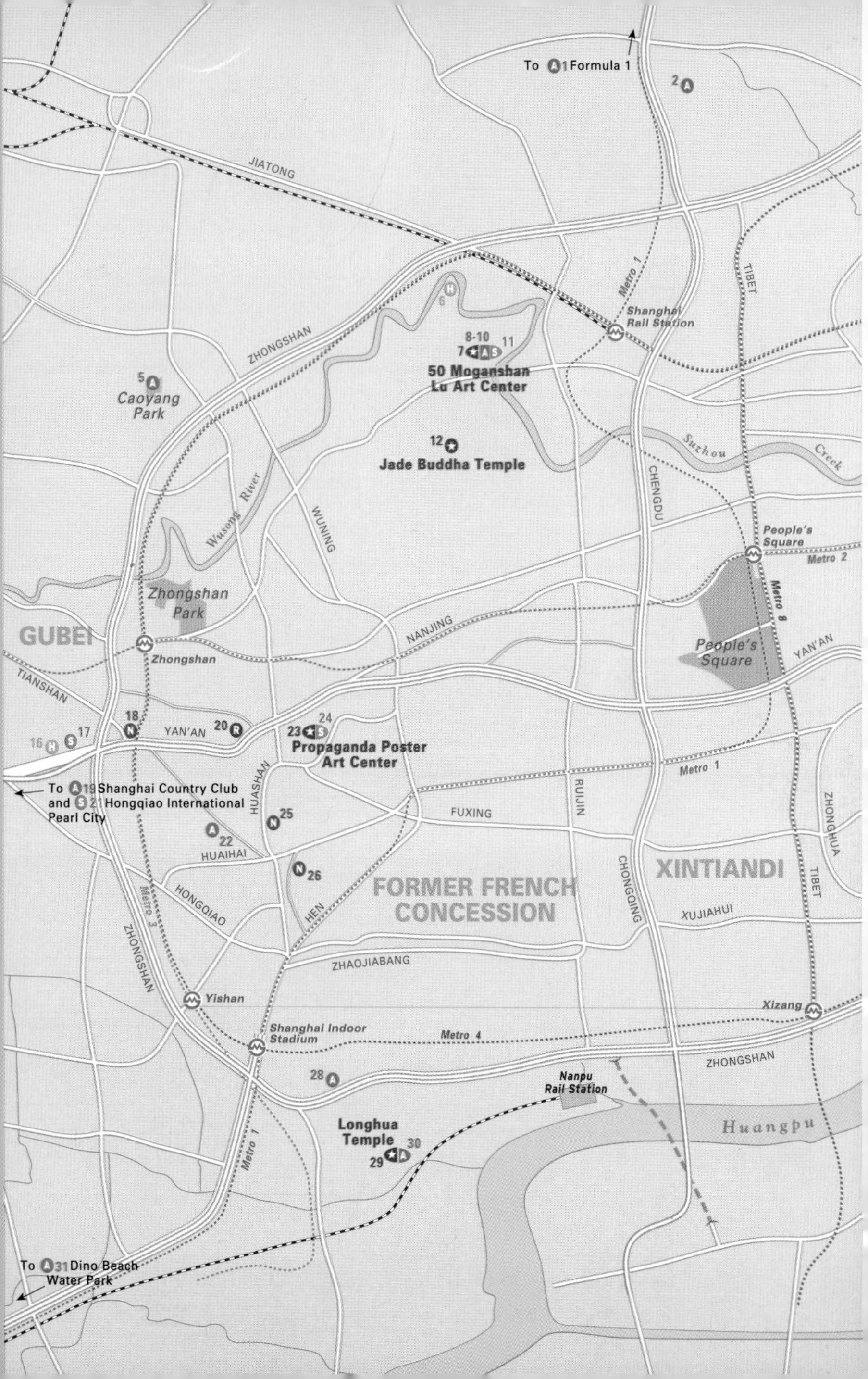

To 1 Formula 1
2
JIATONG
Metro 1
TIBET
6
Shanghai Rail Station
ZHONGSHAN
8-10
7 11
50 Moganshan Lu Art Center
5
Caoyang Park
12
Jade Buddha Temple
Suzhou Creek
CHENGDU
Wusong River
WUNING
People's Square
Metro 2
Zhongshan Park
Metro 8
NANJING
GUBEI
Zhongshan
People's Square
YAN'AN
TIANSHAN
18
20
24
23
YAN'AN
16 17
Propaganda Poster Art Center
Metro 1
To 19 Shanghai Country Club and 21 Hongqiao International Pearl City
HUASHAN
25
RUIJIN
FUXING
ZHONGHUA
22
HUAIHAI
CHONGQING
XINTIANDI
26
TIBET
Metro 3
HONGQIAO
FORMER FRENCH CONCESSION
HEN
XUJIAHUI
ZHONGSHAN
ZHAOJIABANG
Yishan
Xizang
Shanghai Indoor Stadium
Metro 4
ZHONGSHAN
28
Nanpu Rail Station
Huangpu
Longhua Temple
29 30
Metro 1
To 31 Dino Beach Water Park